12-25

To Greg

With love, pride + respect...

Mom + Dad

WORKERS AT WAR

WORKERS AT WAR

LABOR IN CHINA'S ARSENALS, 1937-1953

Joshua H. Howard

Stanford University Press, Stanford, California   2004

Stanford University Press
Stanford, California
© 2004 by the Board of Trustees of the
Leland Stanford Junior University

Printed in the United States of America

Howard, Joshua H.
    Workers at war : labor in China's arsenals, 1937–1953 /
Joshua H. Howard.
        p. cm.
    Includes bibliographical references and index.
    ISBN 0-8047-4896-9 (cloth : alk. paper)
        1. Labor—China—Chongqing—History—20th century. 2. China—
History—1937–1945. 3. China—History—Civil War, 1945–1949. 4.
Chongqing (China)—History—20th century. I. Title
    HD8740.C48H68   2004
    331.7'6234'095138—dc22   2004008533

Typeset at Stanford University Press in 10/13 Sabon

Original printing 2004

Last figure below indicates the year of this printing:
13   12   11   10   09   08   07   06   05   04

For my parents
and
for Xiaoyun

Acknowledgments

The research for this book would have impossible without the generous institutional and financial support I have received over the course of a decade. In particular, I would like to acknowledge a grant from the Committee on Scholarly Communication with China that permitted the bulk of research in Chongqing from October 1993 to January 1995; a write-up grant from the Graduate School of the University of California at Berkeley in 1995; a summer fellowship from the Pacific Cultural Foundation in 1997; research funding from the Croft Institute of International Studies at the University of Mississippi in 2000; and three summer fellowships from the University of Mississippi from 2000 to 2002. I am also extremely grateful for a publication subvention from the Department of History and the Office of Graduate Research at the University of Mississippi.

This book was also made possible with the help of many archival staff and directors. I would like to thank General Hu Chu-sheng, acting director, and Lt. General Fu Ying-ch'uan, former director, of the Bureau of Historical Compilation and Translation, Ministry of National Defense (Taipei); archivists at the Nationalist Party Historical Archives (Taipei); archivists at the National Historical Archives (Taipei); the staff at the Institute of Modern History at Academia Sinica (Taipei); the staff at the Franklin Delano Roosevelt Library at Hyde Park (New York); Director Li Hua, Liu Liqun, and Wang Qinghua of the Chongqing Geleshan Martyrs' Cemetery Archives; and Wan Renyuan, former director at the Number Two (Republican Era) Archives in Nanjing. I am especially indebted to Director Lu Dayue and the entire staff of the Chongqing Municipal Archives for their encouragement and assistance.

I am deeply grateful to the many retired arsenal workers, engineers, and labor activists who shared their wartime experiences with me. I hope I may have done justice to their history. Many of the interviews were made possible with the assistance of the late Dean Yang Guangyan, the Chongqing Federal Trade Union, the Chongqing Retired Engineers Association, and the Chongqing Steel Company Union, for which I am most grateful. In Taiwan, Ms. Cui Lianxiang deserves special mention for arranging interviews with several of her father's colleagues in the arms industry. Thanks, too, to Professor Zhang Ruide for his continuous support and help in arranging interviews and archival visits in Taiwan. General Lei Ying, retired director of the Combined Services Forces Ordnance Production Department, was also most gracious in hosting me and sharing his recollections of the arms industry.

I wish to thank the many friends, colleagues, and teachers who have read and commented on parts of this manuscript or provided other invaluable help in making this a better book: Carlton Benson, Marc Blecher, Ming Chan, Gao Hua, Michael Gasster, Tom Gold, Guo Gang, Mark Halperin, Madeline Hsu, Pierre Landry, Luo Shaodan, Stephen MacKinnon, Mark McNicholas, Mark Metzler, Karin Myhre, Elisabeth Perry, Morris Rossabi, Keith Schoppa, Brett Sheehan, Tang Xiaohui, Tian Ziyu, Wang Guoqiang, Yeh Wen-hsin, Yu Maochun, Zeng Xiaoyong, and Zhan Kaidi.

Let me also express my appreciation to the University of Mississippi. Members of the Department of History and the Croft Institute, led by the fine examples of Bob Haws and Michael Metcalf, have been extremely collegial and supportive of Chinese studies. I am especially indebted to Peter Frost, Sue Grayzel, John Neff, and Joe Ward, who provided perceptive comments and constant encouragement.

I owe a special debt of gratitude to three scholars with whom I worked extensively in Chongqing. Dean Yang Guangyan of Southwest Normal University, whose premature death represented both a personal and professional loss to me and to the many people he touched, shared his expertise on the history of modern China with me and helped me in many other ways. Professor Huang Shujun very generously shared valuable source materials and her vast knowledge of the Chongqing labor movement with me. I also benefited greatly from the guidance of Director Lu Dayue of the Chongqing Municipal Archives who helped me track down numerous sources on the wartime defense industry. I learned much from Professor Huang and Director Lu's work on wartime Chongqing, as will be evident to all readers.

I began this study while still a graduate student at the University of California at Berkeley more than a decade ago. I am particularly grateful to my dissertation advisor, Frederic Wakeman, for teaching me so much about the historian's craft and for his constant support and friendship over the years. I would also like to thank Arif Dirlik for his many invaluable suggestions and criticisms of the book. Professor Dirlik's writings on the Chinese revolutionary experience have been a continuous source of inspiration to me. Charles Postel shared many keen insights on labor history with me and spent countless hours discussing the ideas in this book, for which I am most grateful. My uncle, Gian Carlo Falco, professor of economic history at the University of Pisa, has taken time away from his own hectic schedule to review every draft of this work, to translate relevant German documents, and to make numerous substantive criticisms. This book would have been much poorer without his advice and encouragement. I acknowledge his help with the utmost gratitude and affection.

At Stanford University Press, Muriel Bell and Carmen Borbón-Wu, have my heartfelt thanks for their unwavering support for this project. Special thanks, too, to John Feneron and Peter Dreyer for the rapidity and professional care with which they edited the book. I am indebted to my longtime friend Alessandro Mortarino for his cartographical work. I am most grateful to the two anonymous readers for their meticulous and extremely constructive criticisms of the manuscript. If I have not always followed their wise counsel, it is entirely due to a genetic disposition, "stubborn-mule" mentality. The individuals and organizations mentioned here have all helped me write a better book. Needless to say, any errors of fact or judgment that I may have committed are entirely my own responsibility.

I would like to thank *Asian Studies Review* for permission to reprint excerpts from my article "Yu Zusheng: Organic Intellectuals and the Moral Basis of Class," which appeared in vol. 27, no. 3 (September 2003) of the journal. An article upon which parts of chapter 5 are based appeared as "Chongqing's Most Wanted: Worker Mobility and Resistance in China's Nationalist Arsenals, 1937–1945," *Modern Asian Studies* 37, pt. 4 (2003), reprinted with the permission of Cambridge University Press, for which I am very grateful.

My family has always given me unfailing support, to which a few lines can never do justice. Much of the research for this book was a collaborative effort with my wife, Zhou Xiaoyun. Xiaoyun helped me to gather archival documents and to transcribe the many hours of interviews that we conducted. But beyond this, Xiaoyun has provided me with great joy and support. Finally, I hope some of the passion for history and life that my parents, Angela Falco Howard and Harrison Howard, have given me can be found in these pages. I dedicate this work to my parents and to Xiaoyun with the deepest love.

Contents

Contents   xii

8 pages of photographs follow page 192

Tables

Maps and Figures

Maps

Figures

Foreword

Workers at War brings a much needed perspective to the study of labor in China. Ever since the publication of Jean Chesneaux's *The Chinese Labor Movement* in 1968 (French original in 1962), it seems that historians of Chinese labor have devoted their efforts to refuting Chesneaux's argument that a class-conscious proletariat had emerged in China by the 1920s, which provided the social basis for the Communist revolution. Counterarguments range from the insignificance of class in Chinese society to the lack of class consciousness among Chinese workers to the overshadowing of class by nationalist concerns.

The argument that a fully class-conscious proletariat had emerged in China by the 1920s or, for that matter, in later years, no doubt suffered from a proletarian triumphalism that overlooked not just the complexities of the Chinese social scene but of the concept of class itself. Work since then has offered important correctives as regards the composition of the urban working class, its social dynamics, and its politics—especially with respect to the relationship of workers to the Communist Party. This work, however, has been marked by a tendentiousness of its own, because it has been too eager to jump from evidence of complexity to the conclusion that Chinese workers suffered from a lack of class consciousness, and that class is therefore largely irrelevant to understanding radical politics in China.

The present study brings a new level of theoretical sophistication to issues of class, class consciousness, and class politics in the Chinese revolution. Howard eschews a reductionist Marxist functionalism that deduces class formation and consciousness from the mode, the conditions, or even the relations of production, and that ignores everything else (from gender and ethnicity to places of origin and life trajectories, I am tempted to say) that went into the making of workers' lives. On the other hand, he also refuses to allow the latter to cover up the ways in which workers thought and acted in class ways. Someone observed once that class struggle is first and foremost a struggle for class consciousness. The study here, with its rich documentation, bears witness to this observation. Howard draws on a range of literature that has brought a new sophistication to the understanding of class, which has demonstrated that to think or act in class ways requires the mediation, not only of experience, but also of education and organization. Class is not something out there, as a positivist social science (including Marxist social science) would have it. For the worker, no less than for the scholar, it is a concept with which to grasp and act upon one type of social division among others, albeit a fundamental one. The question in the end may not be whether or not there are classes, but what we stand to gain or lose by denying class as an analytical and political concept. It is a political and ideological question, but one that is crucial to a critical social science, no less than to a radical, and radically democratic, politics. My favorite chapter in the book is the chapter on the "organic worker intellectual" Yu Zusheng, which brings together the concerns of the social and the intellectual historian, pointing us in valuable new directions of historical understanding. It also shows how much Howard and the literature he draws upon are indebted to theorists like Antonio Gramsci, who brought the complexities of everyday experience and consciousness to the elaboration of abstract theory. The Chinese revolution itself has been an indispensable source of such theoretical elaboration.

If class is best understood in its structural overdetermination, which allows for an account of the moments that go into its making (or unmaking), its social, political, and ideological significance as a concept or practice can be grasped only historically. The entanglements of different aspects of consciousness (or existence) in social activity would suggest that their outcome in either consciousness or politics can be grasped only in their concrete historicity. Class may be a function of social structures, and pervasive in social relations, but that does not mean that it is equally salient in consciousness under all circumstances and at all times, or that it is a necessary determinant of politics. *Workers at War* examines an instance in which class consciousness played an important part in workers' politics. It is also remarkable that class politics achieved saliency at a time of national crisis, and in industries that were crucial to national defense against imperialist invasion, which is an important corrective to the me-

chanical opposition some studies assume between class and national consciousness. The workers Howard studies were not necessarily skilled
workers, who, according to theory, might be more inclined to class consciousness and politics, and this makes his findings more intriguing and
generalizable across the working class understood broadly. The workers'
politics dating back to the 1920s also suggest that nationalism and
class—rather than oppositional—consciousness may under some circumstances nourish each other. The question ultimately is a historical one,
and one that deserves further study.

Given the centrality of the issue of class in labor studies, as well as in
the present study, it has drawn all my attention here. Howard provides us
with an argument that is theoretically sophisticated and richly documented. I hope that this study will contribute to stimulating interest in
studies of Chinese labor, which have receded with the decline of interest
in the history of the Chinese revolution as socialism has become "history" in China and elsewhere. Workers are the main interest of *Workers
at War*, but in analyzing the conditions of labor, Howard takes up a
wide-ranging set of questions concerning production and its organization
in Guomindang China during World War II, which offer much of value
beyond issues of labor and class.

Arif Dirlik
University of Oregon

WORKERS AT WAR

INTRODUCTION

In January 1950, several weeks after Nationalist troops had failed to blow up Chongqing's defense industry and had fled their former wartime capital, class struggle gripped the arsenals. Workers dragged factory managers and staff officers down to the banks of the Jialing and Yangzi Rivers and forced them to kneel in the water for several hours. Afterward, they subjected managers to "fatigue interrogations" for three days and three nights. Such actions were highly symbolic, but effective. By humiliating their former oppressors and subverting the Nationalist regime's factory order, arsenal workers began to *fanshen* ("overturn the body"), a term that has been aptly used to describe the revolutionary process whereby peasants destroyed the traditional elite during the land reform movement sweeping across rural China.[1] In the defense industry, workers similarly pursued the overthrow of the existing structure of authority. Allied with the Chinese Communist Party (CCP), they successfully organized unions for the first time since the founding of the arms industry during the second half of the nineteenth century. New channels of upward social mobility, a more egalitarian wage system, and political movements targeting the managerial class also raised the social and economic status of the arsenal workers in an effort to bridge the long-standing divide between mental and manual labor.

These radical measures expressed Mao Zedong's belief in the need for continuous revolution and mass mobilization to construct socialism after the establishment of the People's Republic. The Communist revolution "from above" enjoyed popular support. By actively participating in political campaigns, workers vented pent-up grievances provoked by rapid industrialization, political repression, and over a decade of total war involving three interwoven conflicts—a war of national liberation, a civil war, and a war between social classes—which engulfed China's armaments industry between 1937 and 1953.[2]

That China fought Japan between 1937 and 1945, and was subsequently divided by civil war between the Nationalists and Communists, is common knowledge. But the lines between these two wars were blurred, since national liberation involved not only resistance to Japanese aggression but also the liberation of China from the authoritarian hold of the Nationalist (Guomindang, or GMD) leader, Chiang Kai-shek. It may be even more surprising to suggest that those workers concentrated in the river port entrepôt of Chongqing and employed by the defense industry, a bastion of Guomindang power, engaged in a class war over the course of a decade. For a variety of reasons, stemming from ideological and historiographic trends, class has often been noticeably absent from discussions of Chinese labor.

During the Anti-Japanese War, patriotism conveniently meshed with the Nationalist government's efforts to exclude class from its very own language to maintain social order and stifle political dissent. Fearing its subversive quality, Guomindang officials censored any word that resonated with the labor movement. Even the word "labor" was suspect. By 1940, General Yu Dawei, the director and architect of the Nationalist arms industry, ordered all arsenals to change the name "labor office" (laogongke) to "work administration office" (laozhengke). Ostensibly, Yu argued that the term "labor" had too broad a meaning to describe accurately an institution overseeing the daily administration of workers. But Yu also felt "labor" had a political significance that was best avoided. "The word 'labor' is a term used to connote conflictual labor-capital class [relations]," he warned.[3] In place of a class-based language, officials substituted a discourse based on patriotism and anti-imperialism. According to GMD labor leaders, China's predominantly agricultural economy precluded the formation of distinct social classes, and the country thus did not share the injustices associated with the "abnormalities" of Western capitalism. Imperialism was the real culprit behind whatever oppression and suffering workers endured. And once the union formed between workers and their employers helped defeat the Japanese, the "labor problem" would dissipate.[4]

Ironically, Chinese historians have accepted at face value the wartime Nationalist official discourse, according to which the United Front—a multi-class, multi-party alliance committed to resisting Japanese imperialism—rendered issues of class subsidiary to patriotic goals. Labor historians have widely adopted the view that nationalist sentiment subsumed class tensions during the Anti-Japanese War. In the most authoritative work to date on wartime labor, the historian Qi Wu argues that social contradictions did not emerge during the war because of the relative unity between labor and capital in resisting Japan. According to this interpretation, the wartime labor movement, which Qi defines simply by strike activity, contrasts sharply with an earlier pattern of class formation during the 1920s, which had developed alongside the encroachment of imperialism and foreign capital. China's labor movement derived its strength from workers concentrated in the larger, more capital-intensive foreign-owned factories of the coastal areas. The interplay between workers' anti-imperialist sentiment and class grievances thus spurred much of the labor movement. But with the wartime industrialization of the southwest, industries for the first time became overwhelmingly nationalized or controlled by Chinese capitalists. As a result, workers had difficulty mobilizing an opposition force, since they no longer directly faced a semi-colonial presence. In short, as employers and workers united in the resistance against Japan, nationalist imperatives overrode workers' class interests.[5]

On an experiential level, the devastating air raids on Chongqing no doubt fostered workers' visceral hatred of the "Japanese devils." Management capitalized on these sentiments by using patriotic slogans to spur production over the course of grueling twelve- to sixteen-hour shifts. Qi Wu premises his argument, however, on the relative quiescence of labor during the Anti-Japanese War, compared with the surge in labor militancy during the immediate postwar years. Although persuasive in a general way, this interpretation uncritically takes the ideals supporting the CCP-GMD alliance and the United Front as historical reality and ignores the social dislocation, grievances, and tension created between workers and managers by the war. As the work of Huang Shujun demonstrates, workers also engaged in strikes and sit-downs during the Anti-Japanese War.[6] Building on Huang's study, my own work shows that many of the arsenal workers' demands for better treatment, greater human dignity, and improved social status in the postwar strike waves derived from the war period. Despite evidence to the contrary, many contemporary Chinese historians have avoided class analysis, affirming Benedetto Croce's maxim "All history is contemporary." China's recent market reforms, efforts at rapprochement with Taiwan, and repudiation of the Maoist emphasis on class struggle have reinforced a revisionist trend in mainland

Chinese scholarship that has emphasized the Nationalist regime's contributions to the war effort against Japan and the patriotic unity of the Chinese people.

The tendency to downplay the salience of class to the study of Chinese labor has been even more marked among Western scholars. One important exception was Jean Chesneaux's pioneering 1962 study *Le Mouvement ouvrier chinois de 1919 à 1927*, which argued, in Marxist terms, that Chinese workers instinctively moved from being a "class in itself" to a "class for itself" during the 1920s, under the impact of exploitation, imperialist oppression, and the ideological guidance of the Chinese Communist Party. In echoing the biases of his sources (especially Comintern documents) regarding the "feudal" legacy of peasant culture that informed workers' consciousness, Chesneaux implied that workers cast off their "traditional" shackles, that is, regional rivalries and patron-client relations, as they became ever more conscious of their class interests.[7] A second generation of labor historians intent on reaffirming workers' capacity to affect social change reached more mixed conclusions regarding working-class consciousness. In *Sisters and Strangers: Women in the Shanghai Cotton Mills, 1919–1949,* Emily Honig stresses that regional particularities, the gender gap between male Communist activists and female cotton mill workers, and traditional values rendered class formation more problematic during the 1920s. By contrast, cotton mill workers, the "sisters" in her book title, embraced forms of solidarity during the postwar (1945–49) labor movement. Honig demonstrates that the CCP played a major role in politicizing workers by grafting onto forms of associational culture (sisterhoods) and utilizing networks that YWCA members had previously established with workers. She concludes that workers embraced multiple loyalties by the late 1940s: "Patterns of localism and traditional hierarchical loyalties are perhaps not as antithetical to working-class consciousness as many pre-Liberation Party organizers and contemporary students of working-class history have assumed."[8]

Whereas labor historians have generally treated class fragmentation as a liability for the labor movement, Elizabeth Perry's study of Shanghai strikes contends that the labor movement's political influence derived from divisions within the working class. Perry makes a strong case for linking productive processes, regionalism, and skill levels with political activity, suggesting that skilled workers and artisans formed the backbone of the Communist labor movement. Her focus on the micro-associations of labor clarifies some of the strategies used by labor activists and Communists in building a labor movement, but this approach is more problematic when dealing with periods or strikes of mass action, such as the Three Armed Uprisings of 1927, when issues of class were hotly contested and workers had begun to organize on a mass scale through the city's General Labor Union. As a fall-back position, Perry argues that inflation and nationalism underlay the large-scale strikes, saying, "Such issues appealed to participants as *consumers* or *citizens*, rather than as members of a *class*."[9] By contrast, Steve Smith reintroduces the concept of class in discursive terms. In this interpretation, the language of class became intertwined with workers' sense of anti-imperialist nationalism in 1920s Shanghai.[10]

Given the contested nature of class and its varying usages, it may be useful to highlight the theoretical aspects of class analysis that inform this study. Like patterns of class formation in Shanghai or elsewhere, China's arsenal workers did not participate in an ineluctable, unilinear march toward a revolutionary class consciousness. Framing workers' consciousness in terms of revolutionary class consciousness has often led to all-or-nothing conclusions about the state of working-class formation. Essentialist studies that idealize the working class in this manner tend to reject the concept of class in toto. Bryan Palmer defines essentialism as "the insistence that class exists only when class forces are *uniformly* conscious of their *unproblematic* class place in the society and act *unambiguously* and *persistently* on the basis of that consciousness."[11] Essentialism caricatures class-conscious workers as marching in unison to the Promised Land, even though Marx and Engels fully acknowledged that conflict and ambiguity exist within the working class. "Competition is the completest expression of the battle of all against all which rules in modern civil society," Engels wrote. "This battle, a battle for life, for existence, for everything, in case of need a battle of life and death, is fought not between the different classes of society only, but also between the individual members of these classes."[12]

Rather than emphasize workers' consciousness to the exclusion of other forms of class or give a teleological account of change from objective to subjective states of class, this study builds on recent research that stresses the simultaneous existence of both objective and subjective forms of class. In particular, the social theorist Ira Katznelson introduces four interrelated and contingent levels of class: structure, ways of life, dispositions, and collective action.[13] Structure relates to the position of labor within a capitalist economic system. Ways of life refer to the conditions of work and life off the job that affect workers' daily lives. As regards "class dispositions," Katznelson adopts the British historian E. P. Thompson's definition: "When we speak of *a* class we are thinking of *a* very loosely-defined body of people who share the same congeries of interests, social experiences, traditions, and value-system, who have a *disposition to behave* as a class, to define themselves in their actions and in their consciousness in relation to other groups of people in class ways."[14] Workers' disposition becomes activated into class particularly during collective action.

This approach to class formation emphasizes workers' own agency, but the role of vanguard workers and activists proved just as crucial to shaping workers' class consciousness. To echo David Montgomery, class formation was more than simply a process based on working people's historical agency and unmediated experience, but also a project in which a militant minority organized workers and articulated an alternative politics.[15] Montgomery's approach to class formation builds upon but also departs in significant ways from Thompson's. Labor historians working in the tradition of Thompson have emphasized the historical process of class formation stemming from workers' own daily experience within the community and at work. Thompson distinguished between class experience, as largely determined by the productive relations into which workers are born or enter involuntarily, and class consciousness. Thompson broke new ground in adding a cultural dimension to class consciousness, "the way in which these experiences are handled in cultural terms: embodied in traditions, value-systems, ideas and institutional forms."[16] But in emphasizing the development of class consciousness as arising organically from workers' unmediated experience, Thompson (and his followers) underestimated the crucial role played by "outsiders" during the labor movement.

Finally, class is historically contingent. Several contingent factors worked to shape the class formation of China's arsenal workers. These included workers' interaction with labor activists and underground Communists; workers' experience in the factory; workers' aspirations to greater social status and political freedom; their collective action in the wake of both World War II and the Chinese civil war; and the repressive factory regime, buttressed by military discipline and rigid hierarchy.

Although arsenal workers' consciousness of class was not necessarily revolutionary, their war experiences intertwined with the Chinese revolution. War, as the historian Gabriel Kolko notes, has had profound social and revolutionary effects. "More than any other single factor, the overwhelming and direct consequences of war have shaped the human and political experiences of our century and have become the motor of change within it, creating political and ideological upheavals—revolutions being the most important of them—that otherwise had scant possibility of occurring."[17] Likewise, the War of Resistance against Japan unleashed social changes that set the stage for both civil war and socialist revolution in China. Since the revolution was primarily rurally based, historians have duly explained how the Communists mobilized the peasantry during the pivotal 1937–45 period.[18] This focus has, however, impeded our understanding of social change and conflict in the Nationalist-controlled urban territories, most prominently Chongqing, Chiang Kai-shek's wartime capital between 1938 and 1946. Besides a study of Nationalist labor written over fifty years ago, there has been no published study in English on the social and political history of Chongqing.[19] With their focus on government elites and institutions, the standard explanations for the Nationalist collapse—government factionalism, hyperinflation, military blunders, and malfeasance—have rendered invisible the role of urban social classes as agents of historical change.[20] Even Odd Arne Westad's recent survey on the Chinese civil war, *Decisive Encounters,* while exploring how the Guomindang alienated urbanites during the 1940s, focuses on the loss of middle-class and intellectual support for the regime. Westad concludes that "in general the CCP's efforts at winning influence among the urban proletariat were, if not wasted, then a detraction from the party's successes among students and intellectuals."[21] The role of the working class in the CCP victory of 1949 and its relationship to the two political parties remains understudied.

To address this lacuna, I examine the process of industrial development, social transformation, and labor activism within China's largest and most strategic industry, the arms industry. Since the arms industry was a bastion of Nationalist military and state power, arsenal workers' gradual alienation from factory officials, who were a stratum of the military elite, contributed to the general collapse of state legitimacy. The decline in the Guomindang's legitimacy corresponded to a rise in Communist influence and prestige among workers. Communists and workers frequently had separate interests during the War of Resistance and the postwar labor movement. Nonetheless, the grievances, aspirations, and concerted actions of arsenal workers during the war period converged with the Communist program and class-based political movements of the early 1950s. From their wartime struggles, arsenal workers gained the confidence to demand better treatment and an end to the long-standing divide between mental and manual labor once the Communists gained power. In short, the wartime history of the Chongqing arsenal workers and management confirms recent findings that the Communists rose to national power, not simply because of peasant support and the collapse of Nationalist authority, but also on the basis of their own appeals to the working class.[22]

The structure of this book follows this shifting pendulum of power in the context of the wars (national liberation, civil, and class). I first analyze the emergence of Chongqing's arms industry as a vanguard of China's state-led industrialization, which formed the structural conditions for working-class formation. Beginning in the early 1930s, the Nationalist government's wartime mobilization and its plans for industrial development focused on consolidating state control over and expanding its military-industrial base. State-guided industrialization led to the establishment of the National Resources Commission (NRC), which became the largest government organization managing industry during the war.[23] Of equal importance, and running along parallel tracks with the NRC, the Ordnance Department oversaw the development of the chemical plants, steel mills, and advanced machine factories that made up the arms industry. Much of China's prewar military modernization depended on the close ties between the Nationalist government and Germany. Arsenal officials working in tandem with German advisors promoted technological diffusion, the use of advanced machinery, interchangeable manufacture, and mass production within the defense industry. These changes in the production process coincided with changes in the social landscape of the shop floor. Increasingly, arsenals bureaucratized their employment practices and looked to Western managerial methods for inspiration. These reforms promoted self-sufficiency in the production of small arms, enough to carry on the war of attrition against Japan.[24]

By late 1937, the brutal occupation of the industrial and commercial centers of coastal China by Japanese troops had forced an unprecedented mass migration. Several million migrants fled to the hinterland of southwestern China. Within the year, Chiang Kai-shek designated Chongqing, the longtime commercial hub of Sichuan, as wartime capital. Along with the influx of government and cultural institutions, the city witnessed the rapid and forced expansion of heavy industry. The relocation of industrial plants and arsenals from central China and the coastal cities coincided with the development of new coalfields and the building of blast furnaces, metal-rolling mills, chemical plants, and electric power stations to produce inputs for the defense industry. The buildup of the arms industry, two-thirds of which was based in Sichuan Province, transformed the wartime capital from a commercial center into southwestern China's center of heavy industry. Notwithstanding the devastation it wrought, the war thus also had the constructive economic effect of promoting heavy industry.

The arsenals dominated the industrial landscape of Sichuan and at any given time employed roughly half of Chongqing's male industrial workforce. At the height of wartime mobilization in 1944, fourteen of the Nationalists' twenty-seven arsenals were located in the greater industrial zone of Chongqing.[25] These arsenals employed as many as 60,000 workers, staff officers, and soldiers, with 40,000 employee dependents. Considering that approximately 10,000 arsenal workers left the arsenals each year during the Anti-Japanese War, and that Chongqing's population exceeded one million by the mid 1940s, arguably one in ten inhabitants had either direct work experience in or contact with the defense industry.

Given the vast number of migrant workers and refugees in the wartime capital, from Sichuan Province as well as throughout China, a study of the arsenal workers' social composition and social relations at work sheds light on the dialectical relationship between regionalism, nationalism, and class formation. Much of the scholarship on Chinese labor history has treated workers' regional, national, or class-based identities in mutually exclusive terms, privileging region to evoke the historical absence of class or to downplay its salience. As Elizabeth Perry has stressed, workers throughout East Asia generally "appear to have been more consumed with the politics of 'place'—a quest for social and cultural status entailing a desire to elude, rather than to embrace, the ranks of the proletariat—than with a 'class' struggle to further their interests qua workers."[26] But could workers after all not have class, nationalist, and regional loyalties simultaneously? As Eric Hobsbawm asserts, "Men and women did not choose collective identification as they chose shoes, knowing that one could only put on one pair at a time."[27] Indeed, most recent scholarship on labor, from Brazil to Colorado, has stressed the multiple sources of workers' identity.[28]

The process of class formation was complicated, because the mass migration to Chongqing resulted in a labor force of great regional and skill diversity. Thousands of Sichuanese assembly workers and laborers worked alongside a core of skilled workers from China's central and coastal provinces. At the same time, mass production and the pressing wartime demand for labor accelerated the process of proletarianization, by which numerous workers without resources entered a class relationship by selling their labor power to survive.[29] This process forged increasingly common industrial conditions and experiences for machinists and laborers working in the arsenals. Workers also shared a common goal, in that many perceived their work as a patriotic act. Moreover, the wartime development of internal labor markets, whereby workers were hired at lower-entry-level jobs and eventually trained for new skilled positions, helped bridge regional boundaries once manifest in terms of skill. The arsenal workers thus presented a complex amalgam of regional, national, and class-based identities.

The increasing use of internal labor markets suggests that arsenal management exercised direct control over its workforce and was not beholden to middlemen contractors. In contrast to China's textile and mining industries, where the contract labor system figured prominently, the arsenal labor relationship was primarily based on wage work.[30] This system granted workers greater independence over the sale of their labor power but tore away intermediaries between workers and managers and contributed to the bureaucratization of the workplace because of the rapid increase in staff personnel. Indeed, the arms industry's increasing use of piecework, which Marx termed "the form of wage most appropriate to the capitalist mode of production," drew the line between labor and management ever more starkly.[31] As this study shows, working conditions, wages, and social welfare programs formed one element of class, which Jürgen Kocka defines as "a multitude of persons (and families) who, due to this joint socio-economic position, share structural presuppositions of common interests, in contrast to the related and potentially conflicting interests of at least one other class."[32]

The rapid growth of an industrial proletariat altered the social profile of the defense workforce from a craft- to a class-based one. With thousands of peasant recruits from Chongqing's hinterland entering the workforce, a greater managerial presence curbing artisan autonomy, and hyperinflation eroding real wages, the artisan stratum lost significant social prestige during the war. As a result, workers' collective action changed during the war period in at least two crucial ways. During the strike waves of the 1940s, large-scale factories such as the arsenals, rather than the local community or workshop, became the battlegrounds for labor militancy. The social composition of the labor movement changed accordingly, from being largely a movement of artisans, to include skilled workers, semi-skilled assembly workers, and laborers. Arsenal workers of different skill levels participated in party activities, whether led by the Communists or the Guomindang, and engaged in industrial action.

Studies of the 1920s labor movement have drawn attention to the leading role of artisans in struggling against the incursions of industrial capitalism.[33] Research linking Shanghai working-class politics to occupational or skill categories has made explicit comparisons with the labor movements of nineteenth-century Europe, where artisans rather than industrial workers played central roles.[34] Several reasons explain why artisans in nineteenth-century Britain or France were more prone to organize or become radicalized. Higher wages, fewer working hours, and a greater degree of literacy and mobility enabled artisans to organize more easily than less skilled workers. Artisans also shared a sense of pride in their work—as a craft learned through apprenticeship— and as members of traditional economic organizations, such as guilds. As a result, they had greater expectations of how their employers should treat them. Because of their leverage in the labor market owing to their knowledge and skill, they were more likely to resist threats to their social and economic status.[35] The craft skills involved in small arms manufacture made the Chongqing arsenals conducive to artisan work. Highly trained skilled workers did play an important role in the labor movement, but in general, the artisanal stratum in the wartime capital was numerically and culturally weak relative to factory workers. Consequently, the politics of the arms industry involved workers of various skill levels.

In countries with strong bureaucratic traditions and weak guild and artisan traditions, such as Japan and Germany, the "collar" divide became a more prominent division within industry than demarcations between skill levels.[36] A similar development occurred in China's arms industry, where a military bureaucracy reigned. In helping foster China's military industrial modernization during the 1930s, German military advisors influenced the organization of the Nationalist arms industry. The more complicated organizations of production, technology, and factory bureaucracy that distinguished the arsenals also shaped their social relations and the forms of labor militancy. Factory life—as manifest in regulations, work, status, social welfare, and community life—revolved around the social division between staff officers (*zhiyuan*) and production workers (*gongren*). This social gulf, premised on the division of mental and manual labor, united arsenal workers against their social superiors. Daily reminders of their subjugation and segregation brought production workers from different skill levels into the labor movement.

Because of arsenals' strategic value to the state, employment in the arms industry became intensely politicized, more so than in any other industry in China. Westad notes that during the civil war, "the great majority of the population were passive onlookers, doing their best to stay out of harm's way in the cataclysm that engulfed their country."[37] By contrast, the lives of arsenal workers were invariably swept up in the political currents of national liberation and civil war. Fully aware that labor was essential to war production and to the cause of national resistance, both managers and militant workers, Nationalists and Communists, battled to secure workers' loyalties. For its part, the Guomindang encouraged and mandated arsenal employees to join its ranks and participate in factory cell organizations. Moreover, the wartime government played an important role in arbitrating labor conflict and, in tandem with arsenal directors, shaped social welfare policies.

Such policies influenced workers' status and identities, because the factory became the focal point of workers' community. Several wartime developments lend credence to the idea that social relations within the factory, rather than the destruction of a moral economy in the broader community, played the key role in working-class formation. Most arsenals were isolated from the city proper, located along riverbanks and at the base of foothills to shield them from air raids. Moreover, factory management actively intervened in regulating both the working and off-work hours of its employees in order to maintain a steady supply of labor for war production. Cultural activities and the provision of fringe benefits helped secure workers' loyalty. Hiring practices, whereby workers were employed from the same family, often extending from two to three generations, also reinforced the arsenals' paternalistic managerial style. It is perhaps easy to fall back on interpretations of Chinese authority patterns and social control that stress the efficacy of managerial paternalism, because of workers' filial deference to their employers. But the forging of a factory community through real and fictive forms of paternalism did not necessarily create lasting bonds of deference between workers and management. After all, family feuds have typically been the most deeply divisive, violent, and emotionally fought conflicts.

The pivotal role played by labor in the Nationalist war effort meant that arsenal workers' parameters for thought and action were very much, although not exclusively, shaped and defined "from above." The Nationalist government denied class, in keeping with its ideological appeals to national unity. Yet the very language of managers betrayed their fears that workers as a social category had their own separate interests and a latent capacity for mass opposition. This perception, in tandem with labor-management conflict, informed much of management's elaborate social welfare policies. The distribution of fringe benefits to factory employees, however, privileged management. Intended in part as a form of social control, the arsenals' welfare programs backfired by polarizing the factory community. Repression in the form of severe military discipline, the intensity of the Nationalists' political program, and its total separation from the reality of workers' daily life struggles further alienated workers from Nationalist ideologues.

While the GMD lost support among arsenal workers, the CCP and the militant minority tried to enlist labor in its class project. Through political organizations, activities, and the written word, activists, both underground Communist Party members and non-Communist working-class activists, consciously pursued and shaped workers' class consciousness. Communists moved from mobilizing workers en masse during the National Salvation Movement, a patriotic movement that swept urban China during the mid to late 1930s, to developing a clandestine force.[38] By the early 1940s, underground networks, reading societies, and the Communist press had become crucial links between arsenal workers and the CCP. The Communist daily *Xinhua ribao*, in particular, served as an important forum in which to criticize social relations within the factory and to question the legitimacy of the Nationalist government. Workers' grievances and demands for better treatment, or *daiyu*—a term implying higher pay and social status—stemmed from their own work experiences and the prevalent social stigma associated with manual labor. Arsenal workers' shared experiences in the labor market, factory community, and workplace provided a basis for forging common interests against their employers, as represented by state managers. Class formation—always reconstituted by the shifting composition and attitudes of diverse groups of workers—was heightened during periods of intense conflict and stimulated by Communist organizers and militant working-class activists.

As important as both Communist and Nationalist activities and organizations were in politicizing the arsenals, workers often acted independently of both parties, or used preexisting organizations for their own separate interests. Fueled by their economic grievances and political aspirations, which at times even outpaced Communist party goals, workers engaged in strikes and slowdowns immediately after World War II. Although Communists played an instrumental role in mobilizing workers for the postwar strikes, they lagged behind more militant workers' desire for direct action to effect political change. If there was ever a "revolutionary moment" before the Communists rose to power, it was in 1946, not 1949, when workers were "ready to go." Only by unleashing class struggle campaigns in the early 1950s would the CCP reaffirm its commitment to revolutionary action for workers.

The close but complicated ties between underground Communist activists and arsenal workers is explored here through the life of Yu Zusheng, a radical arsenal worker and revolutionary martyr. Before his execution in November 1949 at the hands of the fleeing Nationalists, Yu became a prolific writer, seeking to build bridges between workers and intellectuals and to break down stigmas ascribed to the working class. The aphorism "Writing is my way of being a free man," attributed to the African American novelist Richard Wright, could just as well have been said by Yu. His poetry and letters offer testimony to the social injustices endured by his fellow workers, as well as to their struggle for dignity within the factory and in the larger society. Yu Zusheng and other worker-writers' quest for better treatment, which they often depicted in highly moral terms, formed an important part of the process of Chongqing's class formation.

Yu Zusheng's life also reveals the ambivalent relationship between the Communist Party and radical workers. He became a writer in part because he feared that the party, dominated by intellectuals, had distanced itself too much from workers. Only by supplanting the traditional role of intellectuals could workers transform the social order. After 1949, it appeared that the way was open for the transformations that Yu sought. Changes in the wage structure, the establishment of unions, and increased social mobility for workers marked significant departures from the past. An analysis of the political campaigns examines how the Communist Party and arsenal workers mutually reinforced the class-struggle campaigns. At the same time, the radical actions and advances made by the arsenal workers posed a dilemma for the new authorities—the Communist Party and the People's Liberation Army. The very meaning of socialism became contested between those who stressed the forces of production and material output against those who emphasized the relations of production and social justice.

Workers at War centers on Chongqing, the heart of the wartime defense industry, yet other Nationalist arsenals were located in southwestern China, and occasional references to these factories are made throughout the book. Despite the often vast geographical distances separating individual arsenals, their employees envisioned themselves as part of a single community, known by contemporaries as the defense industry world (*binggongjie*). Arsenals shared information and technology with one another, divided up production assignments, and had similar political programs. Munitions workers also formed part of a community that transcended the workplace. Workers often moved from one arsenal to another, and in moments of conflict, they sought support across arsenal lines. Workers' feelings of solidarity and loyalty to the defense industry did not generate a sectional consciousness, unity with the *binggongjie*, but rather became identified with the fate of the nation and the working class. The book's jacket, which reproduces Yun Bo's 1938 woodblock print *Guarding Our Factories,* shows a war worker protecting his factory, a symbol of the nation, from Japanese attack. Over a decade later, many of those same workers would identify with the working class in defense of their arsenals against Guomindang plans to destroy the entire arms industry before the Communist takeover of Chongqing. This is the history of that transformation.

1

TO BUY OR TO BUILD?

Economic Development and the Arms Industry

Ordnance Director Yu Dawei in full military regalia during World War II. General Yu was the architect of the Nationalist arms industry between 1933 and 1945 and the Republic of China's defense minister between 1954 and 1965. From Guofangbu shizheng bianyiju, ed., *Yu Dawei xiansheng nianpu ziliao chubian*, vol. 1 (Taipei: Guofangbu shizheng bianyiju, 1996). Reproduced by permission of Mr. Yu Yanghe.

On September 19, 1931, a day after invading Manchuria, the Japanese Guandong Army occupied China's largest war plant, the Shenyang arsenal. Adding insult to injury, Japanese troops posed by the factory gates for photographs standing or kneeling under an ominously worded banner: "With the exception of Japanese, kill on the spot anyone who enters or leaves." The loss of the Shenyang arsenal was devastating. At its peak during the late 1920s, it had employed 17,000 workers and its monthly production surpassed the combined output of all other munitions plants. The value of the factory, estimated in November 1932 to be 330 million yuan (U.S.$61.8 million), almost equaled the Nationalist government's five-year defense reconstruction budget.[1]

The Manchurian Incident and the impending threat of war forced China to initiate several key reforms of the armaments industry. The cornerstone of Chiang Kai-shek's military industrial modernization plan, linked to broader state-making goals, was the extension of central control over independent provincial arsenals and the creation of a more self-sufficient defense industry. If China hoped to increase its arms production, technological reform as an integral part of modernization was critical. Realizing the limitations of importing advanced technology without an adequate base for its use, Yu Dawei, director of the Ordnance Department, which oversaw the arms industry, promoted technical education and research, greatly expanding the number of technical and administrative personnel. Technological reforms also transformed production processes. The Ordnance Department used arms transactions, especially with Germany, to acquire technology that facilitated both interchangeable manufacture and weapons standardization, ushering in mass production before the Anti-Japanese War erupted in 1937.

Yet the political economy of the arms industry rested on several contradictions. The first involved Nationalist fiscal policy, which in rhetoric envisioned growth of the armament industry as a key to national survival, but in substance crippled economic development. During the 1930s, Chiang Kai-shek's government was constrained by massive foreign and domestic debt, and he was obsessed with eliminating his Communist rivals (the so-called "disease of the heart"), so rather than promoting economic "reconstruction," Nationalist ministers of finance directed the bulk of state funding to buying military hardware and sustaining military campaigns against the CCP. In part to redress this imbalance, the Nationalists cultivated close ties to German military advisors, hoping that the ensuing barter arrangements would promote China's mil-

itary industrialization and self-sufficiency. The unraveling of this mutually beneficial relationship ultimately entrapped the Nationalists, forcing
the diversion of resources from economic development to purchase
weapons.

For the arsenal workers, China's particular path of development had
severe long-term consequences. As a latecomer in the process of industrialization, the Nationalist state played a central role in guiding the industry, which also heightened its proclivity to authoritarianism. The increased economic and political importance accorded the ordnance
industry made its factories centers of political control and propaganda.
While the dire economic conditions facing the wartime industry and the
weighty political symbolism of the arsenals exacerbated the siege mentality among managers and government bureaucrats, they remained confident that their tight labor controls would be effective, because both
workers and the state perceived Japan as their primary enemy. Since industry in wartime Nationalist-controlled territory was no longer dominated by foreign capital, the emergence of "class-inflected anti-imperialist nationalism" to spark the labor movement, as had happened in coastal
cities during the 1920s, was all the more difficult.[2] But the high degree of
state industrial management also politicized workers' resistance to their
bosses and raised workers' expectations of the state's obligations to
workers for their wartime sacrifices. The question of how a highly inter-
ventionist state shaped labor relations in the defense industry is pursued
in subsequent chapters.

The Qing Legacy and Industrial Development

Reform and state economic intervention had characterized China's pioneering industry since the late Qing dynasty. Between 1861 and 1895,
seeking to resist the dual threat of Western encroachment and internal rebellion, the imperial state embarked on a program of rapid military industrialization. Arms were crucial to the empire's salvation and future
glory. As Feng Guifen, the leading advocate of the so-called self-strengthening movement, argued, "Eventually we must consider manufacturing,
repairing, and using weapons by ourselves. . . . Only thus will we be able
to pacify the empire; only thus can we play a leading role on the globe;
and only thus shall we restore our original strength, and redeem ourselves
from former humiliations."[3] By the end of the Qing dynasty, the government and its prominent viceroys managed over a dozen large-scale arse-

nals, the most prominent of which were established in Shanghai (by Zeng Guofan and Li Hongzhang in 1865), Nanjing (by Li Hongzhang in 1865), Hanyang (by Zhang Zhidong in 1890), and Tianjin (managed by Li Hongzhang in 1875).

Qing efforts to build a defense industry, however, had mixed results. Munitions plants pioneered the use of steam-powered machinery, and in the span of thirty years, they produced steel breech-loading guns and smokeless powder ammunition, which made possible the use of quick-firing guns and magazine rifles. Yet the civil service exam system continued to be the chief provider of prestige and power to aspiring bureaucrats and thus hindered acceptance of technical managers. "[T]he civil service was the towering institution in China, and duty in the arsenals was only a steppingstone for civil servants," John Rawlinson notes.[4] A combination of high personnel costs for the salaries of foreigners and Chinese officials, conflicting financial and strategic priorities on the part of government and military industrial leadership, and all too frequent encounters with charlatans posing as foreign advisors also thwarted the self-strengthening movement. These problems, compounded by insufficient natural and human resources, impeded military modernization and rendered the industry vulnerable to technological dependence on foreign powers and to imperialist pressures.[5] The Qing rulers' struggle for greater economic autonomy foreshadows the future history of China's arms industry.

Extensive state economic intervention was the most noticeable link between late imperial times and the 1920s. Although numerous small machine shops engaged in repair work and limited production of light arms and gunpowder, the need for large financial resources and the strategic demands of militarists restricted the expansion of privately run arsenals.[6] The bulk of the defense industry continued to fall under state control and ownership, as represented by provincial governments and regional warlords. Arsenals remained dependent on state financing, government orders and loans, and bureaucratic appointments. When the central government drew up production quotas to supply its armies during the early 1930s, it was no surprise that it ignored private weapon manufacturers.

Another important continuity with the late Qing dynasty was the arms industry's isolation from other industrial sectors and its continued dependence on foreign technology. Internecine warfare and the high demand for arms during the warlord era may have "spread a new industry across China's map," but reliance on foreign machinery impeded "spinoff," or technology diffusion from the public to the private sector.[7] The close links between modern armament production and the availability of specialized steel in China help explain why military industrialization did not stimulate economic growth in other sectors. Manufacturing more advanced weapons called for tungsten carbide steel, an extremely hard metal, requiring specialized cutting tools and machinery.[8] Given its technological capacity during the 1920s, it is unlikely that the Chinese metallurgical industry could produce such machine tools. The Shanghai steel plant, a prominent supplier, for instance, smelted steel, using a Siemens-Martin hearth, solely for the production of rifle barrels and gun mounts, but not machine parts or tools.[9] Arsenals continued to import high-quality steel parts, gun tubes, and artillery shells, suggesting a high degree of assembly work and, by extension, greater demand for cheaper and less skilled labor. Importing steel parts also obviated the need to build machine tools to cut and shape steel, thus limiting possible "spin-off" effects on China's machine industry.

Because so much of China's military buildup took place in the late nineteenth century, by the eve of the 1927 Nationalist revolution, the machinery in its arsenals had become dilapidated, exacerbating reliance on labor-intensive technology. With the important exception of the arsenals in the northeast controlled by the warlord Zhang Zuolin, increased production during the 1910s and 1920s derived more from extensive exploitation of the labor force than from "rapid military modernization."[10] The Jinling arsenal exemplified the outdated equipment of most arsenals. Established by the viceroy and self-strengthening proponent Li Hongzhang in 1865 as the Jinling manufacturing bureau, the plant consisted of both gun and cartridge factories. During the next three decades, the Nanjing-based arsenal added two machinery workshops, a steel-rolling factory, and a copper smelter. Much of the expansion occurred in the 1880s with purchases of new machinery and foreign materials. In 1887, a large machinery plant was established, which would eventually be converted to produce guns, and would still be in use in the early 1930s. Managers made a final renovation in 1908, when they purchased twenty-five machines from Germany to manufacture small guns and dies. Besides building a smokeless powder plant in 1927, the 1908 purchase represented the last effort to modernize machinery before the Nationalist reforms in 1934. Small wonder that American observers concluded in 1930 that its machinery was dilapidated and in need of "constant repair."[11]

Even the Taiyuan arsenal, which by the late 1920s had one of China's largest production capacities, reflected a mixture of Western technology and exploitative labor practices, enforced by domineering foremen. Foreign technicians from Krupp and the Danish firm Nielson and Winther were employed as advisors in production departments (large workshops known as *zhizao suo)*, and many of the department heads held technical degrees from the United States. The gunpowder plant had been established as recently as 1926 and equipped with German machinery, allowing the Shanxi warlord Yan Xishan to become self-reliant for munitions.[12] Nevertheless, Taiyuan depended more on manual labor than on mechanical advances. Factories had no systematic examination of products or inspection equipment. The cartridge and rifle workshops lacked gauges, rendering impractical standard practices such as rifling or the examination of initial velocities. Without specialized equipment, standard materials, or inspection molds, the machine-gun plant could not check for quality control. These conditions reinforced the dominant position of older foremen, who relied on their experience to replicate weaponry and machinery. At the height of its production, Taiyuan employed eight thousand workers, including numerous children to load ammunition. The notoriously tight-fisted Yan preferred child labor, because it was cheap, although this did not stop him from paying adult workers lower wages than at most other arsenals.[13]

Long hours and poor working conditions characterized employment at most armories. Jinling workers toiled in dark workshops for fourteen-hour shifts, guided only by a single light bulb hung over their machines. "Practically all machinery is belt driven by overhead shafting, actuated by large electric motors," an American observer noted of the Hanyang arsenal. "The shops are a maze of belting. Lighting is poor." Thirteen-hour work days lasting as late as 10 P.M. worsened conditions, because workers could inadvertently mangle their arms in machine shafting.[14] Abuse of unfree labor compounded these arduous working conditions. Managers used coercion and the threat of conscription to discipline workers. "The [Hanyang] director stated that it was well known among the laborers that if any disaffection was noted the guilty ones would be sent for assignment to the front."[15] The social composition of the workforce probably facilitated managerial control. Many arsenal workers during the warlord era came from the ranks of the army, a practice begun under the Qing dynasty. No doubt, managers hoped to recruit men they considered obedient and of good stock. Of necessity, these recruitment practices were abandoned during the War of Resistance against Japan, but one could still find veteran soldiers listed on the work rolls.

To be sure, the 1920s witnessed production advances. The enforcement of the Arms Embargo Agreement (May 1919–April 1929) was one reason China's arms industry expanded. The United States implemented the unprecedented embargo, in which it was followed by Britain and France, ostensibly to prevent civil war and promote economic stability within China, but also to curb Japan's political influence over Beijing through the sale of arms.[16] Britain's control of key shipping routes led to a sharp drop in China's arms imports, as reflected by its balance of international payments. To offset this decrease, domestic output rose dramatically, especially during the latter half of the decade, coinciding with the 1926 Northern Expedition, Chiang Kai-shek's military campaign to reunify the country.[17]

If the warlord era witnessed a modernization of warfare, what Arthur Waldron has termed a "military revolution," warfare did not necessarily boost the fortunes of the arms industry or stimulate economic growth in other industrial sectors. Warlord battles and changes in political fortunes among contending regional armies often led to partial or complete dismantling of arsenals. The Zhangjiakou, Dezhou, Lihe, Jiaodao, Sichuan, Kaifeng, and Zhengzhou arsenals, for example, were either subsumed under larger plants or shut down.[18] Through the 1920s, the defense industry continued to rely on despotic labor regimes, based on exploitation and abysmal working conditions, and remained relatively isolated from other industries and the private sector. Thus the "military revolution" of the 1920s characterized the scale of warfare more than any qualitative change in the production of weaponry. When the Nationalists came to power in 1928, they found a defense industry in dire need of reform. Superficially, undeveloped technology in the form of human resources and production processes limited China's weapons' production, but the root problem was political. The division of the country, weakened by foreign domination, impeded economic development and the modernization of the arms industry. "In this twentieth century of ours, eagles glare and tigers stalk; the weak fall prey to the strong," *Binggong yuekan* (Ordnance Industry Monthly) warned. "In an era where the mighty are duplicitous, if we lack weaponry, we cannot speak of war; if we are not self-sufficient in arms production, how can we talk of nation building?"[19]

China's weak international status had contributed to the passage of the arms embargo, as well as an unintended outcome of the embargo—the promotion of illegal arms trafficking. After World War I and throughout the 1920s, warlords' voracious appetite for arms and a surfeit of cheap weapons in Europe benefited arms merchants in search of new markets and dumping grounds. Although China may have increased its supply of weaponry at a cheaper cost, most arms were discards from World War I. China's army was "an exhibition gallery for weapons from 10,000 countries," a critic mocked. As much as 80 percent of the one million rifles borne by Nationalist soldiers in 1929 were "old and damaged."[20]

The production and maintenance of so many different weapons delayed the standardization of small arms and impeded mass production. Managers at Shanghai's Jiangnan arsenal, for instance, became exhausted trying to fulfill government orders for eight different rifles and four different machine guns.[21] Repairs caused tremendous backlogs, because machinery had to be coordinated with the various caliber makes. Imprecision and sub par standards also had fatal consequences for soldiers on the battlefield. "There is a deplorable lack of appreciation of exactness and precision (common to all arsenals in China) which results in faulty weapons and munitions turned out to the troops in the field; this is particularly true in the case of small arms ammunition, to the extent that gun jams are the rule rather than the exception," a foreign military observer noted.[22] Artisans continued to rely on their experience to replicate parts and of necessity resorted to cruder production techniques.[23] Hanyang machinists during the late 1920s, for instance, assembled machine guns, rifles, and revolvers with parts and bolts that had been hand-filed to achieve a fit.[24] "Mechanism roughly machined and parts are therefore often not interchangeable," a U.S. consul noted of Chinese-made rifles in 1930 (although production of substitutable parts may have begun during the mid 1920s).[25]

Political rivalries among militarists also influenced the diffusion of arms technology and impeded uniformity in the type of model. By and large, arsenals did not transfer technology between themselves. Their geographical isolation—spread out among various provinces—prevented greater collaboration and convergence. Significant technological innovations occurred during the warlord era, especially the replication and modification of foreign small arms, but these remained loosely coordinated. It often took more time for arsenals to adopt a similar make of weapon than it did for them to replicate a foreign model. Weapons production and competition over the latest caliber model tended to reinforce the political rivalries of provincial militarists. Between 1919 and 1923, for instance, four war plants replicated five different makes of machine guns but refused to share technology.[26] Instead, they used weaponry to compete in a domestic "arms race." During the 1920s and early 1930s, as if to advertise their own expertise and goad their competition, munitions plants even named their gun makes after the specific arsenal.

State Intervention and the Ordnance Department

Military industrial reforms to achieve economic self-sufficiency and military modernization thus quickly followed the ascension of Chiang Kai-shek's Nationalist government in Nanjing. Under the jurisdiction of the Ministry of Military Affairs (Junzheng Bu), the Ordnance Department (Binggong Shu) was established on November 6, 1928, along with other branches of the defense industry: the Army Department, the Aeronautics Department, and the Office of Military Supplies. These measures signaled the Nationalists' desire to intensify state planning and consolidate their control of the defense industry. Although the state had traditionally managed the armament industry, the regional polarization of the country between 1912 and 1927 belied whatever influence the northern-based Beiyang government's Ministry of the Army had exercised over its arsenals. In practice, the ministry had supervised only four arsenals, located at Hanyang, Gongxian (Henan), Shanghai, and Dexian (Shandong). These conditions prompted the Ordnance Department to proclaim its mission to be "ordnance reconstruction and management of the entire nation's arsenals."[27]

Consequently, the politics of arsenal dominance was just as important as rearmament, if not more so. Although the Nationalists had launched their new government in 1928 premised on the elimination of regional militarists and the unification of China, "residual warlordism" continued to rule the provinces. Over the course of the Nanjing decade (1927–37), provincial militarists aggressively resisted the extension of central government control over their arsenals, since these buttressed their own military and political autonomy. The point was not lost on Chiang Kai-shek. By 1930, Chiang was so desperate to eliminate Yan Xishan that he ordered daily bombing raids on his rival's arsenal at Taiyuan. Provincial plants, especially those in the north and central plains, maintained an independent stance against the Nationalist government until the Japanese threat proved too dire. By then, the eleventh-hour change often hampered the government's complete takeover of arsenals, such as at Taiyuan.[28] Nationalist state-building efforts through industrial takeovers achieved greater success in southeastern China. There, too, Chiang faced direct resistance when the military leaders Chen Jitang and Li Zongren rebelled in June 1936 for greater autonomy in Guangdong and Guangxi Provinces. Their abortive uprising, however, allowed the Ordnance Department to consolidate the three major Guangdong armories by the fall of 1936. This takeover proved a major coup for the Nationalist government, since two of the munitions plants had advanced German machinery for artillery production and "secret production designs" for chemical weapons and gas masks.[29]

Chiang's desire to quell civil disorder motivated him, not only to move against his provincial rivals, but also to reorient the location of arsenals. In part, Japan's occupation of Shenyang prompted Nationalist military leaders to reevaluate their industrial planning in light of other arsenals' geographic vulnerability. The chiefs of staff considered war plants in the interior, such as Gongxian and Hanyang, ideal locations and designated them for expansion. Machinery from the Shanghai arms plant, which had shut down after Japanese bombing raids in January 1932, was shipped to Hanyang and Jinling. Machinery from two smaller munitions plants, Dezhou and Kaifeng, was transferred to the Jinan arsenal. In a 1932 memorandum sent to the Ministry of Military Affairs, the chiefs of staff recommended eventually relocating the Jinling and Jinan plants to "safe areas" further inland. Fear that relocation would disrupt urgently needed production of artillery shells to bombard the Communist Jiangxi Soviet prevented an immediate transfer of the two war plants. "From the perspective of national security, the Jinan and Jinling arsenals should be moved to safe areas . . . but because relocation will diminish their supply of ammunition for the purpose of pacification, we should temporarily put a halt to relocation except for what is essential," the memorandum noted.[30]

The central government's desire for tight political control over the ordnance industry thus overrode any economic and strategic rationale. The state mandated that all products from state yards be shipped to and distributed from Jinling.[31] Consequently, rather than being moved to the interior, as the plan had recommended, the Jinling arsenal remained in the capital, along with other industrial research institutes and laboratories, where it was vulnerable to Japanese attack. By late 1932, these mergers and relocations left the Ordnance Department with nominal control of thirteen factories and actual control of six arsenals: Jinan, Hanyang, the Hanyang powder works, Gongxian, Jinling, and the Shanghai steel mill.[32]

Reconstruction, the second component of the arms industry's mission, took as its premise the development of professional managers. From the start, Chiang Kai-shek stressed able leadership, as reflected in the choice of Zhang Qun as director of the Ordnance Department. A member of Chiang's inner circle, Zhang had been his classmate at military academy and also had close ties with the founder of the German advisory mission in China, Max Bauer.[33] Like many in the top managerial ranks, Zhang's close ties to Germany proved crucial to China's military modernization. Yet Zhang left his post soon afterward, in 1929, to become mayor of Shanghai. He was succeeded by Chen Yi and Hong Zhong, both of whom had equally brief tenures. Finally, it fell to Yu Dawei to build up China's defense industry as director of the Ordnance Department between January 1933 and December 1945.

Born in Shaoxing, Zhejiang, in 1896, Yu Dawei came from an illustrious family closely associated with military modernization and the late Qing reform movement in Hunan Province. If Yu was characterized by common denominators among his family, they were a calling to serve the nation and advocacy of reform. His mother, Zeng Guangshan, was a poet in her own right and the granddaughter of Zeng Guofan, dynastic savior during the devastating Taiping rebellion and an early proponent of self-strengthening. Yu Dawei's uncle and father both had some influence in military circles. In the wake of the first Sino-Japanese War of 1894–95, Yu Dawei's uncle, Yu Mingzhen, and his father, Yu Wengming, were commissioned to survey Japan's military education. On their return to China, both men headed military academies. Yu Mingzhen, a former Hanlin scholar and noted poet, became administrator of the Nanjing Naval Academy. Yu Wengming directed the Hunan Army Primary School, where his pupils included future governors of the province, such as Tang Shengzhi and Cheng Qian. By the time of the 1898 Hundred Days reform movement, which he enthusiastically supported because of its promise to restore China's wealth and power, Yu Wenming held the post of Qing military commander.[34]

Such a pedigree might have predisposed Yu Dawei toward a military career, but his schooling suggests the opposite. Precocious and brilliant by all accounts, Yu Dawei began studying the classics at the age of five under the tutelage of Xing Muxiang, a Hunan *juren* degree holder. After his family moved east, he attended middle school at Shanghai, skipping several grades in the process. He then went to St. John's University in Shanghai and graduated in three years with a degree in literature. An interest in English, which he had begun learning as a child at home, took him to

Harvard in 1918. Enrolling in the department of philosophy, while also studying mathematics, he completed his Ph.D. within three years. With a Sheldon Travel Grant to research mathematical logic at Berlin University, Yu Dawei started an eleven-year sojourn in Germany in 1921.

Intellectual excitement marked Yu Dawei's first few years in Berlin. Yu studied philosophy with Alois Riehl (an expert on Nietzsche), attended the lectures of Albert Einstein, and published an article on mathematical logic in *Mathematische Annalen*, the renowned journal of David Hilbert and Einstein. Only gradually did he turn to a vocation in the military and ordnance. Yu Dawei never received formal training in the subject, but as part of his self-education, he began to meet informally with German field staff officers to study ballistics and the related fields of artillery and military strategy. In 1928, when Chen Yi led a delegation to inspect German industry, he appointed Yu to head the Trade Department affiliated with the Chinese Embassy in Berlin. During the next four years, Yu oversaw Sino-German arms negotiations and played a vital role in establishing a framework for the close ties between German industry, the military, and the Nationalist government. Acting on the recommendation of Max Bauer, Chiang Kai-shek's first military advisor, Yu started formal studies in German staff officer education. By 1932, his talents and knowledge of the European military theater so impressed Chiang Kai-shek that he recommended Yu for the post of directing secretary at General Staff Headquarters with the rank of major general. Yu politely declined the promotion, preferring to become chief instructor of weaponry at the Central Training Corps. In January 1933, though, acting on the recommendation of his chief military advisor, General Hans von Seeckt, Chiang appointed Yu Dawei to direct the Ordnance Department and promoted him to lieutenant general.

Yu Dawei immediately began to reform the arms industry as part of a broader military modernization program that the Nationalists spearheaded with German military and technical aid. By 1931, some sixty German advisors resided in China, helping to reorganize the Nationalist army and establish a blueprint for industrial reform. Yu drew on his foreign experience to use as many as ten German advisors in the Ordnance Department. With their help, Yu introduced mass production methods, established research and technological institutes, and reformed management.[35] Engineers were struck by the modern scientific elements they associated with German managerial methods and mechanical advances of the prewar period: "The German managerial style was predominant. . . .

They reformed the engineering designs. This was based on the most recent German ways—the best shortcut to complete work. Productivity
was raised, because less productive forces were used. Relatively good machinery was used; equipment reached scientific standards. From the
standpoint of design, complete sets of equipment were German."[36] Reforms helped cut costs and raised standards of production. According to
American military observers, by 1934, both the Gongxian and Hanyang
arsenals had reduced production costs and improved the quality of output because of "the more efficient management and more honest supervision of the present Director-General of Arsenals and his German advisors."[37]

American military observers lauded Yu's hands-on managerial style:
"Yu Dawei exercises personal supervision over the purchasing, manufacturing, organization and research departments of all the arsenals. He is
making an earnest and conscientious endeavor to better the quality of the
output, improve the installations and methods and to reduce as far as
possible the operating expenses and cost of production. It is believed that
considerable headway is being made in this respect."[38] With Yu at the
helm, the Ordnance Department parceled out responsibilities among
three branches: Technology, Natural Resources and Production. The
Technology branch would play an important role in standardizing
weaponry and procuring technology through reverse engineering, the
practice of buying technology to reproduce it domestically. The Production branch established uniform standards for production and materials
and introduced an audit system. A highly educated staff specialized in engineering, ordnance, and metallurgy oversaw these three branches. Over
80 percent of the 1929 Ordnance Department leadership had university
degrees. Half had studied abroad, chiefly in Japan, and attended elite
schools, such as Tokyo Imperial University, Harvard, MIT, and the Berlin
Technische Hochschule.[39]

Interchangeable Manufacture and
Weapon Standardization

Zhou Zixin is a prime example of how important technically qualified
personnel were to China's military industrialization. After majoring in
German at Tongji University in Shanghai, Zhou studied precision instruments and optics at the Berlin Technische Hochschule between 1929 and
1934. Under his guidance, the Nationalists sponsored the Baishuiqiao

Precision Research Institute in order to achieve parity with Western producers and decrease reliance on imports. Planning began in December 1934 and production two years later. After acquiring extremely advanced precision equipment from Germany, Zhou created the first research center in China able to manufacture gauges (*yangban*), precision tools used for interchangeable manufacture and factory control.

Defense plants used two types of gauges, the master block (*duiban*) and the working gauge. Master blocks tested the tolerance of working gauges, while the working gauge, as its name implies, was used in the workshop to measure the precision of parts. Master blocks were ranked in ascending order of precision as Class A, double-A, and triple-A. Signaling just how far and how rapidly armament technology would develop, the Nationalist arsenals began using double-A blocks during the War of Resistance, an extraordinary feat at the time.[40] Gauge departments assiduously protected the master block from being touched, in order to prevent wear, and only used the tools to test tolerance, the variance in dimension between the original and copied parts. Extremely skilled workmen made working gauges, which they placed alongside the master block to see if they sealed hermetically, a mark of success. The level of precision obtained by these gauges reached up to 1/100,000 of an inch, making them the most precise in China. Their use helped produce bores for weapons, such as the widely used 7.9-mm caliber rifle, that maintained a tolerance level of less than .04 millimeters, thinner than a strand of hair. Workers and technicians in assembly and repair shops used fairly high level working gauges to inspect gun barrels, stocks, and shell parts for factory quality control.

The importance of gauges is difficult to exaggerate. By achieving far greater precision, they facilitated interchangeable manufacturing of guns of standardized caliber, a cornerstone of Western gun manufacturing since the mid nineteenth century and an important precursor to mass production.[41] Mass production in turn rendered the industry more self-sufficient and reduced the constant and severe shortages afflicting the poorly equipped Nationalist army during the early 1940s. Mass production changed the social landscape of the shop floor, creating structural conditions conducive to class formation. Gauges accelerated production and altered power relations on the shop floor by diminishing management's reliance on experienced artisans to check precision. Although the production of gauges required extremely skilled workers, once they had been produced, machine operatives could use them to make individual parts more easily. Widespread use of gauges reduced dependence on highly skilled artisans during the War of Resistance and opened the factory gates to less skilled workers and Sichuan's rural proletariat.

The Ordnance Department's investment in optical instruments was closely linked to the advent of machine tools and the search for greater mechanical precision. Optical equipment served to ascertain the precision of gauges. The working gauge was measured against gauge blocks, which were rectified by calibrators, whose accuracy in turn was initially based on light-wave precision measurements. In December 1934, Zhou Zixin obtained Chiang Kai-shek's approval to establish an optical instrument repair plant near the Baishuiqiao Precision Research Institute, but it would take several years to complete and only after arduous negotiations with the Zeiss optical firm.[42]

The development of precision production and interchangeable manufacture led to greater uniformity of weapons. Whereas political rivalries during the warlord era had impeded uniform advances in military technology, Nationalist unification improved conditions for standardization. Still, in December 1934, Chiang Kai-shek found reason to worry that China's strategic vulnerability stemmed from the indiscriminate use of foreign technology and lack of standardization:

Our country's current armament supply is largely bought from abroad. The dangers this involves the moment an incident [i.e., war] occurs go without saying. The habitual lack of regulations for weapon manufacturing, for organizational drafting, and for the compilation of drill books has resulted in a total absence of definitive standards. We continue to invite any foreign advisor, buy weapons from any foreign country, adopt their organization and drill books, and thus lose the rationale for our own military buildup.[43]

For Chiang and Yu Dawei, weapon standardization was crucial to achieving a self-sufficient and productive arms industry, and hence to modernizing China's military equipment. The Nationalist government's close ties with German military advisors further accelerated the standardization of arms that were predominantly based on German prototypes.

It was precisely during this period that Sino-German military and economic ties grew closer, affecting the dynamics of weapon standardization. Relations between the two countries were shifting from informal ties based on the central role of military advisors as middlemen to more formal, albeit covert, military and economic ties between government-sponsored administrations. The process culminated in the August 23, 1934, drafting of important credit and barter agreements between the Nationalist government and Hapro, the Handelsgesellschaft für Industrielle Produkte, a private trading company that the arms merchant Hans Klein managed in coordination with the German Military and Finance Ministry. German advisors played a critical role in advocating the modernization of China's defense industry. Chiang Kai-shek's second military advisor, Georg Wetzell, brought in the ordnance specialist Lieutenant General Karlowski to help Yu Dawei standardize weaponry. Karlowski's stay of only five months in 1932 cut short the full realization of his mission. But the appointment on November 11, 1933, of General Hans von Seeckt as Chiang's advisor-general marked a turning point for the two countries. Part of Seeckt's appeal stemmed from his advocacy of a self-sufficient arms industry to sustain the Nationalist government's modernized defense forces. But until that was achieved, the elite troops that Seeckt sought to create would have to be supplied with weaponry purchased abroad from the same industrial firms that were aiding China build up its domestic military industry. Only by these means, Seeckt argued, would weapon standardization be ensured.

Seeckt's tacit support for German industrial interests did have an inherent logic and fell on receptive ears. The Ordnance Department achieved considerable success in standardizing weapons through technology transfers that accompanied large-scale armament transactions with Germany between 1933 and 1935. Specifically, the transfer of gauges allowed arsenals to manufacture their weapons based on German models, hence eliminating the plethora of foreign makes. China's military leaders purchased weapons, not only for their immediate use, but also to study their manufacture so that they could eventually produce the same weaponry. Both Chiang Kai-shek and Yu Dawei were forceful proponents of reverse engineering. They accordingly advised Ministers of Finance T. V. Soong and Kong Xiangxi to make sure that they obtained complete sets of gauges, designs, and work charts when negotiating with the Germans over the purchase of a Bofors-style 15-cm mountain gun, a German 20-cm cannon, and the 7.92-mm Mauser rifle.[44]

Chinese Ordnance Department leaders regarded standardization as so critical that it overrode their concerns over the high prices charged for German weapons and equipment. In 1935, the price of German-manufactured tanks was 40 percent higher than world market prices. German steel, ordnance materials, and chemicals were 30 percent more expensive.[45] Hapro, as was customary among arms dealers, skimmed money off the top by raising prices after goods reached China. No surprise that Chiang Kai-shek somewhat bitterly told his ministers, "This merchant is intent on nothing but profit, give him an inch and he'll take a mile."[46]

Nevertheless, reverse engineering allowed China's military industry to standardize and establish prototypes for much of its weaponry prior to the outbreak of war in 1937. Besides both light and heavy machine guns and rifles, after 1931, each factory successively converted to mass-producing wooden-handled hand grenades based on the German E model, which Gongxian had initially replicated in 1922.[47] Finally, the Ordnance Department played a key role in standardizing the mortar. In 1930, after purchasing the French 1930 Boulanger 81-mm trench mortar, Jinling quickly produced a copy. Its subsequent replication and modification of an 82-mm caliber mortar also became a standard national weapon and was produced on a mass scale. Reflecting the armament industry's technological advances and its ability to adapt and innovate, by 1934, Jinling had successfully manufactured a complete set of gauges. In sum, these examples demonstrate an ability to tide over the phase of "technological indigestion," a common ill facing developing countries on the receiving end of technology transfers.[48] The Ordnance Department's ability to standardize armaments and introduce interchangeable manufacture radically improved the quality of weaponry and facilitated mass production of various light weapons.

Centralization and the Five-Year Plan

While standardizing weaponry, the Nationalist government continued consolidating control over the military industry. Centralization involved incorporating arsenals controlled by provincial militarists, reorganizing and merging them under the Ordnance Department's control, and establishing new plants. In 1932, the Ordnance Department articulated these goals and that of increasing production in a Five-Year Plan.[49] Although implementation inevitably diverged from planning, the plan offers insights into how the defense industry began to mobilize for war.

According to the 1932 plan, China's defense industry would expand through both imports and domestic production and gradually become self-sufficient. Ultimately, Chinese military strategists hoped to be able to equip forty divisions within ten years, allotting the first two years to organizing and preparing equipment and the remaining eight years to production.[50] The Ordnance Department anticipated importing foreign weapons for three years and then converting to domestic production.[51] The first two years would require updating machinery, reorganizing factories, and completing construction of new arsenals. By the third year, production would supply four divisions; by the fifth year, arsenals operating at maximum capacity would supply five divisions a year.

Meeting these goals depended on the construction of a large-scale modern arsenal at Zhuzhou in Hunan Province. Consisting of an artillery plant, shell factory, and gun cartridge plant, Zhuzhou was intended to overcome severe deficiencies in the production of artillery and shells, since the Nationalist industry supplied only 10 percent of the current demand for shells. The National Defense Planning Committee also envisioned a daily production capacity of 1.7 million cartridges, an enormous figure, considering the production capacity of China's other arsenals.[52] Li Daichen, assistant ordnance director, estimated a construction cost of U.S.$16 million (Ch$80 million) and advocated constructing ancillary plants for secondary materials (smelted steel, smelted copper, and gunpowder) needed to attain self-sufficiency within five years.[53]

Zhuzhou lay at the heart of the central government's project to develop the military defense infrastructure of central and southern China. Anticipating the 1936 Three-Year Plan promoted by the other state institution spearheading industrial development, the National Resources Commission (NRC), the Ordnance Department chose many of the same sites to develop and supply Zhuzhou with raw and secondary materials.[54] Leaders of the NRC and the Ordnance Department envisioned a geographic reorientation to an "internal economic center" to compensate for the potential loss of coal mines in northeastern China and anticipate probable Japanese control of iron ore deposits in Anhui, Jiangsu, and Zhejiang.[55] Construction at Zhuzhou had several strategic advantages over arsenals situated along the more exposed coastal area. Storage tunnels for protection against enemy bombing or gas attack could be excavated in the continuous stretch of mountains to the east. The nearby cities of Changsha, Xiangtan, and Wuhan provided a large labor pool. Furthermore, the development of transport routes by water and rail, both of which were being promoted for the export of primary materials to Germany, linked Zhuzhou to the rich mineral reserves of antimony, tin, and coal in Hunan and Hubei.[56]

Faith in autarky and fear of total war mobilized GMD military leaders to support the Zhuzhou arsenal. Curiously, though, the planners flirted with the idea of ceding control over the industrial complex to a foreign company. Suggested as an alternative to funding by the Ministry of Finance, and perhaps as a goad to obtain Chiang Kai-shek's financial backing, the 1932 plan envisioned having "renowned foreign industrialists with abundant capital" invest in the new arsenal.[57] In theory, the Nationalist government would gradually buy back shares in the plant and fully nationalize it within eight years. Given the timing of the proposal at the height of the worldwide depression, the scheme was nothing more than a pipe dream.

Ultimately, the Nationalist government retained control of the project, but lack of financial support delayed construction. Soon after the plan had been drafted, Chiang scaled down the ordnance proposal in August 1932. The Generalissimo proposed a construction period of five years rather than the initial two years, reduced funding, and set much more modest goals for production quotas and armament purchases. Chiang proposed equipping ten divisions in five years. Zhuzhou and other arsenals would equip one division per year, while imported weapons would supply another division.[58]

In compliance with Chiang Kai-shek's wishes, Ordnance Director Hong Zhong's new budget extended the plan to five years and decreased ordnance production and imports. Particularly striking, given that so much of China's production capacity had been lost with Japan's annexation of Manchuria, was the extent of reliance on Zhuzhou. The annual production budget for the new arsenal during the last two years of the plan totaled U.S.$7.6 million, which surpassed by $400,000 the combined budget of all other Nationalist arsenals. Despite the inherent risks, Chiang Kai-shek overrode policy recommendations to distribute production of each major weapon among two to three munitions plants. Arms industry leaders sought to prevent the complete loss of a weapons type if an arsenal was destroyed.[59] Chiang, on the other hand, felt that a concentration of technology, machinery, and supplies within one arsenal complex had a greater economic rationale and would also be easier to control politically.

Despite ambitious construction plans, the Zhuzhou arsenal's grandeur was more symbolic than real. Chiang Kai-shek waited until February 10, 1936, four years after the plan had been conceived, to even authorize financial support for the construction project. Protracted negotiations with the Berlin Hapro office over China's industrial development and barter agreements contributed to the delay. These delays impeded the delivery of imported machinery for Zhuzhou. Consequently, managers shelved their plans for an artillery plant, an artillery shell factory, and a cartridge fac-tory.[60] By the time war struck, only the general office, railroad tracks, and road to the colossal 767-acre complex had been completed; the civil engineering project for the various workshops had just begun. Engineers resorted to constructing workshops with machinery from the Shanghai and Gongxian arsenals and the entire artillery plant of Hanyang. By March 1938, mass production of cartridges, at the rate of 400,000 per day, had started and proved critical to the war effort. Yet from the standpoint of the Five-Year Plan, the dream of building a modern arms complex never materialized. At best, the long-awaited machinery for the production of light artillery arrived within the year and would be relocated to Chongqing.[61]

Ordnance Department leaders had more success expanding ancillary industries, such as chemical plants. The legacy of chemical warfare during World War I and the fear that Japan would use poison gas, such as arsenic and mustard gas, in future attacks on China accelerated research into chemical warfare.[62] In 1931, the Ministry of Military Affairs established a Chemical Warfare Arsenal Bureau as part of the Ordnance Department administration in Nanjing. Over eight hundred high school students were recruited and trained in Nanjing to serve in a preparatory gas defense squad.[63] In October 1934, the Ordnance Department established the Applied Chemistry Research Institute to oversee gas defense technology, medical treatment for gas warfare, and chemical warfare. The Nanjing institute trained military officers to propagate defense planning against poisonous gas attack. University faculty throughout China were also mobilized to research gas defense technology and to help produce flares, incendiary bombs, smoke bombs, and canisters.[64]

Research in chemical warfare coincided with an expansion of the chemical industry's productive capacity, relying heavily on American technical assistance. In April 1932, the Nationalist government sent Wu Qinlie—a graduate in chemical engineering of MIT, Chicago, and the Friedrich-Wilhelms-Universität in Bonn, and acting committee member of the Ordnance Research Committee—to order and buy machinery in the United States for a chemical munitions plant. Upon his return to China, Wu oversaw the construction of a chemical plant in Xiao-yi, Henan, near the Gongxian arsenal. By the spring of 1934, engineers from the Lake Erie and Monsanto Chemical companies, working in tandem with Chinese engineers, designed and installed chemical warfare agent plants and assembly plants. On February 1, 1936, Wu Qinlie assumed the post of factory director and formally established the arsenal, the so-called Gongxian arsenal branch factory.[65]

Besides expanding production by building new war plants, the Ordnance Department modernized older ones, such as Jinling. Much of the credit can be ascribed to the Jinling director, Li Chenggan. Born in 1888 in Hunan Province, a center of late Qing reform and revolution, Li became an avid proponent of *shiye jiuguo*—"industrialization for the nation's salvation." As he proclaimed on the eve of the 1911 revolution, "My country cannot achieve order unless we overthrow autocracy; nor can we achieve strength unless we vigorously develop industry." At the time, Li was studying engineering in Japan, sponsored in 1905 by the noted Qing industrialist Zhang Zhidong, founder of the Hanyang Ironworks. Li put aside his studies to return to China and join Huang Xing's revolutionary army battling the Qing. After finally completing a degree in electrical engineering at Tokyo Imperial University and working as an engineer in his native Hunan, as well as at the Hanyang and Jiujiang arsenals, Li found a job in the Works Bureau at Jinling, finally becoming its director in 1931.[66] During the mid 1930s, Li Chenggan invested over U.S.$800,000 to update equipment, buy new machinery, and install new workshops and lodgings.[67] A full third of the construction budget went to build a gauge workshop, reflecting Li's support for precision tools and interchangeable manufacture. New equipment enabled Jinling to become a primary manufacturer of mortars, gas masks, and TNT. The arsenal also substantially increased production of cartridges and Maxim heavy machine guns. Following these reforms, the price of cartridges decreased by a third. Li also spent considerable funds on living accommodations and social welfare for workers. Li's reputation for paternalism followed him in Chongqing, where he implemented elaborate social welfare programs as manager of Nationalist China's largest arsenal.

On balance, the Ordnance Department had a mixed record in meeting the 1932 production quotas. Annual production between 1932 through 1936 surpassed the original quotas in almost all categories of ammunition and light weaponry, enough to supply at least five new divisions per year. The greatest increase in output occurred in 1936, resulting from the modernization of Jinling and Hanyang, the completion of the Gongxian branch arsenal, and the standardization of weaponry.[68] On the other hand, the industry could barely produce artillery and gun shells. Rather than compensate for these glaring deficiencies, caused by delays in the construction of the Zhuzhou arsenal and by difficulties in transferring technology, ordnance management chose to manufacture light weaponry and ammunition, which was also cheaper and more labor-intensive. Arsenal budgets of the mid 1930s reflect this policy. Hanyang, for instance, allocated only 11 percent of its monthly production budget to artillery and shells, while spending the bulk of its funds on rifles, machine guns, and cartridges.[69]

The emphasis on producing light weaponry and ammunition set important precedents for production and strategy during the War of Resistance. Defense industry leaders rationalized their inattention to artillery as a conscious strategy to produce weaponry only if it could be mass-produced. American advisors reached similar conclusions a decade later. "General Yu [Dawei] observed that any weapon that China cannot mass produce is of no value to it. This statement was in partial explanation of why China had concentrated on the smaller, simpler types."[70] China's inability to manufacture artillery led to a selective policy of acquisitions and reverse engineering. According to Lu Zeren, a graduate of the Ordnance School during the war period, Yu Dawei advocated a policy of "buying artillery, manufacturing ammunition" (maipao zaodan). Thus the Ordnance Department sought to buy artillery while acquiring technical materials to manufacture artillery shells.[71]

Budgetary Woes

The failure to rearm in a more comprehensive manner was directly linked to questions of finance. Fiscal policy of the Nanjing decade not only limited spending on economic development but was the root cause of China's hyperinflation crisis during the 1940s. Between 1928 and 1937, Chiang Kai-shek used half of each year's fiscal outlay on military expenses in attempting to exterminate the Communists. Of the remainder, 30 percent went to repay foreign debts and interest on government bonds. The government's own outlay on civilian and industrial programs never exceeded 18 percent of total expenditures, thus crippling potential economic development. Insufficient revenue sources plagued the Nationalists. The outbreak of the Great Depression made it doubly difficult for China to obtain credit from Western countries. With a weak tax base, the other main source of revenue was borrowing either by bank loan or by issuing government bonds. Given the regime's extortion from members of the business community and the low per capita income of most Chinese, society had few incentives and little capacity to absorb large amounts of bonds. Consequently, during the 1930s, the central government increasingly relied on its four banks to sell bonds as a means of raising revenue and as a guarantee for the same banks to issue currency. Although bonds can be used as a counterinflationary mechanism by draining the money supply, in this instance the more bonds were issued, the more currency was issued. By the time the war broke out, the Nationalist government was already debt-ridden to the tune of 2.2 billion yuan. Once the war started, it continued to issue more bonds, leading to an escalation in the number of bank notes and inflation.[72]

Since "reconstruction" fees derived from government outlay, China's arms industry was quickly shortchanged. As a percentage of the Nationalist budget, the ordnance industry never became a top priority. Treasury budgets of the late 1930s indicate that spending on the ordnance industry outpaced that of all other major industries combined.[73] By 1939, the central government allocated seven times more funding to ordnance than to heavy industry (metallurgy, machinery, chemical, fuel, and electric power). This figure, however, attests more to the low economic status accorded to industry in general than to any favoring of the arms industry. The relative weakness of the arms industry becomes more evident when one compares the government ordnance budget with that of other military sectors, particularly within the budget for national defense reconstruction. The government concentrated its expenditures on defense forces, such as the air force in fiscal 1937 and the army in 1940. The navy, no longer controlled by the Nationalist government after its forced retreat from the coastal areas, did not receive funding after fiscal 1937. Although 1939 marked a surge in expenditures for ordnance, it is striking that spending on the production and purchase of military uniforms exceeded that for the ordnance industry in fiscal year 1937 and again in 1940. The army's subsistence needs, which consumed a disproportionate amount of the military budget, thus diverted funds from the more technical needs of the arms industry.

Taken as a percentage of the entire national budget, the share of ordnance was even smaller. While expenditures for national defense reconstruction between fiscal year 1937 and 1940 averaged 12 percent, ordnance spending through 1940 hovered at just over 4 percent. By contrast, the Nationalists spent far more money on armaments and ordnance equipment purchases. In effect, the Nationalists preferred to rely almost exclusively on importing military hardware rather than allocate funds to their own arms industry. Expenditures on weapon imports for fiscal years

TABLE 1.1

Wartime Reconstruction Expenditures, July 1, 1937–December 31, 1940

(1,000 yuan)

Item	1937	1938	1939	1940
National defense reconstruction	191,149	170,555	357,109	748,381
Army and navy	91,149	60,103	120,206	401,129
Air Force	70,000	57,973	95,843	135,134
Ordnance	30,000	52,479	141,060	212,118
Economic reconstruction	96,146	16,012	143,702	127,108
Heavy industry	15,706	8,000	21,500	67,980
Industry and commerce	80,440	3,425	81,074	37,628
Water conservation	0	4,587	8,458	18,500
Other	0	0	32,670	3,000
Communications/Transport	75,897	60,883	238,648	487,174
Railways	57,000	44,615	122,000	216,535
Highways	18,897	11,470	96,413	228,669
Telegraphs	0	4,798	18,043	38,215
Shipping	0	0	2,192	3,755
Army and navy reconstruction	91,149	60,103	120,206	401,129
Navy	1,439	0	0	0
Transportation and telecommunications equipment	20,480	20,000	31,000	77,718
Uniforms	65,000	37,000	84,000	314,661
Barracks' construction and tools	4,230	3,103	5,206	8,750
Ordnance reconstruction	30,000	52,479	141,060	212,118
Arsenal construction	9,000	11,000	50,000	71,760
Ordnance equipment	20,000	40,000	84,000	120,000
Ordnance storage construction	1,000	1,479	7,060	10,358

SOURCE: Second Historical Archives of China, Nanjing, 367 (2), 270 *juan*, zhanshi jianshe fenxi biao 5; zhanshi geniandu jianshe fenxi biao 1, 2.

1937–38 amounted to 17.1 percent and 11.2 percent respectively of total annual expenditures. The following year marked the greatest expenditure on foreign armaments, at 22.6 percent. Costs dropped precipitously in 1940 once Japan cut off transport routes to China. Expenditures for military affairs, defense reconstruction, war operations, and ordnance purchases comprised over half the total budget between 1937 and 1940. Surprisingly, China's spending equaled or even surpassed that of Japan in 1937, yet overhead costs to support the excessive and outmoded armies gobbled up funding from the central government.[74]

Not all military leaders favored concentrating expenditures on arm imports. Yu Dawei for one questioned the wisdom of importing armaments at the expense of promoting domestic production. Yu may not have considered a policy of autarky possible or even desirable, but he did feel that the high rate of dependence was misguided and thus stressed the need for greater self-sufficiency. "Our country's finances over the years

TABLE 1.2

Nationalist Arsenal Production and Imports, 1937–1939

Weapon	Domestic Production	Imports	Ratio
Machine guns	7,092	47,135	6.6
Rifles	205,000	373,446	1.8
Artillery shells	2,705,352	6,815,863	2.5
Cartridges (1,000 rounds)	384,120	1,079,402	2.8
Mortar shells	1,518,952	690,353	0.5

SOURCES: Wang Guoqiang, *Zhongguo binggong zhizaoye fazhan shi* (Taipei: Niming wenhua shiye gongsi, 1987), 299. U.S. Department of State Records, 893.113/1658; 893.24/438; 893.24/470; 893.24/559; 893.24/584; 893.24/587–88; 893.24/595; 893.24/603; 893.24/608; 893.24/644; 893.24/650; 893.24/671; 893.24/673. Second Historical Archives of China, Nanjing, 367 *quan*, 3804 *juan*. Wang Zhenghua, *Kangzhan shiqi waiguo dui Hua junshi yuanzhu* (Taipei: Huanqiu shuju, 1987), 104, 114.

have been insufficient," he noted to Kong Xiangxi. "We are still unable to build, according to plan, a large-scale plant to manufacture machine guns. Consequently, in this War of Resistance, we rely on foreigners, to our detriment. If we compare prices of domestic products with foreign weapons, considering the amount of weapons we are currently buying, the sum of money we could save by relying on our own production would be enough to build two arsenals with money to spare."[75] Despite Yu Dawei's concerns, the government continued relying heavily on imports throughout the initial period of the war.

The rapid escalation of armament prices in 1937 contributed to the discrepancy between spending on domestic production and imports. China relied exclusively on imports of more costly and advanced weapons, such as aircraft and tanks. But even in areas where the Ordnance Department had striven to become more self-sufficient, as in the production of light weaponry, imports far surpassed domestic production. Only the production of hand grenades and mortar shells, which did not require elaborate production processes, exceeded the amount of imports.

Wartime strategy and China's limited production capacity pushed the Nationalists to buy up sufficient arms supplies. The government may have wished to stockpile weapons, anticipating that Japan would impose a blockade. Between July 1936 and June 1937, the Ordnance Department placed numerous orders for ordnance equipment and secondary materials, such as lead, copper, and steel for artillery shells and gun parts, enough to maintain a year's worth of reserves.[76] An army starving for supplies also underlay the scramble for arms. According to Yu Dawei, combat with the Communists prior to the Sino-Japanese war had reduced Nationalist army supplies to only 9,000 heavy machine guns, 32,000 light machine guns, and 5,000 mortars.[77] He Yingqin underscored China's dire need to increase production of ammunition. Although the defense minister's report estimated that one "arranged" division would consume twenty-four million rifle and machine-gun cartridges per month, annual domestic production during 1937 barely surpassed 100 million rifle cartridges.[78]

The German Connection and the Arms Trade

The imbalance between domestic spending and arms purchases abroad had its roots in trade policies that spanned almost a decade. This might seem surprising, since the dominant role that Germany played in China's arms market was premised on German support for Nationalist economic development and military planning. Indeed, the prime attraction of the 1934 Sino-German agreement for the Nationalist government was its ability to acquire armaments and technology through the barter of strategic raw materials. Barter trade would offset China's weak currency and shortage of foreign exchange. In theory, this arrangement worked in China's favor, because it produced over half of the world's output of antimony and tungsten by the mid 1930s. As these raw materials were vital to Germany's war mobilization, China could pay for its own military industrialization and arms buildup by relying on the increasing demand for and escalating price of ore. Tungsten prices in Europe, for example, doubled between 1932 and 1936, and the maximum price of tungsten in 1937 had increased almost ninefold since 1932. British and U.S. restrictions on the marketing of Burmese tungsten, the other main global source, enhanced China's control of tungsten prices vis-à-vis Germany.[79]

Because of China's control of strategic mineral ores necessary for Germany's rearmament, the two countries forged a relationship based on mutual benefit during the Nanjing decade. While Germany sought new export markets and sources of raw materials, China saw an opportunity to industrialize rapidly with German technical aid. Chinese negotiators of the treaty described its benefits as if manna had fallen from heaven. "Now that our country does not have to pay cash, we can obtain an enormous amount of weapons. Money we currently spend on weaponry can be used to fund our defense industry reconstruction and to develop the agricultural and mining products that we shall supply Germany, since we can obtain machinery and equipment on credit, but our country's labor and materials used for industrial reconstruction still require cash."[80] The credit treaty, formally signed on April 8, 1936, for RM100 million (U.S.$ 8 million), enabled the Nationalist government to launch an ambitious Three-Year Plan to develop heavy industry.

Accordingly, 1937 marked the apex of Sino-German economic ties. Orders made in the wake of the barter arrangement began to arrive in Hong Kong, while strategic materials were shipped to Germany. China's economic importance to Germany, both as a recipient of weapon exports and supplier of strategic minerals is indicated by the balance of trade. In 1937, China received 37 percent of Germany's weapons exports. China also became Germany's main supplier of wolfram ore (used in the production of tungsten): 71 percent in 1937 and 63 percent in 1938.[81] At the same time, the Nationalist government increasingly relied on Germany for much of its weaponry. Up through 1937, the Nationalist government's imports of German munitions and armaments constituted 80 percent or more of its total arms imports.[82]

The barter agreement quickly unraveled, however, soon after war struck China. In part, the Nationalists sought to reduce their dependency on Germany by diversifying their sources of military hardware and strengthening their recent alliance with the Soviet Union. Economic ties between China and Germany also suffered from Germany's decision to resolve its diplomatic impasse with Japan. Hitler's prohibition of arms sales to China on May 3, 1938, and the pullout of German advisors from China the following month were politically inspired by the desire to strengthen ties between the Axis allies and to satisfy the pro-Japan faction within the Reich. Although German armaments continued to be shipped to China through 1939, the pro-Japan course significantly reduced German exports to China.[83]

A shift in the financial terms of the barter arrangement between the Nationalist government and Hapro proved equally decisive in curbing German exports. Almost immediately after the war broke out in 1937, Germany dealt a blow to China's favorable trade conditions by charging hard currency for all Nationalist orders for armaments and military supplies. Although technical orders, mainly for the development of NRC industries and the railroad, could continue to rely on barter credit, Hitler stipulated that all military supplies shipped to China after September 4, 1937, had to be paid for in cash. The origins of this policy shift went back to Minister of Finance Kong Xiangxi's visit to Germany in the summer of 1937. China's desperate need for German armaments and fear of Germany's impending alliance with Japan pushed Kong to accept the new policy. Hapro representatives justified their own government's decision as a way to stabilize Germany's weak financial position with respect to foreign funds and to obtain more supplies of strategic materials. They described Kong's compromise as a magnanimous gesture, reaffirming Sino-German friendship.[84]

Given that the Nationalist government in 1936 had funneled almost 90 percent of the barter credit into purchasing military supplies rather than industrial and technical equipment, Kong's acceptance of German demands was a crippling financial blow.[85] Moreover, while orders placed in 1936 and 1937 indicate that the Nationalist government had apportioned relatively equal funding for procuring war supplies and investing in industrial projects, by 1938, technical orders had been reduced to a minimum. China suspended an order of RM55 million (U.S.$22 million) for the steel and copper works, the cornerstone of the NRC development plans. Some 81 percent of the remaining RM16.3 million funding for technical equipment to build China's heavy industry went instead for orders on arsenal equipment and construction. The Nationalist government shelved much of the industrial development program designed to promote auxiliary factories for a self-sustaining armament industry. The lion's share of barter money and hard currency was thus devoted to military and ordnance supplies. The Nationalists paid RM78.3 million for military equipment delivered by October 1938.[86]

By 1938, the Nationalists faced a barter agreement that seemed increasingly unfavorable. The financial agreement favored technical orders, of which there were almost none, and hindered buying urgently needed weaponry and military supplies, which could only be paid for with scarce foreign funds. To offset the agreement's severe financial impact, the Nationalists made their first counterproposal; cash should be paid only for Kong Xiangxi's orders or for new orders. These orders amounted to U.S.$2.2 million dollars and $15 million dollars, respectively, of which $7.2 million would be remitted immediately after Germany's acceptance of the proposal.[87] What the Nationalists implied, and in the following months made explicit, was their desire to pay for "old orders" of armaments, primarily made in May 1936, with credit established under the former barter arrangements. Hapro initially accepted the Nationalist proposal on condition that the $7.2 million sum be paid immediately, but the Germans hedged on the critical financial issue regarding means of payment. Through the summer of 1938, all supplies of war materials based on "old orders" continued to be paid for in hard currency. By September 1938, the value of "old orders" totaled RM118.5 million, roughly six times the value (RM20.6 million) of the "Kong-orders." The magnitude of the old orders indicates why the Nationalists were so intent on using the barter arrangement to pay for them, and why the Germans likewise postponed any final decision.[88] Only in August, because of late payments and a halt in China's shipments of raw materials, did Germany modify its policy and accept U.S.$5.3 million (RM12.3 million) worth of raw materials, especially wolfram and zinc, as collateral for munitions.[89]

The policy change ushered in a new contract between Hapro and the Nationalists.[90] The contract stipulated that the Nationalists could now purchase military materials using the barter account, but all arms purchases still required cash payment. To ensure a constant supply of raw materials and payments, Germany requested that China guarantee that at least $8 million worth of mineral ores and agricultural products be shipped every month. Finally, to balance wartime needs with industrial development and to limit German arms exports, Ministry of War orders were not to exceed 40 percent of China's total orders.[91]

Nationalist officials reacted with dismay to the proposed contract, especially the new barter arrangement. L. T. Chen, an administrator in the Central Bank of China and liaison between Hapro agents and Kong Xiangxi, argued that the barter arrangement had outlived its economic benefits. "The barter is unlikely to work to our benefit as a commercial deal. On general principles, such an arrangement will be beneficial only when the goods exchanged are surplus products. That is not the case for us. We are exchanging goods that are necessary to our economic life for goods that are surplus in Germany."[92] Chen further warned Kong that headquarters should understand that the contract did not apply to arms and ammunition so that "they [headquarters] would not entertain false hopes." Nor was shipping goods, half of which were mineral ores, easy, "in view of our other commitments" (referring to the Soviet Union). At best, Chen argued, the barter arrangement could only serve as a political tool.

Effective October 4, 1938, the new contract proved increasingly difficult to carry out. Japan's control of China's shipping routes, China's delayed payments, and Germany's reluctance to ship war materials without receiving ready cash contributed to the deteriorating political relations between Germany and China. Germany became increasingly frustrated at not receiving prompt payments or shipments of raw materials. In turn, China's efforts to use the old barter agreement to acquire the newly promised military materials were rebuffed in May 1939. A month later, any remaining hopes of using the barter accord to acquire arms were dashed when the German government ordered Hapro to terminate all negotiations, including those regarding war materials.[93]

The overwhelming reliance on imports during the initial stages of the Sino-Japanese war underscored the limitations facing China's state-guided military industrialization. Despite notable progress in production and standardization through the introduction of gauges, such technological gains were insufficient to render China self-sufficient. Arguably, the standardization of weaponry, in large part inspired by German technological transfer, increased dependence on German products. Since such a large part of the Nationalists' light weaponry and ammunition was based on German models, it made sense to continue imports from Germany, despite financial obstacles and deteriorating diplomatic relations.

Several studies of the War of Resistance have emphasized how the early eruption of war caught the Nationalists unprepared. F. F. Liu, for instance, suggests that had the war been delayed two years and German influence allowed to "work and spread in China," the resistance would have been far more effective.[94] Such a hypothesis neglects the structural and fiscal weakness of the Chinese arms industry and the pitfalls of economic dependence on Germany. No doubt, the lack of preparation time devastated the defense industry, since the manufacture of armaments usually involved a much more protracted process than that of most manufacturing industries. Alan Milward notes that three interrelated stages of research and development, mass production, and deployment in combat make weapons production a more lengthy process.[95] Only the first stage had been reached for artillery, one of the Nationalists' most pressing needs. When foreign firms zealously guarded their gauges, it became even more difficult to bypass the initial development stage. With regard to mass production, the Ordnance Department achieved considerable success in mass-producing light arms and ammunition, but only on the eve of the war.

Financial pressures and contradictory means of promoting the defense industry impeded its growth. Beginning in the early 1930s, the Nationalist state took on the dual role of both producer and consumer to guide military industrialization. Ordnance Department policy emphasized the need to import weapons, while simultaneously building up the capability for domestic production. Industrial leaders viewed engagement in the global arms market as a means to greater self-reliance, since technology transfer could accompany arms transactions. The achievements in reverse engineering during the 1930s attest to the success of this strategy. The Ordnance Department failed to meet its primary goal of economic self-sufficiency, however, since the state redirected funding from the arsenals to the arms market. Financial pressures delayed the buildup of an infrastructure for the domestic defense industry, which seemed too costly. To alleviate these fiscal problems, the Nationalists placed their hopes on barter arrangements with Germany, believing that the export of raw materials and German credits could help subsidize both military industrialization and arms acquisitions. This arrangement benefited both countries at first, but it collapsed almost immediately after the war started, when Germany denied export of military supplies on the basis of barter. The abrupt policy shift left the Nationalist government with large orders for predominantly military supplies, which could be paid for only with scarce hard currency. Government leaders' intentions to invest in a domestic defense infrastructure had been subverted in the process when they shifted their orders increasingly to purchase military hardware rather than technical supplies.

The closing of routes through Vietnam in 1940, and the fall of Burma to the Japanese two years later, forced the Nationalist army to rely almost exclusively on the Chinese ordnance industry for its supplies. The dramatic decrease of imports, combined with demands from the war front, radically transformed the role of the arms industry from an accessory industry, geared more to assembling weapons, into the production lifeline of the Nationalist government. The arsenals also became an important symbol of Nationalist unity. Chongqing, the new capital of the Guomindang, would form the center of a military industry that had for the better part of a decade been politically divided and economically fragmented.

2

FORTRESSES OF THE GREAT REAR

The Wartime Economy of the Arms Industry

Zhou Baoquan, "Jianshe guofang zhonggongye" [Reconstruct the national defense industry] (1938). From Su Lin, *Guotongqu heibai muke* (Nanning: Guangxi meishu chubanshe, 2000), 147.

Guomindang executive committee officials marveled at the wartime achievements of the arms industry. Retreating from the cities of coastal and central China, which had been overrun by Japanese troops, the Nationalists had installed their arsenals after hauling machinery and equipment hundreds of miles into the interior. Severe shortages in the imports of raw and secondary materials compounded the problem that only the bare rudiments of a steel industry existed in the wartime capital of Chongqing. Yet by 1943, the annual production of gunpowder and bullets had doubled, three times as many rifles, machine guns, and artillery shells were being produced, and hand grenade output had increased five-fold since the war had begun.[1]

The early years of the war, from 1938 to 1941, witnessed an industrial boom in Chongqing following the massive relocation of heavy industry. Industrial relocation accelerated Yu Dawei's ongoing rationalization program and transformed Chongqing into China's dominant military industrial base. Paradoxically, the outbreak of war also promoted centralization of the armament industry, culminating almost an entire decade of efforts by the state to consolidate control over the defense industry. The transfer of thirteen arsenals to Chongqing allowed the Nationalist government to administer the formerly independent and dispersed war plants. The defense buildup, which complemented and reinforced the industrialization of the city, enabled the Nationalists to become more self-sufficient in the production of small arms and ammunition, enough to carry on the war of attrition against Japan.

Insufficient fiscal support, however, continued to plague the arms industry during the war. Faced with a drastically reduced tax base after moving to Chongqing, the central government diminished funding for all state-run organizations and industries, pitting private against state-owned enterprises and fueling competition for resources between government agencies. Fearful of losing state contracts, the Ordnance Department also shunned industrial plants in the private sector, which were mired in depression by the mid 1940s because of diminished capital investment. The lack of coordination between ordnance and raw material production, with the exception of the coal industry, led arsenals to accentuate their own vertical integration. A vicious cycle ensued: the arms industry operated below capacity because of the limited production of ancillary industries, and as a result, it was less able to promote overall growth in industry and create an industrial system. The arsenals sustained the war effort as fortresses of the Great Rear area (Dahoufang) in unoccupied China, but they remained isolated from other industrial sectors.

The political economy of the arms economy shaped Chongqing's class formation in distinctive ways. The structural weaknesses of the wartime economy reinforced the arms industry's dependence on labor. Large numbers of workers with a wide range of skills were employed in the arsenals. These included skilled workers, but also many laborers engaged in indirect production because of the difficulty of mechanizing certain processes as a result of import limits and scarcity of resources or because of inadequate funding for mechanization. This economic environment underscored the importance of recruiting adequate supplies of labor from the moment all international trade routes were blocked in 1941. The state of war emergency and the need to become self-sufficient explain management's recourse to militarizing the workforce and the high state of factory discipline.

State-guided industrialization also manifested itself in direct managerial control over labor. Influenced by German military officials in the 1930s and by American advisors a decade later, the ordnance industry promoted a professional managerial staff, which undercut the power of middlemen and foremen typical of most industries in China. The development of a modern bureaucracy helped the Nationalists implement new production processes based on mass production. But one unintended consequence of bureaucratization was the polarization of relations between staff officers and workers by increasing stratification and accentuating traditional divisions between mental and manual labor. Although this professional managerial staff had modern trappings, their collective mentality was the product of a cultural legacy that scorned manual labor, resulting in friction between the industrial bureaucracy and labor, a crucial element in Chongqing's class formation.

Industrial Relocation

Although the Nationalist government ultimately chose to develop Chongqing as a center of heavy industry after the war broke out, Chiang Kai-shek had viewed Sichuan as a potential wartime base as early as the mid 1930s. The proliferation of industrial surveys under the auspices of the Ministry of Economics heralded plans to develop the southwest and exploit its rich reserves of coal, manganese, iron, antimony, and tungsten, all essential components of arms production. Sichuan ranked second only to Heilongjiang in pig iron production and third in coal production among all provinces.[2] Moreover, Chongqing's easy access to raw materials via the Yangzi and Jialing rivers and the labor surplus in the surrounding rural counties proved alluring to industrial planners. Chiang's plan in 1935 to increase the production capacity of the southwest arsenals by moving equipment from the Shanghai arsenal suggests that he envisioned building an industrial base there.[3] But the timing of Sichuan's military mobilization, occurring soon after the Nationalists entered Sichuan in pursuit of the fleeing Red Army, involved the immediate suppression of Communist rivals rather than a farsighted plan to mobilize for war against Japan. Chiang's stubborn adherence to the policy of "first internal pacification, then external resistance" *(rangwai bi xian annei)* dictated the political economy of the arms industry.

Chiang Kai-shek's clashes with industrial interests over the issue of local control versus nationalization further delayed developing Chongqing as a wartime industrial base. As a result, only after the war began did the Ordnance Department incorporate Chongqing's three military industrial plants established by the provincial governor and warlord Liu Xiang. Of the three, the Sichuan-Kang pacification commission weapon repair plant was the largest munitions plant in all of southwestern China prior to the war, and not surprisingly, it offered the most resistance to Nationalist takeover. But Chiang was equally determined to nationalize all arsenals, fearful that rapacious middlemen might subvert the central government's ability to procure weapons. After first subcontracting production out to the war plant, Yu Dawei took over its machinery, along with several thousand employees, in 1939.[4]

Such protracted negotiations may have drawn Chiang's attention to central China, rather than Sichuan, as a more suitable military industrial base. If the numerical ranking of arsenals, used for purposes of identification and secrecy, is any indication of strategic priority, then the Nationalist military favored Hubei and Hunan Provinces as destinations for industrial relocation.[5] The establishment in the fall of 1937 of the Ordnance Department's main office in Changsha, in Hunan, with branch offices in Chongqing, Xian, and Hong Kong, is equally telling. Only in March 1939 did the department move its main office to Chongqing in order to supervise the relocation of arsenals and requisition land for factory construction there.

Strategy and weaponry influenced the Nationalist decision to develop the Middle Yangzi macroregion. Following the heroic but disastrous bat-

TABLE 2.1

Relocation and Mergers of the Sichuan Arsenals, 1937–1940

Former arsenal name (and location)	Sichuan arsenal number	Date of production or merger	Location	Main products
Hanyang machinery, rifle, and shell plant	1	1940	Chongqing	rifles, shells, grenades
Gongxian rifle and shell plant	1	1940	Chongqing	
Hanyang gunpowder plant	2	October 1940	Baxian	alcohol, nitric acid, smokeless powder
Guangdong Arsenal No. 1 artillery plant	10			mortars, shells, artillery
Zhuzhou artillery research dept.	10	August 1938		artillery shells
Chuan-Kang suijing gongshu bullet plant (Chongqing)	20	August 1938	Chongqing	cartridges
Jinling bullet factory	20	February 1938		cartridges
Jinan cartridge plant	20	1937–38		
Jinling arsenal (Nanjing)	21	March 1938	Chongqing	rifles, shells, cartridges
Hanyang rifle plant	21	July 1938		rifles
Huaxing machinery plant (Chongqing)	21	July 1938		machine guns
Chuan-Kang suijing gongshu weapon repair (Chongqing)	21	June 1939		
Gongxian Branch Arsenal	23	May 1939	Luxian	chemicals, gunpowder
Gongxian Branch Arsenal	23		Chongqing	gas masks, boots
Chongqing steel-smelting plant	24	January 1939	Chongqing	ordnance steel
Zhuzhou cartridge plant	25	Apr. 1938	Chongqing	rifles, grenades
Hanyang cartridge plant	25			cartridges
Aircraft weapons technical research laboratory (Nanjing)	27	June 1938	Wanxian	bombs, rifle grenades
Hanyang Iron & Steel Works	29	June 1938	Chongqing	steel, tools, grenade launchers
Shanghai steel plant	29	February 1938		
Liuhegou Company iron smeltery	29			
Jinan arsenal	30	Nov. 1938	Chongqing	grenades, fuses, shell cups
Nanchang explosive packing plant	30	Dec. 1938		ammunition
Guangdong Arsenal No. 2	50	1938	Chongqing	artillery, shells
Baishuiqiao precision instrument plant	50	Sept. 1938		gauges
Sichuan Arsenal No. 1	50	Apr. 1939	Chengdu	apprentice training

SOURCES: Wang Guoqiang, *Zhongguo binggong zhizaoye fazhan shi* (Taipei: Niming wenhua shiye gongsi, 1987), 125–54. Wang Dexiu, "Kangzhan shiqi qian Chuan de binggong danwei," in *Kangzhan shiqi neiqian Xinan de gongshang qiye*, ed. Guo Songying, 124–33 (Kunming: Yunnan renmin chubanshe, 1988). Lu Dayue, "Kangzhan shiqi da houfang de bingqi gongye," *Zhongguo jingji shi yanjiu*, no. 1 (1993): 105–6. "Zhongguo jindai bingqi gongye dang'an shiliao" bianweihui, comp., *Zhongguo jindai bingqi gongye dang'an shiliao* (Beijing: Bingqi gongye chubanshe, 1993), 3: 241.

tle of Shanghai in the fall of 1937, which decimated 300,000 of Chiang Kai-shek's elite troops, Yu Dawei advocated a mobile strategy in mountainous territory rather than continued positional warfare.[6] In response to frequent shortages and inadequate firepower, Yu recommended positioning troops and the military industry along the three fronts of Luoyang, Xiangyang, and Hengyang, where light arms could be better deployed in the surrounding hills. Once fighting entered more mountainous areas, Yu reasoned, the topography would play to China's superiority in both the flat and curved trajectory fields, whereas the Japanese army's heavy weaponry would be less effective.[7] The Ordnance Department thus pinpointed Hubei and Hunan as their industrial bases. This reorientation also permitted the Nationalists to continue developing the Zhuzhou arsenal to serve as the nucleus for China's "new economic center."[8]

Despite the continued production of light arms, the *san-yang,* or three-front, battle strategy proved short-lived. By June 8, 1938, Chiang Kai-shek ordered his Wuhan-based administration to move to Chongqing. Following his lead, many arsenal directors who had come to central China fleeing the advancing Japanese army moved their factories again. Whether or not Chongqing was their initial destination (only six arsenals went directly to Sichuan), the eventual move to the wartime capital was of immense proportions.[9] By the early 1940s, two-thirds of the Nationalist government's entire arms industry had settled in eastern Sichuan, and most were located in the greater Chongqing industrial zone. Of the twenty arsenals in southwest China in 1941, fourteen were located in Sichuan, eleven of those in Chongqing (see table 2.1).

The relocation consolidated the rise of heavy industry in Chongqing almost by default, as most owners of light industrial factories proved reluctant to leave more lucrative ventures in the International Settlement of Shanghai and Canton. As Lloyd Eastman has observed, "They did not allow patriotism to dull their business instincts."[10] To be sure, as many as 448 private factories also participated in the exodus to the unoccupied areas, with over half relocating to Chongqing.[11] But in trying to mobilize for war, the government focused on salvaging heavy industry, the machine industry, and, above all, the arsenals. Between 1937 and 1940, over 196,000 tons of arsenal equipment moved from Shanghai, Nanjing, Wuhu, Wuhan, and Yichang to Chongqing (see map 2.1), more than the combined tonnage of all other industrial sectors that was transferred to the entire southwest.[12]

The Ordnance Department oversaw the relocation to Chongqing by allying with the Sichuanese shipping magnate Lu Zuofu, owner of the

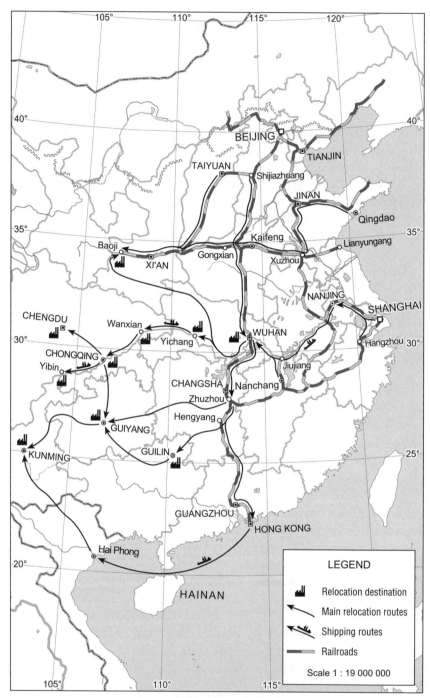

MAP 2.1. Main Transport Routes of Industrial Relocation to Southwestern China, July 1937–February 1940. Redrawn, with permission, from Wu Yuexing, ed., *Zhongguo Kang Ri Zhanzheng shi dituji* (Beijing: Zhongguo ditu chubanshe, 1995).

Minsheng Shipping Company.[13] In October 1937, arms industry officials contacted Lu to move most ordnance equipment to Chongqing and eastern Sichuan. Lu faced additional pressure upon hearing that Chiang Kai-shek sought to annex his company and place it under the Ministry of Military Affairs. To appease Chiang, Lu proceeded to Nanjing, where he joined the War Mobilization Planning Committee. He reduced transport fees to one-tenth the average peacetime rate and transported refugee children and injured soldiers free of charge.

In retrospect, this became a lucrative venture for Lu Zuofu. Within two years, his company holdings expanded from 46 to 116 steamships. The Minsheng Company's domination of the Yichang-Chongqing route derived from having steamships with a lighter draft than those of their main competitors, the large state-run Zhaoshang ju and the Chuanbei Company. As a result, Minsheng boats could navigate the upstream current of the Yangzi, which was especially difficult from late fall through spring, when the water reached its lowest ebb. It was precisely on the eve of the low-water period that much of the relocation took place, in view of the impending Japanese occupation of major industrial cities such as Shanghai (November 1937), Wuhan (October 1938), and Changsha (September 1939). The company also used new shipping techniques and equipment to speed up transportation. Engineers designed booms to lift and unload the enormous machinery, some of which weighed up to thirty tons per piece. New means of transport were put to the test in "China's industrial Dunkirk," the evacuation of material and manpower from the Hubei provincial port of Yichang to Chongqing. Faced with Japanese armies about to attack Wuhan and threatening Yichang in September 1938, Lu Zuofu used twenty-two ships and an accelerated "three-stage navigation" plan to transport 80,000 tons of ordnance equipment from Yichang to Chongqing in little over a month.

The movement of so many arsenals, let alone other industrial plants, to Chongqing was an enormous undertaking. The transport of materials involved tremendous human effort and sacrifice. As Lin Jiyong, the NRC leader in charge of industrial relocation observed, "The move of factories is heroic. Workers of each factory have risked their lives to dismantle and pack machine parts. When the Japanese flights come, they hide on the ground near the machines. . . . Seeing their colleagues die, they simply move the corpse aside and keep working with tears in eyes. Cold machines are painted with warm blood."[14] Minsheng hired over two thousand porters and carriers to load the ships and accessory barges. When porters had to transport the machinery inland, they moved everything by hand. "Coolies by hundreds and thousands hauled at blocks of steel weighing up to 20 tons."[15] Despite efforts to camouflage equipment being transported, boats and sampans were frequently attacked by Japanese bombers. Air raids left at least 117 Minsheng employees dead and 76 wounded.[16]

While Chinese historians have commemorated the exodus to the Great Rear area as an example of Chinese valor and nationalism, Western scholars have been more cautious in their assessment. Lloyd Eastman even cites a case of arsenal workers shooting at one another in their desperation to find a means of transportation inland.[17] The migration to the southwest, as the historian Lu Liu has documented, clearly fostered a sense of working-class nationalism, as evident in the following workers' petition:

We don't worry about minimal payments, or that we might lose our jobs. We have been doing our best to make contributions to wartime transport. We have been sending millions of soldiers to fight the enemy; we have been rescuing industrial equipment and workers; and we have been escorting our refugee compatriots into Sichuan . . . we have been doing all these tasks under the enemy's raids and bombs. Alive or dead, we would prefer to fight for the victory of the Anti-Japanese War rather than eke out an ignoble existence for a meager income.[18]

To be sure, workers aggressively sought self-preservation, but that search was intertwined with their nationalism. A petition by workers at the Jinling arsenal soon after the factory had moved to Chongqing in 1938 illustrates the interrelationship between workers' "rational choice" and nationalism. Addressed to their factory director, Li Chenggan, and signed with over a hundred chops, the petition appealed to Li's Confucian propriety and paternalism, as well as nationalism, to urge providing economic aid for dependents of workers in the occupied areas so that they could join their relatives in the war capital: "Our children in the occupied territory will receive an education of enslavement. As descendents of the Yellow Emperor, we are the future generations of warriors to reconstruct our country, but how can we be used if the talent of youth is buried?" Noting the low wages they were paid, despite inflation, the petitioners asked, "How can workers have enough to save their elders, brothers and sisters from the abyss of misery and deliver them inland? We are dedicating our lives to the cause of the country, but we do not have the economic means to save them. . . . We believe your Excellency treats workers like his family and will prevent workers from worrying."[19]

Relocation to Chongqing and managers' ability to capitalize on work-ers' nationalism boosted the productive capacity of the arms industry. No doubt the constant instability and vulnerability to attack meant frequent stoppages, but production increased through overtime work and the in-troduction of double shifts in factories that were temporarily stable. To the degree that there was an element of planning in war mobilization, the state encouraged private industries to relocate first, so that arsenals could continue producing as much as possible up to the last minute. In October 1937, the Ordnance Department ordered arsenals to "maintain their pre-sent work and increase production to maximum capacity. . . . No factory should relocate unless it has no alternative."[20] Once arsenals moved, however, the tremendous speed of relocation and subsequent assembly minimized disruption of production. Even Yu Dawei was astonished to learn that within sixteen days, the entire Jinling arsenal had been trans-ported from Nanjing to Chongqing. Li Chenggan used patriotic appeals, such as "Go to work as if you were going to battle," to exhort his work-ers and even slept alongside them in an old depot while his arsenal was being rebuilt, and production resumed March 1, 1938, within one hun-dred days of having left Nanjing.[21] Consequently, annual production in 1938 of heavy and light machine guns, mortars, and shells actually sur-passed original quotas.[22]

Increased production also stemmed from the opportunity provided by relocation to streamline production and to continue the rationalization project started in the early 1930s. Rationalization occurred through greater vertical integration and increased specialization of production among individual arsenals. The Ordnance Department set up central and branch factories to coordinate production and the transfer of primary and secondary materials between arsenals. Central factories were gener-ally larger and better equipped, but branch factories played an important role in filling production gaps.[23] Arsenal No. 24 and the Iron and Steel Works Reconstruction Commission also directly controlled iron ore and coal mines to guarantee a steady supply of raw materials for the produc-tion of specialized ordnance steel. Besides supplying their own raw mate-rials, arsenals oversaw purchasing, research and development, finance, and transportation. Vertical integration thus rendered production more efficient.

To foster production specialization, which aided complementary pro-duction among arsenals, Yu Dawei ordered a host of mergers between 1938 and 1939. Arsenal departments and entire factories merged with

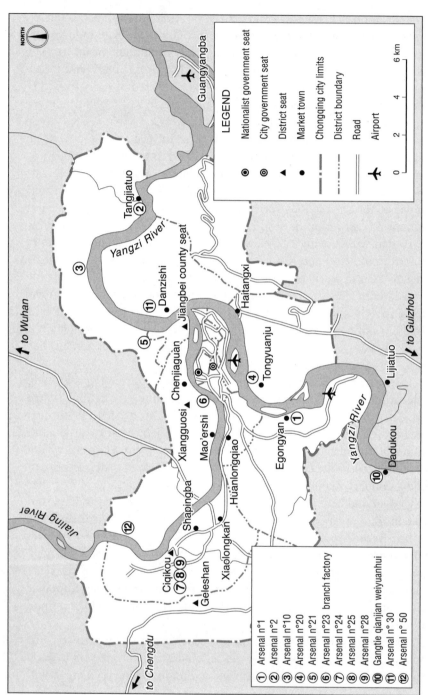

LEGEND

◉ Nationalist government seat
◎ City government seat
▲ District seat
● Market town
▪—▪—▪ Chongqing city limits
▪—·—·— District boundary
—— Road
✈ Airport

0   2   4   6 km

Arsenal n°1
Arsenal n°2
Arsenal n°10
Arsenal n°20
Arsenal n°21
Arsenal n°23 branch factory
Arsenal n°24
Arsenal n°25
Arsenal n°28
Gangtie qianjian weiyuanhui
Arsenal n° 30
Arsenal n° 50

NORTH

Guangyangba

Tangjiatuo
②

Yangzi River

③

Danzishi

Jiangbei county seat

Haitangxi

⑪

⑤

Chenjiaguan

Xiangguosi
⑥
Mao'ershi

Huanlongqiao

Tongyuanju
④

Egongyan
①

Lijiatuo

Dadukou
⑩

Yangzi River

to Wuhan

to Guizhou

Shapingba
⑫

Xiaolongkan

Ciqikou
⑦⑧⑨
Geleshan

Jialing River

to Chengdu

MAP 2.2. Approximate Location of Arsenals in Chongqing, 1943.

larger arsenals in Chongqing. The main producer of ammunition, Arsenal No. 20, incorporated two cartridge factories from Arsenals No. 21 and No. 30. In turn, Arsenal No. 21, which manufactured rifles and machine guns, took over a light machine gun factory from Arsenal No. 20. Arsenal No. 21 handed over its gas mask factory to Arsenal No. 23, which concentrated on chemical production.[24] These exchanges and mergers indicated an important shift in managerial policy. Under warlord control, arsenals had often been comprehensive in their production abilities, manufacturing a variety of weapons and ammunition. During the Nanjing decade, the Nationalist government continued this practice for strategic reasons, apprehensive that an entire type of weaponry might be jeopardized unless arms production was diversified among several arsenals. In contrast, relocation to Chongqing allowed the industry to adopt functional rather than comprehensive specialization. Managers realized that they could only meet the constant demand for arms if arsenals specialized their production.

These economic principles clashed with strategic ones when managers debated arsenal locations. At the height of industrial relocation in 1938, Yu Dawei felt that the concentration of most arsenals around Chongqing rendered them vulnerable to Japanese air raids. Other arsenal directors dissented, arguing that areas further away from Chongqing were too hilly and thus impeded rapid construction. Isolating factories would also disrupt production in those that depended on the city's supply of electricity.[25] Ultimately, the dissenters had their way. The Ordnance Department established all of the arsenals in the new industrial districts of Jiangbei, Dadukou, and Nan'an, located within a radius of ten to twenty kilometers from Chongqing proper (see map 2.2).

Bordering the Yangzi or the Jialing River made it easier to transport coal, iron ore, secondary materials, and machinery necessary for construction and production. To guard against Japanese bombing raids, they took care to place the arsenals close to natural buffers. Arsenal directors often placed their most vital machinery and power plants in caves carved out of the surrounding hillside. As the metallurgist J. K. Stafford observed, the front of the cave was closed in with a heavy concrete wall. "In this wall were hundreds of rectangular shaped holes, the idea of forming these holes was to act as a muffler, so that, in the event of a bomb landing close to the wall the pressure against the wall would be relieved, and prevent the wall from collapsing."[26]

Concern over air raids shaped the physical layout of each industrial compound. These were enormous factory complexes, spanning several hundred acres in area. Under the administration of the National Resources Commission and the Ordnance Department, the Iron and Steel Works Reconstruction Commission (Gangtiechang qianjian weiyuanhui, or Gangqianhui for short) became the largest steel producer in Nationalist China. Located in the industrial district of Dadukou, the plant covered 550 acres, with seven production departments, each the size of an entire factory.[27] In contrast, most arsenals were an assemblage of small plants scattered over the factory complex to minimize the risk of bombardment. This dispersal led to a great deal of extra transportation and was one reason so many laborers were hired.

Because of their proximity to Chongqing, arsenals and especially steel mills controlled by the Ordnance Department faced prohibitive transportation costs for coal, coke, and iron ore. Chongqing's steel mills were over 165 kilometers from its coal and iron ore mines. Transportation remained slow and costly, since it depended on manual labor and tributary navigation. Being unable to use machinery because of firedamp (combustible mine gas) and lack of ventilation, miners extracted coal piece by piece, using hand picks, working stripped and wearing only sandals. Working in the lower shafts, where because of the low headroom, adults could only crawl on all fours, young boys carried baskets of coal up to the surface. At the upper levels of the mines, workers shoveled coal into tubs, which they pushed along rails some fifteen kilometers to the river tributaries. Boatmen then took eighteen days to row five- to fifteen-ton loads of coal 110 kilometers from Pu-ho-chang to Jiangkou and return. At Jiangkou, where a tributary flowed into the Yangzi, workers manually unloaded coal and coke from bamboo baskets and then transported 50-to-80-ton loads by boat to Chongqing in three days.[28]

Metallurgists had considered moving the steel mills closer to the source of coal and iron ore, but when the Gangqianhui steel mill was established on the outskirts of Chongqing, unloading machinery that weighed from 3.5 to 25 tons per piece required wharves and machinery not found further up the small river tributaries leaving Chongqing.[29] Bringing equipment up river in junks towed by laborers, or on their backs, had already required Herculean efforts. As Yu Dawei noted, production was not carried out at the source of raw materials "for the simple reason that we just could not physically carry it [the steel mill] any further than we did."[30] The ensuing transportation bottleneck plagued production and generated enormous costs throughout the war. For every ton of steel produced in Chongqing, six to seven tons of coal and two to four tons of ore had to be transported to the production site.[31] Despite these economic constraints, the relocation of the arms industry fueled the rapid industrialization of Chongqing.

Chongqing's Industrialization

Pockets of manufacturing had existed in Chongqing since the turn of the twentieth century, but trade had always been the main engine of growth. Chongqing catered to light industry and handicrafts prior to the war, in keeping with its role as a commercial hub for eastern Sichuan. The local economy revolved around weaving, tanning, food processing, pottery, and match manufacturing. Exports included cloth, especially raw silk, foodstuffs, spices, and medicinal herbs, as well as hog bristles and tung oil, exported to Britain and the United States.[32]

Mechanized industry spread under the prodding of the warlord Liu Xiang. Soon after taking control of eastern Sichuan in 1926, Liu began building up heavy industry and the armament sector. Within eight years, Liu had established an arsenal, converted a copper-coin mint into a cartridge factory, and set up Chongqing's first electric-powered steel-smelting plant, the largest in southwest China, to supply his arsenals.[33] Although noteworthy, these large-scale modern factories were, however, exceptional. Much of the industrial growth in the early to mid 1930s derived from small workshops and household factories employing from a dozen to fifty workers. For this reason, Chongqing's industrial growth paled in comparison with Shanghai, China's industrial capital. Based on 1933 records, the total number of factories in Chongqing equaled roughly 12 percent of Shanghai's total; Chongqing's labor force was 5 percent that of Shanghai; Chongqing's industrial capital stood at only 4 percent that of Shanghai, and production value was 1.4 percent that of Shanghai.[34]

It was primarily the war and industrial relocation that spurred the rapid expansion of heavy industry. By 1938, close to one-third of some 244 Chongqing factories involved heavy industry, defined as machinery, coal, oil, construction, and the chemical industries.[35] Two years later, the Ministry of Economics had registered 120 chemical factories, 23 electric plants, and 17 steel-smelting plants. Expansion of the machinery industry was especially prominent. Prior to the war, Chongqing had only ten machinery factories, but by 1940, their number had expanded over fif-

TABLE 2.2

Nationalist Arsenal Workforce in Chongqing, May 1, 1945

Arsenal	Staff	Soldiers	Workers	Total employees	Family dependents	Total
1	472	398	4,510	5,380	5,862	11,242
2	305	320	1,482	2,107	1,734	3,841
10	400	200	2,400	3,000	1,600	4,600
20	414	381	3,218	4,013	4,640	8,653
21	534	655	6,883	8,072	—	8,072
21 Qijiang	750	—	2,300	3,050	7,500	10,550
23 CQ	41	25	288	354	452	806
24	332	375	4,190	4,897	2,860	7,757
25	371	308	2,817	3,496	1,614	5,110
26	—	—	—	1,355	604	1,959
28	202	—	1,180	1,382	632	2,014
Gangqianhui	1,226	1,041	10,014	12,281	5,875	18,156
30	348	315	2,156	2,819	3,020	5,839
50	477	417	3,409	4,303	3,105	7,408
Subtotal	5,872	4,435	44,847	56,509	39,498	96,007

SOURCES: Chongqing Municipal Archives, 10 Chang, 3 *mu*, 21 *juan*, Changzhang huiyi, no. 61 (May 1, 1945); 21 Chang, 18 *zong*, 20 *juan* (August 1946).

teenfold.[36] Coal production increased from 770,000 tons in 1938 to 1.2 million tons in 1943, with almost half of the province's total output coming from expanded production at the large-scale, more mechanized mines in the Chongqing area.[37] Unlike the wartime industrialization of other cities under Nationalist control, that of Chongqing was comprehensive, encompassing metallurgy, machinery, chemicals, textiles, transport, and mining. A broad range of occupations and economic sectors coexisted with industry, of which the personal service and commercial sectors were the most important. Yet within a span of only five years, Chongqing employed almost as many industrial workers as those working in commercial enterprises. By the end of World War II, defense production workers comprised one-third to one-half of Chongqing's industrial workforce, which ranged anywhere from 100,000 to 150,000 workers.[38]

The rapid forced industrialization of Chongqing dramatically increased the number of arsenal workers employed in the city and its surrounding districts. Whereas in 1937, roughly 4,500 arsenal workers worked in Chongqing, eight years later, the size of the workforce had leaped to over 56,500 (table 2.2). By August 1945, almost two-thirds of all Nationalist arsenal employees worked in the wartime capital. The rapid growth of the workforce enabled the arsenals to increase production and placed arsenal workers at the forefront of the Nationalist government's industrial mobilization drive.[39]

There were several reasons the arms industry employed so many workers. Complicated work processes required a much higher proportion (roughly 50 percent) of skilled workers than other industries. At the same time, arsenals hired great numbers of unskilled workers. Managers may have tried to compensate for low productivity caused by the lack of schools to train workers in the late 1930s by substituting quantity for quality. Hiring large numbers of laborers was also considered cheaper and more expedient than investing in machinery that would have decreased reliance on porters, but that became almost impossible to import once Japan blocked international routes. Finally, the arms industry needed a dependable supply of labor to meet sudden production assignments or take advantage of the delivery of raw materials. In wartime Chongqing, the pace of work often fluctuated because of various external forces. Bombing raids, power shortages, or a lack of supplies would slow down production, after which work suddenly intensified.

The disproportionate number of workers employed in the arms industry compared to other industries reflected how the military industry dwarfed other industrial sectors and monopolized scarce resources. Financial resources, machinery, technical knowledge, and manpower were allocated to the arms industry. By May 1945, roughly one-quarter of the monthly 75,000 metric tons of coal distributed to Chongqing went to defense production.[40] Arsenals in Kunming and Chongqing consumed a staggering 15 percent of southwestern China's entire electrical output. The 12,000 tons of steel needed each year by the Ordnance Department represented two-thirds of total steel production.[41] Much of the industry's development was based on its almost total control of resources and machinery. "The arsenals have the best equipped plants in China," one American advisor noted. "Due to the necessity for making most everything they needed, some of these plants are self-sufficient. They include melting and rolling facilities, forges, foundries, and machine shops."[42] This advanced state made the industrial economy completely lopsided, with the arsenals controlling most of the machinery and industrial manpower of southwest China, as table 2.3 suggests.

Disparities in machinery contributed to the lack of cooperation between private concerns and the arms industry during the war. Wariness over quality control prevented Yu Dawei from subcontracting out orders

TABLE 2.3

*Comparison of Factories, Employees, and Machinery in Chongqing's
Arms Industry and Other Industrial Sectors, 1944–1945*

	Factories	Staff	Workers	Machines
Arms industry	16	6,188	50,855	15,082
Other industries	1,518	14,517	89,630	6,622
Ratio of arms industry to other industries	1%	43%	57%	228%

SOURCE: Lu Dayue and Tang Runming, *Kangzhan shiqi Chongqing de bingqi gongye* (Chongqing: Chongqing chubanshe, 1995), 269.

to private industries, which generally lacked sufficient precision equipment to achieve the close tolerances required for weapons manufacture based on interchangeability. Financial considerations also made Yu reluctant to contract out munitions orders to private concerns, since he feared state funds would be diverted from his own industry.[43]

Rather than benefiting from increased demand, iron and steel mills in the private sector suffered because of state policies favorable to the arms industry. "The position of private industry is practically untenable from the standpoint of raw materials supply, low production rates, rising costs and established prices for iron and steel being below costs for long periods," an American advisor noted in 1945. "This was largely brought about by the Ordnance and Arsenal plants cornering the market in raw materials and transportation of the same."[44] Compounding this problem, privately owned steel plants depended on commercial banks for financing, which became increasingly difficult under conditions of inflation. By 1944, "iron and steel manufacturing was on a depression level. Orders were unavailable in sufficient amount to provide for anything like capacity operations. Companies were losing money on much of their business and, in the face of irregular and rapidly shifting money values, were experiencing great difficulty in maintaining adequate working capital."[45]

The failure of the metallurgy industry to meet Ordnance Department demand stemmed from the industry's rudimentary conditions prior to the war. The loss of Manchuria, where annual output prior to 1931 had reached 500,000 tons of pig iron and 150,000–200,000 tons of steel, had dealt a mortal blow to the industry. In subsequent years, the Nationalists relied on importing steel and iron, but annual imports after 1937 plummeted from 700,000 to 50,000 metric tons. By the outbreak of the Pacific War, the Japanese blockade had cut off all imports via Canton, Haiphong, and Rangoon. In desperation, the Nationalists set up twenty-eight blast furnaces, ranging in capacity from 5 to 100 tons each, eleven Bessemer converters, thirteen electric furnaces, five small open-hearth furnaces, and twenty-one rolling mills in southwestern China. Most blast furnaces and Bessemer converters used steel plates from wrecked ships. Salvaged marine engines were converted to power units. Total annual production in Nationalist China between 1942 and 1944 only amounted to 30,000–40,000 metric tons of pig iron and steel.[46]

Predominantly under the control of the National Resources Commission, the largest state institution managing industry, over twenty steel mills operated in wartime Chongqing. These mills were established on the premise that they would supply arsenals, yet Yu Dawei remained wary of using NRC steel products. Much of their production depended on the cheaper, but cruder Bessemer process, which converted pig iron into steel. Yu judged the final product unsuitable because its high phosphorus level made steel too brittle for rolling. This defect, in addition to the fiscal tug-of-war and underlying political infighting, prevented greater cooperation between the National Resources Commission and the Ordnance Department during the War of Resistance. According to an American metallurgist, "Dr. Wong [Minister of Economics] was reported as saying that the Ordnance Department could be one of his principal customers, but that they will not purchase from the Government-owned NRC plants under Dr. Wong's Ministry. Dr. Wong apparently believes that there could be no point in discussing with General Yu measures that might be designed to help China on wartime production."[47] Only with the arrival of American advisors in November 1944 did the two government agencies even begin discussing using NRC Bessemer steel.

Consequently, Yu relied on his own iron and steel works for better-quality steel. Arsenal No. 24 produced over 45,000 metric tons of steel and parts between 1937 and 1946. The Gangqianhui operated two open-hearth furnaces with a capacity of 10 tons per heat each, a 100-ton and a 20-ton blast furnace, and two electric furnaces with a total capacity of 4.5 tons per heat. Total production of 56,000 tons of pig iron and 44,000 tons of steel ingots between 1941 and 1947 fell far short of actual capacity, but provided enough steel to maintain production in the arms industry.[48]

In short, the Chongqing ordnance industry was built on unstable foundations, limited by ancillary industries that had either been decimated prior to the war or continued to use primitive means of production. Despite these adverse conditions, there were certain unexpected benefits for the arms industry. The forced and massive industrial relocation to China's interior gave the Nationalist government greater control over formerly independent or dispersed arsenals, especially since most were located in the wartime capital after 1938. Relocation had also brought economic benefits to the defense industry by accelerating the rationalization of production. The advanced state of machinery was also exceptional for the times, even intoxicating for certain employees. One can sense the visceral excitement of a former technician when he first visited Arsenal No. 50: "Relative to the entire industrial world within the country, it was incredible. Although we were not allowed to use our hands, it was addictive and fantastic that we could do our training there, or just watch. Students of mechanical engineering in other schools had never seen such things. The level [of mechanization] was extremely high."[49] The impression that the arsenals symbolized modernity was reinforced by the emergence of a technical and managerial stratum.

Zhiyuan: Formation of an Officer Class

With Yu Dawei at the helm, the arms industry began implementing administrative reforms to modernize and become more self-reliant. These reforms included the use of accounting systems that considered both fixed and variable costs and relied on the principle of "control through statistics," the evaluation of both workers' and managerial performance, and the creation of departments and bureaus based on functional specialization.[50] Administrative reforms at the Gongxian arsenal during the mid 1930s illustrate the expansion of hierarchical levels—departments, sections, and subsections—that occurred throughout the arms industry. Management was subdivided into three bureaus (General Affairs, Works, and Inspection), an Investigation Department, and three commissions: Examination, Construction, and Education. The General Affairs Bureau included a secretarial section in charge of mail and reports, an accounting section, a general office, a purchase section, a medical section, and so forth. The Works Bureau (gongwuchu), the largest bureau, which was central to the management of workers, oversaw production in the various departments. The Inspection Bureau tested raw materials and products. The Investigation Department supervised technological transfer and the study of foreign military technology to improve domestic production. Overseeing labor was the Examination Commission, the forerunner of the personnel department, which tested recently hired workers to decide whether to retain or dismiss them.[51]

Increasing bureaucratization of work changed the social climate of the shop floor, making the role of supervisors more prominent than that of foremen. The use of personnel departments, responsible for recruitment, worker and staff evaluations, and wage rankings reflected the growth of management's direct control over labor. This was a major reason why the contract labor system, a noted means of labor recruitment in China's textile and coal-mining industries, did not play a visible role in the arms industry.[52]

These administrative reforms created a surge in staff personnel, or *zhiyuan*, a term encompassing engineers, technicians, clerks, and managers. Reflecting the expansion of the state bureaucracy in managing industry and the tight bonds forged between the scientific community and government, the ratio of staff employees to production workers more than doubled within a decade. Based on a 1934 survey of six arsenals, 559 administrators and technicians were employed, compared to 9,956 workers, an administrative density of 5.6 percent. By August 1945, the Nationalist arms industry employed 9,056 staff members, roughly 13 percent of the 69,030 arsenal workers.[53] *Zhiyuan* became increasingly important throughout heavy industry and state-owned industries. Among ten nondefense industries surveyed in 1944, staff members totaled some 9,471 members compared to 51,883 workers, that is, an administrative density of 18.2 percent.[54]

These quantitative leaps in the number and proportion of *zhiyuan* working for the defense industry were accompanied by a marked rise in their social status. "During the late Qing and early republic, the main reason our defense was so terrible was not that China lacked technical experts but that those rotten bureaucrats and old warlords who were running the show did not know how to use and respect experts," the diplomat and air force commander Yang Jie said. "They treated technical experts like lackeys, beckoning them here, ordering them there, so that we could not put much of our technical talent to good use."[55] By the 1930s, however, there was a new respect for *zhiyuan*. Engineers, in particular, were the prime beneficiaries of state-guided industrialization plans to create a professional class that would shape and define China's modernity.[56]

The advanced education of *zhiyuan* was a prime reason for their elevated status, as well as a catalyst of the arms industry's modernization. "The staff of the arsenals is made up of engineers who have been educated in Germany, China and/or America in that order of numbers," an American technical engineer noted. "On the whole, individually, they are

TABLE 2.4

The Educational Background of Chongqing Arsenal Personnel, 1948

Educational level attained	Technical staff	Administrative staff	Total	Percentage
Foreign university	26	5	31	1.0%
Chinese university	475	150	625	20.3
Vocational school	150	316	466	15.2
Advanced school	353	101	454	14.8
Senior middle school	36	484	520	16.9
Junior middle school	79	725	804	26.2
Other	37	137	174	5.7
Total	1,156	1,918	3,074	100.0

SOURCES: Chongqing Municipal Archives, 50 Chang, 3919 *juan*; 24 Chang, 3565 *juan*; Gangqian-hui, 117 *juan*; 50 Chang, 2613 *juan*; 24 Chang, 3 *mu*, 240.3 *juan*; Second Historical Archives of China, Nanjing, 774 *quan*, 1658–60 *juan*.

capable men, imbued with a desire to show good production records and consequently have done commendable jobs in getting results from their transplanted equipment under difficult operating and supply conditions."[57] If we subdivide staff into technical and administrative personnel, it is evident that the former reached higher levels of training than the latter (see table 2.4). This education gap may have contributed to the discord between technical staff and administrators, many of them Guomindang functionaries, over the role of the party in industry, a topic discussed in chapter 6. On the whole, however, staff members had received much more formal education than workers.

As part of its wartime mobilization plan, and in an effort to free itself from technological dependence on foreign powers, the Nationalist government launched education reforms in 1932 that promoted science and technology. As a result, the 1930s witnessed a threefold increase in the enrollment of engineering students, many of whom attended newly established or reorganized ordnance research centers.[58] The Specialized Ordnance School (Binggong zhuanmen xuexiao) became the most significant military industrial training center in China. Between 1921 and 1948, 821 students graduated from the armament engineering and applied chemistry departments and assumed technical posts in the arsenals.[59] Tongji University, which emphasized combining applied science with practical training in factories and offered classes taught by German professors and opportunities to study in Germany, was the other leading source of ordnance technicians, and its ample pool of graduates were highly desirable recruits for the defense industry.[60]

Although *zhiyuan* shared with production workers the need to sell their labor to owners of the means of production, and thus shared a common economic class position in the broadest sense of the term, in every other respect they parted company. As contemporaries such as Zhu Bangxing noted, most of the *zhiyuan* came from the rich peasant or landlord classes, whereas laborers derived from the ranks of the poor peasants. Although Zhu, a Communist underground activist, accurately conveys the stark contrasts in social class, he slights the increasingly urban, middle-class origins of staff personnel. By the 1930s, close to 300,000 *zhiyuan* worked for the old-style foreign and Chinese capitalist firms in Shanghai, where they formed one of several urban professional classes.[61] Given the range of their employment, the term *zhiyuan* had broad connotations. As defined by Zhu,

The term *zhiyuan* refers to service employees in economic, cultural, political, and other institutions that perform nonmanual labor. *Zhiyuan* includes many ranks; within factories from the top levels of managers and engineers to the lower ranks of students training in offices, all are *zhiyuan*. . . . Generally speaking, in this society, where manual and mental labor are distinct, *zhiyuan* tend to perform mental labor, thus the ranks of *zhiyuan* all more or less have overtones of the intelligentsia.[62]

This social proximity to the intelligentsia elevated the status of *zhiyuan*. Moreover, all *zhiyuan* employed in the defense industry held military rank. It is thus more accurate to translate *zhiyuan* as "staff officer" rather than "white-collar employee," since the former title better conveys a sense of authority. As a former secretary of the Ministry of Economic Affairs pointed out, "State-owned enterprises . . . treated *zhiyuan* as officials."[63]

Arsenal staff occupied a broad range of positions, but most, if not all, assumed different degrees of authority, thus blurring the lines between management and *zhiyuan*. These lines were even less distinct within the arsenals, since all managerial personnel were distinguished by their military rank under a civilian officer system *(wenguanzhi)*. Sources refer to arsenal personnel as *zhiyuan*, but they more frequently use their specific rank or refer to them as commissioned officers, military civil officers, or military technicians. Approximately 75 percent of all staff personnel (N = 3,074) held ranks between first lieutenant and major.[64] Most likely, a class of officers developed in the arsenals in order to stabilize the technical workforce. Conferring officer rank imparted the power and prestige of management as a whole to staff members. The relative proximity of all staff members to arsenal leadership enhanced their social status. Office staff and management personnel occupied the top echelons of the factory social hierarchy. By contrast, all factory workers occupied the lower two-thirds of the factory "ladder." Starting from the bottom, temporary workers comprised the bottom rung, while in ascending order of status, laborers and skilled workers occupied the broad middle half of the ladder. Acting as mediators between production workers and management were the foremen, who were drawn from the workers' ranks.

Wartime Production

Managerial reforms, the massive influx of workers, and the development of mass production helped the Nationalist arms industry achieve greater self-sufficiency in the production of light artillery, small arms, and ammunition during the War of Resistance. The army continued to face chronic shortages, but the shift to more mobile warfare and the diminished scale of combat during the war of attrition allowed the arms industry to send a steady supply of weapons to the front. In truth, the Nationalist military had few alternatives to self-sufficiency. At the height of government imports in mid 1938, arms depots maintained a minimum reserve of four months' supply of essential military hardware, enough to supply thirty divisions.[65] The army, however, quickly consumed the bulk of supplies in the early stages of the war. With the price of weapons in Europe soaring because of the high demand, the Nationalists were forced to rely increasingly on their own production.

Comparing average monthly production and wastage, the military term for consumption and use of weapons, indicates that small arms and ammunition production generally met the demands of the front. The arsenals produced many more heavy machine guns, mortars, rifle and hand grenades, and rifle-grenade launchers than the average monthly demand. Nationalist armies were using between five to ten million rounds of ammunition each month, while production kept pace at ten million rounds per month. As American advisors noted in September 1944, "production of the arsenals is about sufficient to maintain the number of weapons in the hands of the armies at a constant level."[66]

The arms industry had more difficulty meeting the demand for heavy weaponry. As a matter of principle, defense industry leaders since the 1930s had concentrated on manufacturing mobile weapons that could be mass-produced. Arsenal directors consciously geared production to light

TABLE 2.5

Nationalist Arms Industry Production, 1940–1945

Weapon type	1940	1941	1942	1943	1944	1945[a]
7.9-mm rifles	54,510	39,000	59,200	66,831	61,850	43,354
Heavy machine guns	2,982	2,380	2,290	2,940	3,066	1,363
Light machine guns	1,324	2,440	6,000	9,391	10,749	4,902
82-mm mortars	900	500	760	1,381	1,215	1,084
Rifle cartridges (1,000s)	113,878	120,585	140,010	144,050	150,000	70,960
82-mm mortar shells	651,542	420,006	550,156	738,784	706,100	348,578
75-mm mountain artillery shells	61,614	23,072	62,956	119,638	115,400	—
Rifle and hand grenades	812,962	834,039	983,196	1,004,597	940,987	401,037
Gas masks	101,810	102,000	101,500	71,500	45,900	—
TNT (packets)	1,113	260	1,546	928	460	—

SOURCES: "Zhongguo jindai bingqi gongye dangan shiliao" bianweihui, comp., *Zhongguo jindai bingqi gongye dangan shiliao* (Beijing: Bingqi gongye chubanshe, 1993), 3: 426; Franklin D. Roosevelt Library, Hyde Park, New York, American War Production Mission, box 32, J. A. Jacobson–Chongqing file; box 16, "Annual Munitions Production."

[a]1945 production includes only the first half year.

artillery and small arms, even though this strategy severely limited heavy firepower. The production of tanks and armored cars was therefore not even considered. By 1941, arsenals did successfully manufacture a 37-mm flat-trajectory infantry field gun, which the army used as its main form of heavy artillery. But arsenals had to import the gun barrels, made using a complicated heat treatment process only recently discovered in Germany. With a supply of one hundred barrels for the entire war, Chongqing could manufacture only twenty to thirty guns per year during the war.[67] In general, inadequate machinery and lack of raw materials owing to the Japanese blockade made it difficult to produce artillery, while poor foundry practices, with casting scrap running as high as 50 percent, limited production of artillery shells.[68]

Although the arms industry achieved a modicum of self-sufficiency, production was not uniform, and neither did output progressively increase during the war. Data show that production of most weapons decreased in 1941 but rose sharply over the next few years (see table 2.5).[69]

Insufficient funding was a primary cause of reduced production in 1941. In letters to Finance Minister Kong Xiangxi, Yu Dawei pleaded for money to continue production and maintain adequate provisions for staff and workers:

Because funding is insufficient for domestic production, we are on the verge of halting work, and there is no hope regarding our foreign source. In the future, material assistance to the front will be cut off. The appropriation for purchasing ordnance equipment and for production pertains to each arsenal's operating budget. They depend upon this fund to pay for maintaining workers' wages, to purchase workers' grain supply, and to pay for domestic production. Based on these funds, one hundred thousand employees cry piteously for food. The slightest delay will have a severe impact. Already two months have passed since funds were paid on time. Mass sentiment is terrified.[70]

Funding was all the more urgent, Yu argued, given the escalating world war. Roosevelt still prohibited American sales of small arms to China, and Stalin had diminished aid to the Nationalists after German troops invaded the Soviet Union. The temporary closure in July 1940 of the Burma Road, the last remaining international supply route into China, had an immediate and severe impact on domestic production. Compounding the problem, a shortage of government trucks, and the soaring price of fuel impeded transport of material and explosives that had already reached Yunnan. The location of most arsenals in Kunming and Chongqing, separated by a distance of 750 miles, made it difficult and costly to coordinate exchange of parts and materials. By the spring of 1941, arsenals throughout Sichuan and Hunan were on the verge of suspending production, and as chapter 5 details, workers were exiting en masse.[71]

Ultimately, the import of Lend-Lease materials supplied through Rangoon and airlifts over the Himalayan Hump prevented the closure of the Burma Road from developing into a full-blown crisis. Between 1941 and 1945, America supplied China with $846 million in Lend-Lease materials and equipment.[72] The amount received by the Nationalists paled in comparison to that distributed to European allies of the United States. Nevertheless, much of the outright grants-in-aid was used to provide critical raw materials. A full 80 percent of tonnage directed to Nationalist ordnance consisted of crucial supplies of zinc, copper, and smokeless powder, enabling the arms industry to increase its output during 1943-44.[73]

Paradoxically, American aid contributed to the Nationalist government's tight fiscal policy, which deterred wartime arms production. As the war progressed, Kong Xiangxi and his brother-in-law T. V. Soong, both in control of the levers of finance, increasingly waxed confident that the United States would determine a successful outcome of the war, and that maximum industrial ouput was not warranted. When technical advisors led by Donald M. Nelson, the director of the American War Production Mission, arrived in China in November 1944, they were shocked to find ordnance production operating at an average of 55 percent capacity, and steel output as low as 20 percent capacity. From Nelson's vantage point, officials in the Ministry of Finance assumed that the United States was willing to buy Chiang Kai-shek's support. "Dr. Soong and others would speak soberly of obtaining vast and virtually unsecured loans from the U. S. and would refer to the large sums made available by the U.S. to other allies."[74]

According to Minister of Economics Weng Wenhao, dependence on the Lend-Lease program minimized the expenses of each government department, diverted government investment from industry, and thus lowered production rates. "The Ordnance production is so low because of shortage of money," he explained. "Therefore, the policy of Ordnance is to purchase the least possible amount of things in China. In fact, this is the policy of the whole government."[75] If funding for the arms industry was limited, outlay to other government departments was minimal. A lack of detailed budgets for the 1940–44 years precludes comparison, but the 1945 provisional budget indicates the economic weight accorded to the arms industry. Besides the War Ministry, which received 176 billion yuan, or 72 percent of funding, the Ordnance Department was slated to receive more money (23.4 billion yuan) than any other government institution.[76]

Although the Nationalists devoted most of their budget to the military, subsistence expenditures consumed the lion's share. Military expenditures for Nationalist China reached an estimated 80–90 billion yuan in 1943, less than 10 percent of national income, and half of that was spent on food for the military.[77] This indirectly influenced the production of arms, since the army's requisition of weapons was diminished. Moreover, funding to the Ordnance Department was often delayed or never materialized. "Arsenals continued to operate at about 35 to 40 percent of capacity as they have in the past due to necessary funds never having been made available for full scale operation," Colonel L. B. Moody, the main technical advisor to the arsenals working under Donald Nelson, reported in 1945.[78]

Nationalist fiscal policy, aptly defined by American advisors as the "politics of attrition," had severe consequences for the economy. By 1944, the metallurgical industry was in depression, stifling the supply for the arms industry. Within a year, the head of the American mission reported that budgets had stopped reaching the Ordnance Department, and that General Yang Jizeng (Yu Dawei's successor) "just couldn't go on much longer operating the Arsenals because he was fresh out of money to pay wages!"[79]

By the last stages of the Sino-Japanese War, the Nationalist army faced critical shortages. In their last great offensive to destroy American air bases in southern China, the Japanese launched Operation Ichigo (Operation Number One). In the spring of 1944, Japanese troops suddenly swept into central and southern China and occupied the key rice production provinces of Hunan and Guangxi, inflicting enormous losses on the Chinese military. By late 1944, Yu Dawei related, the roughly three hundred divisions of the Nationalist army (three million men at full strength) were left with one million rifles, 61,000 light machine guns (six per company), 16,000 heavy machine guns, 7,000 trench mortars, and 2,357 cannons.[80] When American technical advisors arrived at Chongqing, they thus faced numerous challenges: unfulfilled production quotas, rising wage costs, internecine rivalries between state and private sectors, and a growing inflationary crisis.

The Americans Are Coming! The War Production Mission

When Franklin Roosevelt selected Donald M. Nelson, chairman of the War Production Board, to lead a fact-finding mission to China in August 1944, he had two broad goals.[81] The first involved understanding how China's economy would support the war. The second concerned the role the U.S. government and private investors would play in China's postwar economy. To what extent would China's industrial economy require public loans or assistance from American companies, and what restrictions would be placed on American investors? These concerns influenced Nelson and his team of technical advisors in trying to improve use of foreign aid and draw up plans for military conversion. While FDR aspired to open up markets, Nationalist military leaders remained committed to state-controlled industry. Ultimately, the technical advisors found common ground with their Chinese counterparts. Both envisioned military conversion to promote economic growth and social stability. In general, relations between the Nationalist military industrial leaders and American specialists thrived on the exclusive but important goal of technical reform. For this reason, the ordnance specialist L. B. Moody had nothing but the highest praise for Yu Dawei, calling him the "best qualified ordnance officer I have met since the beginning of World War I. Unassuming and rather poker faced, which I believe has trapped sundry people into making fools of themselves."[82]

American technical advisors, like their German counterparts a decade before, played a key role in overseeing foreign aid and mobilizing the war economy. Between November 1944 and November 1945, Nelson directed over forty technical advisors to work in heavy industrial plants—ordnance, coal, chemical, and metallurgy. The War Production Mission made several long-standing contributions to the development of Nationalist ordnance. The arsenals and their branch factories improved production processes and raised output. Within three months, Nelson reported, iron and steel production had reached 50 percent capacity, and it would increase shortly to 80 percent. American technicians introduced beehive ovens for metallurgical coke production and improved coal washeries to obtain cleaner coal for the production of blast furnace coke. As a result, coke production quickly doubled from 3,700 tons to 7,500 tons between March and October 1945.[83] American engineers also participated in weapons testing to make them more effective. With the help of one advisor in 1944, Arsenal No. 21 changed from manual to mechanized casting of 82-mm mortar shells and used high-speed steel instead of pig iron. These new methods cut production time by two-fifths, eliminated half the waste, and increased the amount of explosives contained in each shell by 50 percent.[84]

Although relations between American advisors and Chinese ordnance managers eventually flourished, the lingering German influence among Nationalist defense leaders opened the door to critics of the arrangement. Many of the first conversations between American military advisors and Nationalist managers were "carried on in German, as most of the executives have, at one time or another, visited and studied in Germany or have had German instruction."[85] Some members of Nelson's mission even suspected that high-level managers guiding the Nationalist arms industry still kept their political allegiances to Germany, and that Yu Dawei harbored Nazi sympathies well into the 1940s. "Consequently, they desire to operate now in a manner that secures their positions in a post-war China dominated by Axis victors. This attitude is reflected in inefficiency of production and in other activities regarded as tantamount to deliberate sabotage. . . . Direction of China's ordnance department by pro-German personnel distinctly deters China's munitions production."[86] Whether sabotage was practiced is questionable, but the metallurgist Knute Lund's observation that Yu Dawei was "only interested in getting German technical people back into China" once the war ended did hold a kernel of truth.[87] From Yu's perspective, stockpiles of German weaponry were ideal for the Nationalist army, and German technicians could better aid Chinese arsenals, since their production systems had originally been built to German designs.

The greatest frustration for American technical experts arose over their belief that Nationalist China was not pulling its weight in the war. Advisors suspected that they were being manipulated when they saw supplies and products requested from Lend-Lease being sold in small shops. This perception reinforced the American War Production Mission's view that industrial production had become hostage to fiscal restraint and Lend-Lease aid.[88] Determined to reduce reliance on the costly Lend-Lease program and to cut back air transport, American advisors introduced industrial surveys to determine whether manufacture of weapons and ammunition was advantageous from a tonnage standpoint. By July 1945, Moody noted a "gratifying increase" in the substitution of Chinese-produced material for imported materials.[89]

Technical advisors also pressed the arms industry to cooperate with the private sector and the NRC. China's War Production Board, which had been established on December 6, 1944, to coordinate production of munitions and strategic matériel, helped private concerns land substantial orders to produce entrenching tools, land mines, bayonets, and trench mortar shells. But competition for funding provoked bitterness and backstabbing between the arsenals and subcontracting firms. Already by May 1945, private manufacturers were criticizing the defense industry for not having supplied them with master and working gauges, making it impossible to fill orders for mortar shells. According to War Production Board members, arsenals began to withdraw contracts, saying they could do the job for half the price.[90] Even without obstruction, private manufacturers often lacked enough machine tools to carry out the orders, and the program thus fizzled out soon after Nelson's mission ended in November 1945. The case was yet another example of the arms industry's isolated modernization. The Chinese military industry's failure to use subcontracting stands in contrast to the expanding industrial network in Japan that had originated in World War I. Although large firms in Japan initially saw subcontracting as a flexible arrangement to buy cheap parts, the process ultimately drew small producers into a system of modern industry, because large firms imposed their technological standards on the small companies and forced them to modify their technical procedures.[91]

Demobilization and Retrenchment

The historian William Kirby has drawn attention to the conflict between proponents of a free market and those of a state-planned economy that divided the American and Nationalist governments. Since much of the American War Production Mission in China was geared to increasing the production capacity of the arsenals, however, advisors and their hosts rarely disagreed over the continued importance of the state-run arms industry. For a brief period of time in late 1945, both sides pushed to stimulate growth in the urban industrial economy.

During the immediate aftermath of the eight-year war, American specialists envisioned converting much of Chinese military industry to civilian use. In a report advocating civilian conversion, Colonel Moody estimated the value of the annual potential capacity of ordnance plants at U.S.$59.7 million. Only 20 percent would be used for continued military production, storage, and repair needs. Oblivious to the looming civil war, Moody believed that the army should be maintained for "occupation purposes, internal police and contributing a token force to any United Nations operation." Another $10.5 million of the productive capacities of the arms industry, a full third of small arms and ammunition machinery, could not be converted to civilian use because of its specialized nature. Moody proposed, however, that the remaining $37.7 million production capacity be used to build up the civilian sector to produce vitally needed domestic items to accelerate commercial recovery and expand employment.[92]

On the eve of V-J Day, even military brass supported defense reductions and civilian conversion. Seeking to sway Chiang Kai-shek, U.S. General Albert Wedemeyer, General Joseph Stilwell's successor in command in the China-Burma-India (CBI) Theater, stressed the need for limiting production to 40 percent capacity. This would be adequate "for maintenance of internal order and for dealing with the 'Communists' should that be needed."[93] The Nationalists also flirted with the idea of deep cutbacks in the defense industry. In early 1945, the Nationalist Military Commission authorized General Chen Cheng, recently promoted minister of military affairs, to supervise demobilization and the reorganization of the arms industry. Leaders of the military industry shared American planners' commitment to retrenchment, but were divided as to how far to privilege the civilian sector. Immediately after the war, Chen Cheng wanted to continue production of weapons to maintain war readiness, but diminish production or gear production to civilian use. Taking a more hard-line position and vigorously defending the interests of the arms industry, Yu Dawei advocated maintaining the "internal bastion of Chongqing" by continuing production at strategic mines and steel mills. In meetings with American advisors, Yu argued that only a strong defense industry able to support 120 divisions could establish "internal stability." This goal would be achieved if the United States made its munitions plants available to China. Yu was less optimistic about civilian conversion, feeling that this would take considerable time because of the demand for weapons and the inevitable delays in converting production lines.[94] Although Chen and Yu disagreed about the production needs of the Nationalist military, they both sought to improve efficiency by consolidating production. Following Chen's plans for demobilization, the Ordnance Department recommended consolidating and reducing the number of arsenals based on four principles: those producing similar products or products of similar quality that were located in the same area should merge or establish branch arsenals; if several factories produced the same weapon, the larger arsenal should produce according to demand, while smaller arsenals should either stop production and conserve machinery or move and merge; production and storage work were to stop because of limited conservation time; factories should concentrate dispersed workshops.[95] Once Chiang Kai-shek approved Chen Cheng's plans on March 16, 1946, the largest arsenals incorporated machinery of smaller and more geographically isolated arsenals that produced similar products. Arsenals Nos. 2, 26, 28, and 30 shut down and moved machinery and personnel to the larger arsenals. By the end of 1946, retrenchment had reduced the number of arsenals located in the Chongqing industrial area from seventeen to seven main arsenals and two branch arsenals.[96]

Tremendous economic dislocation occurred in the immediate postwar period as industries folded. Chen Cheng had outlined four different policies for arsenal workers, staff, and soldiers premised on the Ordnance Department's ability to provide employment or welfare relief and to regulate the labor market. Roughly two-thirds of all personnel (N = 87,670) would continue working. The remaining third of all arsenal employees would either transfer out to another industrial sector, pursue advanced training, and then work in arsenals once under Japanese control in coastal or northeast China, or, in the case of older and unskilled workers, be discharged with severance pay.[97] But the bulk of retrenchment came

TABLE 2.6

Regional Distribution of Arsenal Employees

(percentage)

Region	May 1945	September 1948	November 1949
Chongqing	58.6%	50.9%	69.9%
Sichuan	70.7	56.6	76.2
S.W. China	13.3	11.3	10.2
Taiwan	—	11.1	9.4
S.E. China	5.3	14.3	13.6
N.E. China	—	17.8	—
Other	10.7	6.6	—
Total	96,474	77,337	46,677

SOURCES: Chongqing Municipal Archives, 10 Chang, 3 *mu*, 21 *juan*, Changzhang huiyi, no. 61 (May 1, 1945); 21 Chang, 18 *zong*, 20 *juan* (August 1946). Second Historical Archives of China, Nanjing, 774 *quan*, 708 *juan* (June 6, 1949). "Zhongguo jindai bingqi gongye dangan shiliao" bianweihui, comp., *Zhongguo jindai bingqi gongye dangan shiliao* (Beijing: Bingqi gongye chubanshe, 1993), 3: 878.

through dismissals of both workers and staff personnel. Between the late spring and early fall of 1946, roughly 16,000 people, one-third of all workers and staff employed in the Chongqing arsenals, were laid off.

The resumption of conflict with the Communists ended the policy of retrenchment. By July 1946, the Nationalists had begun a new production drive. General Yang Jizeng, promoted as director of the Ordnance Department after Yu Dawei became involved in the U.S.-sponsored Marshall negotiations, ordered arsenals to "work hard at increasing productivity" and meet all quotas that were now assigned to each arsenal.[98] The emphasis on productivity and retrenchment in the wake of the eight-year war led to an increase in the intensity of work during the civil war years. This was a chief reason why Chongqing arsenals produced more arms and ammunition per year between 1946 and 1948 than during the War of Resistance, despite the decrease in workers.

During the Chinese civil war, Chongqing retained its strategic importance. Two major geographical shifts occurred, however, reflecting changes in the political and military configurations of northeastern and southeastern China. The Nationalist government regained control over Japanese-occupied arsenals in Shenyang. Starting in February 1948, the Nationalist government also began shifting its resources to the islands of Taiwan and Hainan. The move to Taiwan resulted in the relocation of Arsenal No. 26 from Changshou County, Sichuan, as well as of several arsenals that had already moved to Wuhan and the coastal areas. These shifts and mass layoffs lowered the absolute number of workers employed in the Chongqing arsenals after 1945, despite a relative increase in the percentage of the Nationalist arsenal workers in Chongqing on the eve of the Communist revolution (see table 2.6). This increase reflected the fact that Chongqing remained a bastion of Nationalist military power in China until November 1949.

Conclusion

War is a catalyst for social and economic change. Reacting to the dual threat of foreign invasion and domestic civil war, Chiang Kai-shek and Yu Dawei launched a series of reforms to modernize Nationalist China's arms industry. By achieving centralization of the entire arms industry, standardization of weapons, the creation of a specialized and highly qualified bureaucracy, and a complementary exchange with first Germany and then the United States, the Nationalists demonstrated policies that were both flexible and adaptive. In other respects, however, Chiang Kai-shek shortchanged the armament industry, preferring to allocate most funding to the international arms market.

The Great Migration and development of Chongqing as the center of China's arms industry had spurred a massive social transformation. Not only did industrial relocation between 1937 and 1940 change Chongqing from a commercial haven into a heavy industrial center, but the rapid and concentrated form of industrialization typified by the arsenals developed new and potentially conflictual social relations in industry. While the Nationalists' military industrial drive facilitated the emergence of a class of professional engineers, technical personnel, and office staff, it also accelerated an already unprecedented migration of refugees and working people from the central and coastal regions to southwestern China. The development of mass production and managers' desperate need for manpower and skilled labor also drew on the pool of migrant labor from eastern rural Sichuan. These two migration patterns, from within Sichuan and from outside the province, accelerated the process of class formation in Chongqing as workers from different regions and with diverse or different skills assembled in the gigantic arsenals, where they developed close social networks. We now turn to the interplay between regional and work identity and the changes in workers' social position wrought by industrialization.

3

FINDING WORK

*Origins and Composition of
the Arsenal Workforce*

Luo Qingzhen, "Quanmin zhanzheng" [People's war] (1938). From Su Lin,
Guotongqu heibai muke (Nanning: Guangxi meishu chubanshe, 2000), 111.

The Great Migration to southwestern China (1937–39) led in-migrants and Sichuanese to construct two distinct and opposing identities. Sichuanese came to see "downriver people" (*xiajiang ren*) as suave, but shallow, condescending, and prone to jabber. In-migrants to southwestern China used equally derogatory stereotypes to depict local residents and Sichuanese migrants. "Upriver people" (*shangjiang ren*) were supposedly brusque, boorish, and as hot-tempered as their daily fare of red chili peppers.

"Downriver people" sought to achieve social superiority vis-à-vis local Sichuanese by contrasting images of a more refined outer provincial with the subjugated and backward natives. Such attitudes had formed prior to the war, when non-Sichuanese occupied a small but influential niche in the Chongqing economy. Outsiders, many of them merchants or small restaurant owners, seemed united by their ability to influence local market trends and project the coming wave of commercial development, which they aspired to represent. As one Zhejiang observer noted, "Even though they only constituted 10 percent of the population, their influence was such that they made all market conditions of Chongqing heed their change; all trends became 'downriver' ones; sojourners [*chumen ren*] thus united more easily than the local people."[1]

Sichuanese, however, rejected the subordinate role envisioned for them by sojourners intent on creating self-other dichotomies. They too created identities vis-à-vis the sojourning community. Some local provincials, in following market trends, may have been attracted to the sojourners' savoir faire, while others affirmed their own superiority by belittling non-Sichuanese, going so far as to call them "underfoot people" (*jiao dixia ren*).[2] Resentful local residents blamed the "interlopers" for inflation, swelling population, and descent into decadence. "Chungking disapproved of the lipstick on downriver girls; it disliked their frizzled hair; it was shocked by boys and girls eating together in public restaurants." Sichuanese defended their own customs, those of "traditional" China. Chongqing "clung to the old customs; marriages were still arranged by parents, and husband and wife met on their wedding day for the first time."[3]

To what degree did social relations within the arsenals mirror these cultural and class tensions present in society? What role did native-place ties play in influencing job access and workforce composition? I address these questions by looking at the origins of arsenal workers during the Anti-Japanese War and the formation of the arsenals' internal labor market, defined as "job changes within a firm involving formal and informal training, assignment and reassignment, transfer, promotion, and the like."[4]

Research on the development of labor markets in republican China (1911–49) has stressed the absence of an open competitive labor market and the persistence of particularistic and native-place ties in shaping recruitment and industrial job hierarchies. In her work on Shanghai cotton mill workers, Emily Honig has applied segmented labor market theory to explain how southern Jiangsu (Jiangnan) workers occupied the more skilled and better-paying jobs, in contrast to northern Jiangsu (Subei) people working at casual labor.[5] Lee McIsaac adopts a similar approach, arguing that prejudice and regional differences helped shape a divided labor market in Chongqing. "Downriver" workers dominated the more skilled jobs, even to the point of excluding local Sichuanese, who were relegated to the lower-paying jobs.[6] Besides analyzing labor markets, this research has supported narratives of class fragmentation. As reflected in the title of the recent book *Putting Class in Its Place: Worker Identities in East Asia*, scholars have subsumed class under regional place.[7]

The strength of labor-segmentation theory lies in showing the existence of various labor markets that contributed to social inequities. Expanding on Honig and McIsaac's research, I show that arsenal workers were marked as a group by stratification within an industrial hierarchy structured, in part, along regional lines. Several reasons account for this connection between regional ties and the division of labor. Access to an arsenal job among laborers was in large part influenced by their social origins. Migrants from impoverished regions of eastern Sichuan and Chongqing's hinterland supplied much of the arsenals' demand for cheap labor and thus quickly filled the ranks of the laborers. Conversely, during the initial stages of the war, workers from Hubei and Jiangsu in particular occupied the more skilled jobs, in part relying on their native-place ties and family connections.

Nevertheless, the boundaries that separated workers from different regions were quite permeable and changed over time. Far from being excluded, by the early 1940s, Sichuanese made up a majority of workers in the skilled sector. Sichuanese utilized kinship ties to acquire a foothold in the skilled sector. State and managerial policy also decisively influenced job access. A severe labor shortage of skilled workers coupled with the great demand for arsenal workers caused by the rapid expansion of Chongqing's defense industry pushed management to recruit and train

Sichuanese for skilled positions. Unskilled and inexperienced workers from Sichuan reached the top levels of the labor hierarchy within a few years via the defense industry's internal labor market. Arsenal work thus represented an opportunity for social mobility. In short, these changes in workforce composition suggest a fluidity in the labor market and indicate that regional ties were only one component in the complex process of finding work. Government and managerial policy, workers' connections, and family ties all played important roles. Above all, regional ties took a back seat to the "logic" of production used by managers seeking to stabilize a fluctuating workforce, improve workers' training and thereby integrate workers into the production process.

Agrarian Conditions and Rural-Urban Migration

Sichuan took in two-thirds of the estimated three million war refugees to southwestern China. Whereas 90 percent of Chongqing's 470,000 residents in 1937 had been natives, and sojourners were predominantly from Fujian, Jiangsu, and Zhejiang, by 1945, only 24 percent of the city's population of 1.25 million had been born there, 39 percent were Sichuanese migrants, and 37 percent were non-Sichuanese, primarily from provinces bordering or close to the Yangzi River, most from Hubei, followed by Jiangsu, Zhejiang, Hunan, and Anhui.[8]

Like other enterprises relocating to the wartime capital, the arsenals brought with them their core workforce, predominantly skilled workers from the coastal areas. Non-Sichuanese also occupied jobs on the lowest rungs of the industrial hierarchy, but this occurred more often during the first few years of the war. Many of these workers had helped move the factories to Chongqing and reassemble them there. In general, though, recruitment of non-Sichuanese laborers proved difficult, since they sought higher wages than managers were willing to offer.[9] Limited access to social welfare benefits also impeded large-scale recruitment of non-Sichuanese. Insufficient travel stipends prevented workers from bringing their immediate family to Chongqing unless they borrowed money from the arsenals, which took the form of wage deductions. Unskilled workers could leave their families behind, but it was difficult to support them through remittances, since the allowance for living expenses and cheap rice only sustained themselves.[10] As a consequence, rural migrants from Sichuan consolidated their hold over unskilled positions in the defense industry.[11]

MAP 3.1. Sichuan Arsenal Workers' Primary Counties of Origin. Based on Charles Y. Hu, *The Agricultural and Forestry Land-Use of Szechuan Basin* (Chicago: University of Chicago Press, 1946), figures 7 and 11.

Internal migration within Sichuan actually predated the war. Starting in the 1930s, migrant laborers had flowed in a broad-based movement away from rural areas to the province's two urban centers, Chengdu and Chongqing. According to a 1935 survey of sixty-four counties in the province, roughly 1.1 million people left their rural villages in one year alone. Some 61 percent migrated to unspecified cities as workers, as refugees, or to reside with their families. The composition of Chongqing's population demonstrates the increasing importance of migration. As a guidebook of the late 1930s noted, only 40 percent of Chongqing residents had permanent roots to the city, whereas half of all residents had migrated from various counties within Sichuan.[12]

Rural distress was the primary cause of migration. According to the same survey, 40 percent left their homes because of banditry or natural disasters. Close to a third migrated because of deteriorating agricultural conditions: a bankrupt rural economy, a shortage of arable land, and poverty. Excessive rents, exacting taxes, and levies caused another 18 percent to migrate.[13] Several aspects of the agrarian structure thus worked to push peasants toward the city. Landlord-tenant relations, taxation, and conscription were the most prominent "push" factors. Whether migration in the 1930s stemmed from a significant deterioration in landlord-tenant relations relative to prior decades remains an open question. Nevertheless, the unequal distribution of wealth and the high rate of tenancy in eastern Sichuan contributed to the marginal subsistence patterns of most peasants and propelled them into sideline employment or to the city and factories. Military conscription and levies compounded the pressures influencing peasants' decision to move.

Arsenal workers in Chongqing originated primarily from three areas (see map 3.1): northern Sichuan (Guang'an, Nanchong, Xichong, Pengxi, and Suining), central Sichuan (Zizhong and Ziyang), and, above all, counties in eastern Sichuan and areas contiguous to Chongqing (Baxian, Bishan, Changshou, Hechuan, Jiangbei, and Jiangjin).[14]

Eastern Sichuan was one of the more destitute regions in the province. Rural poverty, endemic among tenant farmers, coupled with political instability and the threat of conscription accelerated migration into Chongqing. These conditions created a cheap labor pool for the arms industry and other expanding industrial sectors and formed the basis of Chongqing's proletarianization. Despite their proximity to Chongqing, the economic life of these counties centered on agriculture. Rural industry consisted mostly of handicrafts, dominated by women spinning and weaving cotton and silk. Working in small teams, men mined coal, sulfur, and iron ore.[15] But these were far from industrialized or even proto-industrialized regions, and so for many male workers, especially laborers, joining the arsenal workforce often constituted their first industrial experience.

There is no way to pinpoint the social origins of the migrant arsenal workers, but anecdotal evidence suggests that they came from both tenant and more affluent peasant households. According to one union leader, the sons of wealthy and middle peasants who entered factories to avoid conscription made up a portion of Chongqing's unskilled industrial workers.[16] Another worker recalls that a large number of steel mill workers were poor peasants driven off the land and forced to sell their labor to the factory. "If you were on the outside working the land, you had to rent the land and pay a deposit, but many people could not afford to rent land. Even though they were poor, they could get by in the factory. It wasn't the worst possible life."[17]

Given that Sichuan had one of the highest, if not the highest, levels of tenancy in China, it is likely that many migrant workers were either tenant farmers or among those who could not afford to rent land. Three surveys, conducted in 1933, 1940, and 1947, estimated provincial tenancy rates at 56 percent, with eastern Sichuan leading the province.[18] The counties from which most Sichuanese arsenal workers came had some of the highest tenancy rates in the province. At Baxian and Zizhong, half of all residents were tenants, and at Jiangbei and Ziyang, roughly 70 percent. Moreover, a high concentration of landownership rights was the norm. At Baxian and Bishan, land distribution was equally distributed among owner-cultivators and tenants, but in Jiangbei, Zizhong, Ziyang, Nanchong, and Pengxi, rented land ranged from 71 percent to 90 percent of the total cultivated. The proportion of landlords ranged from 3 to 5 percent of the total population.[19] Scholars have argued that accelerated marketing coincided with the growth of a new landlord class from official and military circles, intent on investing in cash crops. Several of the counties from which arsenal workers migrated were major rice producers for the urban market. By the 1930s, Baxian and Jiangbei, for instance, supplied Chongqing with over 30 percent of its annual rice supply.[20] Commercial development made possible the accumulation of the capital required for landownership, and by the mid 1930s, a new militarist landlord stratum had become the dominant elite in the Chongqing hinterland, owning up to 60 percent of the land.[21]

Although land may have been a lucrative investment, tenancy was not necessarily favorable to those tilling it. To be sure, tenancy could be associated with economic buoyancy, even an improvement in peasant conditions. Evelyn Rawski's study of Fujian's peasant economy, for instance, demonstrates that increasing commercialization stimulated landlord absenteeism, which, given fixed rents and security of tenure, allowed tenants to increase their productivity and income.[22] Comparable conditions that might have encouraged tenant investment in the land did not exist in eastern Sichuan, however, where the vast majority of landlords surveyed (N = 1,631 households) retained considerable control over leases by residing in the general vicinity, collecting rents in person, and frequently changing tenants. Over half of all tenant leases there were for less than two years, and a third were from three to five years.[23] Intense competition over land and resources is shown by the widespread use of rental deposits, estimated to have been used in over 90 percent of tenant leases in eastern Sichuan.[24] By the mid 1930s, the large number of tenants in eastern Sichuan prompted landlords to raise rent deposits as high as 80 percent of the land rent, causing considerable debt among tenants. According to one survey, 32 percent took a partial loan, and 43 percent were forced to borrow the complete sum.[25] Such tenants often had no choice but to hire out their own labor to pay back the interest accrued. Furthermore, tenants had difficulty making their landholdings economically viable, since they were not using credit to raise their land and labor productivity.

The physical geography of the region exacerbated the land's shrinking productivity. Hilly terrain covered three-quarters of the land in eastern Sichuan.[26] This topography and the limited access to water precluded double-cropping and hindered the development of a controlled irrigation system with small canals. Instead, farmers flooded their rice fields during the winter with rainwater and then used wooden waterwheels to distribute water between terraced fields. Up to 50 percent of terraced rice fields were left fallow during the winter season and used to store water.[27] Unlike farmers in the fertile Chengdu Plain, farmers did not drain the seasonal rainwater from the rice paddies and cultivate winter wheat, maize, and other winter crops. Such practices, they feared, would adversely affect the rice yield, because the ground would lack adequate moisture to transplant rice seedlings in the spring from their small plots into the main fields.[28] Inefficient irrigation methods thus contributed to the unproductive agricultural economy of eastern Sichuan.

Despite being unproductive, these irrigation practices, known as the winter storage water field system (*dong shuitian*) endured. In part, the difficult transport conditions and high cost of transporting fertilizers, typically night soil and oil cake, inhibited reforms. Farmers also allowed water to stand in their fields to kill the larvae of harmful insects, which otherwise survived the temperate winter climate. Above all, landlords sought to guarantee the annual rice harvest, the basis of their rental income. During the war, the allure of profits from rising rice prices precluded much crop diversification on good arable land or the payment of rents in other forms of grain. Onerous rents, among the highest in China, compounded this problem. Tenants paid from 55 to 70 percent of their primary rice crop (*dachun*), but retained the smaller crop (*xiaochun*) of mixed grains.[29] Yet tenant farmers in eastern Sichuan derived minimal income from the non-rice harvest, because they limited cultivation of secondary crops during the winter in order to assure an adequate water supply for the rice crop. If peasants did grow secondary crops, these were restricted to poor or mediocre land.[30]

Numerous miscellaneous levies, known as *tanpai*, introduced in the last decade of the Qing dynasty to support the New Policy reforms, contributed to the tenuous livelihood of peasant households. By the late 1930s, *tanpai* had become the primary, albeit unofficial, source of revenue for local governments. A survey of eighteen Sichuan counties in 1941 estimated that *tanpai* on average brought in twenty to thirty times as much revenue as formal taxes.[31] Local government officials and village headmen most frequently used the levies to finance conscription, but also to support the local police, government administrations, and education, as well as (according to critics) to line their own pockets. Not surprisingly, the greatest burden of the levies fell on the most vulnerable, whereas village headmen and members of the military administration, the Guomindang, and the Gelaohui secret society used their influence to reduce their own rates. In eastern Sichuan, although both tenants and landowners were assessed, property owners frequently passed on the levies to their tenants by raising rents as much as 80 percent.[32]

Once the war broke out, the threat of conscription and the economic havoc it wrought became primary causes of rural-urban migration. Arsenals proved highly attractive, since they were the only industry until 1942 to offer their workers draft-exempt status. Given that "the ordinary Chinese came to regard induction as an automatic death sentence," arsenals had particular appeal.[33] It was also no coincidence that counties supplying large numbers of arsenal workers contributed heavily to the army, because recruiters for the army and the arsenals often worked in tandem. Baxian, for example, supplied the army with 80,000 men between 1937 and 1945.[34] At Xichong, the army drafted approximately two-thirds of all able-bodied men in villages.[35] Since conscription generally occurred in the busiest part of the farming season to take advantage of the available labor supply, efforts to avoid the draft disrupted production. "Those most likely to be conscripted rush about causing the entire village to be swept off its feet; all the able-bodied men are panic-stricken and run off, even to the point where they harm one another. No one dares to go into the fields to farm, completely ruining the planting season."[36] The picture drawn of rural Sichuan may be overly dire, but it helps explain why working the land became less attractive than moonlighting or migrating to the city. The bleak existence of peasants also must have made arsenal work seem a temporary haven, even though factory conditions were far from ideal.

Kinship Ties and Jobs

Although peasant immiseration fueled migration to Chongqing, arsenal management's reliance on social connections and native-place ties favored certain counties over others in the hiring of workers. The intersection of family and native-place ties was especially prominent in Arsenal No. 24, perhaps because its local origins (established by Liu Xiang) made the munitions plant less dependent on recruiting workers outside of Sichuan once the war broke out. A reliance on hiring local employees led Communists in the early 1950s to denounce the steel plant as having had one of the more nepotistic management systems operating in the Nationalist defense industry. Specifically, the arsenal director Yang Jihui utilized both his native-place and family ties to hire managerial staff and workers from Ziyang County in southwestern Sichuan. His successor, Xiong Kewu, who became director in 1948, continued these personalistic practices, but reoriented recruitment to Xichong County, resulting in the formation of two rival cliques, the so-called Ziyang and Xichong *bang*.[37] From the standpoint of the Communist army, which occupied the arsenals in December 1949, particularistic ties impeded Communist managerial reforms and broader political goals. During the 1930s and 1940s, however, the Nationalist arsenal management felt that family ties guaranteed a semblance of stability and loyalty. Moreover, workers viewed kinship ties as a means of coping with industrialization in both psychological and economic terms.

Although it is difficult to quantify, by all accounts, arsenal workers relied heavily on family networks.[38] Feng Junren, a retired machinist, recalled how he had registered for employment because his father was an employee at the same arsenal. Feng remembered employment via kinship ties as "pretty widespread in our factory. Many employees had three generations working in the same factory. Quite a few." Like his father, Li Jiesun made cartridge shells. The arsenal also employed Li's maternal and paternal uncles, a "common" practice. Xie Lin, too, recalled numerous examples of hereditary employment. "Every family had several members who were all working in the arsenal. Only a minority worked outside [the arsenal]. Since 'green hands' [i.e., rookies] knew one another and lived together, it was more convenient."[39] Recruitment through kin thus ensured a certain continuity and stability to the workforce.

Besides facilitating recruitment, kinship ties proved important for job placement and the status of young workers. Feng Junren, for example, learned about the recruiting test from his father, a foreman, who had seen an advertisement posted inside the factory gates. The role played by kinship and patronage in the hiring of Li Jiesun is even more striking. Li's younger brother had been teaching in the middle school associated with the arsenal, but had fallen sick and died. "After he died, my father (a subforeman) had trouble earning a living, so he wrote a letter, signed by other workers, to gather support [for Li Jiesun's employment]." Many new workers achieved permanent status only after a stint as temporary laborer, which paid a lower wage, but Li's family connections won him preferential treatment. "I became a permanent worker ranked as sixth-grade, first-class, somewhat higher than temporary workers. Most laborers could only reach sixth-grade, fourth- or fifth-class."[40] In turn, Li's family had to reciprocate by giving gifts to their patrons. "Personal connections did play a role in the recruiting process. Usually, everyone used methods of personal relations, such as introductions, interceding for someone, and giving gifts. We gave the gifts—wine, chicken, and meat—to the officials."[41]

Once a son was accepted into the arsenal workforce, his father used connections to facilitate training and set up apprenticeships with appropriate "master" artisans:

As my father was in the factory, he knew many people well. He was well acquainted with many masters. He asked them to help out, help bring along his *wawa* [child]. . . . For example, [one reciprocated by] doing chores in the house, helping out on the holiday, or helping out if there was a wedding or funeral. This was frequent. If one wanted to work, one helped the master. When they celebrated the New Year or a festival, apprentices gave two bottles of wine to their master. This was common. It showed the younger generation's respect for the older generation. The father handed out the money and the son delivered [the gift], because it dealt with relations between the master and apprentice and the two men of the older generation were friends. This was *ganqing* [feeling]. We had to respect this. But we were willing to do this, we weren't forced to.[42]

These relations fostered a work culture based on moral and personal ties of dependence between workers of the same generation and across generations. That family ties could also serve as a fulcrum for working-class action was not lost on managers, who threatened to fire the fathers of militant sons in an effort to stop labor disputes.[43]

Even arsenal hiring practices indicate management's emphasis on industrial families. Certain arsenals limited recruitment to family members of employees. Arsenal No. 50, for instance, only recruited women if they were related to arsenal employees.[44] Arsenals also favored recent graduates of their recently established staff and workers' children schools when admitting apprentices to their skilled worker training schools.[45] The institutionalization of family connections demonstrated management's attempt to maintain a close-knit group of workers.

Reliance on family connection had important implications for the internal labor market of the arsenals. Kinship ties among arsenal workers influenced the division of labor when skilled positions became linked to successive generations of working families. Although laborers also utilized family ties, these historically held more significance for skilled workers, since specific skills could, in theory, be passed down from one generation of workers to the next. As a former steel worker, Zhu Rong, recalled: "Some workers' families had worked at a specific trade at the Daye Iron Mill, the Hanyang Steel Plant, or the Shanghai steel smelting plant for several generations. So they grew up in the factory, became workers, and then followed the factory when it relocated. They were truly formidable production workers."[46]

Zhu Rong raises several important issues: the diverse geographic origins of arsenal workers owing to industrial relocation, the fact that workers from central provinces and the east coast represented the core of industrial workers, and the respect accorded to highly skilled workers. One should add that kinship ties did not necessarily solidify the division of labor around local origins but merely contributed to the heterogeneous composition of the skilled workforce. If this sample of interviewees is indicative (most were Sichuanese), skilled workers relying on family connections were just as likely to be Sichuanese as "downriver people."

At the same time, the urgent demand for workers forced arsenals to be more inclusive in their recruitment methods, rather than continue hiring industrial families. Arsenal management adapted to the desperate times in a number of ways. They used informal recruitment methods, relying on native-place ties or word of mouth. Recruiters also disseminated flyers or placed newspapers advertisements. When arsenals needed additional workers, they often sent their own personnel to recruit or relied on agencies, such as the Social Welfare Board, the Youth Association Vocational Introductory Board, and even the Repatriated Overseas Chinese Guesthouse.[47] But Yu Dawei grew increasingly concerned that the lack of standards in wage rankings and worker qualifications demanded centralized control over the recruitment process. In March 1939, he therefore ordered the establishment of a Labor Recruiting Committee, composed of one representative from each Chongqing arsenal. On paper, at least, individual arsenals lost significant control over the recruitment process. Henceforth, when arsenals wanted to increase their workforces, they were obligated to send the Ordnance Department a list of the number and type of workers they sought. The Labor Recruiting Committee would then decide how many workers to allocate to the arsenal. Moreover, the Ordnance Department held formal recruitment drives and an entrance test every three months. Arsenals also continued to hold entrance tests, but the committee evaluated the test and set the worker's wage.[48]

These more formal means of recruitment allowed workers to find employment on their own initiative. Zhu Rong, for instance, successfully applied to the skilled workers' school at the age of fifteen after seeing a notice in the paper.

They were recruiting higher primary students, but I hadn't even graduated from elementary school so I went out and bought a book called "Guide for the Advancement of Learning" [Shengxue zhidao]. It had geography, natural science, history, math—all the curriculum for primary school. I spent a month reading that book over, then I went to take the test at the Tongyuanju [site of Arsenal No. 20]. Many people took the test, about 900, but I still passed. The test consisted of language, math, natural science, history, and geography. It took one day. In the end, they accepted 150 students.[49]

Reliance on more formal means of recruitment signified a shift from the clientelist relations between foremen and unskilled workers, in effect, an attenuation of the foreman's power and control over workers. In contrast to laborers, skilled workers were subject to a broader array of authority figures. Personnel managers directly recruited workers and used rigorous placement tests to select workers. In theory, too, the use of bulletins obviated the need for personal ties. But even here, their format proved advantageous to those with some personal pull. Sometimes advertisements omitted any reference to arsenal work, preferring to say a "certain administration" for fear of disclosing military information.[50] Such practices meant workers required a certain savvy or the right contact in finding out about and getting a job. Social connections, although less reliant on the family, continued to affect one's employment chances.

Laborers

Significant growth in the employment of unskilled operatives and laborers accompanied the expansion of the arsenal workforce, stemming in part from changes in production processes that "deskilled" jobs. Arsenals used the term "common laborer" (*putong gongren* or *xiaogong*) to connote laborers and unskilled operatives. Both held jobs characterized by low wages, few skills, and arduous working conditions. Nevertheless, there were important differences among unskilled workers, since the two groups worked in different types of production. Laborers relied on their strength and endurance to lift and transport; operatives did simple, repetitive, and monotonous tasks in the workshop.

In discussing the composition of the unskilled workforce, it is important to realize that the arsenals distinguished between temporary and permanent status, or *zhenggong*. Permanent laborers received benefits such as rice stipends or room and board. Although the documentation of temporary laborers remains sparse, arsenals probably hired them in greater numbers during the first few years of the war to do construction work. The variability of construction projects caused by fluctuating weather, availability of building materials, and high risk of accident among workers because of the rapid speed of building dissuaded employers from retaining a permanent labor force, which would have increased their wage costs. Temporary laborers were advantageous to management, in that their lower wages could justify decreasing the wages of more stable workers when the labor market turned favorable to the employer.

In contrast to other industrial sectors, especially the textile industry, casual labor was rare. The employment of casual labor remained limited to jobs in inspection, storage, transport, and construction. By the late 1940s, temporary laborers made up only 3 to 15 percent of the total labor force.[51] Demand did not fluctuate on a seasonal basis, because arsenals sought to maintain a steady level or expanding rate of production. This provided unskilled workers with greater stability and prospects for improvement compared to other industries. Moreover, because of the high demand for labor and the expansion of the defense economy, arsenals were hard-pressed to retain workers of all skill levels, and they thus preferred to hire workers on a more permanent basis, regardless of skill level.

While temporary workers remained few in number, the war period witnessed a dramatic increase in the absolute and relative numbers of laborers. Whereas in 1934, arsenals employed almost three times as many skilled workers as laborers, by 1945, the proportions were equal.[52] Simplification of the production process was a primary reason for the increased demand for unskilled labor. Beginning in the early 1930s, under the leadership of Yu Dawei and German technical advisors, arsenals began to implement changes facilitating mass production. When the war broke out, this process was by no means complete. Arsenals often underutilized machinery or lacked equipment and raw materials to maximize their production capacity. Nevertheless, centralized production, interchangeable manufacture, weapons standardization, and self-contained factories all contributed to forming the basis for mass production. Mass production had important implications for the workforce, creating a "division of labor in detail."[53] By the late 1930s, arms production was divided into many different components, with each worker performing a single operation.

Division of labor in detail affected certain production processes, most notably the packing of shells and grenades and inspection work, jobs characterized by speed, repetition, and low skill. These workshops employed a disproportionate number of laborers to fetch and carry, but also assembly operators to do basic machine work. At Arsenal No. 50, for example, laborers exceeded skilled workers by a ratio of four to one in the inspection shop, where workers checked the exterior of the product to see if it passed the mark.[54] Xie Lin, who apprenticed in north China before his arsenal moved to Chongqing, recalls the simplified work process involved in grenade production. "I was thirteen at the time. I was called a laborer. Children were classified as laborers, but actually they were child laborers. When we entered the workforce, a master artisan guided us for about a week because the work was simple. One could quickly learn the specific work process. At the time, I put the fuse inside the wooden handle and set it in place firmly, that was all. I learned it in a week, after which I worked independently."[55]

Such production processes were exploitative and the classification of "laborer" masked the reality of child labor. Even the definition of "laborer" was a misnomer, since it encompassed what would be considered an operative or machine assembler, someone assigned to constant repetition of a task. Whether consciously designed or not, the categorization of an operative as a laborer was a formal means of assigning a low wage, since unskilled workers occupied the bottom of the wage scale.

In other countries, the deskilling of machinists' work during wartime enabled management to lower wages and change the composition of the workforce. In Great Britain, for instance, the demands of the war and technological innovations in machinery, which rendered work processes more automatic, led to a tremendous increase in the number of women and semi-skilled workers employed in munitions factories during World War I.[56] Although "deskilling" disseminated certain jobs among women in China, they remained marginalized. During the prewar period, only the Shenyang arsenal employed women, and they were segregated in the cartridge plant. After 1937, several Chongqing arsenals employed women, but they remained few in number and were restricted to packing shells, stitching canvas, and inspecting products. A 1950 union survey indicates that women made up 3 percent of the arms industry's total workforce.[57] Several factors account for the exclusion of women from the workforce. Cultural prejudices and economic factors perpetuated a division of labor based on gender. As in other cities, women in Chongqing worked in light industry, especially textile manufacturing, and in the domestic service sector, but avoided heavy industry, such as the machinery, metallurgy, and chemical industries, which were central to arms production. Patriarchal conceptions regarding appropriate gender roles merged with the assumption that women were physically unable to do arsenal work.

In the late 1930s, arsenal managers called for the employment of more women in "light jobs," ostensibly to decrease the "excessively heavy family burden of arsenal workers, who lack the means of maintaining their family's livelihood."[58] The opportunity to pay lower wages and find a convenient means of decreasing geographic mobility among workers remained tacit motives. Although management pinpointed the spouses of employees, there was no substantial increase in their employment. A document listing the age and employment of 106 workers' wives, which may or may not be representative, noted only one "employed wife"; the vast majority were classified as "lacking employment."[59] Women did begin working in arsenals in peripheral areas, but this confirms that women were hired as a last resort and only when there were insufficient male workers.[60]

Newfound opportunities for women's work may have clashed with an idealized image of the arsenal as family benefactor, as articulated in a county ditty: "Grow up quickly, Jiangbei girls. When you grow up, marry [a worker from] Arsenal No. 21. Every three days, there'll be a big dish of pork, every half month is payday."[61] For certain arsenal workers, especially those employed by Arsenal No. 21, the wages they earned to support their families were sources of pride and security. Feeling that their jobs brought in sufficient income, many of the better-paid skilled workers assumed that their wives should be homemakers. In part, such attitudes played into patriarchal visions of the home. Workers—and that included women—may have also felt that arsenal work was more drudgery than a means of self-realization, and best avoided.

In reality, the wives of Chongqing arsenal workers both worked and earned income at home out of necessity. Women raised children, went to the market, gathered fuel, did the cooking, and mended and washed clothes—all labor-intensive, time-consuming tasks. Often the wives of arsenal workers did laundry for other families, and those in desperate straits had to "nurse the babies of rich families for pay."[62] A contemporary sociologist observed of Chongqing industry: "Married workers are in the minority. Those with families must take on subsidiary occupations after factory hours, such as peddling, to maintain them. Even then wives must take in washing, and even children must find paid employment or help the family out by spending whole days collecting waste fuel. In other words, no family can live if only one member is employed."[63] A report on the education of arsenal workers' children noted that parents were "too busy" to take care of their children. One can infer that spouses of the predominantly male arsenal workforce worked outside the home. The prevalence of this type of family economy by 1945 helps explain why more than 60,000 women engaged in commercial activity and some 145,000 women worked in Chongqing's "personal service" sector.[64]

Chongqing's demographics played an important secondary role in restricting women's access to arsenal employment. War refugees and rural-urban migration created an urban population explosion and exacerbated an imbalance in the ratio of sexes toward men. Between 1937 and 1945, the number of Chongqing residents increased 162 percent, while the ratio of women to men rose from 1 to 1.44 to 1 to 1.55.[65] Based on household surveys, these sources underestimate the actual number of men in Chongqing, who constituted much of the uncounted population of migrants, unmarried residents, and sojourners. Many men left rural areas either for the army or for the city to avoid conscription and find jobs in industry. Women remained in the countryside, working in the fields and participating in sideline employment (raising silkworms and pigs, spinning cotton and thread, weaving straw sandals and hats), leading to a feminization of the rural Sichuan economy. Between 1937 and 1945, more than 2.5 million Sichuanese men were drafted or forced into compulsory labor, lowering the total provincial population by 5.5 percent. Roughly one-third of all farm households in Sichuan were left without an adult male. [66] As in the experience of industrial workers' wives in the American South during the Great Depression, "the burden of survival fell increasingly upon the shoulders of women, not as paid workers contributing household income directly, but as unpaid producers whose labor ensured the maintenance of the industrial worker."[67]

Many of the Sichuanese migrant laborers took on arduous physical work associated with indirect production: construction, farmwork, and transport. Each arsenal hired several hundred laborers to transport coal and iron ore from the mines in nearby Jiangbei and Nantong Counties to the arsenals. After barges and cargo junks reached the docks along the Yangzi and Jialing Rivers, laborers hauled up supplies to the various workshops. At the steel plants, laborers carried loads of 250 to 285 pounds of coke up a thirty-degree slope to the blast furnaces without the aid of skip hoists.[68] Before American technical aid to arsenals began in 1945, Nationalist arsenals and steel mills had few vehicles, and transport infrastructure, such as a narrow gauge railway, had not yet been developed. The location of arsenals on the steep inclines of the "hill city" further impeded these efforts. Supply work relied to an even greater extent on manual labor using steps and ramps.

Within the workshops, laborers transported products and parts from one machine to another. Although arsenals began using assembly lines with conveyor belts, more often skilled workers ran single automated machine tools and loaded parts into baskets or carts as they finished them, which transport workers and laborers then carried or pushed to another machine tool for the next operation.[69] "Practically all transportation throughout the works is done by workmen carrying the material in two baskets suspended from a stick or beam resting on their shoulders."[70] Such work became especially burdensome when parts were carried to another workshop, since these were dispersed and often situated on different levels owing to the steep inclines.

One gets a sense of the enormous physical strain involved in daily work from the selection process of laborers. All laborers being tested had to carry heavy loads a distance of 100 meters. The arsenal gave the highest score to workers who carried 120 kilos or more, a B rank to those carrying 95 to 120 kilos, and a C rank to workers carrying 70 to 95 kilos. Management also tested whether laborers ran, walked briskly, or walked slowly while carrying 50 kilos.[71] Other arsenals used similar endurance tests, as Feng Junren describes:

Common laborers [were] tested [for] strength. At the time, the lead bars were fairly large. There were four loads, each 50 kilos, which we had to bring up [a 48-step incline] and then back down. It was that type of distance. Some workers couldn't endure. Some people spat blood while carrying the load. There was a worker named Lin Suping. He was only eighteen or nineteen years old, young when he went in for the test. He injured his insides, so he didn't pass. There was also Old Man Wang (Wang Daye), who worked in the [metal-]rolling squad. He carried steel rods. Each steel rod was about 15 kilos. He had to carry ten of them, or 150 kilos, inside the factory and walk in a circle. But he couldn't do it until my father [the foreman] lifted two pieces. Later, Wang told me, "Your old man's good. When I was taking the test, he took hold of two rods, otherwise I wouldn't have passed." This was connections. Other people had to lift ten. He lifted eight and passed. This is what connections meant.[72]

Feng's account illustrates the intense competition for jobs and the reliance on connections to gain employment. Despite the physical hardships of the laborer's job, employment was by no means assured. Arsenal policy granted all of its workers deferment from the draft—an odious prospect for most young men—motivating many laborers to seek employment for reasons besides wage income. The intense search for work provided a more stable labor supply, giving management greater leverage over the hiring process. Mounting concerns over security also prompted management to require that all workers furnish five guarantors, who would be held responsible if the worker "absconded, stole goods, or committed other infractions."[73] Certain arsenals stipulated that the guarantor should be a shop owner or "someone with substance." Presumably, those with fixed capital would be less transient and easier to pin down in case of mishap. If the worker bolted or was heavily fined, the guarantor would be legally and financially responsible, often being made to recompense the factory for training expenses.[74] By the late 1940s, arsenals restricted guarantors to workers or staff or required at least two staff members from within the arsenal to assume sponsorship.[75] Such a policy influenced the type of worker joining the workforce, favoring those who had a broader array of social contacts, while excluding the most destitute. As one former arsenal worker and underground activist recalled with some bitterness, "It was extremely difficult to enter Arsenal No. 23. Honest peasants had no way of joining the workforce. Everyone who joined had connections with factory personnel. . . . Those joining the factory were not naïve in the least. Most carried over vestiges of that petty urbanite or peasant mentality."[76]

The need for connections among laborers promoted the influence of secret societies over the hiring process. Several gangs gained a foothold in Chongqing industries when members of the Shanghai and Wuhan underworlds turned their attention to Chongqing. According to one Communist Party survey, Green Gang members numbered some 20,000 during the 1940s, concentrated among truck and car drivers, auto bosses, boatmen, stevedores, and arsenal workers. Among laborers, branch lodges of the Paoge, otherwise known as the Gelaohui, were especially prominent. The Paoge's historical ties to the transport and river trade, strengthened during the warlord era by transporting weapons for feuding militarists, pulled arsenal transport workers into its fold. By the war period, this "secret" society dominated most strata of society. The same survey estimated that 70 to 80 percent of Chongqing residents were members, and 100,000 of those "professional" members.[77]

Many laborers regarded the gangs as a support mechanism. If one did not join, one became isolated, especially outside the factory community. "Not joining was like a horse being bullied. Joining, you would have friends and you would not be excluded."[78] As one former labor activist and gang member put it, "The masses joined the Paoge hoping it would be an organization they could rely on, a guarantor of employment, a means of help and convenience."[79] The bridge to low-level jobs was supported by the Daye, or leader of each lodge, who served simultaneously as foreman and labor broker. These men, such as Feng Junren's father, fostered ties of personal dependency between workers and foremen by providing jobs to laborers and overseeing wages in return for kickbacks and allegiance to the gang.[80]

In assessing Jiangnan and Subei workers' access to jobs, Emily Honig argues that connections—or lack of them—were both a prominent cause and a manifestation of the divided labor market in Shanghai. Likewise, it can be argued that the limited network cultivated by unskilled workers, the majority of whom were Sichuanese, perhaps perpetuated and reinforced their lowly status. One crucial difference, though, was the expansion of direct managerial controls, which offered laborers the opportunity to rise into the ranks of skilled workers.

The Origins of Skilled Workers

Beyond favoritism or connections, employment in the skilled sector meant demonstrating one's objective skills, the product of training and experience. But notions of skill in China, as elsewhere, have been socially constructed, that is, both historically and culturally defined. As Perry Willson, a historian of women and work in fascist Italy, explains, "The reasons for calling one job skilled and another unskilled often have more to do with the political muscle of certain sections of the labour force or with general cultural values than with some intrinsic aspect of the work itself."[81] Cultural values especially affected women's work, since it was assumed that their jobs did not require skill. As further evidence that definitions of skill are often socially constructed, we have seen that the administrative labeling of skill did not always correspond to the actual job. This was not unique to Chongqing, or to China for that matter, and could be merely a convenient device to determine wage ranks. McIsaac, who accentuates the socially constructed dimension of skill, argues that definitions of skill reinforced Chongqing's segregated labor market, denying most Sichuanese workers access to the skilled sector. Contemporary observers, such as engineers, denigrated Sichuanese as unfit for skilled labor. Consequently, the classification of skill was skewed in favor of "downriver people," allowing non-Sichuanese skilled workers to preserve their privileged position as a labor aristocracy and successfully corner the skilled labor market.[82]

Whether arsenal workers used subjective notions of skill to maintain their own status is another question. Non-Sichuanese skilled workers may have desired to preserve their position at the top of the industrial job hierarchy by accentuating the differences between "upriver" workers and themselves, but they could not restrict access to jobs. They lacked the kind of tradition of craft unions and contracts that has given artisans in other contexts greater control over labor markets.[83] Management, which made the hiring and promotion decisions, did not hesitate to use Sichuanese skilled labor. The basic vulnerability of skilled arsenal workers is evident from the changes in their status over the course of the Anti-Japanese War.

During the initial boom years of the war, migrant skilled workers were paid better than Sichuanese laborers and enjoyed a different lifestyle. An Arsenal No. 23 worker and activist recalls that older skilled workers from Gongxian earned three yuan per day, over eight times the amount earned by a Sichuanese laborer, who had "absolutely no status." "Back then, three yuan was a very high wage. Every Sunday, they went to the Emei athletic club to eat. Food was expensive, but they had a feast. Every evening, they played cards and mahjong. They ate fish and meat and wore Western-style clothes."[84]

Within a few years, the skilled elite saw their economic status plummet. This is evident when one compares the 1945 wage rates of Sichuanese and extraprovincial skilled workers employed in the first department of Arsenal No. 20.[85] Following segmented labor market theory, one would expect extraprovincial machinists, many of whom had formed an artisan elite prior to 1937, to have received higher wages than Sichuanese skilled workers. As applied to Shanghai, the theory correlates skilled work, higher wages, and better working conditions with ethnic domination.[86] Workshop figures indicate, however, that wages were depressed across the board, rather than being aligned along regional lines or based on seniority. This placed non-Sichuanese at a disadvantage, since they were usually older and had been employed longer. Some thirty-nine Sichuanese workers were employed in the cartridge shop; they earned an average of 1.12 *fabi* (1 *fabi* = 1 yuan) for the eight-hour work day, were on average twenty-nine years of age, and had an average employment tenure of 6.2 years. On average, extraprovincial skilled workers earned negligibly higher wages at 1.13 *fabi*, were eight years older, and had worked in the arsenals for 13.2 years, about twice as long as the Sichuanese workers. This same pattern held for the boiling and cleaning shop, where extraprovincial workers had tenures of over eleven years, compared to six for Sichuanese workers, but earned only .03 *fabi* more than Sichuanese. At the copper-shell workshop, where eighty-three Sichuanese and sixteen extraprovincial foremen and skilled workers worked, the average wage rates were identical at 1.2 *fabi*. Here, the Sichuanese were slightly older (thirty-nine on average, compared to thirty-six) and had an almost identical length of service (7.6 years compared to 8.3 years).[87]

Together with dwindling earnings, higher-status machinists suffered a marked deterioration in their quality of life. "[A] skilled worker in heavy industry who had lived in a room with a wooden floor and electric light in a brick house in Shanghai might have had to content himself with a corner of a dormitory, or a mud-floored, unlighted bamboo shed in Chungking," Israel Epstein notes.[88] It was perhaps the diminution of their status in material terms that led non-Sichuanese workers to construct an image of more sophisticated and skilled worker vis-à-vis the "backward" native worker. To echo W. E. B. Du Bois's thesis on race and work, even when the non-Sichuanese migrant workers received low wages, they were compensated by a "public and psychological wage."[89]

Even the terminology describing skilled work reflected the diminished status of "artisans." Technological modernization facilitated direct managerial control by creating more specific jobs among factory operatives. By the late 1930s, skilled workers were no longer identified as artisans, (gongjiang), a term implying a range of skills. Instead, machine operatives—fitters, turners, forgers, and welders—had become specialized and were known for their specific skills.

Emphasizing the socially constructed aspects of skill also underplays the reality that arsenal work, especially metal cutting, entailed learning specialized skills. Operating machinery and tools and manipulating materials was a complicated matter. Metalworking required "genuine skills," not just "socially constructed" ones. According to Robert Gordon, who has studied the metalworking technology of nineteenth-century American armories, genuine skills can be subdivided into four components: dexterity, judgment, planning, and resourcefulness. Dexterity involves an ability to wield tools with ease. Judgment is the skill of gauging the size and shape of a part by eye and relying on touch to determine the fit between mechanical parts. Planning and resourcefulness entail preparing the actual work process and anticipating complications caused by shortage of material or problems with machine tools.[90]

Genuine skill remained essential to armaments production in China. Although the use of gauges in achieving standardized parts decreased reliance on workers' experience, by the late 1930s, this process was still incomplete. On the eve of the war, workers at the Taiyuan arsenal, for instance, continued to rely on their judgment and experience to gauge the precision of parts.[91] In general, machinists required ample skills to operate drill presses, boring mills, grinders, and lathes when cutting metal to high tolerance. The time involved in mastering a craft also illustrates the difficulty of metalworking. One worker studied with a master artisan for two years before he mastered the lathe. Another required at least three years of training to do highly skilled work as a welder or use precision machine tools, such as the milling machine.[92]

While entrance tests for laborers emphasized strength, those for skilled workers required a minimum level of schooling and a demonstration of machinist skills. A skilled metalworker recalled that after the Jinling arsenal relocated to Chongqing in 1937, recruitment tests were held each week testing workers' particular skills.[93] A typical test consisted of an oral interview, in which workers related their work experience and read a mechanical draft. They then demonstrated their operative skills. Turners had to turn a bent axle on the lathe; fitters had to shape a metal piece in the form of a swastika, the symbol of Arsenal No. 21.[94] If accepted, workers underwent a trial period of two weeks or more, after which they were assigned a wage ranking.[95]

Because of the greater degree of training and genuine skills involved in armaments production, arsenals at first employed a higher percentage of skilled workers from the more industrialized coastal region and central provinces. During the late 1930s, the establishment of training schools for local skilled workers did not rapidly resolve the dearth of skilled workers in Chongqing, forcing arsenal managers to recruit skilled workers from cities outside Sichuan. Recruiting agents concentrated their efforts on former defense industry sites at Changsha, Guilin, Hengyang, and Zhuzhou.[96] The provincial distribution of the skilled workforce also reflected the geographical origins of the relocated arsenal, as indicated by Arsenal No. 25's 1939 rolls (table 3.1). Part of the arsenal had belonged to the Zhuzhou complex, and consequently many Hunanese either traveled to Chongqing and helped reassemble the plant or were subsequently recruited. Similarly, Jiangsu workers had ties to the arsenal, since a significant portion of the machinery came from the former Shanghai arsenal.

Recruiters considered provincial origins per se less important than the amount of skill and experience in arms manufacturing a worker brought to the job. Often these criteria proved difficult to match, as Jin Xiesheng, a staff member of Arsenal No. 10, discovered upon arriving in Yuanling, Hunan. Jin could not find skilled workers of "good quality" and bemoaned their "faulty character" and poor skills, which he compensated

TABLE 3.1

Provincial Composition of Arsenal No. 25 Workforce in 1939

(percentage)

Province	Skilled workers	Laborers	Apprentices	Total
Sichuan	18.9%	53.3%	32.8%	34.8%
Jiangsu	44.9	12.2	16.2	27.5
Hunan	6.2	2.9	20.6	7.0
Shandong	11.9	2.5	0	6.4
Henan	1.8	10.6	6.4	6.0
Hubei	6.2	4.7	5.4	5.5
Anhui	3.6	7.7	2.4	5.1
Zhejiang	3.9	3.6	7.8	4.4
Hebei	1.3	0.9	2.0	1.2
Guangdong	0.5	0	5.4	1.0
Jiangxi	0.2	0.9	1.0	0.6
Other	0.6	0.6	0	0.5
Total	612	548	204	1,364

SOURCE: Chongqing Municipal Archives, 25 Chang, 5 *mu*, 10 *juan* (July 1939).

for by reducing their wages. Nevertheless, those workers that eventually went to Chongqing had considerable work experience, and of the twelve who had a recorded job history, all but one had worked in an arsenal.[97] Workers' ties to the defense industry must have proved decisive in the hiring decision. From a managerial standpoint, workers with past experience in the industry would adjust more quickly to the work environment and might prove more loyal to the plant.

At times, arsenal managers' preference for non-Sichuanese workers during the early stages of the war hurt Sichuanese workers. Although Sichuanese constituted the second-largest bloc of skilled workers at Arsenal No. 25, over half (sixty-nine) of the total Sichuan skilled workforce were temporary employees. The ratio of temporary to permanent laborers was even more pronounced among Sichuan employees. In 1939, the arsenal employed roughly three times as many temporary laborers from Sichuan. Granting temporary status enabled management to accommodate an expanding workforce after relocation, when arsenals began to build factory housing and to provide social welfare benefits. While arsenal management emphasized retaining non-Sichuanese workers because of their skills and transient qualities as in-migrants, they considered Sichuanese to be more expendable and more easily rehired. The policy discriminated against Sichuanese, since temporary status generated lower income from wages and rice allowances.

Management was sensitive, however, to charges of discriminating against Sichuanese, fearing that a factious workforce would lower morale, decrease production, and even cause defections to the Communist Party. In 1938, when an internal document circulated to Yu Dawei stating that excessively long work hours and unequal treatment between Sichuanese and extraprovincial workers had caused arsenal workers to migrate to the Communist base in northern Shaanxi, Yu ordered detailed reports from his subordinates. Arsenal No. 20 responded that such claims of discrimination were "sheer fiction."[98]

Both reports, though, probably contained elements of truth. Wage levels during the late 1930s reflected the prewar economic disparities between the more developed areas, such as Wuhan and Shanghai, and the interior, Chongqing. At the Gangqianhui, for instance, on average, the highest wage earned by Sichuanese workers in 1940 was comparable to the lowest wage of incoming workers from the lower Yangzi region, Zhejiang Province, and northwestern China. Managers sought to narrow differentials by pegging wages to the type of product and equalizing wages based on the same work.[99] To prevent feuds between workers arising over real and perceived differences in treatment, the Ordnance Department even ordered a member of the arsenal security force to mediate conflicts arising between workers of different regions. Appealing to local workers, the order specified: "Management shall send a fair and impartial member of the security forces. It is imperative that he be from this province [Sichuan] and that he be responsible for binding together regions and negotiate with workers involved in feuds."[100]

The status of Sichuanese skilled workers changed over the course of the war, in no small part because of state intervention and personnel practices. Data from Arsenal No. 50 suggest the absence of constant and pervasive labor market discrimination against Sichuanese (table 3.2). Starting from a maximum concentration of non-Sichuanese skilled workers in November 1939, by November 1942, close to half of all skilled labor was Sichuanese. Nor was Arsenal No. 50 an exception. Separation data of skilled workers from two other war plants indicate that by the early 1940s, Sichuanese had already procured a strong foothold in the skilled sector, and by the middle of that decade, they comprised a majority of the skilled workers.[101] State support for apprenticeship programs and emerging internal labor markets played an important role in Sichuanese' ability to move up the ranks.

Training programs dramatically increased the number and proportion

TABLE 3.2

Provincial Distribution of Arsenal No. 50 Skilled Workers, 1939–1946

(percentage)

Date	Sichuan	Jiangsu	Hubei	Henan	Zhejiang	Guang-dong	Hebei	Other	Number of workers
Nov. 1939	14.7%	12.6%	8.0%	15.9%	3.9%	10.0%	14.7%	20.2%	510
Nov. 30, 1942	47.2	12.7	5.1	6.7	7.1	5.0	4.3	11.9	1,020
Oct. 31, 1943	50.2	8.4	8.2	8.3	4.9	5.3	4.0	10.7	1,242
Dec. 31, 1944	44.3	9.6	10.1	9.8	5.5	5.5	4.2	11.0	1,275
Dec. 31, 1945	46.2	9.2	10.4	8.6	5.0	4.8	3.4	12.4	1,620
June 30, 1946	62.5	6.6	9.0	3.8	4.0	3.5	2.8	7.8	1,035

SOURCES: Chongqing Municipal Archives, 50 Chang, 3 *mu*, 313 *juan*; 50 Chang, 2 *mu*, 303 *juan*, 6; 50 Chang, 2 *mu*, 304 *juan*, 6; 50 Chang, 2 *mu*, 305 *juan*, 132; 50 Chang, 2 *mu*, 306 *juan*, 205; 50 Chang, 2 *mu*, 307 *juan*, 86.

of Sichuanese holding skilled positions. As the largest artillery producer in southwest China, Arsenal No. 50 stood at the forefront of the defense industry's training programs. By late 1939, the arsenal had accepted over 200 students at its apprentice school in Chengdu.[102] The school eventually formed part of the National Defense Industrial Committee's training program. Begun in 1940, this project funded arsenals throughout southwestern China to train over 1,000 skilled workers within three years. As in the apprentice schools, the students were all male, between the ages of sixteen and twenty, and were required to have a higher primary school education or its equivalent. Training consisted of instruction in math, language, and blueprint design. The plan also envisioned six hours of military training per week to inculcate patriotism and provide physical exercise. During their first year of training, students spent several months learning metalworking, fitting, forging, casting, and carpentry. During the second year, they each specialized in a craft. Wages were a pittance, even less than the lowest-ranking laborer earned, but workers received free clothing and room and board. After completion of their training, apprentices entered the ranks of skilled workers. They still, however, only formally completed their training after another three years of employment.[103]

Several thousand skilled workers were eventually trained. If a report of the Gangqianhui is indicative, some 450 workers received training at the steel mill over a span of four and a half years. Between September 1941 and 1947, over 1,000 workers graduated from training schools at Arsenal No. 21. At Arsenal No. 50, the plan assigned 250 workers for training in shell manufacturing, machinery, and construction. These numbers pale when compared to the more ambitious postwar training programs, which increased the annual quota to 2,500 for the defense industry, but the program nonetheless contributed to the increase in Sichuanese skilled workers between 1939 and 1942.[104] Training programs also significantly improved workers' literacy and increased educational opportunity at Arsenal No. 50. Between October 1943 and December 1947, the proportion of *jixie shi*, skilled workers who had received training, increased from 27 percent to 38 percent. At the same time, the percentage of illiterate workers progressively diminished from 31 percent to 13 percent of the total workforce.[105]

A factory promotion system developed alongside worker training programs. Promotions consisted of jumping in status from laborer to skilled worker or advancing within a skill category. Advancement meant a choice of jobs, in addition to promotion and a wage hike. Skilled workers, in particular, preferred jobs involving genuine skills, so that they could keep the level of drudgery and fatigue to a minimum. Feng Junren's decision to study lathe turning typified this balancing act. Feng had entered an arsenal in 1945, where he studied at the skilled workers' training school for two years before choosing lathe turning as his specialization. "At the time I had thought to become a metal fitter, because it required a few more skills. I was then only seventeen or eighteen years old. But my father told me to pick the lathe because you could sit down while working, whereas you had to stand if you were a metal fitter. Turning depended on one's hands, and once the equipment got started, it was a bit more relaxed, but it also required technique." Feng went on to work as a lathe turner in the tool department, which from his description seems to have been primitive—a workshop containing "clubs, sticks, and files." Excessive repair work prompted a search for another assignment. By means of personal networks, Feng transferred out to a position involving more skill.[106]

Promotions were the other primary form of advancement. Management used periodic evaluations (*kaoji*) to advance workers up a wage scale of thirty-six levels, divided into six classes (*deng*), with six grades (*ji*) per class, introduced in the mid 1930s under the influence of a German technical advisor, M. Bischoff. Wage rates were initially comparatively few and straightforward but were expanded to six classes and a total of fifty-four ranks.[107] Starting in 1937, workers were evaluated on a yearly basis for promotion, but limited to one rank per year.[108] Within two years, the Ordnance Department's Production Board revised the wage scale after critics noted that if an apprentice worked diligently, had superior skills, and did not violate any regulations, it would still take fifty years to reach the top of the wage scale! Consequently, arsenals reduced the wage scale to four classes with a total of twenty-four ranks.[109] By 1939, management had introduced a biannual efficiency-rating system to determine wage rankings. Evaluations gave equal weight to moral character and to physical and technical skills.

By the civil war period, managers emphasized productivity over moral values, perhaps because of American technical support and efforts to increase productivity. Accordingly, 60 percent of test scores were based on workers' skills, 20 percent on an oral test, 10 percent on math, and another 10 percent on language.[110] Total scores were graded A through D (*jia, yi, bing, ding*). Scores in the A range meant a three-rank raise; a B led to a two-rank raise; a C scored a one-rank raise; a D carried no promotion. After 1948, scores below fifty led to a one-rank demotion. Rules formalized in 1947 once again increased the wage scale to six classes with six ranks per class and further emphasized skill differentials among the workforce. Foremen could ascend to the first class first grade; assistant foremen could aspire to first class third grade; and rates of both skilled and unskilled workers were set at a low of fifth class sixth grade. Whereas skilled workers could be promoted to the first class fourth grade, unskilled workers could advance no further than the third class first grade. Wage rates of apprentices were not to exceed the sixth class first grade.[111]

Above all, arsenal management limited promotions by introducing numerous technicalities to maintain the arsenal's social hierarchy and restrict wage increases. Besides testing, length of employment determined promotion. Laborers seeking to become skilled workers, and lower-level skilled workers (*jixiebing*) aspiring to become trained skilled workers (*jixieshi*), required a minimum of two years' work experience in the arsenal. Skilled workers seeking promotion to foreman needed three years' tenure. Hierarchical boundaries were drawn between the four categories of workers, so that apprentices, laborers, skilled workers, and foremen had to first change their status before advancing to the next highest skill ranking. If laborers attained the highest possible ranking, set at fourth class first grade, only 5 percent could have their wages changed to rates usually accorded to skilled workers. And once their wage ranking had reached the third class fifth grade level, those 5 percent were no longer promoted. The alternative method of reward used to compensate laborers who had achieved an average score of A or B on two evaluations was to pay a bonus of 30 or 15 *gong*, respectively. (One *gong* was equivalent to eight hours' pay.) This choice reflected management's desire to limit wage expenditures, since a raise in the wage scale was more expensive over the long run than an immediate bonus.[112]

Judging from the policies of Arsenal No. 50, it is clear that the defense industry had no desire to promote workers more than one grade at a time. The arsenal deliberately restricted mobility to prevent large discrepancies in the wage gap between workers and foster more competition. "In order to avoid gross disparities in wages, if *jixieshi* already earn more than two yuan [per day] and are unexceptional, they will not be given an A. We hope that a minority will be able to advance two grades and the majority advance one grade. We can [in this way] not only put an end to their complaints but also encourage their competitive spirit and thus increase productivity."[113]

This policy was later codified when management limited A grades to 20 percent of workers seeking promotion. For most production workers, bonuses replaced wage promotions.[114]

The highest attainable position for most workers who worked their way up the promotional ladder was that of foreman, which was prized for its higher wages and status but required the patience and fortitude of Job. The long tenure of foremen foreclosed the post to many aspirants. All tenures of artisans promoted to subforemen were much longer than the stipulated minimum requirement of three years. At the rifle department of Arsenal No. 21, for instance, foremen constituted an exclusive elite. Artisans' accumulation of experience and craft skills, coupled with their desire to maintain positions of power and authority, had produced a "foreman's empire."[115] A list of six skilled workers promoted to the ranks of subforemen in 1946 indicates that length of service ranged from a minimum of sixteen years to a maximum of forty-seven years before promotion! Other departments were somewhat less rigid but still required extensive experience prior to promotion. The tenures of rising workers in the molding-sand department ranged, for instance, from ten to nineteen years.[116]

Foremen generally held much longer and more stable jobs than rank-and-file workers, which discouraged promotions by limiting the available positions. Data from a roll of 122 foremen and subforemen employed by Arsenal No. 20 underscore their long tenure and relatively advanced age.[117] Foremen were much older, with a mean age of 42.2, while their average tenure was 14.2 years. Significantly, roughly 60 percent of the foremen came from Sichuan. Age, experience, and skill rather than regional provenance were, however, the main criteria used to choose foremen.

If it was difficult for workers to gain a foothold among foremen, it was nearly impossible to become a staff officer. Conditions had changed significantly within the industrial hierarchy since the 1920s, when artisans and even apprentices had frequently attained the highest positions in arsenal management.[118] By the mid 1930s, most workers were excluded from these avenues of social mobility. In theory, some factories allowed up to 30 percent of all technicians to come from the ranks of skilled workers, but in practice only a minute proportion became management or technical personnel, judging from the number of promotions accorded to skilled workers. At best they could aspire to become second lieutenants, the second-lowest rank among arsenal officers.[119] One reaches similar conclusions when using personnel files of managers to trace their social mobility patterns. Among one hundred staff personnel employed in the Works Bureau at the Jinling Arsenal in 1934, none had any experience as a production worker. All either had military experience or had graduated from technical schools or universities.[120]

Why did arsenals consciously segregate managerial employees and production workers? By the wartime period, the arsenals had changed their organizational structure, adopting managerial components from Taylorism and the German movement for industrial "rationalization." Centralized planning coincided with the emergence of a technical class responsible for the planning of production. The exclusion of skilled workers also reflected the traditional chasm in China between mental and manual labor and a general antipathy toward workers. Most officials running the arsenals felt technical and managerial work required academically educated personnel, even though experienced workers could have done much of the work. This social prejudice in turn perpetuated the large gap in remuneration between workers and managers and technicians, making it more difficult to challenge the industrial hierarchy from within. Nor did proponents of the defense industry's organization, with its elaborate ranking system among officers, envision significant opportunities for those on the bottom ranks. Finally, restrictions on the mobility of skilled workers allowed the defense industry to absorb some of the glut in engineering graduates trained during World War II.

The promotion system thus frustrated more ambitious workers. For enterprising workers, leaving the arsenal and then rejoining the work-force were means to advance more quickly. The experience of Zhou Guoguang reveals these career patterns and also the reactions of his peers. Zhou had entered Arsenal No. 50 in March 1943 as an apprentice to be trained as a lathe operator. After acquiring skills over an eighteen-month tenure, he left the arsenal, but he later rejoined it under the as-sumed name of Zhou Zhouming during a recruiting drive for skilled workers. Zhou was then assigned to the repair and assembly department and paid a daily wage of twelve yuan. Before long, he was transferred to the fuse department, where he was finally apprehended and punished. Significantly, Zhou's wages were said to be "higher than those of old workers who have been employed here for over ten years. This really af-fects the morale of most old workers."[121] The senior workers obviously resented an upstart like Zhou Guoguang. The case also sheds light on how low wages and lack of opportunity prompted Zhou to gamble with the promotion system.

Ultimately, the actual number of promotions diverged from these guidelines. If 1948 statistics on promotions are indicative, the number of workers who were graded with As and Bs surpassed the set quotas of Ar-senal No. 50. Among 2,359 evaluated workers, 29 percent received an A, 36 percent received a B, and 35 percent scored a C or worse.[122] These fig-ures point to a degree of upward mobility among arsenal workers. As one former arsenal worker recalled, "If there weren't many problems, work-ers by and large could be promoted two ranks. If you lagged a bit, you were promoted one rank. Some workers had excellent skills and could be promoted several ranks."[123] Training and promotions allowed many Sichuanese to become skilled workers and eventually replace or augment the largely in-migrant skilled workforce. Promotions ultimately depended on wage policies, however, which involved contradictory interests—a de-sire to reduce inflation by freezing wages and thus limiting the extent of promotions, and the need for incentives to keep workers in the arsenal fold.

If the promotion system and the development of an internal labor mar-ket benefited Sichuanese workers, the demobilization drive after World War II consolidated their dominance. Some workers returned home on their own initiative. Others were discharged after the defense industry called for a 32 percent reduction of the rear-area workforce in 1946. At Arsenal No. 10, roughly a third of all workers left before management re-stricted their movement.[124] Rolls from Arsenals No. 10 and No. 20 indicate that Sichuanese constituted about 80 percent of the entire workforce and held most skilled jobs during the civil war years.[125] The provincial composition of Arsenal No. 10 refutes the view of a static and divided internal labor market along native-place lines. As early as 1942, 69 percent of all apprentices, 58 percent of skilled workers, and 87 percent of laborers were Sichuanese.[126] In part, management efforts to train local workers, as reflected in the high rate of apprenticeships among Sichuanese, promoted access to skilled jobs.

If the divide between in-migrant workers from other provinces and local Sichuanese did not restrict Sichuanese from moving into the skilled sector, perhaps sojourning workers retained more influence over particular crafts and dominated certain workshops. Did native-place ties coincide with the division of labor within particular workshops? Production departments in the Chongqing arsenals do show patterns in the concentration of workers from particular regions, reflecting the composition of the factory workforce prior to relocation, since departments kept on their most skilled and experienced workers. The reorganization of arsenals in Chongqing, however, made the workforce composition of each workshop much more diverse. During this process, management often moved workers from one workshop to another, depending on which department needed their skills. "Workers who had originally been together were broken up," Xie Lin recalled. "According to different types of work, different posts were planned for workers."[127] The recruitment of local workers added a further regional dimension and diluted the concentration of specific regional groups within departments.

Because production was the guiding principle in the organization of departments, arsenal management did not make a conscious effort to divide so-called upriver and downriver people. Workers from various regions worked together, but each department retained a nucleus of skilled veteran workers to guide less skilled workers. Since specific crafts were often based on regional ties, various regional cliques developed within departments. In discussing how native-place ties influenced the work site, Zhu Rong, a machinist in a steel-rolling department, recalled:

Everyone worked together according to production needs. Some smelted steel, some rolled steel. Some were lathe turners, others fitters. As long as there was a demand for the work, everyone could work together. They didn't divide "upriver" and "downriver" people. Of course, there were historical conditions that characterized the workforce. Concerning the skills of outer provincial people, they were the core, the main skilled workers. Our arsenal, for example, included several factories that had relocated to Chongqing during the war. There was the

Shanghai steel works, the Hanyang steel works, and also the Daye iron mill and Liuhe steel works. In the factory, there were many workers from Guangdong. Cantonese had gone to the Hanyang steel plant many years before. There were also a lot of Hubei workers, as well as Shanghainese. In our factory, most Shanghainese worked at steel smelting. Most Cantonese were lathe turners, fitters, and [other kinds of] metalworkers. Hubei workers worked at iron smelting and steel rolling. These men had the most advanced production skills.[128]

Although, as Zhu Rong suggests, particular jobs tended to align along provincial lines, workers sharing native-place ties did not monopolize one particular workshop or department. Almost all production departments required metalworkers such as fitters, machinists, and turners. Consequently, non-Sichuanese workers were dispersed throughout the factory, contributing to the heterogeneity of the workforce.[129]

The division of production processes on the basis of native-place ties has led to two different views of labor activism. Emily Honig emphasizes how regional alliances, which both reinforced and reflected a segregated labor market, impeded class solidarity among Shanghai's cotton mill workers.[130] Elizabeth Perry, on the other hand, underscores the role of worker subcultures in sparking strikes in individual departments. "Because workers from the same geographical areas tended to congregate in particular workshops, local cultures overlapped with work experiences to create a powerful potential for labor activism. Shared lifestyles, dialects, and entertainment choices prepared subgroups of laborers for collective action."[131]

Neither approach fully explains the pattern of protest during the high tide of the labor movement from the autumn of 1945 to the summer of 1946. A more extended analysis of the strike waves is presented in chapter 8; suffice it to say here that labor activists often mobilized several departments, could galvanize the entire workforce, and sometimes even coordinated strikes among arsenals. In March 1946, the entire workforce of Arsenal No. 10 held a slowdown to raise wages for workers of all skill levels, shortly after the Gangqianhui workforce had struck on March 23 for back wages and the right to unionize.[132] When workers at the Arsenal No. 21 branch factory struck for three days in the spring of 1949, "about 10,000 workers at the central arsenal put their machines in high gear without working."[133] The mixed composition of departments diminished the possibility of one clique of workers being played off against another, or of one regional group organizing itself alone. Arguably, too, the workforce was predominantly Sichuanese when strikes occurred, so that "place" was an organizational principle behind protest. But this approach overlooks the economic and political grievances workers shared, regardless of their provenance. Labor activists also came from diverse regions, indicating that at least in the arms industry, the "politics of place" had less impact.

Regionalism and Solidarity

Job access had various dimensions, and regional ties were only one factor. Much of the evidence concerning workforce composition indicates the fallacy in assuming that regional ties structured factory life. Although the numbers reveal how arsenal labor forces were organized, they say little about their internal dynamics. Relations between workers from different regions were also conflict-ridden, but attempts to affirm an ethnic identity or negate a class-based identity risk overlooking workers' feelings of solidarity, the belief that workers should help one another protect their livelihoods.

Over a span of several years, the residential patterns among arsenal workers cut across regional ties, making the workforce more integrated than the population at large. The arsenals thus diverged from the city pattern of segregated communities that Theodore White describes: "A thousand Chungking alleyways darted off down the slopes of the hills from the two main roads; they twisted and tumbled over steps that had been polished smooth by the tramp of centuries of padding straw-sandaled feet. The native Szechwanese lived in these alleys as they had for centuries; they held aloof from the worldly downriver Chinese and were suspicious of them."[134] By contrast, Chongqing arsenal workers from different provinces and skill levels lived together in dormitories, where rooms were allocated on a first-come, first-served basis rather than by production unit or provenance.[135] "Generally speaking, there was no difference between Nanjing workers and local workers, even though it was the old society, and each locale had its clique in the arsenals. As regards housing, if the lodging was small, three to six people lived together. Larger rooms held seven or eight people. These eight workers were not from the same production unit. Even where there were workers from eight units, those eight workers got along on fairly friendly terms. Some of them were from Nanjing, Shanghai, Sichuan, and so forth."[136]

To be sure, cultural affinities were conducive to friendships between workers from the same region. Common foods and similar dialects united workers from the same region. After entering the skilled workers' school, Zhu Rong recalled, "We all lived in a collective dormitory. There were people from each province, but Sichuanese were the majority, because out of the 150 recruited students, from 70 to 80 were Sichuanese. We lived, ate and worked together, but Sichuanese were the majority. Sichuanese felt at ease with their language and shared similar customs, and so it was easier to become close."[137]

At the same time, a tradition of geographical mobility among arsenal workers, especially skilled labor, forced workers to learn different dialects. Tan Zuoren, for instance, learned both Cantonese and Wuhan dialect, because his family was originally Cantonese but had moved to Wuhan, where his father and he worked in the Hanyang arsenal. After migrating to Chongqing and living there for five years, he had learned to understand Sichuanese dialect. His apprentice Zhu Rong understood his "standard" speech. A more telling indicator of the porous regional boundaries among workers was intermarriage. We lack quantifiable data, but even Theodore White acknowledged that marriage patterns crossed regional divides: "Now nature took its way. Men from Peking married girls of Szechwan; daughters of Shanghai families married Cantonese. It was a curious mixing."[138]

One reason that workers' regional identity became more fluid was the diminished importance of native-place associations during the Anti-Japanese War. From the late Qing era until the war, these organizations fostered a strong sense of regional identity by replicating local customs, promoting crucial business networks, and providing welfare services to sojourning communities living in foreign urban environments. As Bryna Goodman, a leading historian of this social organization, notes, "Because they bore native-place labels, brought together sojourners in various activities and represented the 'face' of different native-place communities, they were crucial sites for the construction of a positive idea of native-place identity and community for their sojourning populations."[139] As the war progressed and millions of refugees migrated to the southwest, however, the state expanded its role as a provider of social welfare, thus replacing the traditional intermediary role between state and society played by native-place associations. Once they relocated to Chongqing, native-place associations were also simply strapped for cash. For these reasons, Lu Liu argues, nationalist sentiment became a primary form of identity, displacing the regional identity that had been reinforced by native-place associations.[140]

A work culture associated with machinists that centered on pride of craft was also a unifying force for workers. The Sichuanese machinist Zhu Rong recalled his relationship with his foreman as follows: "My relationship with the old workers was quite good. When I was learning the lathe, the foreman was Cantonese. We had a very close relationship. I had studied the lathe for one year, but my skills weren't very good. Soon after my promotion from apprentice to skilled worker, that subforeman, Tan Zuoren, taught me technical skills. He remained concerned with my development. . . . Later, when he went to Daye, we still corresponded by letter. When I got married, I wrote him the news, and he even sent me a letter of congratulations." Zhu and other workers who recalled a skilled worker's prowess using phrases such as "that worker was really formidable" underscore the respect many workers had for learning a craft and for those who imparted its secrets.

These comments are not made to discount the gulf between Sichuanese and non-Sichuanese workers but to show that workers' loyalties and identities changed and assumed different meanings within an industrial setting. If one places regional ties in a historical context, one quickly notes the capacity of workers to share common interests regardless of provenance. This was true at Arsenal No. 23, where a wide breech developed between Henan skilled workers and Sichuanese laborers soon after the arsenal had moved from Gongxian, Henan, to Luzhou, Sichuan. When Communist activists entered the arsenal workforce, they immediately set out to ally themselves with both groups of workers, because they realized that gaining the respect of older workers would be an "arduous task."[141]

Developing friendships with workers on their own terms was a key part of the Communist success. This meant that activists, many of them students, had to remake their lifestyles. To some workers, they acknowledged that they were not of "worker stock." "We said we were middle school students trying to avoid the draft." But before joining the workforce, they assumed the appearance of workers by discarding their Western hair styles and clothing in favor of crewcuts, workers' clothes, and straw shoes. Once hired by the arsenal, the activists entered into forms of solidarity with some of the poorest laborers by swearing brotherhoods and joining mutual-aid societies. With the help of activists, but also on their own initiative, three to four hundred Sichuanese workers organized revolving credit associations (*dahui*), which they used to buy clothing and blankets. Activists then sought to gain workers' trust by working hard alongside them, frequenting the local teahouse, watching local opera, and gambling. Mediating disputes or relying on charisma, activists like Chen Hualuo (whom workers fondly called Omi, because his large ears reminded them of Omito Fo, the Amitabha Buddha), helped organize a workers' club that spread political literature and rallied workers against the welfare department for deducting welfare funds.

Activists also recruited Henan workers, but the veteran skilled workers were generally much more cautious. As one activist recalled, "At first, they felt we were a bunch of youngsters out for fame, or said it was a matter concerning Sichuanese workers, not themselves." Activists responded by doing chores for the "master" craftsmen, such as carrying water or firewood for them. In this way, as the underground activist Xiao Zekuan recalled, "They also realized that we were struggling for the War of Resistance and in the interests of workers. Many of the old workers had been in strikes and had seen workers sacrificed, thus they had a minimum of consciousness, so they began to sympathize with us and supported us." The militant minority also cultivated friendships with charismatic leaders from Henan, Anhui, Hubei, and Shanghai. In this way, the activists, who were predominantly Sichuanese, could more effectively do party work among each regional group and break down barriers. By 1939, activists recall, they had developed a strong base that crossed regional and skill lines. The 400 workers in the gas mask factory often participated in the CCP-run chorus and theater. Communists used the club and their newspapers to propagate principles of patriotic resistance and socialism.[142]

Organizing was done on separate tracks, because of the various regional cliques within the arsenal, but these converged when workers perceived the advantages of concerted action. This occurred, for example, when workers organized their own communal mess hall and rejected management's offer of a separate skilled workers' dining hall. Initially, the arsenal labor board had accommodated northerners and Sichuanese by providing both wheat staples and rice, but workers were disgruntled by wage deductions for food costs, the high price of wheat, and the often mildewed rice they were served. Increasingly, workers turned to cooking in small groups of five or six, or to tramping five *li* to the nearby town of Luohanchang. But the long commute caused workers to return late for their shifts, resulting in fines. Labor activists responded by mobilizing all workers to establish a communal mess hall. Much to the chagrin of management, which had proposed a mess hall exclusively for skilled workers, both skilled and unskilled workers preferred their own cafeteria, where they could control the price of food. From the account of one memoir, the mess hall succeeded in promoting collective interests. In their spare time, workers helped in the kitchen, bought rice, brought in coal, planted vegetables, raised pigs, and swept up the mess halls.[143]

These experiences are suggestive of how the factory community differed from society at large, and how workers' sense of themselves as a group with common economic interests could transcend regional ties. Differences among skilled and unskilled, native and sojourner workers existed and were reinforced by the factory hierarchy. In contrast to recent studies that stress the fragmentary pull of regional ties, I argue that regional divisions aligned themselves along divisions between workers and management. It was conflict between workers and management, an antagonism based on both class and regional lines, that fueled workers' grievances and their involvement in the labor movement. Understanding the tenacity with which workers fought management over issues like wages, treatment, and unionization requires first looking at the working conditions facing arsenal workers and their quality of life during the 1940s.

4

INSIDE THE ARSENALS

Conditions of Work and Life

Assembly line and conveyor belt for production of 60-mm mortar shells at
Arsenal No. 50 (1940s). Reproduced by permission of the Chongqing
Municipal Archives.

How did war, rapid industrialization, and inflation shape the material conditions of Chongqing's emerging working class? Workers employed in the arsenals during the 1940s remember their experiences with varying degrees of nostalgia and bitterness. According to Zhang Ping, who entered the workforce in the late 1940s, many people "wanted to squeeze into the factory." Employment in the war plants supplemented wages with free or cheap daily goods and provided stability, in stark contrast to the impoverished and precarious livelihoods of other Chongqing workers. "Everyone said, 'You workers in that Arsenal are so lucky.' Each year clothing and cloth was issued, even for one's family members. It was at a low price, very low. Rice and food, you really didn't have to pay money. You just went and got it. For instance, every week, we could get several blocks of tofu. It was fine not to pay even a cent. Oil, salt, matches, rice—there was everything. From this perspective, although earnings were a bit low, workers were satisfied."[1] Yang Jinhua was more critical and recalled that he had gone on strike in 1946 because he could no longer stomach the unappetizing food supplied by arsenal mess halls in place of regular rice supplies sold on the black market. "Think about it, eight years of those difficult days, suffering by eating wheat. It wasn't threshed wheat flour; it was simply boiled wheat. They cooked it like rice, but we were eating wheat. Our shit was streams of wheat."[2]

To an unprecedented degree during the War of Resistance, the emergence of an elaborate social welfare system in Chongqing influenced arsenal workers' quality of life. Under the prodding of the state, which by the early 1930s had expanded its role in industrial legislation and as a welfare provider, the arms industry imposed direct control over its workers. Arsenals controlled, not only the terms of employment, but also housing and food, and even the cultural activities of their workers. One effect of such direct control, as suggested by Zhang Ping, was to heighten employees' dependence on the arsenals as a social safety net. An array of welfare reforms, akin to a social wage, compensated for the marked deterioration in workers' standard of living and thus delayed the slow and insidious process of their alienation from the government. By the early 1940s, workers faced increasingly hard times. Hyperinflation after 1941 eroded real wages, while the demands of wartime production and the greater intensity of work sent industrial accidents and disease rates soaring. Workers toiled excessively long hours throughout the War of Resistance until arsenals introduced a new work regime based on principles of scientific management. By the civil war period, managers had increasingly linked wages to productivity, introduced piecework, and shifted from extensive to intensive forms of exploitation, namely, shorter hours but higher wages for greater production. A wage system based on inherent limits, to curb inflation, and compensated for by less costly social welfare benefits, tied workers to subsistence-level wages. Many workers thus became dependent on the factory compound for their livelihoods; it seemed the only source of stability in an increasingly precarious world.

While welfare helped compensate for low wages and brutal working conditions, it also heightened workers' expectations regarding their proper treatment by the state and management. Consequently, neither position in the ongoing debate about industrial paternalism in East Asia holds completely true. Studies of industrial paternalism have long been divided between those who argue that paternalism deterred workers' interest in labor unionism and scholars who hold a more skeptical view of the de-radicalizing effect of industrial paternalism.[3] Just as workers shared both regional and class identities, they also had multiple identities vis-à-vis industrial paternalism. As Elisabetta Benenati has noted of 1950s Italy, for industrial paternalism to exist, workers must also "'choose' this system of relationships because they believe they can extract advantage from it." Moreover, this degree of acceptance does not signify that workers have "abandoned their class identity."[4] Arsenal workers' reactions to social welfare were equally complex. Given the relative security offered by arsenals in increasingly uncertain times, many of workers' demands were not for greater independence but for greater access to the system. At the same time, notwithstanding the differences in treatment among production workers, the even starker contrasts between their treatment and that of managerial staff (who were ranked as officers in a military hierarchy) further emphasized the shared burdens of work and harsh living conditions. As inflation increasingly eroded real earnings, social welfare programs had the unintended effect of spurring production workers' subjective notions of class divisions between themselves and staff members. Although deteriorating economic conditions served as the context for general labor strife, they bore only an indirect relationship to workers' grievances. Like that of workers in Europe, arsenal workers' sense of moral injustice was highly personalized and often directed against their supervisors, whom they deemed responsible for their plight. Rather than direct their anger at the system or societal relations in general, workers pinpointed the more immediate source of injustice within the factory.[5] For these reasons, conflict in the workplace often focused on administrative and technical staff. Workers' anger was thus not simply derived from economic disaffection, but from feelings of moral injustice, intensified by segregation and economic discrimination felt on and off the job. Paradoxically, industrial paternalism simultaneously reacted to and shaped the labor movement.

Dying for Work

Angela Woollacott's recent study of British munitions workers during World War I suggests parallels between the experience of women's work on the assembly line and their brothers' war in the trenches.[6] Although she may exaggerate the similarities between combat and production, her perspective draws our attention to the artificial boundaries often drawn between the war front and home front. In China, a distinction was also made between the war front and the Great Rear area (Dahoufang), territory in southwestern China controlled by Chiang Kai-shek's Nationalist government. Whatever psychological comfort Chongqing residents may have derived from living in the Great Rear area was soon shattered, however, by the arrival of Japanese bombers.

After occupying Wuhan in October 1938, the Japanese quickly set up air bases in the Hubei provincial capital to mount attacks on Chongqing. Acting upon the directive of Chief of Staff Prince Saijin, a member of the imperial household, air raids began in the spring of 1939 with the intent of "destroying China's will to continue the war." Japanese policy shifted from achieving total military destruction of the Nationalist army to using air raids to force Nationalist capitulation. Wang Jingwei's defection in December 1938 and his establishment of a puppet government in Nanjing convinced Japanese strategists that bombing would destroy Chinese morale, deepen the rifts within the Nationalist government, and quickly bring the war to an end. The devastating bombing attacks upon Chongqing reached their most intense phase between May 1939 and September 1941 (table 4.1). The bombing raids of May 3–4, 1939, two days of terror that Chinese historians have aptly compared to the Nazi bombing of Guernica in Spain, killed an estimated 4,400 people and destroyed almost 5,000 homes.[7] Chongqing was at its most vulnerable. Air raid shelters were still being built, and the range of anti-aircraft guns fell short of the 5,000-meter altitude maintained by Japanese bombers. Government response was limited to guiding mass evacuations, no small matter in itself. Within three days after May 4, a quarter million residents had fled the capital acting on He Yingqin's orders.[8]

TABLE 4.1

Casualties and Damage Inflicted by Air Raids in Chongqing, 1939–1941

Date	Raids	Flights	Bombs	Dead	Wounded	Homes destroyed
1939	34	865	1,879	5,247	4,196	7,199
1940	49	3,092	7,976	2,425	3,686	20,109
1941	81	3,495	8,893	2,448	4,448	5,987
Total	164	7,452	18,748	10,120	12,330	33,295

SOURCES: Xu Chaojian et al., eds., *Chongqing da hongzha* (Chongqing: Xinan shifan daxue chuban-she, 2002), 188, 201; Wen Xianmei, "Riji dui Chongqing de 'zhanlue hongzha' he Chongqing de fan-kong xidongzheng," in *Zhongguo Chongqing kangzhan peidushi guoji xueshu yantaohui lunwenji,* ed. Gu Yueguan (Beijing: Huawen chubanshe, 1995), 224, 231; Wu Yuexing, ed., *Zhongguo Kang Ri Zhanzheng shi dituji* (Beijing: Zhongguo ditu chubanshe, 1995), 152.

Over the next two years, bombing raids intensified and expanded to target the civilian population. The bombing took on a seasonal pattern during the summer and early autumn, when the fog no longer enveloped Chongqing. Between May and September 1940, enemy planes carried out "Operation 101," a series of concentrated carpet-style raids. The following August, Japanese bombers conducted thirty "exhaustion raids" on the wartime capital, each lasting up to five hours. Compared to 1939, when air raids struck strategic military, economic, and political nerve centers, bombing in subsequent years spread to densely populated areas, including commercial and residential areas, schools, and hospitals. Bombing raids intensified on the city center after the Japanese requested that European consulates move to a designated "safe area" in the outlying Nan'an district in June 1940. Beyond this gesture, the Japanese military ignored the fact that the Tokyo government had once signed the 1922 International Naval Treaty, which prohibited the bombing of civilians and nonmilitary installations.[9]

Although Chongqing endured over a quarter of all the raids on China during the War of Resistance, remarkably, it suffered fewer than 3 percent of civilian casualties nationwide, reflecting increasingly successful air-raid defense.[10] To be sure, catastrophes occurred, most tragically on June 5, 1941, when a thousand civilians suffocated and trampled one another to death while trapped in the city's Jiaochangkou tunnel.[11] One should not minimize, though, the government's efforts to extend air raid shelters on a mass and equitable basis. By 1941, enough tunnels, bunkers, air-raid shelters, and dugouts had been built to protect almost half a million residents, roughly two-thirds of the total population.[12] The government also enlisted 20,000 people in bomb raid "service teams" to control the fires in the aftermath of air raids and to rescue victims caught in the rubble.

A shift in Japan's wartime strategy and its expanding role in the global conflict spared Chongqing further destruction. Operation 101 ended in September 1940, when a portion of the Japanese squadron was transferred to prepare for the attack on French Indochina. Similarly, Japanese militarists viewed the air raids of 1941 as a trial run for the campaign in Malaysia and springboard for possible war with the United States and Britain. By 1942, Japan's increasing commitments to multiple fronts and involvement in the Pacific War ended most air raids on Chongqing.

The bombing reduced but never halted industrial production. Arsenal No. 21 was bombed at least fourteen times between June 24, 1940, and August 30, 1941, and forced to decrease production of seven different weapons.[13] Over a hundred employees were killed when eighteen planes bombed the Gangqianhui steel plant and residential area on September 14, 1940. A second attack occurred a year later, on August 23, 1941, when the steel mill was struck forty-three times, damaging workshops, dormitories, and offices and leaving nine men and five women dead.[14] In conjunction with the Air Defense Command Center, arsenals took several measures to protect their plants and employees. The Gangqianhui used a hill-shaped net to camouflage the rolling mill. Smokestacks were made to look like a large tree and towers.[15] Many arsenals used the natural surroundings as buffers. Workers moved valuable machinery and power generators into air-raid shelters carved out from the nearby hills. Preceding an attack, sirens would sound and the arsenals would turn off the power and evacuate the workers to air raid shelters.

Workers and their families reacted to the bombings with trepidation and nationalist resolve. One apprentice, who had been eleven years old at the time, recalled his fear of frequenting the city's movie theaters. "Going to watch the movies was like a death warrant, because there was no place to hide during the air-raid warnings."[16] The bombings left many workers victims, heightening their sense of nationalism. "They bombed the civilian district, killing or injuring many families. My mother-in-law was killed during the first bombing raid. So many workers hated the Japanese."[17]

Such experiences, rather than abstract pronouncements of faith in nationalist ideology, prompted managers to spur production in the name of defeating a common enemy. The fiery nationalist Li Chenggan appealed to his workers' sense of sacrifice: "We must exert that spirit of self-sacrifice like warriors combating the enemy and complete our work with all our might." Yang Jinhua, who worked in a steel mill, recalled how staff had used the Japanese threat and China's national humiliation, especially by the victimization of women and children, to intensify work. Staff officers recounted stories of their experiences in Japan, where they had witnessed Japanese men urinate on their Chinese women classmates. Even without such shameful stories to motivate them, news of Japanese atrocities in northern Chinese villages quickly reached the arsenals. "At the time, we hated the Japanese devils, the Japanese devils' rape and killings, and their 'three-all' ['kill all, burn all, destroy all'] policy, so we were encouraged to produce a lot, to produce as many weapons as possible, or else they would invade us here and then we would really suffer."[18] Thus, although intended to dampen the morale of Chongqing residents, air raids may actually have bolstered their resolve. "[W]hen a population is systematically bombed and otherwise brutalized, it pulls together in new ways that strengthen the state and the will to resist," Diane Lary and Stephen MacKinnon note.[19]

Although workers joined the defense industry for a variety of motives, they perceived employment in the arsenals as a patriotic act. "We work for the War of Resistance," a young worker explained. "As long as everyone undergoes equal hardship, as long as we are in high spirits, we prefer to withstand low wages."[20] That sense of self-sacrifice may explain how they could tolerate poor working conditions and risk the fatal dangers that permeated arsenal work. Reports and surveys conducted by the arsenals indicate the carnage during the war. From available records for seven arsenals, a total of 1,348 workers lost their lives between 1937 and 1946, roughly 2 percent of the workforce. At Arsenal No. 21, sickness and disease accounted for over 90 percent of the worker fatalities during World War II (N = 600); the remaining forty-five deaths were attributed to work-related causes.[21]

Chongqing's physical geography and tropical weather exacerbated industrial pollution, rendering the population vulnerable to disease. Located in a basin surrounded by foothills, the city is trapped under the sweltering humidity of summer and the cold, damp winter fog.[22] The scholar Hu Shuhua described Chongqing in the mid 1930s as "hilly, narrow and densely populated, with residents living in extremely crowded conditions. Because coal is used, the entire city is shrouded in foul odors and dusty air. The air does not circulate for residents living below the mountains, while smoke from the kitchen stoves of the hillside residents rises up to fumigate the hill-top residents."[23] High levels of sulfur and ash found in the coal and spread in the form of sulfide and dust often caused lung disease among arsenal workers.

As in many cities in China, abysmal hygiene in Chongqing spread infectious disease. No sewage or drainage system existed, and people piled garbage on the river banks or in alleys and dumped waste water back into the rivers. Such practices contributed to some of the deadliest scourges of society. The wartime correspondents Theodore H. White and Annalee Jacoby graphically described the city streets: "Sewage piled up in the gutters and smelled; mosquitoes bred in the stagnant pools of water deep in the ruins, and malaria flourished. Dysentery grew worse; so did cholera, rashes, and a repulsive assortment of internal parasites. The smallest sore festered and persisted."[24] Public rest rooms, where flies bred in the excrement, often contributed to the spread of epidemics.

The combined effect of industrial pollution, disease, and the dangerous working environment led to frequent sickness among arsenal workers and their families. Records from the steel mill, Arsenal No. 24, and the artillery plant, Arsenal No. 50, reveal a staggering number of medical visits. Perhaps the availability of free medicine and medical care to all employees and their immediate families inflated these numbers, but the high rates of hospitalization confirm that factory clinics overflowed with sick and injured patients. Health care workers at Arsenal No. 24 treated more than 47,000 first-time visits and over 212,000 follow-up visits during a one-year span starting in July 1948. Arsenal No. 50 had as many as 70,000 first-time visits during this period. Roughly 1,100 employees and their immediate family members were hospitalized at this artillery plant, for a total of 8,500 days.[25]

Workers increasingly directed their medical complaints to the department of internal medicine, suggesting the alarming spread of disease. As many as 3,701 (58 percent) of workers' internal medicine department visits in 1939 at Arsenal No. 24 were reported as malaria cases, of which 111 were diagnosed as malignant. Two years later, increased production and an enlarged workforce quadrupled the rate of illness.[26] Memoirs from the Gangqianhui steel mill recall malaria running rampant during 1940, and in September 1942, over 100 people died from cholera. In one day alone, 50 to 60 people died at the Lu-Han workers' village.[27] Laborers frequently contracted dysentery, diarrhea, or typhoid fever because they drank unboiled water or ate spoiled food. One worker recalled his own traumatic experience as an eleven-year-old apprentice: "My greatest fear was diarrhea. In Chongqing I would shit until I got dizzy. It was so bad that by nighttime I couldn't see anything."[28]

Migrants and older workers fell ill and died more often than Sichuanese workers. Of the 555 workers at Arsenal No. 21 who died of illness between 1938 and August 1945, 118 were Sichuanese, 112 were from Jiangsu, and 111 were from Hubei.[29] Although many former Jinling and Hanyang arsenal workers had relocated to Chongqing from Jiangsu and Hubei, they hardly equaled the number of Sichuanese workers, indicating that death took a heavier toll on the in-migrant workers. Likewise, of the 100 reported deaths incurred at Arsenal No. 20 between 1939 and 1942, 56 struck non-Sichuanese.[30] By and large, these workers were older (over forty), skilled workers with long-standing tenure of over twelve years. Exhausted and malnourished older workers who had migrated to Sichuan were more vulnerable to disease.

The kind of sickness and fatalities varied according to each arsenal and work process, but respiratory disease was widespread. Workers grinding and buffing mortar shells on lathes inhaled particles of dust and ran the risk of being hit in the face by metal shavings. Packing cartridges and shells exposed workers to dust and noxious fumes for prolonged periods of time. The accumulation of dust in the lungs caused scarring and increased susceptibility to trachoma and respiratory infections. Tuberculosis, induced by dust, torrid heat, and sudden changes in temperature, caused the greatest number of fatalities in the steel mills. The large concentration of metallic particles stemming from working with sand molds in the foundries was another source of TB. One arsenal worker who witnessed the effects of such work recounted:

The shell factory was as pitch dark as Zhazidong [the Chongqing site where political prisoners were incarcerated]. The main floor machines were extremely noisy and disordered. . . . Workers' bodies were completely black, covered with iron dust. There weren't any ventilators . . . In the shell factory, workers' hands were always black. They couldn't get rid of that iron soot. Usually, they were given sawdust to scrub their hands, but they couldn't be cleaned well. Only if they used oil could they finally clean themselves, so some workers secretly used oil to clean, even though they would be punished if caught.[31]

Poor working conditions and the intensification of work during wartime weakened and struck down even the young. As a former turner recalled, loaders packed the powder and TNT into the mortar shells without recourse to gloves, gauze masks, or any safety controls. "In the loading section, they used a steel brush to brush the inside of the shell. It was full of iron powder. A typical production day was 2,100 82-mm mortar shells, an average of one every three minutes. The labor intensity was extremely high. Some of the workers died of lung disease because of the dust and because there was no protection."[32]

While work-related injuries became a part of the new mass production processes in the arms factories, risks increased inside the steel mills because of inadequate mechanization. To smelt steel, workers carried and then tossed 30-kilo bars of pig iron into the furnace chamber, making sure the iron was distributed evenly so that it would melt quickly. At the furnace entrance, flames would often spurt out and burn their faces. Rolling steel was also dependent on manual labor and prone to mishap. Workers used large iron drill rods and tongs to turn steel ingots over and draw them out of rollers, which shaped them into large and small billets. "One day a subforeman named Wang used too much force and slipped. The floor was smooth. It was a type of sheet iron on the floor, which had become very slick. He fell down. He still went forward, and as a result his arm was swept immediately into the rolling machine."[33]

Industrial accidents linked to the specific production process in manufacturing munitions posed a constant threat to workers' safety. Production of gunpowder and the packing process could be fatal, because the sweltering summers of Chongqing, for which the city is aptly termed one of China's "three great furnaces," could increase the heat normally applied to bake the gunpowder and raise the temperature above combustion level. Smokeless powder was chemically produced from a base of either nitrocellulose or guncotton. Workers then mixed metallic salts and nitroglycerin with the base to form a colloidal jelly, which was dried and granulated. It was during this drying process, a surviving apprentice related, that intense heat caused a chemical explosion and a section of a packing workshop to burst into flames.[34]

Explosions in the filling workshops were a leading cause of work-related deaths. The risks involved in assembling artillery shells, mines, and grenades were so great that certain managers even downplayed the danger, much to the consternation of an American advisor to the Ordnance Department in the mid 1930s. "The superintendent must always warn the workmen about the danger of careless handling of explosives; it is a bad practice, which can be found in some factories, to diminish the danger in order 'not to scare' the workmen."[35] When packing gunpowder into the shell, workers had to limit any friction in order to avoid igniting the shell or detonator. Explosions caused by packing the shells too vigorously (powder would be rammed into the shell with a wooden mallet) could leave the filler with maimed hands, ruptured eardrums, or missing fingers.[36] Workers packing hand grenades had to be just as prudent to prevent igniting the blasting fuse by hammering in the two pins that attached the grenade shell to its wooden handle too far. Cramped conditions in the jerry-built structures and the intensified speed of production made work treacherous. Xie Lin, whose first job in 1938 was to pack hand grenades, recalls how he worked with others right on the floor in a thatched workshop roughly fifty meters long and two meters wide. Hand grenades lay scattered over the floor, since there was no proper storage place. Two weeks after he joined the arsenal, a grenade explosion blew the entire shop to bits, injuring or killing over 150 of the workers.

Judging from Xie Lin's account, almost nothing was done to recompense the victims, contributing to his perception that management was guilty of callous negligence. "After the explosion, single workers like me whose belongings were all burned received a blanket from the factory, but that was all. At the time, I was lightly injured, and after going to the medical clinic, I was all right. I was lucky. . . . I was a little kid. I ran quickly so I escaped. . . . The factory had the Changsha herbal doctor come over to treat the injured. Some of the workers had broken legs, some were cured, and then it was over, the matter was settled. There was not even a compensation fee. If you died, you were cremated; if you lived, you went back to work."[37]

Working Hours and Wages: From Extensive to Intensive Exploitation

War created a work regime that emphasized discipline, strenuous work, and productivity. Production increases over the 1940s were not simply the result of technological and managerial reforms introduced a decade before, but built on the backs of labor. Sheer exhaustion caused by such a labor regime was one reason so many workers succumbed to disease and injury. "You ate on the job so that the machines kept running," Director Li Chenggan recalled. "You did not sleep until late at night, or volunteered to extend [your] working hours to over fourteen hours with no rest at all. Workers who made concerted efforts and vied to rush through production became sick from not sleeping. Exhaustion spread among those relying on this death-defying, sweat-drenched spirit of dedication to our country."[38]

The workers' sense of patriotic sacrifice that Li captures was most pronounced during the first few years of the war, before American military aid began to supplement domestic production and thus lighten the tremendous burden placed on the arsenals. During this period, the factories practiced extensive forms of exploitation, that is, low wages and long hours. Since the steel mills required continuous operation, they used twelve-hour shifts, "in at seven, out at seven." But whenever work groups changed shifts, the workers on the day shift worked sixteen hours and those on night shift eight hours, until the process was reversed the following week. Weapon-producing arsenals, on the other hand, preferred to work a long day throughout the Anti-Japanese War rather than adopt shifts. When arsenal directors met in the fall of 1942 to improve working conditions, they cited thirteen-hour days as the norm.[39] Even working on Sunday, at least half the day, became compulsory in the initial years of the war.[40]

Most arsenals adopted time wages (*diangong*) based on the monthly accumulation of work points, known as *gong*, hence the term *dangongzi* (unit wages). Monthly earnings were then calculated by multiplying the total number of work points earned by each worker by the value of each *gong* based on the worker's wage rank.[41] One *gong* was equivalent to eight hours, which in principle had been the normal workday since 1932. For the better part of two decades, though, workers toiled under the duress of military emergency, and so the working day was legally extended. Workers could increase their earnings by working overtime at time-and-a-half pay, but if overtime fell short of three hours, workers were paid the normal workday rate. This rule was changed in November 1940, when each overtime hour paid one-sixth of a work point. Still, the severe contraction of wage income that inflation caused after 1940 did not make overtime palatable. The experience of China thus differed from that of other countries, where overtime pay significantly boosted workers' earnings during World War II.[42]

This labor regime relied on coercion, rather than workers' consent, and was buttressed by an array of punishments. Given the high turnover rates and rapidity of Chongqing's industrialization, the prevalence of first-generation workers unfamiliar with the rigors and rhythms of industrial work heightened tensions on the shop floor. These tensions were exacerbated by management's desire to inculcate a regimented work ethic and increase productivity. Arsenal workers were thus subject to numerous rules regarding punctuality and absenteeism. If workers forgot to take their nametags to their workshops, or did not take them in time, they were considered absent. Several absences within a month could lead to dismissal. Punishments were also meted out to workers who might have slacked off five minutes before work was over. Finally, arsenal managers sought to prevent workers from socializing on the shop floor by prohibiting talking, smoking, or eating at work. These regulations were enforced in other industries too, but the draconian measures and lack of incentives in the armaments industry are striking. Indicative of management's deep distrust of their workforce, all twenty articles of Arsenal No. 20's factory regulations concerned behavior subject to punishment; none dealt with behavior meriting reward.[43]

Such rules provoked considerable resistance among workers unaccustomed to factory work, but skilled workers also participated in small-scale acts of resistance. An unidentified fitter "deliberately engaged in absenteeism" and left his workshop during a production rush to smoke, compounding the offense by throwing stones into the workshop. A machinist recalled how workers in the mortar shell foundry created a more relaxed environment by driving away the staff officers. "If a supervisor came, workers would get together to 'treat' him. When he came into the workshop, we would fake an accident and spill grease over him, so he would think twice about coming in again."[44] At the boiler room of the Gangqianhui steel mill, someone stationed at the workshop entrance kept an eye out for approaching supervisors while fellow workers rested. Before the supervisor entered the room, they would quickly resume work. The heat of the boiler rooms often became unbearable during the summer, so workers would stop shoveling coal into the furnaces, even though they ran the risk of setting off the steam whistle whenever the temperature of the boilers dropped too far. The whistle alerted the supervisor, a certain Mr. Wang, racially demonized by workers as half-Japanese, half-Chinese, with cat eyes and hair "the like of hog bristles." Wang took great pleasure in punishing workers, even though he suffered the consequences. After they had been disciplined for dawdling, workers plotted revenge that night by tying a rope in front of the entrance. Once the whistle sounded again, Wang rushed in, tripping over the rope and cutting his head.[45]

These cases all occurred before the mid 1940s, when piecework became more widely practiced and wages were linked to productivity. Lack of piece rates may explain why more skilled workers ignored orders to speed up production, since there was no significant monetary gain in doing so. Incentives and disciplinary fines also began to lose their bite as wages lost their real value and workers came to rely on subsidized rice as their primary recompense. Arsenals began to spend twice as much as they paid in wages on rice subsidies (*mitie* and *daijin*), which had originally been introduced to provide stability for workers and their dependents.[46] The escalation of rice stipends had important consequences for the social structure of the industry and management's leverage. By October 1944, leaders in the arms industry feared that wages were no longer tied to productivity. "In all arsenals under the Ordnance Department, the dependents' rice allowance and rice stipends make up the largest portion of earnings for workers, whereas all bonuses, fines, and overtime comprise a small portion and thus cannot raise workers' morale."[47] Facing a similar predicament in Kunming that same autumn, an arsenal manager put the matter more bluntly, "The rice stipend already amounts to 50 percent of the workers' income. Workers have a great interest in knowing the amount of the rice stipend, but they no longer pay attention to the results of their daily work." Now that workers and their family members received rice stipends regardless of their work performance, workers exerted greater control over their labor by taking numerous leaves of absence. "Workers now look upon the rice allowance as a subsidy. On days of leave, there is no deduction, thus many ask for personal leaves. There is absolutely no economic constraint, and productivity is inevitably lowered."[48]

Rice stipends became more popular among workers as they saw their wage income vanish under the onslaught of the hyperinflation crisis. To be sure, real wages did initially increase during the late 1930s because of the high demand for labor and the limited supply of skilled and experienced workers. As one former labor union leader recalled in a 1950 speech to the All-China Federal Trade Union, "the wages of experienced workers rose dramatically. There was a saying that for one month's work, one could live at home and enjoy three months of a fleeting golden age."[49] The respite was all too brief, because, starting in the spring of 1940, drought and the consequent rise of food prices caused the most pronounced rise in Chongqing's cost of living. Real wages declined so dramatically that by December 1942, industrial workers' actual income had already dropped to 20 percent of its 1937 value.[50] In his study of Chongqing working-class conditions, Qi Wu concludes that by 1945, workers' real wages ranged from 33 to 40 percent of their prewar level.[51] The precipitous drop in real income is confirmed even by statistics from the Nationalist Government's Social Ministry (table 4.2).

TABLE 4.2

*Chongqing Industrial Workers' Cost-of-Living Index
and Wage Index, 1937–1945*

Year	Cost of living index	Average monthly income	Real income index	Real wage index
1937	101	24	103	102
1938	116	41	180	155
1939	192	52	226	118
1940	550	100	437	80
1941	1,840	233	1,018	55
1942	4,135	436	2,082	50
1943	11,498	1,064	4,823	42
1944	39,094	3,854	16,808	43
1945	143,806	14,018	53,025	37

SOURCE: Guomindang zhengfu shehuibu tongjichu diaocha cailiao, *Zhonghua Minguo tongji nianjian* (1948), 385.

But wage caps, the government solution to limit consumer spending and control inflation, hit workers hard. Restrictions on Chongqing workers' wages began when the Executive Yuan passed the "means of adjusting wages" on January 15, 1941. Two years later, the government pegged wages to the cost-of-living index throughout Nationalist territory under the "wartime wage control act." Henceforth, employers of all industrial and vocational workers would use their wages of November 30, 1942, as a standard index for future wage hikes, which would be aligned with the cost of living. Employers were also prohibited from increasing wages in order to hire skilled workers, which they had frequently done to poach skilled labor. Arsenals implemented the wage controls starting on June 3, 1943, by order of Yu Dawei.[52] Government policy seeking to address the problem of steadily eroding income only exacerbated the problem. Some critics pointed out the fallacy in assuming that wage levels rather than monetary policy drove inflation, since wage increases consistently lagged behind skyrocketing prices. Others railed at the choice of November 30, 1942, as a base level for wages, when the standard of living had already eroded dramatically by then since the onset of the war.[53]

All arsenal workers suffered from the effects of inflation to varying degrees, since wages fluctuated depending on the arsenal and type of product. Workers earned higher wages at arsenals with more advanced machinery, and thus greater production capacity, such as Arsenal Nos. 10, 20, and 50. These were factories with machinery recently imported from Germany and with high rates of automation. Conversely, the lowest wages were found at Arsenal No. 25, one of the most poorly equipped. Generally speaking, the average wages of workers employed in the chemical plants and the two steel mills run by the Ordnance Department lagged behind those of other arsenal employees because of the high use of laborers.[54] Transport workers and boatmen had to endure the most difficult conditions. The steel plant's paper, *Taosheng*, noted that "boatmen's wages are meager and sufficient only for food; there is nothing left over to buy clothing, so they wear rags and only short pants in the summer, even to the point where sixteen- to seventeen-year-old women [their daughters?] go naked [both] summer and winter." Since transport workers spent most of their wages on food—plain rice mixed with ground chili peppers—it became difficult for them to pursue their favorite activity, sitting in the teahouses along the docks, shooting the breeze while drinking tea and wine. "At six yuan for tea and ten yuan for a cup of wine, they are unable to savor it; they can only quench their thirst by thinking of plums." Steel mill laborers consoled themselves with black humor, exemplified by their "Three Don'ts": "Kindling, rice, oil, and salt are expensive; don't live! Medicine is expensive; don't get sick! Wood for a coffin costs 10,000 gold pieces; don't die!"[55] By the end of World War II, wages barely supported workers at the subsistence level. Arsenal workers' monthly income, one internal survey noted, "was entirely spent on fuel, seasoning, and vegetables." Without wage raises, they would be unable "to maintain the lowest level of livelihood."[56]

The low earnings brought home by workers forced many into debt. Upon receiving their wages, workers made a mad dash for the shops in the industrial district, where they drank a few catties of wine and then bought daily necessities before their money lost any more of its value. At various shops, they paid off a portion of the debt incurred the previous month. In "balancing the books," workers generally paid back half of their debts, two-thirds on a good day. They never had enough to pay the debt in full, so they borrowed and purchased goods from several stores, "paying a little here and there."[57] Arsenal workers also organized rotating fund or mutual-aid associations, called *dahui*, to buy clothing and other essentials or to help out family members.[58] Each month, groups of five workers pooled money in a common fund to be used by a member in particular need. They then cast lots to decide which of the four other workers would receive the following month's share.[59]

Limited farm production during the War of Resistance adversely affected arsenals' plans to provide employees with cheap food. As a result, by 1945, if not sooner, arsenals began encouraging employees to cultivate their own vegetables to make themselves self-sufficient. At Arsenal No. 24, workers and staff members were allotted small plots in front of their dormitories. Workers at the Gangqianhui grew vegetables, and some found the means to raise ducks and pigs. As one worker put it, "Everyone was looking for a way to survive."[60]

By the last year of the Anti-Japanese War, defense industry leaders under the guidance of American military and technical advisors moved away from reliance on long workdays and instead increased the intensity of work. Americans critical of Nationalist China's low production capacity criticized the widespread failure to adopt double shifts, which necessitated at least twenty-hour workdays. Arsenal managers initially feared that their limited budgets would prevent them from providing the additional housing and training that double shifts required, but Ordnance leadership became receptive to change in late 1944, when the Nationalist army mounted a counterattack to fend off Japan's Ichigo Offensive. By November 1944, Japanese armies had swept through Changsha, occupied the Guangxi provincial air bases of Guilin and Liuzhou, and threatened to advance on Chongqing. Yang Jizeng, vice director of the Ordnance Department, responded with plans for a full-scale production drive that was to have increased machinery and manpower, created two shifts, and doubled output within ten months starting January 1945.[61] Insufficient matériel, electricity, and housing, as well as the high cost of training additional labor, impeded the adoption of double work shifts throughout the arms industry. Nevertheless, Arsenal No. 1 began double shifts that year, which increased production after 1945 and reduced work hours.[62] Arsenal No. 10 followed suit by shortening the workday from ten to nine hours. Workers were working less time now, but arguably harder. As managers confirmed, without diminishing total production, a decrease of one hour would prevent workers from collapsing from exhaustion.[63] Such reforms helped increase munitions production some 25 percent between November 1944 and the spring of 1945.[64]

An overhaul of the wage system ensued, effective January 1945. This reform merged rice subsidies into the general category of wages and cost-of-living supplement, which was attached to the wage scale. One immediate effect was to shift leverage back to management, which could now more effectively use wages to discipline workers. From despairing that they lacked the means to discipline workers only a few months before, certain managers now conceded that wage deductions were too severe, noting that work point fines "heavily influenced workers' income." Considering that most arsenals limited workers' monthly wages to a maximum of sixty work points, fines took an enormous toll on their income. To cite a few examples, workers who lost their name cards had the equivalent of five days' wages deducted. Workers who left work early were fined two work points. Workers caught helping fellow workers append their name tags in order to conceal having been absent were fined three work points the first time, seven points the second time, and fired the third time. Managers thus proposed reducing the severity of the fines, but if the disciplinary measures used by the Gangqianhui are any indication, fines continued to exact a heavy toll. The majority of infractions resulted in a two-point deduction, while the most severe disciplinary measures for fights and defiance of authority resulted in five-point deductions.[65]

The wage reform took place just as arsenals sought to promote piece-rate wages, limit workdays, and intensify work. By the mid 1940s, arsenals increasingly turned to piecework, convinced that payment by result would heighten motivation and output.[66] Rather than rely on the formula of long hours and low wages, managers reached the conclusion that workers would work harder if given the possibility of earning more. Increased competition among workers would also undermine their tenuous control over their productivity. The timing of this shift from extensive to intensive forms of exploitation varied, because each arsenal relied on its own initiative rather than any national guideline, but it began in the early 1940s, accelerated in 1945 in response to the production drive, and became widespread by the end of the decade. By the civil war period, frequent use of piece-rate wages and efficiency schemes matched the emphasis on linking wages with productivity.[67]

The adoption of piecework reflected a widespread interest in scientific management and industrial rationalization. Nationalist arsenals sought to emulate Western management systems. A 1946 wage revision notes: "In order to increase production, encourage work and adapt to military needs, this factory has in the past followed the example of European and American factories using piecework. The trial implementation of the piece-rate system has been in effect for several years, and there has been considerable progress regarding work efficiency."[68] In following principles of scientific management proposed by the American engineer Frederick Winslow Taylor to enhance efficiency, most arsenals had a work evaluation bureau, which sent personnel into the workshops to estimate rates. As a former foundry technician in the early 1940s recalled, "If we had to machine a precise part, they would measure a standard working time. Two workers were used, with one stopwatch per person. We would first determine a time and then see how long the worker would take. Then we established a standard, which we used for production. . . . Every part had a standard time."[69] By 1945, in an effort to coordinate production lines, the American War Production Mission in China set as a chief goal the implementation of time studies—a key aspect of scientific management—within each arsenal department.[70]

Arsenal engineers were aware of several wage systems associated with scientific management, such as the Halsey-Towne premium plan, the Rowan plan, the Emerson plan, and Taylor's differential-piece-rate system, but they favored an offshoot of Taylorism known as the Gantt task-and-bonus system.[71] The Gantt System, named for Henry Gantt, a turn-of-the century associate of Frederick Taylor's, appealed to its promoters for several reasons. A lower level of standardization was needed in production processes than with Taylorism. Moreover, arsenal managers felt that less skilled workers would not be punished under the new wage form, since they would be guaranteed a minimum hourly rate if they failed to attain the production standard. This feature had obvious appeal, because most arsenal workers were paid by the hour. As for workers who did reach the target, they would receive a bonus of 20 to 50 percent, depending on how much time was saved. Despite these differences in earning power, the Gantt plan produced a less stark contrast between superior and inferior workers than Taylorism did. Voices are silent on the actual rates set, or to what extent the Gantt system was even implemented, but the efficiency system as practiced in the United States was known to set rates at double normal output. "This is rather like holding a carrot before the nose of a donkey: the donkey may never reach the carrot, but his progress is nevertheless accelerated."[72]

Piecework and "task-bonus" systems proved attractive to employers seeking to raise the output and quality of products, since they could dangle the carrot of higher earnings before workers or deduct wages for lower production or faulty products. Skilled workers often preferred piecework because production over the set rates brought them higher earnings. At the same time, piecework fragmented the workforce by increasing the income gap among employees. Workers at Arsenal No. 21 remember sometimes earning twice as much as workers on a twelve-hour time shift. Not surprisingly, as a 1948 survey of Chongqing arsenals concluded, "workers receiving time wages resent those on piece rates, while temporary workers suppress their anger."[73] Alongside these monetary incentives associated with the new wage forms, managers used fines to impose discipline and increase productivity. At Arsenal No. 10, where each foundry worker had to produce twenty-five mortar shell molds per day, if defects exceeded 10 percent of the total, wages equivalent to the production of five shell molds were deducted for each defect. As a result, workers lost the equivalent of a half-day's pay.[74] Foundry workers were frequently fined for artillery shell defects, which could sometimes number in the thousands, because of the difficulty of maintaining uniform thickness and hardness and avoiding sandholes or cracks while casting.[75]

The increasing use of piece rates led workers to contest the issue of time and, indirectly, raise questions of control over the labor process. Workers' resistance may have been one reason why many arsenals did not adopt piecework sooner. A workplace culture decrying "rate busters" had sprung up, despite the lack of craft unions in which such a culture could have been more easily practiced and maintained.[76] In a 1939 speech to employees regarding the trial implementation of shorter shifts, Li Chenggan admonished workers for slacking. Li charged that for every twelve hours of the workday, workers' output equaled only four to five hours of actual labor, because workers zealously prevented competition to boost rates. "After we set work deadlines and gave incentives through bonuses and piecework, workers not only continued to lack enthusiasm, but even obstructed other workers from doing more."[77]

Regulations forbidding skilled workers from disputing the time estimated to complete a part suggest that the new wage form pitted workers against management. "Regarding estimated times, skilled workers cannot dispute the work they are allocated, the piece-rate form, or the work order form they receive. Upon receiving the order, they must immediately start working hard. If the actual working time truly exceeds the estimated time, the worker will be paid on the basis of the actual time worked, after technicians or the department director verify that it was not the worker's laziness that entailed the additional time."[78]

Workers exerted greater control over their labor by slowing the pace of work, fearing rate cutting if they earned more than the standard wage scale. This form of resistance is inferred from the frequent references in piece-rate rules to workers' indolence. Workers also learned to pace themselves when they lacked incentives. "If you exceeded the production quota, you'd get a bonus," one turner recalled. "The bonus was minimal, so usually we just fulfilled the production quota."[79] Workers continued to flout the rules during the late 1940s, even when payment by result became more widespread. Workplace infractions such as damaging objects, breaking tools, pilfering, leaving one's post or even the factory, arriving late or leaving early, neglecting work, and ignoring directions had become habitual.[80]

Despite the frequency of workers' passive and active resistance, the civil war period marked an increase in productivity and an intensification of labor. "Weapons of the weak," to use James Scott's phrase, proved ineffective precisely because workers, without resorting to mass action, lacked sufficient leverage to improve their working conditions. Detailed statistical studies, an important by-product of the production drive, indicate the intensification of work and increased productivity after 1945. Table 4.3, a study of Arsenal No. 20's main product, the 79-mm cartridge, shows that work took fewer hours, but occupied more days per month after the Anti-Japanese War. Besides 1946, when production decreased owing to the demobilization drive and the temporary truce between the GMD and the CCP, monthly production increased during the latter part of the decade. By 1948, output had more than doubled the average monthly production of the Anti-Japanese war period, in part because of the expansion of manpower and available machinery. The number of machine sets doubled during 1947 and 1948. While the number of workers engaged in cartridge production leaped 54 percent between 1945 and 1949, work intensified for each individual, since the number of workers needed to produce 10,000 cartridges decreased during this period. The burden of work per person increased, because each worker operated more machines. The pace of work accelerated, demonstrated by the higher rate of hourly production per machine after 1945, as well as the reduction in the number of hours needed to produce 10,000 cartridges. This trend began in 1944, but became most evident after 1947.

The social effects of inflation and wage policies created conditions for both fragmentation and solidarity. An important consequence of inflation and anti-inflationary measures was to create a leveling effect among skilled workers and laborers in the defense industry as well as other industries.[81] At Arsenals Nos. 10, 24, and 28, unskilled workers earned close to 70 percent of what skilled workers did by 1945.[82] Arsenal No. 20 provides the most compelling evidence of convergence between skilled and unskilled workers' wage incomes. Throughout 1946, operatives' wages were over 80 percent of what skilled workers earned, and in the following year, they consistently earned over 90 percent. Average wage

TABLE 4.3

Productivity and Production of 79-mm Cartridges at
Arsenal No. 20, 1938–1949

Items	1938	1939	1940	1941	1942	1943
Machines used (sets)	8	8	8	8	11	11
Number of workers[a]	997	1,819	1,720	1,671	2,042	2,112
Workers per unit machine	125	114	108	209	186	193
Days worked/month	27	26	26	25	26	24
Work hours/day[b]	14	24	24	15	15	12
Cartridge production/ month (10,000)	528	972	699	861	860	530
Number of workers/ 10,000 cartridges	1.9	1.9	2.5	1.9	2.4	4
Cartridge production/ machine set (hr.)	1,746	1,946	1,515	2,361	2,004	1,690
Hours needed/10,000 cartridges	714	584	710	885	927	1,142

Items	1944	1945	1946	1947	1948	1949
Machines used (sets)	7	9	6	12	23	23
Number of workers[a]	1,192	1,406	1,089	1,466	2,588	2,611
Workers per unit machine	170	156	182	122	113	114
Days worked/month	25	26	26	26	26	26
Work hours/day[b]	11	11	11	11	11	11
Cartridge production/ month (10,000)	401	632	414	823	1,618	1,735
Number of workers/ 10,000 cartridges	3	2.2	2.6	1.8	1.6	1.5
Cartridge production/ machine set (hr.)	2,083	2,476	2,413	2,398	2,460	2,638
Hours needed/10,000 cartridges	818	631	752	509	458	430

SOURCE: Chongqing Municipal Archives, 20 Chang, 847.2 *juan*, "Binggongshu di20 chang linian 79 qiangdan zhizao gaikuangbiao."

[a]Number of workers refers to those solely engaged in cartridge production.
[b]The use of double shifts explains the 24-hour workdays during 1939–40.

earnings converged until March 1949, when they dropped from 80 to 65 percent.[83] Rice stipends resulted in income-leveling, because rice was distributed in equal portions to laborers and skilled workers. On the one hand, wage leveling eroded the once privileged position of the skilled machinist, while raising, in relative terms, the standard of living for the unskilled permanent worker. Leveling did not necessarily unite skilled workers and laborers. The collapse of the skilled workers' economic base may have led them to perpetuate socially constructed aspects of skill so as to distinguish themselves from the younger "upstart" workers from Sichuan. The increasing use of piecework, especially during the production drive of the late 1940s, also divided workers. Piecework favored the veteran skilled workers and provoked resentment among the less experienced workers. The wage form thus perpetuated the generational divide, which became a fault line during the labor movement. On the other hand, the process of proletarianization and mass assembly work produced a sense of shared hardship among arsenal workers. The common experience of dangerous working conditions, long working hours, and erosion of wages brought workers together during times of open conflict with management or when trying to cope with economic crisis. Moreover, workers from both skilled and unskilled camps demonstrated their opposition to the production drive through everyday forms of resistance and less overt forms of class struggle. However ineffectively, workers tried to regulate the speed of work and the piece rate.

Welfare and Workers' Livelihood

Without the welfare provisions provided by the defense industry during the civil war period, survival would have been very difficult for workers. The erosion of their real wages grew even more pronounced. Prices by the summer of 1947 were 36,872 times those of July 1937, and 1,335,000 times greater a year later.[84] As inflation slashed into real wages, welfare benefits played an increasingly significant role in maintaining workers' livelihood. By the mid 1940s, basic staples had supplanted wages as workers' primary form of income. Employees recall that by the late 1940s, arsenal jobs and the provision of benefits guaranteed a basic livelihood and offered them a semblance of stability amid the rising tide of business collapse, unemployment, and inflation.

Political pressure from the state was a primary stimulus for the defense industry's promotion of industrial welfare. The government played a vital role in implementing industrial legislation and social policy within the arsenals. Converging with both international and domestic trends in industrial legislation and factory welfare programs, the arsenals' promotion of industrial welfare—compensation plans, savings schemes, housing, factory canteens, cultural programs, factory libraries, and so forth—reached new heights during the war period.[85]

The Nationalist Government Factory Act of 1931 was the most obvious precedent for the defense industry's social welfare schemes. Among its more notable provisions, the act required that all mechanized factories employing more than thirty workers impose an eight-hour day, restrict child labor, establish paid holidays, set up workers' savings and cooperative societies, build workers' housing, and provide compensation for injury, sickness, and death. "Factory councils" were also to be established, with both worker and management representatives, in order to defuse labor strife. The Factory Act had little immediate effect, however, beyond the larger, more capitalized firms already practicing various forms of industrial paternalism. Two years later, the Ministry of Industry established a Central Factory Inspection Bureau to enforce the act, especially the provisions regarding working conditions. Nevertheless, by 1936, only occasional reporting of industrial accidents occurred.[86]

Both the Factory Act and the defense industry's welfare program were premised on a conservative ideological underpinning. First proposed in 1929, the Factory Act arose in the aftermath of Chiang Kai-shek's brutal suppression of the labor movement two years earlier. As in Germany and Italy, the state sought to use welfare and arbitration councils to replace independent unions and foster class conciliation. Although the Ordnance Department and the Nationalist government never explicitly referred to a particular foreign model, such as Germany's Strength Through Joy or Italy's Dopolavoro (after-work "recreational club") programs, its wartime social policy and cultural activities were based on similar ideological grounds. For Zhu Jiahua, head of the GMD Central Executive Committee's Organization Department and an avid proponent of the "New Germany," social welfare would promote production, class harmony, and love of labor. These goals would be met because the cultivation of "affection between industrialists and workers" would lead to "workers' altruism" and "love of the machine." Zhu targeted a potentially adversarial work culture by drawing on the work of the German scholar and supporter of National Socialism Werner Sombart and his maxim of strength, reason, and love as the key to social stability. In keeping with the party line on class harmony, Zhu argued that organization, training, and social welfare would dissipate "class prejudices."[87]

Once the Anti-Japanese War commenced, both the real and perceived threat of labor unrest and CCP activism persuaded defense industry leaders to use welfare as a form of material bribery and substitute for unionism. Ironically, the social welfare program owed much to labor activists. The CCP underground's strategy of organizing social services for workers had the unintended effect of pushing arsenal management to co-opt the very same social welfare programs. In mid January 1939, after bombing raids had damaged the Weapon's Repair Plant and injured twenty workers, Communist members set up an emergency relief fund and collected workers' donations for future disaster relief. When the Nationalist Party Executive Committee of Chongqing noted with alarm that Communists had organized emergency relief and unemployment funds at other arsenals, factory management abolished all emergency relief committees organized by workers, on the pretext that they resembled unions. "We have very clear regulations that arsenal workers are forbidden to organize a union or organizations resembling a union. If workers suffer calamity, the management will take responsibility. Management should organize an emergency relief committee so that the Communists have no pretext to be active."[88]

The immediate catalyst for social welfare programs was workers' flight, the most frequent form of industrial action among workers in search of better working conditions. Extensive labor mobility prompted the Ordnance Department's leadership to devise new means of discipline and to instill a sense of loyalty and duty into its workforce. On June 7, 1939, Yu Dawei mandated the establishment of employee welfare associations (fulishe) to offset hardships and create a labor force of loyal retainers, saying:

Since the start of the war, workers have followed the factories into the interior. Because of daily increases in the cost of living, everyone finds it difficult, especially those with dependent families, who must suffer even greater hardships with no means of support. Moreover, changes in the environment and external enticements have unsettled workers to the point where they abscond and job-hop to other factories. This has occurred repeatedly. If we do not improve the situation, our work will inevitably be greatly influenced.[89]

Responding to Director Yu's order, by 1941, the Nationalist arsenals had established welfare boards to oversee arsenal farms, hospitals, entertainment, children's schools, consumer cooperatives, and resident areas. Welfare involved all aspects of an employee's daily life, from providing a marriage service to overseeing mourning rites. By the mid 1940s, fringe benefits had become increasingly elaborate to compensate for abysmally low wages and to prevent flight. As Colonel Walter Sylvester, liaison with the Chinese Ordnance Department, noted: "The wage scale for these ordinary or unskilled laborers is very low. However to keep them from being attracted to more lucrative jobs, the arsenals have provided gratis, quarters, certain food stuffs, medical care, and educational facilities."[90]

Major W. S. Brewster reached similar conclusions, adding that "this considerate treatment of employees is not customary in China and, of course, increases the man's incentive to remain as an arsenal employee as long as it is financially possible for him to do so."[91]

Brewster's assessment is noteworthy for stressing the distinctiveness of the defense industry's measures to encourage worker commitment. As the leading industrial sector in an increasingly state-driven economy, the defense industry was also among the vanguard in promoting fringe benefits. Welfare services in the arsenals had assumed increased significance for several reasons. The geographic isolation of most arsenals and large workforces necessitated social welfare services such as hospitals and company housing. Management sought to use welfare to discipline an emerging proletariat and overcome its resistance to factory life, but above all to maintain and reproduce a stable workforce as economically as possible. The demands of wartime production pressured state managers to offer incentives other than wages to enhance productivity. Payment in kind was replacing cash wages owing to the currency devaluation caused by the hyperinflation crisis. Finally, conflict between workers and management—as manifested in mobility and other forms of everyday resistance—forced arsenal directors to offer benefits. The making of social welfare packages, as elsewhere, derived from a process of "negotiated loyalty."[92]

Yu Dawei's apprehension about social stability and productivity and the wartime siege mentality that his own language evokes should not cause us to overlook arsenal leaders' genuine concern for their workers' welfare. Among arsenal directors, Li Chenggan exemplified the model paternalistic leader. Called the "big boss" (*da laoban*) by his workers, Li disregarded rank, often wore civilian clothes, and enjoyed entering the workshops to rub shoulders with workers. Admirers noted that all details of the arsenal consumed Li's time, even to the point that he never married, rare for a man of his rank and times. It was thus no coincidence that Arsenal No. 21 became a model of social welfare within the arms industry.[93]

Most arsenal directors remained more distant figures. Managers probably sought to institutionalize paternalism to offset the growing bureaucratic and impersonal feel of labor relations caused by the large size of the arsenals and direct managerial control over workers. Given that many workers had migrated to Chongqing and sought to return home as soon as the war ended, this exacerbated workers' feelings of estrangement. Even foremen, despite maintaining daily contact with workers, had little say over most decisions regarding work. Decisions about recruitment, the setting of piece rates, and the meting out of fines were made in offices off limits to workers and foremen.

To offset the growing gap between workers and their employers, arsenals tried to instill a sense among employees that the factory was a cohesive community. Managers produced visual imagery, such as group photographs of a department's employees, or photographs showing hundreds of mortars laid out in rows, to inspire camaraderie and pride in the product. Titles were changed to evoke a similar communal spirit. By 1940, Yu Dawei had renamed all factory stores from "employee social welfare associations" to "consumer cooperatives."[94] Sport and competitions held within and across arsenal lines were yet another method of allowing workers to identify with their particular factory.

The perception that workers' morale had eroded also prompted management to heighten its powers of persuasion. At Arsenal No. 20, for instance, the Propaganda Instructional Office proposed establishing a library, vocational schools, drama and opera troupes, a literary periodical, and a movie theater to "increase workers' knowledge and to raise the morale of staff and workers for the War of Resistance."[95] After ten thousand booklets had been printed in June 1940, Yu Dawei ordered all arsenal employees to begin practicing resistance songs.[96] Certain factories, such as Arsenal No. 21, even had their own arsenal song. Indicative of his progressive sympathies, Li Chenggan commissioned his old friend from Japan Guo Moruo and the revolutionary composer He Luting to compose the music and lyrics, which underscored international struggle, camaraderie, and fraternal love:

It takes war to stop war, weapons to eliminate weapons, [and] the sword of righteousness will protect the peace. Producing potent weapons, we strive for our national security. This glorious history began at our own Jinling, where we worked hard in pursuit of knowledge, honesty, and fairness. Our work involves unceasing competition with other countries, tackling them head on, exerting our utmost knowledge and ability. We have fraternal love of flesh and blood, our sincerity is made of metal and stone, our enthusiasm is cast from the crucible, we have the persistence of steel. Quantity demands abundance, quality demands precision. Comrades, charge! Charge! Comrades, charge! Charge![97]

The promotion of cultural activities suggests how factory life shaped workers' leisure time. Arsenal employees participated in a drama club, Peking opera, and local Sichuan opera, performing once every two months. Sometimes employees pursued these activities at home and put into practice the ideal of class cooperation envisioned by Nationalist ideologues. "My wife sang Peking opera, and I played the *jinghu*," a former engineer recalled. "Some workers and staff became interested in joining us, so we organized a Peking opera group. My home was fairly spacious, and we had many Peking opera musical instruments; every evening it was very lively."[98]

The most basic policy supervised by the arsenal welfare boards to foster a sense of community and to retain a stable workforce involved factory housing. With such large migrant workforces situated in newly formed industrial districts, housing had become an immediate and pressing problem. Compounding the problem, arsenals had expanded to enormous proportions. The largest of them all, Arsenal No. 21 in Jiangbei district, administered over 30,000 employees and immediate family members, while the smaller arsenals comprised communities of several thousand employees and family members.[99] In order to alleviate housing shortages and high rents caused by the massive influx of war refugees, each arsenal provided free housing—dormitories for single employees and dwellings for employees with family members. By the end of World War II, factory housing was by no means complete, but a substantial portion had been built. To cite one example, a 1945 survey from Arsenal No. 20 estimated that dormitories could house two-thirds of the arsenal's 2,000 single employees. Although arsenals provided most laborers with dormitory housing, some lived outside the factory grounds in makeshift dwellings. Temporary workers, who often faced the most wretched existence, lived in caves or on the riverbank in boat sheds. "Inside they set up a bed and a stove and spent their time there. Some lived in sheds. They used two boards and put them together. Some built a thatched shed between two mounds."[100] Family housing also remained a grave problem, since only 40 percent of the roughly 2,000 employees with family members had been accommodated. The remaining families were forced to live close by the factory or rent private lodgings outside the factory district. As an alternative to factory housing, arsenals offered monthly rent subsidies to their employees if they lived in the district neighboring the factory. Although the subsidy was a pittance (100 yuan by September 1944), these housing arrangements reflected the expanded role of the factory management in workers' daily lives.[101]

Besides the political motives, an economic calculus underlay factory welfare policy. In particular, the defense industry's distribution of daily necessities complemented the government's price and wage control policies. By 1942, the Nationalist government had introduced price ceilings and general rationing of consumer goods in the major cities. These efforts at containing inflation foundered on the rocks of ineffective enforcement, the lack of a comprehensive administration, and the unevenness of prices between different regions. Chongqing had difficulty implementing price controls because it remained dependent on outside supplies from unregulated areas. The government was more successful, however, in buying in bulk commodities, such as rice, salt, cooking oil, fuel, and cotton, and then selling them at fixed prices. Government distribution of rice proved more feasible, for instance, because the collection of land tax in kind generated a greater supply of rice in Sichuan.[102]

Apart from curbing inflation, factory directors found it less expensive to provide social services than to raise wages. In truth, welfare benefits were quite meager. Available data from the mid to late 1940s indicate that monthly welfare expenditures on medical services, compensation fees, and rice allowances hovered between 1 and 2 percent of the monthly payroll. Factories spent the bulk of their money on primary materials, while capping total wages at 20 percent of the payroll.[103] From the perspective of the employer, rationing and discounted products allowed arsenals to economize and maintain a stable labor force. By growing most products on their own farms, which used cheap labor, and then selling them at reduced prices, arsenals maintained the low wages they paid the regular workforce. Earnings spent by workers on food products were, moreover, reintroduced into the arsenal's own budget. An extractive redistribution system also applied to the welfare system. Money from fines imposed on workers who had violated factory rules was pooled in a collective fund and used as a portion of the welfare budget.[104]

The American consular official Julian R. Friedman analyzed this system of control and economy in his survey of labor in Chongqing and Kunming in January 1946. Although he studied manufacturing plants, not arsenals, the logic guiding their social welfare policy was similar to that of the defense industry:

As it would be expected, this system of payment in wages and kind benefited the employer as well as the worker. Management could figure wages in terms of supplemental allotments to real wages. It could provide mass services and facilities at a relatively low cost per worker, less than the amount management would have had to pay each worker to maintain himself on his own earnings at even a subsistence level. The system assured management of a constant labor force. Furthermore, it provided management with stringent control over the productive capacity of the worker. It tended to prevent loss of production resulting from arbitrary absenteeism of the worker.[105]

Prices remained below those of the black market and thus benefited the arsenal workforce, especially after 1946, when prices surged and jobs became scarce. At the same time, these were inexpensive ways of encouraging employee loyalty to the factory.

Whatever its limitations, the arsenals' welfare system did provide a steady source of food in a war-ravaged society. Workers' diet consisted primarily of vegetables and grains. Liu Feng, who apprenticed at a Chongqing arsenal during the earliest and most difficult stage of the Sino-Japanese war, recalled a spartan diet. "From morning till night we ate squash. I ate so much I couldn't bear it anymore. It's true, I'm still afraid to eat it."[106] At the Ordnance Department's steel mills, workers relied on a diet of tofu, cabbage, turnips, carrots, and mustard greens, while eating meat every two weeks.[107] Workers throughout Sichuan ate large amounts of pork, a practice known as *da yaji*, once or twice per month. "Pork was a treat," a former worker said. "We bought pig's feet, which were really top-notch. When we ate meat, we also had the pig's head, a quarter of a pig's head, or we bought the heart and lungs. Nowadays these are used to feed pigs and dogs, and sometimes dogs don't even want them. We ate it with boiled turnips. This was known as *dayaji*."[108]

Mess halls built for single workers distinguished the new welfare system, although not always favorably. Gangqianhui workers dreaded the canteen food. Even the steel mill's own bulletin reported that "[t]he managers of the canteen have created such low costs that everyone eats horribly. There isn't enough nutrition; there are few vegetables and too much rice."[109] Workers fared better at Li Chenggan's Arsenal No. 21, where many ate at the mess halls during their one-hour lunch break. Generally, workers paid a monthly fee for up to four dishes per meal, at costs lower than market price. After entering the canteen, which could hold up to three hundred tables, workers would sign up for a table and eat with seven other workers. Single employees ate there at night as well, whereas employees with families ate dinner at home.

Workers and their families depended to a far greater extent on the low-priced food and rationed staple goods distributed by arsenal cooperatives. Arsenals provided all workers with monthly supplies of free rice, known as *junmi* (military rice), and low-priced salt, oil, firewood, and coal. These services were fairly uniform throughout the industry. Arsenal

No. 24 was typical in that workers received a free monthly supply of 3.23 *dou* of unhulled rice (the equivalent of 72.6 kilos), one *jin* (or catty) of salt, and one *jin* of cooking oil. Adult and child dependents of workers could also buy two *dou* and one *dou* of rice, respectively, at a reduced price. Workers with family members received fifteen kilos of firewood per household, two hundred kilos of soft coal for one adult, fifty kilos for additional adults, and twenty-five kilos per child, with a limit of four people. Workers supplemented these daily necessities by buying vegetables, sugar, tofu, bean sprouts, and soy sauce from the factory cooperative at prices below market (*pingjia* or *lianjia*).[110]

Despite these policies, both laborers and skilled workers with large families had trouble obtaining enough rice. Skilled workers at the steel mills recalled their frustrations with restrictions placed on cheap rice for their family members. "During the War of Resistance, there was only four *dou* of rice for family members, regardless of how many members. There were parents, children, five to six people, and sometimes seven to eight members. Four *dou* of rice was simply not enough food. Of course, workers were given 3.2 *dou* of rice, but there wasn't enough for family members. . . . And the rice was of poor quality, often mildewed, so losses were considerable after you threw out the mildewed rice."[111] Laborers trying to support family members suffered even more, because they could not buy rice inexpensively for their relatives. If this restriction was intended to foster competition for skilled positions, it succeeded. "So at the time, all workers strove to become skilled workers. If you were a laborer, it was no good trying to eke out a living. There was no rice, no low-priced rice. There was rice on the market, but if he relied on his wages, he wouldn't have enough."[112]

Malfeasance underlay problems in the distribution of rice. By the late 1940s, corruption and inadequate provisions were endemic to the management of the arsenals, as noted by Major Colonel Liu Yuansen, head of the managerial section of the Ordnance Department's administrative section. Liu criticized arsenal directors and staff for graft and incompetence in the distribution of goods. Workers' dependents were entitled to subsidies upon registering, but the registration process was onerous. "A worker has four or five members in the family, but those registered cannot exceed one or two people, and sometimes not even one person can register." To make matters worse, managers often hoarded the good rice and later sold it on the black market, or distributed poor-quality rice that they had made heavier by soaking it in water or adding husks. Either way, rice and grain distribution was often delayed as much as six months. Thus, workers concluded, "Besides water and electricity, there's nothing to say about welfare."[113]

Colonel Liu's report underscored the growing alienation of workers from factory managers and, by extension, the Nationalist regime. Because of arsenals' limited budgets and conflicting power interests, the limited welfare benefits were inequitably distributed, creating conditions for conflict between workers and management. The welfare system reinforced a class society in the arsenals. To be sure, as Barrington Moore points out, rigid, steep class divisions do not necessarily breed workers' opposition.[114] But in the Great Rear area, the discord between reality and Nationalist government rhetoric of shared sacrifice—"those who have money give money, those who have labor give labor"—heightened tensions between workers and managerial staff. The welfare and wage system reinforced these divisions among workers and staff and was an underlying cause of social conflict.

The "Collar" Divide

Arsenal workers and managerial and technical staff occupied different social and physical worlds. As we have seen, a range of ranks and functions distinguished the latter. Although staff members were ranked as officers in a military hierarchy, these were differences of degree rather than kind. Staff came from higher class backgrounds, were more educated, and had different aspirations from production workers. On the job, staff employees worked shorter hours, were paid much more than workers, and partook of a different work culture. Fundamentally, because they carried out managerial functions, staff members shared varying positions of authority within the factory. Like foremen on the eve of the Russian Revolution, staff occupied an ambivalent position in relation to the means of production.[115] While they sold their labor power and were dominated by state capital, staff also enforced discipline and managed production, making for an inherently conflictive relationship with labor.

These clashes between staff and workers may have arisen from their structural position within the arsenal hierarchy, but much of their antagonism stemmed from how society at large informed workers and staff's perceptions of their interests. Specifically, enduring perceptions of a natural social division based on mental and manual labor continued to inform management practices and underscored staff members' sense of superiority. "Our country's people have in ignorance retained the long-standing habit of scorning workers," Li Chenggan remarked in a parting speech to the skilled workers' school.[116] Both sides of the political divide explained these social divisions as an immutable cultural divide. Communist underground activists argued in class terms that workers came from predominantly poor peasant stock, whereas staff arose from the ranks of landlords and the rich peasantry, thus influencing their degree of education and social status. "According to traditional social customs in China, one respected the long-gowned class and scorned the laboring class. Consequently, we have virtually divided staff and workers into two different social strata."[117] Although Nationalist officials acknowledged these social divisions, their explanation rested on "natural" causes, such as intelligence. "Owing to dissimilar lifestyles, varying remuneration, unequal status, as well as a wide education gap and unequal levels of intelligence among all ranks of staff and workers . . . it is easy for staff and workers to form prejudices and develop boundaries."[118]

These prejudices were reinforced when arms factories began to hire excess numbers of *zhiyuan* during the war. Sent into arsenals and mechanized plants for "training," these young engineers and supervisors often simply observed workers and shunned production work. At their worst, as the following vignette illustrates, supervisors emulated their literati forefathers' aversion to manual work:

One day when Lt. Kelley was demonstrating the correct process, he noticed strolling about the premises, with an air of polite interest, a very clean Chinese gentleman dressed in fine skirts, with a parasol fastened to his belt and a fan in his hands. Lt. Kelley, himself hot and dirty, asked one of the workers who the gentleman was. "Oh he," the worker said, "is the boss. He supervises our work." Lt. Kelley had a heart to heart and reasonably violent conversation with the boss, Lt. Kelley's remarks being to the effect that it is good practice for a supervisor to pitch in and do a bit of demonstrating. The supervisor replied that he had been to college, and never had he been told anything like that.[119]

The supervisor's reply reflected how divisions between mental and manual labor informed social status. The self-consciousness of staff employees as a more educated and Westernized elite reinforced a cultural divide between themselves and factory workers. For staff, their economic position was linked with their privileged access to social and cultural capital in and out of the workplace. Workers described staff within the factory gates as haughty and condescending. The image of arsenal managers and staff officers depicted in Lo Kuang-pin and Yang Yi-yen's novel

Hong Yan (*Red Crag*) may be an exaggeration, but does ring true to the worst of perceptions held among workers: "He realized that the high-ranking officials, dressed in American military uniforms, were spending most of their time speculating on the stock-market, pulling strings, grafting and hoarding, living on the sweat of the people and sucking their blood. . . . Most of the office staff were slick characters, whose day's work was almost limited to reading the papers, gossiping, commenting on films and women."[120]

Off work, staff did indeed try to practice an elevated lifestyle and to distance themselves from the factory environment and the socially stigmatized production workers. Staff members would "always don Western suits and leather shoes to crash high society *[peng huagui zhi men]*," a reporter for the CCP's *Xinhua ribao* (New China Daily) wrote in May 1940. The *Xinhua* reporter, unsympathetic to the salaried employees' crass sentiments, suggests with some sardonic wit and insight that staff personnel aspired to upper-class status, even though the door was seemingly closed to them.[121] This was written during the "boom" years of the war, and such hopes were probably dashed during the inflationary crisis, which traumatized the middle classes. Sun Zhiguang, a low-level technician during the mid 1940s, recalled using his first month's salary to buy a Chinese tunic suit, which he always wore. "My economic situation didn't allow me other clothing. I used my salary for my family, giving it to my brothers so they could attend school. The rest I used for food."[122] Nevertheless, that staff members aspired to distance themselves from production workers was quite evident to workers. One arsenal worker recalled with some bitterness how bathrooms were segregated among workers and staff not simply because of different shifts but because staff "feared workers were dirty."[123]

These cultural clashes manifested themselves within the arsenal schools attended by children of both *zhiyuan* and workers. At Arsenal No. 10, for instance, 160 children of staff parents, 187 children of worker origins, and 65 students from the outside community attended the arsenal school. Such a diverse student body went against the grain of the arsenal hierarchy, and since the schools were microcosms of the factory community and its social relations, mutual mistrust reigned. As the factory paper reported, "There are quite a few parents who have various types of misgivings: they fear that their children will suffer. Some staff say, 'The sons of those workers are dirty and they have awful habits. I worry about sending my son there to study with them.' Likewise, there are workers who say, 'I'm afraid our children in this school can't avoid being bullied by those young masters of the house.'"[124]

Motivated by idealism and a belief in class harmony, the writer tried to put the best light possible on the school's socializing effects, but much of the essay's findings reaffirmed his elitist views and the reality that students came from vastly different backgrounds. These social divisions manifested themselves in several ways. Indicative of their higher standard of living, the children of staff personnel were found to have fewer health problems. They excelled in their roles as class monitors and patrol members. Because of "frequent family nurturing, the children of staff have enough leadership ability to spare." School problems also were described in terms replicating the divisions at work between management and workers. The children of workers and from the outside community were "unavoidably uncouth and used filthy language," whereas staff children easily became lazy and did not get along with others. Finally, academic results mirrored the factory's social divisions. Staff children scored better in composition, recitation, and speaking, whereas a disproportionate number of working-class children had to repeat the grade. The survey attributed their academic difficulties to several causes, all of which boiled down to poverty. Workers' children started school prematurely because their parents were too busy to take care of them. Since the schoolwork was inappropriate for their age level, they found it too difficult, quickly lost interest, and developed bad study habits. Given the cramped conditions of their homes, children had no place to study. Moreover, many illiterate workers could not help their children in school.[125]

A sense of social superiority informed how staff treated workers. At their worst, staff became agents of social oppression. Although Shih Kuoheng's description pertains to Kunming, his comments shed light on the general mentality of staff officers—a fear of losing social prestige if they became associated with the stigmatized worker:

Chih yuan [zhiyuan] identified themselves with the management and addressed workers familiarly and rudely while insisting on forms of respect for themselves and reacting violently to every real or fancied reflection on their "dignity." Where factories were distant from the town and provided special buses to go there, chih yuan would push ahead of workers in the queues. Workers complained that a chih yuan would speak to them in a friendly way if no one else was around, but would immediately turn his back if another chih yuan appeared. The lowest clerk saw himself as a "gentleman" and shared the Confucian idea of the worker as a "mean man." Many conflicts resulted, and workers often left their employment as a result of insults for which they could get no redress.[126]

The extreme range of material and symbolic criteria heightened workers' sense of injustice. Workers in large-scale industries, such as the arms industry, where staff members were a substantial minority and social welfare practices were more extensive, frequently voiced such grievances. Letters from arsenals workers relate common grievances over unequal "treatment" (daiyu); unequal access to reading rooms, rationing, housing, consumer cooperatives, and entertainment; separate use of canteens and toilets; and disparities in salaries and bonuses, all of which pitted the two groups against each other.[127]

Arsenals' use of status markers distinguished staff employees from workers. Forms of address differed, reflecting the hierarchical relationship. Out of deference to their higher social standing, workers used the polite form xiansheng (Mr.) to address staff members, whereas staff referred to workers by name or ordered them about. Clothing and badges served to distinguish the two different types of employees. Several former arsenal workers recall an overt hierarchical division within the factory. "As soon as you looked, you could tell whether you were a worker or staff." Staff had military uniforms and ranks, but workers had neither military uniforms nor work clothes. Staff carried red round copper badges, while workers carried green square badges.[128]

Segregation defined much of the factory space as well. For one skilled arsenal worker, "the gap between workers and staff was another great difference before the Liberation [of 1949]. Staff and workers had separate washrooms, because their shifts differed and because staff feared that workers were dirty. So the washrooms of staff and workers were separate. The barber and mess halls were also separate. As for the dorms for single men, the staff dorms were at Reconstruction yard. Everyone there was a staff member. Everyone else lived at the Shenyi yuan or other yards."[129]

Within the arsenal compounds, hierarchy and segregation prevailed. The most obvious demarcation was between workers and staff employees, who lived in separate residential areas, known as villages or yards, which maintained the sacrosanct aura of management. The quality of the housing of staff and workers also contrasted sharply. Workers' dormitories typically had bamboo-wattle walls and tile-covered roofs. Most workers with family members lived in straw-thatched huts, with walls made of wheat straw and mud. Staff members, on the other hand, lived in more durable, better-quality housing, often brick buildings with tiled roofs and hardwood floors.[130] According to a retired steel mill worker, "the lodgings of staff were reconstructed into small Western-style houses. They looked like small villas clustered together." The arsenal director, vice director, head engineer, and department heads each had a house for his family. Under them, other top-ranking staff members, such as engineers, lived in small one-story houses, generally occupied by two families. Finally, three to four families of technicians and low-ranking staff shared certain houses.[131]

Space reflected and reinforced an employee's social status. Management personnel enjoyed far greater privacy than workers, who endured cramped conditions in dormitories. "Everything was divided, and divided very clearly," a former steel mill worker recalled. "You couldn't say that staff dorms were wonderful, but each room held two people. When you went to a worker's dormitory, they were more crowded and substandard."[132] Dormitory rooms for workers usually held six to eight people, sometimes as many as ten.

From workers' perspective, these noticeable differences in housing conditions and the use of space to denote hierarchy between workers and management personnel smacked of inequality and provoked resentment against management. Management's investment in housing, which would help increase productivity, had the unintended consequence of fostering a negative type of solidarity among workers, measured by differences in treatment between themselves and management. Frequent reminders of social subordination spurred the sense of injustice of a worker such as Gu Weiyun: "Some of the first-ranking staff directors lived fairly far away. When they came to work or left, they were carried on a sedan [chair]. They had servants at home and there were also laborers who served them. The factory subsidized these staff members' expenses."[133]

For certain workers, moral injustices translated into a consciousness of class. The rationing of consumer goods favored staff and reinforced workers' sense of exclusion and unequal treatment within the factory. Workers expressed their grievances in terms of a producer consciousness, stressing the moral value of work and using the language of rights and class. One anonymous worker questioned the monthly rationing of sugar after being informed that only staff members could purchase a catty. "I'm also human and also Chinese. Why does even the appreciation of food have to be divided by class? Is it possible that workers are constitutionally different from staff officers? Staff officers are people; workers are people, why does one have to make such distinct class divisions as this? The lack of workers' rights to purchase white sugar is only one [form of] inequality between staff and workers. There are countless others."[134]

TABLE 4.4

Provincial Distribution of Arsenal No. 50 Staff, 1942–1948

(percentage)

Date	Sichuan	Guangdong	Jiangsu	Zhejiang	Hubei	Hunan	Total #
10/31/1942	9.6%	22.2%	14.3%	9.6%	12.2%	10.0%	179
10/31/1943	19.3	18.9	12.6	7.5	11.1	7.9	441
6/30/1944	19.4	18.1	12.8	7.6	11.5	7.0	413
12/31/1944	15.5	16.0	17.0	9.7	9.2	9.1	464
6/30/1945	14.6	16.2	15.7	9.9	9.1	9.9	489
12/31/1945	14.8	15.9	16.1	9.7	8.6	9.2	467
6/30/1946	22.9	9.0	13.5	8.5	9.6	10.1	328
9/30/1947	25.6	7.0	12.5	6.3	9.0	9.2	340
12/31/1947	39.1	7.1	9.6	4.9	9.6	5.7	309
6/30/1948	40.1	7.5	8.9	4.6	9.6	5.0	315

SOURCES: Chongqing Municipal Archives, 50 Chang, 2 *mu*, 298 *juan*, 7; 50 Chang, 2 *mu*, 304 *juan*, 9; 50 Chang, 2 *mu*, 305 *juan*, 36, 131; 50 Chang, 2 *mu*, 306 *juan*, 104, 206; 50 Chang, 2 *mu*, 307 *juan*, 85; 50 Chang, 2 *mu*, 299 *juan*, 12, 228; 50 Chang, 2 *mu*, 306 *juan*.

Paradoxically, nonclass relations served to heighten workers' sense of class polarization between themselves and staff members. Although ethnicity has usually been viewed as a barrier to class formation, regional rivalries between extraprovincials and Sichuanese shaped workers' perceptions of class. Throughout much of the 1940s, "downriver people" played the dominant role in Sichuan society, anticipating the quasi-colonial relationship between mainland Chinese and Taiwanese during the late 1940s and 1950s, when mainlanders occupied elite positions in Taiwan and, as Lloyd Eastman points out, attempted "to monopolize the major functions of government and to seize control of banking, trade and the economy generally."[135] The same was true of managerial ranks in Sichuan, as table 4.4 illustrates in the case of Arsenal No. 50 staff.

The fact that many staff came from eastern and central China reinforced workers' sense that they were subject to class domination. "Downriver people didn't make up that many of the workers, but a majority of them were staff. They directly supervised workers, which resulted in antagonisms between staff and workers. This contradiction was not entirely based on regionalism, but a regionalism problem existed. Since there were many high-ranking Shanghai and Cantonese staff, they naturally looked after the interests of the factory director."[136] To be sure, Sichuanese occupied some staff positions, especially after demobilization in 1946 accelerated the out-migration of non-Sichuanese. However, although Sichuanese increasingly dominated the skilled sector, extraprovincials retained their hold on managerial posts. At Arsenal No. 10, for instance, a 1947 survey indicates that while 27 percent of total staff members were Sichuanese (N = 297), over a third came from the Lower Yangzi macroregion, and roughly 18 percent came from the Middle Yangzi.[137]

Given this basic divide based on cultural and structural positions, wage discrepancies, especially perceived and real inequities in wage scales, were a chief cause of dispute between workers and management. Staff members earned more than workers because of their salaries, but also because of additional benefits, including living supplements, overtime pay, and bonuses. This gap seems to have increased during the late 1940s. Liu Yuansen noted that a sharp remuneration gap existed between officers and workers among the five Chongqing arsenals he surveyed. Liu cited the example of a warrant officer in Arsenal No. 24 receiving over 70 million yuan in June 1948. Much of this income derived from supplemental income not available to workers, such as the "technicians' supplement" and subsidies. In contrast, the highest-paid skilled worker received 15 million yuan, and the worst-paid laborer only 2 million yuan. Liu estimated that, on average, workers received even less than one-third the income of staff, leading them to "feel widespread injustice and frequently to hold slowdowns or skimp work [tougong]."[138]

Lack of funding or resources often played to management's preconceived ideas of hierarchy and protocol. As resources dwindled, management distributed welfare benefits on the basis of employees' social status, unintentionally contributing to the polarization of the factory community along class lines. The lack of fringe benefits, their delay or unequal distribution to workers, and other indications that many of the welfare benefits had still not been institutionalized were frequent sources of hostility between labor and management. A work stoppage at Arsenal No. 50 indicates how perceived injustices became a galvanizing issue for workers. On December 4, 1943, gauge, machine-tool, and fuse workers rushed out of the workshops, leaving their machines on, and assembled at the road beside the foundry before going to the welfare office to make their demands.

Analyzing the leadership of the work stoppage indicates how workers identified with their labor. Management cited the incendiary role played by several foremen, known as assistant technicians, and skilled workers. Disgruntled by their low salaries, which did not exceed the wages of skilled workers, certain assistant technicians covertly suggested to workers that they attack the welfare board. Management also blamed the incident on a ringleader, Su Changshi, and seven other skilled workers from the gauge and fuse departments. Called "the Heavenly Club" because of his aggressive behavior, Su had a history of confrontation with management. He had already been fired twice, once as foreman at Arsenal No. 21 and later while working at a shipyard in Wanxian, Sichuan. This time, management blamed Su for mobilizing support throughout each workshop and defaming the welfare board. While it may seem contradictory that an ex-foreman and foremen played leadership roles, this reflects how alliances were built around production labor. As we have seen in previous chapters, because of the scarcity of and high demand for skilled workers, those with superior skills commanded substantial respect. That foremen often participated in leading production accounts for such alliances during times of conflict.

Workers left their machines to protest preferential treatment accorded staff officers, yet accounts differ regarding disparities among nonwage benefits. According to one report, the factory had originally prepared to sell a batch of leather shoes to both staff and skilled workers at a reduced price. But the batch that arrived from Chengdu only sufficed for the staff members. To compensate skilled workers, management sold them cloth shoes. No shoes were sold to laborers, because, management explained, their work "did not require shoes." Workers also felt disgruntled that goods sold at below-market prices to *zhiyuan* far surpassed what they could purchase. While staff could buy cloth, toothbrushes, dental powder, wool, and medicated soap, workers could only purchase five meters of cloth. Inflation had also eroded workers' purchasing power; a *chi* (.33 meters) of cloth had suddenly increased in price from 16 to 26 yuan. These differences in benefits led skilled workers to take their protest to the welfare board office. Workers dispersed only after officials explained to them that although staff officers had greater purchasing power, they had still not received their salaries, unlike workers who had been issued their wages.[139]

A similar incident arose at Arsenal No. 20 in July 1948, when management distributed different types of cloth to its workforce. As one skilled worker recalled, management gave wool to staff members but distributed cheaper indigo cloth to workers. To express their opposition, workers shut down the first and fourth departments for several hours. Both departments were located in the old factory district, making communication and concerted action possible. Management compromised by distributing a higher grade of cotton suiting, two-thirds cotton and one-third wool, to workers.[140] Not only were different departments capable of united action, but by the civil war period, dwindling resources and mismanagement catalyzed workers of different skill levels to protest in unison. At Arsenal No. 10, for instance, the entire workforce held a slow-down in March 1946 to protest official malfeasance, the threat of mass layoffs, and inequities between staff and workers.

In short, workers felt that the gains in material terms and social prestige of management and the salaried employees had been at their expense. This perception was not always entirely objective; some staff members also suffered economically in the late 1940s. In the context of Germany, Hans Speier makes a telling observation in this regard: "[J]ust as the anti-feudal bourgeoisie, in its struggle for social advancement, had painted a picture not of the nobility's impoverished members but of its ruling representatives and strongly provocative life styles of libertines, so the worker focused on those white-collar characteristics that he lacked. This perception was eminently sociological in character, for indeed, every kind of social prestige is founded on differences rather than equalities."[141]

Management was not unaware of these inequities. After meeting in July 1948, arsenal directors expressed the hope that all arsenals would "try their utmost to make welfare equitable for both workers and staff."[142] A proposal the following year recommended that reconciliation be achieved through night schools, literacy courses, and technical lectures. Managers felt these would close the education gap between staff and workers, which they saw as a root cause of friction. The report also recommended mutual aid associations to help the neediest workers.

Inadequate funding, however, remained a recurrent problem facing arsenal management. In part, the source of allocation influenced the amount received by employees. On the one hand, since the Ordnance Department paid all officers' salaries according to the cost-of-living standards of Nanjing or Chongqing, sufficient funds were more often available to it. Each arsenal, on the other hand, determined workers' wages depending on the price obtained for its products. According to Liu Yuansen, these prices fluctuated widely and the difference between staff and workers' pay was "extremely great."

By 1949, wage gaps between office staff and workers had grown, and workers' earnings had dropped to new lows. The situation had reached crisis proportions. As real earnings plummeted, even the best-paid skilled workers could no longer support their families. Workshops increasingly called for slowdowns, and management feared the specter of revolution, eyeing potential linkages between student activists and workers.[143] But work continued until the last days of Nationalist rule, days marked more by widespread demoralization and small-scale resistance, notably slowing piece-rate output, than by open revolt. Managers for their part were reduced to paying wages in kind, giving out blankets rather than cash. Workers would have to wait until the early 1950s, when the urban revolution was deepened, to attack their class enemies.

If resilience and resistance were two options available to workers employed in the war plants, a much commoner solution was simply to exit. At the peak of their exodus during the early 1940s, some ten thousand workers left the arsenals each year to escape the militarized compounds, to search for better work conditions, and in some cases to express political opposition. The compound system and industrial welfare, developed to gain their loyalty, had minimal effect on these workers.

5

CHONGQING'S MOST WANTED

The Mobility and Resistance of Arsenal Workers

Li Hua, "Zhua ding" [Press-ganged conscripts], from the series "Nuchao" [The raging tide] (1946). From Ma Ke, ed., *Li Hua huaji* (Tianjin: Tianjin renmin meishu chubanshe, 1987), 26.

The mobility of Chongqing's arsenal workers became the most contested labor issue facing workers, industrialists, and the Nationalist government. Frequent job changing had persisted throughout China during the entire republican era.[1] But chaos in the labor market, especially the movement of defense industry workers, took on particular significance during the Anti-Japanese War. The exodus of both skilled workers and laborers from the arms industry reached a peak during the early 1940s, pushing the Nationalist state to the verge of crisis. Weapons imports had plummeted, owing to Japan's control of all of China's shipping routes and key transshipment points, and the demand for skilled labor became urgent. As Chongqing's arsenals became lifelines for the state, the mobility of workers out of strategic government-controlled industries constituted a real and well-recognized threat to national interests and wartime production.

There were at least two distinct phases to labor mobility. During the first stage, between 1939 and 1945, Chongqing's defense industry rapidly expanded its workforce to over 50,000, but also experienced heavy turnover among skilled workers and severe labor shortages because of voluntary quits, layoffs, and involuntary separations. Mobility during these years was rooted in arsenal workers' efforts to obtain better jobs and to cope with factory conditions. The development of social welfare benefits barely alleviated oppressive working conditions and low wages, which drove many laborers and skilled workers away from the arsenals. The second phase, between 1946 and 1949, witnessed numerous forced separations, market retrenchment, and fewer opportunities outside the arsenals, making workers much more reluctant to leave their posts.

Structural changes in the defense industry after its move to Sichuan and competition between private and state-run industries contributed to the labor turnover of the early to mid 1940s. Industrial managers frequently poached from each other, a practice that exacerbated mobility across industrial sectors and within the arms industry. Poaching became a quick fix to meet industry's demands for labor, but it had the unintended consequence of alerting workers to their own job market value and pushed them to seek greater control over their own labor power.

With the law of supply and demand on their side, workers used their mobility as a lever to defy arsenal management and to express dissatisfaction with working conditions. Flight reflected workers' desire to improve their material conditions and to attain some form of job control. Skilled workers fled the arsenals to preserve craft autonomy, while laborers left to assert some say over their lives. As a form of resistance, mobility was truly a "weapon of the weak."[2] Denied recourse to unions, or to any association, workers had no alternative but protest on an individual or small group basis. Although workers engaged sporadically in strikes and slowdowns, the harsh authoritarian practices they faced in state-run industries forced them to oppose management on a more subterranean level through their transience. Leaving the arsenals epitomized the survival strategy of many workers, which, in Eric Hobsbawm's words, was one of "working the system to their minimum disadvantage."[3] In contrast to the commonly held view of the docile patriotic worker, I thus argue that workers' grievances and discontent with management spurred mobility, which in turn became a real and perceived form of resistance.

Interpreting mobility as a form of workers' resistance raises questions concerning workers' motives. In general, the paucity of sources left by workers and the fact that people often have mixed motives, which may change over time, make it difficult to gauge the motives of the "weak." James Scott papers over such differences by concluding that everyday forms of resistance prompted by the desire to maintain or improve material interests often meshed with more political acts of resistance. By extension, while Scott reveals an important course of action taken by the subaltern, he conflates conscious political acts of resistance with actions that are significant only at the individual level or not important at all. To preview the evidence presented, it is misleading to equate the actions and motives of workers who left in groups for the Communist base areas with those of workers who job-hopped from one Chongqing factory to another.

From the perspective of government, military, and industrial leaders, frequent job changing was an explosive political issue regardless of the individual workers' motives. Leaving the arsenals meant defying state policy, as the worker went up against a barrage of government regulations designed to control the labor market. The high rates of labor mobility do not indicate a conscious and deliberate intent to oppose the Nationalist regime. At the same time, draconian punishments—ranging from blacklisting to incarceration—instructed workers that the Ordnance Department leadership perceived their act of leaving as a statement of opposition to the state, because high turnover threatened war production and ultimately national security. Paradoxically, government efforts to eliminate the political voice of labor—a process originating in the Nationalists' ascent to power in 1927—helped define and shape Chongqing's emerging working class. The intensified repression of workers during the War of Resistance, coupled with the state's corporatist propaganda, thinly veiled the Nationalists' leadership's fear that working-class action of any kind might destabilize the regime's foundations.

Militarization and Manpower Competition

In all countries affected by the world war, the mobility of workers raised the specter of labor shortages. Industrial and military demands for manpower created tensions between politicians and the military throughout Europe and the United States.[4] In contrast, there was no absolute shortage of potential conscripts in China. Their surplus numbers generated callous neglect on the part of military leaders and, consequently, frequent evasion of conscription. Arsenals, which sought to maintain a steady workforce, served as havens for army recruits by offering them draft exemption. This push-and-pull effect resulted in considerable mistrust between the army and defense industry and prompted the devising of numerous methods to control mobile workers.

Recognition of arsenal workers' critical economic importance to the War of Resistance led to their special military status. On May 26, 1939, the Ministry of Military Affairs decreed all full-time arsenal workers subject to military law but exempt from military combat. Because of the increasing difficulty of importing weapons, arsenal workers' production role became as vital as the role of soldiers at the front. Workers' privileged status coincided with the arms industry's desire to maintain a stable labor force even among transient laborers. "It is neither in our interests to disrupt the work of skilled workers, nor frequently to change laborers who have received training," General Yu Dawei declared.[5] Consequently, during the first years of the war, arsenal workers were the only members of the industrial workforce guaranteed employment.[6]

Deferred military service was a primary reason to join the arsenal workforce. Wartime production was a source of pride and patriotism for many arsenal workers, but improving their material conditions and avoiding conscription was of more lasting importance. Sichuanese peasants and young men with few means shared these motives, since they were prime targets of press gangs recruiting soldiers for the Nationalist army. Brutal treatment, malnourishment, and disease produced catastrophic death tolls among conscripted soldiers. Between 1937 and 1945, an estimated 1.4 million conscripts—or one out of every ten men drafted—died before even reaching their assigned units in the field.[7] By 1941, as the wartime journalist Israel Epstein noted, "the ordinary Chinese came to regard induction as an automatic death sentence, and tried to avoid it by every means." Given the alternative, most recruits tolerated the low factory wages paid throughout the Chongqing arsenals. "Apart from the minority of skilled industrial workers who came from Shanghai and other ports, *most local workers came from rural districts to escape military service* and therefore do not care about the scanty wage. They say: 'To feed oneself in the rear [i.e., Nationalist-controlled territory] is better than to starve in the army.'"[8] Workers frequently joined the arsenal workforce only to leave once army recruitment in their home county or village was over. Such survival strategies explain why arsenals were effective in attracting workers but much less so in keeping them.

Competing demands for manpower created considerable friction between the army and arsenals. Press gangs frequently seized arsenal workers off the streets in Chongqing and permitted their return to the arsenals only after the latter had lodged a formal petition. Conversely, army brigade leaders accused local industries of enticing soldiers to join their workforce, leading the Ministry of Military Affairs to prohibit arsenals from accepting "fugitive soldiers and enticing draftees, to avoid weakening the forces of resistance."[9] Not until a series of labor recruitment laws staggered conscription and recruitment times were both administrations satisfied that they would have ample recruits.[10]

Because of their pressing need for workforce stability, arsenal managers branded transience as a criminal act. Since arsenal workers had the legal status of active soldiers, arbitrarily leaving the factory signified desertion. By April 1939, Yu Dawei ordered that all arsenal workers be subject to military law. "If there are fugitives, they shall be apprehended and managed in accordance with precedents for deserting soldiers."[11] "Fugitive" report charts and arsenal rolls documenting worker separations confirmed the transformation of labor mobility into a criminal act by listing workers who had "deserted" the arsenals. Officials rarely used the neutral term for job-hopping (*tiaochang*), preferring to describe workers as fugitives (*taowang*) or as having stealthily absconded (*qiantao*).

Jostling over manpower and making mobility a crime prompted more bureaucratic control of workers. Labor market controls began shortly before the war when Yu Dawei used blacklisting to prevent discharged workers from moving to other arsenals. Thereafter, employers reported a worker's age, native place, work experience, and skills, and the reasons why he had arbitrarily left the arsenal or been fired. Other arsenals then used these lists, sometimes referred to as "fugitive reports," along with employee pictures to identify workers. Since workers often changed their names to bypass these restrictions, management found photos especially useful, and within a few years had increased their number to as many as twenty-six per worker.[12] Arsenals also kept entry and exit rolls to coordinate recruitment with the army.[13] At the end of each month, starting in January 1939, management compiled elaborate lists of workers detailing their names, ages, provenance (province and county of origin), entry and exit date, department, and occupational status (skilled worker or laborer). Before the tenth day of the next month, the arsenals sent two copies to the Ordnance Department and placed a third in their own files. Subsequently, the department sent a copy to the local county army administration or division headquarters, where army officials examined the lists to verify whether the workers had been conscripts. These sources permit a quantitative study of labor mobility in wartime Chongqing.

In April 1942, labor market controls extended throughout strategic industries of the Great Rear when the Ministry of Economic Affairs issued "Regulations Governing the Control of Skilled Labor in Time of Emergency." Skilled workers were "required to possess certificates issued by the committee for the control of skilled labor of their respective localities"; otherwise, they could not work in any factory, not even in their own business.[14] Further regulations promulgated in the National General Mobilization Act of April 1943 mandated that each employer and skilled worker register with the government before assuming employment. Employers could recruit workers only after receiving a certificate of registration from the government in exchange for copies of workbooks issued to each employed worker. Furthermore, certificates would not be issued to employers hiring workers who had been discharged or who had left employment without authorization.[15] In theory, by July 1943, skilled workers were prohibited from leaving their jobs without justification or the employer's consent.[16] To be sure, it was impossible to enforce the letter of the law. But by the early 1940s, indicative of the defense industry's widening scope, arsenal military police were traversing provinces and prowling both private and state-owned factories in search of fugitive workers.[17] If workers were apprehended, they could be fired and denied employment at all arsenals. Most of the time, arsenal military police brought workers back to the arsenal under armed guard for discipline.

The Scope of Labor Mobility

Labor mobility was a mass phenomenon. Tens of thousands of workers entered and left the arsenals over the course of a decade. The early 1940s represented a peak in the turnover rate attributable to over a thousand incoming and outgoing workers from each munitions plant every year. The sheer density of documentation and numerous injunctions against labor mobility reflect these high rates, as well as the government's sense of impending crisis. High labor mobility rates coincided with the virtual termination of imports and thus increased pressure on the Nationalist arms industry to supply weapons to the front. Numerous workers' leaving when skilled workers were in such high demand compounded the leadership's sense of crisis.

Data from Arsenal No. 10, a large, modern artillery works (table 5.1), and the steel mill known as Arsenal No. 24 (table 5.2) confirm that there was considerable movement through 1944. Entry rates for 1941–42 were extremely high, because the demand for war production spurred industrial expansion. Full-scale production at Arsenal No. 10 began that year after machinery ordered from Germany finally arrived via Burma. At the same time, numerous separations in 1942 coincided with a peak in Chongqing's industrial boom. For workers who sought other jobs, this was an opportune time to leave. Although the figures for 1943 are incomplete, the trend of mobility at Arsenal No. 24 suggests a slight decrease that year. Besides 1946, when exit and turnover rates sharply increased because of massive layoffs after V-J Day, turnover during the civil war period was much reduced.

The end of World War II ushered in a new phase of labor mobility. The steady growth of the workforce stopped by 1946, and there were lower turnover rates thereafter. Turnover during this period primarily involved involuntary separations. The demobilization drive immediately after the war and during the temporary truce with the Communist Party resulted in numerous layoffs. Arsenal No. 10, for instance, reduced its workforce from 2,500 to 1,262 in 1946. Demographic shifts paralleled decreases in the number of arsenal employees. Migration back to central and coastal China accelerated when the Nationalist government reclaimed Nanjing as its political capital in April 1946—an estimated 500,000 people left Chongqing during the first ten months of that year[18]—but the decrease in the arsenal workforce proved temporary. Within a year, production demands stemming from the civil war led to an increase in the Arsenal No.

TABLE 5.1

Annual Labor Mobility Trends Among Full-Time Workers at Arsenal No. 10, 1941–1948

Mobility type	1941	1942	1943	1944	1945	1946	1947	1948
Accessions	1,647	1,199	1,473	1,217	1,152	718	396	442
Separations	1,086	1,071	875	1,299	1,099	1,107	179	351
Avg. employed	1,156	1,373	1,694	1,850	2,172	1,586	1,790	2,048
Entry rate (%)	121.2	87.3	88.7	66.6	53.5	47.7	22.1	21.9
Exit rate (%)	71.3	78.0	53.5	69.5	50.5	65.3	10.0	16.9
Turnover rate (%)	118.2	82.7	71.1	68.0	52.0	56.5	16.1	19.4

SOURCES: Chongqing Municipal Archives, 10 Chang, gongwu lei, 308–9, 311, 364, 379, 404, 418–20, 484–85, 605, 618, 664, 667, 832 *juan;* 10 Chang, 1 *mu,* 544 *juan;* 50 Chang, 3919 *juan.*
NOTE: Turnover rate is derived by dividing the sum total of accessions and separations by two and then by the number of average employed workers. Average employed refers to the total monthly workforce divided by 12.

TABLE 5.2

Annual Labor Mobility Trends Among Full-Time Workers at Arsenal No. 24, 1938–1949

Mobility type	1938	1939	1941	1942	1943	1946	1947	194	1949
Accessions	396	1,398	1,931	1,457	585	643	342	917	505
Separations	265	760	1,795	1,160	839	1801	118	587	1,210
Avg. employed	551	1,177	2,513	2,757	2,581	2,600	2,689	3,001	2,923
Entry rate (%)	71.9	118.8	80.3	54.4	22.8	23.8	14.0	30.3	16.8
Exit rate (%)	48.1	64.6	69.2	42.3	31.2	61.7	4.4	19.2	40.1
Turnover rate (%)	60.0	91.6	74.7	47.5	27.6	42.7	9.2	24.8	28.5

SOURCES: Chongqing Municipal Archives, 24 Chang, ren *mu,* 119, 162 *juan;* 24 Chang, 1 *mu,* 92 *juan;* 24 Chang, *zong,* 249 *juan;* 24 Chang, 3240, 3251, 3565–67, 6394 *juan;* Second Historical Archives of China, Nanjing, 774 *quan,* 1658 *juan.*
NOTE: Data missing for 1940; October–December 1943; 1944–45; January 1946; January–February, December 1947; November–December 1949.

10 workforce to over two thousand.[19] By 1949, with the political collapse of the Nationalists, voluntary separations had almost stopped; workers sought to keep their jobs because of the hyperinflation crisis.[20]

Nationalist government leaders became concerned about workers' mobility for several reasons. They fretted over high rates of flux, that is, the number of changes required per full-year worker, among specific job categories. At Arsenal No. 10, construction workers, utility workers, and laborers moved most frequently in 1942. The flux rate for odd-jobbers and laborers of roughly two, equivalent to a 100 percent turnover rate, in theory indicates a complete turnover of the workforce. In other words, this was the equivalent of having all laborers during 1942 leave their jobs and be replaced by a new group. Despite the lower flux rates among skilled workers, managers were forced to replace at least half of them each year.[21]

High turnover rates among skilled workers proved to be another area of concern for industrial managers. The short-term nature of laborers' work generally leads to higher mobility rates, yet skilled workers proved just as transient. In 1942, a year of high turnover, skilled workers constituted 45 percent of all separating workers (N = 1,465) at the cartridge plant, Arsenal No. 20.[22] Between 1943 and 1946, there was more than one labor change for each skilled and unskilled member of the Arsenal No. 10 workforce.[23] Separations exceeded accessions for most skilled workers, thus contradicting the general trend of workforce expansion. These separations proved most worrisome to the defense industry, because they signaled an absolute shortage of skilled personnel. Despite the development of an internal labor market designed to train and promote laborers to the status of skilled workers within the same industrial plant, the number of workers leaving far outpaced the number of trained apprentices. Skilled workers left for a variety of reasons. Turners and fitters occupied valued trades as metalworkers and responded to the intense demand and higher wages across industrial sectors. Fillers who packed shells and detonators with ammunition occupied dangerous jobs and moved in search of better working conditions. Even apprentices often enrolled for a year or two in specialized training schools at the arsenals before going elsewhere to test their skills and earn higher wages.[24]

With greater leverage on the job market because of the high demand for their labor, most workers left voluntarily. Throughout the mid 1940s, voluntary separations made up a far greater proportion of total separations than discharges. "Absconding" workers, those who left the arsenals without alerting management, topped the list of exiting workers during the early 1940s at factories such as Arsenal No. 50.[25] Given the high demand for skilled workers and the risks involved in leaving the arsenals, skilled workers were more likely to leave than laborers. Laborers, in contrast, were deemed expendable and thus suffered higher discharge rates.[26]

Tenure of Employment

Taken alone, figures on labor turnover may be misleading, because there was much more flux in some jobs than in others. Another problem inherent in quantitative studies of labor mobility is that supervisors determined the causes of separation, ascribing motives often at odds with why workers actually left the factory. Hong Jiaxin, a twenty-three-year-old worker at Arsenal No. 10 was, for example, branded a deserter for slacking, absenteeism, and finally absconding from the arsenal to join the Central Radio Plant. Only later did management acknowledge that they had erred. In reality, Hong had convalesced at his uncle's home for a month after spitting blood and fighting hemorrhoids for over a year. When Hong did find a position at the Central Radio Plant working in food sales and distribution, it was because the job was less physically taxing.[27] Hong's case illustrates the obvious point that statistics do not exactly mirror reality. At best, turnover rates represent trends over time and must be used with other sources, ranging from managerial testimony to rates of worker retention.

Data on workers' ages and employment tenure confirm the high rate of mobility among arsenal workers. Regardless of skill level, permanence and "company loyalty" did not characterize the arsenal workforce. Short tenure among workers compounded arsenal managers' apprehension, because frequent displacement of workers, especially skilled labor, increased costs. To be sure, arsenals did retain a small core of loyal workers. This was an elite group of veteran skilled workers, similar to the Shanghai machinists, whom Alain Roux has identified as part of an "aristocracy of labor."[28] They were older, better-paid, less mobile, and occupied the most craft-oriented of the skilled jobs. This kind of worker composition had been the norm before the War of Resistance. According to a 1936 survey of the Hanyang arsenal's workforce, for instance, the average age was thirty-six, and a quarter of all workers (N = 395) had employment tenures of over ten years.[29] During the initial stages of the war, many of these same machinists and metalworkers migrated to Chongqing. At Arsenal No. 21, one of the largest and oldest arsenals in China, with factories dating back to the Qing dynasty's self-strengthening movement, some six hundred workers had been employed from ten to twenty-five years.[30] Approximately half of these veteran employees worked in the rifle-manufacturing department, while the remaining workers toiled in the machine-gun plants and repair plants, where one needed skills and experience to operate complex machines, cut metals, and make precise parts.

Nevertheless, transience changed the structure of the workforce employed in the arms industry. The industry characterized during the late 1920s by continuity among workers through generational ties, and by artisans who developed their craft over long periods of time, had almost

TABLE 5.3

Ages of Full-Time Workers, 1938–1939

(percentage)

Age groups	Arsenal		
	No. 24	Gangqianhui	Paobingchu
15–20	16.9%	5.9%	21.2%
21–25	29.0	21.6	29.2
26–30	30.6	22.0	30.3
31–35	12.2	13.5	12.0
36–40	8.0	18.5	5.1
41–45	2.7	8.8	1.8
46–50	0.6	6.9	0.4
51–55	0	1.4	0
55–65	0	1.4	0
Total workers	847	422	274

SOURCES: Chongqing Municipal Archives, 24 Chang, zong 1 *mu*, 92 *juan*, 3; 29 Chang, 5 *mu*, 1231 *juan*; 10 Chang, 187 *juan*, 40.

disappeared. Workers employed during the Anti-Japanese War were noticeably younger. While munitions plants that relocated to Sichuan brought with them many of their older skilled workers, deemed indispensable to factory production, these core veteran workers were a minority. The Chongqing-based steel plant, the Gangqianhui, in merging steel works from Shanghai and Hanyang, retained a sizable minority (18.5 percent) of workers over the age of forty. Concepts of age are relative, and at the time, a forty-year-old worker was already considered "old." As indicated by table 5.3, however, the distribution of age groups was weighted toward youth. Arsenal No. 24, a local Chongqing steel plant that began production after the war broke out, employed far fewer veteran workers; almost half of its workers were under twenty-five. At the Paobingchu arsenal (later renamed Arsenal No. 10), most workers were aged between fifteen and thirty.[31]

The relatively young workforce was the result of the large influx of inexperienced workers during the war and the departure of older workers. Recruitment and training of apprentices, who tended to be under the age of twenty, contributed to the youthfulness of the workforce. Young men from the surrounding rural areas filled the need for laborers. Although skilled workers were generally older than laborers, at the Paobingchu arsenal, young men dominated the skilled posts of fillers and inspectors. As a major producer of artillery shells, the factory put a premium on young adults in shell filling, which required dexterity and a good pair of lungs

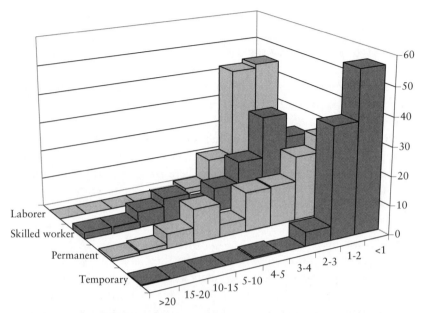

FIG. 5.1. Tenure Distributon of Arsenal No. 20 Workers Leaving in 1943 (percentage). Total number of entries = 1,296. October–December 1943 are missing. Original documents recorded January–June separations only for temporary and permanent workers, and separations for July–September noted only laborers and skilled workers. Data from Chongqing Municipal Archives, 20 Chang, 1012, 1032, 1121 *juan*, "Gongren lichang huaming ce."

to offset the pervasive risk of tuberculosis. Inspectors, who examined parts for shells and mortars, also tended to be much younger than turners and fitters.

Moreover, most workers moved quickly during the war. Low levels of retention indicate the difficulties faced by managers dealing with a shortage of skilled personnel and high turnover rates. As figure 5.1 demonstrates, close to 80 percent of all workers leaving Arsenal No. 20 did so before they had worked three years. Slightly over two-thirds left before two years had elapsed. Length of employment varied according to the status and skill of the worker. Skilled workers and permanent workers (often one and the same) were more stable. Nonetheless, roughly a quarter left during their first year, and half did so before completing two years of work.

Looking at Arsenal No. 20 a few years later from the perspective of tenure confirms the high rate of instability. Approximately half of all workers (N = 4,895) in 1947 had joined the payroll within the past two years. A full 70 percent had been employed for less than five years.[32]

Laborers and skilled workers left during their first year of employment for several reasons. Indicative of the intense disciplinary environment, workers were often fired for infractions or slacking during their first six months on the job. Listless work or sleeping at work probably stemmed from sheer exhaustion and malnutrition, notwithstanding management's conviction that they employed too many lazy workers. Moreover, sheer fatigue and dangerous working conditions caused sickness and pushed workers out of the arsenals. Workers were frequently fired or quit for reasons listed as weak constitution, tuberculosis, venereal disease, or spitting blood. Those seeking exemption from military service also tended to stay for shorter periods of time. There is no direct correlation between draft dodgers and workers who took leaves of absence, but it comes as no surprise that workers granted leave remained clustered in the first six months of employment, and absconders in the first nine months.

Flight was often an extension of shop-floor resistance or a reaction to working conditions. Records on workers struck from the rolls of Arsenal No. 10 and Arsenal No. 20 (table 5.4) suggest that many workers left the arsenals because of conflict. Shop-floor resistance, as measured by the categories "rule violation," "authority conflict," and "work performance," comprised almost one quarter of all cases. Even more workers left the arsenals on extended leaves or were long-term absentees. A legal distinction characterized these two forms of separation; the former was approved through formal channels; the latter was considered a breach of discipline. Not surprisingly, a greater proportion of skilled workers practiced absenteeism, whereas laborers more often asked for extended leave. One may attribute this difference to the leverage of skilled workers, who feared fewer repercussions even though absenteeism was punished by heavy fines and, ultimately, discharge. Despite these differences, workers often used both means to search for other jobs before leaving the arsenals outright.

In large part because of the political repression within the arsenals, workers perceived mobility as the best form of resistance and avoided direct action. If government repression limited the possibility of an organized labor movement during the war, CCP tactics during the early 1940s also influenced workers' preference for small-scale acts of resistance. Following Mao Zedong's policy of "justification, advantage, and restraint"

TABLE 5.4

Reasons for Separations at Arsenals No. 10 and 20, 1941–1942

Reason	Apprentice	Laborer	Skilled worker	Total	Percentage
Death	6	31	52	89	3.0%
Sick leave	22	171	129	322	10.9
Extended leave	31	449	270	750	25.4
Absenteeism	41	224	311	576	19.5
Absconded	13	93	29	135	4.6
Quit	0	4	2	6	0.2
Personal	2	17	29	48	1.6
Rule violation	9	97	61	167	5.7
Authority conflict	4	57	34	95	3.2
Work performance	39	282	117	438	14.8
Fired	3	82	58	143	4.8
Laid off	0	23	8	31	1.0
Promotion	2	62	23	87	2.9
Transfer	0	33	26	59	2.0
Retirement	0	1	6	7	0.2
Total	172	1,626	1,155	2,953	100.0

SOURCES: Chongqing Municipal Archives, 10 Chang, 308–9, 311, 338, 379, 404 *juan*; 20 Chang, 1019, 1049, 1089 *juan*, "20 chang 31 nian 1–12 yuefen lichang gongren baogao biao."

NOTE: Missing data for Arsenal No. 10, August–September 1941 and March–May 1942. "Personal" refers to family and school reasons.

(*youli, youli, youjie*), laid down in March 1940, local underground activists affiliated with the CCP's Southern Bureau (Nanfangju) proposed that workers use only legal and restrained means of resistance: "Our demands should not be excessive or involve many conditions. We should refrain from going too far, accumulate small victories for the bigger victory, avoid senseless sacrifice and refrain from striking unless we have no alternative." To avoid exposure, party members favored slowdowns and foot-dragging rather than open mass opposition. These forms of struggle were well suited to the CCP's shifting views of the arms industry. Communists ostensibly supported arsenal work as part of the patriotic cause, but they nonetheless wanted to disrupt "industries that the Guomindang reactionary clique uses to carry on the civil war."[33] Supporting less overt acts of resistance thus provided a middle ground for the Communists, allowing them to uphold the ideals of the United Front while jabbing away at their ideological rivals. To have openly defied and possibly damaged China's arms industry would merely have played into enemy hands by tarnishing the image of patriotic integrity that the Communists sought to propagate.

Conditions for Separation

Many workers left the arsenals for personal and most likely apolitical reasons. Many workers exploited the new labor market situation to better their individual welfare. The widening discrepancy between an expanding manufacturing sector and the severe shortage of skilled workers formed conditions for the high rates of labor mobility. Pockets of industry had existed before the war, but war and industrial relocation led to the forced and rapid growth of Chongqing's manufacturing base. Rapid expansion increased demand for workers, especially skilled workers, who were in short supply, given the small size of Chongqing's prewar industry. The situation looked increasingly bleak during the initial period of the war, when arsenals faced an absolute shortage of skilled workers. By one account, as few as 8,105 skilled workers migrated to Sichuan, many from Shanghai and the lower Yangtze region, which a leading sociologist estimated to hold 80 percent of China's prewar skilled labor force.[34]

The exceptionally high proportion of skilled workers employed in the arms industry exacerbated the labor shortage. The industry suffered from an acute shortage of skilled workers and machine operators, which manufacturing processes required in large numbers. According to General Zhuang Quan, director of Arsenal No. 10, Nationalist arsenals throughout the southwest employed roughly 100,000 workers in 1945, and at least half were skilled machinists, toolmakers, and tool operators. More than in any other industry, technological innovations and production depended on this select group, creating extensive problems of labor allocation.[35] Moreover, and much to the dismay of arsenal management, the disproportionately large number of arsenal workers formed a convenient labor pool for other industrial sectors.

Imbalance between the supply of and demand for labor led industrial managers to poach skilled arsenal workers with promises of higher wages. Poaching prevailed during the industrial boom of 1939–42. Conspiratorial theories were the rage, and arsenal managers blamed the immoral practices of other industrialists for luring away their workers. Industrialists, though, viewed poaching as an attractive alternative to more costly and time-consuming investment in worker training. Despite their protestations, arsenal managers were not above engaging in poaching themselves. Managers used similar recruitment tactics to allure machinists from other state-run industries, such as the railroads and the aircraft industry.[36] A general shortage of skilled workers in Nationalist-occupied territory accelerated recruitment of skilled workers from central China. For strategic reasons, the Nationalist leadership also sought to strip regions of skilled personnel, fearful that they might be of use to the Japanese. In the spring of 1939, for example, Chiang Kai-shek authorized the recruitment of skilled workers and technicians in Henan, an area soon to be overrun by the invaders.

Once they had had become familiar with arsenal work, many workers also moved within the defense industry, attracted by the higher wages offered at more mechanized plants or seeking to renew ties with friends from whom they had been separated during the relocation. Arsenal management and Nationalist leaders found the poaching of workers from among "friendly factories," or between arsenals, especially troubling. Turnover would create economic disruption, obstruct discipline, and cause a bidding war for labor, escalating wages. Yu Dawei's directive to arsenal directors typifies management's apprehension of the economic and social crisis brought on by labor mobility. Yu became frustrated when his own efforts to control the labor market by administrative decree diverged radically from the practices of his subordinates. "You must temper yourself through severe trials. Exert yourself in traversing this crisis together. Competing in the enticement and recruitment of workers disrupts group organization and inflames workers' emotions. [Workers'] submissiveness and obedience is swept away leading both sides [workers and managers] to lose."[37] Whereas Yu viewed transient workers as the passive victims of conniving agents, more often than not, workers took the initiative in searching for other jobs. Poaching had the unintended effect of raising workers' consciousness of their own market value, thereby promoting further mobility.

For the majority of workers who left arsenals for other industrial jobs, a primary motive was the promise of higher wages. Comparative wage surveys of factories in the private sector and the arms industry indicate that arsenal workers earned less than workers employed in either large joint state-private firms or small privately run workshops (see table 5.5).

Skilled workers' monthly actual income (total income from wages, overtime, and bonuses) at Arsenal No. 20 was about half that of nonarsenal workers. Piecework provided much more income to those employed in the small machine shops of Danzishi and Longkan districts. Skilled workers employed by large state-private concerns (e.g., the Minsheng Shipping Company), large private firms (e.g., the Shunchang Iron Mill), and small shops (e.g., the Longkan workshops) also earned higher wages

TABLE 5.5

Comparative Income and Conditions of Chongqing Skilled Workers, 1942

Enterprise	Hours	Minimum wage/hr	Maximum wage/hr	Actual monthly income (yuan)	Other forms of remuneration
Arsenal No. 20	12	0.4	0.8	650–850	Stipend; possible wage increase of Ch$200; cheap oil, salt, matches, vegetables; housing; bonuses also for indirect producers
Minsheng Shipping Company	9–12	0.9	1.7	1,000–1,500	Wartime stipend 30% of wages; Ch$1.2 daily rice stipend, overtime and bonus; cheap rice at Ch$16 per deciliter; housing
China Xingye	12–13	0.4	1.2	1,000–1,500	Ch$150–400 living stipend; Ch$150 overtime night shift; housing
Shunchang Iron Mill	13	—	—	1,300–1,800	Wartime stipend 100% of wages; housing for single workers and minority of relatives
Danzishi workshops	—	piece	work	1,300–1,500	Housing, water and electricity provided
Longkan workshops	12	2.7	3.1	1,300–1,500	Meals and monthly bonus, housing for single workers

SOURCE: Adapted from "Yushi fujin shu gongchang jigong daiyu ji gongzuo qingxing jianming biao," Chongqing Municipal Archives, 29 Chang, 5 *mu*, 1119 *juan*, 5 (October 31, 1942).

on overtime shifts. At these three firms, a full day's pay was based on the first nine hours' work, with the next three based on overtime rates. Overtime pay was equivalent to 4.5 hours, that is, a half-day's wages. In contrast, workers at Arsenal No. 20 put in long hours without being paid overtime rates. Arsenal surveyors viewed low wages as the main economic motive for job switching. This explains why the Shunchang Iron Mill, which offered rice subsidies equivalent to 100 percent of wages and higher monthly income than any other factory, had such low turnover rates.

Other qualitative reports indicate that wages in the arms industry consistently lagged behind those of other industrial sectors.[38] During the late 1930s and early 1940s, wage differentials were a product of competition for the scarce supply of skilled workers. Although poaching raised wages for a select few, management may intentionally have kept wages low for the bulk of the workforce, knowing full well that workers valued draft deferment even more than wage income. After 1942, other sectors in heavy industry granted deferment, making the arsenals less attractive to prospective workers. Arsenal wages continued to be kept low throughout the entire decade because of the increasing emphasis placed on fringe benefits in light of inflation. By the war's end, the erosion of real income through inflation exacerbated the wage gap between arsenal workers and workers employed in privately managed industries, as well as in the state-owned NRC plants.[39]

Although arsenal workers received housing subsidies and food and fuel priced below market, by the early 1940s, other large-scale plants began to offer comparable supplementary benefits, such as rice stipends.[40] Even the small workshops provided some form of housing. Given the convergence of nonwage benefits, the depressed wages earned by arsenal workers relative to other industrial workers during the early 1940s became the primary economic motive for leaving.

Low wages even turned away laborers, who were otherwise in great supply. Arsenal managers became caught in a vicious cycle. They preferred to cut costs by maintaining low wages, but guaranteed laborers nonwage benefits to keep a constant supply of labor. Increasingly, by the mid 1940s, housing and food costs provided to laborers forced management to reduce the number of employees. "Unskilled workers formerly were one of the arsenals' chief assets, but now provide a real problem," Major W. S. Brewster noted. "Living costs have climbed to the point where it is more and more necessary to displace hand labor with machinery, which unfortunately is not readily available, to avoid very high labor costs. There is a tremendous supply, of course, of unskilled labor but it cannot be taken advantage of because of the low salaries which the arsenals can afford to pay."[41]

Besides job-hopping, skilled arsenal workers tried to better their situation and to exert some degree of control over their own labor by setting up small machine shops, printing houses, electrical repair shops, or weaving workshops. Itinerant machinists often subcontracted their labor to raise sufficient money before purchasing spare parts from other factories. They then employed two or three workers to assemble and sell the products. Poorer workers unable to purchase the necessary equipment used personal connections to become brokers or middlemen.[42] The amount of criticism that this phenomenon provoked suggests the proliferation of petty capitalists during the first few years of the war. A journalist depicted the rise of such entrepreneurs in apocalyptic terms. "If the government does not consider fair means to ban the small plants, the future will be severely crisis-ridden."[43] Critics accused petty capitalists of depriving larger factories of workers and contributing to the speculative climate of the inflation-driven economy. Moreover, since many workshop tools and parts came from the black market or through pilfering, disparate production equipment led to products of dubious quality. Even the Communist underground chimed in, bemoaning the political effects of petty capitalism. Activists blamed enterprising workers and their new lifestyles for abandoning the working class and sapping its spirit.

Whether these charges were accurate or not, the "golden age" for enterprising workers lasted only a few years. By the mid 1940s, workers seeking to escape the proletariat faced an uphill battle, as many of their small businesses had collapsed. According to Israel Epstein, they faced grim prospects: "As is usual in such situations, the less bold and less lucky majority of fortune-seekers joined the procession after the circumstances that produced the early windfalls had already lapsed. Many invested their small savings in new businesses at the beginning of the wartime depression that was to wipe out practically all minor enterprises and affect large ones as well. When they tried to return to factory jobs these were no longer available."[44]

Resistance and the Politics of Labor Mobility

Although workers' search for a better livelihood may have been apolitical in motive, their flight soon threatened war production and thus was transformed into a gesture of opposition to the state. Whereas material conditions often motivated workers to leave, the army command perceived labor mobility as an overt political statement. Minister of Military Affairs He Yingqin considered poaching and flight to be subversive. "According to reports in the vicinity of all munitions plants, other administrations frequently send their people to loiter and use high wages to lure our workers into absconding or establish ties to pilfer materiel. This conduct is extremely disruptive of the social order and moreover undermines workers' morale. Therefore, you must ban and eliminate these practices. Pay close attention to all factory neighborhoods, habitually investigate, make arrests and deliver [perpetrators] to the authorities. Post this."[45] He Yingqin's orders reflect the Nationalists' wartime siege mentality, in which everyday forms of life became political. In other words, people's private actions came under public scrutiny, were often legally proscribed, and were categorized on the basis of political loyalties.

The Nationalist government thus perceived workers' out-migration as a form of political opposition. Workers' exodus to the remote Communist base area of Yan'an constituted the most threatening form of mobility. "Recently, the Communist Party has been wantonly advocating that workers go to northern Shaanxi. In the past two weeks, over 400 have fled and left the arsenals. From our investigations, we now know that they recruited 500 technical personnel to go to northern Shaanxi to manufacture weapons," Yu Dawei reported in 1938.[46] Half a year later, General Yu's associate, Yang Jizeng, director of the Ordnance Production Board, confirmed that arsenal workers were leaving in droves of ten for Yan'an.

Rather than focus on stereotypes of Communist agitators and manipulated workers, Yang Jizeng candidly underscored the arsenals' exploitative conditions and workers' desires to improve their livelihood as the main reason for leaving the arsenals. "Under the influence of the Communist Party, countless workers are demanding to go to northern Shaanxi for training, chiefly because they feel factory life is abysmal." Poor working conditions, low wages, long hours, and arbitrary discipline were forcing workers out of the arsenals. "Treatment within the factory is humiliating, and workers feel tormented, so when the Communist Party stirs them up, it is all the more motive for workers to go to northern Shaanxi."[47] Given the increasing dearth of information from the Communist base areas and the difficulty of passing through the Nationalist-imposed blockade, it is unlikely that arsenal workers continued to stream out of Chongqing. But the Communist base areas became a symbolic political alternative for workers in the Nationalist territory precisely because they had no political association with the Communists. Hence workers often recited the following doggerel upon encountering oppression in the workplace or if dissatisfied: "If this place won't keep me, there's still a place for me; if no place will keep me, I'll join the Eighth Route Army."[48]

The Nationalists responded to workers' movement to the Communist base areas by increased use of carrot-and-stick tactics. Yu Dawei directed his arsenal managers to heed workers' welfare and curb any political activities. "The mission of workers in the arms world is to bury themselves in hard work and struggle hard for production. We cannot allow them to join any political activity and must make this absolutely clear."[49]

Dissatisfaction over working conditions, political repression, and loss of autonomy resolved workers to flee, even at the cost of changing their political allegiance. Especially for skilled personnel, moving had become the only means of resistance. Israel Epstein observes:

The authorities replied to all complaints by repression, and absence without leave from military plants was punished by arrest. But the worker had no way of manifesting protest except to move. Complete obedience was expected in state industries at the same time as workers were maltreated, something skilled men from the coast, with their craft pride and tradition of organization, could not tolerate. In May 1942 alone, 600 skilled workers deserted Chungking. There appeared guides who guaranteed to get them back to occupied areas for a fee of $800, or $1,500 including a puppet "Good Citizenship Identity Card" so that they could travel there without hindrance.[50]

Although movement to the Communist base areas decreased, scores of workers were thus packing their bags for the Japanese-occupied coastal region by 1942.

Legal Measures Against Labor Mobility

In response to the high political and economic costs that workers' mobility imposed, the arms industry mobilized state resources to crack down on them. Arsenal management's use of stringent laws to deter mobility signaled the beginning of government intervention in the labor market. These controls proved ineffective during the peak period of labor mobility in the early 1940s, however, because of the continuing high demand for labor. In the short term, the laws were arguably even counterproductive, because workers resented such restrictions on their freedom to choose jobs. Designed to enhance stability and wartime production, the new laws only lowered workers' morale and decreased output.

High turnover continued until the last stages of the War of Resistance, indicating that the industrial decline of the mid 1940s had a more immediate impact than draconian legislation. Nevertheless, industrialists welcomed the laws, hoping that they would ensure an adequate labor supply, prevent job-hopping, and thus decrease wages. Moreover, arsenal managers were now given license to impose a range of punishments on "fugitive workers." Sometimes management punished apprehended workers and made an example of them, the proverbial "killing a chicken to frighten the monkey." One such victim was Xu Guoqing, who was sentenced to ten years' imprisonment by the military tribunal for having left the Aviation Weapons Technical Research Bureau. In his directive to all arsenal directors, Yu Dawei commanded them to post up the case in detail, so that "workers would be vigilant and never defy the law again. . . . You must deal strictly with workers who have been arrested. Do not be lenient. This is of the utmost importance. This is an order!"[51] Arsenals often fired workers and coordinated among themselves to prevent their being rehired.[52] Many cases do not specify the punishment but state that discipline was meted out according to factory regulations. Punishments ranged from wage reductions and denial of overtime pay to trial by military tribunal and potentially three to thirty days in prison.[53]

Besides legal restrictions, managers depended on a mutual responsibility system to promote stability and guarantee workers' reliability, but the guarantor system often proved to be a double-edged sword. Recruitment or sponsorship by someone already employed might deter labor mobility. As one worker put it, "If five workers were acting as mutual guarantors, and one of us ran off, the other four would be implicated and that would spell trouble."[54] But the fear of punishment could also motivate the guarantors, especially if they were all workers, to leave together. "At the time, to enter the factory workforce you needed five guarantors, other mutual guarantors," one arsenal worker recalled. "Workers would sponsor each other; you'd sponsor me and I'd sponsor you. If you ran off, we'd go together."[55] Paradoxically, the guarantor system thus increased the likelihood that workers would leave the factories together.

The frequency of group separations complicates hard and fast distinctions between individual acts of resistance and collective action. Among Arsenal No. 20 workers, group separations accounted for a quarter of absentee cases (N = 402) and some 39 percent of extended leaves (N = 476). In 1942, 55 percent of all "absconders" (N = 246) left arsenal No. 50 in small groups. These groups usually consisted of two to three workers, but sometimes as many as twelve. Native-place ties were an important component of group solidarity for workers leaving on the basis of mutual guarantor groups. When workers had to come up with mutual guarantors upon arrival at the arsenal, they chose friends, acquaintances, or other workers whose recruitment experience was similar. Yet, in more than half of the separation cases at Arsenal No. 50, workers chose guarantors from provinces other than their own.[56] Management's policy of having guarantors come from different social strata aimed at preventing networks from forming.

Other arsenals used both carrot and stick to curb absenteeism, a frequent corollary of labor mobility. Because many workers lived in the factory compound with their immediate families, management used the families as a wedge in its drive to enforce factory discipline. Starting in 1942, management fined steel workers a day's wages for each day they were absent. More severe punishments included deducting one-third of the worker's and his family members' low-priced rice for that day. If a worker was absent for two days, an additional third was deducted. The steel plant eliminated the rice subsidy for an entire month if a worker was absent for three or more days. This must have been hard on workers with dependents in an inflation-ridden economy.

Management introduced several bonuses to reduce frequent turnover and promote longer employment. In the compensation plans for injured workers and the victim's family, workers with longer tenure were rewarded. Similarly, pension plans benefited senior employees. Workers over the age of sixty were required to retire, and for the most part the rule was honored. Arsenals distributed pensions of 200 yuan per year to workers with over ten years' employment experience, and an extra 50 yuan for every additional five years of seniority. The regulation is significant for its omission of workers with less than ten years' experience. Issued first in 1932 and then again in 1937 prior to the war, the regulation was devised when the arsenal workforce was older and more stable, and it thus failed to address the short tenure of most wartime workers.[57]

A similar logic pertained to the higher severance pay accorded to longer-tenured workers. According to the 1947 regulations, workers laid off with less than a year's tenure were to receive two months' wages. An additional month's wages was accorded for each additional year of work experience. These "rewards," however, barely compensated for the traumatic experience of the layoff, especially in the late 1940s, when unemployment became severe. Since these funds were allocated after the worker had left the arsenal, they did not effectively promote a stable labor force.

The Legacy of Mobility

Labor mobility had two important consequences. The immediate economic effect of high turnover rates was to disrupt production. An assessment of the arsenals' production capacities cannot isolate labor turnover from the availability of raw and secondary materials, machinery, or working conditions. Nevertheless, it was no accident that output was in inverse proportion to the rate of turnover. Generally speaking, armament production was much higher during 1946–47 than during the early 1940s, when mobility peaked. Limited production capacity during the early 1940s, before American military aid and the Lend-Lease program, severely affected wartime strategy. A war of attrition and the policy of trading space for time became the only available options for the Nationalist government.

As chapter 4 has demonstrated, workers' transience also forced arsenal management to increase social welfare benefits. These benefits contributed in part to the relative stability of the workforce during the late 1940s. Of even greater consequence, restrictions in the labor market had a disciplining effect. Options narrowed for arsenal workers as privately run factories increasingly shut down and the masses of unemployed grew. Labor mobility ground to a halt by the mid to late 1940s as industrial depression in other sectors made job-hopping too great a risk. In April 1944, even before the War of Resistance ended, the Social Ministry reported an unemployment rate as high as 42 percent. By the eve of the Communist takeover, some seven thousand industrial and business concerns had shut down, leading to 120,000 unemployed people in Chongqing.[58]

If one focuses on the development of fringe benefits from workers' perspective, these measures, however sophisticated for their time, still left much to be desired. During the Anti-Japanese War, thousands of workers "voted with their feet," leaving the arsenals in search of better working conditions or to assert their own autonomy and dignity. Seeking better "treatment," machinists and laborers imparted their own meaning to factory paternalism, which differed from the hierarchical ideas of the factory authorities. While arsenal directors during the 1940s had sought to bolster the status of their staff personnel in the interests of stability by maintaining some of their privileges, these policies reinforced the divisions between mental and manual labor that still persisted in society at large.

Workers' mobility and flight from the arsenals was one method of resistance that avoided open confrontation with management. High turnover testifies to tense work relations, confirmed by convergent phenomena: fringe benefits, punishments and fines, efforts to cut production times through piecework, and increased discipline enforced by military law. Arsenals thus became a breeding ground for dissident workers armed with a consciousness of class, informed by visions of equality, and mobilized in the strike waves of 1946 and the ensuing civil war. For the workers who remained in the arsenals, organizing and concerted action became the best way to express discontent with arsenal conditions.

If the concern of management and labor for job security provided the groundwork for the Nationalist promotion of social welfare practices during the 1940s, an equally important influence was the labor movement. Nationalist arsenal leaders saw labor mobility and social conflict, in the form of slowdowns, strikes, petitions, and individual protest, as two sides of the same coin. Both had to be suppressed in the interests of social order, production, and national security. The Nationalists thus constructed their own project; they politicized the arsenals to win the hearts and minds of defense workers.

Top: The "neoclassical" façade and main gate of the Jinling arsenal in Nanjing, built during the late Qing self-strengthening movement. After relocating to Chongqing in 1937 and merging into Arsenal No. 21, the arsenal became the largest munitions plant in unoccupied China. Reproduced by permission of the Chongqing Municipal Museum. *Bottom:* During the Anti-Japanese War, the arsenals cut caves into the hillside to store machinery and power equipment, as well as to serve as air defense shelters. Reproduced by permission of the Chongqing Municipal Archives.

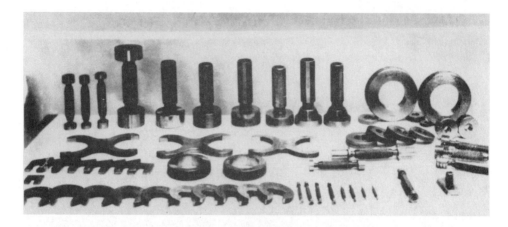

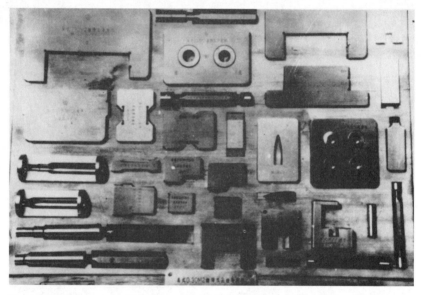

Top: A set of gauges used by Arsenal No. 50 to measure tolerance of parts and to ensure that specific parts of rifles, machine guns, and cartridges were finished correctly. These were necessary precision instruments for achieving interchangeable manufacture and mass production during the war. Reproduced by permission of the Chongqing Municipal Archives. *Bottom:* A set of gauges used to measure tolerance of the American-style 30-mm rifle bullet. Reproduced by permission of the Chongqing Municipal Archives.

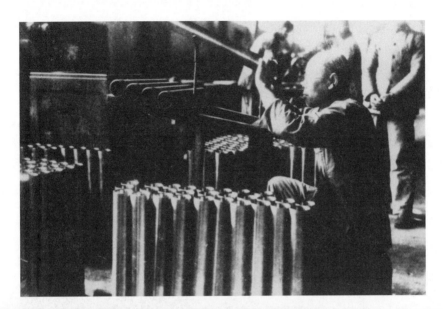

Top: Worker inspecting the barrel for a 60-mm mortar at Arsenal No. 50 (1940s). The "headless" figure in the background is a foreman, distinguished by his cotton-padded clothing. Reproduced by permission of the Chongqing Municipal Archives. *Bottom:* Compressed-air press used in the forge shop of Arsenal No. 50. Arsenals were equipped with state-of-the-art machinery, much of it imported from Germany prior to the Sino-Japanese War. The German firm SMS Eumuco GmbH was and continues to be an important producer of press and forging machines. Reproduced by permission of the Chongqing Municipal Archives.

Easily produced in quantity and light enough to be carried on the back, the 60-mm mortar was a key light infantry weapon of the Nationalists during the War of Resistance. Reproduced by permission of the Chongqing Municipal Archives.

An array of 60-mm mortars produced at Arsenal No. 50. The aesthetics of production and standardization was used to instill pride in workers' product and their arsenal. Reproduced by permission of the Chongqing Municipal Archives.

Top: Although severely limited in their production capacities, Nationalist arsenals were able to manufacture the mobile 37-cm anti-tank field gun as one of their main forms of heavy artillery. Reproduced by permission of the Chongqing Municipal Archives. *Bottom:* Group photo of foremen at the Smeltery of the Gangqianhui, Nationalist China's largest wartime steel mill. Photograph taken on New Year's Day, 1948. Reproduced by permission of the Chongqing Municipal Archives.

Top: A jerry-built arsenal workshop of Arsenal No. 21 in wartime Chongqing. Reproduced by permission of Southwest China Teachers' College, Department of History, Local History Research Room. *Bottom:* An arsenal workers' dormitory at Arsenal No. 21. Reproduced by permission of Southwest China Teachers' College, Department of History, Local History Research Room.

Top: Peking opera troupe members at Arsenal No. 50. The Welfare Board of each arsenal organized such troupes. These cultural activities served to break the monotony of the war and promote class conciliation between workers and staff officers, since participants hailed from both sides of the production divide. Reproduced by permission of the Chongqing Municipal Archives. *Bottom:* Arsenal theater troupe at Arsenal No. 50. Like Peking opera, theater was a main form of entertainment at the arsenals. Troupe members were arsenal employees. Reproduced by permission of the Chongqing Municipal Archives.

Top: Workers in a Sichuan teahouse. *Bottom:* Basketball team of Arsenal No. 50. Each arsenal organized sport teams and competitions as part of their social welfare activities, but also in line with popular social Darwinist views that physical fitness was necessary for national survival. Reproduced by permission of the Chongqing Municipal Archives.

6

THE NATIONALIST
PROJECT

Coercion, Consent, and Conflict

Li Hua, "Ye de kongbu" [Terror during the night] (1947). From Ma Ke, ed., *Li Hua huaji* (Tianjin: Tianjin renmin meishu chubanshe, 1987), 36.

Political controls and propaganda permeated the defense industry because it played such a strategic role in both the resistance effort and civil
war. Guomindang ideologues sought to remind workers that they were
working for a greater patriotic cause, using slogans like "One more drop
of sweat exerted on the shop floor means one less drop of blood on the
battlefield." And frequent visits by the most powerful state officials, including Chiang Kai-shek, as well as prominent foreign emissaries, such as
U.S. Vice President Henry Wallace, underscored the weighty political status of the arsenals.

Fearful that their Communist rivals might recruit workers, Nationalists tried to build a social base and foster workers' allegiance to the state
by means of social welfare, militarization, and "partification" (*danghua*).
Militarization changed arsenal workers' legal status from civilian to soldier and thereby heightened factory discipline. Partification involved
mass inductions into the Guomindang and holding party cell meetings to
mobilize and educate workers in the virtues of nationalist ideology.
Through these initiatives, Nationalist officials sought to homogenize
workers' rough culture, much like the partification of higher education
during the Guomindang's so-called Nanjing Decade (1927–37).[1] These
political activities had similar effects. Workers and many staff personnel
proved unresponsive to the appeals of the Guomindang. Arguably, the
very intensity of the political program further alienated workers from the
Nationalists and their appeals to spiritual unity and the national interest.
Rather than shunning party ideology, however, workers mediated GMD
propaganda for their own purposes, using the ideology of common sacrifice for the national good to criticize their own working conditions and
demand more political rights. This tactic was most evident in the demands and grievances of workers involved in the strike waves of the mid
to late 1940s, but it had already become prominent during the War of
Resistance.

Mobilizing Mind and Body

In theory, the Nationalist regime sought to control and stifle political
discourse. The GMD injunction "Don't speak about national affairs" often hung on the walls of the popular teahouses that workers frequented.
In practice, arsenal directors advocated a sweeping physical, military, and
political regime that would strengthen their employees' work ethic and
commitment to the Nationalist cause. Fearful that "a minority of weak-

willed elements" had come under "external influence" (from the CCP), arsenal directors resolved in 1939 to strengthen factory organization through military training corps. Henceforth, factories would be organized along military and managerial lines. Experienced workers led squads of ten workers, which provided the basis for larger military units—platoons, detachments, and the regiment—controlled by staff officers and the director. Three weeks of training with soldiers in the open country would impart basic military tactics, weaponry use, and political indoctrination. Lectures on staples of Nationalist ideology—the New Life Movement, Three People's Principles, and National Spiritual Mobilization Campaign—would "unify the will of employees and help protect the arsenals." Through these experiences, each squad would be enlisted alongside the arsenal's guard battalions to counter threats to security. Equally important, directors hoped that this spiritual mobilization campaign would raise the patriotic mood and foster good habits among workers. Women work squads were to investigate workers' family situations in order to rectify their private lifestyles.[2] After initial military training of the workforce, defense industry leaders proposed using both military-style management and the traditional household registration system (baojia) to regulate residential areas. "In this way, there will be no difference between family and factory. Everyone can maintain order in each other's private lives; enticements from the outside will have no means of invading."[3]

Like other spiritual mobilization campaigns throughout East Asia, the government's reorganization of the labor force was meant to instill a sense of community into factory employees. Whereas in Japan, the Sanpō movement's emphasis on mutual respect began to break down social hierarchies between blue- and white-collar workers, preexisting hierarchies based on the collar divide were superimposed on the new political organizations of Chongqing's armament factories.[4] Both military training and political education via Nationalist party cells reinforced the defense industry's social divisions.

Like many of their ambitious projects, the Nationalists found military training of arsenal workers difficult to put in practice. Realizing that production demands necessitated their workers' full attention, Li Chenggan and other managers quickly abandoned much of the military training regime, which had also begun to hamper arsenal recruitment. Potential recruits who initially sought munitions work to avoid the draft now began to view joining the arsenal workforce as tantamount to enlisting.

Peasants, as one arsenal officer concluded, "did not dare be recruited" by the arsenals for fear that they would become soldiers.[5] However accurate this perception may have been, during the late 1930s, as the demand for conscripts escalated, the military did view arsenal boot camp as a stepping-stone into the army. To distinguish between arsenal and military service, Li thus rejected the Chongqing militia's efforts to enlist workers in their training corps, on the grounds that training was interfering with production.[6]

Despite the short-lived nature of such training regimes, employees' legal status as officers and soldiers lent a distinctly military ambience to the defense industry. Starting in mid 1939, all full-time arsenal workers became subject to military law, albeit exempt from combat in recognition of their critical economic importance to winning the war. This new status proved a double-edged sword. Some of the more outspoken workers flaunted their status and thought of their uniforms as a source of pride and distinction. One worker, for instance, dressed up in his Nationalist army uniform to watch "soldier commemoration" movies that were shown at the downtown Guotai theater, honoring wounded veterans.[7] More often, the law was used to impose military discipline on the workforce, especially new recruits in the skilled worker training schools. As one former student recalled, a regimented lifestyle pervaded training:

We all wore military uniforms. As soon as we got up, we would have morning exercises and then we went to the factory for training. When we went to the classroom, we had to line up. When we ate, it was as a group. They would set the table and only when they shouted, "Start!" could we begin eating. . . . These military officers all supervised very strictly. They just loved military discipline.[8]

The arms industry had traditionally been one of the most, if not the most, politically disciplined in China. Since at least the 1920s, arsenal directors had used the threat of conscription to deter labor activists. The high demand for arsenal workers diluted such threats during the war, but managers continued to bank on draft deferment to secure workers' compliance. Moreover, the government increased its control over labor through legal means. The Labor Union Law of 1929 prohibited unionization and banned strikes in all military industrial establishments. A decade later, the defense industry used arsenal workers' status as soldiers to once again prohibit organizing unions or other associations.[9] To prevent workers from joining the National Salvation Movement, Chiang Kai-shek instructed arsenal workers to bury their bodies and minds in work to serve the national cause.

There is no job as important in the War of Resistance as that involving the production, maintenance, and transport of arms and ammunition. If the workers and staff of all factories and arms depots administered by the Ordnance Department work hard, resist the enemy, and dedicate themselves to defending the country, there is no particular need to join any organization or political group to resist the enemy. Eliminate those who use the pretext of a group to resist the enemy or use other pretexts to harm the employees' work. If any personnel join this type of group, or if their speech and action is inflammatory to the point of harming the workers of said Department, it is imperative that you discipline them and immediately have them resign.[10]

The military ambience of the arsenals created a "state within a state," in which punishment for crimes was meted out on the basis of military law. Management codified factory laws to enforce military punishments, either by detention, corporal punishment in the form of "military canings," or adjudication by military tribunal. Infractions of moral norms, such as swearing or taking liberties with women, led to solitary confinement for one day. Managers confined workers for three days if they fought with fellow workers. Punishments became even harsher if workers impeded production and challenged authority. Those who slowed down production, disobeyed an officer's directive, or spoke back to an officer received thirty blows of the cane. Theft of factory property or the destruction of tools or machines led to fifty blows and a fine equal to the value of the property. Leading strikes or encouraging unrest led to eighty blows and an investigation by the military tribunal.[11]

Besides punishing the perpetrator, the rules functioned to deter other workers, as the following adjudication suggests. "The apprentice Lin Jiaxu intentionally swore at many artillery shell machinists and impeded production many times. He has violated factory regulations and there was talk of brawling. This type of behavior betrays the factory's principle of mass production. Request submitted to punish him severely and place him in detention for one month as a warning to others." The department chief responded, "Detain for ten days and then fire him."[12]

One should not underestimate the use of indiscriminate and arbitrary terror to deter working-class activism. Du Liang, who apprenticed at a Chongqing chemical plant and became a labor activist, recalled how he and other chemical workers often drank tea and conversed with workers from the neighboring Arsenal No. 10. "One turned pale at the mere mention of the investigation section's controls within the arsenal. It was terrifying. Many people disappeared for no reason. They were frequently arrested." A former turner in Arsenal No. 21 remembers how he and a fellow worker, Xu Yundong, had gone to the canteen for lunch. The doors were still shut, and Xu began yelling out for them to open up. "By that afternoon, secret agents belonging to the investigation section had arrested him and beaten him up badly. A twenty-year-old who was a bit bigger than me was beaten to death." In another case, Wang Zhiping, a soldier working at the arsenal was arrested for having danced a folk jig, the *yanggewu,* popular in Yan'an.[13]

It might be argued that these memories were shaped by post-1949 political campaigns and Recalling Bitterness meetings encouraged during the Maoist era. Yet the written record confirms the picture of heavy-handed repression. In a major operation uncovering several party branches and over one hundred Communist members and activists at Kunming's Arsenal No. 52, the military tribunal sentenced workers to death for carrying seditious literature. The continuation of the so-called White Terror after the Nanjing Decade instilled fear into workers. Armed agents often entered the workshops to inspect workers, who fell silent when they saw the agents' weapons. During the civil war period, when Communists became the overt enemy, the use of paid informants among workers reinforced this repressive regime.[14]

By January 1941, the Ordnance Department had established a more formal security and spy network that effectively promoted a climate of terror and arbitrary violence. Each arsenal had its own guard and investigation squad, typically made up of two dozen men, and a guard battalion of from two hundred to four hundred soldiers. The guard battalion, accountable to each arsenal director, oversaw matters of general security, such as bomb threats, fires, theft, and discipline. The investigation squad played a much more visible political role, because it was under the control of Chiang Kai-shek's henchman Dai Li and his 100,000-strong secret service, euphemistically named the Military Bureau of Investigation and Statistics (Juntongju). Most squad personnel had also received intelligence training from the Juntongju. Established during the anti-Communist wave of early 1941, the squad ferreted out labor activists, underground Communists, and spies working for the Japanese. Despite their differences, a high degree of coordination existed between the investigative squads and guard battalions because of an overlapping leadership structure.[15]

The numerous methods used by underground Communists to maintain their cover and avoid persecution attest to the reach of the Nationalist spy system within the arsenals. Underground activists went to great lengths to devise disguises and elaborate codes to carry on covert communications. Communists identified each other using secret signs, such as triangular handkerchiefs, square pieces of cloth folded into three, or white bands worn under their watches. Greetings included clapping the left elbow with one hand and then extending the right hand outward using the hand symbol for the number eight. Fellow activists would acknowledge the password by signaling nine on their right elbows and extending their left hands to their comrades. Or one activist would feel the nape of his neck twice, while the other comrade would touch his ear with one finger. According to Nationalist spies, communication was limited to four phrases during these initial encounters: fight to the death, never be taken prisoner, disregard your father or mother, simply do your public duty.[16] This reflected the Nationalist government's perception of Communist activists as ruthless terrorists lacking in any feeling for their own kith and kin. But they also suggest the isolated and dangerous path activists chose in joining the underground movement.

In line with Albert Hirschman's model of exit, voice, and loyalty, one can suggest that arsenal workers responded to political repression in three ways.[17] Facing a repressive terrain that limited the possibility of an organized labor movement during the Anti-Japanese War pushed activists into ever more clandestine forms of resistance. Other workers perceived mobility as the best form of resistance and avoided direct action all together. Finally, many workers who continued to toil in the arsenals adopted a more consensual relationship with the state by joining the Guomindang.

Nationalist Party Factory Cells

The spiritual mobilization's goal of ethical and political training was a prelude to workers' political participation in Nationalist party factory cells. Patriotic propaganda, recruitment into the Nationalist Party, and party cell meetings functioned to contain workers and steer them away from the labor movement. The recruitment of numerous GMD members in the arsenals suggests considerable success on the part of the party faithful, but to what extent did arsenal workers support or identify in a positive manner with the Guomindang?

The wartime defense industry became a key site for partification. In December 1939, the GMD formally established a special party bureau attached to the Ministry of Military Affairs, and within several months the

Ordnance Department had its own district party branch. At its peak, in 1941, the Seventh District party branch supervised eighty-four subdistrict branches and included 40,000 party members, about half the total party membership working for the ministry.[18] Several reasons account for the pronounced party recruitment efforts in the defense industry. In part, this was a legacy of the Nationalist Revolution of the 1920s when the GMD developed a social base in the military.[19] More immediate causes, such as high labor turnover and the unraveling of the United Front, also forced the GMD to foster ideological cohesion in an industry so vital to the state's survival.

In theory, party membership served as a means of political indoctrination and maintained workers' loyalty to the state. Starting with the induction ceremony, arsenal employees were introduced to the symbols and ideology of the Nationalist Party. Once dignitaries had taken their place, inductees sang the party song, bowed three times to the national flag and Sun Yat-sen's portrait, and then stood in silence for three minutes to honor the latter's memory. After taking the oath, members shouted slogans: "Obey the will of the president and orders of the director-general [Chiang Kai-shek]! Implement the Three People's Principles! Overthrow Japanese imperialism! Long live the Guomindang! Long live the director-general!"[20]

Beginning in the summer of 1939 in the wake of the National Mobilization Act, weekly cell meetings served as the primary source of political education.[21] As one arsenal director remarked, "Our greatest priority in implementing training is spiritual training. In other words, we train correct thought and proper behavior."[22] Cells retained the basic factory organization by dividing staff, soldiers, and workers. The size of cells for staff officers had a minimum of ten participants, and those for workers ranged from thirty to forty members. Each cell chose a group leader; for workers, these would typically be a foreman or experienced skilled worker. The GMD thus sought to use the personal ties of loyalty among workers by replicating the same divisions of authority present in the factory. Furthermore, a political instructor guided the meeting and met regularly with a chief political instructor to determine each meeting's content. Members alternated in giving short reports on political treatises, such as the Three People's Principles, and neo-Confucian texts. Members spent up to thirty minutes reading the selected text out loud and then discussing it. The cell leader would then summarize the lecture and allow time for self-criticism.[23]

A paucity of documents makes it difficult to gauge the frequency and impact of such meetings throughout the war years. Judging from the recommendations of the arsenal director Ding Tianxiong, members had trouble sustaining interest in cell meetings. The imperatives of production impeded even holding meetings. Ding thus established new guidelines in 1945 that would be used throughout the defense industry. Meetings were now to be held each Monday at seven in the morning, when workers' spirits reached "a high point."[24]

Sagging employee morale continued to plague the Nationalist party propagandists throughout the 1940s. Compounding the problem of arousing workers' involvement, many arsenal staff members proved just as apathetic. Political instructors reported that most officers pleaded ignorance or viewed party membership as perfunctory. "When I asked the staff members their view of the party [all] twenty answered that they did not know about the party, did not know what the ideology (ism) was, or had joined the party because they had been ordered to do so."[25] Lack of interest in party activities was the most striking recollection of a former arsenal technician. "There were cells, but it was a formality. . . . what the party meeting discussed was absolutely absurd. I rarely participated in the cell meetings. I would just sign my name when needed. . . . Anyway, it was just those on top directing."[26]

Among staff officers, technicians proved less receptive than administrators to the Nationalist project. An aversion to political involvement and self-serving ends affected technical personnel's distaste for the party. Conversely, since the party became an adjunct to management, its influence was proportionately greater among administrators. A speech to the leaders of district party branches and over three hundred cadres by the assistant GMD bureau director remains telling, despite his emphasis on national unity: "Our country's scholarly and technical circles in the past misunderstood the party's significance. They held the traditional view that 'a gentleman does not join a party' [junzi budang]. This is mistaken. We should understand that party membership is not for the sake of gaining promotion or wealth, but rather to save the country and the people."[27] And yet, as one skilled worker suggests, a quid pro quo relationship prevailed between the Guomindang and arsenal management. "Administrators had to join the GMD. They had to fill out a party card application; otherwise, their promotional form would be rejected. As a result, relatively more [administrative] staff joined, but the proportion of engineers and technicians who joined was limited."[28]

Friction between party functionaries and technocrats arose from the Nationalists' desire to influence the political direction of the arsenals. The resultant factionalism rendered party work increasingly difficult. Speaking at the same assembly for party leaders convened in April 1943 to improve party work in the defense industry, Yu Dawei noted that, "All district party bureaus should now follow the principle of cooperation between party and administration." Yu focused on two challenges facing the GMD. "First, in the past there was no shortage of administrative personnel or ardent party workers, but some of these people were not interested in party work. They developed a belittling attitude, which influenced the progress of the party and hurt it. Henceforth, we must spare no effort to rectify this matter. Second, party workers in promoting party work must respect party discipline and not meddle with the administration."[29] Compounding these problems, rifts developed between the GMD and its fledgling organization, the Sanqingtuan (Three People's Principles Youth Corps). The Youth Corps had been established in 1937 to revitalize the revolutionary spirit of the GMD, but turf battles developed between the two organizations over jurisdictional authority. By August 1943, conflict between Nationalists and Youth Corps members at Arsenal No. 1 led the Ordnance Department to ban the Sanqingtuan from all arsenals.[30]

These types of problems led to calls for reform within the party. Critics like Zheng Jiayi, a special GMD envoy to the defense industry, recalled that in the early 1940s, the Seventh District branch was "limited by its organization, having many problems carrying out its work, and achieving few results."[31] Reforms enacted in April 1943 shifted policy making from the Seventh District branch to a special party branch at the Ordnance Department in order to make the party more responsive to the needs of arsenal management. The arrangement coincided with a streamlining of party subbranches and members.

Judging from the Nationalist Party's lukewarm reception among workers, the reforms made little headway. One reason to doubt that workers held deep commitment to the Guomindang was the way in which they were recruited. Although Chiang Kai-shek stressed that members should not be coerced into joining, since that would prompt them to "feign compliance," local party leaders preferred mass recruitment methods.[32] By the early 1940s, it was common for anywhere from a few hundred to over a thousand workers to take a collective oath of loyalty to the party and sign party cards.[33] Financial pressure at the local level prompted such tactics. All members paid monthly "contributions" deducted from their wages and salaries to support subdistrict party branches, since the top party administrations swallowed the lion's share of the annual budget.[34] Recruiting large numbers of workers also played into the hands of opportunistic party zealots. As the number of recruits increased chances of promotion, party personnel compiled lists of workers, sometimes even without their direct knowledge.[35]

Many workers perceived party membership in highly instrumental terms. One skilled worker put it bluntly, "If you wanted your job, you had to join the Nationalist Party."[36] During the civil war period, the threat posed by the Communist underground and the upsurge of labor strife pushed management to demand increased controls and safeguards ensuring the political loyalty of workers. CCP underground reports underscored how political litmus tests became the primary focus of recruitment, even to the neglect of a worker's skill. "Starting in July 1946, management recruited skilled workers in order to increase production, but before hiring them, it used extremely strict ideological controls to make sure these workers were backward, had not previously joined labor struggles, and were ignorant of current events. Otherwise, regardless of how skilled a worker was, he could not join the workforce."[37]

The difficulty of motivating workers dampened the enthusiasm of even the most zealous political instructors. Numerous instructors blamed workers' poor schooling and widespread illiteracy for their difficulty in learning the party song, not to speak of party ideology. The following report illustrates the chasm between workers and the political instructors:

I asked them about the relationship between the soldiers fighting the enemy at the front and us, and no one answered. I then asked a worker where he was from. He answered "Anju." I asked him who administered Anju. After thinking about it, he answered, "Tongliang." I asked who administered Tongliang. He answered, "Sichuan." Who administered Sichuan? He didn't know. He didn't know what other provinces existed besides Sichuan, and he wasn't the only one at this level. I asked them to raise their hand if they had graduated from elementary school. Only one did. From this one can see they really do not know what the country is and what the relationship is between the country and themselves. Of course they don't understand patriotism. Isn't explaining to them about the party and isms like playing the lute to cows?[38]

Such scenarios prompted instructors to advocate new methods of teaching, such as, for instance, narrating stories to make lecture materials more accessible. The party also promoted a literacy campaign, although instructors readily admitted that teaching one word per day had minimal effect.

The problem of illiteracy was real, although it was also exaggerated by cadres on both sides of the ideological divide, but the belittling attitude of political instructors masked a deeper problem. Many workers simply found party materials irrelevant. This gap between nationalist ideology and daily concerns revealed itself in an exchange between workers in a party cell and Wang Guozhang, a leading party instructor and German-trained engineer. In demonstrating how health was essential "to be a good citizen," Wang appeared miffed when one worker asked how one could achieve this goal without adequate nutrition. Wang replied that nutrition was only one component of good health, and that it was even more important to curb "careless eating."[39]

When party propagandists recognized daily hardship incurred under the stress of war, they sought to inculcate patriotic values and deflect responsibility from their own policies by projecting Japan as the root cause of workers' hardships. A political tract entitled *Who Is Inflicting Pain on Our Country?* noted the fall in real wages because of inflation, but castigated Japan for invading China, cutting off ports, denying access to international aid, and occupying the industrialized coastal areas. "It is inevitable that our poor country and our people are having a hard time fighting the war," the tract declared. "We must increase production, especially military defense production, to end our suffering. Replenishing our munitions will accelerate the collapse of our enemy. Once our enemy collapses, prices will naturally stabilize. Our working lives will be joyful and prosperous and the country's people will all enjoy prosperity."[40]

A recent study has shown that labor propaganda in Nazi Germany was more effective when it resonated with workers' own cultural values and symbolic practices, rather than being manipulated "from above."[41] In contrast, Guomindang propagandists found little to commend in what they saw as workers' culture. Political instructors obsessed over tearing down workers' culture, imploring workers to "discard their inherently boorish qualities and to develop a friendly disposition at all costs."[42] Propaganda typically relied on injunctions rather than affirmation of workers' practices, for fear that workers might become an autonomous force. These anxieties are revealed in the GMD political tract *Workers Should Have Self-Management*. Although the party argued that "self-management" meant an end to capitalist exploitation, its program was no more than a litany of commands designed to enforce industrial discipline.[43]

In evaluating how they felt about official propaganda, workers' own testimony reveals that a chasm had developed between factory ideologues and workers. As early as 1940, one notes the dissatisfaction of an arsenal machinist in his letter to the Communist daily *Xinhua ribao*. He effectively adopts a humble tone to make a stinging critique of the factory hierarchy, tight political controls, and the irrelevance of Guomindang cell meetings to workers' daily needs:

Because our factory is government-owned and because we workers are frequently called soldiers, our method is extremely moderate and our report offers mild requests. . . . We work for the War of Resistance. As long as everyone undergoes equal hardship, as long as we are in high spirits, we are content to endure lowly treatment. But even this little hope was dashed! What was their response? They mobilized security guards to investigate and make arrests. Usually the political cadres who are running back and forth are able to follow their keen sense of smell to dig into our team and get some people fired. Sir, we could never have imagined this! It seems many people want to commit suicide to show their sincerity. We also have a small group council, but they force us to discard our own problems and discuss the European war. Naturally the European problem is related to us, but there are still many more immediate problems, such as improving our leisure life, organizing a reading hall, setting up a wall newspaper. In short, they force us to avoid discussing our immediate problems and to research distant problems far off into the clouds. . . . most of us young workers are middle school students and thus increasingly look for other jobs and run off, even at the risk of arrest for leaving and despite the importance of our work for our country. Sir, there have been many people who have left sadly, because this type of work is what we really want to do. We sincerely cherish our factory and our work, but we bitterly detest this reactionary system and the sinister parties involved.[44]

The machinist's sorrow at being forced to flee the factory reflects a genuine feeling of loss in no longer being able to participate in arms production and by extension the cause of resistance. At the same time, the onus is placed squarely on the factory officials for creating such politically repressive conditions. The machinist justifies his actions through nationalist appeals, subverting Nationalist ideology in the process.

Although the Communist press was the most popular means for workers to express their discontent, arsenal workers also wrote to management in order to effect social change within the factory. Workers in the branch factory of Arsenal No. 50 wrote the following anonymous letter, quoted at length to show the linguistic and thematic similarities with the previous letter. Signed "Society for peace and temporary aid," the authors appeal to fellow workers for solidarity, while indicting their labor supervisors:

We are the masses and laborers of the Chengdu branch factory of Arsenal No. 50. We have toiled throughout the eight years of the War of Resistance, burying ourselves in hard work. Your honor said that once we beat back the enemy, the government would raise workers' treatment and improve workers' livelihood. Who would have thought that to this day we laborers [would] continue to live amid terror and are still abused by most supervisors? We laborers are like the slaves of a conquered nation, like cattle and horses. Jin Shenglei, the section chief of inspection, Feng Jihe, the technician for mortar shell tails, and Chen Dexiang, the shell technician, are among the most evil elements oppressing and coercing workers. Workers frequently run the risk of being fined work points. Workers earn very few wages each month, and they must still support parents, wife, and children. Life is extremely difficult. The technicians fine a minimum of eight or ten work points. We do not dare say a word lest they deduct wages again or place us in detention. We laborers have no recourse from heaven or earth; we can only endure the pain and wait it out. The Chengdu branch factory, the dark Chengdu branch factory, is under fascism. The Chengdu branch factory is a henchman of Mussolini. We request that the factory director quickly sanction the powerful and evil and appease the workers. What kind of democracy, nationalism, or people's livelihood does China now have? It is a complete sham. It is nothing like the genuine democracy of comradeship. Workers hold enormous grievances; they have no hope. Their only hope is for genuine democracy. We shall realize it soon, and then workers will eat their fill and dress warmly. Everything will be settled, and they will avoid this façade. The supervisors wallow in the mire with each other and bully people by flaunting their powerful connections. Workers of the entire factory quickly become conscious! The glorious road at last will belong to us. We must wipe out the reactionary clique's effective strength. We shall only have a way out and a reliable guarantor of livelihood if we beat back the reactionary clique's desperate attack. The Chinese government has had an awful effect on us. We can only be dissatisfied and resist because the administrators are corrupt and embezzle profits. Due pay for example. They promote wage scales for those who work for them privately, while we have sweated and poured our blood out for the public. We still receive no respect. Every time there is a promotion, it is never our turn. We cannot write everything at once. Afterward, we shall slowly write the ugly inside story of the factory.[45]

The letter, delivered in August 1946 to the factory director of Arsenal No. 50 in Chongqing, conveys the grievances and nationalist rhetoric used by arsenal workers during the postwar labor movement. One of the metaphors—"like cattle and horses"—bears a striking resemblance to the anti-imperialist, class-inflected discourse of the 1920s. Whereas that discourse was directed against foreign imperialism, however, the authors of the letter direct their wrath against the Nationalist government, comparing it to a colonizer. The writer indicates widespread feelings of betrayal because the Nationalist Party had not honored workers' sacrifices during the war. While linking the factory regime with fascism, and referring to the unfulfilled promises of the Three People's Principles, the worker is obviously sympathetic to the goals of the CCP's New Democracy, which would, Mao wrote in 1940, be a "democratic republic under the joint dictatorship of all the anti-imperialist and anti-feudal people."[46]

Much of the letter condemns factory supervisors and corrupt officials who had appropriated from workers their rightful postwar gains and continued to lord it over the workers they supervised. These charges of official malfeasance and inhuman treatment stemmed from workers' shop-floor experiences with their supervisors and a repugnance of the military officers who oversaw them. The letter signifies a desire to shape the social climate of the workshops and pressure management to remove the supervisory personnel. The radical writer thus demands more humane treatment and social recognition. The message is double-sided. Workers demanded an end to being treated like animals, but their tone was still one of deference to the factory director. In part, workers' humble tone was an acknowledgment of their own mean status. But this supposed submissiveness was also a rhetorical tool, since it reminded employers of their social obligations to dependent workers and the corrupting nature of their power if not exercised in a decent fashion.

In short, even though numerous arsenal workers joined the GMD, there was no necessary correlation between their party affiliation and political attitudes. Workers' participation and motives varied, and few shared a burning commitment to the party. One can be sure, though, that Guomindang members differed from their CCP counterparts. Participation in Guomindang activities offered potential rewards, but it involved little personal responsibility or commitment and absolutely no risk. Although a core of GMD activists existed among arsenal workers, perfunctory rituals associated with collective membership do not suggest that the Nationalist Party had galvanized a more moderate social base within the arsenals. If skilled arsenal workers comprised a "labor aristocracy," the term, as Lenin defined it, can only be used to describe workers' relatively privileged economic status within the working class, but not to characterize a segment of workers with more reformist political beliefs.[47]

Nevertheless, arsenals had become politically contested sites, because they stood at the heart of Guomindang power. Nationalists tried various means of garnering the loyalty of arsenal workers, ranging from patriotic appeals to blanket condemnation of Communists as "Han traitors." These appeals coincided with an intensification of repressive force, often used in arbitrary fashion to deter dissent. Nationalists also tried to organize workers into factory cells, hoping to boost workers' morale, deflect the blame for wartime deprivation onto the shoulders of Japanese imperialism, and propagate class harmony. When the Nationalists failed to integrate workers into their party project, in part because of management's own divided reaction and rifts between GMD activists and technocrats, the unresponsiveness of workers became cause for alarm.

Numerous official sources attest to the arsenal authorities' uncertainties and fear of their workforce. Although arsenal authorities sought to bury the language of class and thus deny the formation of a working class, however fragile, their very actions and perceptions of the labor force said otherwise. The political activities centered on arsenal workers reflected the special status accorded to workers. This status derived from a realization and apprehension on the part of management and state officials that workers had their own interests and capacity for mass opposition. These perceptions on the part of the elites had profound consequences. Such fears had informed the arsenals' social welfare policies, and they would shape the industry's response to workers' organizations and the open social conflict of the immediate postwar period.

7

ORGANIZING,

1937-1946

Xin Yi, "Kaihui qu" [Going to a meeting] (1947). From Su Lin, ed., *Guotongqu heibai muke* (Nanning: Guangxi meishu chubanshe, 2000), 225.

The question of why China's labor movement failed to produce a revolutionary working class has long dominated scholarly inquiry. Certain historians have concluded—correctly, I believe—that the structure of economic and political power during the 1920s crushed labor, and this would have lasting consequences for the next twenty years. A more recent historiography has focused instead on how internal rifts within the working class based on gender, skill, and region impeded the formation of working-class consciousness, defined as revolutionary class consciousness.[1] For all their insights into intraclass divisions, and these were at times real and deep ones, these histories have suffered in their analyses of labor politics from trying to "explain not what is or has been empirically present, but rather the failure of people to behave correctly according to a [Marxian] theoretical prediction."[2]

To avoid some of the pitfalls of class formation studies, which Margaret Somers faults for being "rooted in an epistemology of absence," let us turn our initial question around. Instead of implicitly asking why the labor movement was not more radical, it is more fruitful to ask how the labor movement could become as radical as it actually did during historical periods such as the mid 1920s or two decades later. This was particularly true in Chongqing's wartime arsenals, which promoted and enforced some of China's most militarized and disciplined work regimes. Political controls weighed heavily on the back of arsenal workers because of their strategic role in the national wartime economy. The constant fear among arsenal authorities that workers had their own interests and might manifest them in opposition led to policies that combined repression and ideological appeals to the national interest. At the same time, the work site became an intensely political arena, precisely because workers began to appropriate some of the organizations and ideology espoused by the militarized management and turn them against the Guomindang.

Like their archrivals, the CCP approached arsenal workers as part of a distinct social class to secure their loyalty. But organizing the arsenal workers was fraught with challenges and moral ambiguity. For one thing, the CCP's exile to the countryside since 1927 had rendered urban mobilization a decade later even more challenging. Moreover, the CCP's adherence to the United Front, defined by its multi-class, multi-party alliance united in resisting Japanese aggression, raised questions about organizing in an industry so vital to achieving national liberation. For this reason, when party activists mobilized en masse by supporting the National Salvation Movement during the early stages of the Anti-Japanese War, the party did not openly advocate extending the patriotic movement to the defense industry. Ideologically, the United Front emphasis on appealing to the urban middle class also raised questions for the CCP. Although winning over, or at least neutralizing, staff officers would weaken the Nationalists' power base, rapprochement with the middle class might alienate workers from the party, given the worker-staff divide in the arsenals.

Whereas previous studies have concentrated on the ideology and high politics of the United Front,[3] I focus instead on how the CCP's understanding of the United Front influenced its mass work, show the links that party activists forged with workers, and examine their shared goals, as well as points of discord. After the initial euphoria of the National Salvation Movement had subsided by mid 1939, Communists were increasingly forced to operate in semi-legal forums and underground organizations. By its very nature, clandestine work makes it difficult to locate, leading some historians to dismiss and thus underestimate the scope and influence of the CCP, which was far greater than its membership rolls might suggest.[4] An evaluation of the CCP's significance during the War of Resistance depends to a great extent on the specific time period, because the party alternately expanded and contracted. Communists also made their presence felt in much more intangible ways. With the party forced underground by the early 1940s, *Xinhua ribao* (New China Daily), the CCP's only legal outlet, took on important symbolic and organizational functions. The paper disseminated the Communist party line and provided literate workers with a forum in which to reassess factory social relations and to express their grievances. The participatory form of journalism involved in the production of *Xinhua ribao,* whereby certain columns were expressly written by and for workers, facilitated the growth of workers' class consciousness.

As important as both Communist and Nationalist activities and organizations were in politicizing the arsenals by treating workers as a critical force, workers often acted independently of both parties or used preexisting organizations for their own separate interests. This was also the case with two other labor organizations, the so-called strongholds (*judian*) and the government-sponsored Chinese Association of Labor (CAL). In the former instance, workers formed small organizations, based on an ethical code of mutual aid, to address workshop grievances and create a political forum. In the latter case, industrial workers and leaders of CAL united to work for independent unions. Under the guidance of the militant minority, these organizations fueled social conflict and created politically charged communities in the arsenals during the 1937–49 period.

From Communist Mobilization to Consolidation

The eruption of the Sino-Japanese war generated a flurry of Communist activism throughout Sichuan. Following a strategy of urban mass mobilization, the CCP rapidly expanded by participating in the National Salvation Movement, while using the United Front as political cover. From literally a handful of active members at the start of the war, by July 1939, the CCP had mushroomed to 50,000 members in southern China as a whole, some 14 percent of them in Sichuan.[5] Under the guidance of Qian Shaoyu (alias Wang Ming) and the Wuhan-based Yangtze Bureau, the party regained a base within the province by mobilizing on a mass scale.

The initial impetus for mobilization came from the party leaders in Yan'an, who reestablished a foothold in Sichuan by placing members with long-standing ties to the province there. Many of these activists also had both international experience and loose ties to the Wang Ming faction in the CCP. The most prominent was Luo Shiwen, who arrived in Chongqing from Yan'an as formal representative of the CCP to forge relations with Liu Xiang and to start mobilizing party members. Helped by his extensive party and native-place ties to Sichuan, dating back to the early 1920s, Luo played a decisive role in the organization of the Sichuan party apparatus by establishing a Chongqing Municipal Working Committee in October 1937.[6] Subsequently, Luo acted as intermediary between the Sichuan Provincial Working Committee and the Yangtze Bureau, which replaced the Central Committee in April 1938 as overseer of Sichuan party affairs. Acting on Luo's request for more experienced cadres to join him, the Central Committee responded by sending the veteran labor organizer Cheng Zijian, a Communist Party member since 1925, with experience abroad as well as in Chongqing, to Sichuan. Cheng would play an important role in the labor movement as secretary of the Provincial Committee's labor department.[7] Cheng was soon joined by another Sichuanese revolutionary and Long March veteran, Liao Zhigao. Leaving his post as director of the Central Party School in Yan'an,

Liao guided the Chongqing-based Eastern Sichuan Special Committee as secretary from 1938 to 1943.[8]

Given the rampant factionalism among CCP members prior to the war, relying on veteran local cadres made perfect sense. By the mid 1930s, only a handful of Communist members in Sichuan had survived the onslaught of warlord repression. They remained isolated, because mutual mistrust reigned among activists, and could only take defensive measures to ensure their political survival. These conditions gave rise to small-scale organizations, which participated in the prewar National Salvation Movement, involving nonparty activists, members who had lost contact with the party, or former members lacking identification. As Liao Zhigao recalled, "They all called themselves true Communists and they did not trust anyone. Each [organization] followed its own policy, so they could not have a concerted anti-Japanese National Salvation Movement."[9]

The years 1938 and 1939 marked the high point of open political mobilization for the CCP in Sichuan. This political resurgence marked the brief flowering of Wang Ming's urban policy, for which he would be criticized at the Sixth Plenum of the Central Committee in October 1938. These criticisms more likely reflected the ongoing power struggle between Wang Ming and Mao Zedong, since both the Yangtze Bureau and the Central Committee launched activist policies in tandem during the fall of 1937. None other than Zhang Wentian, secretary-general of the party, endorsed the transfer of leadership from the Central Committee to the Yangtze Bureau, mass mobilization, and a tenfold expansion of Sichuanese party members. According to the plan, Chongqing, Chengdu, and Zigong (Sichuan's salt capital) would each mobilize up to one thousand members within three months.[10]

If recruitment at Chongqing is any indication, the CCP quickly met these quotas. By October 1938, the Eastern Sichuan Special Committee directed the work of over 800 party members in Chongqing and the surrounding districts.[11] Liao Zhigao estimates that total membership in the province had by then surpassed 3,400, and by July 1939, the CCP had 7,000 members in Sichuan, a major achievement considering that just two years earlier, there had been only 30 members in Chengdu and only 5 in Chongqing.[12]

The effectiveness of patriotic appeals and the more tolerant political climate of the initial war years contributed to the Communists' rapid expansion in Sichuan. Tan Jianxiao, a prominent labor activist, exemplifies the route many militant arsenal workers took before joining the CCP, in that he had extensive ties to the peasantry and his rural experience influenced his turn to labor militancy.[13] Like many activists, Tan had received some education. Born in 1912 to a relatively prosperous peasant family living in Guang'an County, Sichuan. Tan attended an old-style "private academy" (*sishu*) while helping his father farm. At fourteen, he entered the public middle school. In 1929, Tan began working for his uncle, a pharmacist, to support his education. Inspired by his teacher, a former May Fourth movement activist in Beijing, Tan organized a secret reading group with fellow students, including a Communist Party Youth League member, who introduced him to Marxism.

Japan's occupation of northeastern China in 1931 marked a turning point in Tan's commitment to radical politics. By then a local schoolteacher, he became involved in the county's national salvation society, raising contributions for the patriotic movement and participating in village and small town theater to reach a broader audience. The local school authorities did not, however, take kindly to Tan's outspoken political views and his criticism of the status quo. Over the next three years, he was repeatedly fired from his various teaching posts and moved from one village school to another. He returned to till the land, but his efforts to earn a living that way only earned him the ridicule of his peers, who felt that farmwork was beneath someone of Tan's intellectual stature. Ostracized and searching for better employment prospects, Tan left Guang'an for Chongqing with several of his classmates in the fall of 1935. Ever defiant, Tan changed his first name "xiao" from "filial piety" to a homophone meaning "roar."

In Chongqing, Tan Jianxiao both pursued his patriotic ideals and sought to improve the working conditions of arsenal workers. After joining the Huaxing machine plant, which later merged into Arsenal No. 20, Tan became a leading spokesman for apprentices. Faced with a reduced demand for arms after Nationalist troops entered Sichuan and put an end to warlord feuding, the arsenal sought to reduce costs. Management thus prolonged apprenticeships, which had minimal wage costs, even though workers had already fulfilled the requirements to become artisans. Representing other apprentices, Tan demanded a guarantee that upon finishing their apprenticeship, they would promptly become artisans; rejected the use of badges that connoted the lowly status of apprentices; and, with Liu Zonglin, an underground activist, succeeded in establishing a study group for machinists. Engineers and technicians began instructing apprentices in math, drafting, design, and English during the two evenings a week when there were no night shifts. There was nothing radical in such an organization, but it did provide a base for many of the fifty to sixty participants who went on to join the Chongqing Anti-Japanese Society for National Salvation, in which Tan and Liu played leading roles.

A variety of personal experiences informed the motivations and political views of underground activists. The experience of Liu Zonglin illustrates how Communist activists joined the CCP because of family ties and the political climate. As with Tan Jianxiao, anti-Japanese sentiment pushed Liu into the political arena. In 1931, Liu formed a native-place association with twenty of his middle-school classmates. Liu used the cover of the association to read works of leftists like Guo Moruo. Liu's formal education abruptly ended the following year, when the school shut down for fear of the growing influence of the Red Army base in northern Sichuan. Without a job, Liu began working as a courier for his Communist uncle, who captivated his nephew with revolutionary tales. "He had directly participated in Chongqing's March 31 [1927] struggle at Daqiangba. He had engaged in heroic struggle and only escaped danger by jumping over the city walls. He also frequently told us stories about revolutionary struggle and his own personal experiences. In this way I personally received education and encouragement."[14] From his uncle, Liu also received his first impressions of Marxism at the age of fifteen.

Like many of his fellow activists, Liu's family ties propelled him to join the CCP-led rural insurrections. In 1932, Liu joined a "peasant pacification squad," organized by his uncle, who began planning a rural insurrection to link up with the Red Army. The expansion of the CCP in northern Sichuan had driven the local elite from the village, leading to a proliferation of local bandits, and Bai Zhouxi used the pacification squad as a local militia to patrol the area. Liu recalls how his squad defeated local toughs and acquired weapons in the process. These experiences would serve Liu well in the late 1940s, when he smuggled arms out of the Nationalist arsenals and joined in the rural insurrections at Huayin mountain near Guang'an.

Although the Left did not monopolize patriotic sentiment, Communists played a leading role in organizing national salvation societies. After establishing the Chongqing Workers' Anti-Japanese Society for National Salvation in January 1937, several party members used demonstrations, theatrical troupes, and songs to mobilize workers on the basis of anti-imperialist sentiment. After work, Tan Jianxiao and Liu Zonglin brought banners of the Anti-Japanese propaganda troupe to key intersections of the city. Members galvanized support by singing patriotic songs such as "Raise Your Arms and Do Battle," which denounced Japanese war atrocities and urged national resistance: "The water of the river runs yellow, oh, so yellow; [the] eastern foreign devils are too savage; today they burn Wang's hamlet, tomorrow they will burn Zhang's village. What good is it living like this? Raise your arms and do battle!"[15]

Young workers under the age of twenty-five were most receptive to the calls for national resistance. "We repeatedly stressed that everything was for national salvation, so we won over quite a few enthusiastic young workers, who joined the National Salvation Movement," the activist Cheng Zijian recalled.[16] Involvement in the patriotic movement correlated with party membership, which through 1939, consisted of increasingly young workers rather than older, experienced skilled workers.[17] The dramatic influx of workers into the CCP also changed it into a party centered on workers and young intellectuals. Here, one should probably distinguish between members and cadres, because working people increasingly made up the rank-and-file party members. By November 1939, the Chongqing Municipal Committee estimated that 34 percent of all party members were industrial workers, and another 12 percent were artisans in the handicraft industries.[18] Regarding cadres, a local Communist report ascribed to 1941 suggests that an equal number of cadres were either politically trained intellectuals or had a working-class background. A remaining third of all cadres came from Shanghai and Hankou, but their class background is unclear.[19] These social changes within the party had implications for the CCP's own policy toward labor, and for which type of cadre was most suited for party work.

In the early 1940s, Sichuan Communist Party members involved in the labor movement expressed considerable ambivalence over the role played by intellectuals, since they ultimately desired a "purer" working-class base. They acknowledged the difficulty involved in forging links between workers and intellectual cadres, especially idealistic youth, noting: "Chongqing cadres predominantly come from the National Salvation Movement, thus, although they are enthusiastic, they lack experience, especially in terms of organization and struggle. The base of cadres for the labor movement is still in a transitional phase. Intellectuals make up the majority of cadres, thus our cadres still lack sufficient contact with the mass of workers." On the other hand, comrades of middle-class origin not only had more theoretical grounding in Marxism but experience in dealing with staff and workers; they could thus "truly merge with the masses' lifestyle and thus play an exemplary role."[20]

Nonetheless, contradictions persisted in using *zhiyuan* as cadres. How could staff mobilize workers when the status differentials between the two groups in the arsenals, and in industry in general, loomed so large? As the Communist labor activist Du Yanqing remarked, "the working masses have traditionally thought of staff as running dogs of the capitalists. Most staff really do look down on workers, making it impossible for these two forces to complement each other in the struggle against capitalists and thus allow workers to achieve greater success in improving their lives." In slightly more restrained style, the sociologist Shih Kuoheng reached similar conclusions regarding unoccupied China's state-run industries: "Anyone in the factory who is not a manual worker or a guard is a Chih Yuan *[zhiyuan]*. And this Chih Yuan group enjoys an immense feeling of social superiority over the manual workers. In the eyes of the latter, everyone who belongs to Chih Yuan represents the management (Chang Fang, or the factory side), and his interests are directly opposed to those of the wage earners."[21]

Given the extent of the friction between staff employees and production workers, it is important to understand how radical intellectuals articulated the problem, whether they devised solutions, and what effect worker-staff conflict had on labor organizing. Surprisingly, party theorists offered little analysis of this problem, perhaps because they envisioned an eventual convergence of the two social groups. In this respect, the CCP diverged from a more classical Marxist analysis offered by German sociologists, who viewed white-collar employees as part of the working class, defined in a broad sense of the term. According to this interpretation, low-level supervisors, foremen, technicians, and office clerks did not own their means of production, worked for either private employers or the state, and received wages in the form of salaries. It was thus to be expected that white-collar employees would eventually come to regard themselves as part of the emerging working class.[22]

In theory, Chinese Communist labor organizers acknowledged that staff personnel, if not necessarily of the working class, did have affinities with workers, since both were exploited in producing surplus value. The Communist Zhu Bangxin argued that:

Workers and staff are indivisible in terms of social status and welfare. Consequently, they can belong to the same stratum and should pertain to the same class. Workers are direct producers of value. Besides a minority of top-ranking staff, such as managers and engineers, who can participate in distributing the surplus value produced by workers, the common staff member either produces value in subsidiary production processes or guarantees the capitalist's partition of surplus value. Thus, the labor of staff is an indivisible part of this society's economic construction, while they remain exploited.

Rather than predict a proletarianization of the white-collar stratum, however, Chinese Marxists hoped to harness staff members' technical skills and knowledge for future economic development:

At the moment, staff have a fairly high cultural level and technical knowledge, which helps the capitalist profit, but they also aid social production. Tomorrow the same culture and education will help guide social welfare and eliminate or reduce the current cultural and technical deviation between staff and workers.[23]

If this prognosis relied on a certain amount of voluntarism, it did conform to the multi-class alliance envisioned by United Front policy. In this respect, Zhu was inspired by the achievements of European popular fronts, citing the 1935 and 1937 general strikes in France, in which both white- and blue-collar workers had participated.[24] Although Zhu recognized that the social divisions between the two strata loomed larger in China, he derived hope from the recent involvement of *zhiyuan* in the Shanghai National Salvation Movement to press for class unity in the interests of the nation.

The emphasis on the acquisition of technical skills by workers as the key to ending social divisions was echoed by a *Xinhua ribao* editorial in May 1940, which offered specific solutions, such as further education to broaden workers' cultural horizons, and called on workers to adopt staff demands as their own.[25] Responding to workers' sense of inequality, the paper advocated equal access to clubs and entertainment for both workers and *zhiyuan*.

Despite the fact that it urged unity, the editorial was keenly aware of the conflict between workers and staff personnel and highly critical of the latter's social aspirations, since their elitism repudiated working-class values. The writer largely attributed the chasm between staff and workers to status consciousness and differences in educational background and lifestyles. Whereas staff members were mostly advanced technicians or literate office personnel, workers were uneducated and illiterate. Unlike scholars, the editorial intoned, using a traditional metaphor, workers had "white stomachs without a trace of ink." Preferential treatment of staff permitted them to aspire to an upper-class lifestyle, whereas boorish workers frequented teahouses with grease smeared on their clothes and faces. The lowly position of workers, who had "not even reached the lowest level of social status," only strengthened staff members' sense of superiority. This feudal perspective, the editorial explained, contributed to staff members' haughtiness and harassment of workers. Seeking to unite staff and workers, the Communists felt frustrated that different lifestyles and demands prevented the two groups from relating to each other. "Workers' struggle in any select enterprise is a constant, but because workers' demands are completely different from those of staff, staff members have become totally separate from workers."

Ultimately, local party leaders viewed cadres of intellectual and staff origins as transitional figures, laying the basis for a labor movement led by workers themselves. "Although these cadres are not the most effective," noted a Sichuan Communist report of 1941, "this is the only method before workers become cadres themselves." Nevertheless, the report added, "these cadres have played a very important role in the Chongqing labor movement, paving the way in some of the national defense factories and cotton mills."[26] The CCP mobilized different social strata within the defense industry, seeking to exploit any potential rift. Sichuan party authorities quickly realized they could not rely on workers only to oppose the government within the cities but had to expand their alliances with other classes and social strata. The formulation and practice of this theory began in 1937 with the United Front, whereby the party constructed alliances in terms of objective class position, while also considering peoples' attitudes to its politics. In theory, this strategy enabled the party to polarize the Right (those deemed hostile to the CCP) by winning over the Left and those in the middle.[27]

Communist activists used a number of ways to establish footholds, generally relying on contacts with party members already employed in the arsenal. Mobilization of workers remained a priority. At Arsenal No. 20, for instance, over thirty Communists and over a hundred activists had been organized at the gun and cartridge factories. It was here, too, that Liu Zonglin and Tan Jianxiao had organized workers. But the CCP also sought to penetrate different strata within the industrial hierarchy, especially the top echelons of each arsenal, to gain valuable military intelligence and protection for other Communists. The strategy of using managerial staff as bridges between the party and workers was used at several arsenals in the late 1930s. At the Daxigou machine-gun plant, the personnel board director, Wang Minggang, who according to police reports had "built a reputation in industrial circles," and therefore had been "roped in" by the CCP, played a leading role in organizing workers, led the Communist Party branch in the factory, and oversaw subbranches in each workshop.[28]

Similarly, Arsenal No. 23 became one of the most active sites for establishing party branches and cells because of the activities of a middle-level manager, Zhang Yintang, who was responsible for recruitment and labor allocation at the plant and hired party activists, many of them students. Zhang had joined the CCP in 1925 while studying engineering at Tongji University in Shanghai. He later found work at Gongxian arsenal and assumed the post of labor subsection director when the explosives plant, later renamed Arsenal No. 23, relocated to Luzhou County, Sichuan. In May 1938, Cheng Zijian, by then a member of the CCP's Provincial Committee leadership, introduced nine party activists to Zhang to be employed in the arsenal.[29] Zhang's wife, Gao Yuying, also a party member since the late 1920s, recalled using fictive kinship ties to maintain their secrecy. "In name they were our relatives. Through Zhang's position, we found work for them. Three of them lived in our house. Every day, they wrote wall newspapers and pamphlets for the resistance against Japan. Jiang Haoran [also a Communist] and I pasted them up."[30] In October, the Provincial Committee introduced a second batch of workers to join the arsenal, followed by another dozen members in the spring of 1939. Activists also recruited workers within the factory, so that by the latter half of 1940, over seventy party members worked in the arsenal, organized on the basis of two subbranches.[31]

Activists forged ties to arsenal workers by working alongside them and participating in the same organizations, building their trust and friendship. This merger of worker and intellectual lifestyles was informed by the party dictum "Only when cadres go amid workers will they launch the work of labor." In May 1938, at Arsenal No. 23, the provincial party committee sent seven party members, two university and five middle school students, into the arsenal to begin organizing workers. Working as laborers, the students hauled stones, moved concrete slabs, and "merged with the working masses."[32] The students made conscious efforts to adopt aspects of workers' culture, shaving their scalps like other laborers, frequenting teahouses, playing cards, and gambling with their fellow workers. "In terms of daily life, they completely merged with the workers, eating and sleeping together. They taught them reading and helped them resolve disputes. When they drank in the teahouse, they [the activists] contributed tea money, or if both parties did not pay, they would settle the matter. These activities allowed them to gain greater trust from the native (coolie) workers, but it was still not a higher form of organization, only a way of bonding brotherhood."[33]

When gaps between intellectuals and workers resurfaced and impeded mobilization, the CCP quickly replaced labor movement leaders. A Nationalist government report on Chongqing's Communist labor movement indicated that its leaders were not originally workers, and were thus "unfamiliar with workers' livelihood and could not merge with them." Accordingly, the party sent Rao Zuobao, director of the practice workshop at the workers' training school of the Tongyuanju (the predecessor of Arsenal No. 20) to replace them in 1939.[34]

Another means of bridging the gap between intellectuals and workers lay in the party's efforts to improve the material conditions of arsenal workers. According to surveillance reports, Ye Jianying and Liao Zhigao emphasized infiltrating the defense industry en masse. Their strategy consisted of establishing workers' organizations, such as consumer cooperatives, at all arsenals to win over defense workers.[35]

Although the late 1930s were a period of rapid growth for the CCP, patriotic fervor and the pressure for rapid mass mobilization did not bode well for the ideological basis and organizational cohesiveness of the party. In certain cases, patriotism had become the chief qualification for membership. Liao Zhigao recalled that loose admissions policy had lowered standards among party members:

Some [members] were only anti-Japanese activists and were accepted on that basis. Some only needed to have peasant status and their political views and consciousness would be ignored. Some were accepted simply for supporting the party, regardless of other factors. Some joined the party via group induction. Some applied for membership without having their history carefully examined, even to the point where we accepted a few opportunists and bad elements. Some alternate party members also introduced other applicants to join before completing their own trial period.[36]

From the CCP's perspective, the rush to accept activists and inadequate training prevented the formation of a cohesive, disciplined group of cadres. The rapid expansion of party cadres employed in the arsenals coincided with a lack of secrecy and discipline necessary for survival. Reputedly, certain cadres were so thrilled about joining the Communists that they boasted among friends, "Hey, are you [a member]? I am!" Withdrawal by new members after they had belonged to the party for

only one or two months, and a general lack of prudence, frequently compromised discipline and secrecy.[37]

Part of the problem lay in the inadequate training of cadres, which
forced the party to organize training sessions to build cohesiveness. Hundreds of cadres were trained throughout Guangdong, Hunan, and
Sichuan during 1939–40. When Liao Zhigao established the Chongqing
City Committee in January 1940, he held training sessions, especially for
arsenal workers who had joined the party.[38] Likewise, training cadres to
work in the labor movement was taken as the "most pressing duty of the
Eastern Sichuan Committee" in 1940. Training lasted for one week and
touched on the history of the specific industry's labor movement and its
current situation, the nature of party branch work, the function of the
party, and an outline program for the labor movement. By late 1940, the
adverse political climate changed the format of training sessions.
Whereas cadres had previously received instruction in group settings, individual research was now stressed and simplified to emphasize the labor
movement platform and practical lessons to be learned from the Shanghai labor movement. This focus on Shanghai may have been in response
to the large influx of Shanghai cadres, but more likely it was because
Shanghai's tragic experience in the early 1930s offered practical lessons
in underground work.[39]

Despite these initial attempts at training, the CCP perceived workers'
class consciousness as deficient. Huang Gang, who was an apprentice at
the Fuxing iron mill and branch secretary of Chongqing's Caiyuanba district, began recruiting party members in July 1938. By June 1939, he had
recruited nine members, most of them at Fuxing iron mill, which had become the center of the National Salvation Movement within the district.
Huang recalled:

At the time, education within the party was terribly weak. New party members
joined for ill-conceived reasons, and after they joined, there was no timely education to help them raise their consciousness. Some had joined to resist the Japanese; others had joined because they saw that Soviet workers were doing better
and they hoped to go to the Soviet Union; some joined to fight the GMD and the
capitalists; and a few even joined to share the limelight. In an environment dominated by underground work, one could neither read party journals together nor
establish training courses. Although I talked to them several times, the content
was mainly "What is Marxism" and other types of education to raise consciousness. Because we had limited contact, this type of education was necessary, but
many of our members had minimal, if any, knowledge of organizational principles or policy. Later, when the going got rough, many party members did not

know what to do. Some acted in a rash and foolhardy manner; others became passive and stopped working.[40]

Huang's recollections underscore the internal weaknesses facing the CCP, which, as we shall see, provided a historical justification for the ensuing purges within the party that began in the fall of 1939. In addition, Huang notes contradictions between party activists and workers. Whereas ensuring its political survival and maintaining a cohesive organization became the overriding concerns of the CCP, workers had a variety of different concerns. Their consciousness simply differed from the one party cadres envisioned.

The demands of party organization could also lead to unemployment, which was especially threatening to cadres of working-class origin. In 1940, when cadres working in the arsenals risked exposure if one of their leaders was arrested, the party sought to transfer out the remaining cadres. Yet working-class cadres sometimes preferred to risk political suicide and remain in the arsenals, fearing that they would be unable to support their families if unemployed. These problems would not be addressed until 1941, when the CCP guaranteed a fund for comrades at risk and their families, but only on condition that the cadres immediately transfer out of danger.[41]

The CCP's lack of internal cohesion also made it vulnerable to mounting pressure from the Nationalist government. Not only did the Japanese attack Communist bases after occupying Wuhan in October 1938, but the Nationalists also launched a campaign of political repression against the CCP. The Guomindang's Fifth Plenum, held in January 1939, marked a turning point by signaling a course of simply holding the line against the Japanese while pursuing an aggressive campaign against the CCP. "How to actively struggle against the Communists" was the central theme of the plenum, which decided that "guarding against Communists, restricting Communists, and dissolving Communists" (*fanggong, xiangong, ronggong*) would be the Nationalists' fundamental policy. The plenum was followed by a series of measures to restrict activities of the "alien party" (*yidang*).[42] Thereafter, the GMD reorganized unions under state control and began a campaign to win over CCP members, known as "*zhengqu yiren*," with punishment of all GMD members who failed to turn in at least one Communist.[43] A second wave of political repression, highlighted by the Chengdu "rice-riot incident," followed in March 1940. The destruction of rice depots belonging to the Banks of Chongqing and Sichuan sparked mass arrests of CCP members in Chengdu, including Luo Shiwen. This marked the first arrest of an openly public United Front Communist representative.[44] By March, the authorities had increased their surveillance of *Xinhua ribao* and shut down *Xinhua* offices in Guilin and Guangdong. These actions all manifested the breakdown of the United Front months before the New Fourth Army incident of January 1941, when the Communist army was ambushed by Chiang Kai-shek's troops, effectively ending cooperation between the two political parties.

By mid 1939, government repression and party schisms resulted in a renewed emphasis on the underground movement, which remained the dominant Communist urban strategy until the mid 1940s. While the internationalist wing of the CCP and the Returned Students (from Moscow) developed much of the framework for the United Front in Sichuan, the transition to clandestine work took place under the auspices of the Southern Bureau, led by Zhou Enlai, in conjunction with Party Central in Yan'an. Established in January 1939, the Southern Bureau undertook party work in the south and southwest, effectively replacing the Yangtze Bureau and the leadership of Wang Ming. Southern Bureau leaders operated on two separate levels. While conducting United Front work with the Guomindang through the open channels of *Xinhua ribao* or the office of the Eighth Route Army, they also supervised underground work. In theory, party members were to follow Zhou Enlai's formulations, expressed as the "three diligences" (*san qin*), "work hard, study hard, and be diligent in making friends" and the "three transformations" (*san hua*), "socialize, be professional, and be legitimate in political activities."[45]

At the same time, the CCP recognized the need to promote ideological harmony and curb the "storm membership drive," the prevailing policy since the outbreak of the war. In April 1939, Zhou Enlai called for "quality over quantity, consolidation over mobilization," leading to the August 25, 1939, resolution on party consolidation, which highlighted several problems endemic to party work in Nationalist-controlled territory.[46] Communist leaders criticized weak organization and poor recruitment practices, such as holding group inductions and improperly screening members for admission. The rush to raise party membership levels had diluted the quality of its members. Local party branches had uncritically accepted members who were sympathetic to the resistance movement against Japan but lacked ideological commitment to the party. In the process, "members of other classes, opportunists, and even spies" had infiltrated the party.

Following the resolution, each provincial party organization began consolidation (*zhengdui*). Between late 1939 and 1941, three to four hundred CCP members renounced their membership. By January 1941, the recruitment drive in eastern Sichuan had stopped.[47] Overall, party members working under the auspices of the Eastern Sichuan Special Committee diminished from roughly 3,500 to 1,900 members.[48] To ensure that local bureaus were entrusted to reliable cadres, members of the landlord, rich peasant, and merchant classes suspected of infiltration and spying were purged. The number of party members working in Chongqing industries, especially the defense industry, thus dramatically decreased; only 25 party members remained in the defense industry in 1941, down from 130 prior to the investigation that year.[49] In the early 1940s, the underground lacked a strong organizational basis within the arsenals. Any open political space was further constricted when the party stressed minimizing organizations within the defense industry or other industries where there was extensive spy surveillance. Within the arsenals, party members would each only retain contact with one other party member. Party cells were forbidden in the war plants, and in other industries, they were limited to no more than three members and organized on parallel lines.[50]

Instead, the party outlined a more moderate strategy, designed to ensure the long-term survival of the underground, while waiting to capitalize on the opportune moment for open class struggle. In this approach, the Southern Bureau followed the general policy set by Mao Zedong in March 1940, known as "justification, advantage, and restraint." In the face of growing military clashes with the Nationalist armies that had begun the previous year, Mao had sought to resist the Nationalist government without exceeding the limits of its tolerance and impairing United Front work and the image of the Communists as loyal patriots.[51]

Communist labor policy in Nationalist-controlled territory was defined as "justification," which meant a platform calling for minimum living standards for workers. By the early 1940s, the underground focused on neutralizing labor bosses, employers, and managerial staff to gain economic advantages for workers. Workers were to cooperate, that is, "change their former attitudes toward labor bosses and staff," so as to gain their sympathy and support in improving their livelihoods. But if employers did not raise wages, Communists instructed workers to resist by lowering productivity.

Tactics involved the same mix of restraint, legality, and struggle.

Workers were to proceed with caution and use legal forums. On the other hand, cadres adopted struggle tactics reminiscent of Mao's rules for guerrilla warfare. As Cheng Zijian wrote in a 1942 report, "Be sure not to expand; there will be advances and retreats, soft and hard areas. If you encounter a hard spot, do not get stuck and destroyed. If you encounter a soft area, do not sacrifice workers' minimum livelihood." When working in labor unions, party activists were to adopt a "white skin and red heart"—Nationalist in appearance but Communist in spirit—approach. Rank-and-file members would abide by the Nationalist government's laws but use contradictions among the unions to "shield the lower levels and to penetrate and usurp authority."[52]

The use of double-faced tactics led the CCP's leadership to issue several directives on whether underground activists should join the Guomindang. In response to a deadline of April 1, 1940, for all civil servants to join the GMD, the CCP allowed activists working in GMD institutions to join the Nationalist Party immediately, without prior approval. It was imperative to protect party members' vocation and legal standing. However, exposed members who were ordered to join the GMD should refuse to join. In that case, it was better to sacrifice one's position and flee to another job. Underground members who joined the GMD should henceforth frequently receive "profound class education, so that they clearly understand the differences between Marxism-Leninism and the Three People's Principles. Activists should also receive education in work methods, so that they can lie low for the long term, [and] carefully and tactfully conduct liaison work with the masses."[53]

Now that the CCP espoused extreme prudence in expanding, it was more circumspect in choosing its enemies and friends. By 1943, local party leaders stressed recruitment of older skilled workers in strategic industries. "Those who are skilled, charismatic leaders of the revolution among the older generation should be the main object for developing [the party]."[54] Attention to veteran workers arose from having scorned them in the past for their "backward" ways, while relying on idealistic youth during the National Salvation Movement and falling victim to their recklessness. "Young workers constituted the majority of participants in the National Salvation Movement," Cheng Zijian noted. "Enthusiastic, pure, and active, they were warmly received by society, but they were also glaringly exposed, one-sided, and naïve, and sowed the seeds of their own destruction."[55] Veteran skilled workers were generally more reluctant to become politically active. Older workers had families to care for and did not relish the thought of revisiting the White Terror, a point the Communists underscored in promoting a more moderate labor policy during the early 1940s.

In the span of only a few years, the CCP had built a base within the defense industry by mobilizing workers through patriotic appeals. From the party's perspective, the class project remained unfulfilled while the nationalist struggle took center stage. But with consolidation in late 1939, and the shift to the underground movement focused on workers' economic conditions as a precondition for political struggle, class issues were now given equal weight with nationalism. Tactically, the party underground now linked economic with nationalist goals. Writing in 1942, Cheng Zijian explained, "With regard to their ideology, we must bit by bit raise workers' consciousness of their intertwined class and nationalist interests."[56] Previously, the CCP had subordinated workers' economic grievances to the goal of patriotic resistance, believing that only victory against Japan would improve workers' livelihood, but now it reversed its emphasis. Improving workers' standard of living, or at least maintaining it, was a precondition to strengthening the forces of national salvation. This change formed part of a crusade to win the allegiance of veteran skilled workers, as the party believed that its prior emphasis on patriotism had ignored their experiences and demands. Underground leaders, such as Cheng Zijian, also sought to link the unraveling of the United Front in the early 1940s with the plight of workers, arguing that political repression had intensified the exploitation of workers.

The CCP may have renewed its emphasis on economic issues, but the retreat underground forced it to contend with the objective difficulties of lacking open labor organizations. Party work would have to be conducted in a gray zone, using existing GMD organizations, in the hope of subverting their leadership and rank and file. These types of survival strategies necessitated using much more indirect ways of forging alliances with workers. The tactical shift to underground work also pushed local working-class activists (some party members, others only with loose ties to the CCP) to the forefront of the labor movement. The development of this subelite, together with the Communists' adherence to the United Front, helps explain why worker militancy during the strike waves of the mid 1940s would outpace the CCP.

The Communist Press and the Subculture of Opposition

When the CCP reverted to underground work, *Xinhua ribao* assumed vital importance in articulating the party's message and garnering public support in the Great Rear. Communists considered the paper a "dagger pointing at the heart of the GMD," for *Xinhua ribao* offered its readership a public forum to express grievances and propagate moral standards by which to judge the government. The reading and writing of *Xinhua ribao*, especially by workers, thus became a form of political participation. If Barrington Moore is right in equating obedience and revolt with the degree of political space needed to express workers' moral outrage, the legalization of the opposition paper opened up political space in a period of general political retrenchment.[57] As one of the few legal fronts for the CCP in wartime Nationalist territory, the paper and its press agency became a key organization, in which workers and Communists interacted. Not surprisingly, it is said that Chiang Kai-shek recalled this conferral of legality as his "biggest mistake vis-à-vis the Communists."[58]

Xinhua ribao was established on January 8, 1938, at Hankou, under the editorial direction of Pan Zinian, but moved to Chongqing in October 1938 and remained in circulation until February 28, 1947, when the Nationalist government suppressed all legal Communist channels in the city. During this period, the CCP used the paper to reach a mass audience in the wartime capital. By January 1945, Chongqing garrison headquarters reported that at least 22,000 copies were being printed, with a projected distribution of 50,000 copies.[59] Considering the extent of government press controls, the parity of these circulation figures with those of other prominent newspapers attests to the popularity of *Xinhua ribao*.[60] Furthermore, these figures greatly underestimated the paper's appeal, since workers often shared copies among "at least five or six people, and even over ten people," thus ensuring a broader readership.[61]

The paper successfully targeted a widespread audience through its reportage covering the masses and innovative approach. Zhou Enlai, Dong Biwu, and other CCP leaders often wrote editorials in *Xinhua ribao* calling for patriotic resistance. Pan Zinian emphasized populist aspects by printing political satire and features, such as the "life of youth" and "women's chronicles." The "reader's garden" (*duzhe yuandi*) was notable for printing workers' letters dealing with their trials and tribulations. Simple, direct language made reading *Xinhua ribao* more accessible to literate workers. Articles covering labor issues concerned the experiences of daily life and working conditions, rather than more abstract theoretical issues. Frequent reports on the labor movement, both within China and abroad, were calculated to strengthen workers' solidarity, especially during a period when trade unions, such as they were, lacked autonomy and underground activists faced the constant threat of arrest. Many of the letters and proletarian literature, which described inequalities in the workplace, must have aroused readers' anger and sense of injustice against the employer. Militant workers found *Xinhua ribao* appealing because its advocacy of social justice resonated with their consciousness of class. Shen Qichang, for instance, read the paper on a daily basis and often copied down articles from the paper. When asked by his interrogators to describe its strengths, he responded: "*Xinhua* stands on the side of workers and speaks for us."[62]

The paper proved especially popular among working-class readers, who may have comprised up to 70 percent of the readership, according to the daily's own internal survey.[63] The occupational status of its subscribers was likely more varied than the paper proclaimed. Government-affiliated sources, for instance, indicate that "students, clerks in government offices and business firms, and literate workers form the bulk of its readers."[64] Still, workers became an important constituency of the paper, because it paid attention to their needs. As the Nationalist propaganda journal *China at War* admitted: "[T]he life of students and workers is more fully reported in the newspaper *[Xinhua ribao]* than in any other."[65]

To understand why *Xinhua ribao* became so popular among arsenal workers, let us first examine the educational background of workers and the symbolic importance workers and industrial elites placed on reading. Given how both Nationalists and Communists often belittled workers for being either illiterate or lacking "consciousness," it may seem surprising that most workers, at least in the defense industry, had received some form of education and achieved functional literacy. At Arsenal No. 24, for instance, as a 1939 survey attests, only a minority of the workforce were illiterate (table 7.1). To be sure, artisans had higher literacy rates than laborers, and a significantly greater proportion of them had either studied at or graduated from middle school. But even among laborers, almost half had attended private or family academies (*sishu*), the main form of rural education.[66] Relative to other plants, one would expect higher rates of illiteracy, for the munitions plant had recruited heavily among first-generation industrial workers in Sichuan. As a local steel

TABLE 7.1

Workers' Educational Level at Arsenal No. 24, December 1939

(percentage)

Educational level	Foremen	Artisans	Apprentices	Laborers	Total
Illiterate	0.0%	17.3%	1.2%	37.5%	21.8%
Discontinued elementary school	23.1	28.0	22.1	11.5	22.1
Elementary school graduate	46.1	12.1	33.7	3.7	12.2
Discontinued secondary school[a]	7.7	7.3	25.6	0.4	7.0
Graduated from secondary school[a]	15.4	6.3	4.6	0.0	4.3
Private academy	7.7	29.0	12.8	46.8	32.7
Total numbers	13	479	86	269	847

SOURCE: Chongqing Municipal Archives, 24 Chang, 1 *mu*, 92 *juan*, 4.
[a]Junior secondary schools.

mill, the arsenal also received less capital and technology than coastal arsenals that had relocated to Chongqing.

In comparison, a 1947 survey of Arsenal No. 10 and No. 20 indicates that only 18 percent of the total combined workforce (N = 6,760) were illiterate. Most workers were functionally literate or had received some education, primarily at the elementary level.[67] In light of the average age of students attending primary school, such an education was one that a nine-to-thirteen-year-old child received. On the other hand, factory-training programs proved to be a major conduit for social advancement and education. In one worker's view, skilled workers received the modern-day equivalent of a junior secondary school education in terms of math, Chinese, and mechanical design.[68]

Besides these formal avenues of education, workers developed a "subculture of opposition," "an interlocking network of formal institutions and informal practices based on an ethic of social equality, cooperation, mutual trust, and mutual assistance."[69] This subculture had a symbiotic relationship with the Communist daily and expressed itself in several organizations and activities. In 1942, when the Southern Bureau's youth wing halted the expansion of most party cells and branches, organizations known as "strongholds" (*judian*) emerged, which were sympathetic but not beholden to the CCP, and within three years, they had spread from the universities to schools, businesses, and factories. Flexible organization and the fact that their members predominantly lacked party affiliation distinguished strongholds from party cells. The Communist underground considered them bridges between the party and the masses, whereby individual party members or nonparty cadres could maintain contact with the people through groups of three to five members. Linking up with strongholds, party members developed an expanding network of connections, described by the underground as a "chain of rings." Each member in turn maintained single-line contact with another stronghold member, thus building an invisible network of strongholds that spanned across industrial sectors.

Workers involved in strongholds shared a commitment to solidarity and raising political consciousness. As outlined by the Youth Organization, their goals included advocating mutual aid so that friends could help each other in their daily lives, work, and study. Strongholds thus overlapped with mutual-aid associations, such as the *dahui*, used by workers to cope with debt and economic deprivation. In their conception and practice, strongholds promoted political education. At meetings, stronghold members concentrated on their professional activities and areas of common knowledge, but touched on politics, economics, and the dreaded spy system. Strict guidelines were enforced to ensure their secrecy. With the encouragement of CCP organizers, stronghold members read *Xinhua ribao* and the progressive literature of Lu Xun, Zou Taofen, Gogol, Romain Rolland, and Henri Barbusse.[70]

Paradoxically, extensive wartime labor mobility became strongholds' greatest asset. Although rapid job turnover impeded transient workers from establishing permanent organizations in any one factory, job mobility accelerated the spread of preexisting networks and strongholds, which had no set organizational structure, throughout Chongqing and also to the surrounding rural counties. For these reasons, when the CCP began to mobilize again after the War of Resistance, it first looked to the strongholds in recruiting cadres for the labor movement. Strongholds at other factories served as nuclei for labor disputes involving arbitrary firings, spy surveillance, and leadership struggles in company-sponsored unions.[71]

A closely related form of opposition subculture involved the proliferation of reading societies among Chongqing factories.[72] To be sure, some reading societies gathered to discuss work issues rather than political tracts. One steel mill mechanic recalled that his reading society preferred to study mechanical drafts each Sunday to supplement their instructor's teaching. These groups offered individual advancement and a safeguard against unemployment. "We wanted to learn things, because in those days, during the Guomindang period, no one knew when there would be any food to eat. No one knew if we would be fired or dismissed. To learn a skill meant [buying] food would no longer be a problem."[73] But self-betterment through education and radicalization were often indivisible. Starting in the late 1930s, reading societies and other cultural associations frequently established political ties with the CCP. According to Nationalist reports, "Their method of action is to organize National Salvation groups—reading societies, wall newspaper societies, theatrical groups, chorus—and in this way gradually attract leftist-inclined workers to read their outline and become acquainted with Communist ideology."[74]

One such leftist, who would become a leader of the postwar labor movement, was Xie Wanquan. Like so many of Chongqing's nascent proletariat and other labor activists, such as Liu Zonglin and Tan Jianxiao, Xie came from Chongqing's rural hinterland—the county of Dianjiang, in eastern Sichuan—and his family's experience with landlords proved a lasting influence on him. As he would relate in a deposition after being arrested in 1946 for leading the strike at Arsenal No. 10, the harsh experience of class oppression had forged his social identity:

A person's ideology is very much related to his social standing and social environment. I grew up in a family of the poor. From early on, the seeds of hatred had been planted within me against the rich and powerful landlords. After graduating from primary school, because of my family environment, I joined the 28th Group Army stationed in Chongqing and worked as an orderly in their office. I thus have a profound understanding of officialdom's seamy side. In 1942, this factory recruited apprentices, so I tested into the factory. I served for four years in the engineering office. During these years, as I grew older, I became discontented with too many aspects of society. I prepared to join the political party [the CCP] because grumbling by itself had no effect.[75]

Xie attributed his anger with power holders to a deprived emotional childhood. "Maternal love is the yeast that nurtures humanity. I obviously was lacking this. I was an unsociable and eccentric child who from early on was pessimistic. Among the boundless sea of people, I had no direction or boat and just went blindly forward. Communism finally provided me with the wave."

Xie's work experience proved decisive in fostering his working-class consciousness. A leading cause of his radicalization was his opposition to the stigma attached to menial labor and a desire for respect, a recurring theme in the Chongqing labor movement: "Menial labor such as [that of] an orderly and laborer occupied my innocent youth and contributed to my extremist thought. . . . In the fall of 1939, I was a laborer in the telecommunications bureau. I was ridiculed, and this hurt me both physically and mentally. I often wondered, was I not a person? I also wanted to enjoy people's rights. Why did I have to do corvée labor like a beast of burden and be yelled at to work? At the time, I truly had no answer."[76]

Marxism and the factory experience would provide the answer. In a training class at Arsenal No. 10, where he began an apprenticeship in 1941 at the age of sixteen, Xie developed a passion for Marxist thought. "Within the factory I had a vigorous thirst for knowledge, which no one surpassed. Besides studying drafting and design, under the guidance of Lu Dailian [an instructor of Chinese], sociology books, like a tidal wave, gushed into my bosom. Marx stimulated me." The congruence between Western industrial capitalism and China's arms industry, where workers entered a wage relationship subordinate to state capitalism, was not lost on Xie. "He [Marx] spoke of all types of morbid social problems existing in all the thriving capitalist countries of Europe. There was no denying the fact that the production methods of Arsenal No. 10 were in the same category as capitalist ones."[77]

Xie's desire to learn and an ambition to read Marxist literature, which was fostered by the party, and *Xinhua ribao* in particular, helped bridge the gap between the radical intellectuals and himself. Before joining the party, Xie met frequently with individual party members, most of them fellow Sichuanese. He would often go to the editorial board of *Xinhua ribao* for guidance from Wang Shenhua. "I often went to ask him to explain problems I didn't understand, such as the 'Asian mode of production.'"[78] His first contact, Wang Dihua, editor of the underground paper *Qingnian shenghuo* (Young Lives) introduced him to the *Communist Manifesto* and Lenin's *Left-wing Communism, an Infantile Disorder*. Wang also gave Xie Mao's report *On Coalition Government* (published by Liberation Press in May 1945) to read. From Ma Xilin, a *Xinhua ribao* editor, he obtained Mao's report *Economic and Financial Problems* and Engels's *Anti-Dühring*. Upon joining the CCP, Zhang Yunxi, who had formally introduced him to the party, got him to read Lenin's *State and Revolution* and Chen Boda's *A Critique of* [Chiang Kaishek's] "*China's Destiny*." Only after joining the party that fall did Xie begin reading explicitly about labor, a three-volume set of *Workers' Vanguard*.

One can only speculate why these specific books were given to Xie and what he learned from them. Mao's works were among the most current books he read, indicating the rapidity with which they were promoted among Communist Party members. *Economic and Financial Problems*, with its stress on the development of producer cooperatives in the Communist base areas, may have influenced Xie Wanquan's advocacy of collective production. Other choices, such as the *Communist Manifesto*, provided the most succinct expression of Marx's themes of class struggle and social transformation and could be grasped in fairly short order. Similarly, *Left-wing Communism* and *State and Revolution* were basic introductory texts by Lenin. With their emphasis on tactical approaches to political action and criticism of undisciplined left-wing communists, these texts were well suited to clandestine activists operating under an authoritarian regime. They appealed to organizational discipline and ideological unity and induced militants to consider that action that might seem morally right could be politically counterproductive. In expounding Lenin's theory on the united front, *Left-wing Communism* also resonated with the CCP's urban political line. The CCP leader Wang Ming had previously adopted this theory to reconcile resistance to Japan, which meant forming a united front with the Guomindang, while still conducting mass work and preserving the CCP's interests under such an alliance.[79]

Radical workers' passion for study paralleled their reverence for the written word. The book became a sacred icon for the militant minority. The underground activist Liu Zonglin recalls how he was willing to sacrifice his life to protect Communist tracts.[80] Xie Wanquan was equally determined. "*Qunzhong* and *Xinhua ribao* were my main food for thought. I placed them beside my pillow and often read them. My faith was steadfast and my admiration resolute, almost as if I had taken a magic potion. The reality dismayed people. I firmly believed in Communism as a miracle cure for the world. . . . At the time, the money I spent on books was double my monthly wage."[81]

Not all workers were interested in left-wing literature. Reading tastes varied to include both weighty political tracts and trashy novels. But apart from what workers read, those who held power deemed the very acts of reading and writing to be subversive. Li Chenggan, manager of the largest arsenal in wartime China, grew exasperated at seeing so many of his workers take time off to read novels on the sly or to scribble on work desks, machines, and the factory walls.[82] In trying to maximize production, managers became concerned about the uses and abuses of time. At another level, workers' involvement with reading and writing helped overturn social stigmas ascribed to them and raised questions about traditional prejudices against manual labor. Thus, workers were attracted to *Xinhua ribao* because it reflected and nurtured their desire for greater human respect. Conversely, industrial leaders felt that their very authority was threatened, since that authority was premised on a division of labor.

For some of these very same reasons, although United Front arrangements had accorded *Xinhua ribao* legal status, by 1941, Yu Dawei found cause to prohibit its circulation among all the arsenals. The paper's political message and the political participation it generated among readers and press workers convinced the Nationalist government that it threatened the social order, a sentiment that fed into widespread anticommunist hysteria, especially after the January 1941 New Fourth Army Incident. Yu Dawei expressed the leadership's fear of the Communist daily when he prohibited subscriptions. "The thought of *Xinhua ribao* is biased, the writing extreme. It is truly a great threat to the future prospects of the [War of] Resistance and reconstruction. We are now actively vigilant to prevent it from running rampant. There are many national defense industrial workers. If they become influenced, the momentum will be difficult to stop."[83] Government officials used both carrot and stick to dissuade arsenal workers from reading Communist literature. Violators of the ban on the paper were generally fired. To avoid appearing heavy-handed, though, arsenal managers offered discounts or reimbursed workers who read the army-sponsored paper *Saodang bao,* established in support of Chiang Kai-shek's military campaigns against the Jiangxi Soviet during the early 1930s.[84]

But as a low-ranking engineer recalled, "Most of the time we didn't read *Saodang bao.* Its content was dull and dry and didn't appeal to us. We felt the content of *Xinhua ribao* was innovative." Paradoxically, government vigilance and suppression had the unintended effect of promoting the Communist daily. Government controls piqued readers' curiosity and indignation. As the same engineer remarked, "The more they censored it, the more we wanted to read it."[85] Controls over distribution even increased circulation. To avoid confiscation, couriers started their routes before dawn, thus ensuring a greater share of the morning readership for *Xinhua ribao.* Feeding into the subculture of opposition, the teenagers sometimes flaunted authority by clever wordplay when hawking the paper: "Selling papers, selling papers, New China sweeps up [a reference to *Saodang bao*] Central Daily!"[86] Such forms of resistance against the Nationalist regime probably contributed to the popularity of the Communist daily. Of equal or more importance, though, was the actual message of *Xinhua ribao.*

There were several ways in which *Xinhua ribao* formed a class discourse, or, to play on Benedict Anderson's phrase, created class as an "imagined community."[87] The paper addressed workers as a class with its own self-interests. Editors usually devoted half of page 3, and sometimes the entire page, to labor issues. The letters of workers printed on this page reinforced the idea that industrial workers in general had similar experiences, a shared sense of injustice, and a shared social identity—epitomized by the words "we workers"—based on their production value. As the historian Reinhart Koselleck has noted, "it is possible to articulate or linguistically create a group identity through the emphatic use of the word 'we.'"[88]

Underlying friction between labor and management during the War of Resistance can be traced through letters published in the *Xinhua ribao* and petitions. At issue was workers' desire for greater respect and dignity. This quest for membership, which workers sought to define on their own terms, underlay their demands to better their lowly status within the factory community, as well as in society at large. As staff officers represented their immediate social superiors within the arsenals, production workers directed much of their vitriol against management and supervisors in demanding equity.

Of course, these letters did not represent all workers. Supporters of the Sanqingtuan or Guomindang are not to be found among the writers, nor did the critical anti-management tone of the articles reflect the sentiments of every worker. Moreover, despite the CCP's policy of encouraging alternative viewpoints, editors probably screened articles.[89] Nevertheless, since workers lacked other legal organizations and were forced to traverse a repressive terrain, they welcomed the opportunity to express their hopes and grievances in the Communist daily.

Workers frequently used rhetorical devices, such as first-person plural references, to underscore their shared suffering and foster class solidarity. One worker questioned the competence of an engineer and his abusive practices, and denounced managerial supervisors, who were identified by badges, for their hypocrisy in using nationalism and paternalism to spur production:

Our managing engineer has no hands-on knowledge. He does not understand that it takes time to finish the work. But he frequently curses at us, and we do not dare say anything. Besides formal working hours, we still have endless private chores for these gentlemen carrying badges. We make bathtubs, washing basins, teapots, woks, even the piss pots for their wives and sisters. Even if most of them are made from factory materials, it's all right as long as they can be used in their homes, just like home-style cooking. Is this what is called production to save the nation!? Not at all, this is production to save the family![90]

The writer emphatically uses "we" to identify his tribulations with those of the entire workforce. This sense of victimization was a means of strengthening group solidarity and made all the more effective by contrasting the workers in positive terms with a coterie of evil authority figures presiding over the factory community.

Another arsenal worker recounted his grief as an apprentice. Like many of his peers, he found the opportunity to learn a craft in the defense industry and serve the national cause alluring. Yet the apprentice's patriotic fervor soon dissipated when supervisors treated him like a menial servant. The apprentice conveys his alienation at being exploited and stripped of his human dignity and sense of self-worth:

I came from difficult family circumstances and could not continue my education. After graduating from elementary school, I entered a certain factory as a skilled apprentice. I was so excited to think I could learn a few skills and serve the country. But in reality, I just did chores for the engineer, managers, and staff and brought them tofu. Later I replaced another factory apprentice and swept the floor, rang the bell, and cleaned the spittoon. In name, I am a skilled apprentice, but in their eyes, I am really an animal.[91]

Workers frequently expressed their grievances in terms of the unjust treatment they received relative to supervisory personnel. Whereas management used the term "treatment" (*daiyu*) to refer to benefits other than wages, workers invested the word with their quest for higher social standing and respect. An arsenal machinist demanded a more egalitarian workplace after being criticized by the manager's sultry wife for inviting a friend to the factory canteen, a privilege reserved for staff officers. "Why is the status of workers lower than [that of] staff? We cannot support this kind of thinking! What could you do without workers? We firmly demand equal treatment and oppose this unjust thought!"[92]

These letters manifest a growing awareness among workers that they formed a group of producers, and that their labor for the war effort entitled them to proper dignity and respect. The authors were quick to acknowledge their lowly status, but commonly and emphatically spoke of themselves as "we workers," thus reinforcing their sense of class and national identity. Workers played on nationalist sentiment by implying that managerial self-interest, as opposed to the public good of the country, had lowered workers' morale and production. These letters, testimony to workers' discontent with management, illustrate that antagonism between labor and management coexisted alongside workers' nationalist sentiments. Workers' nationalist sentiment did not simply serve as a moderating influence on the labor movement; rather, workers used nationalism to press their demands for better treatment. Demands for an egalitarian work site were also made more effective by contrasting the diligent and aspiring worker with either parasitic managers, staff members who upheld an undemocratic order by parroting the official line, or the manager's wife, portrayed as a vixen wielding power, with a cigarette in her mouth. The writers, representing a broad spectrum of the workforce, became increasingly self-assertive, alternately mocking and criticizing authority. In essence, *Xinhua ribao* gave these workers a political voice and a forum in which to reassess social relations within the factory.

Party activists also circulated clandestine papers among the arsenals. *Xuexi* (Study), one of the few such papers of which copies survive, reveals the political messages popularized by the underground. Most likely, writers followed the CCP's political line, since the paper's organization, the Chongqing Study Society, had direct links to the Southern Bureau.[93] As suggested by its title, *Xuexi* sought to promulgate study as a means of raising young workers' consciousness and organizational discipline. Subject matter included basic Marxist principles and theoretical literature, such as a primer on dialectical materialism, as well as the CCP's advocacy of "New Democracy." The paper called for a more democratic government instead of a "bureaucracy for minority fascist rule." Editorials attacked the Nationalists for ruling a "feudal semi-colonial country in league with fascist countries, which used spies to oppress people and suppress their freedom."[94] Activists also used the paper in a didactic way, warning intellectuals against the pernicious effects of bureaucratism, that is, "scorning masses who are not enlightened," and advocating education and developing friendships with workers before organizing.[95] But the paper made workers its main audience and thus, like *Xinhua ribao,* used simple, accessible language, with articles covering workers' experience and struggles with their employers.

Whether it was *Xinhua ribao* or *Xuexi,* the Communist press forged closer ties between the CCP and workers. This was an interactive process between the party and readers. Workers for their part contacted journalists so that their grievances could be publicized. The actual writing of the paper thus became a form of political participation and consciousness-raising, and shop clerks, workers, and government office employees contributed a quarter of the articles.[96] Their letters might in turn elicit responses from the editor, thus serving to disseminate socialist propaganda.

Besides uniting workers through their reading and sharing of *Xinhua ribao*, the Communist press agency secretly organized workers during the strike movement of 1945–46. Labor activists frequently discussed strategy with Communists at the paper's headquarters or its business office. They also used *Xinhua ribao* as a propaganda and mobilization tool. Workers throughout Chongqing expressed solidarity, for instance, with striking steel-mill workers by writing letters and petitions to *Xinhua ribao*.[97] Journalists reported factory arrests, exerting pressure on the government to reach a compromise. Given the risks faced by the militant minority, however, the Communist press had its greatest impact on workers' consciousness and in fostering their subculture of opposition. For more traditional means of organizing, arsenal workers utilized the legal forum of the Chinese Association of Labor (CAL), subverting it from within.

The Chinese Association of Labor and Arsenal Workers

By the end of World War II, the Chinese Association of Labor (Zhongguo laodong xiehui) emerged as an outspoken representative of labor's independent interests. Its founders could not have imagined a less likely scenario. The Nationalist government had originally conceived of CAL as an organization to foster labor control and class harmony. Established in 1935 as a "labor cultural group," the Shanghai association's mandate was to "research labor theory, develop labor culture, assist in planning labor welfare, and promote the labor movement." Espousal of the labor movement was to be strictly contained within the harmonious and mediated labor-capital process. As its own platform declared, CAL was to "promote a labor policy based on the Three People's Principles to eliminate Bolshevik class struggle."[98]

December 1939 marked a shift to a more moderate leadership when the government granted CAL the preliminary status of national labor union so that it could represent China on the international stage. On the pretext that only union leaders had the legal right to represent labor organizations, the former postal union leader Zhu Xuefan replaced the more conservative director Lu Jingshi of the Ministry of Social Affairs. Thereafter, CAL and Zhu Xuefan were allowed to represent China on the International Labor Organization executive, press for better treatment of Chinese seamen on foreign ships, and, most important, obtain financial assistance from American labor organizations. Donations from the American Federation of Labor totaling over U.S.$600,000 per annum between 1943 and 1945 provided welfare services to workers employed in the unoccupied territories.[99] Although CAL aroused the jealousy of the more powerful Ministry of Social Affairs, the Nationalist government looked favorably on the arrangement, because American funding supplied it with hard currency, while it in turn provided depreciated Chinese currency to CAL. The state also derived a certain amount of legitimacy from CAL, especially when the association endorsed its labor policy, such as the 1942 wage-fixing regulation.[100]

By the mid 1940s, however, the worsening economy led CAL to take a more independent political stance, bringing it into conflict with the government. Increasingly, workers used the association to mediate labor disputes and strikes, much to the chagrin of the Ministry of Social Affairs. Between September 1945 and February 1946, CAL mediated 173 labor disputes.[101] Moreover, the association moved leftward as a result of increased contact with Communist labor leaders from Yan'an and members of the Democratic League during the Marshall-mediated Political Consultative Conference (January 6–February 1, 1946). Government tolerance reached its limits when CAL issued a twenty-three-point "platform" during the conference. The declaration placed the association within the mainstream of the CCP's New Democracy politics, because it called for a speedy resolution to the political impasse, greater representation for all political parties, reduction of land rents, the right to strike and organize, and guaranteed employment for industrial workers. CAL also led organizing and petition drives to aid unemployed workers and guarantee severance pay. In March 1946, the Chongqing municipal court arraigned Zhu Xuefan on charges of "disturbing peace and order," and on August 6, police arrested over twenty CAL employees and members of the government-controlled "General Labor Union" and occupied all the CAL buildings. Bureaucrats from the Ministry of Social Affairs replaced the association's leadership. Zhu, who had fled to Hong Kong and revitalized the organization, narrowly escaped with his life from an abortive assassination attempt.[102]

The political jousting and rift between Zhu and the Nationalist government signaled the failure of the Guomindang's corporatist labor policies. After the assassination attempt, Zhu, despite a checkered past in the Shanghai underworld, rose to even more prominence in the eyes of the World Federation of Trade Unions and the CCP, which he eventually joined. At the same time, the growing popularity of Zhu and CAL among arsenal workers implicitly challenged the state's labor policy. By the eve of V-J Day, arsenal workers comprised the largest portion of Chongqing's CAL membership, estimated at over 15,000 members. (A few years earlier, such numbers had meant nothing, because as Nym Wales explains of "labor front" methods, "all workers in a particular factory or category are considered union members *ipso facto*.")[103] However, one should read membership rolls with an eye to whether they originated from before or after the ban on all CAL membership. By V-J Day, membership was a risky business and had political costs. Indicative of their workers' prominence in the labor organization, arsenals were the only individual factories to contribute "activity funds" to CAL; otherwise, funding was apportioned by district.[104]

The association garnered support from a broad spectrum of arsenal workers by providing social welfare for unemployed workers or workers living on the edge of subsistence. A report issued after a certain Zuo Jue was arrested for corresponding with the labor organization and recruiting other workers noted that "many workers compete for membership, believing that this will provide them with security or help them find another job if unemployed."[105] The view that CAL could guarantee employment is confirmed by numerous workers' testimonies. Li Bing, a thirty-nine-year-old worker at Arsenal No. 10 joined CAL "after hearing that it could safeguard our jobs." Long Ming, a worker in Arsenal No. 10's rifling department, joined because he believed that CAL could "mutually help and benefit" workers, and because of its legal status. Long Ming apparently left the organization for fear that its growing militancy, "agitating for unrest and mobilizing strikes," would compromise workers' efforts to gain welfare.[106]

To meet the growing demand for its social services, CAL set up sixteen welfare stations throughout the city's industrial sectors, including teahouses, reading rooms, night schools, barbershops, clinics, and showers. Ultimately, the association proved unable to cope with rising unemployment, which by October 1945 had reached 60,000 industrial workers, but its reputation as provider of unemployment relief and social welfare benefits continued to attract workers. The stations received an estimated 290,000 visits in one year alone.[107]

In addition to economic motivations, workers looked to the association as a proxy for union representation. The CAL member Zuo Jue, for instance, had previously worked at the Gangqianhui, where he had earned a reputation as "troublemaker." He had fought with foremen and had encouraged workers to join a union, contrary to government orders. In typical fashion, managers branded Zuo as subversive, "crude and violent," indicating that his behavior was beyond the pale. Nevertheless, given CAL's advocacy of unions, many of its members shared Zuo's aspirations. Similarly, the government viewed CAL as a conduit to unionization, as demonstrated by the frequency of its prohibitions of union organizing, uttered alongside its restriction of the association.

By early 1946, Ordnance Department authorities accused CAL members of recruiting arsenal workers en masse and using their bulletin *Zhongguo gongren zhoukan* (China Workers Weekly) to incite labor unrest. Citing as precedent the 1939 prohibition of all political and organizational activity among arsenal workers, the Ministry of Defense asked the Social Ministry and Chongqing Municipal Government to ban the association from all arsenals. By February 1946, all arsenal employees were ordered to withdraw their membership or be fired.[108]

Government suppression of CAL led to the formation of four national friendship societies during the spring of 1946. Members intentionally chose the name "friendship society" to avoid registering with the local Department of Social Affairs or Ministry of Economics, legal procedure for all unions. Although they were quickly suppressed, the emergence of such societies indicated workers' desire to unionize on an industrial and national basis with international support. In February 1946, for instance, workers deliberately chose the trucking industry as the first in which to establish a friendship society so as to take advantage of its international connections and mobility. According to a former trucking industry friendship society member in charge of propaganda, since many truck drivers were overseas Chinese from southeast Asia, their status helped protect them. Their mobility also enabled workers to quickly set up branches in Beijing, Shanghai, and Wuhan.[109] The second society, consisting of printers, also had strategic value, since workers were able to promote their message through the printing houses. Du Liang supervised a newsletter and was ready to start printing before the government crackdown on the Chinese Association of Labor. The third society, comprising workers employed in the military clothing industry, established itself in May 1946.

Arsenal workers provided the greatest number of members and leaders in the fourth society, the Chinese Machinists Friendship Society (Zhongguo jiqi gongren lianyihui), founded on May 20, 1946. As declared in its charter, unionization remained the main goal. "This society depends on mutual affection between workers of the same trade to promote a national machinists' union and be engaged in the goal of industrial and national reconstruction."[110] Both the CCP and CAL played visible roles in the organization, confirming Nationalist fears that CAL had become an "outer organization" of the CCP. The Bureau of Social Affairs reported that Communists had used their status as social welfare group organizers at the Daliangzi welfare society to organize the Machinists Society.[111] Because the GMD authorities called for the organization's immediate suppression, we know little of its social dynamics. But the large number of unemployed workers that the organization reputedly convened, and its emphasis on unionization, social welfare, and national reconstruction resonated with two of the labor movement's chief goals, greater job security and collective organization.

Given the repressive terrain workers faced in the defense industry, labor organizing challenged even the most stalwart of the militant minority. Forbidden to assemble, let alone join unions, arsenal workers promoted the class project through subterfuge and indirect methods. They used the corporatist Chinese Association of Labor as a front for unionizing; they joined clandestine "strongholds" to forge links across industries; and they imagined class via the Communist daily, *Xinhua ribao*. Arguably, only a militant minority, those who envisioned a radical restructuring of society, promoted the Communist press in wartime Chongqing. But the popularity of *Xinhua ribao* among workers indicates that their ideas did resonate with many workers' sense of injustice and desire for equal treatment. By the mid 1940s, the impulse toward a class movement and class organization among Chongqing workers underlay this process. Through the dynamic of the labor movement, workers' view of the world increasingly made class their point of reference. This was most evident in the concentrated, violent, and often coordinated struggles of workers in various factories, the subject of chapter 8. It was also apparent in workers' increasing demands for unionization and the leftward push of labor organizations, most notably the Chinese Association of Labor.

At the very least, this reading of *Xinhua ribao* and its relationship to workers may cause us to rethink our view of wartime Chongqing politics. From the very first press reports issued from the hilly city, journalists described the Nationalist regime's inexorable decline as a result of its own endemic sicknesses—corruption, bungled fiscal policies, and factionalism.[112] Conversely, while historians continue to debate how the Communists mobilized peasant support and rose to power in the countryside, they have unwittingly minimized the CCP's popular appeals in urban China prior to 1949. To be sure, Chongqing was not "Red Chongqing," but its political colors were undoubtedly more vivid than its infamous gray fog.

8

THE LABOR MOVEMENT,
1946-1949

Wang Daofeng, "Nan Zhongguo de huaxiang—fennu de gongliu" [The furious torrent, from the series South China images] (1947). From Su Lin, ed., *Guotongqu heibai muke* (Nanning: Guangxi meishu chubanshe, 2000), 226.

As economic crisis struck, and factories collapsed or left Chongqing, maintaining a livelihood became the central concern of workers. The erosion of real wages under hyperinflation and the alarming threat of unemployment by the mid 1940s, until dissipated by the resumption of military production during the Chinese civil war, formed the context of the postwar strike waves. Strikes and slowdowns reflected workers' defensive stance. Their demands called for stopping the downward spiraling of real wages, salvaging jobs, and, at the very least, receiving severance pay. Yet the formation and dynamics of the postwar labor movement did not simply or directly respond to the economic deprivation and increasing poverty facing workers. The strongly felt issue of injustice, revolving around discrimination against production workers, fueled disputes of the postwar period. Invoking both nationalist rhetoric and a sense of pride in their production, workers articulated a critique of the factory hierarchy that implicitly challenged their own lowly status and the legitimacy of their superiors by seeking to eliminate distinctions between status groups.

In pressing these demands, workers recognized that their status had suffered a long-term decline because of structural changes in production processes and wartime labor mobilization. On the one hand, changes in the organization of production dating back to the early 1930s had transformed the shop-floor milieu. The prestige of veteran skilled workers had diminished in inverse proportion to the ascending authority of staff members. These changes in the power balance were reflected in the segregation of workers and unequal treatment between staff and workers, even to the point of demarcating separate access to toilets. On the other hand, a factory proletariat had rapidly emerged in Chongqing because of the wartime demand for labor. Increasingly direct managerial controls over jobs, production, and wages starkly highlighted arsenal workers' status as wage laborers. Although management tried using welfare measures and benefits to fragment the workforce and render workers more quiescent during the war, these buffers between the state, management, and labor did not deflect the harsher reality of industrial life. When workers did vent their grievances, they had no recourse but to criticize management directly. Workers of all skills vented their anger as they shared the social stigma attached to manual labor. The articulation of their grievances thus helped foster an incipient working-class consciousness, in the sense that workers acquired an "us versus them" mentality. Workers recognized that they were mistreated, and that this mistreatment stemmed from unequal social relations.

Throughout the 1937–49 period, both Communists and labor activists befriended and organized workers. The relationship between Communists and workers was not, however, a one-sided affair, with the CCP as "vanguard party" leading workers on a trajectory from "economism" to revolutionary class consciousness. The relationship between Communists and workers remained a close but contradictory one. The Communist newspaper *Xinhua ribao* played an important role in stimulating the class impulse of arsenal workers and fostering a militant minority. But this class impulse was distinct from the goals of the Communists, who vacillated between adherence to the United Front and commitment to social change. By the late 1930s, the deteriorating United Front and its own self-imposed consolidation forced the regionally based CCP to resume underground work. To be a Communist in Chongqing was unenviable. Success was measured by political survival and the slow accretion of revolutionary forces, but maintaining secrecy often came at the price of political impotency. As a consequence, militant labor activists, often "outer party organization" members, were pushed to the foreground of the labor movement.

Building upon factory "strongholds" and reading groups, the militant minority assumed leadership roles in the strike waves of the mid 1940s. A conjuncture developed during the slowdowns and strikes at the Chongqing arsenals between the more radical message preached by working-class activists, on the one hand, and the desires among the rank and file for more humane treatment, on the other. Different strata of the labor movement shared the goals of job security, unionization, and better treatment, that is, higher pay and social status. Contrary to labor studies that have emphasized workers' local demands, it would seem that Chongqing arsenal workers saw themselves as participants of a broader social and economic transformation. Arsenal workers came to know themselves as a class through the violence that wracked the factories in the aftermath of the Anti-Japanese War.

Battles in the Arsenals

Although the sudden wave of strikes in 1946 suggests an almost elemental and spontaneous reaction to economic crisis, the labor movement had its roots in the Anti-Japanese War. Increasing state intervention and factory controls over labor during the war had pushed the labor movement underground and forced workers to adopt less overt forms of resistance than the strike. The relative absence of labor strife during the Sino-Japanese War has led Chinese historians to argue that workers under the guidance of the CCP subordinated class struggle to the nationalist resistance against Japan. Although this view conveys the tenor of the CCP's United Front policy and helps explain the expectations of workers after the war ended, one should note that industrial action erupted in isolated incidents and in individual factories. In 1944, the same historians note, as many as 300 labor disputes took place in Chongqing.[1] A quantitative difference remains between the postwar strikes and earlier labor disputes, but continuity is apparent in workers' consciousness; workers sought greater respect and better treatment throughout the entire decade.

Wartime arsenal workers carried out several strikes and slowdowns over wages, working conditions and social equity—prominent issues that resurfaced during the postwar labor movement. Two labor disputes, in which economic and moral grievances converged, occurred at Arsenal No. 21. In the first instance, workers challenged management's use of a compulsory savings plan when Chiang Kai-shek began consolidating control over Sichuan. Prior to the local Chongqing machine-gun plant's merger with the Jinling arsenal, management had deposited 3 percent of workers' wages in individual savings accounts. The plan proved unpopular with workers who demanded their full wages and proceeded to strike for three days. Management's ability to divide workers along economic and regional lines and fire workers' representatives temporarily defused the conflict.[2] Workers were further appeased when the director of the machine-gun plant agreed to return employee savings if his successor consented. But when Li Chenggan took control over the arms plant and merged it with Jinling to form Arsenal No. 21, he refused to terminate the plan. Li argued that the savings plan was an incentive for workers to stay put, because they would lose their savings if they left their posts. His stance prompted Communist activists to capitalize on widespread dissatisfaction among the workforce by threatening a slowdown if the savings were not repaid. Police reported that activists threatened a factorywide strike if management did not respond to workers' demands within a week of the slowdown. Apparently, the issue was resolved in favor of the arsenal workers without recourse to violence.[3]

Perhaps buoyed by their success, workers at the same arsenal challenged social welfare policy regarding subsidies for family members. In 1940, workers from six departments coordinated a four-day slowdown to protest the selective distribution of ten yuan as a provisional subsidy to workers with dependent family members. Workers perceived the measure as a form of economic discrimination designed to divide the workforce. The coordination among departments needed to mount the slowdown suggests the rancor caused by economic discrimination stemming from managerial policies intended to favor one segment of the workforce over another. Ultimately, management acquiesced and distributed the ten yuan to the entire workforce.[4]

While the collective actions of arsenal workers during the Anti-Japanese War remained isolated, they formed part of broader strike waves that struck Chongqing and major urban centers throughout China after V-J Day. From October 1945 through 1946, the wartime capital witnessed at least 423 labor disputes, including 80 strikes, involving close to 100,000 workers, employed at over 450 factories.[5] Disputes occurred in practically all sectors of the dual economy, ranging from the handicraft industry and small-scale industries to the mechanized, capital-intensive chemical and machine industries.

Economic collapse and workers' demands for greater economic security precipitated most labor disputes. Press reports suggest that over 40 percent of all factories had shut down by April 1946, while another 35 percent had partially stopped production. Economic collapse was the result of an overabundance of factories no longer needed to produce for the war demand. The mass exodus back to the coastal areas further contracted the local market. Industrialists and state managers sought to regain control over industries among the richer coastal cities and anticipated new opportunities brought by the resumption of foreign trade. But for working people, losing jobs became a living nightmare. Over 70,000 workers were unemployed or working part-time. By year's end, the number was over 100,000.[6]

Workers' economic demands fused with their political demands, which was no surprise to the authorities. As a representative from Chongqing Garrison Headquarters acknowledged at a July 20, 1945, meeting regarding the prevention of labor strife, "Labor unrest is not entirely caused by economic problems, but other complex reasons."[7] A mid-1946 managerial report on the arsenal labor disputes indicates that workers had four interrelated demands: union recognition, keeping wages in line with the cost-of-living index, increasing grain stipends and monetary wages, and eliminating the "dark aspects" of the factory, that is, abuses and corruption. The politicized nature of the labor movement was obvious to the authorities. Several reasons account for the merger of political

and economic issues in the strike wave of 1946. Ongoing negotiations between Chiang Kai-shek and Mao Zedong mediated by General George C.
Marshall indirectly opened up political space for social movements, since
the Nationalist government wanted to avoid appearing too heavy-
handed. The connection between social movements and the unfolding political drama was not lost on the industry's leaders. "They [student
demonstrations and labor strikes] were especially active during the Political Consultative Conference," Ordnance Director Yang Jizeng noted.[8]
Second, the government became a magnet for workers' resentment, since
it managed all strategic industries, regulated wages, and allocated benefits. Although state intervention in the economy might provide social cohesion and stability, its mismanagement pushed workers' economic demands into the political arena. Workers expected to receive social welfare
amenities, yet the incapacity of the government and state-owned industries to fulfill their promises and the widespread perception of government corruption caused workers' attitudes toward the government to
harden. Finally, the authoritarian response of the government, as exemplified by its quick resort to armed force, further polarized labor and
management.

Just as economic and political demands fueled workers' participation
in labor disputes, emotional issues of fairness and sacrifice often underlay their demands, as exemplified by the conflict generated over "Victory
bonuses." Starting in September 1945, state-run industries began issuing
these bonuses in recognition of their employees' wartime sacrifices. Delays in payment, unequal distribution of the bonuses, and poor timing—
coinciding with massive layoffs after the war—reinforced workers' perception that they were on the receiving end of a cruel hoax. Writing in
Xinhua ribao in December 1945, a worker at Arsenal No. 25 articulated
the widespread sense of betrayal among arsenal workers after the war,
saying: "All we thought of was how to make more guns for the War of
Resistance, to kill one more enemy. We waited until the war would be
won, thinking we would have good days ahead. Now look at the result.
The government is truly harsh to us workers."[9]

This issue subsequently provoked a strike at the same factory. Based
on the rigid military hierarchy among arsenals, the distribution of "Victory bonuses" had the unintended effect of polarizing workers against
management. Large gaps existed between the bonuses of officers and
workers. Whereas most workers, depending on their skill level, received
between 1,400 to 8,000 yuan, bonuses for lower-ranking staff started at

a minimum of 25,000 yuan. Middle and high-ranking management received from 60,000 to 100,000 yuan, and the arsenal director got as much as 120,000 yuan. Workers responded by appropriating nationalist rhetoric and using it against management. They appended slogans at each office, insulting the factory director by branding him a "Han traitor."[10] Workers struck on October 26, 1945, but were quickly suppressed when additional guard battalions were deployed; 39 workers were arrested, and over 400 were fired.[11]

The strikes and slowdowns at the arsenals were marked by their militancy and emotional fervor. The strike at the Gangqianhui, better known as the Dadukou steel mill, on March 23, 1946, was one of the most dramatic. The entire narrative of the strike became contested in a war of words between labor and management, with each side working to impose its own version of events. To avoid a possible reprimand from his superiors in the central government, Yang Jizeng, the acting steel mill director, and newly promoted head of the Ordnance Department, sought to justify his use of force. Workers tried to sway public opinion by using the Communist and liberal press to portray themselves as martyrs in a righteous cause, and the Xinhua news agency, always keen on building its political capital, supported and propagated the strike as it unfolded. Not surprisingly, discrepancies arose regarding the actions and motives of strike participants, reaffirming the factory's class divisions. The context of the strike, though, should be seen as a response to deteriorating economic conditions, in both absolute and relative terms, and a push for unionization. A reconstruction of the related strikes demonstrates the dialectical relationship between workers' organization and the spontaneity of conflict. The strike also illustrates workers' aspirations, as well as the diverging demands and tactics of militant workers and Communists.

Delays in the readjustment of wages and distribution of welfare benefits precipitated the strike.[12] The previous year, management had stopped selling rice to workers' dependents and begun distributing a rice stipend. The change dismayed workers, who saw the stipend's value plunge relative to the market value of rice. Moreover, the ensuing conflict was yet another instance in which social welfare policies rendered management vulnerable to charges of neglect and graft. "Welfare benefits do not reach workers, but are monopolized by the director and section leaders," angry workers wrote *Xinhua ribao* that March. "Since last November, we have still not received oil, salt, or matches. Rationed cloth has not been issued for a long time. Who is it that has been taking over the welfare budgets?"[13] In short, workers perceived the delays as the latest in a long list of injustices perpetrated by corrupt managers.

On March 21, over a thousand workers assembled outside the factory office and submitted a list of twelve demands.[14] These included a 100 percent wage increase, an eight-hour workday, increased compensation in case of injury or death, the right to unionize, workers' election of supervisors and foremen, participation in factory meetings, freedom to read books and newspapers, and freedom of speech and assembly.

For the director, Yang Jizeng, workers' efforts to send representatives to participate in meetings and their demands to organize unions were the two most explosive demands. The desire to be represented at all future factory meetings indicates that workers wanted more than just a representative to resolve the immediate wage dispute. These demands (workers used the word *yaoqiu* for demand, rather than the less deferential *qingqiu*, or request) constituted a more daring and permanent change in the way factory decisions would be made and how power would be structured. They also reveal how the very process of collective action had spurred workers' efforts to unionize and thus politicized their demands. Reflecting the deep divisions between labor and management, Yang Jizeng viewed the two demands as outlandish and an affront to the natural order of things. "Obviously, besides the adjustment of wages, these were side issues raised to create obstacles. But this committee [the steel mill] is a military institution where discipline is of the greatest importance. We cannot accept these clauses, especially if we are restricted to answering within twelve hours as if it were an ultimatum. Their abnormal behavior was totally preposterous."

In a meeting convened by Yuan Shizhong, chief of the guard battalion, negotiations ensued between the workers and department heads. According to Director Yang, department chiefs explained to workers that the steel mill had already decided to increase wages and had petitioned the Ordnance Department, which had authorized wage hikes. Workers "could rest easy" on this matter. Other clauses might also be accepted, but those detrimental to discipline, that is, "joining all internal factory meetings and freely organizing a union" could not be promised. Yuan then instructed workers to "go back to work peacefully." By 5 P.M., Yang reported, they had begun to disperse.

The following day, management tried to secure the loyalty of the workforce by appealing to foremen, whom they viewed as informal labor representatives. Although foremen constituted the bottom link in the management chain, most had risen from workers' ranks, and subforemen continued to work on the production line. Consequently, management felt confident that they had a certain amount of respect among workers and could pacify the labor force. Department heads thus convened all foremen and discussed the steel mill's "deep concern and care" for the workers with them. That afternoon, arsenal security guards reassembled the foremen and discussed the arsenal's decision to increase wages and to assist workers desiring to return home. But just as the meeting adjourned with the foremen, who appeared satisfied with management's proposals, five workers' representatives, chosen and led by Xiang Dingshan, a twenty-one-year-old graduate of the skilled workers' school, convened a closed meeting. Apparently, the foremen had lost their credibility (already signaled when workers demanded to elect their own foremen), because Xiang and his fellow workers rejected management's proposals and decided to strike the morning of March 23.

If Yang Jizeng's report was accurate, the workers' tactics demonstrated a well-thought-out plan rather than a spontaneous riot, as official reports later characterized the strike. Strikers would first force the power station to shut off electrical power, thus immobilizing the entire steel mill. If guards protected the power station, workers would threaten to use hand grenades. After the power was shut off, strikers would march in protest into the city (a distance of ten miles) and petition the Ordnance Department. Contemporary sources are not very explicit, but workers may also have begun organizing a union prior to the strike. Oral histories compiled in the 1950s indicate that after workers first met with Yuan Shizhong on March 21, they selected forty-six representatives (many of them CAL members) and formed a union. Xiang Dingshan was elected chairman.[15] Yang Jizeng's mention of the closed meeting led by Xiang may have been an allusion to the union, but management's refusal to accredit unions barred the issue from even being mentioned in official sources.

What transpired that night changed the dynamic of the confrontation and helped transform the strike into a bloodbath. Press reports later in *Xinhua ribao* and *Minzhu bao* speak of the arrest of the workers' representatives and the imposition of martial law, enforced by the transfer of several hundred soldiers to the factory at midnight on March 22. Yang Jizeng, on the other hand, justified the arrests and martial law as a necessary deterrent. Xiang Dongshan and others "went everywhere convening meetings, actively manipulating, coercing, threatening. . . . We learned not only about the strike but also about their decision to destroy this factory's vital equipment. This method demonstrates their desire to destroy the national defense industry." Even if Yang's accusation expresses his genuine fear of an armed insurrection, there is a fair amount of hyperbole here, since workers had planned to stay within legal avenues by going over the heads of the factory management and appealing directly to the Ordnance Department. Some of the workers' propaganda activities must have transpired, though, because slogans were posted up throughout the factory complex and workshops the next morning. Among these were: "Demand to organize unions!"; "Demand an eight-hour day!"; "No more arbitrary dismissals!"; "We want fair wage adjustments!"; "Improve workers' livelihood and welfare!"[16]

The arrests enraged the workers, who felt betrayed in light of Yuan Shizhong's promise. A desire for vengeance added fuel to the fire and led workers into a confrontation with the armed guards stationed in the arsenal. On the morning of March 23, up to 700 workers headed toward the power station. Yang's official report emphasizes the willful nature of the strikers coercing fellow workers into following them. This supposed lack of active and widespread support for the strike was in accord with Yang's view that most of his employees were "extremely pure" workers, who were otherwise manipulated by agitators. According to Yang, the minority of "extreme elements" shut down the water and electrical departments and then forced other workers to proceed to the investigation section. There, the strikers severely beat and humiliated the fire brigade chief. One worker took a steel rod and beat the leader of the third guard section on the head with it until he lost consciousness. When a guest of the garrison headquarters tried leaving the factory compound, workers blocked the jeep and beat up the driver and the passenger. An officer who tried driving to Chongqing on business was dragged out of his car and severely beaten up. "He was covered with bruises and blood ran over his entire face. Workers were still not reconciled. They tried to entice, surround, and arrest Yuan, chief of the guard battalion. He fled from the top of a hill and began to escape. The extreme elements seized a machine gun. The guards were forced to fire their guns into a clear space to strike fear into them. Workers gradually began to disperse."

Yang's description captures the emotional fervor underlying workers' militancy. But who were these workers? Both sides describe them as an undifferentiated mass, probably because both laborers and skilled workers participated in the strike. But many of the strike leaders and workers' representatives came from the skilled workers' school. Yang Jinhua, a former steelworker, recalls that students in the training school and underground activists mobilized workers from each department (the small furnace workshop, the steel rod plant, the small and large rolling plants, the foundry and machine factory) to join the strike.[17] Skilled workers, such as Xiang Zhongshan, made more natural leaders because of their degree of urbanization, literacy, and pride of craft. As beneficiaries of considerable investment by management, the students of the training school may have also felt less threatened by possible reprisals. Political connections further facilitated their mobilization. The CCP underground, which was reportedly working behind the scenes to mobilize workers, had contact with the skilled workers' school students. Moreover, CAL committee members, such as Sun Zhicheng, were involved in the strike leadership.[18]

Conversely, the only group of workers who did not strike were some of the least skilled, the transport workers employed by the steel mill. Skill level per se may not have been the determining factor in strike involvement, since laborers involved in direct production also joined the strike. Rather, the geographical isolation from the production workers who initiated the strike and the fact that some of the transport workers were war veterans made it more difficult for them to challenge the military authorities. The Gelaohui, which generally had a good deal of say in the hiring of transport workers and porters, may have also played a part in securing their discipline.[19]

Considerable evidence suggests that the conflict stemmed from management's refusal to recognize workers' demands for collective representation and wage increases, coupled with its prompt use of heavy-handed tactics. In the early morning hours of March 23, close to 500 soldiers were transferred to the steel mill. Ten machine guns were set up on hilltops around the factory complex. In the war of words that followed the strike, workers quickly pointed out that management's use of the military had inevitably led to conflict. As one fleeing worker later told *Minzhu bao* reporters, "There obviously was a plan to massacre workers. At the time, management's troops surrounded all the workers. We carried no weapons. We were unable even to flee. Who was even going to counterattack?"[20]

In contrast to the official report, sources more sympathetic to the workers noted that the strike had been fairly well organized. Because of the arrests, the strike began sooner than workers had originally planned. Workers stopped their machines at 6 A.M. when their night shift was over and proceeded to shut off the power and water. Once the strike started, three teams of workers marched in demonstration to the guard section office. By 8 A.M., they had assembled and begun to demand the release of their representatives. Workers grabbed hold of the security guard Wu Xiaoxi, a suspect in the arrest of the workers' representatives, and had him lead the group of workers to Yuan Shizhong. Accounts vary as to what happened next, but all accuse the guard battalion leader of murder. In the most graphic account, after workers demanded the prisoners' release from Wu, military police blew a bugle. Soon afterward, Yuan came riding up on a horse, followed by a coterie of guards. Yuan opened fire first, killing one worker. As workers began to flee, machine guns placed on the surrounding hills opened fire.[21]

The strike was rapidly suppressed, leaving casualties on both sides.[22] In its aftermath, management stopped all production, imposed martial law, and restricted movement. Guards from Arsenal No. 1 transferred to Dadukou district, and a battalion of soldiers was stationed at nearby Zamawang . Workers were forbidden to go into staff's residential area, perhaps to render managerial space sacrosanct again, or to prevent further conflict. Workers were prohibited from moving between workers' residential areas or from leaving the factory complex. *Minzhu bao* headlines flared, "Troops stationed at factory threaten workers: 'If anyone takes a step outside the factory, they will immediately be shot dead.'" In this way, the entire affair would be covered up, as critics of management contended. Meanwhile, leading activists who had participated in the "riot" were either fired or brought before a military tribunal and imprisoned.

Yang Jizeng also sought to foster dependency on the factory and to restore the pre-strike social fabric through an elaborate registration process that forced workers to state their loyalty to the factory. The strike had battered its authority so much that management felt constrained to fire and then rehire the entire workforce. Production was thus delayed until April 4, ten days after the strike. For their efforts and sacrifice, workers had gained the full 100 percent wage increase. It had taken the workers' struggle to once again alert management to the need to dissipate further conflict by conceding wages and benefits to their workers. As one official report, which the Ordnance Department authorized to circulate among all arsenals, concluded: "If we desire to prevent future turmoil, we must do our utmost to improve workers' treatment and welfare so that workers trust the authorities and a feeling of affection is created toward all personnel ranks."[23]

Management made these concessions convinced that the strike was the handiwork of a few "bad elements," an allusion to Communist activists. No doubt the CCP played an important subsidiary role by galvanizing public opinion after the strike and placing pressure on management to meet workers' demands. Between the outset of the strike and imposition of martial law, *Xinhua ribao* published more than a dozen articles on the steel mill strike critical of management or expressing solidarity on the part of other Chongqing factory workers.[24] The end of the war had also stimulated underground members to renew mobilizing. By October 1945, the Southern Bureau established a labor movement leadership cell, which took as its mission: "setting the current task of the labor movement as opposition to civil war and dictatorship, support for workers' reasonable demands, and linkage between political and economic struggle."[25]

Yet workers acted independently and in certain crucial respects were at odds with Communist underground activists. It was precisely on the issue of unionization where Communist activists diverged from the more militant workers, as is evident in Du Yanqing's January 1947 report to Party Central. With the advantage of hindsight, Du argued that the working class had committed subjective errors, that it had been overly militant during the strike. Whereas the CCP had not been "overly active demanding workers' own organizations," the steelworkers had gone beyond voicing "reasonable demands" in seeking a union and representation for workers at factory directors' meetings.[26] Given the relative weakness of labor organizations in the strictly controlled arsenals, workers had suffered huge losses. The arrest of progressive workers, an increase in spying, and prohibition of *Xinhua ribao* had made underground work even more difficult after 1946.

Although Du placed some of the responsibility for political defeat on workers' "subjective errors," he acknowledged that wartime deprivation and conflict with the Guomindang had politicized workers, especially the younger and more militant generation. Despite weak organizational forces and a repressive terrain to cover, "the struggle continues to explode unabated between workers, who seek to survive, and the Guomindang and capitalists. This situation proves that during the War of Resistance, class consciousness was greatly raised among workers in the Great Rear. The class consciousness of the workers I got to know, especially young workers who experienced the war, is even more evident. They detest the Guomindang."[27] His realization suggests that like-minded other CCP activists had felt compelled to respond to workers' militancy and mobilize mass industrial action. But because of its lingering adherence to

United Front politics, the CCP found itself playing catch-up with the workers.

Contradictions between militant workers and party strategists, stemming from their differing approaches to class struggle and their competing priorities, emerged during the strikes of 1946. Whereas workers sought to protect their own interests, the CCP, in somewhat contradictory fashion, sought to strike a devastating blow at the Nationalists but maintain a secure base. While the party insisted on operating in the gray political zone of the United Front, radical workers advocated a more clear-cut class struggle.

A position paper (*zibaishu*) by Xie Wanquan, a leader of the Arsenal No. 10 strike, held within days of the Gangqianhui strike, illustrates the diverging interests of militant workers and the CCP.[28] The document, written shortly after Xie's arrest, sheds light on the motivation and goals of radical activists, as well as on the different political lines within the Communist party. Xie was one of those who bridged the divide between the intelligentsia and the workers and served as intellectual agents within the arsenals helping to carry out the class project. A more problematic question is to what degree the duress of the interrogation forced Xie to criticize the Communist Party and stress its undemocratic nature. Perhaps Xie thought he would receive a lighter sentence if he were to criticize the CCP, since in his second and last interrogation, he recanted his involvement with the CCP, saying: "If I could be released, I would plan to tell other workers at this factory not to be deceived by the Communist Party."[29] The position paper, I would suggest, does nonetheless reflect Xie's genuine grievances against the party. At the same time, whatever misgivings Xie had about the CCP did not deter him from following through with the strike or continuing his involvement with the party. Moreover, despite having criticized the CCP, Xie neither renounced his radical beliefs nor felt constrained to withhold criticism of authorities, whether on the Left or on the Right. Xie maintained his support of and sympathy for other workers even during his interrogation, saying: "I was influenced by the suffering of many workers with families during this strike."

Despite their frequent intellectual exchanges, tension existed between Xie Wanquan and the Communist activists. On the one hand, Xie's job as a twelfth rank technician, a drafter in the engineering office, must have exposed him to the manners and speech of more educated intellectuals, which he sought to emulate. For this, he would be criticized by party members, who believed Xie's role in the labor movement required embracing what they saw as the culture of the working class. The criticism worked both ways, since Xie also chastised party members for unwittingly looking down on workers. For example, Xie challenged Tang Yun, a fellow Sichuanese and Communist leader who worked at Arsenal No. 20 for having discarded his working-class clothes: "One Sunday [in] October [1945], while I was waiting at the station to take the bus into Chongqing, I saw Tang Yun waiting for the bus. When Zhang introduced me to Tang, he had been wearing workers' clothes. When I saw him this time, Tang was wearing a Western-style suit. The style was something a worker would never wear. I used this to question him."

After Xie submitted an application to the party in the spring of 1945, he frequently met with Tang Yun to discuss politics. Xie recalled frequent discussions with *Xinhua* journalists about Chiang Kai-shek's speeches. It was in one such discussion, after Tang had asked him to express his criticisms of the CCP freely (standard fare for party applicants), that Xie Wanquan voiced his dissent:

(1) If the Communist Party is a political party implementing Marxism and Leninism, why does it have to recognize the Three People's Principles? Otherwise, the Communist Party might as well dissolve itself and join the Nationalist Party.

(2) With regard to Maoism, isn't it dictatorial to take Mao Zedong thought as the guiding and central ideology of the party?

(3) The news that Madame Mao Zedong came to Chongqing to get medical treatment for tooth trouble contradicts the party's effort to unite its members and instruct them to bear hardships and put up with hard work. Madame Mao is not a well-known figure. Among over a million Communist Party members, there are those who have made important contributions and whose achievements are brilliant, and those stricken with serious illness. Is it possible that they do not suffer as much as Madame Mao? Yet Madame Mao can fly to Chongqing for medical treatment.

I feel the Communist Party also blindly submits itself. The upper strata are corrupted; the lower strata are enslaved.[30]

Xie's outspoken views bear striking resemblance to those of the intellectual dissident Wang Shiwei at the Communist base of Yan'an.[31] Both sought to strengthen the party by exposing its undemocratic and authoritarian qualities. In criticizing Jiang Qing (Madame Mao), Xie accuses the party of cosseting a privileged elite divorced from its social base and contrary to the revolution's egalitarian goals. However, Xie differed from Wang Shiwei in one important respect. Because of his social background, Xie viewed questions of inequality and revolution through the prism of class analysis. This approach is exemplified in his more manichaean approach to revolution and his defense of workers' class interests, issues that he debated with Communist activists.

Tang Yun's response and his directions to Xie Wanquan exemplified the dissonance between party strategists and radical militant workers over means and ends to revolutionary action. Whereas Xie saw the CCP's adherence to Sun Yat-sen's thought as a betrayal of Marxist-Leninist practice, Tang Yun tried to justify the Three People's Principles in light of the United Front. "When Tang answered me, he said that recognizing the Three People's Principles was a revolutionary means." They did not resolve the issue, but it would seem that the Communist Party's 1940 injunction that cadres should receive "profound class education" so as to be able to distinguish between the ideologies of the GMD and CCP had influenced Xie more than it had Tang. On the question of Maoist hegemony, Tang responded that "the expansion of the Communist party's forces proves the correctness of Mao Zedong's leadership, thus the Communist party took Mao Zedong's thought as its leading center." Unfortunately, Xie did not elaborate on what alternatives to Maoist thought he supported. With regard to Xie's criticism of Jiang Qing, Tang Yun justified her treatment as part of a political strategy. "When Madame Mao came to Chongqing to treat her teeth, she had another special mission. It was not for people like us to make improper comments."[32]

Although Xie continued to meet with underground party members, he became frustrated with Tang Yun's adherence to clandestine tactics. By March 1946, Tang was working in *Xinhua ribao*'s typesetting room and directing the labor movement. Xie's newfound role was to investigate arsenal conditions, and Tang gave him Mao's *Village Investigations* as a reference for this assignment, in addition to documents on the rectification campaign. To facilitate his work, Xie was to penetrate enemy ranks. "He urged me to go into hiding and to rope in the less advanced [people in terms of consciousness] by using the Youth Corps. . . . Avoid by all means getting dragged into politics. When you are talking with workers, do not bring up Chiang Kai-shek, Mao Zedong, the Nationalist Party or the Communist Party to avoid exposing yourself and scaring off worker masses." But Xie disagreed. "If one was not exposed, this demonstrated one had not done any work . . . Tang then criticized me saying I was a phony revolutionary, that my theory did not match reality, and that I had committed the error of indulging in exaggerations." Tang espoused Zhou Enlai's underground party strategy of lying low and building up one's strength. In contrast, Xie feared he would be emasculated as a radical if he cooperated with the arsenal's power brokers. How was one to build up strength without exposing oneself, and if one didn't expose oneself, could revolutionary work continue to have any meaning?

Whereas Xie describes Tang as a more cautious clandestine activist in his strategy, by the eve of the Arsenal No. 10 strike, Tang and Xie had reversed positions. Now it was Tang who fanned the fires of labor unrest. Tang's espousal of a more militant position and open mobilization strategy reflected CCP efforts to take advantage of the escalating labor movement and respond to widespread anger among workers. The government and managers' inability to pay wages on time, corruption, mass layoffs, and the widespread feeling among workers that they were treated with disrespect increased their frustration, anger, and disillusionment. For Tang Yun, the time for a mass offensive had arrived, and he was determined to grab the opportunity. Xie now describes Tang as an advocate of adventurism, pressing for a militant strike wave even at the cost of sacrificing workers' interests. Whereas Xie cautioned that "the environment of Arsenal No. 10 and its distinct managerial style make it extremely difficult to start a struggle," Tang exuded optimism. "In a revolution, only develop the circumstances, do not heed the difficulties. I hope you embolden yourself to do the work." Tang enjoined Xie to "mobilize a struggle" at Arsenal No. 10 in response to the Gangqianhui strike while he stirred up all the arsenals and used *Xinhua* to shape public opinion. Xie was still wary. "You need to see the situation, if we can mobilize, we'll mobilize. If we can't mobilize, we won't mobilize, to prevent workers from getting the worst of it." Tang continued to pressure Xie noting that it wasn't good to be faint-hearted. "I don't have high hopes of you. If you don't mobilize, there are other people who can mobilize."

Tang Yun's transformation to advocacy of mass industrial action illustrates the psychology and motivations of underground activists. As soon as the political opportunity presented itself, party members proved eager to shed their clandestine tactics and guise to strike a blow at the authorities by leading open mass struggle. This changeover to militancy validated working underground to serve the end of open revolutionary struggle, but as Tim Mason has noted of the Italian Resistance, the dilemma for activists was the timing and form of the future struggle.[33] Miscalculation could easily incriminate militants among the rank and file, leading to the arrest of underground members and dooming the entire enterprise.

Despite his differences with Tang Yun, Xie Wanquan followed through with the strike. His growing radicalization and sense of loyalty to the CCP were strong motivating factors. Perhaps he was encouraged when the party had commended him for investigating factory conditions before the slowdown. Xie may have also been inspired by Tang Yun's goal of supporting the steel mill workers and striking a blow at the government by mobilizing the strike. Nevertheless, Xie kept the CCP at arm's length by trying to protect the workers' interest rather than that of the party. Xie and his fellow activists were careful to avoid making direct ideological appeals in favor of the Communist Party. The militant minority emphasized the need for workers to maintain their political autonomy and class interests. "We workers need to fend for ourselves to bring about our own happiness, our own well-being, and to improve our lives," a militant worker named Peng Ji'an said. Xie underscored that political representation was necessary if workers were to gain an equal footing in society: "I frequently asked them why we workers had no clout? I answered, 'because there is no official minister among us workers. If workers are to have an influence, workers must engage in politics. We must first seek improvement in our economic livelihood and then seek equality in our political status.'"[34] Finally, Xie retained a flexible policy going into the slowdown with a view to damage control. If the go-slow had no effect, a strike would be called. If workers could achieve their most pressing demands, work would resume. If not even the bare minimum could be realized, workers would see the attitude of management. If management used force, Xie and other activists would bring the strike to an end and not "fight recklessly with management."[35]

As with the strike at the Gangqianhui steel mill, a combination of economic and moral grievances fueled conflict at Arsenal No. 10. At 2 P.M. on March 25, only two days after the strike at Dadukou, several departments in the arsenal staged a slowdown, following the lead of department 8. Over the next two days, workers throughout the arsenal downed their tools to protest wage cuts and official malfeasance. The strikers accused Shen Gengzu, the arsenal's labor board director and acting proxy for the arsenal director, of having raised wages only 20 percent for skilled workers, 15 percent for apprentices, and 10 percent for laborers, despite an Ordnance Department order to raise wages by 80 percent across the board. The parallels to the steel mill are striking, although in this case, the different wage rates seem to have been consciously designed to divide and fragment the workforce. Workers responded to management in various ways, and their grievances changed over the course of the ensuing conflict, but during the slowdown, workers put forward three main demands: that management increase wages by 50 percent; that it distribute production bonuses on a monthly basis; and that the government pay the transportation costs of workers who had been dismissed and were returning home.[36]

That much of the arsenal workforce could stand idle by their machines starting at 2 P.M. that day suggests considerable coordination on the part of workers. In contrast to the strike at Dadukou, where workers acted autonomously, at Arsenal No. 10, the CCP underground and militant workers organized and coordinated the go-slow. Prior to the strike, Xie Wanquan was in frequent contact with Tang Yun discussing how best to mobilize workers. From these discussions, Xie developed a twofold strategy. Xie hoped to "win over semi-open and open organizations," such as the Green Gang, the basketball team, and the literary and artistic discussion group, by having members swear brotherhood among themselves. In turn, Xie would develop a core of leaders from the brotherhoods. The second part of Xie's plan involved placing two to three activists in each department to mobilize other workers for the slowdown. According to the sources, the latter tactic was the more successful of the two.[37]

Xie used his contacts and friendships to develop a growing network of committed activists, who formed a secret labor organization. Although we lack details of the organization's role, its name—the Workers' Mutual-Aid Society—suggests the subculture of opposition. These men do not seem to have joined the CCP, but their interrogators branded them as leftists because of their outspoken political views. Xie first won over Liu Zhenglin, who worked in the inspection office, and then "absorbed" several other workers employed in various departments who knew the fitter Peng Ji'an, a former classmate. Before the slowdown, Xie instructed them to gather information about factory conditions and personnel, which he then passed on to the CCP. Above all, Xie's group was to research social relationships within the arsenal to understand what rifts could be exploited during a strike and the basis of management's support. In accordance with Tang Yun's recommendation, Xie spoke to workers about the reasons for their misery: "I tried my utmost to explain why workers suffered, as well as the various types of management oppression, and that workers' conditions stimulated their hatred of management."[38]

To initiate the slowdown, Xie directed Peng Ji'an to contact various workers: Lin Daoxin in the eighth department; Wu Bodong, a skilled worker in the second department; Cui Wenbin, a worker in the mortar department; and Liu Zhenglin, an inspector. Peng and his friends raised their three demands with department chiefs, and each led workers to follow the slowdown.[39] Then to mobilize public opinion, Xie delivered an article to the *Xinhua* news agency on the evening of March 25, which Tang Yun published the following day.

CAL members backed the action by organizing Arsenal No. 10 workers to support the strikers at the Gangqianhui. Shen Yongfa, a skilled worker originally from Shanghai, had joined CAL in July 1945 and quickly became responsible for accepting application cards and transmitting them to the central CAL office. After the steel mill strike, Shen elicited donations of 3,700 yuan from fifty of his fellow workers in departments 5, 7, and 8 on March 25 and enlisted thirty other workers to collect money. For Shen, this expression of solidarity exemplified workers' class feelings and sense of shared destiny. "Because we are all workers, we share the same interests. Everyone is on the same line. . . . The strike [at Dadukou] was abortive, and people were shot there, so we are in the same boat. Facing disaster, we asked everyone to make a small contribution to show our support and sympathy."[40]

Besides these activists, how conscious were rank-and-file workers that their impending struggle was linked to that of the steel mill workers? Recent scholarship on the politics of labor has emphasized the locally oriented quality of strikes, premised on the view that "the factory workshop was often a world unto itself."[41] In this particular case, though, the arsenal workers were well aware of the Dadukou strike. According to Xiao Jiazhu, a twenty-year-old apprentice and Youth Corps member, "before the slowdown, I heard many workers on the playing field discussing the fact that Factory No. 3 had already gone on strike, and that many people had been beaten to death." Xiao was not terribly sympathetic to the strikers (probably because other workers mistakenly viewed him as a GMD spy, as he later noted), and he considered the steel mill strike and the exhortations of *Xinhua ribao* to have precipitated the arsenal strike.[42] Probably the leading piece of evidence linking labor-management conflict at Arsenal No. 10 to other workers' struggles is the timing of the strike. Arsenal No. 10 went on strike, for the first time in its history, only two days after the strike at Dadukou. Lastly, the Arsenal No. 10 workers made a conscious decision not to appoint representatives so as to avoid arrests like those that had occurred at the steel mill.

The slowdown could not have taken place so rapidly and effectively without prior organizing, but some workshops, such as department 3, did not participate that day. To try and mount a factorywide offensive, workers who were participating in the slowdown went to the dormitory of department 3 to tell the workers there that they had already stopped their machines. The next day, according to Chen Jiafu, a twenty-year-old laborer in the department, the workers all entered the workshop at the start of the shift and turned over their attendance tags. Then Tian Yabo and Hu Zhiseng came running out holding a paper on which they had written seven conditions and called on all workers to sign it with their seals. Over a hundred workers stamped it with their seals, after which everyone in department 3 left the workshops and returned to the dormitory.[43]

Chen Jiafu's account does not explain why workers went into the workshop in the first place, only to come out suddenly. Did workers believe turning over their attendance cards, even without starting the machines, would appease management? More likely, many workers only realized that there was a strike on once they had reached the factory. Tian Yabo, the leader of the department 3 walkout, may have also influenced them to down their tools. Tian denied any leadership role, however, saying that he had only found out about the slowdown when he read about it that morning in *Xinhua ribao*, and that he had proceeded to the factory despite encountering hostile workers outside the plant who threatened to beat up anyone entering the factory to work.[44] No one was working at the factory, despite the department head's order to resume work. When the department director, Zhang, saw that he was making no headway, he told Tian and other workers to submit a written report rather than confronting him with their requests face-to-face. Tian and some thirty other workers discussed their proposals and then wrote down their conditions.

The way Tian and other workers protested was in keeping with moral and legal customs. The widespread use of the seal, reflecting literacy and solidarity on the part of the workers, was typical of petitions to government authorities. Workers proceeded with caution and deference, choosing the word "request" rather than "demand" in their list of conditions. No doubt department 3 workers feared being sacked, because over 600 of their fellow arsenal workers had recently joined the ranks of the unemployed.[45] This abiding fear may also help explain why Tian Yabo emerged as a labor activist, since his Nationalist Party membership and his father's position as a cadre in the central GMD administration might lessen the degree of punishment.

Tian Yabo's list of demands gives us clues as to the state of mind among the striking workers. Only one condition was identical to the three demands made the previous day: distribution of bonuses on a monthly basis. Whereas the previous day's demands had focused on the wage dispute, workers in department 3 raised this issue in a more general way, seeking payment of wages based on the city's standard-of-living adjustments. The issue of severance pay preoccupied department 3, as reflected by two of the strikers' conditions. Workers desired job security, or at least the guarantee that some social insurance would be provided in case of dismissal. The most important change in the workers' demands concerned injustice in the workplace. The workers' final condition spoke to the unequal wage and benefit distribution among factory employees. "No matter whether staff or worker, everyone should receive equal treatment."[46]

For Xie Wanquan, workers' deep resentment of managerial discrimination was the driving force behind the strike. "Because of management's treatment of workers, the oppression is too great, and all aspects of their treatment are just too unequal, so that workers usually feel hatred in their hearts. As a result, workers completely gave vent to their feelings in this strike."[47] When asked to specify what he meant by oppressive management, Xie recounted a litany of complaints documenting the unjust relationship between workers and staff. Among Xie's nine listed grievances, four focused on the disparities between conditions at the residential areas of managerial staff and workers, known as Village No. 1 and Village No. 2. In terms of entertainment, the club in the latter had only "one newspaper, a few books, and no equipment worth mentioning." By contrast, the staff village had a more complete collection of books, newspapers, and equipment. Water and electricity supply also varied. In the Village No. 1 bathhouse, hot water was supplied at designated times, whereas in the workers' village, "they frequently supply only cold water, most shower nozzles are broken, and no one repairs them." Xie also felt disgruntled that the staff residential area had electricity throughout the night, while the power in Village No. 2 was cut off at specified times. Food was another problem. "The meals for workers at Village No. 2 are bad. To save money, they serve leftovers, rather than increasing the courses."

Xie's grievances also spoke to authority relations within the arsenals and the feeling that workers did not receive adequate respect from management and other employees. Xie described personnel at the accountant's office and the facilities office as having an "incredibly arrogant attitude when giving out money to workers." The guard battalion chief and his soldiers added to workers' feeling of being disrespected by frequently and deliberately adjusting the position of workers' badges. These daily reminders to workers of their subordination must have been all the more humiliating in that the workers considered the soldiers, many of them originally poor Sichuanese peasants, to be of lower social status. Rather than denouncing working conditions, Xie limited himself to attacking the arbitrary and brusque manner in which workers were fined. "Management fines workers so impolitely. If they want to fine you, they go ahead, without leaving workers any leeway for appeal." Finally, Xie criticized the prisonlike atmosphere of the arsenal, citing the time limits imposed on workers seeking to enter or exit the factory, as well as the numerous trivial procedures for guest registration.[48] These feelings were not his alone, but widespread among workers, as evidenced by certain symbolic actions taken during the ensuing strike at Arsenal No. 10.

As in all labor disputes, the actions of management shaped both the process and the eventual outcome. To defuse the mounting tension, the acting director, Shen Gengzu, convened all department and section heads on the evening of March 25 and issued a response to the workers' three original demands. Supplemental wages would be raised by 20 percent, and workers would also receive a raise of half a work point, but daily overtime would have to be increased by two hours in return. Regarding workers' demands for the monthly distribution of bonuses, Shen promised that the March bonus would be distributed by April 8, and that the April, May, and June bonuses would all be paid before July 8. Finally, Shen tried to assure workers that no one would be dismissed. If future discharges occurred, workers would be granted severance pay. But on this concession, Shen argued that as acting director, he lacked the authority to make any guarantees.[49]

The general level of mistrust between workers and management stemmed in part from administrative changes that had occurred after V-J Day. In October 1945, the former arsenal director Zhang Quan had transferred out to supervise the takeover of northeast China's arsenals from the surrendering Japanese. Ding Tianxiong had replaced Zhang as director of both Arsenal No. 50 and its branch factory, Arsenal No. 10. Because of the distance between the arsenals, as well as their administrative complexity, Ding had delegated authority to Shen when he was not residing at Arsenal No. 10. These changes heightened workers' uncertainty about their arsenal's management. Ding's sacking of over 600 workers that fall compounded workers' impressions of an uncaring and irresponsible director, distant from the daily functioning of the arsenal. To make matters worse, Shen had eroded any remaining trust when he reduced movie showings, allegedly to pocket the 70,000 to 80,000 yuan needed for movie expenses.[50] The unequal wage scale was one further reminder of Shen's malfeasance. His lack of a definite answer to their demands regarding severance pay added insult to injury. Finally, despite Shen's assurances that workers could retain their jobs, the proposed work hour increase in exchange for higher wages must have been extremely provocative. Coming as it did in a period of reduced production, the proposal signaled open license for mass layoffs. Workers pushed to strike the following day.

The strike started uneventfully, perhaps because it was a Sunday. Workers either remained in their dormitory rooms, outside the factory complex walls or went to work. In the latter case, as we have seen, these workers quickly returned to the dormitories, confirming investigative and guard section reports that the strike became factorywide. Only workers in the mess hall, acting upon instructions of the strikers, remained on the job, so as to provide food to the strikers. Until that afternoon, the greatest commotion arose over a symbolic act of defiance. Mao Ren'gan, a Sichuanese draft worker in the engineering office, broke the steel-plated bell used to signal work shifts, located near a workers' dormitory.[51]

The strike forced Ding Tianxiong to meet with skilled workers in hope of winning over the most influential members of the workforce. (Ding's actions resembled the steel mill officers' appeals to the foremen at Dadukou.) Ding then assembled workers at an athletic field in the first residential village to "instruct and persuade," but without apparent success. Even before the meeting, trouble was brewing. A Sichuanese forge worker in training saw the director leave his office and began shouting from a distance, "Shoot him, drag that son of a bastard out, shoot him!" Once workers assembled on the field, more disruption occurred when Director Ding had his bureau director represent him on a makeshift platform and speak to the assembled workers. Workers clamored for and challenged the director to speak instead, saying: "We want Factory Director Ding to get on stage himself, to speak on stage, and to express his views to us all and let everyone listen."[52]

Not that everyone would listen, because workers expressed their discontent, despair, and hatred. When Ding Tianxiong finally addressed the crowd, one worker in the audience swayed back and forth brandishing a cudgel. A construction laborer demanding greater respect yelled out, "Are laborers not people?" Another worker grew exasperated with the director and shouted, "Fucking fart! Let's go, let's go. Whoever doesn't leave is a cuckold." The war of words continued after Ding finished speaking. Guards reported that workers yelled out, "Let's go, beat him, grab him!" The trainee forge worker yelled out, "It's too unfair!" Anticipating conflict, Xian Ziqiang, an ammunition loader from Hebei, shouted from the back of the crowd, "If we are going to die, everyone is going to die!"[53]

After the meeting broke up at dusk, Ding returned to the home of the proxy arsenal director, Shen. "All the workers [according to the trainee forge worker], wanted to go into the street, enter the residence, and beat up the factory director." Several hundred workers then surrounded Shen's residence and began hurling insults, before presenting ten demands. These demands were never listed, but clues are offered by the interrogation record of Liu Wenqing, a seventeen-year-old Sichuanese laborer. Liu indicated that he had led the entire group and become a spokesman for the workers. Speaking in front of the window, Liu discussed his grievances with a guard section leader and a personnel officer, both of whom remained inside. "I proposed that they should show more movies. Everyone picked me to be in charge to say that we wanted to eat, to be paid more, to see movies, to go into the city to watch them."[54] It was at this point that workers accused Shen of embezzling movie fees. When the security chiefs came out of the building and explained that management would post a response the next morning, most of the workers retreated. No issue had been resolved, though, and in fact the class violence escalated when several dozen workers began throwing stones and clods of dirt at the house, breaking the windows before the guard section leader chased them away.[55]

By the morning of March 27, management had responded to the ten demands, but workers remained dissatisfied. Workers now demanded an across-the-board 80 percent raise, more than what they had originally asked for and in keeping with the Ordnance Department's mandate. Workers also opposed Shen Gengzu's proposed two-hour work increase, now scheduled to start on April 1. Their fourth demand, as guard reports note, concerned the issue of "guaranteed employment" and an end to arbitrary firings.[56] To make sure Shen would not double-cross them, workers insisted that they would only resume work once the factory director responded in a public notice. Indicative of the workers' suspicion, they refused to accept the conditions of the previous day, because the document lacked the factory seal. Although the March 27 notice did include the factory seal, workers rejected it, among other reasons, for lacking the factory director's personal seal.[57]

To beef up support for management's plans, the investigation section leader, Yan Guowei, and his guards entered the workers' village, where they assembled small groups of workers and tried to persuade them to appoint representatives and resume work the following morning. If the resolve of some workers was beginning to crumble, others "fanned the flames and threatened, 'Whoever goes to work tomorrow will be beaten up.'" Suspecting representatives would be arrested as at Dadukou, a skilled worker blurted out, "No one wants to be used by spies." Shen Qichang, a thirty-two-year-old apprentice from Zhejiang, addressed the entire crowd, protesting the additional two hours' overtime that management was asking for.[58]

Faced with continued resistance to negotiations, Yan Guowei proceeded to call in the troops and mobilize gang members to break the strike. On March 27, Yan contacted Green Gang leaders in the factory to assemble some two hundred workers to resume work the following day. In case of "tumult," gang members and guard squads would prevent disturbances. Troops were to be stationed at storage areas, explosives caves, and the artillery room within the factory compound, and local army units were posted 600 meters outside the factory, ready to enter the factory grounds and suppress violent workers.[59] That night, the authorities imposed martial law on the factory district to quell the industrial strike, which increasingly resembled a prison uprising. By 11:45 P.M., an artillery battalion platoon from the 25th Division, armed with machine guns and Generalissimo rifles, joined the four hundred soldiers permanently guarding the arsenal.

Under the threat of force, arsenal workers went back to work on March 28. The choice was not easily made. According to the investigation squad, gang workers began to walk into the factory compound, as planned, but found their way blocked when they reached a bridge leading from Village No. 2 into the factory workshops. Anticipating the resumption of work, by 6:30 that morning, strike leaders had convened over two hundred workers to stand on each side of the wooden bridge and prevent workers from passing. Supporters of the strike appealed to their fellow workers' sense of nationalism and also relied on intimidation, saying: "Whoever goes forward to work is a Han traitor, and we'll execute him."[60] Gang leaders hearing the bell signal the start of the shift called on their followers to come forward and go to work, but most stayed behind, fearing conflict with their fellow workers.

At this point, the guard squad leader ordered workers to resume work, threatening severe punishments. Demonstrating their pivotal position in factory politics once again, many skilled workers crossed the bridge, followed eventually by an estimated 80 percent of the workforce. The walk across the bridge must have been brutal, because the two hundred workers remained at the bridge, cursing the squad leader and workers. To avoid the humiliation, one thirty-nine-year-old cement worker from Nanjing and a fellow worker had tried to reach their department by way of a back route, only to encounter some twenty workers from the rifle-cleaning department. As the two men entered the workshop, workers standing alongside the department cursed them as "fucking things, all afraid of breaking our rice bowls. 'You fucking cunt. The old man wants to die. You fucking scabs with family.' We didn't dare say anything and lowered our heads while entering."[61]

The violence of the language reflected the intensity of the struggle against management. From the rifle workers' perspectives, the scabs had clearly violated their own collective interests. Even the scabs acknowledged this by lowering their heads in shame and fear. There was a logic to workers' defense of their class interests, similar to that depicted in Arif Dirlik's analysis of conflict between strikers and scabs during the 1927 Guangzhou uprising: "And yet, it is easy to overlook that, to the radical workers, the scabs were part of a structure of oppression that sought to take away from them the privileges that they had won through difficult struggles—not just against the oppressors, but for their own hard-earned class consciousness."[62]

The strikers' hostility toward management had now turned inward among themselves. As the militant rifle-cleaning worker's language suggests, the older workers' fear of risking job security and family livelihood overrode their commitment to the strike action. On one level, workers' attitudes toward returning to work reflected the generational divisions within the working class, with the older workers prone to greater caution. Strike leaders tended to be in their early twenties, clearly much younger than the thirty-nine-year-old cement worker who was subject to such vitriol. Tang Yun's suggestions to the twenty-one-year-old Xie Wanquan regarding future strikes provide another hint of this fault line along generations. "If the strike is successful, you should not willfully have another unnecessary strike (even if there has been conflict between staff and workers to cause a strike). Because old workers will easily become dissatisfied."[63]

In the immediate aftermath of the strike, divisions among militant and more moderate workers manifested themselves, while investigation squad personnel, aided by department supervisors, arrested workers in the workshops. "The workers of each department made no response, remained silent and continued working as normal, as if they felt this lot of workers should be arrested and kept under guard."[64] There is a generous amount of self-interest generated in Yan Guowei's report, since he sought to earn a commendation for bringing the strike to an end, pacifying the workforce, and bringing workers to heel. Surely, workers' attitudes must have also been shaped by the fear inspired by the arrests taking place before their very eyes.

With the enforcement of martial law, troops quickly brought the strike to an end. Still, there were pockets of resistance, forcing the squad leader by 10 A.M. to proceed to the political education office and broadcast orders to resume work over the loudspeaker system. A platoon of soldiers under the command of the squad chief and guard leader Tang then entered the workers' village, only to find workers from department 3 scattered nearby or in their rooms. At this point, Tian Yabo and seven other workers were arrested, while other workers were forced back into the workshops at gunpoint. Guard and investigation squads immediately brought the arrested men to the Ordnance Department's central office in Chongqing to avoid a recurrence of the Dadukou experience. At the Gangqianhui, the arrest of representatives and imprisonment within the factory compound had provoked further conflict between management and workers seeking their release. In the afternoon, another twenty-six workers, including Xie Wanquan, were arrested inside the workshops and then escorted to the investigation squad's office for questioning and detention. For the next several days, investigation squad personnel worked feverishly into the night and early morning hours interrogating the arrested workers.

There was a range of punishments, fitting the gravity of the crime. The inspection squad leader, who seems to have commanded the fate of all workers, classified his prisoners as primary and secondary offenders. Primary offenders were deemed to have led other workers, instigated the slowdown and strike, and turned openly against the factory authorities and, by implication, the government. The variety of experiences defies neat categorization, but most of the eight primary offenders were relatively young (aged twenty-one to thirty-two), highly literate, technically skilled, and politically leftist. Strike leaders came from a variety of regions: eastern Sichuan, Nanjing, Shanghai, and Hunan. All were skilled workers, except for Zhao Baoshu, a staff member of the research room, and Liu Wenqing, a laborer. Their actions were considered to have incited the strike or provoked unrest. Xie Wanquan, Long Ming, and Shen Qichang had worked behind the scenes to promote the strike. Zhao Baoshu, Long, and Shen covertly did labor movement work for the CCP and had "frequently raked up the government's misdeeds, slandering the central government in articles given mass distribution." The trainee forge worker, Wu Jiujiang, had publicly insulted the arsenal director and, along with Liu Wenqing, had led workers in wrecking the arsenal director's residence. Mao Ren'gang, a draftsman in the engineering office, had demolished the steel-plated bell that signaled work shifts in the workers' village. Shen Yongfa, the CAL leader, had gathered funds for injured workers at Dadukou. As of April 19 (the date of the investigative squad's last report), all eight were still detained and awaiting a verdict and possible trial by military tribunal. Secondary offenders, an equal number of laborers and skilled workers, were either released after posting bail or detained for several days in the factory prison. By April 19, all secondary offenders had been fired for having "blindly followed and committed relatively minor offenses."[65]

Although the military tribunal ultimately sentenced Xie Wanquan to three years' imprisonment, investigative section reports suggest he had become more expendable, since he was not a full-fledged Communist party member, which prevented him from informing on other members. "This worker is an element in the Communist Party's outer organization. He has only vertical relations, and absolutely no horizontal links; therefore, I fear, he is of not much use." Xie's recanting of party ties on April 5 may have also worked in his favor. By April 19, the investigative section contemplated releasing Xie on bail and letting him return to work.[66] Eventually, Xie was released in March 1947 under a general amnesty proclaimed by the government. Yet two months later, he was back in prison, along with six other Communist suspects, for organizing workers, sabotage, theft of munitions, and intelligence work in the arsenals. Xie, according to a fellow suspect's deposition, had been gathering factory intelligence from Arsenal No. 24.[67]

The strike's impact on the arsenal's labor relations was generally unfavorable to the arsenal workers. Besides the replacement of the temporary arsenal director Shen Gengzu, the major adversaries of the strikers worked to consolidate their power. By mid April, the Ordnance Department's investigative section recommended rewarding the squad for bringing the strike to a "smooth resolution." In prior reports, Yan Guowu also lauded the Green Gang leaders for their bravery and "enormous contribution to the resumption of work." "We request that the factory director individually honor each of the above personnel and workers to encourage them!"[68]

Given such encouragement, political controls inevitably tightened, frustrating the efforts of CCP activists like Du Yanqing, who regarded the strike as a political fiasco. *Xinhua ribao* suggested, however, that management had consented to six of the strikers' conditions. Starting April 1, wages would be raised 100 percent; leaves of absence (for private business) and extended leaves of absence would be treated differently; movies would be shown three times per month; severance pay would be granted; the December 1945 and February 1946 bonuses would be distributed immediately; monthly bonuses between March and June would all be distributed before July 8; and welfare benefits would be distributed equally, with the exception of those distributed by the Ordnance Department. It is unclear whether these conditions were actually implemented, given the grudging attitude of so many arsenal managers. But the proposed settlement indicates how social conflict pushed management to respond with higher wages and fringe benefits, which were still not formalized. One should not exaggerate workers' clout, though, as evidenced by the ensuing mass layoffs. On April 23, the arsenal began to dismiss workers in accordance with the Ordnance Department's projected goal of reducing the labor force by 40 percent to 800 workers by the end of May.[69]

Layoffs and the manner in which they were conducted increased many arsenal workers' hostility to and resentment of their superiors. The case of Arsenal No. 30 well illustrates how arsenal closures exacerbated workers' sense of alienation from the defense industry, since many workers had been staunch supporters of the Nationalist government. As recently as March 1, 1946, arsenal workers had "felt gratified" upon hearing that if they took extended leaves, they would receive a month's wages for each half year they were employed in the arsenal. Wages would be doubled for workers wishing to remain with the factory and not return to Shandong, the place of origin of most northern immigrant workers.[70] And a week later, under the guidance of the Nationalist Party political director and their native-place association, over 700 Shandong employees assembled at the Experimental Theater, along with arsenal workers from throughout Chongqing. They then marched to the Nationalist government seat, where they petitioned the government in support of liberating Shandong Province and preventing an "illegal occupation" by the Communists.[71] Yet two weeks later, Juntong agents began writing a flurry of reports that workers were discussing plans to strike and smash machines. (Although no connection was made, these rumors coincided with the ongoing strikes at the Gangqianhui and Arsenal No. 10.) By late May, the Chinese Association of Labor was actively recruiting workers, and "everywhere, workers were reading *Xinhua ribao*."[72] Reports now circulated that Arsenal No. 30 workers were producing hand grenades and plotting to mount an insurrection within the factory and blow up the Ordnance Department![73]

The insurrection never transpired, but how had the situation become so volatile? The fear of unemployment was an obvious reason, and workers who wished to return to their homes in Shandong grew increasingly frustrated when management would not increase the travel stipend, or set arbitrary stipends that discriminated against northerners. Despite establishing a "return home committee," which estimated an individual worker's needs at 140,000 yuan to return home, the factory director would only grant 52,000 yuan, leaving it up to workers to pay the balance themselves.[74] To add insult to injury, the factory director distributed bonuses worth four months' wages to foremen to get them to "persuade workers to leave quickly and prevent an insurrection." "The foremen were extremely satisfied and used repressive means and enticements to accomplish this goal."[75] Upon hearing that the foremen had been bought off, workers could only curse them. It was at this point that they began to gravitate toward the Chinese Association of Labor.

By the summer of 1946, the strike wave had ended. Several factors account for its demise. Authorities stabilized the situation by increasing the severity of their labor controls, while at the same time appealing to workers' sense of loyalty by compromising on social welfare policies. As demonstrated elsewhere, it was precisely during the civil war period that fringe benefits began to heighten dependence on the factory. Increased production during the civil war also salvaged workers' jobs and tempered some of the distrust that had arisen in the aftermath of the War of Resistance. Nevertheless, this was an uneasy truce; the renewed production drive created a backlash of foot-dragging and individual acts of resistance.

Certain arsenals, it is important to note, had also been shielded from overt conflict due to the influence of gangs working with arsenal authorities. Nationalist officials periodically condemned the gangs, while arsenal management, for its part, treated them with considerable caution, fearing the rise of an independent power base within the arsenals and abuses of that power. Nevertheless, gangs were also found to be convenient allies when needed to suppress labor strife, as the case at Arsenal No. 10 demonstrated. Similarly, at Arsenal No. 24, the leader of the security forces had recruited gang members to deter spies and traitors aiding Japanese bombers. In his view, before the guard and investigative section had been established in 1941, such covert methods had effectively eliminated traitors. To justify gangs' continued use, a security official reported to the factory director that despite the strike wave after V-J Day, there had been no disputes in the vicinity. "Although we have had numerous discussions at the factory, in the end we have safely pulled through. As can be amply seen, this leader's use of the gang has not been inappropriate. Nor has the use of gangs led in any way to his own personal power."[76]

Another factor that abruptly halted the labor movement was the diminished influence of the Communist underground. According to one Nationalist government report, CCP Central Committee leaders expressed utter dissatisfaction with the Sichuan Provincial Committee leader Wu Yuzhang's inability to guide the labor movement. Despite Wu's sterling revolutionary background, dating back to the 1911 Revolution, his efforts had led to "defeat and absolutely no results in the latter half of 1946." Consequently, the CCP strategy for the following year changed. Resources were to be diverted from the student movement to the labor movement. Henceforth, the outer party organization, the Chinese Association of Labor, which had witnessed a resurgence after its leadership fled to Hong Kong, would use "surprise attack methods" to penetrate all factories in the outlying districts of Chongqing.[77] Relatedly, CCP leaders, such as Du Yanqing, advocated resuming United Front tactics—maintaining workers' minimum economic interests while co-opting legal organizations. By expanding their presence in factory schools, reading rooms, and athletic and music groups, as well as welfare organizations, the party could "unify workers, organize workers, link up with workers and educate workers about the party's work."[78] Echoing the thesis of Lenin's *Left-wing Communism*, Du cautioned moderation: "We absolutely should not come under the sway of leftist disorders, and assume that the Left is always better than the Right, or that we need more revolution. This point of view amid the workers' struggle is a terribly dangerous mistake. Because as soon as the Nationalists and capitalists find out that workers have committed this error, they will use all their force to overthrow workers' reasonable demands and cause their reasonable demands to meet utter failure."[79] It was another question whether moderation would appeal to workers.

On the Eve

The disruption of the fiscal administration that caused hyperinflation had forced an excess printing of money to meet public expenses, but difficulties of production, speculation, and hoarding rendered inadequate the supply of goods and services. The social tensions created by these manifestations of hyperinflation provided the context for the strike waves of the mid 1940s. By the spring of 1949, the economy of the arms industry was in complete shambles, leading to further social unrest. Managers from model factories, such as Arsenal No. 10, reported extreme shortages of materials and feared that production would have to stop. Workers' morale had sunk to even greater depths. Approximately 40 percent of the workforce receiving mid-level wages, it was noted, "desire to maintain the lowest standard of living, but it is extremely difficult." Half of the workforce was paid even less, the equivalent of 3–4 *dou* of coarse rice. Arsenal funding to pay wages was delayed or distributed several times over the month, making it more difficult to keep pace with inflation. Not surprisingly, managers reported increases in workers' leaves and absenteeism, as well as reluctance to work overtime.[80]

Even more threatening, Ordnance Director Yang Jizeng reported, the inflationary crisis was leading to strikes, slowdowns, petitions, and a buying panic throughout the arms industry. Reports that "traitorous bandits had infiltrated and incited labor unrest" confirmed the worst of Yang Jizeng's fears that a fifth column was emerging. With Communist forces advancing south and labor strife spreading throughout the arms industry, Yang called on all arsenals to improve distribution of daily necessities and increase surveillance and security forces.[81]

Yang's subordinates did not completely heed his entreaties. In part, delays in budget allocation from the central government severely constrained the ability of arsenals to act promptly. The impending collapse of the Nationalist government must have also weighed heavily on the minds of Chongqing managers, such that the workers' plight took a distant second place to their own political survival. This concerned top Ordnance Department officials in Sichuan and Nanjing when they discussed events at the former Gangqianhui, now renamed Arsenal No. 29: "According to the report of this factory's investigative squad, recently the price of goods has increased enormously. The living standard of employees is severely threatened and their morale is low. This situation is widespread. . . . An undercurrent has been brewing among workers to organize and petition to demand relief and improve treatment. Management does not care in the least about them."[82] Out of desperation, workers had perfected the art of disrupting production to push management into concessions. As one official remarked, "The workers feel that if they do not have slowdowns, the management will not give them their wages. They use slowdowns as a means of coercion. It has become their only customary tactic."[83]

Given that these slowdowns took place at Dadukou, the first labor battle in 1946 offers some basis for comparison with the grievances and goals of workers over the course of three years. By 1949, workers' demands focused on retaining or expanding welfare provisions to tide them over the subsistence crisis. Although workers still sought some form of representation, the political edge of the unionization drive had been tempered. These goals were evident in a list of demands presented to management on March 17 by workers in department 4, a steel rod factory, who had struck the previous week over unmet demands.[84] Specifically, workers had sought to be paid their February wages and obtain their family members' rice stipend several days in advance. With promises by management that accounts would be settled when the Ordnance Department remitted funds, and that family members' rice would be allocated on March 11 and 12, workers resumed work that afternoon. By March 14, workers halted work again as the Ordnance Department had delayed distributing the rice stipend. "People's emotions are surging and they can be stirred up at any time," the investigative squad reported in alarm. In contrast to the 1946 strike, though, workers stopped working for calculated periods of time and used legal means, posting up a list of twelve demands in the factory director's office and the office of personnel and welfare, as well as on the walls of each department. Although one department initiated the demands, a factorywide shutdown was threatened if there was no response that afternoon.

The demands indicate that subsistence during the economic crisis had become workers' paramount concern. Deprivation was the underlying theme of most of their clauses and is reflected in the heading of the demands: "At present no worker can make a living . . ." In desperation, arsenal workers had begun raising animals as a sideline. Workers demanded thus that factory-owned livestock (pigs and cattle) not be subject to outside taxes. At least three demands centered on allocating wages and income other than wages so that workers could survive the inflationary crisis. Workers sought wage adjustments according to the monthly price index, and allocation of wages twice a month. To ensure prompt payment, workers demanded that wages be paid no later than the fifth day of the following month. Real wages, according to workers' eleventh demand, had also fallen to the bare minimum. "This month the maximum wage cannot even buy one *dou* of rice. It is truly difficult to endure the pain." Workers demanded that their annual wages be based on their (short-lived) prosperity immediately after V-J Day, "when the minimum daily wage could purchase three catties of pork."

Because of the erosion of wages under inflation, the distribution of rice to family members had become a crucial component of workers' incomes. Two of the demands focused on achieving a more equitable distribution of rice stipends. First, workers implied that the storage office was retaining 30 percent of their allotted rice by using a different standard than the one used for the guard battalion. Second, workers sought an equal apportionment of rice, regardless of skill or position. "No matter whether skilled worker or laborer, they have worked many years and have several children. None of them can earn a living. Management must properly distribute the family members' rice so that they can eke out subsistence."

Three of workers' demands concerned benefits other than wages, reflecting the economy of scarcity and the ongoing institutionalization of social welfare. Workers demanded that the factory farm allocate vegetables rather than sell them to workers. Clothing should be given to workers each season. Other arsenals had adopted similar policies, and it is likely that Arsenal No. 29 workers were trying to achieve parity. Finally, workers sought the construction and repair of factory-owned housing. As with their wage demands, which sought parity regardless of skill, workers wanted an end to housing allocations along skill lines, preferring that it be allocated in terms of workers' proximity to the factory.

A key issue driving workers' militancy during the 1946 Dadukou strike had been workers' demands that they be allowed to unionize and have factory representation. Three years later, workers broached this overtly political issue with much more caution. This time, workers sought representation in a more roundabout manner, demanding that all foremen "freely participate in all factory meetings." This demand reflected workers' aspirations for representation, even if only indirectly, given management's and the state's consistent hostility to unionization.

No further reports on the threatened strike were issued, suggesting that management had resolved the dispute. Within a month, though, delayed payment of wages resulted in another slowdown among workers at the steel mill's department 7. These recurring conflicts centered on workers' demands for wages and benefits. As the following account of a rice riot and slowdown at Arsenal No. 21 indicates, however, civilian strife affecting the entire city pulled workers' concerted actions out of an isolated industrial context. The widening of labor unrest can be seen in the timing of protest to coincide with the student movement and the participation of both workers and community residents in rice riots.

Arsenal workers' anger at merchants for hoarding and profiteering led to several rice riots during the Chinese civil war. One of the most dramatic of these occurred in the Jiangbei district, near Arsenal No. 21, where a confluence of economic and political issues sparked labor strife. The issuance of wages typically prompted workers to rush off to buy goods before their earnings became worthless. But on April 20, 1949, when Arsenal No. 21 issued wages and rice stipends to its 30,000 employees and their family members, the city government had imposed martial law. April 20 was the same day the "acting president" of the Republic of China, Li Zongren, rejected the CCP's ultimatum for surrender. City officials had enacted the prohibition in response to student demonstrations over the continuation of the civil war. On April 15, Chongqing students had called for a three-day all-student strike starting April 18 in sympathy with the Nanjing students who had been suppressed on April 1. Rumors now spread that workers were seeking to ally with students. Arsenal workers were thus banned from crossing the Jialing River and entering Chongqing to purchase goods. That same day, over 3,000 rifle-plant workers and ten representatives responded by threatening a slowdown on April 21 if they were not allowed to join the student demonstrations.[85]

When Chongqing arsenal directors convened on April 19 for their bimonthly meeting, they viewed the crisis with growing alarm. As their official report queried: "If, in the days ahead, the value of the currency continues to sink, how can we endure this danger and risk?" Directors lacked cash to pay their workers or to purchase "secondary materials in a timely manner, causing a large part of the arsenal to stop work." Workers were growing increasingly resentful of the higher wages paid to the soldiers patrolling them, a frequent practice, since all Sichuan arsenals had been placed under martial law at the start of the year.[86] Workers began to engage in concerted action across arsenal lines through slowdowns and had come under the sway of the student movement. "What is even more alarming is that the Chongqing student movement is turbulent and surging with student strikes, teacher strikes, petitions, and demonstrations. It has already been let loose and affected those working in the factories, and [it] will immediately explode and not be contained."[87]

Chongqing garrison headquarters reported that a slowdown was already in progress at the Arsenal No. 21 branch factory in Egongyan, Chongqing. Protesting "poor treatment," workers had begun a slowdown on April 18, forcing the central factory director to leave the Jiangbei district. Whether in support of the branch factory workers or believing that the conjunction of student and labor movements made it ideal to take action and pressure management, roughly ten thousand workers at the main plant stood still while their machines went into high gear on the afternoon of April 20. Workers selected twenty-seven representatives, who issued four demands to resolve their subsistence crisis: increase benefits severalfold, according to the March cost of living, and pay wages in kind; allocate a continuous supply of welfare; increase rice for family members; and supply family members of workers who had not received rice stipends.[88]

Faced with management intransigence (the arsenal director had still not returned from the branch factory) and widespread currency panic, several thousand workers streamed into the main street, Liujiatai, of the neighboring Chenjiaguan district to buy rice and other goods. Within the hour, several rice and cloth shops threatened legal action against the military institutions, because arsenal workers had damaged their property, injured several clerks, and stolen some 275 bushels of rice.[89] Like other food riots, both in China and abroad, participants deliberately chose their targets rather than engage in spontaneous mob violence. In this particular case, workers directed their outrage at the Yang Zhaocheng rice shop for having increased the price of rice per *shidou* from 23,000 to 40,000 yuan, and then severalfold more within an hour. Although arsenal officials had negotiated with rice stores to maintain fixed prices for rice, local shops commonly participated in wartime profiteering. As police reports noted, the shop owners in the Chenjiaguan district were "petty entrepreneurs who rapidly escalate prices whenever the opportunity arises."[90] Workers resented the fact that merchants did not engage in productive labor or honor their social obligations.

To make matters worse, the Yang Zhaocheng shop owner infuriated workers and residents by barring entrance to the shop. The shop owner may have been frightened that the growing crowd was threatening to barge into the store. But in the view of the four hundred arsenal workers and three hundred local residents who had assembled outside, the owner had closed the shop in order to ship rice out for sale. Arsenal workers and community residents promptly broke down the door, stormed into the shop, and pillaged the rice after someone wearing a military uniform had entered the shop. This may have been an arsenal worker, since police and arsenal security personnel had retreated upon encountering a mass of workers and were noticeably absent from the scene. Ostensibly, they were guarding the arsenal storage facilities and had "no power to supervise workers' activities after work."[91] By and large, workers did not target the other ten rice shops in the area, which had maintained fair prices. An official from the Bureau of Social Affairs explained that these shops "had coped with the situation in a considerate manner and had not raised prices. Although it was unavoidable that some people did not pay, their losses were far fewer, and five or six rice stores did not even suffer any damage."[92] Instead, workers targeted the most egregious price gougers.

The Factory Protection Movement

Workers' desire and desperation to earn a living was evident in the factory protection movement during the Nationalist regime's final hours. A convergence between the CCP's political strategies and workers' efforts to keep their jobs thwarted the Guomindang's plan to destroy Chongqing's strategic industries and infrastructure. The underground CCP played a critical role in the movement by organizing workers and winning over managers to minimize the damage of industrial sabotage.

Before fleeing Chongqing, the Nationalists' final plans involved destroying their own arms industry. Committed to retaking the mainland and to preventing the CCP from controlling a military industrial base in southwest China, the government sponsored a guerrilla force, known as the "Resolute Sichuan-Kang Army to Extinguish Bandits" (Jianqiang

jianfei budui) to continue fighting against the Communists. Under Major
General Du Changcheng, the Nationalist army drew up plans in mid November to destroy Chongqing's key bridges, the Baishiyi airport, broad-
casting stations, and strategic industries. These included chemical and
steel plants, the Minsheng shipbuilding plant, two textile factories, and
all arsenals. General Du leaves few details in his report but indicates that
in the last days of November, over three thousand workers organized factory protection teams and obstructed his fifteen squads from carrying out
the sabotage at Arsenals Nos. 20, 21, 24, and 50. Fighting ensued before
the army executed the workers' leader, surnamed Yang, and proceeded to
"accomplish" its mission.[93] Most arsenals, however, were only partially
destroyed. If Du's report is accurate, the army destroyed few workshops,
focusing instead on the arsenals' power generators. At the steel mills, the
cupola furnace at Arsenal No. 29 and the electric furnace and smelting
section at Arsenal No. 24 were destroyed.

The CCP minimized the extent of damage by winning over key figures
in the arsenal management, as well as mobilizing workers into factory
protection squads. Mass defections in the Nationalist army, estimated at
one-fifth of all military personnel, proved crucial to the Communist rise
to power. The arms industry proved no exception, as the case of Arsenal
No. 21 illustrates.[94] At the mass level, CCP members secured the allegiance of over two hundred trainees at the skilled workers' training
school to form a workers' self-defense squad. In appealing to workers'
need for job security, the underground members deliberately couched
their propaganda in nonpartisan terms: "No matter whether Nationalist
or Communist, workers have to protect the factories." "The factory and
[its] machines are workers' clothes and rice bowl; if we lose it, we'll go
hungry."[95]

Underground work to sway management proved a more complicated
task. Party members were concentrated in the low to middle ranks (technicians and assistant engineers), making it difficult to influence the arsenal management directly. Fortuitously, the arsenal director, Li Chenggan,
had resigned in March 1947 for reasons of health, before being promoted
to assistant director of the Ordnance Department. Li subsequently led an
arms industry survey team to the United States and then on his return to
China worked for the Yongli chemical company. Despite having left the
defense industry, which was done perhaps for political reasons, Li continued to enjoy considerable prestige among acting arsenal directors.
When Li attended the first meeting of the Chinese People's Political Con-

sultative Congress at Beijing in October 1949, he wrote back to Yu Zhuozhi, his former secretary and successor at Arsenal No. 21. Li urged Yu to save his political skin and ally with the Communists: "The situation is already settled. . . . Conduct yourself carefully."[96] Moreover, the Communist Lai Zongyu worked to sway Yu Zhuozhi through his connections with the director of the skilled workers' training school. A meeting was then arranged between Lai and Yu. Yu made several guarantees that prevented the complete destruction of the arsenal. He promised not to leave the arsenal for Taiwan and ordered employees to stay at their positions. When necessary, he would also open up the armory and allow the factory protection squad to arm themselves. Yu also strategically removed explosives from the arsenal depot and thus impeded sabotage plans. Even before the meeting, Yu had organized workers into a factory protection squad and began concealing valuable equipment from the gauge room and power station.

It is unclear whether the workers who clashed with General Du Changcheng's troops used these arms. One memoir speaks of eighty-four workers being injured and one worker being rifle-butted to death for impeding guards' efforts to transport and set the explosives. Conflict and the impending arrival of PLA soldiers, who entered Chongqing the following day (November 30), delayed and frightened the Nationalists enough to prevent proper placement of dynamite in several workshops. As a result, only the power room was blown up, damaging the turbine and generator. The following day, assured of a monetary reward by Yu Zhuozhi, workers removed 147 cases of explosives from the machine, gun-repair, and rifle departments and dumped them from a barge into the Jialing River. Wu Shenshan, a sixty-three-year-old Hubei rifle worker who led efforts to remove the explosives, would become the arsenal's union leader in 1950. Thus, workers' demands of the entire decade, in the course of their efforts to keep their jobs and gain a more equal footing in the factory community, culminated in their protection of the arsenals from the Nationalist army, often at the risk of death.

It is frequently noted that the Chinese revolutionaries only succeeded by mobilizing the peasantry and steered away from orthodox Marxist prescriptions regarding the vanguard role of the proletariat. One result of this stereotype has been a concentration of scholarship on the process by which Communists mobilized the peasantry, and a small but influential number of works on the causes of the Nationalist debacle, but almost no study of the popular sources of urban support for the CCP. Debunking the common assumption that there was little if any tangible urban support, Joseph Yick persuasively argues that the CCP's mobilization of urban forces in Tianjin during the civil war complemented the ongoing social revolution in the countryside, and thus played a crucial role in the Communists' ascension to power. Yick's book *Making Urban Revolution in China* underscores how the Communist alliance with intellectuals and the student movement, in particular, eroded the authority of the Nationalist regime. Consistent with the mainstream interpretation, though, Yick dismisses the political role of workers, arguing that the CCP underground rarely targeted workers, and that its "almost exclusively economic struggle" did not lead to the government's loss of authority or generate political gains for the Communists.[97]

This argument is problematic for several reasons when applied to the case of Chongqing. There, the CCP underground frequently targeted workers but, in adhering to United Front tactics, followed a much more elastic conception of class alliances. Within the arsenals, this form of political struggle translated into party organizers either being put in staff positions or Communist activists allying with other members of the managerial ranks. These methods had been used since the Anti-Japanese War, but they were articulated most clearly in January 1947, when Du Yanqing called for a United Front between workers and staff to further labor's cause. "If we work well among staff, we can understand the factory's economic conditions, the contradictions between each rank of the leadership, and find out who is progressive, die-hard, or even reactionary."[98] Cooperation across the occupational divide, which had also been a trademark of European leftist movements and "popular fronts" since the mid 1930s, appealed to staff employees and technicians of the middle class, since this social group shared with workers the burdens of the economic crisis in urban China. Most staff officers continued to identify strongly with factory authorities and thus did not join workers in any strike or slowdown. But by 1949, when forced by circumstances to take a political stance, a significant minority of staff members and high-ranking managers chose to work with the CCP to protect the factories.

Workers also played an important political role in the revolutionary transformation of 1949. But rather than judge their role in terms of revolutionary rhetoric, and thus facilely castigate the working class for failing to meet its ostensible vanguard role, a more accurate standard is one based on the perspective and goals of contemporary Communist organizers. Their vision was utterly practical in 1949. The overriding concern shared by both workers and the underground party was to preserve the productive capacity of industry and salvage jobs. The continued supply of goods and investment for reconstruction would ease the transfer of political power and maintain military supplies to the CCP. This meant downplaying class struggle and pursuing cross-class alliances, as illustrated by the factory protection movement.

The development of common interests between workers and Communists on the eve of the revolution should not gloss over the fact that workers and Communist organizers did not always share congruent interests. In this respect, it would be wrong to characterize labor activism as the "Communist labor movement." During the mid 1940s, militant workers engaged in political struggle at times even outpaced the Communist Party, forcing it to participate in political battle or risk losing its own credibility. Nonetheless, from the perspective of both militants and workers in general, political goals were not defined solely in terms of revolution. In a context of harsh authoritarian rule, arsenal workers' desire for independent unions was in itself political. It is thus not surprising that after assuming control of the Nationalist arsenals, the PLA established unions as one of its very first measures.

The issue of unionization, which had always been only one of several worker demands, receded in the last months of Nationalist rule. Job security and wage demands became the paramount issues as hyperinflation and the irreversible crisis facing the Nationalist government and the Guomindang engulfed the lives of arsenal workers and the entire civilian population. Workers responded by engaging in collective action, knowing that slowdowns, as in the spring of 1949, rather than individual solutions, were the most effective way of obtaining their hard-earned income. The fact that such action had become, in the words of one official, "a customary tactic" was startling, given the repressive environment of the arsenals and the relative lack of a collective political tradition of protest among first-generation workers. Workers' actions were one of multiple fronts undermining the legitimacy of the regime, and they were aware of this. "Workers also knew that the sun was setting in the west for the Nationalists, that they were breathing their last gasp."[99]

9

YU ZUSHENG

Organic Intellectuals and the

Moral Basis of Class

The radical worker-writer Yu Zusheng. Photo from Chongqing Geleshan lieshi linyuan bian, ed., *Hongyan hun* (Beijing: Qunzhong chubanshe, 1997), 106. Reproduced by permission of the Chongqing Geleshan Martyrs' Cemetery Archives.

Despite their brevity, the 1946 strikes opened social fissures along class lines. Conflict deepened the chasm between workers and management, while exposing rifts between party members and militant workers and, in a broader sense, between workers and intellectuals. How to bridge the gap between mental and manual labor and carry out the class project became a lifelong quest for the revolutionary martyr Yu Zusheng. Shifting our lens from the mass participants of the postwar strikes, and arsenal workers in general, we now focus on the mental and moral world of this radical worker-writer.

Yu Zusheng was born in Hukou, Jiangxi Province, in 1927, and his experience with industry began when his father joined the Hanyang arsenal shortly before the Sino-Japanese war. After Japanese troops occupied Wuhan in 1938, Yu's family migrated to Chongqing, where his father and brother worked at Arsenal No. 21, the largest arms plant in wartime China. Through the late 1940s, Yu's life was punctuated by brief, intense experiences, highlighted in chronological order by an apprenticeship, training at the arsenal school for skilled workers, unemployment, and news work for the Communist underground paper *Tingjin bao* (Forward). Soon after formally joining the CCP, he was arrested and imprisoned in the former SACO (Sino-American Cooperative Association) penitentiary in Chongqing in April 1948. On November 27, 1949, Yu was executed, along with over three hundred Communists and partisans, when Nationalist troops fled Chongqing, their last bastion of defense in the Chinese civil war. Posthumously, Yu became a revolutionary hero, helped in part by the fictionalization of his life in the popular novel *Red Crag* (1961).[1]

Here, though, I am more concerned with Yu's ideas and values for what they tell us about a politicized worker and how he envisioned liberation on the eve of the revolution. Few of his writings were published during his lifetime, but he left over forty poems, several short stories, articles, and personal letters, from which it is possible to probe his state of mind. Yu's ideas converged with those of radical militants. As a literate and articulate worker, he articulated themes of suffering and moral indignity common to working people and voiced workers' demand to be treated like human beings. His poems were not restricted to factory life but expressed a class consciousness about the human condition and workers' role in transforming society. Nevertheless, their focus on injustice and the hidden injuries of class resonated with his working-class audience. In short, he played an important role among arsenal workers in

Chongqing by trying to raise their class consciousness, or, to use his own term, "awaken" them to their plight. Like other members of the militant minority, Yu mediated between the educated and the masses, often at the margins of both worlds, moving in several social spheres, ranging from the poverty-stricken areas of Chongqing's Jiangbei district to the skilled workers' school. His contact with intellectuals revolved around both the officially sanctioned schools and illegal reading societies. From these positions, he transmitted ideas, words and, dreams about the larger society and its injustices.

If Yu wrote poetry of the poor, an anthem to survival, he did not explicitly speak a language of class. Perhaps this is not surprising, because to talk about class in straightforward terms would not have made for much poetry! Instead, moral and ethical norms informed his sense of class relations. His concern with questions of justice and inequity, suffering, and humane treatment pervaded his writing. Moral concerns, as elsewhere, were an integral part of working-class formation. As Mark Steinberg, a historian of Russian labor, has argued, "For individual workers to perceive that they are members of an exploited class usually requires that they do more than simply recognize that they are poor or poorly treated; they also need to believe that their personal hardships reflect unjust social relationships."[2]

Yu Zusheng's life and writings also give ample testimony to the close but contradictory relationship between intellectuals and workers. To close the chasm between mental and manual labor, Yu attacked social hierarchies through writing and by writing about "the people." Writing was both a form of personal liberation and a vehicle to express Yu's conviction that working people were not downtrodden "beasts of burden" but active participants in society. Working-class opposition to the social order and the transformation of that order could be achieved only if intellectuals arose organically from the subaltern classes. As a writer of working-class origin and a radical committed to social activism, Yu redefined the concept of intellectuals who were not only committed to the written word as avid readers and propagandists, but also activists, as in Antonio Gramsci's notion of "organic intellectuals" arising from a specific social group and expressing positions coherent with their own social sphere. "The mode of being of the new intellectual can no longer consist in eloquence, which is an exterior and momentary mover of feelings and passions, but in active participation in practical life, as constructor, organizer, 'permanent persuader' and not just a simple orator," Gramsci believed.[3]

Important differences nonetheless separated Yu and Gramsci. In line with a tradition of twentieth-century Chinese radicals and revolutionaries, of whom Mao Zedong is the most prominent example, Yu criticized ivory tower intellectuals for distancing themselves from practical work and the people. His own ethical and political needs, melded together with his personal experiences, led him to advocate a new role for intellectuals, a role that was both socially and politically critical and militant. Gramsci focused more attention on the ties that bound intellectuals to a dialectic between preservation and subversion of the existing social order in a more developed industrial society. Despite such differences, both were sensitive to the relationship between intellectuals and society and thus between intellectuals and politics.

Yu's ideas invariably collided with the Communist Party's attempts to ally with the "traditional" intellectuals. Gramsci contrasted organic intellectuals with traditional ones, such as teachers, bureaucrats, and doctors, who were disseminators of high culture and could mediate between state organs and the public, either accepting or challenging the dominant system. In Gramsci's view, the key role of the revolutionary political party was to weld together organic and traditional intellectuals.[4] In his study of the CCP's "New Democracy" platform during the 1940s, Thomas Lutze convincingly shows how it achieved its hegemonic project by allying itself with the urban middle forces, whom he considers akin to Gramsci's "traditional" intellectuals.[5] What is less clear is the degree to which these class alliances between traditional intellectuals and the party offset attempts by organic intellectuals to create a more democratic party and society. The intellectual biography of Yu Zusheng may provide some answers to this question.

Seeds of Bitterness

Neither official histories nor contemporary sources fully explain what radicalized Yu Zusheng. A union-sponsored biography underscores that the "seeds of bitterness" were sown in his first encounter with the police at the age of ten. The arrest of his teacher at the "poor people's night school" for teaching patriotic songs and the closure of the school prompted Yu and his classmates to skirmish with police, leading to battles and stone-throwing. Yu responded with a song of defiance: "Dark conscience, truly detestable. They captured Teacher Zhou and forbid us to attend school. Remember, classmates, arise in the middle of the night and strike the dark conscience!"[6] From the start, Yu's political discourse was expressed in moral terms.

The wartime immiseration of his family contributed to Yu's dissatisfaction with society and the status quo. Like many artisans whose status plummeted during the Anti-Japanese War, Yu's father suffered a reversal of fortune. Yu Guixi worked as a fitter in the rifle plant of the renowned Hanyang arsenal. The post carried prestige among workers, but tragedy struck the family after the arsenal relocated to Chongqing and merged with Arsenal No. 21. The devastating Japanese air raids of May 3–4, 1939, left his elder brother blinded. Shortly afterward, his father fell sick and died. In desperation, his mother gave away her one-year-old child.

Forced to find a job, Yu became an apprentice at the age of thirteen in the machine-gun factory of Arsenal No. 21. His semi-autobiographical story "My First Master" conveys how traumatic the experience was. Metaphors of oppression and servitude fill the narrative. Writing of one trip to a village outside Chongqing, the apprentice, who is also the narrator, contrasts the relative freedom of peasant life with the prison atmosphere of the factory. Farmers on their way home from work sing:

> April rains
> Bring an abundant supply
> We thrash the wheat as the sun comes out,
> Water fills the paddies to plant the seedlings.

The song "made me envious of how free and lucky their lives were. Such songs would never be heard in a factory. Our songs were bitterly sad, squeezed out of the people's strangled throats," the apprentice notes:

> No sight of the sky in the morning
> No sight of the ground at night
> Breathing in the greasy smoke
> Tolerating the leather whip.[7]

Yu's sense of oppression, conveyed vividly by the image of the whip, resulted from his relationship with his master. The story's central event lies in the apprentice accidentally damaging a machine tool and being fined two hundred work hours, an enormous, and exaggerated, amount, considering that most fines ranged from one to five work hours. The apprentice shows a mixture of defiance and pity toward his teacher. The master's frequent lateness in getting to work, resulting from his addiction to gambling and alcohol, may have indirectly led to the accident, since the milling tools had not been tested before the apprentice began work that fatal day. The apprentice therefore stands his ground:

"Stupid pig, get back." Because I stood firm, he became even angrier. He held a hammer in his right hand as if he were getting ready to hit me.
"Are you going to beat me? I'm not budging. I'm not afraid of dying."
"Who taught you to argue? Tell me, or I'm going to beat you to death. You're incompetent."
"Well, I'm your apprentice, not your slave."
"Yes. . . . What do you know about slaves?"

In another scene, in which several apprentices commiserate over the brutal treatment of a dead worker, the seeds of revolt are sown. "You all saw how brutally he died. They wrapped him up in a straw mat, dug a hole, and threw him in. His wife and son were crying their eyes out. How are they going to survive now? This is the fate of the poor, the poor! I know no one pities him. Brothers! Do you know that his manager said, 'He worked too slowly, and he deserved to die!'" And one of the apprentices sings:

> This chaotic world
> Our ancient China
> We have still not overturned
> We are still slaves, still slaves . . .

Such scenes hint at the need for revolution, and the degradation of the work that is killing his master fills the apprentice with despair when he draws the analogy with his recently deceased father. "The managers treated him [the master] with indifference. Life gave him a heavy load and smothered him to the point where he had no breath left. . . . A ceaseless torment lay buried in his silent face. This suffering flowed slowly to my brain and I unconsciously recalled my father. At this point, I could only lower my head and weep. I cried for my father, who had died three months ago."

The monotony of factory life aggravated these conditions of oppression and psychological anguish. Yu suggests that the roots of his militancy lay more in boredom than in his absolute poverty:

There wasn't any cooking oil, still my family always felt satisfied. We were used to this lifestyle; we didn't feel it was bitter in the slightest. After we had eaten our fill, we often went to the teahouse to listen to people recount novels of gods and spirits. Our lives unfolded like this page by page. I grew dissatisfied with our monotonous lives. I wanted to leave this living hell, but there was no way out. I was never satisfied, always dissatisfied with something. I hated myself. I hated my friends. I became desperate and terribly upset.[8]

Such feelings spurred Yu to continue attending night school. In 1944, he tested into the prestigious skilled workers' school. Two years later, his formal education ended when sickness left him hospitalized and he was dismissed.

While unemployed, Yu shared a makeshift twelve-square-meter room made from mud bricks with his brother and sister-in-law. In "My Home," written in 1947, he describes the hardships and anxieties his family experienced living like water buffalo amid the leaking water. The poem underscores the suffering entailed by a working-class existence and the family's struggle against poverty and the elements:

> Mother worries that the matches are damp
> Little sister rubs her eyes in front of the kitchen stove.
> How easy it is to borrow half a liter of rice
> Past nine and we still haven't filled our bellies.
>
> Stinking gutter water churns out bubbles
> Water from the rat hole floods the room.
> A broken basin spins on top of the water
> My home is nothing but a watery prison![9]

Yu's letters suggest that he felt wracked with guilt on having to depend on his family and burdening them. "How can I feel at ease! I can't help my family, and my family has to support me. This is too embarrassing to talk about. When outsiders look at us, it is most unseemly." He then asked his close friend Zhong Bin, who had recently moved to Wuhan, whether jobs were available and if he could help him. "How much money doesn't matter. It's best if I can work for less than ten hours a day. This would only be short-term. Come next spring, I want to find a way to go back to school."[10] Although idealism motivated Yu, concern for his family's welfare and his own sense of filial duty may have also driven him into the arms of the CCP, which offered him material support and the opportunity to study.

Participation in the subculture of opposition also fostered Yu Zusheng's radicalism. Like other members of the militant minority, he had a passion for learning. "I have a good feel for mechanics, so that even during break I still ponder over problems," he wrote Zhong Bin after taking an examination at the skilled workers' school. "There is no end to my interest, and this makes me do more exercises than my classmates."[11] Education, both formal and informal, was often a conduit to political organizing. As a student at the skilled workers' school, and then while unemployed, Yu formed reading societies with other workers and edited a bimonthly wall newspaper, *Flame,* which the authorities quickly suppressed.

The poem "Flame," published in the first and only issue, draws an analogy between fire and socialist ideals. Prone to moralizing, Yu uses the words "dark, selfish, and immoral" to portray the enemies of socialism, while as in Buddhist symbolism, the flame purifies and strengthens. The fire's light, a recurrent imagery in writings associated with social movements in China as elsewhere,[12] represents guidance to truth and liberation:

> Flame! Flame!
> Burn a warm flame!
> You blaze and shine with boundless radiance
> Lighting up dark and remote places of the earth.
>
> Your powerful flame burns the demons,
> warms the spirits of all our fighters.
> For the truth . . .
>
> We want to wake up the drunk
> You beautiful bright flame,
> How many people admire you!
> Only the diehard selfish
> think of cruel and immoral ways to destroy you!
>
> How many youths fall madly in love with you.
> Your love granted to the people
> widespread like the celestial sun
> You point out the correct path amid the dark.
> They raise their solid arms.
> Saluting you,
> They throw themselves into your arms![13]

Yu Zusheng left no record of exposure to Marxism per se, but his favorite works manifest a class consciousness. He was fascinated by the iconoclastic Lu Xun, translator of the Russian writer Maksim Gorky's autobiographical trilogy, *My Childhood, My Apprenticeship,* and *My Universities,* and on his notebook he inscribed Lu's celebrated dictum from his 1932 poem "Self-Ridicule": "Fierce-browed, I coolly defy a thousand pointing fingers. Head bowed, like a willing ox, I serve the children."[14] Yu's choice of the couplet is extremely suggestive, because of its various political interpretations. As found in the *Zuo zhuan,* a classical text, it originally referred to Duke Jing of Qi, a devoted father who lost a tooth while playing ox with his son. Pretending to be the ox, the father placed a rope in his mouth to serve as reins and let his child hold them.

When his son accidentally fell, he yanked at the rope, pulling out a tooth or two. Jon von Kowallis notes that, writing under repressive political conditions, Lu Xun expanded the meaning to "encourage young writers and to stand up for the interests of the oppressed and downtrodden." In his celebrated "Talks at the Yan'an Forum on Art and Literature" in 1942, which yoked art and intellectual autonomy to the revolutionary cause, Mao Zedong offered yet another interpretation, saying: "All Communists, all revolutionaries, all revolutionary literature and art workers should learn from the example of Lu Hsun [sic] and be 'oxen' for the proletariat and the masses, bending their backs to the task until their dying day."[15]

It remains an open question whether Yu Zusheng was taking his cue from Mao. What is certain is that these ideals of altruism and unwavering discipline in pursuit of social justice were continuing themes in Yu's writings and life. In August 1947, Yu reenlisted under an assumed name as a temporary worker at the arsenal, where, as an unofficial CCP activist, he distributed the underground party newspaper *Tingjin bao* and organized a reading society with a fellow worker and party member, as well as continuing to write. He was encouraged when the legal Communist daily *Xinhua ribao* published his poem "Rising Sun" and an article by him critical of the Guomindang. "I must study even harder, like progressive poets who have not completed their road, and run forward quickly," he noted in his diary.[16]

Although his efforts at self-betterment and advancement through education were widely shared, his passion for reading and the written word was not a goal in itself but a means to social activism and change. This is what characterized him as an organic intellectual. Like the other workers who created a subculture of opposition, he had an ethical vision of greater human dignity, expressed in demands for better treatment and to be considered a human being.

Schisms Between Intellectuals and Workers

Yu's desire to learn, and his conviction that theory should not be divorced from praxis, contributed to his rather tense relationship with intellectuals, in the broad sense of teachers, writers, and students. Paradoxically, while intellectuals kindled his desire to become an activist, Yu's commitment to underground work reflected a self-conscious act of distancing himself from them. From Yu's perspective, intellectuals could not understand the grievances or aspirations of workers, because they lacked factory experience. Yu questioned the use of theory, perhaps alluding to Marxism, if intellectuals had no practical understanding of workers. Moreover, if intellectuals understood workers only on the basis of a sterile bookish knowledge, inevitably they would lack sympathy for workers. These ideas are evident in a letter from Yu to Ye Weicai, a former classmate at the skilled workers' training school who had left the world of workers to study at a technical school. In it, Yu criticizes Ye and other intellectuals for their limited understanding of industrial life, saying:

I have rejoined the factory. I work together with those nameless heroes. Their labor has written a new page in history. Although this ancient China has produced some new men of letters, they still have not entered the factories. The life of the laborer is too bitter. Sunshine does not enter the factory. They will mildew and rot. Who cares about these matters? Who? Some readers are armed with theory, but I have yet to see anyone apply themselves at a basic level. If we don't make a new route for those laborers, they will continue to carry a heavy burden of oppression and be mired in misery. The fault of intellectuals lies in their lack of empathy. Your last criticisms of me were not factual, but I can't blame you for this old shortcoming. This is a harmful tradition, to misunderstand the context of a person's life and add criticism and commentary. I feel I have a tragic destiny, but I just want to live alongside good people. Now can you finally understand me? I still want to say so much to you, but I am too stupid to put it in words. I still have ten hours of work waiting for me tomorrow.[17]

Yu ends the letter on a humble and heartfelt note. Like other worker-writers, he was constantly reminded of his torturous experience with writing. But his implied apology was also a rhetorical ending used by workers speaking truth to power. His letter challenges intellectuals and traditional social hierarchies and, in a Marxist vein, underscores the potential historical destiny of the working class. Through his own activism, he would work to end the oppression of workers and in the process serve as a role model for intellectuals. As a writer and organizer from the working class, he would supplant the authority of the traditional Chinese intellectual and give workers a voice.

In truth, the CCP was quite cognizant of the social divisions between mental and manual labor. As Maurice Meisner has shown, the issue became a leitmotif of Mao Zedong's thought and practice.[18] In his "Talks at the Yan'an Conference on Literature and Art," Mao recounted his personal experience in stressing the need for intellectuals to live and work among peasants and laborers in order to achieve a "transformation in feelings, changing over from one class to another."[19] And in the cities under Nationalist control, the CCP used its popular legal organ *Xinhua ribao* as a forum to bridge the divide. Propaganda in the paper aimed to reinforce workers' sense of pride, as the following exchange of letters illustrates. A worker, Min Xian (People First), describes how his piecemeal education and dire straits forced him to apprentice in a shipyard. Although he aspired to pave a future as a writer for himself, the long workdays prevented him from self-betterment. In reply, the editor does not discourage the worker's ambition, but exhorts him to be proud of his role as a worker and reject traditional thinking, saying: "The feeling that holding a pen is loftier than wielding an axe, in other words, [Mencius's dictum] 'Those who work with their minds govern; those who toil with their labor are governed [to be dominated],' is an entirely outdated perspective, resulting from the ruling class's monopoly on learning." The editor proposed that the apprentice try to improve study conditions in the factory by joining forces with his fellow workers to pressure management to allot time for remedial education.[20]

Rectifying Working-Class Culture

While his relationship to other intellectuals may have been strained, Yu had an equally complicated rapport with other workers as he gravitated in a gray zone between the worlds of the educated and the masses. In his study of the 1920s Chinese labor movement, Steve Smith suggests that *bangong-banxue* (semi-educated, semi-worker) types, exemplified by Yu Zusheng, occupied a "liminal" position. Their training rendered them distinct from most other workers, yet their incomplete "education" and working-class roots made it difficult for them to be fully accepted by party intellectuals.[21] Moreover, Yu's weak constitution probably contributed to his sense of alienation from other workers, which he confides to Zhong Bin. Yu relates feeling physically weak and, at first, somewhat isolated from his classmates at the skilled workers' school, because he does not measure up to them. "My classmates all struggle enthusiastically with the steel and iron, but your little brother is nothing but a weakling." Heightened psychological sensitivity and loneliness compounded his sense of physical weakness. Yu had a predilection for dreaming, and in the same letter he describes his visions at school: "My eyes gazed through the window at the tree beaten by the cold rain and strong winds. The Chinese scholar trees shake by the side of the gutter. Bin, I never thought I would meet such disaster. To make a true friend is so difficult!"[22] He then relates how he had become a guarantor for a fellow worker who had left the factory and saddled him with the bond, dealing his idealism and faith in the brotherhood of workers a severe blow.

Feelings of weakness and alienation recur throughout Yu's writings. In the autobiographical "My Second Year in the Factory," he describes being taunted and verbally abused by a neighborhood "aunty" jealous of his family's modest social standing and good health. "Second Mother often came to encroach upon us. She often used unfeeling, treacherous language to abuse us naïve children. Her hideous grin made me fear for my life, as if I lived in a demon's lair. [My brother] De and I were weak and feeble. The entire heavy burden fell on Mother's shoulders. Only she was able to bear life's difficulties."[23] In a 1947 poem, "Leaves," Yu uses a combination of images and identities. He is simultaneously a proud rose physically threatened by an immoral society and a weakling enslaved to that society:

> Pond reflects golden ripples of grease.
> Willow's branch lowers her head.
> Wind shakes the boneless body.
> Golden leaves drop silently.
> A solitary rose stands in the field of weeds.
> Filth splashes the blue petal.
> Stains can deprive it of beauty,
> yet its spirit cannot perish.
> She will never be sullied.
> Come on wind and rain!
> Wash away this stain
> I pray like this in silence.
> Proud and aloof, the petal stares at me,
> condemning me for my slavelike appearance.
> What is filth?
> This is the mark of evil.
> Leave me alone!
> You are a weakling.[24]

For Chinese workers, as for revolutionary workers in Russia, radical identity entailed a rejection of the "rough culture" associated with rank-and-file workers. Moral condemnation of oppressors went hand in hand with a moral crusade against workers' customs. Chongqing workers' rough culture involved a strong sense of machismo—physical prowess, blood oaths, and fraternal orders—which could provide solidarity but could also prove divisive.[25] Domestic violence, theft, whoring, gambling, and opium and alcohol abuse were, moreover, not uncommon among arsenal workers. Yu thus became a moral evangelist, trying to rectify the hearts and minds of workers. Ironically, "conscious" workers like Yu Zusheng shared the same moral values as the Guomindang cadres in the factories. Both were critical of workers' personal lifestyles, albeit for different reasons. While the Nationalists condemned workers' habits for preventing them from fulfilling their patriotic and civic duties, Yu felt such "vices" impeded political organizing and weakened the will of workers to resist their oppression. From a moral perspective, Yu believed that rough culture reinforced public perceptions of workers as beasts of burden, a stigma of their subordination.

Yu's antipathy to workers' rough culture had a variety of sources, both personal and political. His interest in discussing social injustices at work did not go unnoticed, and his supervisor got a thug to beat him up. Yu grabbed a wrench, however, and fought back. Although enraged with the manager, he felt just as disturbed at his own lack of self-control, as he angrily noted in "Lan wairen" ("Outside the Pen"), which described workers as animals.[26]

A decisive break with rough culture followed Yu's experience with gambling at the age of fifteen. His repulsion was based on a deep sense of shame that he had betrayed the love of his widowed mother by following in the footsteps of his elder brother, a compulsive gambler. "I got swept up into a gambling whirlpool. De could gamble even more than I could, so much so that he would play until no one was left. He wanted to win everything, but would always leave depressed. He would then sleep at home for several days and skip factory work. Mama's fate was to be doomed to have two sons who couldn't help her."[27]

Yu may have internalized these feelings of degradation and guilt over gambling, making his desire to attain a higher social standing all the more urgent. Thus, he pursued learning not only for its practical advantages but to overcome the cultural stigmas associated with workers. Cultural development was essential to achieve equality with people of higher social rank. Like vanguard workers elsewhere, however, Yu did not subscribe to the mores of the upper class because of its cultural hegemony, but approached it in a spirit of defiance. As Mark Steinberg has argued in the case of Russian workers, "Paradoxically, though, it was precisely this feeling of moral estrangement from both their own class and the larger society—their marginality—that attracted them to the idea of a class movement that promised to erase the boundaries of class."[28]

Yu was not alone in rejecting these negative stereotypes. A worker writing in *Xinhua ribao,* for instance, accused the Guomindang propaganda machines of trying to divert attention from the growing economic crisis and the government's own failings by using workers' culture as a scapegoat:

In the several meetings they have held, the wise gentlemen often instruct us that more work and lower pay is the only way to resolve the present crisis. They believe the present industrial problems are entirely caused by workers' natural dispositions of negligence and laziness. They are unwilling to do more work and frequently ask for wage hikes. If they have a little money, then they go eating, drinking, whoring, or gambling, to the point where they undermine small factories and leave large factories without the means to survive. So now we must work more and receive less pay to save us. But is this really true? Working people always have to depend on their work to support themselves. In these conditions of high costs, who wants to go hungry by stirring up trouble? Many skilled workers have been forced out of the factory gates and now line up on the road of unemployment. In the past, workers went through thick and thin together, but now they are abandoned.[29]

Moreover, in keeping with his view that workers should be the moral voice of society, a role traditionally occupied by intellectuals in China, Yu viewed the relationships he eventually forged with other workers as ethically uplifting, for they represented honesty, purity, and innocence. They had become the "good people" whom he often juxtaposed with their oppressors—the political manipulators, pot-bellied merchants, factory supervisors, and wily landlords. Yu thus came to evoke an idealistic view of workers as morally superior when he describes the factory compound of Arsenal No. 21:

Jingong Village really does have its merits. Here you can see the living conditions of all of China's laboring workers. For this reason, I love the place, but I also hate it. I pity their fate, which is far worse than my own hard lot. They are not hypocritical. They never play games like those aspiring politicians. They have the purest of hearts. If there is some gathering, it's not like the big shots. They don't just talk without action. They are the true vanguard. You can experience their trust and honesty in this place. I can't find such honest people anywhere else.[30]

Yu felt that his daily contact with workers made him more empathetic, a prerequisite for revolutionary organizing and action that he found lacking in fellow intellectuals. "Sometimes we get talking, and I tell [workers] my opinion about our reality. They mull it over and then, after a while, they smile sadly. Because I understand their pain, I feel even more tormented. After talking with them, they want me to be careful! Who will take pity on them, these pitiable people?"[31]

Yu's belief in the innate moral goodness of workers, their rough culture notwithstanding, may have intersected with machinists' tradition of craft pride. Skilled machinists formed part of an elite group and looked down on workers with less skill. Arguably the wartime pauperization of skilled workers caused by the physical toil of arsenal working conditions, disease, and hyperinflation prompted them to mount a defense of their "moral economy." But this interpretation remains speculative, because Yu's writing on factory work does not evoke craft pride as much as a sense of overwhelming fatigue.

Anarchism was another important ideological source for workers' moral concerns. Chinese anarchists challenged the traditional subordination of manual to mental labor by introducing the concept of "labor as sacred" in political discourse. "Ethically, labor was 'the greatest obligation of human life,' and 'the source of civilization.' Morally, labor was 'the means to avoid moral degeneration and help moral growth, it was a means of forging spiritual will-power.'"[32] Anarchists stressed the moral virtues and humanity associated with labor, "an expression of the natural goodness and beauty of the human spirit," Arif Dirlik writes.[33] Anarchism was most influential among the intelligentsia in China during the New Culture movement of the late 1910s, and by the 1940s, Marxists had appropriated one of its central issues, namely, the sacredness of labor. CCP members were thus acutely sensitive when using cadres from intellectual backgrounds to mobilize workers about reinforcing the traditional mental-manual divide.

Despite his odes to workers as the moral and political vanguard, Yu faced a repressive terrain in the factory, which impeded his organizing efforts. At best, his official history notes, Yu was able to lead worker slowdowns, although contemporary sources leave no trace of his actions. Impeded by these objective obstacles, and in trying to awaken society to its plight, Yu devoted much of his time to writing essays and poetry. The pen would serve as his primary political weapon.

Writing and Power

Authorship became a form of empowerment for Yu Zusheng and other members of the militant minority because their writing challenged the divisions between mental and manual labor. In a culture that had traditionally accorded status and moral authority to the educated, or conversely, relegated the illiterate to the lower classes, the very act of writing overturned workers' ascribed status. Although Yu's writing was replete with word misusages, a mark of the self-educated man, his writing style—a complex mixture of local Sichuanese dialect and classical Chinese, poetry and prose—transgressed and subverted accepted cultural boundaries. Yu had a more explicit political message than the Saint-Simonian worker-poets whom Jacques Rancière has studied, but in both cases, "what imperiled the existing order was to make aesthetic the life of the masses. The workers' poetry exercises its social impact neither through its descriptive content nor in raising demands, but actually from its very existence. . . . Poetry addresses neither the misery nor the conflict of workers, but the capacity to express the aesthetic of the people."[34] This concern with the aesthetic side of poetry as a challenge to social hierarchy was one reason Yu, like many activists, preferred writing poetry to any other genre. Traditionally, too, poetry was considered the apex of Chinese literature; it most easily conveyed the gamut of human emotions and could be wielded as a veiled form of dissent. Yu and other prisoners in the former SACO building who formed what they called the "Iron-barred-window Poetry Society" (Tiechuang shishe) were able to leave a legacy of prison poetry even under these arduous conditions.[35]

Although Yu did not record his thoughts on writing and style, the interest among worker-writers in the aesthetics of their craft politicized the issue. The experience of the labor activist Xie Wanquan, Yu's contemporary, illustrates that workers and the CCP contested the adoption of a proletarian writing style, because style raised the question of how radical workers should communicate effectively with other workers and what class stance to adopt. In his deposition to Guomindang authorities, Xie Wanquan relates how a Communist organizer questioned and criticized his writing style as too bourgeois. "Tang [the organizer] told me, 'Although you are a worker you have the deep-rooted bad habits of the petty bourgeoisie, especially in your articles, which by and large employ expressions often used by the capitalist class. You must exert great efforts and be more introspective. Strive hard to use the language of the masses. Use the common experiences of the masses to explain why workers are oppressed and exploited."[36] Tang's criticism, which may reflect the growing imposition of Maoist dogma and the party line on the role of art and literature, nevertheless reveals both the attraction and repulsion that upper-class culture had for worker-writers. Xie's emulation of bourgeois culture in his writing style, which indicated the power of cultural hegemony, coexisted with workers' critical attitudes toward the upper classes.

This amalgam of admiration for upper-class culture and populist ideals informs Yu Zusheng's "Ode to Pushkin," written in the spring of 1947. Besides reflecting the fact that Chinese writers were familiar with Russian literature, thanks to probable Soviet influence, the work is the clearest indicator of how Yu used poetry as a political weapon. His object of attack, like that of his revolutionary hero Lu Xun, was the stupefying numbness of Chinese society. Imagery of awakening and light—recurrent metaphors in Yu's poetry and a leitmotif of class discourse during the 1920s[37]—was linked to raising workers' self-awareness so that they could cast off their traditional shackles of deference and filial piety, and by extension strive for national liberation and human equality. Yu saw his role as continuing Lu Xun's work of awakening society to its own ills, which had also been Pushkin's, he believed:

> You are the clarion call of Russia
> Bounding over the barren desert
> Floating over the dark green grasslands
> Awakening China's dying grass.
>
> Although the road is long
> your sound is like sonorous waves.
> as poet you passed away over a century ago
> But your sacred spirit lives on.
>
> Seeds sown during the bitter cold winter
> germinate come spring.
> The dead revived again.
>
> In sacred battle
> for liberation!
> You shed blood
> and fall over!
>
> Yet your blood is not shed in vain!
> Fallen!
> Your spirit lives on.
> The despotic tsar
> has now become a fool.
>
> History is tried by fire.
> Here, no false existence
> Only true existence.
> Good metals must turn into good household tools.
>
> Let my naïve voice rage
> and ripple without boundaries.

> Wherever people live lies a shore.
> Pushkin!
> Let me help you cry out and awaken the slumbering.
>
> This is my reward.
> I do not need a silver medal
> nor cling to that spiritless gold.
> I only wish for human equality.[38]

Yu also challenged the power structure by taking alienated and outcast members of society as his subject matter. Most of his remaining forty-odd poems date from 1946–47 when Yu was either unemployed and wandering the streets of Chongqing or had resumed work in the arms factory. His poems describe stonemasons, boatmen, fishermen, cobblers, machinists, prostitutes, factory workers, and farmers, whose lives are frequently juxtaposed with those of their oppressors—foreign competition, merchants, and landlords—to underline social divisions.

In "Workers," Yu describes the sacrifices and abuses workers endure at their exhausting jobs. Paternalist relations all too thinly veil their exploitation when workers are obliged either to donate part of their wages for a birthday present to the factory director's son or face dismissal. Ironically, while workers support the manager's family, they must abandon their own kin to survive. The poem ends on a sardonic note, praising the factory director for his generosity in supplying workers their jobs and dormitory beds—planks of wood:

> They melt their lives in pools of machine oil.
> Grease-stained tattered clothing hangs from their bodies.
> That oil spreads on their faces.
> On seeing that, even Mr. Supervisor says "Filthy!"
>
> For the birthday of the director's son, one has to bring an "envelope"
> Or else disaster will strike.
> You'll be requested to leave the factory.
> They can only swallow hard and give the "envelope."
>
> After the night shift, they still have to help out their wives.
> The week over, we are still busy planting rice and carrying kindling!
> There's nothing I'm not adept at.
> It's tragic, but I fear I'll come down with TB or exhaustion
>
> Abandoning wife and children away from home.
> Still, four boards of wood are the factory director's benevolence![39]

More often than not, Yu's language of class expanded beyond factory social relations to criticize the gap between rich and poor in society at large. In his poem "New Year's Night," although the setting is a modern movie theater, the theme of class divisions plays on traditional Confucian representations of merchants as parasites leeching the blood out of commoners:

> The movie song lures pedestrians.
> Potbellied merchant holds a banknote and walks up to the box office.
> Round-faced boy, a young girl
> exchanging a coquettish smile for a heart-shaped diamond ring.
>
> How much sadness and distress?
> How much hunger and misery?
> Creating delight for the pot-bellied merchants
> When will the light sweep away these bloodsucking bedbugs?
>
> Sweep away! Sweep away! Sweep away!
> Sweep away humanity's bloodsucking bedbugs.
> We shall have our serenity only after the crimes of the world are
>   wiped out.
>
> The person moaning in the dark
> Don't feel sad!
> Shed your own tears
> Over your own suffering;
> Your own happiness
> you must create yourself.
> We countless hungry people
> Must distinguish the world's ugliness.
>
> Singing our song
> Awaken the honest farmers.
> Smash the rich merchants' pipe dreams.
> Welcome the happy radiance![40]

The poem juxtaposes individual agency, as in the phrase, "you must create your own happiness," with visions of collective good, exemplified by the hopeful "We shall have our serenity." There is a tension, reflecting Yu Zusheng's own internal contradictions, between the individual and class. Ultimately, self is submerged in a group identity forged by the frequent use of "we" or "our," as in "we countless hungry people" and "singing our song." The poem ends with a call for class struggle against the merchants so that light will finally radiate. As in many of his poems, the sun and light represent the socialist revolution that will sweep away the dark, immoral side of a corrupt society.

"Giving Charity" also contrasts ostentatious greed and conspicuous consumption with the misery of child poverty:

Rain falls on the bodies of the porters and beggar children.
A hand extends out of the car awning.
Oh, such extravagance:
A watch and dazzling diamond ring
Two fingertips throw out a 500-yuan bill,
which falls into the filthy hand of the child beggar.
In front of the dance hall,
Jin Bangbang stands in his military uniform.
Pot-bellied merchants loaf here and there
their hands shake banknotes.
It is not cash that they wave,
but the lives of the poor![41]

Yu's exploration of self encouraged his sense of class oppression. Like the worker-poets in France for whom "the poetic act was a movement of individualism," or Russian poets concerned with exploring the self, Yu used poetry to convey his own feelings.[42] His heightened sensitivity to the social environment and to nature intensified his awareness of personal suffering. In his 1947 poem "Rough," Yu describes the constant suffering one must endure, especially if undertaking the road of revolution:

The rough road of life
Will it ever be smooth?
Having walked the lonesome sandy banks
I face the rugged mountain.

An endless road
Is it really broad and smooth up ahead?
Hollow like a dream,
Distant and indistinct like the ocean.

The whole day I could not feel the warm sunlight
or the gentle breeze.
So bleak and barren, not even one flower
Such a desolate picture.

Suffering and depressed,
my whole body marked by misery.
The rough road of life
Will it ever be smooth?[43]

Despite his overwhelming pessimism, Yu viewed suffering as critical to revolutionary struggle. Even before his arrest, he envisioned becoming a martyr to the cause: "I feel I have a tragic destiny," he declared, but said that working beside "good people" was worth the sacrifice.[44] In the essay "On Life and Struggle," which he wrote that same month, April 1947,

Yu lauds radicals with whom he identifies and lashes out at former activists who had abandoned radicalism for material gain:

They do not believe in anything, they "take things philosophically" and hold themselves aloof from the world. Compared to those who were never radical, this type of person is even more hollow and pitiable. Day by day they degenerate. They cannot stand the test of time. Moreover, they are only interested in material things. This type of personal life directly shapes their character and willpower. How could they forget everything? Their former oaths that they would "never be subdued by force" have become nonsense. This is the type of person most easily lured by profit.

By contrast, true radicals immersed themselves in the world of struggle. Although Yu realized that he might not survive the struggle, future generations would reap the benefits. Yu portrays a utopian society shaped by his moral values:

These types of people understand the genuine meaning of life and struggle. Although they meet with defeat, they absolutely never yield. Why are they like this? Because justice and truth must yield ample fruit. I myself won't be able to enjoy these fruits, but we believe that the next generation can enjoy them to the full. This proves that our sweat and blood have not flowed in vain. In this respect, every progressive thinking person can experience this through his or her trials. They have not the slightest hesitation, the slightest doubt that the future will be an ideal state. They are optimistic about the world's progress. I look to a humanity that will no longer deceive and oppress. All will move toward the true, the good, and the beautiful. Friends! Let us use our final willpower to strive for our ideal garden.

Before that stage could be reached, Yu believed, society would degenerate further. He uses the metaphor of darkness to describe this process. It would be the responsibility of radicals such as he to create a new historical era. "We should firmly believe that the people's suffering will become even worse [darker]. This is nothing but the historical era. It is also a new page in our history. Our task of constructing a new history is extremely weighty. At that time, an even heavier load will fall on our shoulders. We must advance the wheel of time toward the light."[45]

Utopian Visions

The symbols of light, especially the sun, used in many of Yu's poems are suggestive of how radical workers envisioned socialism on the eve of the revolution. Whereas his official biography notes that his 1947 poem "Tomorrow" expresses workers' desire for liberation under the Communist mantle, there is no explicit reference to politics. At best one can suggest that Yu juxtaposed the darkness of present-day society with the future brightness of socialism:

> I bend over my desk in the dark night
> listless, I hold a pen.
> Let this dark night quickly go by.
> The dreams I wish for—
> I never can fulfil.
>
> My trembling hand opens the quiet night.
> A night without the stars or moon.
> The pitch dark encloses me even deeper
> I cannot see any light in the world.
>
> Sad and vexed, I close my heart.
> Turn off the lights.
> Darkness come!
> Surround me
> Pitch-black night!
> No walls on either side, no roof above and no ground below.
> I curse the magic power of the pitch-black night.
> You always have an end.
> I can see you vanishing and destroyed.
> You will yield to daylight
> yet we welcome your new life.
> Sincerely receive her love
> yet who will take pity on your destruction?
> The darker the night, the brighter the day.
> I pray!
> I wish!
> Tomorrow will be a beautiful day.
> My happiness lies in tomorrow![46]

"Tomorrow" describes a Manichaean struggle between the forces of dark and light. In this vision, the forces of revolution, as represented by daylight, will vanquish the night, the old political order.

Another aspect of socialist ideals among workers was a faith in collective ownership. Xie Wanquan, for instance, summarized his belief in socialist ideals by saying: "I hoped for political democratization to achieve a dictatorship of the peasants and workers. I hoped that economic democratization could become linked to a collective economy." The idea of an economy based on collective production captivated Xie. When asked soon afterward by Communist activists to explain the meaning of the Communist Party, Xie defined it in terms of collective production and collective existence.[47]

Yu Zusheng's own aspiration for collective life is revealed in his "Basking in the Sun." The poem reflects a consciousness of poverty and exploitation, an analysis of a society divided into the poor and the powerful, and visions of social revolution in which "we" the people may one day share the sun's splendor:

> Sunshine pours down on to the stones, warming our bodies.
> What? Does this warmth also break those bloodsuckers' law?
> They have no sense of shame! Their eyeballs roll, glaring eyes stare
>   ahead.
> In this fortress where people and animals live together—
> morality, law, force, money . . . are all like wild, man-eating beasts!
> Spring has come, but they coerce and rob us. The poor shall forever
>   live in winter.
> As I stand in anger on top of this rock, I want to respond—
> the day will come when we shall stand up on the wall and shout, "This
>   is our sun!"[48]

In seeking to embody a new type of intellectual and dissolve the hierarchical distinction between mental and manual labor, Yu Zusheng experimented with metaphors to create an emotionally charged language. These moral signifiers may have had a powerful impact on lower-class readers, because they describe a social order in which the oppressed are armed with moral righteousness. Arguably, Yu Zusheng was simply echoing a long-standing tradition in using poetry to express his personal grievances and political criticism. "The odes can stimulate your emotions, broaden your observation, enlarge your fellowship, and express your grievances," Confucius had remarked, after all.[49] But in the radical context of his times, Yu was not seeking to ensure proper rule or social harmony. Rather, he envisioned the apocalyptic struggles of revolution, as well as a new social order and ethical system that would emanate from those struggles.

Exploring the mental and moral world of Yu Zusheng opens new vistas on the politics of labor and worker identity in modern China. Although historians have addressed workers' class consciousness, such studies have generally relied on inference, owing to the paucity of documentation giving voice to workers' own perspectives. One school of thought has stressed workers' regional identity, suggesting that segregated labor markets, the division of labor within particular factories, and gang affiliations reinforced the importance of workers' native-place ties and impeded workers' sense of class consciousness. Lee McIsaac's work on Chongqing wartime labor is representative in insisting that particularistic ties and working-class relations characterized by sectional competition and violent conflict prevented workers from developing a national or class identity. Building on the assumption that workers were divided because of their particularistic ties, other scholars link working-class politics to occupational or skill categories in arguing that artisans formed the backbone of the Communist labor movement.[50]

By contrast, questions of regional or craft identity never entered Yu's consciousness. Rather, he wrote prolifically to build bridges between workers and intellectuals and to break down stigmas ascribed to the working class. Writing became a form of personal liberation for Yu and other workers by imparting a sense of positive identification as workers, an integral part of the process of Chongqing's class formation. Although previous chapters have stressed workers' material conditions and organization as components of class formation, these factors did not necessarily bear a *direct* correspondence to consciousness. Yu Zusheng's writings suggest that cultural discourse (words, metaphors, and emotions) played a prominent role in shaping his understanding of material conditions and his consciousness of class.[51]

Yu Zusheng's life also reveals the ambivalent relationship between radical workers and the Communist Party. He became a writer in part because he feared that the party, still dominated by intellectuals, had distanced itself too much from workers. Only by supplanting the traditional role of intellectuals and breaking down intellectual prejudices against labor could workers transform the social order. Thus Yu typified Gramsci's conception of an organic intellectual in trying to create a counterhegemonic view among the workers with whom he toiled. To achieve this goal also meant criticizing workers' rough culture, which Yu felt was a fetter hindering their emancipation. As Yu was a "conscious" worker, dedicated to the revolution and a class struggle that would tear down social hierarchies, it would be inaccurate to suggest that a desire to "elude" the working class precluded an awareness of workers' own class interests.[52] Yu's relationship to members of other social classes was much more ambiguous, holding elements of both attraction and repulsion. He often occupied a "liminal" position between intellectuals he aspired to emulate, at least in terms of their political training, and workers with whom he viewed himself as sharing the moral high ground.

In the main, Yu Zusheng and other worker-writers' quest for dignity and humane treatment was a decisive part of the formation of Chongqing's working class during the 1940s. To be sure, Yu's writings may not have reached a wide audience, given that so few were published at the time. Nevertheless, his poetry and prose conveyed imagery that formed part of a broader intellectual discourse among workers. Metaphors of servitude, freedom, darkness, light, fire, and awakening served at least two important functions: they imparted a sense of self-esteem to workers often scorned by society, and they allowed participants in the labor movement to imagine their liberation.

Tragically, Yu's execution cut short his struggle to create a more just society and a new kind of human being. There are hints in his writing too of the apocalyptic views of past Chinese visionaries who felt that society would pass through horrendous times before reaching a more beatific state, and like them, Yu Zusheng made the ultimate sacrifice. His beliefs were not, though, a futile manifestation of a personal idiosyncrasy. Rather, Yu's concerns that theory not be divorced from practice, that intellectuals not retreat to ivory towers, and that art be practiced for and by the people resonated with many of Mao Zedong's writings during the Rectification campaigns of the early 1940s. Although not a theoretical writer by any means, Yu sought to live his life as a worker-writer in order to bridge the hierarchical division between mental and manual labor. These convictions also foreshadowed a fundamental policy of Chinese socialism that became prevalent within a decade of Yu's death, namely, the participation of intellectuals and cadres in manual labor.

10

DEEPENING
THE REVOLUTION,
1950-1953

A forge worker laboring under a large-character poster reading "Respond to Chairman Mao's contract to increase production." Reproduced by permission of the Chongqing Municipal Archives.

Like other members of the militant minority, Yu Zusheng eagerly anticipated a revolution, proclaiming: "The day will come when we shall stand up on the wall and shout out, 'This is our sun!'" Yet the antagonism between arsenal workers and management, which had been a recurring theme of the entire decade, did not suddenly dissipate after 1949 with the changing of the guard. On the contrary, as noted by A. Doak Barnett, an astute observer of the Chinese revolution, the 1949–55 period was one of "intense social revolution, in which the Communists, through a series of emotional mass campaigns, worked steadily to break down the fabric of traditional Chinese society in order to lay the foundations for socialization."[1]

Scholars have subsequently diverged on how to interpret the factory campaigns of the early 1950s. Kenneth Lieberthal, for instance, argues that political campaigns helped the CCP break down traditional social relations and parochial political consciousness among urban Chinese. These movements constituted a revolution "from the top down" that "would at all times be guided by, and serve the interests of, the Chinese Communist Party."[2] Deborah Kaple, on the other hand, contends that the political movements were an ideological construct modeled on High Stalinism. China's industrial relations, as characterized by mass campaigns, mass organizations, and the primacy of the party, were modeled on managerial methods developed during Stalin's Fourth Five-Year Plan (1946–50).[3] More recently, Mark Frazier has posited that the party used campaigns to counter morale problems and achieve social control over a recalcitrant and mistrustful workforce.[4] Although these interpretations are useful in clarifying the intent of the party in promoting mass mobilization, they neglect the active role played by participants themselves. In contrast, I would argue that the campaigns are better explained as a continuation of the social struggles stemming from over ten years of war, a culmination of long-standing ideological battles between the Nationalists and the Communists, and a response to the emergence of a new bureaucratic class that threatened the vitality of the revolution. The movements may have been initiated as a "revolution from above," whereby the party sought to radically transform society, but their effectiveness hinged on their being based on longer unresolved processes of social conflict that preceded 1949.

The "revolution from above" perspective suggests that the CCP imposed these movements on a largely unreceptive public. Without denying the instrumental role of the party, it is also true to say that many working people were active and enthusiastic participants in these campaigns, even though they often brought unanticipated results. In short, the party successfully tapped into a politics of revenge simmering at the mass level. Thus, the revolutions "from above" and "below" interacted and mutually reinforced each other. Mass mobilization would not have succeeded otherwise. "The Party has always paid attention to combining its leadership with broad mass movements, guiding the masses to raise the level of their revolutionary consciousness constantly, and to organize their own strength to emancipate themselves step by step, instead of imposing revolution on the masses or bestowing victory on the masses as a favor," Zhou Enlai contended in 1959.[5]

As a result of this dynamic between "state" and "society," the political movements and union policies of the early 1950s brought about radical transformations in the status of workers and the industrial hierarchy, marking a break with the pre-1949 regime in both policy and personnel. The transformations of the arsenals' social hierarchy confirm Franz Schurmann's thesis that a social revolution necessitates new forms of organization and leadership.[6] The Nationalist industrial leadership based on staff officers was brought to its knees. Conversely, the early 1950s heralded significant opportunities of social mobility for workers, thus ensuring the Communist Party's ability to maintain and broaden its popular support. To be sure, industrial planners emphasized production over egalitarian goals, unions were not autonomous, and the traditional stigmatization of manual labor remained a constant obstacle. These impediments to a more democratic workplace and society were in part legacies of the pre-1949 era, but the context in which unions, workers, and the Communist Party continued to struggle over these social issues was radically different.

Legacies and the Quest for Legitimacy

The rapid establishment of unions throughout the arms industry is the strongest evidence that arsenal managers were responding after 1949 to the social conflicts of the Nationalist era. After meeting on December 27, 1949, the city's general preparatory union began organizing all Chongqing workers and sent organizational teams into each factory to establish preparatory unions. Within two months, the China Southwest Ordnance Union Committee (Zhongguo binggong gonghui xinanqu weiyuanhui) began operations. Study committees were quickly established to promote study and set up employee representative committees, followed that summer by the establishment of unions within each arsenal. Workers initially greeted the unions with great anticipation, reflecting their long-standing demands for unionization. At Arsenal No. 21, for instance, over 97 percent of workers and staff members joined preliminary workshop committees in preparation for the union. Arsenals No. 21 and No. 50 had already organized the cores of their unions, known as staff-worker federations, during the factory protection movement. These preexisting organizations suggest the active role of workers in forming the unions and their genuine desire for representation.

In keeping with the CCP's New Democracy platform of the early 1950s, union organizers stressed the democratic process of union elections. The employee representative committees of each arsenal supervised elections for the preparatory unions. The representative committees first made nominations in each section and department. To emphasize the choice of candidates, the number of nominees was double the number of those to be elected. A factorywide meeting was then held to introduce the candidates, whereupon the entire factory voted for union committee members, that is, the union leaders. Former staff officers were noticeably absent from the list of candidates, having been banned from joining the preparatory unions for fear that their participation would replicate the hierarchy of the Guomindang era.[7] Over 80 percent of the committee members, many of them worker activists, were elected from within the factory. The other 20 percent were nominated from outside the factory. New elections to select formal union committee members followed within months.[8]

While unions were being established, the party and unions allowed workers to vent their long-standing resentment against staff officers. But the class struggles within the factories involved much more than a manipulation by the party for its own political ends. Grievances that had simmered throughout the previous decade boiled over when workers were allowed to attack managerial personnel and members of the guard and investigation squads, whom they had regarded as their political oppressors. Staff officers became primary objects of workers' wrath because of their past association with the Nationalist military. As one skilled worker recalled, "After Liberation [the term for the Communist victory and establishment of the PRC], they [staff] often were placed on the opposing side and attacked during the class struggle. All the staff members who remained, and did not go to Taiwan or leave the arms industry, were attacked because of their military rank."[9]

At one level, these struggle sessions resembled the ongoing land reform movement, in which, according to one historian, class struggles against landlords were based more often on moral and symbolic categories than objective class position.[10] This discrepancy between objective class position and representational reality was never apparent, however, to workers participating in the arsenal struggles in the immediate aftermath of the revolution. The preferential treatment accorded to staff members, distinguished by their predominantly middle-class origins, diverged considerably from that received by most workers, making one's objective class position an unavoidable fact of everyday life. As Barry Richman, an authority on China's industrial management, has noted, "industry in old China was characterized by sharp cleavages between managers and workers, educated intellectuals and workers who were illiterate and barely literate, white-collar and blue-collar employees, and mental and physical labor. Class distinctions, including income differentials and living standards, were strong, large, and very real."[11] The growth of a managerial class during the war period had given staff personnel considerable authority and punitive powers. The suffocating militarism, as reflected by the command structure, military tribunals, and the widespread presence of soldiers and staff wearing military uniforms had all buttressed political repression within the arsenals. In turn, the use and abuse of power galvanized unity and opposition among production workers.

It is no surprise, then, that, encouraged by cadres who sought to wipe out the vestiges of counterrevolution, workers engaged in "speak-bitterness" campaigns, "confession and accusation" meetings, public executions, and class struggle, going so far as to drag department supervisors into the river, and killing one arsenal director. As the union reported:

Most workers are very happy about Liberation, believing that they have *fanshen* [i.e., overthrown the old order]. Workers gave vent to their anger through struggle and by settling accounts with some of the staff officers. Arsenal No. 10 workers dragged the factory director and the manager of the cooperative to the riverbank, where they forced them to kneel for two hours. After that, they locked them up for several days. . . . In February 1950, they subjected upper-ranking staff officers and those they deemed corrupt to fatigue interrogation methods lasting three days and three nights. The other factories shared this tendency toward settling accounts and struggle.[12]

By bringing former authority figures down to the river, workers were overturning former hierarchical roles. Whereas prisoners under the Nationalist regime had been forced to kneel in public, now factory directors were humiliated. Now staff officers had to endure "fatigue" interrogations similar to the treatment that had been accorded labor activists rounded up after the strikes of 1946. In these cases, class struggle took on highly symbolic forms, but there was a fine line between symbolic and real violence. A total of 516 "counterrevolutionaries," mostly GMD members, Youth Corps leaders, and investigative squad personnel, were arrested in 1951 throughout the arms industry of southwest China.[13] The violence would have escalated had the party and unions not reined in the movement. "Leaders must avoid a leftist inclination," the Southwest Ordnance Union exhorted party members. "Let us give counterrevolutionaries the chance to confess their crimes and start anew. We need to avoid executions. We should not rashly pass judgments and simply label them."[14]

The arsenal unions faced several immediate challenges in the wake of their establishment and the heady atmosphere of class struggle. The first involved sheer power politics. What would be the functions of the party, the military administration temporarily occupying the arsenals, and the unions? Who should replace the previous power holders in authority? How would these three institutions meet workers' rising expectations in the wake of such momentous political change?

Although the party was to severely circumscribe the autonomy and power of industrial unions, the early 1950s in Chongqing, and most likely throughout China, were years of great flux and uncertainty. The local CCP was still on the rebound after the defection of Ran Yizhi and Liu Guoding, assistant secretary of the Chongqing City Committee, in the spring of 1948. Although by January 1949, the Eastern Sichuan Special Committee had been established and would guide an estimated ten thousand cadres on the eve of the Communist takeover, they were concentrated in the rural periphery of Chongqing. When the Nationalists fled the city, as few as 2,379 party members were active in Chongqing. These were joined by an estimated 5,000 cadres from eastern China as part of the Nanjing-based Second Field Army that arrived to liberate Chongqing in December 1949.[15] Many of these cadres would occupy the arsenals and comprise the military administration during 1950–51. Limited knowledge of local Sichuanese society exacerbated their suspicion that the arsenals remained bastions of Nationalist power and counterrevolution. Although arsenal workers' political support for the former ruling party had been tepid at best, the large number of working-class GMD members aroused the suspicion of the newly arrived Communist cadres. Such fears translated into hostility toward the putative representatives of the working class, the unions.

If distrust marked the psychology of the newly arrived cadres, much the same could be said about workers' attitudes toward the Communists. Although many workers sought revenge for past injustices suffered under the Nationalists, these sentiments did not automatically translate into unconditional support for the Communists. After October 1950, the CCP made a concerted effort to expand membership in Chongqing factories, but it was slow going. By November, the former Gangqianhui had only 70 new party members, little over 1 percent of the 6,100 employees. Workers hesitated to join the CCP because of a variety of practical concerns and misconceptions. Some workers adopted a "bystander mentality," believing that the Communist regime would last no more than three months; others feared that they would lose their jobs, having heard rumors that the defense industry would shut down in peacetime, and thus adopted a politically neutral stance; in the eyes of many, party membership meant jeopardizing rations for family members or having dues deducted from wages, as the GMD had done; and a few feared losing face if other workers rejected their applications.[16]

The unions saw themselves as genuine political players. During the first two years of their existence, unions retained considerable autonomy from the factory administration and gave workers some voice in political decisions. As one lower-ranking union official recalled, "During the 1950s, the unions had a greater purpose. They put words into action. . . . In 1950–51, they established the staff-worker representative council, which had a lot of power. Everything had to pass through the council."[17]

The second major challenge facing the unions, interrelated with the question of factory authority, was improving the dire living conditions of the arsenal workers. The inflation crisis, severe shortages of daily necessities, inadequate housing, and unequal social relations all had to be resolved if the unions were to gain legitimacy in the eyes of workers.

The initial role of the unions was highly contested and created a breech between workers, the party, and the unions. "The party is deficient in its leadership of the union and training of cadres," it was said. "Some party branches and unions are in opposition, or they monopolize the union's work."[18] Specifically, the CCP accused certain union cadres of ignoring party directives to raise workers' political consciousness during the Korean War. Many union cadres regarded securing economic and social welfare benefits for rank-and-file members to be a more pressing task. Workers for their part felt disillusioned that the first factory committee meetings, which they attended en masse, "lacked substance," leading to a "chilly atmosphere."[19]

Diverging views on the proper role of unions were highlighted during the December 1951 Democracy Reform Investigation Movement. During the three-week campaign, which had been designed to impart self-management techniques to workers, attack old-style bureaucrats, and rectify the faults of certain staff members, union leaders indicated that labor activism was running out of control, in ways beyond what they had initially conceived. Some of the branch union leaders "did not dare manage their workers." "Extreme democratic phenomena" resulted when workers tried using their newly founded unions to determine job allocation, in effect, taking over a power previously vested in the personnel office.[20] Judging from the tone of its paper, the union leadership considered such actions to be too radical and quickly stopped them once the campaign ended.

One reason workers began to take such action on their own initiative was a loss of faith in the unions' ability to serve their best interests. At the root of the unions' declining prestige was their own tenuous relationship with the defense industry administration, which military representatives dominated during 1950. According to union reports, many administrators saw little use for the unions and did not take them seriously. "The administration relies on the working class but neglects the union. They don't firmly support the union, because they believe the union just means trouble. Even without unions, they can maintain good production."[21]

The relationship between arsenal unions and military representatives varied from resistance to accommodation, but invariably the unions' stance alienated workers. Some unions sought advice from the administration, but when the administration ignored the union, procrastinated, or passed on troublesome matters to the union, the union "became a substitute for the administration." The consequences were sometimes dire. At former Arsenal No. 20 (each arsenal changed its code number after the Communist ascension to power), for example, it was noted: "The union runs the whole show without suiting the needs of the masses and without resolving practical problems. Very quickly the union lost popular trust."[22] Other unions, like that of the former Arsenal No. 31, were "at the beck and call of the administration. If the administration calls for beating people, they will beat people."[23] Likewise, as the Southwest Ordnance Union reported, "The union lacks a definite stance; nor does it raise demands to realize solutions representing the workers' interests. If it encounters unfair practices or inappropriate measures taken by the administration, the union does not voice dissent or raise opinions. It has always gone along with the administration and acted as its tail."[24]

Workers thus grew frustrated with what they deemed to be ineffective unions. When arsenal authorities delayed issuing bonuses or providing material support, workers saw union defense of the administration's position as a capitulation. An incident at Factory 454 during 1951 offers a telling example of how union prestige rapidly declined. Tensions arose when the factory administration decided to stop night school classes because they lacked tables and chairs. Refusing to accede to the union director's plea for further deliberation, the military affairs representative notified him that any further complaints should be directed to the superiors. Dumbstruck, the union chairman only smiled. To add insult to injury, the factory director began to humiliate the union leader, "Chairman Ren, if you have something to say, speak up. Are you a mute? If you don't speak up, everybody will call you Chairman Mute." Before the union chairman had received an answer from the administration, workers directly went to find the military representative, who agreed to their demands. As a result, workers lost faith in the union and demanded that the union chairman (also director of the night school) be dismissed and replaced. "This greatly decreased the union's prestige. Generally speaking, relations between the administration and the union are not very good, to the point where it decreases their capacity to cooperate, to allocate work, and to mutually supervise. Or the administration does not respect the union and does not value the union's ability to resolve problems, so it does not give the union these responsibilities."[25]

Rather than cooperate, the administration rode roughshod over the unions regarding personnel decisions. Tension arose when the administration unilaterally transferred or hired new personnel, while rebuffing the unions' efforts to maintain influence over hiring decisions. As the vice factory director at Factory 791 chided union representatives, "If hiring needs to go through the union, are we also going to have to discuss the matter with the union when factory directors and military representatives join the factory?"[26] Breaches of contract between the union and the administration were another source of contention. According to the union, "Most administrators have not recognized that a contract is between two sides. They believe that all they have to do is give workers their production assignments. As a result, they made many empty promises." The most glaring violation of contracts occurred when the administration arbitrarily increased shifts and work hours. Factories that had completed their production task as outlined in the contract were allocated "crash jobs," which increased shifts and work time. When the union protested, the administration told workers that they could do the extra shifts on a voluntary basis. This was no compensation for the union. "At Factory 791 last year, because the production task was so heavy, workers even brought suitcases and food into the workshop. Workers felt dazed. The administration thought the workers had done the work voluntarily, but they didn't respect the workers' opinions."[27]

Long-standing prejudices against workers and their capacity to participate in factory affairs beyond production work exacerbated the divisions between the union, labor, and the administration. For instance, factory management councils that were established to discuss production problems, were, as the union reported, "more form than substance." They rarely met to discuss production problems, and when they did, committee members would not be notified to solicit opinions from workers. Some of the factory management councils had organizational problems. At Factory 451, the committee had only one worker committee member besides the committee chair. "As a result, this worker management committee has become an administration cadre meeting. It doesn't reflect the opinions of workers regarding production, but just remains a formality."[28]

Seeking to salvage their dwindling popularity, unions reexamined their work methods in accordance with the newly promulgated Union Law of 1951 and accepted criticisms from rank-and-file union members. The Southwest Ordnance Union acknowledged that it "has not truly become the voice for workers. The union does not do enough to sustain workers' demands or its own position. Some of the unions are insufficiently democratic. They do not announce their agenda publicly; they do not regularly announce their work. And a democratic structure was not adequately built."[29] To offset the inexperience of union cadres, each arsenal union organized work committees to supervise training of over 5,000 cadres between January and September 1951.[30] New elections were also held to enable union members to voice their displeasure with union leadership. Although sources do not reveal the extent of turnover, the South-west Ordnance Union anticipated that two-thirds of the present cadres in one arsenal would lose their jobs during the summer of 1952.[31]

In fairness to the union, officials were sensitive to workers' concerns and keen to win their allegiance. They tried to improve workers' living conditions, recognizing their aspirations and their struggle during the preceding war period. The very candor of the union reports regarding their failings is ample testimony to their idealism. To reverse their declining prestige and to demonstrate their commitment to upholding workers' interests, the unions focused on improving workers' standard of living.

Wage reforms were an important element in fostering worker support. The new factory administrators stabilized the dizzying hyperinflation crisis by pursuing a low-wage policy and providing workers with a "sustenance stipend" (*weichi fei*) at arsenals where production had been disrupted. Most important, they moved quickly to tear down the long-standing occupational divide between production workers and office personnel. Wage adjustments in July 1950, followed by a "second wage reform" in January 1951 eliminated unfair subsidies and other nonsalary income of high-ranking staff members.[32] A comparative wage survey of seven Chongqing arsenals taken in December 1950 indicates that workers' average income was 93 percent that of administrators and office staff. A greater gap existed between workers and technical staff, since the administration rewarded technical staff with a pay raise in 1950. Still, when compared to the mid 1940s, workers had narrowed the wage gap, earning roughly two-thirds as much as technicians and engineers.[33]

The reduction of wage differentials continued through 1952, despite changes in the classification of staff members and workers. At Factory 791 (the former Arsenal No. 20), wage statistics between July 1950 and December 1952 show an emphasis on rewarding technical and production work. Engineers and technicians continued to earn much more than any other kind of employee. Regular workers earned from two-thirds to four-fifths of their income, still a significant proportionate increase for production workers compared to pre-Liberation days. Regular workers made the greatest strides in earnings vis-à-vis staff members. Staff members, defined as section chief, section staff, administrators, and office workers, received on average only 4–5 yuan more than "regular" workers during the early 1950s. By 1952, "regular" workers actually earned more than *zhiyuan* did. This radical shift in the factory's distribution of

TABLE 10.1

Comparative Wage Survey of Factory 152 Employees,
June 1948–September 1952 (averages in yuan)

Date	Regular workers	Staff	Workers' pay as % of staff pay
1st half 1948	593	22,513	2.6
2d half 1948	150	599	25.0
1st half 1949	3	17	19.5
2d half 1949	12	16	72.6
1st half 1950	39	63	61.6
2d half 1950	69	66	105.2
1st half 1951	48	59	82.0
2d half 1951	135	159	84.8
1st half 1952	215	200	107.2
2d half 1952	215	200	107.2

SOURCE: Chongqing Municipal Archives, 1032 *quanzong,* 5 *mu,* 113 *juan,* "Jiefang yilai gongzi shuiping biandong qingkuang diaochabiao."

income was not an anomaly. As the comparative wage survey of Factory 152 (the former Arsenal No. 10) indicates, workers in late 1950 and then again in 1952 were earning more than staff (see table 10.1).

Although one should take into account that there were at least three different categories of workers (regular workers, assistants, and apprentices) after 1949, the earnings disparity between assistants and regular workers was quite small. The pronounced division between permanent and temporary workers that would fuel labor strife in 1957 and during the first years of the Cultural Revolution was not yet apparent.[34] On average, assistant workers, who were permanent workers, earned between 78 to 99 percent of what regular workers did.[35]

Besides these redistributive wage policies, the new authorities improved the material conditions of workers, and propaganda stressed the positive impact of the new regime by comparing workers' standards of living before and after 1949. Surveys and interviews confirmed for the union that its wage reforms had benefited workers. A survey comparing the living standards between September 1949 and September 1952 of one hundred arsenal worker families noted an array of improvements. After Liberation, all workers ate three meals a day, primarily rice and vegetables, and most now also had an egg before going to work and consumed 6–7 jin of meat per month, which, the survey noted, had been "impossible" before 1949. Income and consumption had increased dramatically. The average pre-Liberation income (converted into the price of buying rice) was 248 *jin* of rice per family. By September 1952, it had more than doubled to 513 *jin* per family. With the additional income, workers could now purchase close to five times more clothes.[36]

The most pressing social welfare problem of the early 1950s involved factory housing. Many of the workers' dormitories and arsenal housing built during the War of Resistance had fallen into disrepair. Bamboo-thatched houses leaked when it rained. Inadequate plumbing in workers' villages led them to drink water from the fields and the river.[37] Most residential bathrooms were open-air toilets, forcing some employees to walk a quarter of a mile to relieve themselves.[38] Conditions inside the houses were no better. Over 800 families at the former Arsenal No. 20 lacked kitchens. At former Arsenal No. 10, the housing crunch was so severe that "five to six people often live in a single bedroom, and sometimes two to three generations live in one room."[39] The severe housing shortage forced half of all arsenal employees to live outside the factories. Among four arsenals surveyed in October 1950, over 2,500 families were still waiting for their housing problem to be resolved.[40]

The authorities adopted several means to cope with the housing crisis. The Department of Industry subsidized rents for employees living outside the factory compound, while factory officials began construction projects. A shortage of masons and materials led some arsenals to mobilize workers to renovate and repair factory lodgings and to hire employees' spouses in construction teams. Moving women into the public sphere of production was in keeping with the socialist slogan "Women hold up half the sky," but such jobs perpetuated a form of exploitation practiced under the Guomindang, because they kept the women's husbands' wages low. At former Arsenal No. 50, for example, "women have assumed much of the construction work, because there are no transport workers. This has helped most people's livelihood for those with low wages."[41] Seeking to equalize social relations and provide employees with housing, factories assigned houses that staff officers had once occupied to workers' families. Although such measures often led to cramped quarters when three- to four-room houses were converted for the use of several families, the unions succeeded in desegregating the factory compounds. After 1952, staff and workers lived together.

Cooperatives were the other significant measure implemented by the Communists to improve the livelihood of arsenal employees. Cooperatives became popular because they sold everyday necessities at 10–20 percent below market price. Initially, though, union and party authorities faced a dilemma, since they did not want workers to view the cooperatives as mere replicas of the Guomindang-era welfare associations. The CCP regarded the old welfare system as an opiate that had fostered class collaboration. As union cadres explained in meetings, "Welfare was a method used by reactionaries to rope in and numb workers, but in reality it was taken entirely from the sweat and blood of workers' labor and converted into a subsidy wage *[jintie gongzi]*."[42] Workers, on the other hand, viewed the co-op as an extension of the social welfare benefits that they had fought for over the past decade. Some workers, according to union reports, thus remained dissatisfied with a perceived regression in welfare services under the new regime. "A few workers felt prices at cooperatives were not much lower than the market price. They wanted the co-op to be based on the principle of 'buy one, get one free.'"[43] Other workers asked, "Why were firewood, rice, oil, and salt free during the reactionary period?"[44]

The unions countered with several measures to win over skeptics. In March 1950, they established "labor insurance committees" to replace the former cooperative welfare organizations. Whereas the Guomindang had stripped welfare associations of their class connotations, the Communists changed the name in honor of labor. More substantively, they created a new administration by recruiting worker activists and worker cadres to manage the new committees. This made for a stark contrast with pre-1949 days, when staff had run the cooperatives. Certain factories also held numerous meetings to make workers realize that the cooperative was a characteristic of a "semi-socialist society."

These competing conceptions of social welfare formed part of a larger debate among workers and union and party officials over "extreme egalitarian tendencies" among workers. The authorities had two conflicting agendas in reforming wages and welfare. While the unions tried to eliminate the unfair and unequal practices of the past, they sought to use material incentives to maximize productivity. This required eliminating welfare subsidies or forms of "disguised wages," which had fostered egalitarian tendencies. As the Southwest Ordnance Union reported, "On the eve of Liberation, workers depended on disguised forms of wages for their livelihood. [Welfare benefits] became a kind of supply system, and a phenomenon of extreme egalitarianism arose."[45] As the currency devaluation and government policy caused forms of welfare subsidies to surpass wage income by as much as 200 percent, a leveling of skilled workers and laborers' income occurred during the 1940s. Workers with more dependents and personal connections had thus benefited under the old system, since they had received relatively more welfare subsidies.

Not surprisingly, the new policy of displacing welfare benefits based on household members with wages aligned to skill levels encountered resistance. After workers received a maintenance stipend pegged to their wage rankings in 1950, those with many household members and low wage rankings struggled to maintain their livelihoods. "A minority of workers felt that this was worse than the Guomindang period," a union report noted. "Not even rice was given anymore. They now have to use their wages and buy it. The CCP was good in all respects except this one. Everyone wanted to preserve the past system of distributing supplies on the basis of household members, a simple economic welfare mentality."[46] Other workers responded by demanding across-the-board wage increases and the elimination of past injustices. One can sense the union's discomfort in its description of the situation. "At the time, workers' main concern was to completely overhaul past inequalities and unfair practices and to raise wages. Consequently, during the entire readjustment period, we had an unceasing struggle with egalitarian thought."[47]

Workers' demands for leveling manifested themselves in several ways when union officials began to readjust wages. Most workers preferred that wages be determined on the basis of cost-of-living criteria rather than skill levels. According to a union report on workers' grievances, "if a certain person had so many family members or if the past ranking was very low, this person would have suffered for a long time. Everyone felt we should redistribute by increasing the person's ranking." Some felt the new wage rankings imposed too wide a span between the wages of the highest and lowest grades of operatives. "The differences were never this great under the Guomindang. It wasn't as if some [workers then] ate meat, while the others ate soup." Finally, certain workers became disgruntled because they viewed skill rankings as meaningless. "A minority of experienced workers felt that everyone handled these machines and knew the secrets of the machines, thus there was no need for differences in skill, while laborers believed they worked harder than anybody else."[48]

Military representatives began the process of reforming the wage system in mid 1950. Under their orders, arsenal unions tried to win over rank-and-file workers by first eliminating unfair practices left over from the Guomindang era. As advocates of the new policies argued, in the past workers without connections and laborers often had not received welfare benefits. Unions also alleviated the harshest living conditions of low-ranking workers with numerous family dependents by giving relief aid from labor insurance committees and money from workers' mutual aid. Nevertheless, wage adjustments "affected the work morale of a minority of workers. Individual workers whose rankings have been lowered have become passive, and those who have had their wage rankings increased are now afraid of others' sarcasm and blows." At Arsenal No. 20, during the allocation of critical jobs, low-ranking workers frequently let higher-ranking workers do the job.[49]

By the summer of 1951, factory officials decided to institute a full-scale reform of the wage system to eliminate egalitarianism. Notwithstanding prior adjustments, union officials were convinced that the wage system had lost its capacity to "motivate workers in production." The gap between wage rankings, whether for the thirty-six worker ranks or the twenty-three ranks used by technical and administrative personnel, was too narrow. Excessive wage ranks, a carryover from the Guomindang era, had made it increasingly difficult to set technical standards. Finally, varying wage standards caused workers in large plants to earn lower wages than those employed in smaller branch factories, and assistant workers to earn more than principal workers. Implicitly criticizing the previous policies intended to break down the staff-worker divide, the report noted that wages of technicians and administrators were relatively much lower than those of workers. The union concluded that, "egalitarianism still pervades, impeding the enterprising spirit of staff and workers. The rank system has lost its utility."[50]

Following the August 1951 "wage regulations" established by the Labor Board and All-China Federation of Trade Unions, arsenals implemented an eight-rank wage system. Under the new system, managers stopped "disguised wages," such as subsidized rent, water, and electricity, provided during the Guomindang period, and deducted these expenses from the monthly wage.[51] Wages would be based on workers' skill levels and functions. Workers' wages would be pegged to eight ranks (eight being the highest wage), with a ratio of three to one between the highest and lowest wage.

What were the effects of the new eight-rank wage system? Unions were quick to point out the net gains made by workers. According to a 1952 survey of seven Chongqing arsenals, approximately 98 percent of the 12,148 workers received pay hikes. Except for one arsenal, the average wage increases per worker ranged from 33 percent to a high of 44 percent. About 72 percent of the workers were concentrated in the middle range, ranks three through five. Limited data make it difficult to compare wage rankings before and after 1949. But if one considers that in the spring of 1949, 40 percent of the workers at Arsenal No. 10 received the lowest wage rankings, for instance, the new rankings helped workers. Although workers benefited from a net gain in income, however, the eight-rank wage reforms increased the income gap between workers and technical staff. The reforms cut back on some of the gains made by workers relative to staff members or, from another perspective, tried to compensate for the wage cuts suffered by staff members in the first two years of Communist rule. At Factory 296 (the former Arsenal No. 1), for instance, although workers' average wages increased by 44 percent after the eight-rank wage system was implemented, they lagged behind the wages of administrators and technical personnel.[52]

Another noticeable change brought about by the unions was a full-scale campaign to promote literacy. Surveys of the defense industry taken after the Communist victory found that approximately one-third of arsenal employees was illiterate.[53] Seeking to eradicate illiteracy within five years, the Southwest Ordnance Union mobilized employees into accelerated literacy classes. By the summer of 1952, some sixty-five instructors in seven Chongqing arsenals were teaching 125 literacy classes to more than 5,700 students.[54] These adult literacy programs were part of a national effort that led to the enrollment of forty million adults by 1958. By all accounts successful, the percentage of illiterate and semi-illiterate employees plummeted in China from over 70 percent during the early 1950s to only 20 percent in 1964. The importance of literacy in solidifying working-class support for the CCP cannot be underestimated. The literacy campaign raised workers' self-esteem, increased their motivation and involvement in their jobs, offered the prospect of better jobs and more education, and sparked increased political participation.[55] Literacy was the basis for a program stressing cultural and technical education. Union cadres actively sponsored education for staff and workers, as a survey of six Chongqing arsenals in 1951 indicates (see table 10.2).[56]

The factories provided most of the educational opportunities themselves, but over 1,700 employees continued their studies outside the factory. Most enrolled at the Southwest People's Revolutionary University in Chongqing, while others attended the Workers' Political School, the Youth League School, or the Public Security School. China's shortage of technical staff motivated the new regime to provide opportunities for workers to learn engineering skills at the newly founded people's universities.[57] A far greater number of employees attended "spare-time classes" during the evening, typically spending four hours a week in class. Hun-

TABLE 10.2

Educational Enrollment of Employees in
Six Chongqing Arsenals, 1951

Political training classes	3,739
Spare-time cultural classes	5,224
Spare-time technical classes	2,100
Southwest People's Revolutionary University	1,334
Workers Political School	249
Youth League School	32
Public Security School	97
Total number enrolled	12,775
Total number of employees	16,416

SOURCE: Chongqing Municipal Archives, 1032 *quanzong*, 5 *mu*, 100 *juan*, 28.

dreds of workers at each arsenal enrolled in the political training classes sponsored by the party, while even more took cultural and technical classes offered after working hours. Between late 1951 and June 1952, the Southwest Ordnance Union sponsored 203 spare-time cultural classes for over 7,500 arsenal workers.[58] These numbers greatly exceeded the union's initial goal, set in 1951, of having 50 percent of all employees enrolled in night school. The figures are an impressive illustration of the extent of the educational opportunities offered after the Communist rise to power. These educational initiatives reflected the party's and unions' efforts to tear down social barriers in the factory by offering avenues of social mobility to workers, albeit reaffirming the traditional bias that education was the true mark of social status.

Increased opportunities for workers were replicated in affirmative action programs for children of working-class background. We lack figures for Chongqing, but at the national level, reports from 1953 claimed that 57 percent of all middle school students were of worker-peasant origin.[59] If Shanghai is illustrative, working-class children continued to be favored throughout the decade. By mid 1957, more than 70 percent of the city's primary school students came from either working-class or peasant families.[60] Furthermore, the proportion of students from such families enrolled in universities, technical secondary schools, and regular high schools increased dramatically between 1951 and 1958. In higher education, the percentage rose from 19 to 48 percent; in technical secondary schools, the proportion rose from 57 to 77 percent; and in regular senior high schools, the percentage increased from 51 to 75 percent.[61]

These schools and classes gave the party a forum in which to unveil its political program and solidify its social base in Chongqing. The intensive campaign of political education must have struck a responsive chord among workers, many of whom were as ambitious about learning and self-betterment as they were in advocating revolution. Training sessions soon quelled workers' anxieties about the party. At the former Gangqian-hui alone, the CCP instructed over 850 activists in basic Communist principles during 1950 by organizing intensive political training classes of ten days' duration. Between November and December 1951, four classes were held, training over 500 activists, of whom 171 asked to join the party. An additional two weeks of classes, meeting each evening for two hours, were required for activists considering party membership. The curriculum explained the origins of the CCP, its relationship to the working class, and its history of struggle. When workers heard this lesson, the union reported, "they become very excited and are interested. It is easiest to arouse workers' praise for the CCP." These initial forays in political education were followed in September 1952 by the establishment of a political school for workers, which trained 2,500 students its first year.[62]

Such sessions by themselves would have achieved more modest results, since not all workers were enthralled with the barrage of indoctrination. According to union reports, by November 1951, some workers had grown tired of the constant political study, especially when they believed that the counterrevolutionary threat had been resolved. As one worker remarked in a small group meeting, "We study every day, and my butt now hurts from sitting. Isn't it better to work and make machinery?"[63]

But when combined with opportunities for social mobility, especially party membership, the training sessions helped forge patron-client relationships between the party and activists that formed the linchpin of factory authority under the CCP.[64] A more practical concern in recruiting workers was to resolve the scarcity of Chongqing-based party members. For this reason, the city committee had declared in January 1950 that its most pressing problem was weak organization among workers and the lack of leaders at the basic level in industry. The party subsequently defined as its main task developing cadres among industrial workers, and by May 1951, it had organized over 1,600 new members, chiefly among industrial workers.[65] More impetus to recruitment came when Deng Xiaoping, at the time political commissar for the Southwest Department, set the goal of recruiting 5–8 percent of all factory employees into the party during the latter half of 1951. Illustrative of the CCP's response, membership at the Gangqianhui increased ninefold, to roughly 5 percent of the workforce, by the end of that year. Up through 1952, 895 Chongqing arsenal employees were admitted into the CCP, and 2,924 joined the Communist Youth League.[66] Recruitment of arsenal workers matched the spurt in party membership among employees in the industrial and mining sectors of the city. Between 1951 and 1952, there was a tripling of party members who worked in the industrial sector, and membership doubled (N = 16,599) the following year.[67] By 1953, approximately 60 percent of new party members came from these two sectors, far surpassing sectors such as public security, city government, education, and mass organizations. By 1956, when Chongqing convened its first meeting of CCP representatives, the party had expanded to 46,000 members, with workers constituting 55 percent of total membership.[68]

The newly formed unions offered other means of social advancement for workers, especially via education. In 1950, the fledgling union of Arsenal No. 21 sent over 500 union cadres and activists to the Revolutionary University and 150 cadres to the Workers' Political School for political training before working in the union.[69] For workers such as Wang Xianglong, who joined an ordnance steel mill in 1950, political study and union work offered new possibilities and inspired lifelong gratitude:

After becoming a cadre in August 1951, I was sent to the Southwest Revolutionary University. Upon graduating I began working in the union as a political instructor. My work involved propaganda and education. I slowly received the party's nurture. I rose step by step to become a cadre. From my standpoint, I had been an uneducated youth, and the party trained me to take on responsibilities in my work, from everyday work to leadership work. It was all because of party and union support. I worked in the Chongqing Steel union for thirty-seven years. I slowly rose up through the ranks.[70]

Structural reforms of the factory administration provided workers with more opportunities for upward social mobility into the managerial ranks. By April 1951, the union of Arsenal No. 21 abolished lower-level management positions—supervisors, foremen, and subforemen—once occupied by veteran workers during the Guomindang era. In their place, 219 workers were promoted to the ranks of office worker, supervisor, assistant department director, and note taker. This change can be interpreted as an increased bureaucratization of the factory, but it also marked an important recognition on the part of union and party authorities that manual workers could now advance directly into the lower and mid-level managerial ranks and occupy offices formerly reserved for *zhiyuan*. These changes resulted from a concerted effort by the CCP to recruit workers into the cadre structure. In February 1951, the factory party committee at the former Gangqianhui issued a draft statement to promote proletarian cadres. That same month, the party appointed 26 workers as assistant department directors. By late 1953, more than 1,200 steel mill workers within the plant had been promoted to the rank of cadre.[71] Among all the Chongqing arsenals, 627 worker cadres rose to administrative or political positions in 1950. By 1952, the numbers had increased to 2,196 worker cadres.[72]

Many of the promoted cadres were activists, whom the party and unions sought to foster and materially reward for their role in spearheading political campaigns. The party consciously recruited activists of working-class origin during political movements, knowing that such "organic intellectuals" had closer ties to the masses than CCP or Youth League members. "To explain policy we need to rely on activists," a union report noted. "Our demands cannot be too high, but activists should be assembled in meetings to relate the situation, reiterate policy, and adjust erroneous tendencies. We should use activists to convey the leadership's intentions."[73] In tearing down the old guard, as well as a minority of newly minted union leaders, movements ushered in numerous activists, of whom "many excellent workers were promoted to become cadres and assume positions of leadership." During the Three Antis campaign, which peaked in the spring of 1952, Chongqing arsenals promoted a total of 537 workers to become cadres. Some 53 workers were promoted to the upper ranks of the union, achieving positions equal to or above that of section chief.[74] Similar to the effects of the Five Antis campaign in Shanghai during 1952, the creation of a new "subelite" of cadres enabled the leadership to "increase its legitimacy in the urban areas by providing urban workers with enhanced opportunities for advancement on condition that they actively support the policies of the regime."[75]

The convergence of increased social mobility for workers with their replacement of former personnel or "class enemies" during the political campaigns led to a fundamental break in ordnance personnel. During the first year of Communist rule, most personnel of the administrative and technical offices remained in place.[76] Scholars of China's industrial development have underscored the retention of such personnel as a significant mark of continuity with the Nationalist era.[77] But one would hardly expect otherwise, given the expertise required for arms manufacture, the

scarcity of skilled personnel, and the renewed emphasis on wartime production by late 1950. More surprising was the speed with which managers were replaced. At the former Gangqianhui, for instance, all the
leadership positions in the engineering and managerial ranks changed
hands within two years, marking a real and symbolic break with the old
order.[78] Even committed supporters of the Communists prior to 1949
were demoted, and their talents went unrewarded for extensive periods
of time. Yu Zhuozhi, the factory director who had saved Arsenal No. 21
from destruction, was demoted to department director. Only in 1956 did
he join the CCP, and he would wait until the late 1970s to become chief
secretary of the China Ordnance Committee.[79]

The social transformations that took place in the arsenals reflected the
high degree of social mobility between 1952 and 1956, "a time of class
creation and rearrangement." Mobility was both upward and downward; workers took managerial posts, and former "bourgeois" members
assumed jobs as workers. These changes elevated former peasants and
workers into managerial and administrative positions. By the mid 1960s,
one survey of large state-run factories throughout China noted that 40
percent of the managers and 31 percent of the party secretaries were of
worker origins. Another 33 percent of the managers and 45 percent of
the party secretaries claimed to be of peasant origins.[80] Barry Richman
also notes in his extensive study of China's modern industrial relations
that the vast majority of enterprise directors and party secretaries came
from either the working class or poor or middle-peasant families.[81]

Many managers who continued working for the defense industry after
1949 were put under surveillance, and their powers had been curtailed
within a few years. To maintain the old power structure intact would
have prevented the CCP from keeping the allegiance of workers, who as
it is began questioning the retention of personnel. During the anti-traitor
movement of 1951, for instance, over half of the thirty "counterrevolutionaries under surveillance" in one department of Factory 791 (former
Arsenal No. 20) retained their posts as administrative cadres. Three were
department heads and three were section heads, causing some workers to
feel that "those under surveillance are actually supervising us." A construction section chief was reported to have said, "You place us under
surveillance, but aren't you the ones supervised by us? Let's see who is really supervising whom!" Such attitudes were easy targets for political
movements and led to the displacement of the administrators.[82]

A New Class

A much more pressing issue for union and party members than leadership continuity over the 1949 divide was how to retain the revolutionary élan of cadres while preventing the emergence of a new bureaucratic elite. The problem of a "new class" of cadres, identified by the Yugoslav Communist leader Milovan Djilas, was endemic to all Communist countries.[83] What would be the effect of promoting thousands of workers into positions of administrative, political, and industrial leadership? Unions reported widespread anxiety that cadres from working-class backgrounds were increasingly aloof from the masses. "The grass-roots union cadres have not forged close ties with the workshops and the masses and scorn the workers. Workers complain that cadres do not promptly meet their needs and ignore their livelihood and production. They have become divorced from the masses."[84]

Already by 1950, this negative perception of union cadres had spread among workers dissatisfied with the preparatory unions' meager accomplishments. Although, as the Southwest Ordnance Union argued, committee members had at first actively tried to solve workers' problems, the inexperienced unions lacked organization, "had no work methods, and resolved few problems." Union cadres quickly became dejected and lost interest in their work after bearing the brunt of workers' criticism. "They were cursed at by the workers and thus felt that it was a thankless task." The divide between union cadres and rank-and-file workers grew when cadres assumed administrative airs and scorned production work. "The masses have made known that the [preparatory] committee members they elected have become like officials. They don't care about coming to the factory; they don't care about visiting the dormitories. It is difficult for them to see us."[85] In a candid assessment of its own failings, the central union reported a lack of democracy among union leaders, caused in part by their refusal to investigate problems in the Maoist "mass-line" tradition. "Some cadres do not enter the workshops to connect with the masses or do not explain work to the masses in a timely fashion. Cadres are too involved in meetings. Their understanding of the situation and attention to problems are sorely lacking."[86]

Indicative of the growing disaffection between workers and cadres, several union leaders were accused during the Three Antis campaign of embezzling union dues and office fees. "Based on our present knowledge, corruption among the union cadres is truly a widespread and serious problem. It is truly evil, and workers are furious." Complicating matters, whereas previous reports on union graft had blamed nonproduction cadres (administrative staff, secretaries, and mimeograph workers) for the growing rift between cadres and workers, charges were now leveled against union cadres who were still production workers.[87] In part because of their class status, and because most cases of corruption involved going after petty advantages, they would go unpunished. The alleged corruption impeded the effectiveness of union cadres, however, and soured relations between workers and the union.[88] Halting the growth of a new class would require continuous revolution.

Movements: Continuing the Revolution

As the historian Chen Jian has recently shown, Mao's fear that the revolution would be stopped in its tracks was a major impetus behind the Chairman's constant push for political movements, as well as his adroit joining of international crises with domestic mobilization.[89] The lingering influence of the old order and the potential rise of a new class among cadres were important motivating factors in calling for political campaigns during the 1950s. The outbreak of the Korean War gave the party a window of opportunity to mobilize workers on a nationalist platform and continue the revolution.

Once China entered the Korean War on October 25, 1950, the party and PLA leaders supervising the arsenals tried to galvanize the labor force in support of the war effort. But political morale among workers sagged. Union leaders at the former Arsenal No. 20 suggested that employees "lacked a correct understanding of the nationalist and internationalist spirit. Some did not understand the slogan 'Resist America, Aid Korea' or the relationship between China and Korea, while others were afraid of the United States's atomic bomb."[90] Such sentiments are not surprising, given that workers had come into direct contact with American advisors who had strengthened the arsenals' productive capacities during the 1940s. Former Nationalist employees more vividly remembered the role of the United States as an ally during the War of Resistance than as an enemy of the CCP.

Labor's reluctance to actively support the Korean War prompted the CCP to fan the flames of discontent within the factories by merging campaigns of class and nationalist struggle in March 1951. Moreover, party cadres were concerned that vestiges of Nationalist influence remained.

FIG. 10.1. Cartoon of a "Tiger Hunt" During the Five-Antis Campaign.
The slogan on top reads, "Do not retreat until we achieve total victory!"
From *Gangtie huakan* 5 (Apr. 5, 1952).

Party cadres expressed concern that the "pernicious influence of counter-revolutionaries" had still not been eliminated. The old administrative system and management remained, "greatly restricting positive development." The solution was to suppress "counterrevolutionaries," deepen democratic reform work, and on this basis develop the Resist America and Aid Korea campaign. During two weeks of March 1951, 136 alleged counterrevolutionaries were arrested at a single arsenal. Nine hundred employees in the seventh department confessed past actions to political cadres, presumably detailing their relationships with the Guomindang. Others distanced themselves from "counterrevolutionary organizations," that is, the Nationalist Party and the Three People's Principles Youth Corps, through declarations in *Xinhua ribao* and the newly established labor papers circulating within the defense industry, *Laosheng bao* (Voice of Labor) and *Gongren bao* (Workers' Daily).[91]

To win the support of workers, political movements quickly assumed multiple purposes. Unlike two prior political campaigns—the anti-counterrevolutionary and anti-spy movements—which had been explicitly directed against the old guard, the third and most extensive campaign to date, the Three Antis campaign, targeted members of the new elite, such as union committee members and even workers. Starting in late 1951, the movement attacked waste, bureaucratism, and corruption, primarily among cadres. But political mobilization, as Mao frequently reiterated, could help construct socialism by changing the relations of production. If movements targeted class enemies, an equally important dimension was their ability to change the political consciousness of participants through praxis, their involvement in struggle.

The Three Antis campaign was intended to fan the flames of class opposition and thereby raise workers' political consciousness through political participation. Beginning in December 1951, and raging throughout the following spring, workshops organized "tiger-beating" squads that ferreted out alleged perpetrators of corruption and waste. In order to mobilize all factory employees and their family members, the party launched a propaganda war using loudspeakers, newspapers, big-character posters, and cartoons (see figure 10.1). Study sessions were held in which the thinking of participants was classified according to big capitalist, petty capitalist, and worker or peasant mentality. The goal of changing workers' consciousness was articulated most clearly when arsenal unions declared the movement a resounding success. "The movement shattered the leaders and masses' numbness, allowed workers to realize the evil side of capitalism and that capitalists for the past two years had committed vicious crimes against our working class. At the same time, workers realized that corruption was a crime and waste was shameful. . . . The Three Antis made the masses clarify the dividing line between the capitalist and working classes."[92]

The Three Antis campaign effectively tore down the old power structure through largely nonviolent means. Among seven Chongqing arsenals, 142 workers and staff officers were branded as "big tigers" (those with assets of 100 million yuan), "medium tigers" (between 10 to 100 million yuan), and "small tigers" (between 1 to 10 million). More than 3,200 employees were considered "corrupt elements," with holdings under 1 million yuan. Although as many as 2,800 workers were accused of petty corruption, their class designation exempted them from any criminal and administrative sanction. Staff members bore the brunt of the anti-tiger campaign. Most punishments, and these included terms of five years' imprisonment, labor reform, firing, demotion, and surveillance, were imposed on staff members.[93]

As with many of the political movements incited by the CCP, Three Antis struggle sessions took on a dynamic of their own. Workers used the campaign to vent their hatred of managers and administrators. The Southwest Ordnance Union reported that anti-corruption squads relied on "fierce attacks," inevitably leading to the extortion of confessions and use of torture. At one arsenal, workers stripped the chief director of the worker cadre committee naked and interrogated him with his hands raised for hours on end. While authorities did not condone torture, they allowed workers to take revenge. As one military representative put it, "Just let the masses do the torturing. We shouldn't be the active ones."[94]

Conclusion

Movements to strike down rising elites that played on a politics of revenge, the various wage reforms, and the ensuing debate over egalitarianism all formed part of a broader theme in China's efforts to build socialism. Suddenly faced with the urgent need to staff an expanding industrial bureaucracy, the CCP would be forced to balance constantly competing visions of development. On the one hand, proponents of social justice who believed that the relations of production formed an integral part of China's industrial development focused on recruiting cadres and managers with working-class and peasant backgrounds who had the potential to be technical "experts" and, above all, were politically and ideologically "red." The extensive social mobility after the founding of the PRC, coupled with political campaigns that attacked the old guard and broke down traditional social relations seemed to validate Mao Zedong's efforts to keep alive a revolutionary spirit and deepen the revolution. On the other hand, the equally felt desire to modernize through industrialization, a goal that was inseparable from the history of the arms industry, and that had its roots in the nineteenth-century self-strengthening movement and subsequent development under the Nationalist regime, made it almost inevitable that professionally trained "experts" would occupy a prominent place in the industrial bureaucracy.

The continued importance of technical experts and managers in the arms industry was not, however, a mere continuation of prerevolutionary industrial relations. Industrial practices of the 1950s were a direct response to the long-standing divide between mental and manual labor that had generated so much conflict between staff officers and workers. This explains why even the term for managers changed to "service personnel." And, according to some workers, "the main job of these service personnel should be labour, and their subsidiary job, performance of their official or professional duties, and a principal part of 'labour' should consist of making beds for the workers and bringing them tea and hot water."[95] Although carried to an extreme at this one factory, by 1958, the participation of cadres in labor had become national practice. During the Great Leap Forward, factories implemented the "three-in-one method" whereby cadres, technicians, and workers exchanged functions in an effort to resolve contradictions among the three groups. In theory, one could create a unity of opposites by having workers become technicians, technicians become workers, and cadres become both workers and technicians.[96]

Scholars sympathetic to the Chinese revolution have traced the origins of such industrial practices to the CCP's rural revolutionary experience and the anti-urban bias of Mao's political philosophy. The Yan'an spirit, which combined a revolutionary ethos of self-sacrifice and self-reliance with practices that tried to bridge the gulf between leaders and followers, put a premium on cadre participation in physical labor.[97] Similarly, as Maurice Meisner points out, Maoist utopianism condemned bureaucratic rationality, occupational specialization, and formal higher education, elements conducive to urban industrialization. As a consequence, "cadres were called on to practice and glorify the rural revolutionary tradition of 'the fine work style of leading a hard and plain life' and to condemn those corrupted by city life who indulged in extravagance and waste and adopted the 'bureaucratic airs' of lethargy, conceit, and effeminacy."[98]

Examining the urban social context of the Chinese revolution adds another dimension to understanding post-1949 cadre policy and practice. As this book has taken pains to show, much of the class struggle that wracked the arsenals during the 1940s and early 1950s resulted from the deep gulf between workers and managerial staff. Communist leaders presiding over the factories were conscious of this "contradiction," in no small part because many cadres had once been the object of popular scorn for working with their hands. They thus tried to eliminate the disdain for manual labor among managerial, technical, and professional people. From an economic standpoint, such policies may have given managers more knowledge and experience with daily work problems, but the attacks on professional managers also wasted talented people, who were in short supply. Nonetheless, the policies of the early 1950s proved immensely popular among workers. The destructive nature of political campaigns gave workers the opportunity to vent long-standing grievances and carry out a politics of revenge. The massive social restructuring that followed the campaigns also provided a great reservoir of popular support for the Communist Party. The rise in living standards; expansion of educational opportunities and literacy campaigns; and the promotion of workers into more prestigious administrative, political, and technical positions all generated enthusiasm for the party. The paradox was that the creation of more avenues of social mobility for workers looking to improve their social status inevitably fostered a new bureaucratic class that might have had its roots in the working class but ultimately came to dominate the working class. As Djilas notes, "It has always been the fate of slaves to provide for their masters the most clever and gifted representatives. In this case a new exploiting and governing class is born from the exploited class."[99]

CONCLUSION

The premise of this book has been that China's arsenal workers formed part of a broader process of class formation during the war years, 1937–53. Perhaps one would not expect class formation to occur in an industry that was under such tight military control and political repression. The military authoritarian regime presiding over the munitions plants during the Guomindang era made itself felt in numerous ways, starting from the first day of a worker's employment, when one had to submit twenty-six identification photographs (rationalized as a deterrent against labor mobility), followed by a month of military training and indoctrination, and ending with one's participation in bimonthly Guomindang Party cell meetings. Faced with armed guards and spies patrolling the war plants, as well as prohibitions against unions or any association for that matter, workers were impeded from openly organizing and developing class links. Notwithstanding these obstacles to organizing, workers developed a sense of class through their ties to underground activists, through the development of mutual aid associations, and by imagining class. Via the Communist press and their own prose and poetry, workers created a discourse of class that affirmed their positive identification of themselves as manual laborers. Building on these organizations and subjective factors, it was above all through class struggle that workers came to know themselves as a class.

These conclusions may also be unexpected because historians have downplayed the salience of class in wartime Chongqing. In accord with much of the literature on Chinese labor during the Republican era, Lee McIsaac argues that the diverse social and geographic origins of Chongqing's wartime workers promoted regional particularism at the expense of class solidarity. Tensions between "downriver" and "upriver" workers not only exacerbated intraclass conflict but also mitigated workers' sense of nationalism. Along another line of argument, Chinese historians have stressed how labor's quiescence during the War of Resistance resulted from the fact that foreign capital had little or no presence in the Nationalist-controlled territories. Unlike in the coastal areas during the 1920s, when workers involved in the labor movement directed their class grievances and nationalist aspirations against their foreign bosses, Chongqing workers united with their Chinese factory managers against a common enemy, the Japanese. According to this perspective, workers' nationalism trumped class solidarity during the War of Resistance against Japan. As Qi Wu asserts, "class struggle and nationalist struggle had to be united and subordinate to the demands of nationalist struggle. This situation inevitably functioned to restrict labor struggles."[1]

This book has challenged several of the assumptions underlying such arguments. In his seminal work on the Chinese Communist revolution, Chalmers Johnson demonstrated how the Communists capitalized on the Anti-Japanese War by mobilizing the peasantry on the basis of mass nationalism.[2] Arsenal workers identified themselves no less strongly with the currents of nationalism. The experience of the Great Migration, the constant threat of Japanese aggression, the view among workers that munitions work was patriotic, and factory use of nationalist propaganda to heighten war production were all factors contributing to workers' nationalism. Rather than nationalism overriding class-based demands, nationalism and class sentiment were mutually reinforcing. Workers appropriated nationalist propaganda to demand better treatment and human respect from factory supervisors, the state, and society at large.

Although the Great Migration and the rapid and forced industrialization of Chongqing created an extremely diverse workforce, a countervailing force of proletarianization shaped working-class formation. This process transformed arsenal workforces in at least two ways. First, peasant migrants from Chongqing's hinterland supplied much of the demand for laborers and factory operatives. Unlike workers in China's textile mills or coal mines, the arsenal workers retained only peripheral ties to the land. Migrants joined the defense industry and maintained a foothold in urban industry both to join the resistance and to avoid the dreaded draft. Conversely, management's constant demand for a stable labor force resulted in minimal use of temporary contract laborers who might have periodically returned to the countryside. By the civil war period, the only time arsenal workers worked the land was when they cultivated vegetable plots inside the factory grounds as a means of survival. Second, proletarianization accelerated the transformation from craft to a class. Skilled workers from coastal and central China who had once occupied an elevated status among workers suffered a deterioration in their quality of life and limited opportunities for upward social mobility. Their status was further threatened by the development of internal labor markets, which promoted local Sichuanese laborers into positions of skill.

Workers experienced proletarianization in different ways, depending on their social origins. Advances in automated machinery and mass production led to a loss of autonomy in skilled crafts. Likewise, however imperfect their implementation, Taylorist management techniques, such as time-wage studies, had the effect of deskilling work and eroding skilled workers' autonomy, as Harry Braverman's classic work established long ago.[3] On the other hand, Sichuanese regarded moving up the factory ladder into newly created skilled jobs as progress, especially when compared to their former economic status as tenant farmers or laborers. Once employed in the massive state-owned enterprises, all arsenal workers, however, suffered the hardships of factory life. Yu Zusheng's poem "Youchi de tiexie" (Greasy Pool of Iron Shavings) captures the relentless demands of production:

> Sun at high noon
> Greasy pool of iron shavings emits soot
> Burnt stench stimulates your nerves.
> Smoke!
> Won't you ever extinguish the smog?
> The factory keeps producing iron shavings
> all fuel for the raging fire![4]

Regardless of skill or provenance, arsenal workers shared the degrading conditions and wartime intensification of work, the risks of disease or death during the Japanese air raids, and various forms of exploitation—long hours, low wages, poor working conditions, and severe disciplinary measures.

Although these structural conditions—rapid and concentrated industrialization—were conducive to class formation, there was no direct or inevitable link between "objective" and "subjective" forms of class. If we instead employ Ira Katznelson's framework of four levels of class—structure, ways of life, dispositions, and collective action[5]—the history of China's arsenal workers provides ample evidence of a class in formation. Workers' ways of life, both at work and away from it, reinforced the class hierarchy imposed by the arsenals. The advent of mass production and introduction of Western management techniques increased stratification between managerial staff and production workers. The principle of separate and unequal also defined workers' ways of life off the job. Rigid segregation between workers' and staff communities, most evident in their living accommodations, but even affecting their access to restrooms, caused workers to experience the same class relations whether at the factory village or inside the workshop.

These forms of residential segregation and social hierarchy mutually intensified the social stigma that manual labor carried in Republican China. The brutal degrading nature of industrial work confirmed stereotypes of industrial workers as beasts of burden and contributed to their lowly status. Institutional barriers in the defense industry, most notably sharp differences in wages between staff and workers, reinforced the administrative and technical staff's sense of superiority and condescension to production workers. Their prejudices were further buttressed by a host of symbolic and cultural practices, ranging from the sharp distinctions in clothing to different forms of address. As elsewhere in East Asia, where the Confucian value placed on education had traditionally determined social status, workers internalized feelings of subordination and shame at being uncultured.[6] Conversely, arsenal managers and staff took pride in having attained a much higher degree of formal education and thus saw no reason to question the sharp divide between mental and manual labor.

The hierarchical relationship between workers and staff officers shaped arsenal workers' sense of a shared class disposition. In response to unequal remuneration and war-induced material hardships, workers organized a "subculture of opposition" based on the principles of mutual aid and equality. Organizations comprising loose networks of activists, most notably reading societies and strongholds, formed nuclei for the militant minority to pursue its class project in the defense industry. These networks were popular for instilling a sense of solidarity among workers and providing opportunities for them to better themselves through education and earn more respect from society at large. No doubt, the need to organize on a clandestine basis made it difficult for workers to act as a class. But paradoxically, political repression increased the importance of symbolic and linguistic resources at workers' disposal to express their shared disposition of class. The writings of workers, most notably Yu Zusheng, and their published letters in *Xinhua ribao* helped Chongqing arsenal workers imagine a community of class.

This literature played a key role in class formation by allowing the arsenal workers to identify positively with themselves as workers, no small feat given the disdain for manual labor. The language of class that workers used in the 1940s was heavily grounded in moral terms that bolstered workers' quest for dignity and humane treatment. By expressing their aspirations and grievances in ethical language, workers were also able to hold the moral high ground in struggling against their primary adversaries, industrial managers and the state. Ironically, the Nationalists unwittingly helped workers overcome their feelings of degradation. Munitions workers took pride in serving the country as production soldiers, a belief spread by Nationalist official propaganda that frequently compared war workers employed in the Great Rear with soldiers fighting at the front. Arsenal workers also began to construct a counterhegemonic discourse by turning patriotic propaganda against the Nationalists.

The CCP and the militant minority facilitated the link between class disposition and collective action. Forced underground by 1940, the Southern Bureau maintained its links with labor through outer party organizations, reading societies, education classes, and the press. The CCP's need to retain political cover, however, pushed more militant workers with loose ties to the party to the forefront of labor organizing. If the histories of Xie Wanquan or Yu Zusheng are any indication, like-minded organic intellectuals sometimes had agendas that competed with those of local Communist leaders. The CCP's retention of intellectuals in leadership positions was one cause of friction when organizing among workers. That these intellectuals often held the same prejudices against labor as non-CCP elites aggravated party-worker relations. Moreover, although Communist adherence to the United Front proved an effective strategy for gaining control of the factories in 1949, it had a downside. By maintaining the multi-class United Front, cultivating the support of managerial staff, and downplaying the need for independent unions, the CCP unwittingly led more militant workers in 1946 to question the legitimacy of the party in representing their best interests. Ironically, by the end of the War of Resistance, the underground party's fame had probably grown as a result of the Nationalist government's authoritarian stance vis-à-vis labor and its repression of the Communists. As in Japanese-ruled Korea during World War II, "the mass suppressions built up the image of the Communists, because the authorities designated every instance of labor trouble a Communist plot."[7] Not to have pursued direct action in 1946, even if strikes and slowdowns risked harming labor's interests, might have jeopardized the CCP's reputation. Thus while the CCP played a central role in mobilizing workers during 1946, it was often one step behind more militant workers.

Workers identified themselves most clearly as a class in periods of intense conflict during the postwar strikes of 1946. Participation in the labor movement depended on a complex of reasons. Disillusionment with the Nationalist regime spread after the victory against Japan, since workers expected more recognition for their role in the War of Resistance. Perhaps, too, workers believed that the CCP would play more of a visible role in organizing the movement. Whether or not Communists directed the strikes, arsenal workers engaged in class struggle to salvage their economic livelihood and to pursue political aims. At war plants such as the Gangqianhui, workers sought to form autonomous trade unions and have a say in running the factory. These economic and political motives resonated with workers' sense of injustice, their desire to be treated with human dignity. This process of class formation, though, also had its lulls and reverses. In the aftermath of the 1946 strike, an intensification of political repression, the tactical retreat of the CCP, and divisions among workers along generational lines impeded a more sustained and coordinated front on the part of the arsenal workers. The temporary lull in the labor movement gives credence to Jürgen Kocka's observation that "classes are always in the process of becoming or disappearing, of evolution or devolution."[8]

The issues raised by workers during the mid 1940s were not fully resolved and continued to affect labor relations after the 1949 revolution. In response to workers' political aspirations, the Communists quickly established unions to give workers more representation. The most important policies of the new regime, however, involved ending, or at least closing, the traditional divide between mental and manual labor. Through political movements directed against staff officers, wage and welfare reforms, and new avenues of social mobility for workers, the Communists sought to regain the trust of labor and establish a new social base for their own legitimacy in urban China. One of the profound consequences of the revolutionary upheavals that transformed Chongqing during the early 1950s was the re-formation of the working class, with a significant minority of workers forming a "new class." Already by the early 1950s, critical voices had emerged, warning that increasing bureaucratism and embourgeoisement of cadres of working-class origin threatened factory democracy.

A more immediate legacy of class formation in the arsenals involved the development of industrial social welfare. Under the pressure of worker-staff conflict and in reaction to the crises created by hyperinflation and extensive labor mobility, the arms industry implemented elaborate social welfare programs for workers. From the early 1940s on, arsenals began offering a wide range of social services and nonwage benefits to employees. These included medical care, injury compensation, retirement pensions, housing, subsidized daily goods, schooling for employee children, and a host of athletic and cultural activities based on the factory compounds. The defense industry's social policies and paternalism would seem to confirm recent scholarship that suggests that the origin of the Chinese Communist welfare and social organization known as the work-unit system predates the 1949 revolution.[9]

In its industrial form, the work unit refers to China's urban residential and work communities administered by state enterprises. As part of the socialist project during the Maoist era, work units offered their employees many lifetime benefits: social welfare packages, education facilities, health services, and free housing. Significantly, and unique among countries with command economies, China's state agencies allocated jobs that, until recently, were permanent and guaranteed.[10] The provision of fringe benefits by enterprises rather than local municipalities, the permanence of employment, and the absence of labor markets created a high degree of worker dependence and identification with the workplace. Patron-client relations between labor supervisors and workers, especially activists, were buttressed by numerous political campaigns within the enterprise to raise output or attack political enemies, by a dossier system that detailed employees' political records, and by a promotional system that was based in part on employees' political activism.

In a sophisticated analysis of the work unit's origins, Mark Frazier stresses the institutional continuities between China's pre- and postrevolutionary workforce organizations. Various aspects of labor management institutions and norms involving hiring practices, compressed seniority wages, welfare provisions, and dominant factory floor supervisors evolved as a process between the 1930s and the early 1960s.[11] In particular, the Chinese civil war years (1946–49) witnessed the growth of enterprises offering welfare services to sustain workers' standard of living during the hyperinflation crisis that afflicted the Nationalists. In assuming power, the Communists continued enterprise-based welfare practices, albeit under a different name, as we have seen, to diminish consumption, rein in inflation, and meet workers' expectations.[12] The history of labor relations in China's defense industry further indicates that the Communists were not promoting industrial policy on a tabula rasa, or to use Mao's metaphor for the peasantry, a "blank piece of paper." The Communist regime continued the long-standing practice, dating to the mid nineteenth century, but accelerated during the Nationalist era, of state ownership and management of strategic military industries. Other obvious similarities in industrial practices that carried over the 1949 revolutionary divide include the promotion of party activities in the factory and the preference for hiring employees' children to replace their retired parents.

Nonetheless, the management of arsenals and their social relations witnessed profound changes between the Nationalist era and the early 1950s. These ruptures suggest a significant break rather than continuity in state and society relations across the Nationalist and Communist regimes. If, for instance, one considers permanent employment and the absence of labor markets to be hallmarks of the work-unit, the question of continuities over the 1949 divide is a moot point. Economic historians date lifetime employment and the lack of job mobility only to the mid 1960s, when the threat of starvation forced the CCP to halt the migration of rural people to cities and the state replaced individual enterprises as the hiring agent.[13] By contrast, workers moved constantly from one job to another through 1945. Mobility rapidly decreased in the late 1940s, primarily because of the unemployment threat facing thousands of workers, rather than an institutionalization of social welfare practices. Restrictions in the labor market had a disciplining effect. Options narrowed for arsenal workers as privately run factories shut down and the masses of unemployed grew. The importance of the economic crisis in curbing mobility is demonstrated by the resumption of high job turnover during the 1950s, when urban labor markets were extremely fluid.

Until Deng Xiaoping's economic reforms stimulated the reemergence of labor markets, employment stability defined the work-unit system. By contrast, arsenal jobs during the 1940s, although more secure than those in any other industry in China owing to the war, were nonetheless at the mercy of employers. Managers were quick to cut the workforce by 30 percent after the War of Resistance. The Gangqianhui factory, which at its peak in 1942 had employed as many as 15,699 employees, reduced its labor force to 11,553 by late 1946. Further retrenchment and voluntary separations left only 3,122 employees by the time the PLA occupied the factory three years later.[14] Such figures warn us to be wary of assuming that an "iron rice bowl" was already in place during the late 1940s.

A third criterion of the work-unit system used to stress continuities has been the use of social welfare practices and fringe benefits. Arsenals, often under the direction of the central government, provided a whole gamut of services, ranging from sport competitions to medical provisions. One can attribute these social welfare practices and fringe benefits to both Confucian benevolence and Machiavellian strategy. These measures involved a high degree of social control and coercion, since officials sought to curb job mobility, deter militancy, and cement workers' loyalty to the Nationalist regime. None of the fringe benefits were handed to workers on a silver platter, however. With workers calling for equal treatment and a greater participatory role in the functioning of the factories, demanding unions, and clashing with management, the labor movement took on class dimensions during the 1940s and early 1950s. Chongqing's arsenal workers thus fought three interlocked conflicts over the "long decade" from 1937 to 1953: a war of national resistance, a civil war, and a war of class.

Appendix: The Sources

This book would not have been possible without access to the extensive collection of wartime documents from the Chinese defense industry's own archives, now deposited primarily in the Chongqing Municipal Archives. This collection alone holds over 30,000 fiches pertaining to the Chongqing arsenals.[1] The attention that managers paid to every detail of their arsenals attests to the urgency of the war effort, as well as to the self-consciously modernizing mission of the defense industry leadership. Their missionary zeal in collecting data—a managerial principle known as "control through statistics"—stemmed from both foreign influence and domestic needs. A strong ideological dimension shaped the industry's devotion to record keeping. The highly autocratic labor regimes practiced in the arsenals required keeping track of any trace of workers' dissent. Furthermore, from the early 1930s up through 1938, German advisors collaborated with the defense industry leadership in spurring fiscal, technical, and administrative reforms. Subsequently, by the end of World War II, American technical aid played a prominent role in modernizing China's defense industry. American engineers sought to raise the productive capacity of the industry and understand in greater detail the extent to which China should depend on U.S. aid. Intrinsic to the production of advanced metallurgical and machine industries, the arsenals required a high technological base, which in turn depended on sufficient data regarding resources and labor.

These archival documents fall into several categories: (1) quantitative data on arsenal production, finance, equipment, and resources; (2) security reports and interrogation records on the labor movement and the Communist underground; (3) surveys and records of social welfare programs; (4) lists on labor turnover, personnel files on administrative and technical staff, and rolls listing workers' places of origin, ages, skills, and wage levels; (5) Guomindang membership lists and reports on their political meetings; (6) management regulations regarding workers and general administration; (7) annual work reports on production output and managerial and technological problems encountered by each department; (8) minutes from the meetings of arsenal directors; (9) bulletins and technical journals printed by individual arsenals; (10) work reports from the China Southwest Ordnance Union Committee dating from the early 1950s.

These archival records, which focus on the day-to-day workings of the Chongqing arsenals, were supplemented by use of the Number Two Archives in Nanjing and the National Defense Archives in Taipei, where one can study the national policies of the Ordnance Department and its relationship to the Nationalist government. Chiang Kai-shek's personal archives located at the National Historical Archives (Guoshiguan) in Taipei indicate his plans for military industrialization. I also used the technical reports of the 1944–45 American War Production Mission to China, held at the Franklin D. Roosevelt Library in Hyde Park, New York. These sources are rich in information and provide perceptive analyses of the Chinese arms industry's production capacities and related problems.

Inevitably, the type and availability of sources have shaped my questions and methodology. The large amount of quantifiable material raises issues that have traditionally concerned labor economists. These regard the material conditions of workers during wartime, the issues surrounding labor mobility and labor markets, the structure of job employment, and the forms of wages and social welfare. These sources thus provide a wealth of information on workers' daily lives. A better understanding of workers' material conditions may also serve as a basis for study of their actions and attitudes.

By contrast, the archival sources are more limited with regard to understanding working-class culture and the communities surrounding the arsenals, subjects that could draw on the insights of the "new" labor history with its focus on both work and community as the key to working-class formation.[2] A related caveat is the source records' relative lack of attention to the working conditions and the shop floor. Studies of Chinese labor in other cities or industries have often relied on the surveys written by reporters, social reformers, or officials to reconstruct an ethnography of the workshop. In contrast, the arms industry banned such parties, even other government ministry officials, from investigating any facet of the arsenals, ostensibly for reasons of national security. Nevertheless, a partial reconstruction of working conditions can be achieved. Health records and compensation records for victims of job-related disease or accidents reveal the hidden traumas of mass-production work. Disciplinary records attest to the relationship between production drives, resistance, and fatigue. Letters published in the Communist press also speak to workers' attitudes and their views of the workplace.

Oral history can fill in many details regarding the conditions of work and life inside the munitions plants. With that aim in mind, my wife and I conducted twenty-three interviews with former arsenal employees residing in the PRC and Taiwan. Most of the interviews, all of which were taped, were conducted in a round-table format, with three to four participants speaking for three hours. We were given the opportunity for a follow-up interview of the same duration. Rather than try to probe the participants' subjective feelings, which the political environment could more easily influence, questions focused on details of everyday life. We asked each participant similar questions regarding his family background, education, recruitment into the arsenals, work position, working and living conditions, political activity, and associational culture. Following the Bibliography, I have listed the names and positions of the interviewees cited in this book.

With regard to periodization, the vast majority of the relevant documents in the Chongqing Municipal Archives date from the 1937–49 period. Although the war period is the focus of the book, certain questions cross these temporal boundaries and precede the Anti-Japanese War. Specifically, the war changed the social profile of the workforce from a craft- to a class-based one. Sources from the 1940s demonstrate the end result of this process, but ideally one would have wished for more documentation of the lives of arsenal artisans prior to the war. Unfortunately, a trip to the various Wuhan archives to examine documents pertaining to the Hanyang arsenal proved fruitless. Historians of contemporary China often lament their inability to research the history of the People's Republic. The availability of arsenal union reports, however, permitted a preliminary study of the unions' role in fostering the radical changes of the early 1950s.

The relative paucity of workers' own sources makes it doubly difficult to study workers' subjectivity or consciousness. This problem was compounded by the Nationalist government's prohibition of unions or any form of independent labor organization within the defense industry. But documents on the labor movement tell us a great deal about workers' attitudes, aspirations, and feelings. Disciplinary records, reports, and interrogation records conducted in the aftermath of strikes reveal the mind-sets of both workers and managers. Recently published reports of Communist activists shed light on the relationship between workers and party members, as well as on how the militant minority sought to carry through the class project. These sources include the six-volume series *Nanfangju dangshi ziliao* (Historical materials of the Southern Bureau) and the collection *Sichuan gongren yundong shiliao xuanbian* (Selections of historical materials on the Sichuan labor movement).

I also use memoir literature on working-class activists and party militants to complement the archival record. Since the late 1970s, the political rehabilitation of former Communist underground members (accused during the Cultural Revolution by Jiang Qing and Kang Sheng, among others, of having defected to the Guomindang) has produced a steady stream of published memoirs on the United Front period (1936–47). Moreover, Professor Huang Shujun of Southwest Normal University, in coordination with the Chongqing General Trade Union, has directed an oral history project on Chongqing's labor movement leaders. These unpublished materials, which at times are critical of the CCP and not simply hagiographic, shed light on the politics of the arms industry.

Notes

Abbreviations in the Notes

Published Books
(see bibliography for full references)

KHYGS   Chongqingshi dang'anguan, Sichuan sheng yejin gongye ting "yejinzhi" bianweihui, comp., *Kangzhan houfang yejin gongye shiliao*

NFJDS   Nanfangju dangshi ziliao zhengji xiaozu, ed., *Nanfangju dangshi ziliao*

SGRYD   Sichuansheng dang'anguan, ed., *Sichuan gongren yundong shiliao xuanbian*

ZJBGS   "Zhongguo jindai bingqi gongye dang'an shiliao" bianweihui, comp., *Zhongguo jindai bingqi gongye dang'an shiliao*, vols. 1–4

ZSWJ   *Zhonghua Minguo zhongyao shiliao chubian—dui Ri kangzhan shiqi xubian*

Archival References

To facilitate archival searches, I have provided full details based on the archival cataloging system. Pre-1949 archival files for all the Chongqing arsenals were transferred to the Chongqing Municipal Archives, where they are still organized separately. In the notes, I identify each arsenal by number—for instance, Arsenal No. 10 as "10 Chang." I subsequently provide record number *(mulu,* or *mu)*, file number *(juan)*, page number, and date. In certain instances, the Chongqing Municipal Archives retained the original record heading, such as *ren* for personnel, rather than substituting a number. In these cases, I have retained the wording. Regarding pagination, only the verso (b) of Chinese pagination is distinguished; otherwise, the recto side (a) is meant.

AWPM   American War Production Mission
BGS   Ordnance Department (Binggongshu)
CQA   Chongqing Municipal Archives, Chongqing, PRC
CQGLS   Chongqing Geleshan Martyrs' Cemetery Archives, Chongqing, PRC

FDR   Franklin D. Roosevelt Library, Hyde Park, New York

IMH   Academia Sinica, Institute of Modern History, Taipei, Taiwan

MIR   U.S. Military Intelligence Reports: China, 1911–41, University Publications of America, Inc. Microfilm

MND   Bureau of Historical Translation and Compilation, Ministry of National Defense (Guojun dang'an, Shizhengju), Taipei, Taiwan

NHA   National Historical Archives (Guoshiguan), Taipei, Taiwan

NPHA   Nationalist Party Historical Archives (Dangshihui), Taipei, Taiwan

RDS   U.S. Department of State, Records of the Department of State Relating to the Internal Affairs of China, 1910–29; 1930–39. Microfilm.

SHA   Second Historical Archives of China, Nanjing, PRC

Introduction

1. Hinton, *Fanshen: A Documentary of Revolution in a Chinese Village.*

2. This theme of three interrelated wars was inspired by Claudio Pavone's masterful study of the Italian Resistance, *Una guerra civile: Saggio storico sulla moralità nella Resistenza.*

3. "Binggong Shu wei jiang ge chang laogongke gaiming gongzhengke xunling" (Sept. 7, 1940), in *ZJBGS*, 3: 824.

4. On Lu Jingshi, Pan Gongzhan, and other Nationalist labor leaders' discussion of class, see *Zhongyang ribao* (Chongqing), May 1, 1940, 3–4; *Zhongyang ribao* (Chongqing), May 1, 1941, 2. These views formed part of the Nationalist regime's corporatist ideology, described in Perry, *Shanghai on Strike: The Politics of Chinese Labor,* 106.

5. Qi Wu, *Kang Ri Zhanzheng shiqi Zhongguo gongren yundong shigao,* 209–13.

6. Huang Shujun, *Chongqing gongren yundong shi, 1919–1949.*

7. Chesneaux, *The Chinese Labor Movement, 1919–1927.*

8. Honig's methodology follows E. P. Thompson and the "new" labor historians in demonstrating workers' agency through the study of their experience at work and in the community. Whereas Thompson emphasizes the changes in class consciousness brought about during conflict, Honig devotes less analysis to the role of women mill workers in the labor movement, especially during the 1920s. Honig, *Sisters and Strangers: Women in the Shanghai Cotton Mills, 1919–1949,* 249.

9. Perry, *Shanghai on Strike: The Politics of Chinese Labor,* 251. Emphasis in original.

10. Smith, *Like Cattle and Horses: Nationalism and Labor in Shanghai, 1895–1927.*

11. Palmer, *Descent into Discourse: The Reification of Language and the Writing of Social History,* 253. Emphasis in original.

12. Engels, *The Condition of the Working Class in England,* 87.

13. Katznelson, "Working-Class Formation: Constructing Cases and Comparisons," 14.

14. E. P. Thompson, "The Peculiarities of the English," in *Socialist Register*

1965, ed. Ralph Miliband and John Saville (London: Merlin Press, 1966), 357. Emphasis in original. Quoted in Katznelson, "Working-Class Formation: Constructing Cases and Comparisons," 18.

15. Montgomery, *The Fall of the House of Labor: The Workplace, the State, and American Labor Activism, 1865–1925*, 2.

16. Thompson, *The Making of the English Working Class*, 9–10.

17. Kolko, *Century of War: Politics, Conflicts, and Society Since 1914*, 220.

18. Some of the most important studies on the Communist mobilization of rural support include Chen, *Making Revolution: The Communist Movement in Eastern and Central China, 1937–1945*; Johnson, *Peasant Nationalism and Communist Power: The Emergence of Revolutionary China*; Selden, *The Yenan Way in Revolutionary China*; and Wou, *Mobilizing the Masses: Building Revolution in Henan*.

19. Epstein, *Notes on Labor Problems in Nationalist China*.

20. Ch'i, *Nationalist China at War: Military Defeats and Political Collapse, 1937–1945*; Eastman, *Seeds of Destruction: Nationalist China in War and Revolution, 1937–1949*; White and Jacoby, *Thunder Out of China*.

21. Westad, *Decisive Encounters: The Chinese Civil War, 1946–1950*, 143.

22. Lutze, "New Democracy: Chinese Communist Relations with the Urban Middle Forces, 1931–1952"; Pepper, *Civil War in China: The Political Struggle, 1945–1949*; Yick, *Making Urban Revolution in China: The CCP-GMD Struggle for Beiping-Tianjin, 1945–1949*.

23. Kirby, *Germany and Republican China*; Kirby, "The Chinese War Economy," 185–212.

24. Lu and Tang, eds., *Kangzhan shiqi Chongqing de bingqi gongye;* Wang Guoqiang, *Zhongguo binggong zhizaoye fazhan shi*.

25. In keeping with the usage of historians who have employed this more expansive definition, "Chongqing" refers to both the city proper and the outlying counties of Baxian, Jiangbei, Qijiang, and Changshou. Lu and Tang, eds., *Kangzhan shiqi Chongqing de bingqi gongye*, 29.

26. Perry, *Putting Class in Its Place: Worker Identities in East Asia*, 3.

27. Hobsbawm, *Nations and Nationalism Since 1780: Programme, Myth, Reality*, 123.

28. Jameson, *All that Glitters: Class, Conflict, and Community in Cripple Creek*; Wolfe, *Working Women, Working Men: São Paulo and the Rise of Brazil's Industrial Working Class, 1900–1955*.

29. My definition of proletarianization is adapted from Tilly, *Politics and Class in Milan, 1881–1901*, 9.

30. Honig argues that the contract labor system hurt the interests of both mill owners and workers, because it entrenched the power of contractors in league with Green Gang members. The resultant insecurity and dangers of such an arrangement reinforced workers' particularistic consciousness and deflected antagonisms between labor and capital. Honig, *Sisters and Strangers: Women in the Shanghai Cotton Mills, 1919–1949*, ch. 5. For a more comparative economic approach to labor contracting, see Wright, "A Method of Evading Management: Contract Labor in Chinese Coal Mines Before 1937," 656–78.

31. Marx, *Capital*, 1: 698.

32. Kocka, "Problems of Working-Class Formation in Germany: The Early Years, 1800–1875," 282.

33. Shaffer, *Mao and the Workers: The Hunan Labor Movement, 1920–1923*.

34. Elizabeth Perry, for instance, concludes that skilled workers and artisans were often more activist and prone to ally with the Chinese Communist Party, while semi-skilled workers gravitated toward the Guomindang, and unskilled laborers remained politically apathetic, at least in the sense of party affiliation. Perry, *Shanghai on Strike: The Politics of Chinese Labor*, 232–33; id., "Labor Divided: Sources of State Formation in Modern China," 144–45.

35. Sewell, "Artisans, Factory Workers, and the Formation of the French Working-Class, 1789–1848," 45–70; Thompson, *The Making of the English Working Class*.

36. Kocka, "Problems of Working-Class Formation in Germany: The Early Years, 1800–1875," 321–22; Nimura, *The Ashio Riot of 1907: A Social History of Mining in Japan*, 215–16.

37. Westad, *Decisive Encounters: The Chinese Civil War, 1946–1950*, 69.

38. For an overview of the national salvation movement, see Coble, *Facing Japan: Chinese Politics and Japanese Imperialism, 1931–1937*, 289–97.

Chapter 1. To Buy or to Build? Economic Development and the Arms Industry

1. For a photograph of the arsenal occupation, see Lin Sheng, *"Jiu-Yiba" shibian tuzhi*, 87. For production figures, see Chan, *Arming the Chinese: The Western Armaments Trade in Warlord China, 1920–1928*, 111; MIR, reel 6, report no. 360, "Report on the Capacity and Product of the Main Arsenals at Mukden" (Sept. 27, 1926). For economic value, see "Binggongshu baosong guofang binggong wunian jianshe jihua yusuanshu gei Junzhengbu chengwen gao" (Aug. 6, 1932), in *ZJBGS*, 3: 91–92. In August 1932, the Nationalist government projected a budget of 375 million huabi (U.S.$75 million) for the Five-Year Plan.

2. The term is from Smith, *Like Cattle and Horses: Nationalism and Labor in Shanghai, 1895–1927*, 9, 190.

3. Feng Guifen, "On the Manufacture of Foreign Weapons," in Teng and Fairbank, *China's Response to the West: A Documentary Survey 1839–1923*, 54.

4. Rawlinson, *China's Struggle for Naval Development, 1839–1895*, 108.

5. Kennedy, *The Arms of Kiangnan: Modernization in the Chinese Ordnance Industry, 1860–1895*.

6. Chan, *Arming the Chinese: The Western Armaments Trade in Warlord China, 1920–1928*, 110.

7. Rawski, *Economic Growth in Prewar China*, 10–11.

8. On the production and use of tungsten carbide, see Williams, ed., *The Twentieth Century, c. 1900 to c. 1950*, vol. 6, pt. 1, of *A History of Technology*, ed. Singer et al., 181. CQA, BGS 1 *mu*, 762 *juan*.

9. "Yan Zhenbing guanyu yong liangang zaoyao waiguo zhuanmen rencai zhi Dayuanshi michen" (July 29, 1915), in *ZJBGS*, 2: 468.

10. For the latter view, which offers a more positive assessment of China's arms industry, see Waldron, *From War to Nationalism: China's Turning Point, 1924–1925*, 61.

11. MIR, reel 6, report no. 396, "Arsenals in General" (July 28, 1930).

12. MIR, reel 6, report no. 410, "Data on Chinese Arsenals" (Apr. 30, 1930).

13. "Yang Jizeng shicha Taiyuan binggongchang qingxing gei He Yingqin baogao" (Sept. 1, 1936), in *ZJBGS*, 3: 397; MIR, reel 6, report no. 392, "The Taiyuanfu Arsenal" (Dec. 10, 1930).

14. MIR, reel 6, report no. 398, "Additional Reports on Various Arsenals" (July 28, 1930); RDS, 893.2421/28, Richard P. Patrick, May 13, 1930.

15. MIR, reel 6, report no. 398, "Additional Reports on Various Arsenals" (July 28, 1930).

16. Chen Cungong, "Minchu lujun junhuo zhi shuru," 253–54.

17. The embargo's greatest impact occurred between 1919 and 1924, when the average annual value of imported weapons dropped to 1.6 million yuan, from a high point of 22 million yuan in 1918. Increased demand stemming from the Northern Expedition prompted a rise in imports to an average annual value of 9.7 million yuan during the 1925–29 period. Still, this escalation represented only 44 percent of the annual average for 1930–34, 21.5 million yuan, when the embargo was lifted. Zheng Youkui, "Wo guo jinshi nianlai guoji maoyi pingheng zhi yanjiu: 1925–1934," 555. On domestic arms production, see Wang Zhenghua, *Kangzhan shiqi waiguo dui Hua junshi yuanzhu*, 12.

18. MIR, reel 6, report no. 409, "Chinese Arsenal Activities" (Apr. 30, 1930).

19. *Binggong yuekan*, July 15, 1929.

20. "Binggong dashi Li Daichen," *Zong Heng* (Beijing), 1992, 29. Wang Zhenghua, *Kangzhan shiqi waiguo dui Hua junshi yuanzhu*, 17.

21. MIR, reel 6, report no. 398, "Additional Reports on Various Arsenals" (July 28, 1930).

22. MIR, reel 6, report no. 392, Lieut. Col. (Field Artillery) Nelson E. Margetts, "The Taiyuanfu Arsenal" (Dec. 10, 1930).

23. Zhou Weihan, "Shanxi binggong shiliao," 29.

24. MIR, reel 6, letter no. 430, military attaché, Peking, to Washington, "The Mukden Arsenal" (Feb. 14, 1929).

25. U.S. Consul Richard Butrick in RDS 893.2421/28 (May 13, 1930).

26. Wang Zhenghua, *Kangzhan shiqi waiguo dui Hua junshi yuanzhu*, 52.

27. "Junzhengbu Binggongshu tiaoli" (Dec. 11, 1928), in *ZJBGS*, 3: 12.

28. Howard, "Workers at War: Labor in the Nationalist Arsenals of Chongqing, 1937–1949," 41–42.

29. For analysis of the 1936 revolt in the southwest, see Eastman, *The Abortive Revolution: China Under Nationalist Rule, 1927–1937*, 255–61; "Guangdong huaxuechang heyue" (Sept. 8, 1934), in *ZJBGS*, 3: 353–55; "Guangdong di'er bingqi zhizaochang jianchang heyue gao" (July 1933), in *ZJBGS*, 3: 363–66.

30. Huang Liren, "Kang Ri Zhanzheng shiqi Zhongguo bingqi gongye neiqian chulun," 127.

31. MIR, reel 6, report no. 396, "Arsenals in General" (July 28, 1930).

32. "Canmou benbu jiansong binggongchang zhengli jihua cao'an gei Jun-zhengbu gonghan" (Aug. 29, 1932), in *ZJBGS*, 3: 94–96.

33. On Zhang Qun, see Wakeman, *Policing Shanghai, 1927–1937*, 384. On Bauer's ties to the Nationalists, see Kirby, *Germany and Republican China*, ch. 3.

34. Yu Dawei's aunt, Yu Mingshi, provided the closest link to the Hundred Days reform movement through her marriage to Chen Sanli. Chen Sanli assisted his father, the Hunan governor Chen Baozhen, in carrying out the Hundred Days reforms. In the process, Chen Sanli developed close ties with the radical reform-ers known as the "six Wuxu gentlemen" and even sent a telegram to the Guangxu Emperor calling for the Empress Dowager's death. A recent biography suggests that Chen's frankness and "search for truth" rubbed off on Yu Dawei. His influ-ence may have been considerable, because Yu Dawei married his cousin, Chen Xinwu, Sanli's daughter. Yu Dawei's family influence continued to rise after 1949, when Yu Yanghe, his son from a prior relationship in Germany, married the daughter of Jiang Jingguo. Guofangbu shizheng bianfanju, ed., *Yu Dawei xian-sheng nianpu ziliao chubian*, 1: 1–4, 23–37.

35. Kirby, *Germany and Republican China;* Fu, "The German Military Mis-sion in Nanking, 1928–1939." A description of these advisors' role is provided in Huang Qingqiu, ed., *Deguo zhu Hua junshi guwentuan gongzuo jiyao*, 82–86.

36. Interview with Sun Zhiguang (Kunming).

37. MIR, reel 6, report no. 511, 515, "The Hanyang Arsenal/The Kunghsien Arsenal" (Nov. 6, 1934).

38. MIR, reel 6, report no. 509, W. S. Drysdale, "List of the Central Govern-ment Arsenals" (Nov. 14, 1934).

39. "Binggongshu zhiyuan lu" (Apr. 1, 1929), in *ZJBGS*, 3: 53–56. XuYou-chun et al., eds., *Minguo renwu da cidian;* Liu Guoming et al., eds., *Zhongguo Guomindang jiuqian jiangling*.

40. Interview with Qian Rui (Taipei). Lu, "Yu qianbuzhang binggongshu shiji," 146.

41. On the relationship between military technology and the "American sys-tem of manufacture," see Smith, *Harpers Ferry Armory and the New Technology: The Challenge of Change*, ch. 8; McNeill, *The Pursuit of Power: Technology, Armed Force, and Society Since a.d. 1800*, 233.

42. Qin Dequan et al., eds. *Erjiuba changzhi*, 67–71, 80.

43. "Guomin zhengfu junshi weiyuanhui wei zhaokai bingqi zhishi taolun huiyi xunling" (Dec. 12, 1934), in *ZJBGS*, 3: 461.

44. "Binggongshu jishu si 23 niandu gongzuo baogao gaiyao," in *ZJBGS*, 3: 147–48; Chiang Kai-shek, telegram to Song Ziwen, Jul. 4, 1933, NHA, Jiang Zhongzheng choubi, 2010.0/4450.01, 42 *juan*, no. 6546.

45. Ma Wenying, "Deguo junshi guwentuan yu Zhong-De junhuo maoyi guanxi de tuizhan," 158.

46. Chiang Kai-shek, telegram to Weng Wenhao, Dec. 7, 1936; Zhongguo di er lishi dang'anguan, ed., *Zhong-De waijiao midang, 1927–1947*, 249.

47. Wang Guoqiang, *Zhongguo binggong zhizaoye fazhan shi*, 54; *Zhongguo junshi shi*, vol. 1, *Bingqi*, 230.

48. The term "technological indigestion" refers to the inability of a produc-

tive system to assimilate new and different embodied technology over a short period of time. See Smith, *Harpers Ferry Armory and the New Technology: The Challenge of Change*, 283.

49. "Canmou benbu jiansong binggongchang zhengli jihua caoan gei Junzhengbu gonghan" (Aug. 29, 1932), in *ZJBGS*, 3: 94–96.

50. General Joseph Stilwell estimated Chiang Kai-shek's forces in 1937 at thirty-six divisions of about 10,000 men each, closely corresponding to these goals. MIR, reel 6, report no. 1, "The Organization of the Chinese Army" (Aug. 5, 1937).

51. CQA, Binggongshu mulu, 70 *juan*, 2, 49.

52. "Guofang sheji weiyuanhui niju binggong shengchan kuangchong jihuashu" (1932), in *ZJBGS*, 3: 101–8.

53. CQA, Binggongshu mulu, 70 *juan*, 90 (July 19, 1932).

54. Ibid., 30–32.

55. Kirby, "Kuomintang China's 'Great Leap Outward,'" 48.

56. CQA, Binggongshu mulu, 70 *juan*, 30–32 (July 1932).

57. Ibid., 34–35.

58. "Binggongshu baosong guofang binggong wunian jianshe jihua yusuanshu gei Junzhengbu chengwen gao" (Aug. 6, 1932), in *ZJBGS*, 3: 91.

59. "Canmou benbu jianshong binggongchang zhengli jihua caoan gei Junzhengbu gonghan" (Aug. 29, 1932), in *ZJBGS*, 3: 94–96, 102–7.

60. "Binggongshu wei zai Zhuzhou xinjian binggongchang gei Jiang Jieshi qiancheng" (Apr. 10, 1936), in *ZJBGS*, 3: 280.

61. Wang Guoqiang, *Zhongguo binggong zhizaoye fazhan shi*, 129.

62. RDS, 893.2424/1 (May 1932). The government's apprehension proved well founded. The Japanese Guandong army surgeon and chemical weapons specialist Ishii Shiro began research plans in Wuchang and Zhaodong counties, Heilongjiang Province, in 1932 to produce microbial cultures and bacteriological weapons. By 1935, the Japanese Guandong army had established two secret installations, code-named No. 100 and No. 731, to research germ warfare using "human guinea pigs." See Jiang Niandong, et al., eds., *Wei Manzhouguo shi*, 223; Harris, *Factories of Death: Japanese Biological Warfare, 1932–45, and the American Cover-Up*. On Japan's chemical warfare during the Wuhan campaign of fall 1938, see Bi Chunfu, "QinHua Rijun Wuhanzhan qijian Hua'erzhan shishi gaikuang," 134–38.

63. Wang Guoqiang, *Zhongguo binggong zhizaoye fazhan shi*, 96; "Binggongshu huaxue binsi yange" (1946), in *ZJBGS*, 3: 30.

64. Wang Guoqiang, *Zhongguo binggong zhizaoye fazhan shi*, 98.

65. MIR, reel 6, Memo no. 496, "The Chinese Chemical Warfare Arsenal" (May 14, 1935); report no. 504, "The Chemical Warfare Arsenal at Konghsien, Honan" (Apr. 10, 1935); "Gongxian binggong dierchang choujian jinkuang baogao" (Apr. 17, 1934), in *ZJBGS*, 3: 310; "Di 23 Chang changshi" (1948), in *ZJBGS*, 3: 1210.

66. Zheng Hongquan, "Binggong zhuanjia Li Chenggan," 351; Jiang Hong, "Yangwu yundong he jindai junshi gongye: Jiangsu sheng jindai binggongshi zongshu," 10.

67. "Yu Dawei wei Jinling binggongchang yi jieyu jingfei gaijin changwu gei Jiang Jieshi qiancheng gao" (October 3, 1934), in *ZJBGS*, 3: 769.

68. For quota and actual production figures, see Howard, "Workers at War: Labor in the Nationalist Arsenals of Chongqing, 1937–1949," 76.

69. Monthly budgets are for January to March 1935. CQA, BGS, 1 *mu*, 1156 *juan*, 3–6.

70. FDR, AWPM, box 16, Ordnance, "Notes on the conference held on September 11, 1944 with General Yu Ta Wei, Chief of Chinese Army Ordnance."

71. Lu Zeren, "Yu qianbuzhang binggongshu shiji," 146. In Taiwan, Lu Zeren became president of the Zhongzheng ligong xueyuan, formerly known as the Ordnance School.

72. Liu and Tang, eds., *Zhongguo gongren yundongshi*, 426; Eastman, *The Abortive Revolution: China Under Nationalist Rule*, 229–34; Jiang Liangqin, *Nanjing Guomin zhengfu neizhai wenti yanjiu (1927-1937): Yi neizhai zhengce ji yunzuo jixiao wei zhongxin*, 299.

73. SHA, 367 (2), 270 *juan*, zhanshi ge niandu suichu shumu biao, 16; zhanshi jianshe zhichu fenxi biao, 18; zhanshi ge niandu jianshe suichu fenxi biao zhiyi/zhier, 1.33, 1.34; zhanshi ge niandu tebie suichu fenxi biao zhier (gouxie yihuo ji yunfei), 1.37; FDR, AWPM, Microfilm Roll no. 2, "Wartime Annual Expenditures," 14, table 3.

74. SHA, 367 (2), 270 *juan*, "zhanshi geniandu suichu fenxi," table 3. For Japan's production, see Milward, *War, Economy and Society, 1939–1945*, 30.

75. SHA, 367 (2), 3812 *juan*, Nov. 1937.

76. MND, 109.3/3750.4, "Junzhengbu gongzuo baogao 26 nian" (July 1936–June 1937).

77. FDR, AWPM, box 16, Ordnance, "Notes on the conference held on September 11, 1944 with General Yu Ta Wei, Chief of Chinese Army Ordnance," 3.

78. "He Yingqin buzhang dui wuqu sanzhong quanhui junshi baogao" (Feb. 1937), in *ZSWJ*, 3: 386; Wang Guoqiang, *Zhongguo binggong zhizaoye fazhan shi*, 299.

79. Kirby, *Germany and Republican China*, 107, 208–9.

80. Gu Zhen telegram to Weng Wenhao (Feb. 26, 1936), in Zhongguo di'er lishi dang'anguan, ed., *Zhong-De waijiao midang (1927–1947)*, 360.

81. Ibid., 221. Ma Wenying, "Deguo junshi guwentuan yu Zhong-De junhuo maoyi guanxi de tuizhan," 163.

82. Wang Zhenghua, *Kangzhan shiqi waiguo dui Hua junshi yuanzhu*, 62; Howard, "Workers at War: Labor in the Nationalist Arsenals of Chongqing, 1937–1949," appendix tables 1.1, 1.2.

83. RDS 893.24/492; 893.24/559.

84. SHA, 367 quanzong, 3807 *juan*, 1, report from Hapro to Kong Xiangxi, June 15, 1938.

85. Wu Taichang, "Guomindang zhengfu de yihuo changzhai zhengce he ziyuan weiyuanhui de kuangchan guanzhi," 85.

86. SHA, 367 quanzong, 3807 *juan*, 1–9, "List of Obligations," Oct. 5, 1938.

87. Ibid., Hapro report to Kong Xiangxi, June 15, 1938.

88. Ibid., 2. Hapro "List of Obligations," Sept. 19, 1938.

89. Ibid., Hapro letter to Kong Xiangxi, Aug. 19, 1938.
90. Ibid., 3804 *juan*, memorandum regarding Hapro settlements, Sept. 30, 1938, from Wong Wenhao, Chang Pingchun, and L. T. Chen to Kong Xiangxi.
91. Ibid., "ZhongDe yihuo an: Huahuo yunDe zongbiao" (Sept. 1, 1939).
92. Ibid., 3807 *juan*, Oct. 15, 1938, L. T. Chen to H. H. Kong, confidential memorandum regarding the German barter contract.
93. Ibid., Preu to L. T. Chen, May 25, 1939; H. Koon to L. T. Chen, June 3, 1939.
94. Liu, *A Military History of Modern China*, 102.
95. Milward, *War, Economy and Society, 1939–1945*, 180.

Chapter 2. Fortresses of the Great Rear: The Wartime Economy of the Arms Industry

1. NPHA, Zhongguo Guomindang zhongyang zhixing weiyuanhui xuanchuanbu bianyin, *Kangzhan liunian lai zhi junshi* (July 1943).
2. Lu and Tang, *Kangzhan shiqi Chongqing de bingqi gongye*, 256.
3. Tang Runming, "Shishu Sichuan Kang Ri genjudi de ceding," 117–29. "Jiang weiyuanzhang zhi Yu Dawei shuzhang zhishi ge binggongchang shangwei zhuangcheng zhi jiqi ying jinliang shefa gaiyun yu Chuan Gui liangchang dian," in *ZSWJ*, 3: 338.
4. "Binggongshu shang di50 gongchang jieshou wuxiusuo quanbu jiqi gongju xunling" (June 17, 1939), in *ZJBGS*, 3: 402.
5. Yu Dawei, "Binggongshu wei genggai binggongchang mingcheng xunling" (Feb. 2, 1938), in *ZJBGS*, 3: 240.
6. Chi, *Nationalist China at War: Military Defeats and Political Collapse, 1937–1945*, 54.
7. Lu Zeren, "Yu qianbuzhang binggongshu shiji," 147. Although the speed with which Japan occupied China's coastal areas in 1937 has led historians to dismiss the quality and firepower of the Nationalist army, China's weaponry was superior in quality to its Japanese counterparts in both the flat and curved trajectory fields. Japan's strength lay in its ability to mass-produce a greater variety of weapons, especially artillery and ammunition. The approach of China's Ordnance Department, on the other hand, resembled the German policy of "armament in width," in that both countries produced a narrow range of weapons for immediate use rather than invest in research and development of technologically advanced weapons. See Milward, *War, Economy and Society, 1939–1945*, 29–30. The Czech light machine gun, "the backbone of Chinese fighting strength" was easy to manufacture, durable, and considered by many countries the best of its type. China had adopted the French system for the curved trajectory field, whereby hand grenades were used up to 50 meters, rifle grenades between 70 to 170 meters, and 82-mm mortars for distances up to 2,200 meters. The 82-mm mortar, which served as China's primary form of artillery, had two advantages: it could be mass-produced and was light enough to be carried on the back. Beyond 2,000 meters, field artillery was used. For Yu Dawei's appraisal of weaponry, see FDR, AWPM, box 16, Ordnance, "Notes on the conference held on Sept. 11, 1944 with General Yu Ta Wei, Chief of Chinese Army Ordnance."

8. Lu and Tang, *Kangzhan shiqi Chongqing de bingqi gongye*, 40.

9. Wang Dexiu, "Kangzhan shiqi qian Chuan de binggong danwei."

10. Eastman, "Nationalist China During the Sino-Japanese War, 1937–1945," 563.

11. Wei Yingtao, *Jindai Chongqing chengshi shi*, 215.

12. Hu Zi'ang, *Minsheng gongsi shi*, 175.

13. The following sketch of the Minsheng Shipping Company is based on ibid., 173–84.

14. Cited in Liu, "A Whole Nation Walking: The 'Great Retreat' in the War of Resistance, 1937–1945," 145.

15. White and Jacoby, *Thunder Out of China*, 57.

16. Wang Dexiu, "Kangzhan shiqi qian Chuan de binggong danwei," 128.

17. Eastman, "Nationalist China During the Sino-Japanese War, 1937–1945," 563.

18. Liu, "A Whole Nation Walking: The 'Great Retreat' in the War of Resistance, 1937–1945," 161.

19. CQA, 20 Chang, 1352 *juan*.

20. Huang Liren, "Kang Ri Zhanzheng shiqi Zhongguo bingqi gongye neiqian chulun," 130.

21. Zheng Hongquan, "Binggong zhuanjia Li Chenggan," 353–54.

22. MND, 109.3/3750.4, "Junzhengbu Binggongshu zhizaosi 27 niandu gongzuo shikuang jianming biao."

23. Lu and Tang, *Kangzhan shiqi Chongqing de bingqi gongye*, 93.

24. Ibid., 61, 99.

25. Ibid., 64.

26. FDR, AWPM, box 13, Steel Production, memorandum, J. K. Stafford to H. LeRoy Whitney, Apr. 26, 1945.

27. Lu and Tang, *Kangzhan shiqi Chongqing de bingqi gongye*, 59–61.

28. NHA, National Resources Commission 291/2897, report "Report on Inspection of Iron and Steel Plants, Raw Materials and Transportation Facilities in Chungking District" (May 8, 1946), 5; FDR, AWPM, box 4, "Production of Coal and Coke in Chungking Area" (Apr. 1945); Gragg, ed., "History of the American War Production Mission in China" (MS), 90; FDR, AWPM, box 13, Steel Production, memorandum, M. T. Archer to James A. Jacobson, "Ki Kiang Iron Mine and Nan Tung Coal Mine" (October 18, 1945).

29. FDR, AWPM, box 12, Inspections, folder 5, "Report on Works and Mines of Iron & Steel Works Reconstruction Commission."

30. FDR, AWPM, box 7, memorandum, L. B. Moody to J. A. Jacobson, October 18, 1945.

31. FDR, AWPM, box 22, "Progress Reports, Second Mission," Henrik Ovesen Progress Report, Feb. 25, 1945.

32. Wei Yingtao, ed., *Jindai Chongqing chengshi shi*, 125.

33. Lu Dayue, "Kangzhan shiqi da houfang de bingqi gongye," 104.

34. Wei Yingtao, ed., *Jindai Chongqing chengshi shi*, 26, 47.

35. Chi, *Wartime Economic Development of China*, 21; Zhou Yong, *Chongqing: Yi ge neilu chengshi de jueqi*, 256, 259, 333.

36. Zhou Yong, *Chongqing: Yi ge neilu chengshi de jueqi*, 330–31.

37. FDR, AWPM, box 4, Coal Mines: Physical Outlay and Related Subjects, "The Coal Industry in Chungking," translated from an article by C. N. Shen, Sept. 5, 1945.

38. See the various estimates in Howard, "Workers at War: Labor in the Nationalist Arsenals of Chongqing, 1937–1949," table 2.8 and 2.9, 137.

39. Lu and Tang, *Kangzhan shiqi Chongqing de bingqi gongye*, 6–7. For figures for all Nationalist arsenals, see Howard, "Workers at War: Labor in the Nationalist Arsenals of Chongqing, 1937–1949," 136.

40. FDR, AWPM, Gragg, ed., "History of the American War Production Mission in China" (MS), 96.

41. Figures from Lu and Tang, *Kangzhan shiqi Chongqing de bingqi gongye*, 116.

42. FDR, AWPM, box 19, Post-war Industrialization, Planning and Reconstruction II, Sept. 1944–45, M. T. Archer, "Steel and Comments on Arsenals."

43. FDR, AWPM, box 16, Ordnance, "Notes on Conversation Messrs. Locke and Jacobson had with General Yu Ta Wei" (Sept. 8, 1944); FDR, AWPM, Gragg, ed., "History of the American War Production Mission in China" (MS), 147.

44. FDR, AWPM, box 13, Steel Production, memorandum, G. M. Yocom to A. T. Kearney, June 1, 1945.

45. FDR, AWPM, box 13, Steel Production, "Report of the First Steel Group of the Nelson Mission to China," Nov. 1944–Feb. 1945.

46. FDR, AWPM, box 23, "China Mission Data Report: A Summary of Facts Obtained by the First Nelson Mission, Sept. 1944: Ferrous Metallurgy," 1; Tsang, *The Post-War Market of China: A Preliminary Estimate*, 29.

47. FDR, AWPM, box 13, Steel Production, "China's Iron and Steel Industry" (notes by James A. Jacobson during conference with Knute Lund, Chinese representative of H. A. Brassert and Co., Sept. 13, 1944).

48. *KHYGS*, 126, 176–77.

49. Interview with Qian Rui (Taipei).

50. These managerial methods were introduced in Europe and North America during World War I and its aftermath. See Glenn Porter, "Management," in Williams, ed., *The Twentieth Century, c. 1900 to c. 1950*, vol. 6, pt. 1, of *A History of Technology*, ed. Singer et al., 79.

51. MIR, reel 6, report no. 506, "The Kunghsien Arsenal" (Apr. 9, 1935).

52. On contract labor in the cotton mills, see Honig, *Sisters and Strangers: Women in the Shanghai Cotton Mills, 1919–1949*, ch. 5; on the coal industry, see Wright, "A Method of Evading Management," 656–78.

53. For 1934 figures, see CQA, Binggongshu 1 *mu*, 762 *juan*, "23 nian shangban nian yuanliao laiyuan chupin nengli ji renshu tongji biao" (Aug. 11, 1934). For 1945 figures, see MND, 381/3750.2.

54. Chinese Ministry of Information, comp., *China Handbook, 1937–1945: A Comprehensive Survey of Major Developments in China in Eight Years of War*, 364.

55. Liu Huamian, *Zhongguo jindai junshi jingji yanjiu*, 302.

56. Kirby, "Engineering China: Birth of a Developmental State, 1928–1937," 147–49.

57. FDR, AWPM, box 16, Ordnance, "Report, W. S. Brewster Major Ordnance Asst. Theater Ordnance Officer to J. A. Jacobson," Sept. 17, 1944.

58. Kirby, "Engineering China: Birth of a Developmental State, 1928–1937," 147.

59. Wang Guoqiang, *Zhongguo binggong zhizaoye fazhan shi*, 97; Zhang Zhicun, "Sanshi nianlai benxiao dashi ji," *Binggong yuekan*, Sept. 15, 1948, A19.

60. Weng Zhiyuan, ed., *Tongji daxue shi, 1907–1949*, 1: 47.

61. Zhu Bangxing et al., eds., *Shanghai chanye yu Shanghai zhigong*, 621–22; Xu, *Chinese Professionals and the Republican State: The Rise of Professional Associations in Shanghai, 1912–1937*, ch. 2.

62. Zhu Bangxing et al., eds., *Shanghai chanye yu Shanghai zhigong*, 619.

63. Cited in Bian, "The Sino-Japanese War and the Formation of the State Enterprise System in China," 89.

64. Howard, "Workers at War: Labor in the Nationalist Arsenals of Chongqing, 1937–1949," 133.

65. RDS 893.24/446, "Louis Johnson Report," June 15, 1938; Lu and Tang, *Kangzhan shiqi Chongqing de bingqi gongye*, 260.

66. FDR, AWPM, box 16, Ordnance, "Chinese Munitions Production." For a comparison of maximum annual supply and demand of weaponry and ratio of supply to wastage, see Lu and Tang, *Kangzhan shiqi Chongqing de bingqi gongye*, 278.

67. Lu and Tang, *Kangzhan shiqi Chongqing de bingqi gongye*, 135; Wang Dexiu, "Houfang binggongchang de huopao zhizao," 254–55.

68. FDR, AWPM, box 12, Inspections, folder 5, memorandum, J. F. Schnur to J. A. Jacobson, Aug. 1, 1945. For figures on casting, see ibid., folder 6, "Report, Ralph Strang, regarding Arsenal No. 21 82-mm trench mortar," Mar. 14, 1945; FDR, AWPM, box 16, Ordnance, "Chinese Munitions Production."

69. Howard, "Workers at War: Labor in the Nationalist Arsenals of Chongqing, 1937–1949," table 2.13, 143. Wang Guoqiang, *Zhongguo binggong zhizaoye fazhanshi*, 299.

70. SHA, 367 *quan*, 2196 *juan*, Yu Dawei, report to Minister of Finance Kong Xiangxi (July 1, 1941).

71. SHA, 367 *quan*, 2195 *juan*, Yu Dawei, report to Minister of Finance Kong Xiangxi (Mar. 19, 1941).

72. Kirby, "The Chinese War Economy," 200.

73. FDR, AWPM, box 16, Ordnance, report, W. S. Brewster to J. A. Jacobson, Sept. 17, 1944.

74. FDR, AWPM, Gragg, ed., "History of the American War Production Mission in China" (MS), 189.

75. FDR, AWPM, box 19, Post-war Industrialization, Planning and Reconstruction II, Sept. 1944–45, "Summary of conversation held in Chungking on Sept. 12, 1944 between Wong Wen-hao and Mr. Nelson."

76. FDR, AWPM, box 32, China Reports 1–35, J. A. Jacobson–Chungking file.

77. FDR, AWPM, box 9, memorandum, R. W. Goldsmith (acting director, General Planning Staff) to James A. Jacobson, Oct. 16, 1944. Goldsmith reported

that the United States and Britain devoted fully half, and the USSR, Germany, and Japan about three-fifths of their national income to military expenditures, but that food represented only a minimal portion.

78. FDR, AWPM, box 34, memorandum, James A. Jacobson to E. A. Locke, 54th report of the American War Production Mission.

79. FDR, AWPM, box 6, Correspondence from E. A. Locke to Mission members, memorandum, J. A. Jacobson to Locke, Aug. 14, 1945.

80. FDR, AWPM, Gragg, ed., "History of the American War Production Mission in China" (MS), 144.

81. FDR, AWPM, letter, Franklin D. Roosevelt to Donald M. Nelson, Aug. 18, 1944, in Gragg, ed., "History of the American War Production Mission in China" (MS), 11.

82. FDR, AWPM, box 7, Correspondence between Mission members, letter, Lucien B. Moody to J. F. McManmon, October 21, 1945.

83. FDR, AWPM, box 4, "Production of Coal and Coke in the Chungking Area," Apr. 21, 1945; FDR, AWPM, box 13, letter, Donald M. Nelson to Walter Tower, Mar. 22, 1945.

84. Wang Dexiu, "Houfang binggongchang de huopao zhizao," 257.

85. FDR, AWPM, box 16, Ordnance, "Observations of Lt. Col. H. A. Arronet during visits at the 10th, 21st, 24th and 50th Chinese Arsenals," Mar. 17, 1945.

86. FDR, AWPM, box 9, China Finance and Foreign Trade, folder 1, "China Ordnance Department," May 1, 1944.

87. FDR, AWPM, box 13, Steel Production, "China's Iron and Steel Industry" (notes by James A. Jacobson during conference with Knute Lund, Chinese representative of H. A. Brassert and Co., Sept. 11, 1944).

88. FDR, AWPM, box 22, progress report, James A. Jacobson, Sept. 25, 1944.

89. FDR, AWPM, box 16, memorandum, L. B. Moody to J. A. Jacobson, July 26, 1945.

90. FDR, AWPM, Records of the American War Production Mission, memorandum, Ralph Strang to A. T. Kearney, May 31, 1945.

91. Morris-Suzuki, *The Technological Transformation of Japan: From the Seventeenth to the Twenty-first Century*, 133, 136.

92. FDR, AWPM, box 19, Post-war industrialization: Planning and Reconstruction, II, memorandum, L. B. Moody to J. A. Jacobson, Aug. 12, 1945.

93. FDR, AWPM, box 6, letter, J. A. Jacobson to E. A. Locke, Aug. 8, 1945.

94. FDR, AWPM, box 36, master conference file, James A. Jacobson, "Notes on a Conference with General Yu Ta-wei, October 3, 1945"; box 6, J. A. Jacobson to E. A. Locke, "Notes on a Conference with General Yu Ta-wei, Vice Minister of War" (Aug. 16, 1945).

95. Lu and Tang, *Kangzhan shiqi Chongqing de bingqi gongye*, 245.

96. Ibid., 246.

97. MND, 381/3750.2, Junshi wieyuanhui gebumen fuyuan jihua (Aug. 1945).

98. "Yang Jizeng xiada Chuanqu ge chang 35 nian xiaban nian chupin shuliang gei Li Chenggan dian" (July 13, 1946), in *ZJBGS*, 3: 435.

Chapter 3. Finding Work: Origins and Composition
of the Arsenal Workforce

1. Lu Sihong, *Xin Chongqing*, 37.

2. Ibid.

3. White and Jacoby, *Thunder Out of China*, 9.

4. Taira, "Economic Development, Labor Markets, and Industrial Relations in Japan, 1905–1955," 624.

5. Honig, "Native-Place Hierarchy and Labor Market Segmentation: The Case of Subei People in Shanghai," 271–94.

6. McIsaac, "The Limits of Chinese Nationalism: Workers in Wartime Chongqing, 1937–1945," ch. 3.

7. Perry, ed., *Putting Class in Its Place: Worker Identities in East Asia.*

8. Feng Zuyi, "Kangzhan qijian neiqian renkou dui Xinan shehui jingji yingxiang," 851.

9. CQA, Gangqianhui, 315 *juan*, 68b (Feb. 12, 1940).

10. Ibid., 99–100.

11. At Arsenal No. 50, for example, throughout the seven years for which statistics are available, Sichuanese comprised about 90 percent of the laborers. CQA, 50 Chang, 3 *mu*, 313 *juan*. A 1942 Arsenal No. 10 roll also indicates that 87 percent of laborers came from Sichuan. See CQA, 10 Chang, gongwu, 471 *juan*.

12. Lu Sihong, *Xin Chongqing*, 37.

13. Cheng and Li, eds., *Jindai Sichuan renkou*, 187, 345.

14. See Howard, "Workers at War: Labor in the Nationalist Arsenals of Chongqing, 1937–1949," table 3.5, 181.

15. Jin Dingcheng, "Jiangbeixian jingji gaikuang," 403.

16. Liu Shi, "Kang Ri Zhanzheng zhonghouqi Chongqing de zhigong yundong" (Apr. 27, 1950), *NFJDS*, 5: 295.

17. Interview with Yang Jinhua (Chongqing).

18. A 1933 survey estimated Sichuan's tenancy at 59 percent, or 10 percent more than any other province besides Guangdong. Lu Pingdeng, *Sichuan nongcun jingji*, 171. A wartime study also estimated Sichuan tenancy as second only to Guangdong. Guo and Meng, *Sichuan zudian wenti*, 155. For eastern Sichuan surveys, see Cheng and Li, eds., *Jindai Sichuan renkou*, 318, 339; Guo and Meng, *Sichuan zudian wenti*, 8.

19. Guo and Meng, *Sichuan zudian wenti*, 8, 17.

20. Lu Pingdeng, *Sichuan nongcun jingji*, 261.

21. Ibid., 191; Gunde, "Land Tax and Social Change in Sichuan, 1925–1935," 31.

22. Rawski, *Agricultural Change and the Peasant Economy of South China*, ch. 4.

23. Guo and Meng, *Sichuan zudian wenti*, 87, 154.

24. Ibid., 61. For an excellent discussion of rent deposits, see Zelin, "The Rights of Tenants in Mid-Qing Sichuan," 483–526.

25. Zhang Xiaomei, *Sichuan jingji cankao ziliao*, M-3.

26. Zuo and Ye, "33 niandu Sichuan zhi nongye," 44.
27. Hu, *The Agricultural and Forestry Land-Use of Szechuan Basin*, 42.
28. Barnett, *China on the Eve of Communist Takeover*, 112.
29. Guo and Meng, *Sichuan zudian wenti*, 94–95.
30. Chen Pengzuo, "Xia Chuandong de nongye dili," 87.
31. Wu Dange, "Sichuan sheng de difang tanpai," 193. For the significance of *tanpai*, see Eastman, *Seeds of Destruction: Nationalist China in War and Revolution, 1937–1949*, 56.
32. Wu Dange, "Sichuan sheng de difang tanpai," 188–90.
33. Epstein, *Notes on Labor Problems in Nationalist China*, 32.
34. Barnett, *China on the Eve of Communist Takeover*, 145.
35. Zhuan Jintao, "Xichong jingji gaikuang," 330–31.
36. Liu Qiuhuang, "Zhanshi Sichuan liangshi shengchan," 156.
37. On clique formation, see CQA, 24 Chang, 6397 *juan*, 57. Data on worker separations between 1940 and 1942 confirm the importance of Ziyang workers, who made up 12 percent of total separations, second only to Baxian workers at 15 percent (N = 460). CQA, 24 Chang, 1 *zong*, 248 *juan*, §§ 2–7, 250 *juan*, §§ 1–8.
38. Rolls were organized on the basis of department, skill level, and worker number and only give clues to the existence of family ties if workers shared generation names. I have located a few examples of shared generation names in the Arsenal No. 24 rolls of newly employed workers, which indicate the recruitment of brothers, but underestimate family ties, since siblings did not necessarily share generation names. The more likely situation where employment occurred across generations is not traceable. See CQA, 24 Chang, 1 *mu*, 253.1 *juan*.
39. Interview with Xie Lin (Chongqing).
40. Interview with Li Jiesun (Chongqing).
41. Interview with Feng Junren and Li Jiesun (Chongqing).
42. Interview with Feng Junren (Chongqing).
43. Such was the case in an eleven-day slowdown at Arsenal No. 21 in April 1949. Despite the threat of being fired, workers continued the slowdown and won a wage increase. Changshi bianji weiyuanhui banshishi, ed., *Chang'an chang changshi ziliao chugao*, 34.
44. CQA, 50 Chang, 3 *mu*, 186 *juan*, 9–10 (1939).
45. CQA, 29 Chang, 3 *mu*, 1230 *juan*, 74b, "Kangzhan qijian binggongchang gongren fenzu xunlian fangan" (Apr. 21, 1939); "Paojichu xunlian putong jigong yijian shu" (1940), in *ZJBGS*, 3: 1032.
46. Interview with Zhu Rong (Chongqing).
47. CQA, Gangqianhui, renshi, 315 *juan*, 86.
48. CQA, 20 Chang, 902 *juan*, 158–59 (Mar. 4, 1939); CQA, 50 Chang, 3 *mu*, 190 *juan* (Mar. 25, 1939).
49. Interview with Zhu Rong (Chongqing).
50. CQA, 50 Chang, 3 *mu*, 187 *juan*, 4.
51. CQA, 20 Chang, 1121 *juan*, "Gongren tongji yue baobiao" (Aug. 1948); SHA, 774 *quan*, 2111 *juan* (June 1949); CQA, 24 Chang, 3565 *juan* (July 1948); CQA, 50 Chang, 3919 *juan* (July 1948).

52. See Howard, "Workers at War: Labor in the Nationalist Arsenals of Chongqing, 1937–1949," 170, tables 3.2 and 3.3.

53. Marx, *Capital*, 1: 471.

54. CQA, 50 Chang, 2 *mu*, 304 *juan*, 4, "Binggong Shu di 50 gongchang quanti zhigong renshu baogao biao" (Oct. 1941).

55. Interview with Xie Lin (Chongqing).

56. Woollacott, *On Her Their Lives Depend: Munitions Workers in the Great War*.

57. CQA, 1032 quanzong, 5 *mu*, 100 *juan*, 22, "Nugong gongzuo zongjie."

58. CQA, 29 Chang, 5 *mu*, 743 *juan*, 17, "Anding gongren shenghuo fang'an ji shishi chengxu" (May 6, 1939).

59. CQA, 20 Chang, 1161 *juan*, "Fangkong fuwu dui renkou diaocha biao" (1942)

60. See the description of women workers in a Guilin arms plant in Epstein, *Notes on Labor Problems in Nationalist China*, 43–45.

61. Interview with Gu Weiyun (Chongqing).

62. CQA, 1032 quanzong, 5 *mu*, 123 *juan*, Zhongguo binggong gonghui xinanqu weiyuanhui, gongren shenghuo gaikuang diaochazu, "Chongqing binggong xitong 100 hujia tongji diaocha" (Oct. 24, 1952).

63. Epstein, *Notes on Labor Problems in Nationalist China*, 24.

64. Chongqing zhengfu, ed., *Chongqing yaolan*, 17, chart 3.

65. Zhang Xiaomei, *Sichuan jingji cankao ziliao*, B23, Y1; *Chongqing youlan*, 15.

66. Xie Fang, "Kangzhan shiqi Sichuan xiaonong jingji yu shehui bianqian," 794, 802–3.

67. Kelley, *Hammer and Hoe: Alabama Communists During the Great Depression*, 59.

68. Strain, "More Steel for Free China," 11.

69. Interview with Li Guosun (Chongqing).

70. FDR, AWPM, box 13, J. K. Stafford to H. Leroy Whitney, Apr. 26, 1945.

71. CQA, 50 Chang, 3 *mu*, 95 *juan*, 4–6, "Kaoyan xiaogong biaozhun" (Oct. 21, 1943).

72. Interview with Feng Junren (Chongqing).

73. CQA, 50 Chang, 3 *mu*, 187 *juan* (Aug. 1937).

74. CQA, 10 Chang, 391 *juan* (May 4, 1942).

75. The arsenal laid down certain requirements for employees becoming guarantors. Skilled workers had to have at least three months' employment experience, apprentices at least half a year, and laborers at least a year. See CQA, 10 Chang, 3 *mu*, 78 *juan*, 226; 20 Chang, 1180 *juan*.

76. Xiao Zekuan, "Chuandong ji Chongqing diqu gongren yundong de huiyi," 1–7.

77. Zhonggong Chongqingshi weiyuanhui zhengce yanjiushi, ed., *Jiefang qian Chongqing gaikuang*, 101–2, 79. Both retired workers and the survey used the names "Gelaohui" and "Paoge" interchangeably, suggesting common identity.

78. Interview with Wang Pufu of the Dadukou steel mill, from "Lishi diaocha

fangwen ziliao zhengli kapian" [Collated notecards of oral history transcripts], comp. Xinan shifan xueyuan lishixi (1959).

79. Interview with Du Liang (Chongqing).

80. Interview with Feng Junren (Chongqing). It remains unclear the extent to which gang leaders served as labor brokers, because of limited archival documentation. I suspect they played a less prominent role than the contract laborers of Shanghai textile mills, because the labor market in Chongqing was more fluid during the war.

81. Willson, *The Clockwork Factory: Women and Work in Fascist Italy*, 105.

82. McIsaac, "The Limits of Chinese Nationalism: Workers in Wartime Chongqing, 1937–1945," 114–16.

83. See, e.g., Licht, *Getting Work: Philadelphia, 1840–1950*, 158, on the role of AFL craft unions in early twentieth-century Philadelphia.

84. Shi Hua, "Xiao Zekuan tongzhi tan Chuandong dixiadang"; Xiao Zekuan, "Chuandong ji Chongqing diqu gongren yundong de huiyi," 1–7.

85. We lack information on arsenal workers' wages for the years immediately preceding the Sino-Japanese war. But a 1930 document concerning the Tongyuanju, the predecessor of Arsenal No. 20, indicates that non-Sichuanese skilled workers comprised a third of the workforce and earned three to four times more than Sichuanese, who were typically apprentices or laborers. *SGRYD*, 123.

86. Honig, "Native-Place Hierarchy and Labor Market Segmentation: The Case of Subei People in Shanghai," 271–94.

87. CQA, 20 Chang, 1783 *juan*, 38–43, "Diyi zhizaosuo gongyou xingming qingce" (Rolls of the No. 1 Production Department) (Jan. 1945).

88. Epstein, *Notes on Labor Problems in Nationalist China*, 10.

89. As cited in Roediger, *The Wages of Whiteness: Race and the Making of the American Working Class*, 12.

90. Gordon, "Who Turned the Mechanical Ideal into Mechanical Reality?" 769.

91. "Yang Jizeng shicha Taiyuan binggongchang qingxing gei He Yingqin baogao" (Sept. 1, 1936), in *ZJBGS*, 3: 397.

92. Interview with Xie Lin and Feng Junren (Chongqing).

93. Interview with Zhang Ping (Chongqing).

94. Changshi bianji weiyuanhui banshishi, ed., *Chang'an chang changshi ziliao*, 1.

95. CQA, 50 Chang, 3 *mu*, 185 *juan*, 14 (Mar. 15, 1945).

96. CQA, 10 Chang, 1 *mu*, 339 *juan*, 206 (June 27, 1939).

97. CQA, 10 Chang, gongwu, 251 *juan*, 16, "Chang-Yuan yidai zhaokao jigong huaming qingce" (Dec. 26, 1940).

98. CQA, 20 Chang, 1441 *juan*, 10b–11 (Oct. 2, 1938).

99. CQA, 24 Chang, 1 *mu*, 30 *juan*, 83–84 (Oct. 31, 1940).

100. CQA, 24 Chang, 1 *mu*, 69 *juan*, 57 (June 20, 1939).

101. CQA, 20 Chang, 1012, 1019, 1032, 1049, 1089, 1121 *juan*; CQA, 24 Chang, 1 *zong*, 248 *juan*, §§ 2–7, 250 *juan*, §§ 1–4.

102. "Di 50 gongchang yitu xuexiao shourong zhanshi ertong baoyu hui xuesheng banfa" (Apr. 24, 1939); "Di 50 gongchang yitu xuexiao gongzuo bao-

gao" (1939); "Jiang Biao gei Yu Dawei de chengwen gao" (Mar. 14, 1940), in *ZJBGS*, 3: 1024–28.

103. "Yu Dawei wei jianfa jigong xunlianban zhaosheng jianzhang daidian" (Sept. 3, 1940), in *ZJBGS*, 3: 1035–38.

104. "Gangqianhui di 38 jigong xunlianban gaikuang" (1945), in *ZJBGS*, 3: 1040; Zhao Zhizhong, "Li Chenggan zhuanlue," 126; Lu and Tang, eds., *Kangzhan shiqi Chongqing de bingqi gongye*, 170; CQA, 10 Chang, 3 *mu*, 10 *juan*, 28, "Di 16 ci zaiYu ge chang changzhang huiyi yicheng" (Aug. 12, 1940); CQA, 20 Chang, 1144 *juan*, 353b, "Kuochong jigong xunlian shishi banfa" (Feb. 13, 1947).

105. CQA, 50 Chang, 2 *mu*, 304 *juan*, 10 (Oct. 1943); 50 Chang, 2 *mu*, 299 *juan*, 230 (Dec. 1947).

106. Interview with Feng Junren (Chongqing).

107. CQA, 50 Chang, 417 *juan*, 4–13, letter from Hans Klein to General Tang Yen Chuen, Aug. 18, 1936.

108. "Junzhengbu gongbu Binggongshu zhixia gechang gongren daiyu zhanxing guize ling," in *ZJBGS*, 3: 896.

109. Liu Yuansen, "Gaijin gongren gongzi dengji yijian" (June 28, 1939), in *KHYGS*, 701.

110. CQA, 50 Chang, 3 *mu*, 125 *juan* (Feb. 19, 1947).

111. "Binggongchang gongren daiyu guize" (May 14, 1947), in *ZJBGS*, 3: 929.

112. CQA, Gangqianhui, 1048 *juan*, 15–16 (1948).

113. CQA, 50 Chang, 3 *mu*, 120 *juan*, 128.

114. CQA, 50 Chang, 3 *mu*, 125 *juan* (Jan. 11, 1946). For similar caps on promotions at Arsenal No. 10, see CQA, 10 Chang, 6 *mu*, 664 *juan* (July 24, 1947).

115. Nelson, *Managers and Workers: Origins of the Twentieth-Century Factory System in the United States, 1880–1920*, ch. 3, uses the term "foreman's empire" to describe the foreman's dominance before the introduction of Taylorism, which led management personnel to gradually displace foremen's authority in the United States. I use the term for its evocative quality, since Yu Dawei's managerial reforms delegated more power to managerial staff, who now controlled labor recruitment, hiring, and wages, thereby undercutting the authority of foremen.

116. CQA, 21 Chang, 4 *ren*, 83 *juan*, 2, "Gongyou jinsheng lingban, fulingshou" (Nov. 1946)

117. CQA, 20 Chang, 1547 *juan*, "20 Chang ge bufen linggong, lingshou xingming nianji ce" (Dec. 1948).

118. Zhou Weihan, "Shanxi binggong shiliao," 23.

119. CQA, 10 Chang, 2 *mu*, 116 *juan*, 5, "Binggongshu di 50 gongchang Zhongshu fenchang gongren tisheng banfa" (May 5, 1947). Of 1,134 skilled workers struck off the rolls at Arsenals No. 10 and 20 during 1941–42, only 23 were promoted to *zhiyuan* status. See Howard, "Workers at War: Labor in the Nationalist Arsenals of Chongqing, 1937–1949," 337–38.

120. CQA, 21 Chang, 1–1 *mu*, 1–2 *juan*, "Jun guanzuo luli biao."

121. CQA, 50 Chang, 2 *mu*, 71 *juan* (May 15, 1945).

122. CQA, 50 Chang, 3 *mu,* 124 *juan,* "37 niandu quanchang gongren kaoji renshu tongji zongbiao."

123. Interview with He Qiuping (Chongqing).

124. MND, 381/3750.2, Chen Cheng, "Junshi weiyuanhui binggongchang ku zhengli jihua" (unpublished archival report) (Aug. 20, 1945); CQA, 10 Chang, 1 *mu,* 523 *juan,* 61 (Nov. 1946).

125. CQA, 10 Chang, 1 *mu,* 832 *juan,* 16 (Dec. 9, 1947); 20 Chang, 846 *juan,* "Di 20 gongchang 36 nian gongren jishi tongji biao."

126. CQA, 10 Chang, gongwu, 471 *juan,* "di 10 Chang 1942 xia bannian quanchang gongren mingce."

127. Interview with Xie Lin (Chongqing).

128. Interview with Zhu Rong (Chongqing).

129. See, e.g., the dispersal of Shandong workers at Arsenal No. 20. CQA, 20 Chang, 846 *juan,* "Di 20 gongchang 36 nian gongren jiguan tongji tu."

130. Honig, *Sisters and Strangers: Women in the Shanghai Cotton Mills, 1919–1949,* 71–73.

131. Perry, *Shanghai on Strike: The Politics of Chinese Labor,* 142.

132. CQA, 10 Chang, 12 *mu,* 33 *juan,* 19, 23, report of Chongqing Municipal Police Tenth District Chief Jiang Zhongqi (Mar. 29, Apr. 2, 1946); Huang Shujun, *Chongqing gongren yundongshi, 1919–1949,* 357–66.

133. "Chongqing jingbei silingbu wei gongren bagong shijian gei di 21 gongchang daidian" (Apr. 21, 1949), in *ZJBGS,* 3: 1114.

134. White and Jacoby, *Thunder Out of China,* 6.

135. Interview with Xie Lin (Chongqing).

136. Interview with Zhang Ping (Chongqing).

137. Interview with Zhu Rong (Chongqing).

138. White and Jacoby, *Thunder Out of China,* 17.

139. Goodman, *Native Place, City, and Nation: Regional Networks and Identities in Shanghai, 1853–1937,* 9.

140. Liu, "A Whole Nation Walking: The 'Great Retreat' in the War of Resistance, 1937–1945," 197, 297, 300.

141. Unless noted otherwise the following account is from Xiao Zekuan, "Chuandong ji Chongqing diqu gongren yundong de huiyi," 1–7.

142. Shi Hua, "Xiao Zekuan tongzhi tan Chuandong dixiadang."

143. "Luzhou di 23 gongchang dixiadang zuzhi lingdao de gongren yundong dashiji" (MS compiled by Xinan shifan xueyuan lishixi), 68–69.

Chapter 4. Inside the Arsenals: Conditions of Work and Life

1. Interview with Zhang Ping (Chongqing).

2. Interview with Yang Jinhua (Chongqing).

3. For the former view, see Large, *Organized Workers and Socialist Politics in Interwar Japan,* 83. For the latter view, see Gordon, *Labor and Imperial Democracy in Prewar Japan,* 218.

4. Benenati, "Americanism and Paternalism: Managers and Workers in Twentieth-Century Italy," 6.

5. For comparative examples, see Moore, *Injustice: The Social Bases of Obe-*

dience and Revolt, 203, and Smith, "Workers and Supervisors in St Petersburg, 1905–1917, and Shanghai, 1895–1927," 150.

6. Woollacott, *On Her Their Lives Depend: Munitions Workers in the Great War*.

7. Wen Xianmei, "Riji dui Chongqing de 'zhanlue hongzha' he Chongqing de fankong xidongzheng," 223; Wu Yuexing, ed., *Zhongguo Kang Ri Zhanzheng shi dituji*, 151.

8. Wen Xianmei, "Riji dui Chongqing de 'zhanlue hongzha' he Chongqing de fankong xidongzheng," 233.

9. Xu Chaojian et al., eds., *Chongqing da hongzha*, 124–25.

10. Zhou Yong, *Chongqing: Yi ge neilu chengshi de jueqi*, 290. According to Wu Yuexing, ed., *Zhongguo Kang Ri Zhanzheng shi dituji*, 152, Japanese air raids resulted in 335,934 civilian casualties in China.

11. Zhou Yong, *Chongqing: Yi ge neilu chengshi de jueqi*, 288.

12. Wen Xianmei, "Riji dui Chongqing de 'zhanlue hongzha' he Chongqing de fankong xidongzheng," 233.

13. Lu and Tang, *Kangzhan shiqi Chongqing de bingqi gongye*, 221. On weapons production, see *ZJBGS*, 3: 207.

14. Chonggangzhi bianjishi bian, *Chonggang zhi: 1938–1985*, 49; NPHA, 522 lei, 16 hao Chongqing weishu zongsilingbu diaocha diji zha Yu qingkuang ji shangwang sunhai biao (Sept. 1, 1941).

15. Interview with Ye Xiuquan (Chongqing).

16. Interview with Liu Feng (Kunming).

17. Interview with Ye Xiuquan (Chongqing).

18. Zheng Hongquan, "Binggong zhuanjia Li Chenggan," 358; interview with Yang Jinhua (Chongqing).

19. Lary and MacKinnon, *The Scars of War: The Impact of Warfare on Modern China*, 10.

20. Factory machinist, "Shoubuliao feili yapo, hanlei likaile gongchang," *Xinhua ribao*, June 15, 1940, 4.

21. Mortality records are compiled from CQA, 10 Chang, gongwu lei, 419, 484–485, 605, 667 *juan*; CQA, 20 Chang, 1096, 1783 *juan* (gongren siwang zheng); CQA, 21 Chang, *ren*, 31 *juan*; CQA, 23 Chang, 3 *mu*, 321 *juan* (gongren siwang zheng); CQA, 24 Chang, 4010–14, 4016–17, 4019–24 *juan* (gongren shangwang biao); CQA, 50 Chang, 3 *mu*, 73, 88, 254–55 *juan*; IMH, Jiguan 24–13–01; jiguan 2–(1–3), 3–(1–2), 4–(1–3), "Gangtiechang qianjian weiyuanhui yuangong fuxu shengqingshu."

22. Chongqing's summers are notoriously hot and humid. Chonggangzhi bianjishi bian, *Chonggang zhi: 1938–1985*, 3, indicates that temperatures in July and August frequently range from 36.1 to 38.5°C for up to forty days. Average annual humidity is 79 percent.

23. Wei Yingtao, ed., *Jindai Chongqing chengshi shi*, 509.

24. White and Jacoby, *Thunder Out of China*, 16.

25. CQA, 24 Chang, 3565–66 *juan*; CQA, 50 Chang, 2612–14 , 4070 *juan*; SHA, 774 *quan*, 708 *juan*.

26. CQA, 24 Chang, 3599 *juan*, "Binggongshu 24 gongchang 28 niandu gongren jibing diaocha biao"; CQA, 24 Chang, 1 *mu*, 250 *juan*.

27. Xinan shifan xueyuan lishixi and Chonggangshi bianxie xiaozu, eds., *Chongqing gangtie gongsi de ershi nian*, 26.

28. Interview with Liu Feng (Kunming).

29. CQA, 21 Chang, 31 *juan* (Apr. 1946).

30. CQA, 20 Chang, 1783 *juan*.

31. Interview with He Qiuping (Chongqing).

32. Interview with Zhang Ping (Chongqing).

33. Interview with Zhu Rong (Chongqing).

34. Zhang Zhichun, "Jieshao di 21 Chang," *Binggong yuekan* 1, no. 3 (1941): 68.

35. G. Larikov, "'Explosive Train' in Bombs and Shells and Its Separate Elements" (Nanjing, Nov. 29, 1935), in the official technical papers of General Yu Dawei, compiled as *Zhanshu yu jishu*, vol. 10, MND 155.2/8022.3.

36. See CQA, 10 Chang, 336 *juan*, "Gongwuchu di 5 suo gongren zuogong shoushang biao" (Nov. 30, 1942).

37. Interview with Xie Lin (Chongqing).

38. Li Chenggan quoted in Lu and Tang, *Kangzhan shiqi Chongqing de bingqi gongye*, 224.

39. CQA, 24 Chang, zong 57 *juan*, 86, 35th arsenal directors' meeting (Sept. 27, 1942).

40. CQA, 20 Chang, 904 *juan*, 7b, Di 51 ci chang wu huiyi jilu (Mar. 1938).

41. "Binggongshu chongxing fa zhixie gechang gongren daiyu zhanxing guixe" (Nov. 1940), in *ZJBGS*, 3: 908. "Junzhengbu gongbu Binggongshu zhixia gechang gongren daiyu zhanxing guize ling" (Jan. 1937), in *ZJBGS*, 3: 894.

42. Milward, *War, Economy and Society, 1939–1945*, 238.

43. CQA, 20 Chang, 88 *juan*, 5–6 (Apr. 10, 1941).

44. Interview with Zhang Ping (Chongqing).

45. *Sichuan gongchang shi zuopin xuan*, 11–12.

46. CQA, Gangqianhui, 1486 *juan*, 4 (Nov. 11, 1944).

47. "Binggongshu banfa xiuzheng gechang gongren gongzi ji shenghuo buzhufei banfa xunling" (Nov. 1944), in *ZJBGS*, 3: 918.

48. Tang Zhong, "Mou gongchang zhi gongzi zhidu diaocha baogao," 23–24.

49. Liu Shi, "Kang Ri Zhanzheng zhonghouqi Chongqing de zhigong yundong" (Apr. 27, 1950), in *NFJDS*, 5: 294.

50. Actual income was calculated as wage index divided by retail price index multiplied by 100. Gong Yunshi, "1937 nian–1945 nianjian Guomindang gongzhiqu gongren jieji de zhuangkuang," 15.

51. Qi Wu, *Kang Ri Zhanzheng shiqi Zhongguo gongren yundong shigao*, 220.

52. Ibid., 221; "Binggongshu zhuanfa zhanshi guanzhi gongzi banfa xunling" (June 3, 1943), in *ZJBGS*, 3: 914.

53. "Cong gongzi yu wujia shuo dao laogong fuli," *Xinhua ribao*, Mar. 14, 1943; "Xian jiahou zhi gongzi," ibid., Mar. 22, 1943.

54. CQA, 20 Chang, 1101, 1121 *juan*; SHA, 367.2/393 (Aug. 1947).

55. Xinan shifan xueyuan lishixi and Chonggangshi bianxie xiaozu, eds., *Chongqing gangtie gongsi de ershi nian*, 23, 26.

56. CQA, 20 Chang, 34 *juan*, 57–59 (Mar. 2, 1945).

57. Interview with Li Jiesun and Feng Junren (Chongqing).

58. "Luzhou di 23 gongchang dixiadang zuzhi lingdao de gongren yundong dashiji" (MS compiled by Xinan shifan xueyuan lishixi), 67.

59. Interview with Feng Junren (Chongqing).

60. CQA, 24 Chang, 3166 *juan*, 21b, di 24 Chang 34 nian fuli shiye zuoye ji-hua. Interview with Ye Xiuquan (Chongqing).

61. Arsenal No. 50, e.g., called for an increase of 120 staff members, 1,012 skilled workers, and 650 laborers; CQA, 50 Chang, 3485 *juan*, 7–13 (Nov. 28, 1944); CQA, 24 Chang, *zong*, 6 *juan*, "Zai Yu gechang changzhang huiyi jilu, di 58 ci" (Jan. 28, 1945).

62. CQA, Binggongshu, 24 *juan*, 1, "gechang 34 niandu jianshe jihua gaiyao."

63. CQA, 10 Chang, 406 *juan*, 7 (Feb. 28, 1949).

64. Kirby, "The Chinese War Economy," 202; FDR, AWPM, box 6, "Corre-spondence from J. A. Jacobson to E. A. Locke"; ibid., box 12, memorandum, L. B. Moody to J. A. Jacobson, "Visit to 20th Arsenal" (July 10, 1945).

65. CQA, 50 Chang, 3 *mu*, 108 *juan*, 12, report from Guo Muliang (Jan. 4, 1945).

66. The important exception was the steel industry, which continued to use time wages until the early 1950s. Almost all wages at the Gangqianhui in No-vember 1948 were paid at time rates. See CQA, Gangqianhui, 117 *juan*. During the first five-year plan, Chongqing Steel (formerly known as the Gangqianhui) in-troduced piecework, and by 1955, 36 percent of workers were paid by the piece. Chonggangzhi bianjishi bian, *Chonggang zhi: 1938–1985*, 370.

67. CQA, 50 Chang, 4 *mu*, 511 *juan*, 20 (Dec.21, 1944); CQA, 10 Chang, 406 *juan*, 1 (Feb. 28, 1949); CQA, 20 Chang, 846 *juan*, "Di 20 gongchang 36–37 niandu quanchang gongren gongzi bijiaobiao"; CQA, 21 Chang, Cai, 114b, "37 nian 5 yuefen gongren gongshi ji fuli qingkuang tongjibiao."

68. CQA, 50 Chang, 3486 *juan*, 3 (Apr. 31, 1946).

69. Interview with Zhang Dongqiang (Taipei).

70. FDR, AWPM, box 12, inspections folder 6, memorandum from Roy M. Jacobs to A. T. Kearney (Apr. 12, 1945).

71. Hao Hong, "Gongzi zhidu tan," 19–20.

72. Dobb, *Wages*, 63. For analysis of these wage systems in the United States during the early twentieth century, see Montgomery, *The Fall of the House of La-bor: The Workplace, the State, and American Labor Activism, 1865–1925*, 227.

73. Liu Yuansen, "Binggongchang gongren gongzi fasheng jiaofen de yuanyin" (Sept. 1948), in *KHYGS*, 708.

74. CQA, 10 Chang, gongwu lei, 618 *juan*, 17 (1945).

75. CQA, 21 Chang, cai, 33–2 *juan*, 26 (Sept. 1, 1944), "Xinding gongzi tiaolie caoan." Interview with Xie Lin and Zhang Ping (Chongqing).

76. In other contexts, experienced artisans or modern-day assembly line

workers instruct younger initiates in the art of slowing down work to avoid exceeding the daily stint. Deviations from the ethical code are met with scorn and invective. See, e.g., David Montgomery's analysis of the ethical code of American craftsmen in *Workers' Control in America: Studies in the History of Work, Technology, and Labor Struggles*, 13.

77. Li Chenggan, "Shixing suoduan gongzuo shijian tigao gongzuo xiaolu zhi xunhua" (July 7, 1939), in Li, *Zhigong jia yan lu*, 39.

78. CQA, 50 Chang, 4 *mu*, 511 *juan*, 20 (Dec. 21, 1944); 50 Chang, 3486 *juan* (Apr. 31, 1946).

79. Interview with He Qiuping (Chongqing).

80. This discussion is based on infractions cited in the bulletin *Gangtiechang qianjian weiyuanhui mishuchu tongbao* (1946), nos. 866, 877, 879–81, 885–86, 890–91, 893, 901, 904, 907, 911, 926–29, 934–35, 937, 941; (1947), nos. 946, 950, 955, 957, 962, 966, 972, 976–77, 980, 985, 987, 995, 1008–9, 1021–23, 1026, 1035, 1041–43, 1052–53. Since archival holdings are incomplete, these records best express trends in the kinds of violation and the severity of punishment.

81. Howe, *Wage Patterns and Wage Policy in Modern China*, 46–47.

82. CQA, 10 Chang, 1 *mu*, 832 *juan*; 24 Chang, 1 *mu*, 250 *juan* (3–4); 28 Chang, 1 *mu*, 315 *juan*.

83. CQA, 20 Chang, 1085 *juan*, gongzi tongji yuebaobiao; CQA, 20 Chang, 139 *juan*, L1–2, 9, 66–67, 73 (1946).

84. Kolko, *Century of War: Politics, Conflicts, and Society Since 1914*, 316.

85. For analysis of the state's role in shaping European industrial relations, see Rimlinger, "Labour and the State on the Continent, 1800–1939," 549–606.

86. Porter, *Industrial Reformers in Republican China*, 25. Porter includes a full translation of the 1931 Factory Act. For a similar appraisal of early industrial welfare schemes, see Frazier, *The Making of the Chinese Industrial Workplace: State, Revolution, and Labor Management*, 37.

87. Zhu Jiahua, *Zhongguo gongyun yu gongxun*, 9–10. For Sombart, see Riefs, "Werner Sombart Under National Socialism," 202.

88. CQA, 20 Chang, 1441 *juan*, 31 (Feb. 27, 1939), report of Hong Lanyou.

89. Ibid., 960.

90. FDR, AWPM, box 16, Munitions Production, Major Walter G. Sylvester (Ordnance Dept.), "Notes on Chinese Arsenals" (1945).

91. FDR, AWPM, box 16, Ordnance, "Report on Chinese Arsenal Situation—17 September 1944," from Major W. S. Brewster to Jacobson.

92. Zahavi, *Workers, Managers, and Welfare Capitalism: The Shoeworkers and Tanners of Endicott Johnson, 1890–1950*, 105.

93. Zhao Zhizhong, "Li Chenggan zhuanlue," 129; Lai Zongyu, "Jiefang qian 21 binggongchang de yixie qingkuang," 23. The term *da laoban* (big boss) contrasts with *changzhang* (factory director), more commonly used in the large-scale arsenals. Li Chenggan's stature in the defense industry has soared since his death in 1959, when he headed the Department of Measurements. Some Chinese scholars suggest that Li himself joined the Communist Party on the eve of 1949, and that his politics influenced his paternalism. His younger sister, Li Luping, was

definitely a county party secretary in the Shaan-Gan-Ning base area during the War of Resistance.

94. "Binggongshu wei ge chang zhigong fulishe gaizu xiaofei hezuoshe gongling" (Nov. 3, 1940), in *ZJBGS*, 3: 965.

95. CQA, 20 Chang, 1669 *juan*, 1 (July 17, 1940).

96. CQA, 29 Chang, 5 *mu*, 439 *juan*, 62 (June 16, 1940).

97. Zhao Zhizhong, "Li Chenggan zhuanlue," 128.

98. Interview with Li Jiesun (Chongqing).

99. CQA, 21 Chang, Fuli, 61 *juan*.

100. Interview with Li Jiesun (Chongqing).

101. CQA, 20 Chang, 942 *juan*, 47, Fulichu 34 niandu 1 zhi 4 yuefen gongzuo baogaobiao; CQA, 10 Chang, 1 *mu*, 19/2 *juan*, 77 (Apr. 1942), zhigong changwai zhuzhai zudian banfa.

102. Chang, *The Inflationary Spiral: The Experience in China, 1939–1950*, 342–49.

103. CQA, *Gangtiechang qianjian weiyuanhui mishuchu tongbao* (1946–49), nos. 442, 476, 493, 516, 540, 572, 604, 667, 689, 713; "Fenbu yingkui jisuan ge kemu shouzhi zongbiao," CQA, Gangqianhui, 117 *juan*; "Zhizaofei shouzhi yuebaobiao" (July, Aug., Dec. 1948, Jan.–July, Nov. 1949); CQA, 24 Chang, 3565–67 *juan*; CQA, 20 Chang, 932 *juan*, 111, "36 niandu caiwu jiantao"; CQA, 20 Chang, 846 *juan*, "Di 20 gongchang 37 nian ge yue jingfei kaizhi yu juesuan chengben baifenshu tongjibiao"; SHA 774 *quan*, 1660 *juan*, "Zhizaofei shouzhi yuebaobiao."

104. CQA, 21 Chang, cai, 33–2 *juan* (Sept. 1, 1944).

105. Enclosure in Dispatch 117 from Shanghai (Consul General Josselyn) to secretary of state, Feb. 28, 1946, in RDS, 893.504/2–2846.

106. Interview with Liu Feng (Kunming).

107. Interview with Yang Jinhua (Chongqing).

108. Interview with Li Jiesun (Chongqing). A survey of Sichuan apprentices indicates that *dayaji* occurred on the second and sixteenth days of every month. Liao T'ai-ch'u, "The Apprentices in Chengtu During and After the War," 97.

109. Tong Zhicheng, "Mantan fuli," *Taosheng tekan*, Jan. 1, 1945, 4.

110. CQA, 24 Chang, 6397 *juan*, 18–19 (n.d. [1949?]), Yuangong benshen shiwu peigei ji fuli; SHA, 774 (1658), 20 Chang, June 1949 fuli yuebaobiao; CQA, 50 Chang, 4 *mu*, 340 *juan*, 13 (n.d.).

111. Interview with Zhu Rong (Chongqing).

112. Interview with Ye Xiuquan (Chongqing). See CQA, 24 Chang, 1888 *juan*, 1b (Aug. 23, 1947).

113. Liu Yuansen, "Binggongchang gongren gongzi fasheng jiaofen de yuanyin" (Sept. 1948), in *KHYGS*, 709.

114. Moore, *Injustice: The Social Bases of Obedience and Revolt*. See, e.g., ch. 2 on why victims may submit to oppression and degradation.

115. Smith, "Workers Against Foremen in Late-Imperial Russia," 113.

116. Li Chenggan, "zai gaobei jixiao shisheng shu" (May 16, 1947), in Zheng Hongquan, ed., *Huainian yu zhufu: Jinian Li Chenggan xiansheng tingchen 110 zhounian ji gonghe Yu Zhouzhi xiansheng 90 huating zhuanji*, 61.

117. Zhu Bangxing et al., eds., *Shanghai chanye yu Shanghai zhigong*, 620.

118. SHA, 774 *quan*, 625 *juan* (Sept. 1949).

119. FDR, AWPM, Gragg, ed., "History of the American War Production Mission in China" (MS), 94.

120. Lo and Yang, *Red Crag*, 40.

121. *Xinhua ribao*, May 18, 1940, 4.

122. Interview with Sun Zhiguang (Kunming).

123. Interview with Ye Xiuquan (Chongqing).

124. "Sanzhong xuesheng," *Zhongshu* 2, no. 2 (1945): 5.

125. Ibid., 5–8.

126. Shih Kuo-heng quoted in Epstein, *Notes on Labor Problems in Nationalist China*, 26.

127. See *Xinhua ribao*, Feb. 28, 1944, 3; July 21, 1944, 3; Oct. 30, 1945, 4; Nov. 26, 1945, 4; Dec. 4, 1945, 4; Dec. 28, 1945, 4. Several of these cases are discussed more fully in chapter 7.

128. Interviews with Zhang Ping and Ye Xiuquan (Chongqing).

129. Interview with Li Jiesun (Chongqing).

130. SHA, 774 (1658), "1948 20 Chang, fang dichan tongji nianbaobiao" (Jan. 16, 1949).

131. Interview with Zhu Rong (Chongqing).

132. Interview with Ye Xiuquan (Chongqing).

133. Interview with Gu Weiyun (Chongqing).

134. *Xinhua ribao*, Feb. 28, 1944, 3.

135. On Taiwan, see Gates, "Ethnicity and Social Class," 241–81. On Chongqing, see Eastman, "Nationalist China During the Sino-Japanese War, 1937–1945," 565.

136. Interview with Du Liang (Chongqing).

137. CQA, 10 Chang, 1 *mu*, 832 *juan*, 16.

138. Liu Yuansen, "Binggongchang gongren gongzi fasheng jiaofen de yuanyin" (Sept. 1948), in *KHYGS*, 708.

139. CQA, 50 Chang, 2 *mu*, *juan* 3, 2, 5, 6b.

140. Interview with Li Jiesun (Chongqing).

141. Speier, *German White-Collar Workers and the Rise of Hitler*, 61.

142. CQA, 20 Chang, 595 *juan*, 16 (Jul. 27, 1948).

143. "Bingongshu liuYu changzhang di 26 ci huiyi guanyu yuangong gongzi de taolun he jueyi" (Apr. 19, 1949), in *ZJBGS*, 3: 944–45. For a similar report of impending catastrophe because of inadequate money to pay wages and low worker morale, see SHA, 774/706 (n.d.).

Chapter 5. Chongqing's Most Wanted: The Mobility and Resistance of Arsenal Workers

1. For discussion of labor mobility in other cities, see Chesneaux, *The Chinese Labor Movement, 1919–1927*, 85–86; Hershatter, *The Workers of Tianjin, 1900–1949*, 58–60; Wright, *Coal Mining in China's Economy and Society 1895–1937*, 24–26.

2. The phrase echoes Scott, *Weapons of the Weak: Everyday Forms of Peasant Resistance*, which argues that to express their discontent with conditions that they had generally entered into involuntarily, and that were difficult to alter, peasants preferred everyday forms of resistance, such as flight and foot-dragging, to open confrontation.

3. Hobsbawm, "Peasants and Politics," 7.

4. Milward, *War, Economy and Society, 1939–1945*, 217–18.

5. "Binggongshu jiu ge binggongchang gongren shi wei junshu yi junfa guanli bing zhunyu huanyi xunling" (May 26, 1939), in *ZJBGS*, 3: 816.

6. Exemption from military service was extended to skilled workers in twenty other industrial sectors by means of the April 1941 "Provisional Order on the Suspension from Military Service of Skilled Workers and Staffs Employed in the Vital National Defense Mines and Industries." *International Labor Review* 46, no. 6 (Dec. 1942): 706–7.

7. Eastman, *Seeds of Destruction: Nationalist China in War and Revolution, 1937–1949*, 152.

8. There were, of course, those desperate enough to earn a living by selling themselves as substitute conscripts. Xiao Yunxi, "Guomindang shiqi Jiangbei xian binyi nuemin jianwen," 26; Epstein, *Notes on Labor Problems in Nationalist China*, 32 (emphasis in original).

9. CQA, 24 Chang, 85 *juan*, 13b–14a (Aug. 25, 1938).

10. By January 1943, for instance, the Conscription Department (Bingyi Shu) prohibited arsenals from recruiting workers in a county within two months of when conscription was to occur. CQA, 28 Chang, 1 *mu*, 336 *juan*, 65–66.

11. CQA, 24 Chang, 1 zongmu, 47 *juan*, 24b (Apr. 18, 1939).

12. For Yu Dawei's injunction, see SHA, 774 *mu*, 3090 *juan* (Nov. 16, 1936). For an example of a wartime report, see CQA, 10 Chang, gongwu, 500 *juan*, 2–4 (Jan. 15, 1944). For photos, see CQA, 29 Chang, 5 *mu*, 743 *juan*, 3 (May 29, 1940).

13. CQA, 28 Chang, 1 *mu*, 338 *juan*, 149–50 (Aug. 3, 1942).

14. Chinese Ministry of Information, comp., *China Handbook, 1937–1945: A Comprehensive Survey of Major Developments in China in Eight Years of War*, 384.

15. *International Labor Review* 48, no. 6 (Dec. 1943): 767–68.

16. *International Labor Review* 49, no. 2 (Feb. 1944): 234.

17. The Central Automobile Assembly Plant, Central Textile Plant, Shunchang Steel Mill, China Machinery Plant, and Zhendan Iron Mill all entered into negotiations with the arms industry over contested employees. CQA, 10 Chang, gongwu, 391 *juan*, 71 (1942); CQA, 10 Chang, gongwu, 621 *juan* (July 16, 1945), "benzu qiati taogong jingguo qingxing biao." For cases that extended beyond Sichuan borders, see CQA, 10 Chang, gongwu, 391 *juan*, 9 (Mar. 13, 1942).

18. Cheng and Li, eds., *Jindai Sichuan renkou*, 232.

19. CQA, 1 *mu*, 523 *juan*, 61 (Nov. 1947).

20. CQA, 20 Chang, 1121 *juan* (1949).

21. For data on occupational mobility in Arsenal No. 10 (1942), see CQA, 10 Chang, gongwu, 364 *juan*, 15.

22. CQA, 20 Chang, 1019, 1049, 1089 *juan*.

23. Calculations based on CQA, 10 Chang, gongwu lei, 418–20, 484–85, 605, 667 *juan*.

24. On footloose apprentices, see CQA, 20 Chang, 1019 *juan*, 64, 1049 *juan*, 147. Adapted from "20 Chang 31 nian 1 zhi 8 yuefen jishu gongren jintui yilan biao."

25. CQA, 50 Chang, 3 *mu*, 85, 87, 2011–12, 2014, 2016, 2018, 2020, 2022 *juan*.

26. CQA, 10 Chang, gongwu, 419, 484–85, 605, 667 *juan*.

27. CQA, 10 Chang, gongwu, 391 *juan* (Oct. 19, 1942).

28. Roux, *Le Shanghai ouvrier des années trente: Coolies, gangsters et syndicalistes*, 98.

29. "Hanyang binggongchang zhipaochang gongren mingce" (Nov. 1, 1936), CQA, Binggongshu, 1 *mu*, 225 *juan*.

30. CQA, 21 Chang, zongmu, 14–10 *juan*, 4, "Di 21 gongchang 3/1/48 qingzhu qian Chuan fugong shi zhounian jinian zhi fuwu man shinian gongren tongji biao." To put this number in perspective, Arsenal No. 21 employed a total of 11,350 workers during 1947.

31. For Arsenal No. 10 age-group patterns among workers in 1943, see Howard, "Workers at War: Labor in the Nationalist Arsenals of Chongqing, 1937–1949," 357.

32. CQA, 20 Chang, 846 *juan*, "Di 20 gongchang 36 gongren nianzi tongji biao."

33. "1938 zhi 1943 nian Chuandong zhigong yundong de qingkuang," in *NFJDS*, 5: 91. Editors ascribe authorship to the Eastern Sichuan Special Party Committee representative reporting to Yan'an in 1943.

34. Sun Benwen, *Xiandai Zhongguo shehui wenti*, vol. 4, *Laozi wenti*, 193.

35. FDR, AWPM, box 36, memorandum of Lester L. Bosch, July 16, 1945.

36. See Lu and Tang, *Kangzhan shiqi Chongqing de bingqi gongye*, 117–18.

37. CQA, 10 Chang, 336 *juan*, 42 (Mar. 5, 1942). Yu Dawei issued a similar directive in Oct. 1939. See CQA, 29 Chang, 5 *mu*, 1231 *juan*, 69.

38. Epstein, *Notes on Labor Problems in Nationalist China*, 7. See also Zhu Songwei's petition in CQA, 20 Chang, 34 *juan*, 57–59 (Mar. 2, 1945).

39. IMH, National Resources Commission archives, 24–03 jiguan, 48, no. 1 (Apr. 6, 1945).

40. See also Epstein, *Notes on Labor Problems in Nationalist China*, 7.

41. FDR, AWPM, box 16, Ordnance, "Report on Chinese Arsenal Situation—17 September 1944," from Major W. S. Brewster to Jacobson.

42. Liu Shi, "Kang Ri Zhangzheng zhonghouqi Chongqing de zhigong yundong," in *NFJDS*, 5: 295. Liu's text was originally delivered as a lecture to union cadres on April 27, 1950, at the National Federation of Unions.

43. Zhou Maobo, "Houfang jiqi gongye ji qi tiaozheng wenti," 11.

44. Epstein, *Notes on Labor Problems in Nationalist China*, 27–28.

45. CQA, 24 Chang, zong 1 *mu*, 45 *juan* (May 1942).
46. CQA, 20 Chang, 3 *mu*, 235 *juan*, 40 (June 18, 1938).
47. CQA, 20 Chang, 1441 *juan*, 84–88 (Feb. 14, 1939).
48. Liu and Tang, eds., *Zhongguo gongren yundongshi*, 5: 438.
49. CQA, 20 Chang, 1441 *juan*, 28b–29 (Feb. 18, 1939).
50. Shu Hua quoted in Epstein, *Notes on Labor Problems in Nationalist China*, 24.
51. CQA, 20 Chang, 1441 *juan*, 25b (July 4, 1939).
52. CQA, 20 Chang, 1017 *juan*, 36.
53. CQA, 10 Chang, 3 *mu*, 9 *juan* (Dec. 12, 1939).
54. Interview with Feng Junren (Chongqing).
55. Interview with Gu Weiyun (Chongqing).
56. The actual number of workers leaving in groups was probably larger as it was safer to stagger the days of exit. Calculations for Arsenal No. 20 based on CQA, 20 Chang, 1019, 1049, 1089 *juan*, "20 Chang 31 nian 1–3, 4–6, 7–9, 10–12 yuefen lichang gongren baogao biao." For Arsenal No. 50, see CQA, 50 Chang, 3 *mu*, 85, 87, 2014, 2016, 2018, 2020, 2022 *juan* (Jan.–May, Sept.–Dec. 1942), "Tuizhi gongren yi lan biao."
57. See "Junzhengbu Binggongshu zhihai ge chang gongren daiyu zhanxing jianzhang" (Jan. 20, 1932); "Xiuzheng Junzhengbu binggongshu zhihai gechang gongren daiyu zhanxing guize" (Jan. 1937); and "Binggongshu banfa bing-gongchang gongren daiyu guize xunling" (May 14, 1947), in *ZJBGS*, 3: 892, 896, 932, respectively.
58. For 1944 figures, see Liu and Tang, eds., *Zhongguo gongren yundongshi*, 5: 432. For November 1949 figures, see Cheng and Li, eds., *Jindai Sichuan renkou*, 232.

Chapter 6. The Nationalist Project: Coercion, Consent, and Conflict

1. Yeh, *The Alienated Academy: Culture and Politics in Republican China, 1919–1937*, ch. 5.
2. CQA, 20 Chang, 888 *juan*, "Kangzhan qijian binggongchang gongren fenzu xunlian fangan" (June 7, 1939).
3. "Binggongshu jianfa zhigong fuli shiye choushi huiyi jilu ji anding gongren shenghuo fangan xunling" (July 10, 1939), in *ZJBGS*, 3: 961.
4. Gordon, *The Evolution of Labor Relations in Japan*, chs. 11–15.
5. CQA, 50 Chang, 3 *mu*, 185 *juan*, 9 (Sept. 14, 1939).
6. Lu and Tang, *Kangzhan shiqi Chongqing de bingqi gongye*, 118.
7. Interview with Feng Junren (Chongqing).
8. Interview with Ye Xiuquan (Chongqing).
9. CQA, 21 Chang, zong *mu*, 23–1 *juan*, 6 (Feb. 9, 1946).
10. CQA, 20 Chang, 1441 *juan*, 34 (Nov. 1939).
11. CQA, 50 Chang, 3 *mu*, 96 *juan*, 3.
12. CQA, 10 Chang, gongwu, 486 *juan*, 1 (Feb. 27, 1944).

13. Interview with Du Liang (Chongqing); interview with He Qiuping (Chongqing).

14. CQA, Juntongju Yu tequ (henceforth abbreviated as "te") 2, 1 lei, 26 *juan*; interview with Zhang Ping (Chongqing); CQA, 29 Chang, 5 *mu*, 369 *juan*, 65 (Oct. 22, 1947).

15. Zhongguo Renmin Jiefangjun yanjiushi, ed., *Xinan zhi binggong* (Aug. 1949), 77.

16. CQA, 21 Chang, jingji, 36 *juan*, 51–52 (Oct. 4 [194?]).

17. Hirschman, *Exit, Voice, and Loyalty: Responses to Decline in Firms, Organizations, and States.*

18. CQA, 50 Chang, kuaiji, 3981 *juan*, 11. ZJBGS, 3: 1059; Cao Haosen, *Zhongguo Guomindang junzhengbu tebie dangbu di er zhounian gongzuo gaikuang* (1941), in NPHA, 495 lei, 95 hao.

19. Ch'i, *Nationalist China at War, Military Defeats and Political Collapse, 1937–45,* 183–84.

20. CQA, 50 Chang, 1 *mu*, 15 *juan*, 25 (Apr. 6, 1944).

21. CQA, 20 Chang, 1428 *juan*, 103–4 (June 9, 1939).

22. CQA, 50 Chang, 1 *mu*, 2 *juan*, 13.

23. CQA, tedang, 1 *juan*, 54, 59, 63.

24. CQA, 50 Chang, 1 *mu*, 5 *juan* (June 12, 1945), "Disan Guomindang ganshi lianxi huiyilu"; CQA, 50 Chang, 1 *mu*, 8 *juan*, 2.

25. CQA, 50 Chang, 1 *mu*, 2 *juan*, 16.

26. Interview with Qian Rui (Taipei).

27. CQA, Reference Materials Room, 4 *mu*, 382 *juan*, 6 (Apr. 2, 1943). The reference is to the Confucian *Analects*.

28. Interview with Li Jiesun (Chongqing).

29. "Binggongshu tebie dangbu diyici dangwu huiyi jilu" (Apr. 2, 1943), in ZJBGS, 3: 1060.

30. "Binggongshu tebie dangbu fengzhuan chexiao ge binggongchang sanqingtuandui daidian" (1943), in ZJBGS, 3: 1064; Eastman, *Seeds of Destruction: Nationalist China in War and Revolution, 1937–1949,* ch. 4.

31. "Binggongshu tebie dangbu chengli ji tepaiyuan deng xuan zhan jiuzhi dianli jilu" (Apr. 2, 1943), in ZJBGS, 3: 1058–59.

32. CQA, 23 Chang, 2 *mu*, 5 *juan* (Nov. 9, 1939).

33. CQA, 24 Chang, 1 *mu*, Guodang, 33 *juan*, "24 Chang Zhongguo Guomindang Junzhengbu tebie dangbu di7 dangbu di 16qu fenbu dangyuan mingce"; CQA, 24 Chang, 1 *mu*, Guodang, 31 *juan*; CQA, bingdang 22, 29 *juan*, 11; CQA, 50 Chang, 1 *mu*, 4 *juan*, 1 (May 10, 1945).

34. In response to the pressing budget difficulties of most subdistrict party branches, reforms passed in January 1944 allowed the lowest-level party branch to retain a considerable portion of membership dues for its own operating budget; 50 percent of dues went to the subdistrict party branch, 30 percent to the district party branch, and 20 percent to the special party branch. CQA, 25 Chang, 2 *mu*, 18 *juan*, 29 (June 1944).

35. Interview with Du Liang (Chongqing).

36. Interview with Li Jiesun (Chongqing).

37. Du Yanqing, "Chongqing gongyun," Jan. 24, 1947, in *SGRYD*, 382.

38. CQA, 50 Chang, 1 *mu*, 2 *juan*, 16, "di 5 ci zhidaoyuan jian ganshi lianxi huiyi" (Sept. 15, 1945).

39. Ibid., 9.

40. CQA, 24 Chang, Guodang, 9 *juan*, 29 (Oct. 15, 1944).

41. Alf Ludtke, a leading practitioner of the *Alltagsgeschichte* ("everyday history") school, argues that Nazi labor propagandists' emphasis on the "honor of labor" resonated with workers because of their own symbolic practices and sense of dignity associated with manual labor. Ludtke, "'The Honor of Labor': Industrial Workers and the Power of Symbols Under National Socialism," 67–110.

42. CQA, 24 Chang, Guodang, 9 *juan*, 177 (May 24, 1945).

43. CQA, 24 Chang, Guodang, 9 *juan*, 57 (Oct.15, 1944).

44. Factory machinist, "Shoubuliao feili yapo, hanlei likaile gongchang," *Xinhua ribao*, June 15, 1940, 4.

45. CQA, 50 Chang, 2 *mu*, 22 *juan*, 29–35 (Aug. 18, 1946).

46. Mao, "On New Democracy," in Cheek, *Mao Zedong and China's Revolutions*, 89.

47. See Lenin, *Imperialism, the Highest Stage of Capitalism*, preface to the French and German editions, 14: "This stratum of bourgeoisified workers, or the 'labor aristocracy,' who are quite philistine in their mode of life, in the size of their earnings and in their outlook, serves as the principal prop of the Second International, and, in our days, the principal *social* (not military) *prop of the bourgeoisie*. They are the real *agents of the bourgeoisie in the labour movement*, the labor lieutenants of the capitalist class, real channels of reformism and chauvinism." Emphasis in original.

Chapter 7. Organizing, 1937–1946

1. For the former view, see Shaffer, *Mao and the Workers: The Hunan Labor Movement, 1920–1923*. For the latter view, see, e.g., Honig, *Sisters and Strangers: Women in the Shanghai Cotton Mills, 1919–1949*; Roux, *Le Shanghai ouvrier des Années trente: Coolies, gangsters et syndicalistes*.

2. Somers, "Workers of the World, Compare!" 325.

3. Shum, *The Chinese Communists' Road to Power: The Anti-Japanese National United Front, 1935–1945*; Van Slyke, *Enemies and Friends: The United Front in Chinese Communist History*.

4. McIsaac, "The Limits of Chinese Nationalism: Workers in Wartime Chongqing, 1937–1945," 169.

5. According to a report presented at a central political committee meeting in July 1939 by Qin Bangxian (alias Bo Gu), 10,000 members had been recruited in Jiangsu, 7,500 members in Guangdong, 6,000 members in Hunan, and over 5,000 members in the Fujian-Guangdong border region. Bo Gu (1907–46) was concurrently a member of the Southern Bureau's standing committee and director of its organizational bureau. Before being recalled to Yan'an in November 1940, he was second in charge to Zhou Enlai. *NFJDS*, 2: summary, 2.

6. Born in Weiyuan, Sichuan, Luo Shiwen (1904–46) attended a commercial school in Chongqing before joining the Chinese Socialist Youth Corps in 1923. In 1925, he joined the Communist Party and began attending the Moscow Far Eastern University. Upon returning to China in 1928, Luo led peasant movements in Sichuan. Luo became involved in the factional dispute with the CCP leader Zhang Guotao and subsequently went to northern Shaanxi in 1936. In Yan'an, he taught at the Red Army University before returning to Sichuan. The Nationalist authorities arrested Luo in March 1940, imprisoned him at the SACO prison Zhazidong in Chongqing, and executed him on August 18, 1946. Cheng Min et al., eds., *Zhongguo Gongchandang dangyuan dacidian*, 447–48.

7. In 1924, Cheng Zijian (1902–73) joined the Chinese Communist Youth League as a work-study student in France. After returning to China, he assumed various posts in Sichuan from the mid to late 1920s, including that of secretary of the Sichuan Provincial Committee. Zhonggong Sichuan shengwei tongzhanbu, comp., *Sichuan tongyi zhanxian renwu lu*, 303.

8. Ibid., 325.

9. Liao Zhigao, "Kang Ri Zhanzheng shiqi Sichuan dixiadang de chongjian he Sichuan dongdang zuzhi fazhan, konggu de zhuyao qingkuang," 74.

10. Ibid., 70; *Zhonggong Sichuan difang dangshi dashi nianbiao 1921–1949*, 75.

11. Nanfangju dangshi ziliao zhengji xiaozu zuzhi, ed., "Zhonggong Nanfangju zuzhi xitong gaikuang," 21.

12. Liao Zhigao, "Kang Ri Zhanzheng shiqi Sichuan dixiadang de chongjian he Sichuan dongdang zuzhi fazhan, konggu de zhuyao qingkuang," 77–80.

13. Xiao Shaobin et al., "Baizhe bunao, zhandou buzhi: Tan Jianxiao tongzhi zhuanlue," 23–27.

14. Liu Zonglin, "Wo canjia Chongqing gongren yundong de huiyi," 8. The March 31 Incident occurred in 1927 when Liu Xiang ordered troops to disperse 20,000 people assembled to protest the British shelling of the Nanjing assembly hall. In the course of the suppression, 137 people were killed and over 1,000 injured.

15. Xiao Shaodin et al., "Baizhe bunao, zhandou buzhi: Tan Jianxiao tongzhi zhuanlue," 26.

16. Cheng Zijian, "Sichuan zhigong yundong de jingyan zongjie," May 1, 1942, in *SGRYD*, 348.

17. "Chuandong zhigong yundong zongjie," in *SGRYD*, 354. Editors tentatively date this document to 1943 and ascribe authorship to an Eastern Sichuan Special Committee representative in Yan'an.

18. Ibid., 353–54.

19. "Yuqu bannian lai gongyun gaikuang," in *SGRYD*, 309. Editors tentatively date this document to 1941 and ascribe authorship to the Eastern Sichuan Special Committee.

20. Ibid., 309–11.

21. Du Yanqing, "Chongqing gongyun" (Jan. 24, 1947), in *SGRYD*, 398; Shih, *China Enters the Machine Age: A Study of Labor in Chinese War Industry*, 117.

22. See Kocka, "Marxist Social Analysis and the Problem of White Collar Employees," 137–51.

23. Zhu Bangxing et al., eds., *Shanghai chanye yu Shanghai zhigong*, 620–21.

24. Ibid., 619.

25. *Xinhua ribao*, May 18, 1940, 4.

26. "Yuqu bannian lai gongyun gaikuang," in *SGRYD*, 309.

27. Van Slyke, *Enemies and Friends: The United Front in Chinese Communist History*, 100–101.

28. CQA, 20 Chang, 1441 *juan*, 87b–88 (Feb. 12, 1939), letter from Yang Jizeng to Li Chenggan.

29. "Luzhou di 23 gongchang dixiadang zuzhi lingdao de gongren yundong dashiji" (MS compiled by Xinan shifan xueyuan lishixi), 65.

30. Chongqingshi zonggonghui gongyunshi ziliao yanjiuzu and Xinan shifan xueyuan lishixi, eds., "Gao Yuying tongzhi jianghua jilu," 5.

31. "Luzhou di 23 gongchang dixiadang zuzhi lingdao de gongren yundong dashiji" (MS compiled by Xinan shifan xueyuan lishixi), 65.

32. "Yuqu bannian lai gongyun gaikuang," in *SGRYD*, 309.

33. "Chuankang gongren yundong," Dec. 5, 1939, in *SGRYD*, 232–33. Editors tentatively ascribe the document to the Chuan Kang (Western Sichuan) Special Committee.

34. CQA, 1441 *juan*, 84–88 (Feb. 14, 1939).

35. CQA, 29 Chang, 2 *mu*, 2–6 *juan*, 125 (Oct. 29, 1940).

36. Liao Zhigao, "Kang Ri Zhanzheng shiqi Sichuan dixiadang de chongjian he Sichuan dongdang zuzhi fazhan, konggu de zhuyao qingkuang," 86.

37. "Yuqu bannian lai gongyun gaikuang," in *SGRYD*, 278.

38. Zhonggong Sichuan shengwei dangshi gongzuo weiyuanhui, ed., *Zhonggong Sichuan difang dangshi dashi nianbiao, 1921–1949*, 76.

39. "Yuqu bannian lai gongyun gaikuang," in *SGRYD*, 311. For the early 1930s Shanghai underground, see Stranahan, *Underground: The Shanghai Communist Party and the Politics of Survival, 1927–1937*.

40. Huang Gang, "Wo zai Caiyuanba diqu gongzuo de qingkuang," 7.

41. "Yuqu bannian lai gongyun gaikuang," in *SGRYD*, 279.

42. Xu Chaojian et al., eds., *Chongqing da hongzha*, 32.

43. Zhonggong Sichuan shengwei dangshi gongzuo weiyuanhui, ed., *Zhonggong Sichuan difang dangshi dashi nianbiao, 1921–1949*, 80.

44. *NFJDS*, 2: summary, 5.

45. Ibid., 9.

46. Ibid., 6–7. For the full text, see Saich, ed., *The Rise to Power of the Chinese Communist Party*, 888–90.

47. Liao Zhigao, "Kang Ri Zhanzheng shiqi Sichuan dixiadang de chongjian he Sichuan dongdang zuzhi fazhan, konggu de zhuyao qingkuang," 85, 102.

48. *NFJDS*, 2: summary, 7, 12.

49. *SGRYD*, 274.

50. Cheng Zijian, "Sichuan zhigong yundong de jingyan zongjie" (May 1, 1942), in *SGRYD*, 352.

51. Van Slyke, "The Chinese Communist Movement During the Sino-Japa-

nese War 1937–1945," 660. The Southern Bureau's labor policies in Chongqing may have followed the strategies articulated slightly earlier by Liu Shaoqi for Shanghai. For Liu's policies, see McQuaide, "Shanghai Labor: Gender, Politics, and Tradition in the Making of the Chinese Working Class, 1911–1949," 299–302.

52. Cheng Zijian, "Sichuan zhigong yundong de jingyan zongjie" (May 1, 1942), in *SGRYD*, 351.

53. "Zhongyang guanyu mimi dangyuan jiaru Guomindang wenti di zhishi" (May 5, 1940), in *NFJDS*, 2: 24.

54. "Chuandong zhigong yundong zongjie," in *SGRYD*, 358. This was a report of the Eastern Sichuan Special Committee sent to Yan'an in 1943.

55. Cheng Zijian, "Sichuan zhigong yundong de jingyan zongjie" (May 1, 1942), in *SGRYD*, 347.

56. Ibid., 349.

57. Moore, *Injustice: The Social Bases of Obedience and Revolt.*

58. Both quotations are from Shum, *The Chinese Communists' Road to Power*, 122.

59. Chongqingshi dang'anguan, Zhongguo di'er lishi dang'anguan, comp., *Baise kongbu xia de "Xin Hua ribao": Guomindang dangju kongzhi Xinhua ribao de dang'an cailiao huibian*, 588.

60. Chang Hung-tseng, "The Chungking Press: I," 74. The circulation of *Xinhua ribao* was comparable to that of other prominent wartime newspapers in Nationalist territory. The official *Zhongyang ribao* (Central Daily News) distributed 50,000 copies daily; the liberal *Dagongbao* had a circulation of 91,000 and 30,000 for its morning and evening editions. The military paper *Saodang bao* had an estimated readership of 40,000 for Chongqing and Kunming; *Xinminbao* boasted a circulation of 50,000 for its combined morning and evening editions. See Chang, "The Chungking Press: II," 60–64.

61. "Yuqu bannian lai gongyun gaikuang," in *SGRYD*, 279. "*Xinhua riba* Dadukou fenxiaochu," in Chongqingshi zonggonghui gongyunshi ziliao yanjiuzu and Xinan shifan xueyuan lishixi, comps., *Zhou Haoliang huiyi cailiao* (1981), 7. Although I focus on *Xinhua ribao*, one should note that it shared close ties to the Yan'an-based Communist daily, *Jiefang ribao* (Liberation Daily). Communists were using Eighteenth Route Army trucks to transport copies of the *Jiefang ribao* from Yan'an to Chongqing, where they were printed in bulk at the Xinhua press offices and then distributed to strategic factories. Workers shared *Jiefang ribao*, like *Xinhua ribao*, so the paper had a broader readership than implied by its circulation of a few dozen to at most a few hundred copies per factory. See CQA, 50 Chang, 2 *mu*, 90 *juan*, 113 (June 21, 1942).

62. CQA, 10 Chang, 8 *mu*, 158 *juan*, 170, Shen Qichang interrogation record.

63. Huang Shujun, *Chongqing gongren yundong shi, 1919–1949*, 197.

64. Chang Hung-tseng, "The Chungking Press: I," 74.

65. Ibid.

66. Liao, "Rural Education in Transition: A Study of Old-fashioned Chinese Schools (Szu Shu) in Shantung and Szechuan," 28–63.

67. CQA, 10 Chang, 1 *mu*, 832 *juan*, 19 (Dec. 8, 1947).

68. CQA, 10 Chang, 2 *mu*, 116 *juan*, 2–7 "Binggong Shu di 10 Chang gongren tisheng banfa" (May 5, 1947). Interview with Feng Junren (Chongqing).

69. Oestreicher, *Solidarity and Fragmentation: Working People and Class Consciousness in Detroit, 1875–1900*, xv.

70. *NFJDS*, 2: 199, 215.

71. Strongholds provided mobilization support for the anti-spy demonstrations in the wake of the electrician Hu Shihe's killing in 1945. Participants in the Chongqing workers' democratic work team and the New Democracy Youth Society also had previously organized strongholds, which they used as a basis for the new organizations. Finally, stronghold members provided cadres who went to eastern and northern rural Sichuan and participated in the rural uprisings of the late 1940s. Huang Shujun, *Chongqing gongren yundongshi, 1919–1949*, 216–18.

72. Ibid., 189, 213.

73. Interview with Zhu Rong (Chongqing).

74. CQA, 20 Chang, 1441 *juan*, 86b, Feb. 14, 1939.

75. CQA, 10 Chang, 8 *mu*, 159 *juan*, 39–44 "Xie Wanquan zibaishu chaojian." I analyze this "position paper" in more depth in chapter 8.

76. CQA, te 1, 4 *mu*, 2 *juan*, 29. Xie Wanquan interrogation record (October [1947?]).

77. Ibid., 34.

78. Ibid., 34b.

79. Shum, *The Chinese Communists' Road to Power, 1935–1945*, 116.

80. Liu Zonglin, "Wo canjia Chongqing gongren yundong de huiyi," 8.

81. CQA, te 1, 4 *mu*, 2 *juan*, 34b. Xie Wanquan interrogation record (October [1947?]).

82. Li Chenggan, "Gao ge gongyou shu," in *Zhigong jia yan lu*, 35.

83. "Binggong Shu yanjin ge chang gongren dingyue *Xinhua ribao* daidian" (Mar. 11, 1941), in *ZJBGS*, 3: 1100.

84. CQA, 24 Chang, zong 1 *mu*, 81 *juan*, 23 (Sept. 1944).

85. Interview with Sun Zhiguang (Kunming).

86. Wen and Xiao, eds., *Kangzhan shiqi Chongqing de xinwenjie*, 205. Sao can be translated as "to sweep."

87. Anderson, *Imagined Communities: Reflections on the Origin and Spread of Nationalism.*

88. Cited in Zelnik, "Before Class: The Fostering of a Worker Revolutionary: The Construction of His Memoir," 68.

89. Hung, *War and Popular Culture: Resistance in Modern China, 1937–1945*, 247.

90. Yu Gang, "Women ye yao yanyan xi changchang ge," *Xinhua ribao*, Jan. 26, 1944, 3.

91. Qing Jun, "Zhe shi xuexi ma?" *Xinhua ribao*, Feb. 18, 1944, 3. Workers frequently referred to arsenals as a "certain factory" to avoid exposure.

92. Ke Zhi [Overcome It], "Buxu kai kefan" *Xinhua ribao*, May 25, 1944, 3.

93. The Southern Bureau youth group organizers Liu Guang and Zhang Fo-

fan helped organize the Study Society in 1943. Leadership consisted of four party activists, but most participants were workers from printing factories, cotton mills, arsenals, the upper Sichuan industrial company, and radio plants. Huang Shujun, *Chongqing gongren yundongshi, 1919–1949*, 214.

94. Editorial, "Zhankai gongrenzhong de minzhu yundong"; "Shenma shi 'faxisi,'" *Xuexi* 3, no. 4 (Mar. 6, 1945).

95. Liu Ming, "Zenyang zuo qunzhong gongzuo," *Xuexi* 3, no. 5 (1945).

96. Huang Shujun, *Chongqing gongren yundong shi, 1919–1949*, 198.

97. Interview with Zhu Rong (Chongqing).

98. Zhonggong Chongqing shiwei dangshi gongzuo weiyuanhui bian, ed., *Zhongguo laodong xiehui zai Chongqing*, 1; Huang Shujun, *Chongqing gongren yundong shi*, 243.

99. Perry, *Shanghai on Strike: The Politics of Chinese Labor*, 127.

100. Epstein, *Notes on Labor Problems in Nationalist China*, 96–99.

101. Zhonggong Chongqing shiwei dangshi gongzuo weiyuanhui bian, ed., *Zhongguo laodong xiehui zai Chongqing*, 23.

102. For a fuller discussion of the platform and subsequent government repression, see Epstein, *Notes on Labor Problems in Nationalist China*, 104–7; Pepper, *Civil War in China: The Political Struggle 1945–1949*, 101–4.

103. Zhonggong Chongqing shiwei dangshi gongzuo weiyuanhui bian, ed., *Zhongguo laodong xiehui zai Chongqing*, 10; Wales, *The Chinese Labor Movement*, 123.

104. CQA, 50 Chang, 2 *mu*, 95 *juan*, 64 (Feb. 9, 1946); SHA, 774 quanzong, 3282 *juan* (Nov. 22, 1946).

105. CQA, 50 Chang, 2 *mu*, 95 *juan*, 59 (Oct. 18, 1945).

106. CQA, 10 Chang, 8 *mu*, 158 *juan*, 125, Long Ming interrogation record (Apr. 2, 1946); CQA, 10 Chang, 8 *mu*, 158 *juan*, 177, Li Bing interrogation record.

107. Zhonggong Chongqing shiwei dangshi gongzuo weiyuanhui bian, ed., *Zhongguo laodong xiehui zai Chongqing*, 11.

108. See CQA, 21 Chang, zongmu, 23–1 *juan*, 6 (Feb. 9, 1946); 50 Chang, 2 *mu*, 95 *juan*, 67 (Feb. 26, 1946).

109. Interview with Du Liang (Chongqing).

110. CQA, 21 Chang, jingji *mu*, 35 *juan*, 13 ("Zhongguo jiqi gongren lianyihui zhangcheng caoan").

111. SHA, 774 quanzong, 3282 *juan* (Sept. 3, 1946).

112. The classic account remains White and Jacoby, *Thunder Out of China*.

Chapter 8. The Labor Movement, 1946–1949

1. Liu and Tang, eds., *Zhongguo gongren yundongshi*, 5: 424.

2. Liu Zonglin, "Wo canjia Chongqing gongren yundong de huiyi," 10.

3. CQA, 20 Chang, 1441 *juan*, 84–88 (Feb. 14, 1939).

4. "Chang'an zhi lu," in *Jiangbei qu wenshi ziliao*, 7 (1992): 24.

5. Yang Jixuan, "Fuyuan qizhong Chongqing de gongchao," 63–64.

6. Qi Wu, *Kang Ri Zhanzheng shiqi Zhongguo gongren yundong shigao*, 315; Huang Shujun, *Chongqing gongren yundong shi, 1919–1949*, 389.

7. CQA, 29 Chang, 5 *mu*, 371 *juan* (June 28, 1946); Liu and Tang, eds., *Zhongguo gongren yundongshi*, 5: 440. For a more "economistic" analysis of the Tianjin labor movement, see Yick, *Making Urban Revolution in China: The CCP-GMD Struggle for Beiping-Tianjin, 1945–1949*, ch. 6.

8. CQA, 29 Chang, 2 *mu*, 2–6 *juan*, 144 (Jan. 26, 1946), order of Yang Jizeng.

9. *Xinhua ribao*, Dec. 28, 1945, 4.

10. CQA, 1 Chang, 1 *mu*, 1 *juan*, 28 (Oct. 26, 1945).

11. *Xinhua ribao*, Dec. 28, 1945, 4.

12. Unless otherwise noted, the following narrative is based on Yang Jizeng's report in "Gangtiechang qianjian weiyuanhui bugao" (Apr. 2, 1946), in *ZJBGS*, 3: 1103–5.

13. *Xinhua ribao*, Mar. 25, 1946.

14. No existing document provides the entire list of demands, but several sources confirm the reconstruction in Huang Shujun, *Chongqing gongren yundong shi, 1919–1949*, 358. *Shishi xinbao*, Mar. 25, 1946; *Xinhua ribao*, Mar. 25, 1946; and a memoir of the 1950s included in Sichuan shinian wenxue yishu xuanji bianji weiyuanhui, ed., *Sichuan gongchang shi zuopin xuan*, 18.

15. "Chongqing gangtie gongsi de 20 nian" (1959), 38.

16. The slogans are recorded in the factory history "Chongqing gangtie gongsi de 20 nian" (1959), 40. Much of this unpublished manuscript is based on the steel mill workers' oral histories as related to university history students in training.

17. Interview with Yang Jinhua (Chongqing).

18. Chonggangzhi bianjishi bian, *Chonggang zhi: 1938–1985*, 52.

19. Lack of source materials makes it difficult to ascertain the level of gang involvement among arsenal employees. Shortly after Yu Dawei prohibited staff and workers from joining gangs in 1941, one of his subordinates reported that only a "minority of staff and workers had joined gangs *[banghui]*." See CQA, 29 Chang, 2 *mu*, 2–6 *juan*, 61, 69 (Oct. 23, 1941).

20. *Minzhu bao*, Mar. 26, 1946.

21. *Chongqing gangtie gongsi de 20 nian*, 44; *Xinhua ribao*, Mar. 26, 1946. For variants on the same theme, see articles of Mar. 25 and Apr. 4.

22. *Xinhua* reported that machine-gun fire left four workers killed and eight workers seriously wounded (Mar. 24–25). According to Yang Jizeng's report, two guards were severely and one slightly wounded. Three workers suffered heavy injuries, and three light injuries. One worker died from severe injuries.

23. CQA, 10 Chang, 8 *mu*, 159 *juan*, report of Zhang Xiujing (Apr. 21, 1946).

24. See *Xinhua ribao*, Mar. 27–29, 3.

25. Huang Shujun, *Chongqing gongren yundong shi, 1919–1949*, 339.

26. Du resided in Chongqing up to 1945 before attending the CCP's Seventh Congress in Yan'an. This report was written after Du's return to Sichuan and based upon a ten-month sojourn in Chongqing. Starting April 30, 1946, Du held the post of organizational chief of the labor movement under the newly estab-

lished Sichuan Provincial Committee. Du Yanqing, "Chongqing gongyun" (Jan. 24, 1947), in *SGRYD*, 394.

27. Ibid., 396.

28. The document was written in early April 1946 after the investigation section of the arsenal arrested Xie for his role in leading a strike the previous month. Unless otherwise noted, quotations from Xie derive from this source. Security force personnel later recommended "editing" his paper and circulating it for reference purposes, but I have not been able to find the edited version, if it indeed exists. CQA, 10 Chang, 8 *mu*, 159 *juan*, 39–44, "Xie Wanquan zibaishu chaojian."

29. CQA, 10 Chang, 8 *mu*, 158 *juan*, 112–13, Xie Wanquan interrogation record (Apr. 5, 1946).

30. CQA, 10 Chang, 8 *mu*, 159 *juan*, 42, "Xie Wanquan zibaishu chaojian." On Jiang Qing's visit to Chongqing in the summer of 1945 during the Chiang-Mao negotiations, see Terrill, *Madame Mao: The White-Boned Demon*, 174.

31. For Wang Shiwei's writings in translation, see Benton and Hunter, *Wild Lily, Prairie Fire: China's Road to Democracy, Yan'an to Tian'anmen, 1942–1989*, 69–77. For analysis of Wang's role in the rectification movement, see Cheek, "The Fading of Wild Lilies: Wang Shiwei and Mao Zedong's Yan'an Talks in the First CPC Rectification Movement," 25–58.

32. CQA, 10 Chang, 8 *mu*, 159 *juan*, 42, "Xie Wanquan zibaishu chaojian."

33. Mason, "The Turin Strike of March 1943," 286.

34. CQA, 10 Chang, 8 *mu*, 158 *juan*, 89–90, 84 (Apr. 3, 1946), Xie Wanquan interrogation record.

35. Ibid., 88, 95.

36. CQA, 10 Chang, 8 *mu*, 158 *juan*, 1 (Mar. 30, 1946), report of Guard and Investigation squad.

37. CQA, 10 Chang, 8 *mu*, 158 *juan*, 85 (Apr. 3, 1946), Xie Wanquan interrogation record.

38. Ibid., 91.

39. CQA, 10 Chang, 8 *mu*, 158 *juan*, 22 (Apr. 5, 1946), report of Guard and Investigation squad.

40. Ibid., 189 (Apr. 1946), Shen Yongfa interrogation record.

41. Perry, *Shanghai on Strike: The Politics of Chinese Labor*, 60.

42. CQA, 10 Chang, 8 *mu*, 158 *juan*, 135, 138 (Apr. 1, 1946), Xiao Jiazhu interrogation record. Arsenal No. 3 was a former Shanghai steel mill that had merged in January 1940 and become department 7 of the Gangqianhui steel mill. Workers commonly called the steel mill Arsenal No. 3.

43. CQA, 10 Chang, 8 *mu*, 158 *juan*, 46 (Apr. 1, 1946), Chen Jiafu interrogation record.

44. Ibid., 58, Li Zhaoxiao interrogation record.

45. Huang Shujun, *Chongqing gongren yundong shi, 1919–1949*, 364.

46. CQA, 10 Chang, 8 *mu*, 158 *juan*, 64.

47. Ibid., 99 (Apr. 3, 1946), Xie Wanquan interrogation record.

48. Ibid., 100–101.

49. Ibid., 1 (Mar. 30, 1946), report of Guard and Investigation squad.

50. Ibid., 17 (Apr. 5, 1946), report of Guard and Investigation squad.

51. Ibid., 32 (Apr. 1, 1946), Mao Ren'gang interrogation record.

52. Ibid., 181–82 (Apr. 1946), Wu Jiujiang interrogation record.

53. In order of citation, these quotations are from CQA, 10 Chang, 8 *mu*, 158 *juan*, 23 (Apr. 8, 1946), report of Guard and Investigation section; Shen Qichang interrogation record, 164; Wu Jiujiang interrogation record, 182; Xian Ziqiang interrogation record, 40.

54. Ibid., 27 (Apr. 1, 1946), Liu Wenqing interrogation record.

55. Ibid., 2 (Mar. 30, 1946), report of Guard and Investigation squad; Wu Jiujiang interrogation record, 184.

56. Ibid., 3 (Mar. 30, 1946), report of Guard and Investigation squad.

57. CQA, 10 Chang, 12 *mu*, 33 *juan*, 19, 23 (Mar. 29, Apr. 2, 1946), report of the Chongqing Municipal Police Tenth District chief, Jiang Zhongqi.

58. The quotations in this paragraph are from CQA, 10 Chang, 8 *mu*, 158 *juan*, 4 (Mar. 30, 1946), report of Guard and Investigation squad and Shen Qichang interrogation record, 162.

59. Ibid., 4 (Mar. 30, 1946), report of Guard and Investigation squad.

60. Ibid., 5.

61. Ibid., 176, Li Bing interrogation record.

62. Dirlik, "Narrativizing Revolution: The Guangzhou Uprising (11–13 Dec. 1927) in Workers' Perspective," 376.

63. CQA, 10 Chang, 8 *mu*, 159 *juan*, 41, "Xie Wanquan zibaishu chaojian."

64. CQA, 10 Chang, 8 *mu*, 158 *juan*, 9 (Mar. 30, 1946).

65. Ibid., 68 (Apr. 12, 1946), report of the Guard and Investigation squad.

66. CQA, 10 Chang, 8 *mu*, 159 *juan*, 5 (Apr. 19, 1946), report of Ordnance Department Guard and Investigation section.

67. CQA, 26 Chang, 1 *mu*, 121 *juan*, 82 (June 9, 1947), report of Ordnance Director Yang Jizeng.

68. CQA, 10 Chang, 8 *mu*, 158 *juan*, 18 (Apr. 8, 1946), submitted to directing secretary Li.

69. "Binggongshu di 50 gongchang zhongshu fenchang yange shi," in *ZJBGS*, 3: 1186.

70. CQA, te 2, 1 *mu*, 58 *juan*, 68, report of Wang Zizheng (Mar. 3, 1946).

71. Ibid., 100, report of Wang Zizheng (Mar. 11, 1946).

72. Ibid., 43 (May 20, 1946), report of Zhang Yixian.

73. Ibid., 53–55 (May 22, 1946), report of Zhou Hanbo.

74. Ibid., 58 (Apr. 1946), report of Zhou Hanbo.

75. Ibid., 43 (May 20, 1946), report of Zhang Yixian.

76. CQA, 24 Chang, 1 *mu*, 47 *juan*, 44 (June 5, 1946), Cheng Yizhong, report to Yang Jizeng.

77. CQA, 24 Chang, 1 *mu*, zong 164 *juan*, 117b (Feb. 18, 1947).

78. Du Yanqing, "Chongqing gongyun," Jan. 24, 1947, in *SGRYD*, 396.

79. Ibid., 400.

80. CQA, 10 Chang, 3 *mu*, 31 *juan*, 45–47, "Di 10 Chang zhongyao shilei baogaoshu" (May 1949).

81. CQA, 21 Chang, jingji, 36 *juan*, 68–69 (May 1949).

82. "Xue Kegang gei Chen Zhesheng de qingbao" (Mar. 14, 1949), in *ZJBGS*, 3: 1112.

83. "Chuanban dudao zugei Chen Zhesheng de dachen" (Apr. 28, 1949), in *ZJBGS*, 3: 1114.

84. The following discussion of workers' demands is based on "Xue Kegang gei Chen Zhesheng de qingbao" (Mar. 18, 1949), in *ZJBGS*, 3: 1112–13.

85. CQA, 10 Chang, 16 *mu*, 3233 *juan*, 30 (Apr. 22, 1949).

86. Under martial law, workers were subject to inspections between 9 and 10 P.M. and curfew from 11 P.M. to 6 A.M. See CQA, Qujiang tiekuang, 1 *mu*, 78-2 *juan*, 24.

87. "Bingongshu liuYu changzhang di26 ci huiyi guanyu yuangong gongzi de taolun he jueyi" (Apr. 19, 1949), in *ZJBGS*, 3: 944–45. For a similar report of impending catastrophe because of inadequate money to pay wages and low worker morale, see SHA, 774/706 (n.d.).

88. "Chongqing jingbei silingbu wei gongren bagong shijian gei di 21 gongchang daidian" (Apr. 21, 1949), in *ZJBGS*, 3: 1114.

89. CQA, 10 quanzong Shi zhengfu [Municipal government], 2 *mu*, 493 *juan*, 62.

90. Ibid., 61.

91. CQA, 10 quanzong, 16 *mu*, 3233 *juan*, 30 (Apr. 22, 1949).

92. CQA, 21 Chang, zong 23-1, 50 (June 6, 1949), report of the Social Affairs Department chief, Chen Quhuo.

93. MND 543.9/2010, "Chongqingshi gongchang ji dongli pohuai an" (Nov. 1949).

94. The following account is based on Wang Qitai, "Huchang ying jiefang," 283–87; Lu Guangte, "Jiefang Zhanzheng houqi Chongqing gongyun gaikuang," 395–400. Joseph Yick calculates that more than one thousand Guomindang generals and 1.77 million troops defected to the Communists during the Chinese civil war, *Making Urban Revolution in China: The CCP-GMD Struggle for Beiping-Tianjin, 1945–1949*, 47.

95. Wang Qitai, "Huchang ying jiefang," 284; Lu Guangte, "Jiefang Zhanzheng houqi Chongqing gongyun gaikuang," 396.

96. Yu Zhuozhi, "Wo zai 21 binggongchang de yixie jingli," 29.

97. Yick, *Making Urban Revolution in China: The CCP-GMD Struggle for Beiping-Tianjin, 1945–1949*, 145.

98. Du Yanqing, "Chongqing gongyun" (Jan. 24, 1947), in *SGRYD*, 398.

99. Interview with Xie Lin (Chongqing).

Chapter 9. Yu Zusheng: Organic Intellectuals
and the Moral Basis of Class

1. Luo Guangbin (Lo Kuang-pin) and Yang Yiyan (Yang Yi-yen) based their character Yu Xinjiang, the protagonist of *Hong Yan (Red Crag)*, on Yu Zusheng. For an analysis of government influence on the writing of *Hong Yan*, see Shen, "SACO: An Ambivalent Experience of Sino-American Cooperation During World War II," ch. 1.

2. Steinberg, "Vanguard Workers and the Morality of Class," 66.

3. Gramsci, *The Antonio Gramsci Reader: Selected Writings, 1916–1935*, ed. Forgacs, 321.

4. Gramsci, *Selections from the Prison Notebooks of Antonio Gramsci*, ed. and trans. Hoare and Smith, 15.

5. Lutze, "New Democracy: Chinese Communist Relations with the Urban Middle Forces, 1931–1952."

6. Chang'an chang changshi bianji weiyuanhui bangongshi, ed., "Geming lieshi Yu Zusheng," 45.

7. CQGLS, Yu Zusheng file, Yu Zusheng, "Wo de diyi ge shifu" [My First Master] (n.d.).

8. Ibid.

9. Yu Zusheng, "Wo de jia" [My Home] (Feb. 2, 1947), in Wang and Li, eds., *Heilao shibian: Baigongguan, Zhazidong geming lieshi shiwenji*, 214.

10. CQGLS, Yu Zusheng file, Yu Zusheng, letter to Zhong Bin, Sept. 3, 1946.

11. CQGLS, Yu Zusheng file, Yu Zusheng, letter to Zhong Bin, n.d. (Spring 1945?).

12. For an extended analysis of light imagery in Japanese opposition movement writings of the late nineteenth century through the Taisho period, see Mackie, "Liberation and Light: The Language of Opposition in Imperial Japan," *East Asian History* 9 (1995): 121–42.

13. Yu Zusheng, "Huoyan" [Flame] (Apr. 1, 1948), in Wang and Li, eds., *Heilao shibian: Baigongguan, Zhazidong geming lieshi shiwenji*, 217–18.

14. Chang'an chang changshi bianji weiyuanhui bangongshi, ed., "Geming lieshi Yu Zusheng," 46.

15. Mao quoted in Kowallis, *The Lyrical Lu Xun: A Study of His Classical-Style Verse*, 207–8.

16. Ibid.

17. CQGLS, Yu Zusheng file, Yu Zusheng, letter to Ye Weicai, Aug. 24, 1947.

18. Meisner, "Marx, Mao, and Deng on the Division of Labor in History," 79–116.

19. Mao Zedong, *Selected Readings from the Works of Mao Tse-tung*, 255.

20. "Gongren zenyang anpai zixiu shijian?" *Xinhua ribao*, Feb. 18, 1944.

21. Smith, *Like Cattle and Horses: Nationalism and Labor in Shanghai, 1895–1927*, 119.

22. CQGLS, Yu Zusheng file, Yu Zusheng, letter to Zhong Bin, Nov. 27, 1945.

23. CQGLS, Yu Zusheng file, Yu Zusheng, "Jinchang de di'er nian" [My Second Year in the Factory] (1942).

24. CQGLS, Yu Zusheng file, Yu Zusheng, "Ye" [Leaves] (Spring 1947).

25. Tong Zhicheng, "Mantan fuli," 4; McIsaac, "Righteous Fraternities' and Honorable Men: Sworn Brotherhoods in Wartime Chongqing," 1641–55. For Russian worker-writers' rejection of rough culture, see Steinberg, "Vanguard Workers and the Morality of Class," 69, 82.

26. Chang'an chang changshi bianji weiyuanhui bangongshi, ed., "Geming lieshi Yu Zusheng," 46.

27. CQGLS, Yu Zusheng file, Yu Zusheng, "My Second Year in the Factory" (1942).

28. Steinberg, "Vanguard Workers and the Morality of Class," 67.

29. Zhe Sheng, "Rang women shuo ji juhua," *Xinhua ribao*, May 15, 1944, 3. Writers often used pen names to protect themselves from retribution and to engage in political jabs by means of double entendre and play on words. In this case, *zhe* probably refers to *mei zhe*, that is, "to be at the end of one's rope." *Sheng* means "voice."

30. CQGLS, Yu Zusheng file, Yu Zusheng, letter to Zhong Bin, Oct. 15 [194?].

31. Ibid.

32. Dirlik, "Radical Culture and Cultural Revolution," 191.

33. Ibid., 186.

34. Rancière, "Ronds de fumée (Les Poètes ouvriers dans la France de Louis-Philippe)," 46. My translation.

35. Interview with Yang Yiyan (Chongqing). Yang, the co-author of *Red Crag*, was Yu Zusheng's prison cell mate in late 1948. Yang recalls how Yu and other prisoners made ink by burning cotton from their mattresses and mixing it with water. For brushes, they used bamboo sticks, and their paper was cigarette paper. Unfortunately, none of Yu's prison poetry remains, but the works of other prisoners were either transmitted orally to visitors or buried and found after the CCP takeover. On poetry of the "Iron-barred-window Poetry Society," see Wang and Li, eds., *Heilao shibian: Baigongguan, Zhazidong geming lieshi shiwenji*, 219.

36. CQA, 10 Chang, 8 *mu*, 159 *juan*, 43 (Apr. 1946), "Xie Wanquan zibaishu chaojian."

37. Smith, *Like Cattle and Horses: Nationalism and Labor in Shanghai, 1895–1927*, 117–18.

38. CQGLS, Yu Zusheng file, Yu Zusheng, "Huai Pushigen" [Ode to Pushkin] (Spring 1947).

39. CQGLS, Yu Zusheng file, Yu Zusheng, "Gongren" [Workers] (Oct. 29, 1946).

40. CQGLS, Yu Zusheng file, Yu Zusheng, "Xinnian de ye" [New Year's Night] (Jan. 3, 1947).

41. Yu Zusheng, "Shi She" [Giving Charity], published in Wang and Li, eds., *Heilao shibian: Baigongguan, Zhazidong geming lieshi shiwenji*, 216 (Mar. 13, 1947). Jin Bangbang refers to the Nationalist general Jin Lingzhang. "Bank notes" *(guanjin)* refers to a type of negotiable securities issued by the Nationalist Central Bank and replaced by currency in 1942.

42. Rancière, "Ronds de fumée (Les Poètes ouvriers dans la France de Louis-Philippe)," 34.

43. CQGLS, Yu Zusheng file, Yu Zusheng, "Kanke" [Rough] (Spring 1947).

44. CQGLS, Yu Zusheng file, Yu Zusheng, letter to Ye Weicai, Aug. 24, 1947.

45. CQGLS, Yu Zusheng file, Yu Zusheng, "On Life and Struggle" (written in Jiangbei, Chongqing, Aug. 4, 1947).

46. CQGLS, Yu Zusheng file, Yu Zusheng, "Mingtian" [Tomorrow] (Spring 1947).

47. CQA, te 1, 4 *mu*, 2 *juan*, 34 (October 1947?), Xie Wanquan interrogation record.

48. Yu Zusheng, "Shai taiyang" [Basking in the Sun], in Wang and Li, eds., *Heilao shibian: Baigongguan, Zhazidong geming lieshi shiwenji*, 215.

49. Chan, *A Sourcebook in Chinese Philosophy*, 47.

50. For the former view, see Honig, *Sisters and Strangers: Women in the Shanghai Cotton Mills, 1919–1949*; McIsaac, "The Limits of Chinese Nationalism: Workers in Wartime Chongqing, 1937–1945." For the relationship between skill and collective action, see Perry, *Shanghai on Strike: The Politics of Chinese Labor*, 232–33.

51. My emphasis on cultural discourse has been influenced by Steinberg, *Voices of Revolution, 1917*, 4.

52. Perry, ed., *Putting Class in Its Place: Worker Identities in East Asia*, 3.

Chapter 10. Deepening the Revolution, 1950–1953

1. Barnett, *Communist China: The Early Years 1949–1955*, Preface, 8.

2. Lieberthal, *Revolution and Tradition in Tientsin, 1949–1952*, 7.

3. Kaple, *Dream of a Red Factory: The Legacy of High Stalinism in China*.

4. Frazier, *The Making of the Chinese Industrial Workplace: State, Revolution, and Labor Management*, 114.

5. Quoted in Gardner, "The Wu-fan Campaign in Shanghai: A Study in the Consolidation of Urban Control," 477.

6. Schurmann, *Ideology and Organization in Communist China*, passim.

7. CQA, 1032 quanzong, 5 *mu*, 100 *juan*, 63.

8. "Zhongguo binggong gonghui xinanqu weiyuanhui gongzuo zongjie" (Oct. 1950), CQA, 1032 quanzong, 5 *mu*, 100 *juan*, 4.

9. Interview with Ye Xiuquan (Chongqing).

10. Huang, "Rural Class Struggle in the Chinese Revolution: Representational and Objective Realities from the Land Reform to the Cultural Revolution," 119, 137.

11. Richman, *Industrial Society in Communist China*, 228–29.

12. "Zhongguo binggong gonghui xinanqu weiyuanhui gongzuo zongjie" (Oct. 1950) CQA, 1032 quanzong, 5 *mu*, 100 *juan*, 4.

13. Zhongguo binggong gonghui xinanqu weiyuanhui, "Yi nian ban lai gongzuo zongjie" (Jan. 1951–June 1952), CQA, 1032 quanzong, 5 *mu*, 106 *juan*, 1.

14. Zhongguo binggong gonghui xinanqu weiyuanhui, "Minzhu gaige da jiancha yundong chubu zongjie" (Dec. 29, 1951), CQA, 1032 quanzong, 5 *mu*, 97 *juan*, 73.

15. Li Chengwen, ed., *Zhongguo gongchandang Chongqingshi zuzhi shi ziliao*, 1: 89–90.

16. "Zhongguo binggong gonghui xinanqu weiyuanhui gongzuo zongjie"

(Oct. 1950), CQA, 1032 quanzong, 5 *mu*, 100 *juan*, 4; Chongqing nianjian bian-jibu, ed., *Jianguo chuqi de 29 binggongchang yu 101 Chang*, 123.

17. Interview with Wang Xianglong (Chongqing).

18. "791 Chang weiyuanhui 1951 gongzuo zongjie," CQA, 1032 quanzong, 5 *mu*, 106 *juan*, 26.

19. Zhongguo binggong gonghui xinanqu weiyuanhui, "Yi nian ban lai gongzuo zongjie" (Jan. 1951–June 1952), CQA, 1032 quanzong, 5 *mu*, 106 *juan*, 1.

20. Zhongguo binggong gonghui xinanqu weiyuanhui, "1950 nian gonghui gongzuo zongjie" (Jan. 30, 1951), CQA, 1032 quanzong, 5 *mu*, 156 *juan*.

21. "791 Chang weiyuanhui 1951 gongzuo zongjie," CQA, 1032 quanzong, 5 *mu*, 106 *juan*.

22. "Di 20 binggongchang gongchouhui gongzuo jingyan" (approx. Sept. 1950), CQA, 1032 quanzong, 5 *mu*, 106 *juan*, 26.

23. "Zhongguo binggong gonghui xinanqu weiyuanhui gongzuo zongjie" (Oct. 1950), CQA, 1032 quanzong, 5 *mu*, 100 *juan*, 4–4.

24. Zhongguo binggong gonghui xinanqu weiyuanhui, "Xinan binggong hechang gonghuifa jiancha qingkuang zongjie baogao" (Sept. 20, 1951), CQA, 1032 quanzong, 5 *mu*, 102 *juan*, 1.

25. Ibid., 3.

26. Ibid., 2.

27. Ibid., 3.

28. Ibid.

29. "Zhongguo binggong gonghui xinanqu weiyuanhui bageyue gongzuo zongjie" (Sept. 6, 1951), CQA, 1032 quanzong, 5 *mu*, 106 *juan*.

30. Ibid.

31. "Zhongguo binggong gonghui xinanqu weiyuanhui" (postdates May 1952), CQA, 1032 quanzong, 5 *mu*, 105 *juan*, 28.

32. Chonggangzhi bianjishi bian, *Chonggang zhi: 1938–1985*, 369; "454 Chang jiefang qianhou gongzi gaikuang," CQA, 1032 quanzong, 5 *mu*, 113 *juan*, 75.

33. "1950.12 gechang gongzi qingkuang tongji," CQA, 1032 quanzong, 5 *mu*, 113 *juan*.

34. Perry, "Labor's Battle for Political Space: The Role of Worker Associations in Contemporary China," 308–12.

35. "Jiefang yilai gongzi shuiping biandong qingkuang diaochabiao" (Oct. 30, 1952), CQA, 1032 quanzong, 5 *mu*, 113 *juan*, 35.

36. Zhongguo binggong gonghui xinanqu weiyuanhui, gongren shenghuo gaikuang diaochazu, "Chongqing binggong xitong 100 hujia tongji diaocha" (Oct. 24, 1952), CQA, 1032 quanzong, 5 *mu*, 123 *juan*.

37. "451 Chang shenghuo juzhu fangmian de qingkuang" (1951?), CQA, 1032 quanzong, 5 *mu*, 96 *juan*, 1.

38. "791 Chang weiyuanhui juzhu shenghuo qingkuang" (Sept. 10, 1951), CQA, 1032 quanzong, 5 *mu*, 96 *juan*, 75B.

39. "152 Chang gonghui shenghuo juzhu weiyuanhui baogao" (Aug. 4, 1951), CQA, 1032 quanzong, 5 *mu*, 96 *juan*, 68.

40. "Laobao gongzuo zongjie" (1951?), CQA, 1032 quanzong, 5 *mu*, 100 *juan*, 18; "152 Chang gonghui shenghuo juzhu gongzuo de qingkuang"; "791 Chang weiyuanhui juzhu shenghuo qingkuang," CQA, 1032 quanzong, 5 *mu*, 96 *juan;* "Zhongguo binggong gonghui xinanqu weiyuanhui gongzuo zongjie" (Oct. 1950), CQA, 1032 quanzong, 5 *mu*, 100 *juan*, 32.

41. "497 Chang shenghuo juzhu fangmian de qingkuang" (Dec. 6, 1951), CQA, 1032 quanzong, 5 *mu*, 96 *juan*.

42. "21 Chang 1950 shenghuo juzhu gongzuo baogao," CQA, 1032 quanzong, 5 *mu*, 96 *juan*.

43. "Xinan 21 Chang gonghui laobao weiyuanhui," CQA, 1032 quanzong, 5 *mu*, 96 *juan*.

44. "21 Chang 1950 shenghuo juzhu gongzuo baogao," CQA, 1032 quanzong, 5 *mu*, 96 *juan*.

45. "Xinan qu gechang gongzi qingkuang," CQA, 1032 quanzong, 5 *mu*, 113 *juan*, 91.

46. "Laobao gongzuo zongjie," CQA, 1032 quanzong, 5 *mu*, 100 *juan*, 18.

47. "Xinan qu gechang gongzi qingkuang," CQA, 1032 quanzong, 5 *mu*, 113 *juan*, 91.

48. Ibid.

49. "Gongchang zhong jixiang da de yundong zhong gonghui suo zuo de yiban gongzuo, ping gongzi gongzuo zhong suo zuo de gongzuo," CQA, 1032 quanzong, 5 *mu*, 100 *juan*, 24.

50. Xinan binggongju, "Binggong chanye shixing baji gongzizhi zhi chubu jihua," CQA, 1032 quanzong, 5 *mu*, 113 *juan*, 79.

51. "Binggong chanye shixing baji gongzizhi zhi chubu jihua," CQA, 1032 quanzong, 5 *mu*, 113 *juan*, 80.

52. "Jiefang hou gongzi biandong qingkuang," CQA, 1032 quanzong, 5 *mu*, 113 *juan;* "Xinan binggongju suoshu ge gongchang gongren an baji gongzizhi pingding jieguo" (1953?), CQA, 1032 quanzong, 5 *mu*, 123 *juan*.

53. "1951 4–6 yuefen tongjibiao bao fenxi baogao" (Sept. 1, 1951), CQA, 1032 quanzong, 5 *mu*, 105 *juan*, 78.

54. Zhongguo binggong gonghui xinanqu weiyuanhui, "3 nian lai xinan binggong gonghui gongzuo zongjie" (Oct. 31, 1952), CQA, 1032 quanzong, 5 *mu*, 104 *juan*, 7.

55. Donnithorne, *China's Economic System*, 188; Richman, *Industrial Society in Communist China*, 135–37.

56. "Zhigong xuexi renyuan tongji biao" (1950?), CQA, 1032 quanzong, 5 *mu*, 100 *juan*, 28.

57. Donnithorne, *China's Economic System*, 193–94, notes: "The new government put in hand a programme of rapid development of higher education, so that the total number of graduates (new and old) of institutions of higher learning increased from around 150,000 in 1949 to an estimated 625,000 by 1960. Engineers constituted over a quarter of the 1960 total, compared with about one-sixth in 1949." I have not found figures indicating how many arsenal workers were retrained after 1949 to become technicians and engineers. Although by no means representative, my interview pool suggests that such avenues of social mo-

bility were common. Seven interviewees who were production workers during the 1940s eventually became engineers after 1949. One even attended Qinghua University.

58. "Zhongguo binggong gonghui xinanqu weiyuanhui yinianban lai gongzuo zongjie" (Jan. 1, 1951, to June 1952), CQA, 1032 quanzong, 5 *mu*, 106 *juan*.

59. Cited in Pepper, *Radicalism and Education Reform in Twentieth-Century China: The Search for an Ideal Development Model*, 209.

60. White, *Careers in Shanghai: The Social Guidance of Personal Energies in a Developing Chinese City, 1949–1966*, 16.

61. Richman, *Industrial Society in Communist China*, 298.

62. Chongqing nianjian bianjibu, ed., *Jianguo chuqi de 29 binggongchang yu 101 Chang*, 117–18; Chonggangzhi bianjishi bian, *Chonggang zhi: 1938–1985*, 56, 59.

63. 791 Chang weiyuanhui, "Fante yundong wenjiao zongjie" (Jan. 11, 1952), CQA, 1032 quanzong, 5 *mu*, 97 *juan*, 79.

64. Walder, *Communist Neo-Traditionalism: Work and Authority in Chinese Industry*.

65. Li Chengwen, ed., *Zhongguo Gongchandang Chongqingshi zuzhi shi ziliao*, 1: 90.

66. "San nian lai xinan binggong gonghui gongzuo zongjie," CQA, 1032 quanzong, 5 *mu*, 104 *juan*, 6b.

67. "Zhonggong Chongqingzhi dangyuan tongjibiao," in Liu, ed., *Zhongguo gongchandang Sichuansheng zuzhi shi ziliao*, 37.

68. Li Chengwen, ed., *Zhongguo Gongchandang Chongqingshi zuzhi shi ziliao*, 1: 91.

69. CQA, 1032 quanzong, 5 *mu*, 100 *juan*, 124 (1950).

70. Interview with Wang Xianglong (Chongqing).

71. Chonggangzhi bianjishi bian, *Chonggang zhi: 1938–1985*, 56.

72. "San nian lai xinan binggong gonghui gongzuo zongjie," CQA, 1032 quanzong, 5 *mu*, 104 *juan*, 6B.

73. Zhongguo binggong gonghui xinanqu weiyuanhui, "Minzhu gaige da jiancha yundong chubu zongjie" (Dec. 29, 1951), CQA, 1032 quanzong, 5 *mu*, 97 *juan*, 72.

74. "Xinan binggong gechang 'sanfan' yundong gongzuo zongjie," CQA, 1032 quanzong, 5 *mu*, 104 *juan*, 34.

75. Gardner, "The Wu-fan Campaign in Shanghai: A Study in the Consolidation of Urban Control," 530.

76. CQA, "456 Chang gonghui 1951 nian gongzuo zongjie," 41.

77. Frazier, *The Making of the Chinese Industrial Workplace: State, Revolution, and Labor Management*, 92; Kirby, "The Chinese War Economy," 206.

78. Chonggangzhi bianjishi bian, *Chonggang zhi: 1938–1985*, 55, 614–15.

79. Yu Zhuozhi, "Wo zai 21 binggongchang de yixie jingli," 29.

80. White, "Bourgeois Radicalism in the 'New Class' of Shanghai, 1949–1969," 150, 162.

81. Richman, *Industrial Society in Communist China*, 295–96.

82. Zhongguo binggong gonghui xinanqu weiyuanhui, "Minzhu gaige da jiancha yundong chubu zongjie" (Dec. 29, 1951), CQA, 1032 quanzong, 5 *mu*, 97 *juan*, 70.

83. Djilas, *The New Class: An Analysis of the Communist System*. For the classic study of workers' social mobility and the resultant social basis for Stalin, see Fitzpatrick, *Education and Social Mobility in the Soviet Union, 1921–1934*.

84. "Xinan 497 Chang dierqu gonghui weiyuanhui gongzuo zongjie" (Nov. 1951–July, 1952), CQA, 1032 quanzong, 5 *mu*, 104 *juan*, 196.

85. "Zhongguo binggong gonghui xinanqu weiyuanhui gongzuo zongjie" (Oct. 1950), CQA, 1032 quanzong, 5 *mu*, 100 *juan*, 4–3.

86. "Zhongguo binggong gonghui xinanqu weiyuanhui yinianban lai gongzuo zongjie" (Jan. 1, 1951–June 1952), CQA, 1032 quanzong, 5 *mu*, 106 *juan*.

87. At the Southwest Ordnance Union's request, the administration had hired nonproduction cadres on a temporary basis to strengthen union organizations. Among ten arsenals in the southwest, approximately one-third of all union committee members (N = 193) were nonproduction cadres. By 1951, the unions began to doubt the wisdom of using so many nonproduction cadres in excess of the sixteen stipulated by the Union Law. "51 nian di er jidu (4 yue–6 yuefen) tongjibiao bao fenxi baogao" (Sept. 1, 1951), CQA, 1032 quanzong, 5 *mu*, 105 *juan*, 77.

88. Zhongguo binggong gonghui xinanqu weiyuanhui, "Chongqing binggong gechang jiceng zuzhi zai 'sanfan' yundongzhong de qingkuang" (Feb. 29, 1952), CQA, 1032 quanzong, 5 *mu*, 104 *juan*, 41.

89. Chen, *Mao's China and the Cold War*, passim.

90. "791 binggongchang gonghui weiyuanhui 1951 nian gongzuo zongjie," CQA, 1032 quanzong, 5 *mu*, 106 *juan*, 29.

91. CQA, "456 Chang gonghui 1951 nian gongzuo zongjie," 41.

92. "Xinan binggong gechang 'sanfan' yundong gongzuo zongjie," CQA, 1032 quanzong, 5 *mu*, 104 *juan*, 35.

93. Ibid., 32.

94. Ibid., 36.

95. Donnithorne, *China's Economic System*, 201.

96. Richman, *Industrial Society in Communist China*, 251.

97. Meisner, *Mao's China and After: A History of the People's Republic*, 48–49.

98. Meisner, "Utopian Socialist Themes in Maoism," 69.

99. Djilas, *The New Class*, 42.

Conclusion

1. Qi Wu in Liu and Tang, eds., *Zhongguo gongren yundong shi*, 310.

2. Johnson, *Peasant Nationalism and Communist Power: The Emergence of Revolutionary China*.

3. Braverman, *Labor and Monopoly Capital: The Degradation of Work in the Twentieth Century*.

4. CQGLS, Yu Zusheng file, Yu Zusheng, "Youchi de tiexie" [Greasy Pool of Iron Shavings], Feb. 7, 1947.

5. Katznelson, "Working-Class Formation: Constructing Cases and Comparisons," 14–18.

6. Hagen Koo deftly analyzes the influence of educational ideology on workers' quest for social status in Korea and Japan. Like Koo, I believe that arsenal workers struggled for higher social status while they developed a consciousness of equal rights and class. The common separation in the social sciences between status and class is thus less appropriate to understand workers' identity. See Koo, *Korean Workers: The Culture and Politics of Class Formation*, 127, 130–33.

7. Park, *Colonial Industrialization and Labor in Korea*, 42.

8. Kocka, "Problems of Working-Class Formation in Germany: The Early Years, 1800–1875," 283.

9. For various approaches to the historical origins of the work unit, see Lü and Perry, eds., *Danwei: The Changing Chinese Workplace in Historical and Comparative Perspective*.

10. For a description of the work unit as it developed by the early 1960s, see Frazier, *The Making of the Chinese Industrial Workplace: State, Revolution, and Labor Management*, 5. For a concise overview of the work unit's various functions during the 1970s, see Whyte and Parish, *Urban Life in Contemporary China*, 25–26, 72, 82, 240–41.

11. Frazier, *The Making of the Chinese Industrial Workplace: State, Revolution, and Labor Management*.

12. Ibid., 67, 129.

13. Naughton, "*Danwei*: The Economic Foundations of a Unique Institution," 172–73.

14. Chonggangzhi bianjishi bian, *Chonggang zhi: 1938–1985*, 12.

Appendix

1. For a full description of the Chongqing Municipal Archive holdings, see Lu Dayue, *Chongqingshi dang'anguan jianming zhidao*.

2. In the United States, the new labor history was a reaction to the long dominant institutional focus pioneered by John R. Commons, who underscored labor economics and the study of labor institutions (unions, collective bargaining practices) to the neglect of social forces and working people. Regarding China, the methodology inspired by the new labor history is most evident in the work of Emily Honig, Gail Hershatter, and Shiling Zhao McQuaide, with their attention to working-class culture, neighborhoods, family patterns, and ethnicity.

Select Bibliography

Anderson, Benedict. *Imagined Communities: Reflections on the Origin and Spread of Nationalism.* 1983. Rev. ed. London: Verso, 1993.

Barnett, A. Doak. *China on the Eve of Communist Takeover.* Boulder, Colo.: Westview Encore Reprint, 1985.

———. *Communist China: The Early Years, 1949–1955.* New York: Praeger, 1964.

Benenati, Elisabetta. "Americanism and Paternalism: Managers and Workers in Twentieth-Century Italy." *International Labor and Working-Class History* 53 (Spring 1998): 5–26.

Benton, Gregor and Alan Hunter, eds. *Wild Lily, Prairie Fire: China's Road to Democracy, Yan'an to Tian'anmen, 1942–1989.* Princeton, N.J.: Princeton University Press, 1995.

Bi Chunfu. "QinHua Rijun Wuhanzhan qijian Hua'erzhan shishi gaikuang" [A brief account of chemical weaponry used by Japanese aggressors during the Wuhan Campaign]. *Minguo dang'an* 26, no. 4 (Nov. 1991): 134–38.

Bian, Morris L. "The Sino-Japanese War and the Formation of the State Enterprise System in China: A Case Study of the Dadukou Iron and Steel Works, 1938–1945." *Enterprise and Society* 3 (Mar. 2002): 80–123.

Board of Governors of the Federal Reserve System. *Banking and Monetary Statistics.* Washington, D.C.: National Capital Press, 1943.

Boorman, Howard L., et al., eds. *Biographical Dictionary of Republican China.* 5 vols. New York: Columbia University Press, 1967–71, 1979.

Braverman, Harry. *Labor and Monopoly Capital: The Degradation of Work in the Twentieth Century.* New York: Monthly Review Press, 1974.

Brissenden, Paul Frederick, and Emil Frankel. *Labor Turnover in Industry: A Statistical Analysis.* New York: Macmillan, 1922.

Chan, Anthony B. *Arming the Chinese: The Western Armaments Trade in Warlord China, 1920–1928.* Vancouver: University of British Columbia Press, 1982.

Chan, Wing-tsit. *A Source Book in Chinese Philosophy.* Princeton, N.J.: Princeton University Press, 1963.

Chang'an chang changshi bianji weiyuanhui bangongshi, ed. "Geming lieshi Yu Zusheng" [The revolutionary martyr Yu Zusheng]. In Chongqingshi zonggonghui gongyunshi ziliao yanjiuzu and Xinan shifan xueyuan lishixi, comps., *Chongqing gongyunshi yanjiu ziliao huibian*, vol. 5 (Oct. 1983), 45–46.

Chang Hung-tseng. "The Chungking Press: I." *China at War* 14, no. 4 (1945): 69–74.

———. "The Chungking Press: II." *China at War* 14, no. 5 (1945): 60–64.

Chang Kia-ngau. *The Inflationary Spiral: The Experience in China, 1939–1950*. Cambridge, Mass.: MIT Press, 1958.

Changshi bianji weiyuanhui banshishi, ed. *Chang'an chang changshi ziliao* [Materials regarding the history of the Chang'an factory]. Chongqing, 1983.

Cheek, Timothy. "The Fading of Wild Lilies: Wang Shiwei and Mao Zedong's Yan'an Talks in the First CPC Rectification Movement." *Australian Journal of Chinese Affairs* 11 (Jan. 1984): 25–58.

———. *Mao Zedong and China's Revolutions: A Brief History with Documents*. New York: Palgrave, 2002.

Chen Cungong. "Minchu lujun junhuo zhi shuru" [Arms imports during the early Republic]. *Jindaishi yanjiusuo jikan* 6 (June 1977): 237–309.

———. *Lieqiang dui Zhongguo de junhuo jinyun: Minguo banian-shibanian* [The foreign powers' arms embargo of China, 1919–1929]. Taipei: Zhongyang yanjiuyuan jindaishi yanjiusuo, 1983.

Chen Hongjin. "32 nian zhi Sichuan nongye" [Sichuan agriculture during 1943]. *Sichuan jingji jikan* 1, no. 2 (Mar. 15, 1944): 243–58.

Chen Jian. *Mao's China and the Cold War*. Chapel Hill: University of North Carolina Press, 2001.

Chen Pengzuo. "Xia Chuandong de nongye dili" [The agricultural geography of lower eastern Sichuan]. *Sichuan jingji jikan* 2, no. 4 (Oct. 1, 1945): 70–91.

Chen Qihua. "Wu nian lai zhi Sichuan liangshi zengchan" [Increased production of grain in Sichuan during the past five years]. *Sichuan jingji jikan* 3, no. 1 (Jan. 1, 1946): 150–56.

Chen, Yung-fa. *Making Revolution: The Communist Movement in Eastern and Central China, 1937–1945*. Berkeley: University of California Press, 1986.

Cheng Min et al., eds. *Zhongguo Gongchandang dangyuan dacidian* [Biographical dictionary of the Chinese Communist Party]. Beijing: Zhongguo guoji guangbo chubanshe, 1991.

Cheng Xianmin and Li Shiping, eds. *Jindai Sichuan renkou* [The demography of modern Sichuan]. Chengdu: Chengdu chubanshe, 1993.

Chesneaux, Jean. *Le Mouvement ouvrier chinois de 1919 à 1927*. Le Monde d'outre-mer passé et présent, 17. Paris: Mouton, 1962.

———. *The Chinese Labor Movement, 1919–1927*. Translated by H. M. Wright. Stanford: Stanford University Press, 1968.

Chesneaux, Jean, and Richard C. Kagan. "The Chinese Labor Movement: 1915–1949." *International Social Science Review* 58, no. 2 (Spring 1983): 67–87.

Chi, Ch'ao-ting. *Wartime Economic Development of China*. New York: Garland, 1980.

Ch'i, Hsi-sheng. *Nationalist China at War: Military Defeats and Political Collapse, 1937–1945.* Ann Arbor: University of Michigan Press, 1982.

Chinese Ministry of Information, comp. *China Handbook, 1937–1945: A Comprehensive Survey of Major Developments in China in Eight Years of War.* New York: Macmillan, 1947.

Chonggangzhi bianjishi bian. *Chonggang zhi: 1938–1985* [Gazetteer of the Chongqing steel mill, 1938–85]. Chongqing: Chonggangzhi bianjishi, 1987.

Chongqing nianjian bianjibu, ed. *Jianguo chuqi de 29 binggongchang yu 101 Chang* [Arsenal No. 29 and Factory 101 during the early reconstruction period]. Chengdu: Chongqing shi Dadukou Lizilin Chonggang dang'anchu, 2000.

Chongqing zhengfu, ed. *Chongqing yaolan* [An important guide to Chongqing]. Chongqing: Chongqing Municipal Government, 1945.

Chongqingshi dang'anguan, Sichuan sheng yejin gongye ting "yejinzhi" bianweihui, comp. *Kangzhan houfang yejin gongye shiliao* [Historical materials regarding the metallurgy industry in the Rear Area during the Resistance War]. Chongqing: Chongqing chubanshe, 1987.

Chongqingshi dang'anguan, Zhongguo di'er lishi dang'anguan, comp. *Baise kongbu xia de "Xinhua ribao": Guomindang dangju kongzhi Xinhua ribao de dang'an cailiao huibian [New China Daily* under the White Terror: Collection of archival materials regarding Guomindang authorities' controls over *New China Daily].* Chongqing: Chongqing chubanshe, 1987.

Chongqingshi qu zhengxie wenshi ziliao weiyuanhui, ed. "Chang'an zhi lu" [The history of Chang'an factory]. In *Jiangbei qu wenshi ziliao* [Jiangbei County historical materials], 7: 21-28. Chongqing: Chongqing wenxian chubanshe, 1992.

Chongqingshi zonggonghui gongyunshi ziliao yanjiuzu and Xinan shifan xueyuan lishixi, comps. *Chongqing gongyunshi yanjiu ziliao huibian* [Research materials on the Chongqing labor movement]. Vols. 1–13. Chongqing, 1981–83.

———, comps. *Gao Yuying tongzhi jianghua jilu* [Interview with Comrade Gao Yuying]. Chongqing: n.p., 1981.

———, comps. "*Xinhua ribao* Dadukou fenxiaochu" [The New China Daily newsstand at Dadukou]. In *Zhou Haoliang huiyi cailiao* [Zhou Haoliang's memoir documents], 1-22. Chongqing: n.p., 1981.

Chou, Shun-hsin. *The Chinese Inflation, 1937–1949.* New York: Columbia University Press, 1963.

Coble, Parks M. *Facing Japan: Chinese Politics and Japanese Imperialism, 1931–1937.* Cambridge, Mass.: Council on East Asian Studies, Harvard University, 1991.

Dirlik, Arif. "Radical Culture and Cultural Revolution." In *Anarchism in the Chinese Revolution,* edited by Arif Dirlik, 148–96. Berkeley: University of California Press, 1991.

———. "Narrativizing Revolution: The Guangzhou Uprising (11–13 December 1927) in Workers' Perspective." *Modern China* 23, no. 4 (Oct. 1997): 363–97.

Djilas, Milovan. *The New Class: An Analysis of the Communist System.* New York: Praeger, 1957.

Dobb, Maurice. *Wages*. London: Nisbet; Cambridge: Cambridge University Press, 1938.

Donnithorne, Audrey. *China's Economic System*. New York: Praeger, 1967.

Eastman, Lloyd E. *The Abortive Revolution: China Under Nationalist Rule, 1927–1937*. Cambridge, Mass.: Harvard University Press, 1974.

———. *Seeds of Destruction: Nationalist China in War and Revolution, 1937–1949*. Stanford: Stanford University Press, 1984.

———. "Nationalist China During the Sino-Japanese War, 1937–1945." In *The Cambridge History of China*, vol. 13, edited by John King Fairbank and Albert Feuerwerker, 547–608. Cambridge: Cambridge University Press, 1986.

Engels, Friedrich. *The Condition of the Working Class in England*. Edited by David McLellan. New York: Oxford University Press, 1993.

Epstein, Israel. *Notes on Labor Problems in Nationalist China*. New York: Institute of Pacific Relations, 1949.

———. *The Unfinished Revolution in China*. Boston: Little, Brown, 1947.

Fairbank, John K. *Chinabound: A Fifty-Year Memoir*. New York: Harper & Row, 1982.

Fang, Fu-an. *Chinese Labour: An Economic and Statistical Survey of the Labour Conditions and Labour Movements in China*. Shanghai: Kelly & Walsh, 1931.

Feng Zuyi. "Kangzhan qijian neiqian renkou dui Xinan shehui jingji yingxiang" [The socioeconomic effects on the southwest of the internal migration during the War of Resistance]. In *Qingzhu kangzhan shengli wushi zhounian liang an xueshu yantaohui lunwenji* [Collected papers from the cross-straits symposium celebrating the fiftieth anniversary of the War of Resistance victory], edited by Qingzhu kangzhan shengli wushi zhounian liang an xueshu yantaohui choubei weiyuanhui, 849–59. Taipei: Zhongguo jindai shi xuehui, Lianhebao xi wenhua jijinhui, 1995.

Fitzpatrick, Sheila. *Education and Social Mobility in the Soviet Union, 1921–1934*. Cambridge: Cambridge University Press, 1979.

Frazier, Mark W. *The Making of the Chinese Industrial Workplace: State, Revolution, and Labor Management*. Cambridge: Cambridge University Press, 2002.

Fu Pao-Jen. "The German Military Mission in Nanking, 1928–1939: A Bridge Connecting China and Germany." Ph.D. diss., Syracuse University, 1989.

Gardner, John. "The Wu-fan Campaign in Shanghai: A Study in the Consolidation of Urban Control." In *Chinese Communist Politics in Action*, edited by A. Doak Barnett, 477–539. Seattle: University of Washington, 1969.

Gates, Hill. "Ethnicity and Social Class." In *The Anthropology of Taiwanese Society*, edited by Emily Martin Ahern and Hill Gates, 241–81. Stanford: Stanford University Press, 1981.

Geary, Dick. "Identifying Militancy: The Assessment of Working-Class Attitudes Towards State and Society." In *The German Working Class, 1888–1933: The Politics of Everyday Life*, edited by Richard J. Evans, 220–46. London: Croom Helm, 1982.

Gillin, Donald. *Warlord: Yen Hsi-shan in Shansi Province 1911–1949*. Princeton, N.J.: Princeton University Press, 1967.

Gong Yunshi. "1937 nian–1945 nianjian Guomindang kongzhiqu gongren jieji

de zhuangkuang" [Working-class conditions in the Nationalist-party-con-
trolled area]. *Lishi Yanjiu* 3 (Mar. 1960): 9–25.

Goodman, Bryna. *Native Place, City, and Nation: Regional Networks and Identities in Shanghai, 1853–1937*. Berkeley: University of California Press, 1995.

Gordon, Andrew. *The Evolution of Labor Relations in Japan: Heavy Industry,
1853–1955*. Cambridge, Mass.: Council on East Asian Studies, Harvard University Press, 1988.

———. *Labor and Imperial Democracy in Prewar Japan*. Berkeley and Los An-
geles: University of California Press, 1991.

———. "Conditions for the Disappearance of the Japanese Working-Class Movement." In *Putting Class in Its Place: Worker Identities in East Asia*, edited by
Elizabeth J. Perry, 11–52. Berkeley: Institute of East Asian Studies, University
of California, 1996.

Gordon, Robert B. "Who Turned the Mechanical Ideal into Mechanical Reality?"
Technology and Culture 29, no. 4 (Oct. 1988): 744–78.

Gragg, Mabel T., ed. "History of the American War Production Mission in
China." MS. Franklin D. Roosevelt Library, Hyde Park, N.Y.

Gramsci, Antonio. *Selections from the Prison Notebooks of Antonio Gramsci*.
Edited and translated by Quintin Hoare and Geoffrey N. Smith. New York:
International Publishers, 1971.

———. *The Antonio Gramsci Reader: Selected Writings, 1916–1935*. Edited by
David Forgacs. New York: New York University Press, 1999.

Gu Xiuyan and Lu Manping. *Minguo jiage shi* [History of prices during the Re-
public]. Beijing: Zhongguo wujia chubanshe, 1992.

Gunde, Richard. "Land Tax and Social Change in Sichuan, 1925–1935." *Modern China* 2, no. 1 (Jan. 1976): 23–48.

Guo Hanwu and Meng Guangyu. *Sichuan zudian wenti* [The rent question in
Sichuan]. Chongqing: Shangwu yinshu guan, 1944.

Guofangbu shizheng bianfanju, ed. *Yu Dawei xiansheng nianpu ziliao chubian*
[First draft of materials in chronicle form of Mr. Yu Dawei]. Vol. 1. Taipei:
Guofangbu shizheng bianfanju, 1996.

Guomindang zhengfu shehuibu tongjichu diaocha cailiao. *Zhonghua Minguo
tongji nianjian* [Statistical yearbook of the Chinese Republic]. 1948.

Han Suyin. *Destination Chungking*. Boston: Little, Brown, 1942.

Hao Hong. "Gongzi zhidu tan" [Discussion of the wage system]. *Binggongshu
zai Dian gechangchu kuaiji tongxun*, no. 1 (Sept. 1, 1944): 19–20.

Harris, Sheldon H. *Factories of Death: Japanese Biological Warfare, 1932–45,
and the American Cover-Up*. New York: Routledge, 1994.

Hershatter, Gail. *The Workers of Tianjin, 1900–1949*. Stanford: Stanford University Press, 1986.

Hinton, William. *Fanshen: A Documentary of Revolution in a Chinese Village*.
New York: Vintage Books, 1966.

Hirschman, Albert O. *Exit, Voice, and Loyalty: Responses to Decline in Firms,
Organizations, and States*. Cambridge, Mass.: Harvard University Press, 1970.

Hobsbawm, Eric J. "Peasants and Politics." *Journal of Peasant Studies* 1, no. 1
(1973): 3–22.

———. *Nations and Nationalism Since 1780: Programme, Myth, Reality.* Cambridge: Cambridge University Press, 1990.

Hoffmann, Charles. *The Chinese Worker.* Albany: State University of New York Press, 1974.

Honig, Emily. *Sisters and Strangers: Women in the Shanghai Cotton Mills, 1919–1949.* Stanford: Stanford University Press, 1986.

———. "Native-Place Hierarchy and Labor Market Segmentation: The Case of Subei People in Shanghai." In *Chinese History in Economic Perspective,* edited by Thomas Rawski and Lillian M. Li, 271–94. Berkeley: University of California Press, 1992.

Howard, Joshua H. "Workers at War: Labor in the Nationalist Arsenals of Chongqing, 1937–1949." Ph.D. diss., University of California, Berkeley, 1998.

———. "Yu Zusheng: Organic Intellectuals and the Moral Basis of Class in Wartime Chongqing" *Asian Studies Review* 27, no. 3 (Sept. 2003): 289–316.

———. "Chongqing's Most Wanted: Worker Mobility and Resistance in China's Nationalist Arsenals, 1937–1945." *Modern Asian Studies,* 37, no. 4 (Oct. 2003): 955–98.

Howe, Christopher. *Employment and Economic Growth in Urban China, 1949–1957.* Cambridge: Cambridge University Press, 1971.

———. *Wage Patterns and Wage Policy in Modern China, 1919–1972.* New York: Cambridge University Press, 1973.

Hu, Charles Y. *The Agricultural and Forestry Land-Use of Szechuan Basin.* Chicago: University of Chicago Press, 1946.

Hu Ziang. *Minsheng gongsi shi* [The history of the Minsheng Company]. Beijing: Renmin jiaotong chubanshe, 1990.

Huang Gang. "Wo zai Caiyuanba diqu gongzuo de qingkuang" [My situation working in the Caiyuanba district]. In Chongqingshi zonggonghui gongyunshi ziliao yanjiuzu and Xinan shifan xueyuan lishixi, comps., *Chongqing gongyunshi yanjiu ziliao huibian,* vol. 4 (May 1983), 6–8.

Huang Liren. "Kang Ri Zhanzheng shiqi Zhongguo bingqi gongye neiqian chulun" [A preliminary account of the relocation of China's arms industry during the Anti-Japanese War]. In *Kangzhan shiqi dahoufang jingji shi yanjiu* [The study of economic history in the Great Rear Area in the Resistance War against Japan], edited by Huang Liren, 122–43. Beijing: Zhongguo dang'an chubanshe, 1998.

Huang, Philip C. C. "Rural Class Struggle in the Chinese Revolution: Representational and Objective Realities from the Land Reform to the Cultural Revolution." *Modern China* 21, no. 1 (Jan. 1995): 105–43.

Huang Qingqiu, ed. *Deguo zhu Hua junshi guwentuan gongzuo jiyao* [Summary of the German military mission in China]. Taipei: Guofangbu shizhengju, 1969.

Huang Shujun. *Chongqing gongren yundong shi, 1919–1949* [History of the Chongqing labor movement, 1919–49]. Beipei: Xinan shifan daxue chubanshe, 1986.

Hung, Chang-tai. *War and Popular Culture: Resistance in Modern China, 1937–1945*. Berkeley: University of California Press, 1994.

International Labor Review (Chongqing). 1940–45.

Jacoby, Sanford M. *Employing Bureaucracy: Managers, Unions, and the Transformation of Work in American Industry, 1900–1945*. New York: Columbia University Press, 1985.

Jameson, Elizabeth. *All that Glitters: Class, Conflict, and Community in Cripple Creek*. Urbana: University of Illinois Press, 1998.

Jiang Dexiu et al. "Kangzhan shiqi qian Chuan de binggong danwei" [Ordnance units which relocated to Sichuan during the War of Resistance]. In *Kangzhan shiqi neiqian Xinan de gongshang qiye,* edited by Guo Zongying, 124–33. Kunming: Yunnan renmin chubanshe, 1989.

Jiang Hong. "Yangwu yundong he jindai junshi gongye: Jiangsu sheng jindai binggongshi zongshu" [The self-strengthening movement and the modern armaments industry: A historical account of modern ordnance in Jiangsu province]. In *Jiangsu wenshi ziliao* [Historical materials of Jiangsu], vol. 28, *Binggong shilue* [History of the armaments industry], 1–15. Jiangsu: Jiangsusheng zhengxie wenshi ziliao weiyuanhui, 1989.

Jiang Liangqin. *Nanjing Guomin zhengfu neizhai wenti yanjiu (1927-1937): Yi neizhai zhengce ji yunzuo jixiao wei zhongxin* [Research on the Nanjing Nationalist government's domestic bonds (1927–1937): A focus on domestic bonds policy and its consequences]. Nanjing: Nanjing daxue chubanshe, 2003.

Jiang Niandong et al., eds. *Wei Manzhouguo shi* [History of the puppet Manchukuo]. Dalian: Dalian chubanshe, 1991.

Jin Dingcheng. "Jiangbeixian jingji gaikuang" [Survey of Jiangbei County's economy]. *Sichuan jingji jikan* 1, no. 4 (Sept. 15, 1944): 402–4.

Johnson, Chalmers. *Peasant Nationalism and Communist Power: The Emergence of Revolutionary China*. Stanford: Stanford University Press, 1962, 1967.

"Junxie duli" [Independent weaponry]. *Binggong yuekan* [Ordnance industry monthly] 1, no. 1 (July 15, 1929): 1.

Kaple, Deborah A. *Dream of a Red Factory: The Legacy of High Stalinism in China*. New York: Oxford University Press, 1994.

Katznelson, Ira. "Working-Class Formation: Constructing Cases and Comparisons." In *Working-Class Formation: Nineteenth-Century Patterns in Western Europe and the United States,* edited by Ira Katznelson and Aristide R. Zolberg, 3–41. Princeton, N.J.: Princeton University Press, 1986.

Kelley, Robin D. G. *Hammer and Hoe: Alabama Communists During the Great Depression*. Chapel Hill: University of North Carolina Press, 1990.

Kennedy, Thomas. *The Arms of Kiangnan: Modernization in the Chinese Ordnance Industry, 1860–1895*. Boulder, Colo.: Westview Press, 1978.

Kirby, William C. "Kuomintang China's 'Great Leap Outward': The 1936 Three-Year Plan for Industrial Development." In *Essays in the History of the Chinese Republic,* 43–66. Urbana: University of Illinois, Center for Asian Studies, 1983.

————. *Germany and Republican China*. Stanford: Stanford University Press, 1984.

————. "The Chinese War Economy." In *China's Bitter Victory: The War with Japan, 1937–1945*, edited by James C. Hsiung and Steven I. Levine, 185–212. Armonk, N.Y.: M. E. Sharpe, 1992.

————. "Engineering China: Birth of a Developmental State, 1928–1937." In *Becoming Chinese: Passages to Modernity and Beyond*, edited by Wen-hsin Yeh, 137–60. Berkeley: University of California Press, 2000.

Kocka, Jürgen. "Marxist Social Analysis and the Problem of White Collar Employees." *State, Culture, and Society: An International Journal of the Social, Cultural, and Political Sciences* 1, no. 2 (1985): 137–51.

————. "Problems of Working-Class Formation in Germany: The Early Years, 1800–1875." In *Working-Class Formation: Nineteenth-Century Patterns in Western Europe and the United States*, edited by Ira Katznelson and Aristide R. Zolberg, 279–351. Princeton, N.J.: Princeton University Press, 1986.

Kolko, Gabriel. *Century of War: Politics, Conflicts, and Society Since 1914*. New York: New Press, 1994.

Koo, Hagen. *Korean Workers: The Culture and Politics of Class Formation*. Ithaca, N.Y.: Cornell University Press, 2001.

Kowallis, Jon Eugene von. *The Lyrical Lu Xun: A Study of His Classical-style Verse*. Honolulu: University of Hawai'i Press, 1996.

Lai Zongyu. "Jiefang qian 21 binggongchang de yixie qingkuang" [Some details regarding the liberation of Arsenal No. 21]. In Chongqingshi zonggonghui gongyunshi ziliao yanjiuzu and Xinan shifan xueyuan lishixi, comps., *Chongqing gongyunshi yanjiu ziliao huibian*, 4 (May 1983): 22–27.

Large, Stephen S. *Organized Workers and Socialist Politics in Interwar Japan*. Cambridge: Cambridge University Press, 1981.

Lary, Diane, and Stephen MacKinnon, eds. *The Scars of War: The Impact of Warfare on Modern China*. Vancouver: University of British Columbia Press, 2001.

Lenin, Vladimir I. *Imperialism, the Highest Stage of Capitalism*. 1916. Reprint. New York: International Publishers, 1939.

Li Chenggan. *Zhigong jia yan lu* [Collected speeches of Li Chenggan]. N.p., n.d.

Li Chengwen, ed. *Zhongguo Gongchandang Chongqingshi zuzhi shi ziliao* [Historical materials regarding the organizational history of the Chinese Communist Party of Chongqing]. Vol. 1. Chongqing: Chongqing chubanshe, 1999.

Liao, T'ai-ch'u. "Apprentices in Chengtu During and After the War." *Yenching Journal of Social Studies* 4, no. 1 (Feb. 1948): 89-106.

————. "Rural Education in Transition: A Study of Old-Fashioned Chinese Schools (Szu Shu) in Shantung and Szechuan." *Yenching Journal of Social Studies* 4, no. 2 (Feb. 1949): 28–63.

Liao Zhigao. "Kang Ri Zhanzheng shiqi Sichuan dixiadang de chongjian he Sichuan dongdang zuzhi fazhan, konggu de zhuyao qingkuang." [Major features in the development and consolidation of the Sichuan underground during the War of Resistance against Japan, Dec. 1937–Sept. 1943]. *Zhonggong dangshi ziliao* 12 (1984): 69–104.

Licht, Walter. *Getting Work: Philadelphia, 1840–1950.* Cambridge, Mass.: Harvard University Press, 1992.

Lieberthal, Kenneth G. *Revolution and Tradition in Tientsin, 1949–1952.* Stanford: Stanford University Press, 1980.

Lin Sheng. *"Jiu-Yiba" shibian tuzhi* [Historical atlas of the September 18 incident]. Shenyang: Liaoning renmin chubanshe, 1991.

"Lishi diaocha fangwen ziliao zhengli kapian" [Collated notecards of oral history transcripts]. Compiled by Xinan shifan xueyuan lishixi. 1959.

Liu, F. F. *A Military History of Modern China, 1924–49.* Princeton, N.J.: Princeton University Press, 1956.

Liu Guoming et al., eds. *Zhongguo Guomindang jiuqian jiangling* [Nine thousand generals of the Chinese Nationalist Party]. Tianshui: Zhonghua gongshang lianhe chubanshe, 1993.

Liu Huamian. *Zhongguo jindai junshi jingji yanjiu* [Research on modern China's military economy]. Beijing: Junshi kexue chubanshe, 1992.

Liu, Lu. "A Whole Nation Walking: The 'Great Retreat' in the War of Resistance, 1937–1945." Ph.D. diss., University of California at San Diego, 2002.

Liu Mingda and Tang Yuliang, eds. *Zhongguo gongren yundongshi* [History of the Chinese labor movement]. 6 vols. Guangzhou: Guangdong chubanshe, 1998.

Liu Qiuhuang. "Zhanshi Sichuan liangshi shengchan." [Grain production in wartime Sichuan]. *Sichuan jingji jikan* 2, no. 4 (Oct. 1, 1945): 145–58.

Liu Xiaoyan, ed. *99 zhong zhiyebing fangzhi shouce* [Handbook to prevent 99 types of occupational disease]. Beijing: Haiyang chubanshe, 1990.

Liu Zhouyuan, ed. *Zhongguo Gongchandang Sichuansheng zuzhi shi ziliao* [Materials on the organizational history of the Chinese Communist Party in Sichuan Province]. Chengdu: Sichuan renmin chubanshe, 1994.

Liu Zonglin. "Wo canjia Chongqing gongren yundong de huiyi" [Recalling my participation in the Chongqing labor movement]. In Chongqingshi zonggonghui gongyunshi ziliao yanjiuzu and Xinan shifan xueyuan lishixi, comps., *Chongqing gongyunshi yanjiu ziliao huibian,* vol. 10 (Nov. 1983), 8–14.

Lo Kuang-pin and Yang Yi-yen. *Red Crag.* Beijing: Foreign Languages Press, 1978. Originally published as *Hong Yan* (Beijing: Zhongguo qingnian chubanshe, 1961).

Lu Dayue. *Chongqingshi dang'anguan jianming zhidao* [Concise guide to the Chongqing Municipal Archives]. Chongqing: Kexue jishu wenxian chubanshe, 1990.

———. "Kangzhan shiqi dahoufang de bingqi gongye" [The Great Rear Area's arms industry during the War of Resistance]. *Zhongguo jingji shi yanjiu* [Chinese economic history research], no. 1 (1993): 103–9.

Lu Dayue and Tang Runming. *Kangzhan shiqi Chongqing de bingqi gongye* [Chongqing's armaments industry during the War of Resistance]. Chongqing: Chongqing chubanshe, 1995.

Lu Guangte. "Jiefang Zhanzheng houqi Chongqing gongyun gaikuang" [The Chongqing labor movement in the latter part of the Liberation War]. In *Chuandong dixiadang de douzheng* [Struggles of the Eastern Sichuan underground], edited by Zhonggong Chongqing shiwei dangshi gongzuo weiyuan-hui, 395–400. N.p., n.d.

Lu Pingdeng. *Sichuan nongcun jingji*. [Sichuan's agrarian economy]. Shanghai: Shangwu yinshuguan, 1936.

Lu Sihong. *Xin Chongqing* [New Chongqing]. Chongqing: Zhonghua shuju, 1939.

Lü Xiaobo and Elizabeth J. Perry, eds. *Danwei: The Changing Chinese Workplace in Historical and Comparative Perspective*. Armonk, N.Y.: M. E. Sharpe, 1997.

Lu Zeren. "Yu qianbuzhang binggongshu shiji." In *Yu zizheng wei gong jiu xu jin wu hua dan jinian wenji* [Collected papers in commemoration of Yu Dawei's ninety-fifth birthday]. Taipei: Guofangbu shizheng bianzeju, 1990.

Ludtke, Alf. "'The Honor of Labor': Industrial Workers and the Power of Symbols Under National Socialism." In *Nazism and German Society, 1933–1945*, edited by David F. Crew, 67–110. London: Routledge, 1994.

Lutze, Thomas D. "New Democracy: Chinese Communist Relations with the Urban Middle Forces, 1931–1952." Ph.D. diss., University of Wisconsin-Madison, 1996.

Luzhou di 23 gongchang dixiadang zuzhi lingdao de gongren yundong dashiji [Chronicle of the Luzhou Arsenal No. 23 underground organization's leadership of the labor movement]. Compiled by Xinan shifan xueyuan lishixi. N.p., n.d.

Ma Wenying. "Deguo junshi guwentuan yu Zhong-De junhuo maoyi guanxi de tuizhan" [German military advisors and the push for Sino-German arms trade]. *Zhongyang yanjiuyuan jindaishi yanjiusuo jikan*, no. 23 (June 1994): 133–65.

Ma Zhendu. "Deguo junhuo yu Zhongguo Kang Ri Zhanzheng" [German armaments and China's War of Resistance against Japan]. In *Qingzhu kangzhan shengli wushi zhounian liang'an xueshu yantaohui lunwenji* [Collected papers from the cross-straits symposium celebrating the fiftieth anniversary of the War of Resistance victory]. Edited by Qingzhu kangzhan shengli wushi zhounian liang an xueshu yantaohui choubei weiyuanhui, 619–57. Taipei: Lianhe bao xi wenhua jijinhui, 1995.

Mackie, Vera. "Liberation and Light: The Language of Opposition in Imperial Japan." *East Asian History* 9 (1995): 121–42.

Mao Zedong. *Selected Readings from the Works of Mao Tse-tung*. Beijing: Foreign Languages Press, 1971.

Marx, Karl. *Capital*. Translated by Ben Fowkes. New York: Vintage Books, 1977.

Mason, Timothy W. *Social Policy in the Third Reich: The Working Class and the "National Community."* Edited by Jane Caplan. Translated by John Broadwin. Providence, R.I.: Berg, 1993.

———. "The Turin Strike of March 1943." In *Nazism, Fascism and the Working Class: Essays by Tim Mason*, edited by Jane Caplan, 274–94. Cambridge: Cambridge University Press, 1995.

McIsaac, Mary Lee. "The Limits of Chinese Nationalism: Workers in Wartime Chongqing, 1937–1945." Ph.D. diss., Yale University, 1994.

———. "'Righteous Fraternities' and Honorable Men: Sworn Brotherhoods in Wartime Chongqing." *American Historical Review* 105, no. 5 (Dec. 2000): 1641–55.

———. "The City as Nation: Creating a Wartime Capital in Chongqing." In *Remaking the Chinese City: Modernity and National Identity, 1900–1950*, edited by Joseph W. Esherick, 174–91. Honolulu: University of Hawai'i Press, 2000.

McNeill, William H. *The Pursuit of Power: Technology, Armed Force, and Society Since a.d. 1800*. Chicago: University of Chicago Press, 1982.

McQuaide, Shiling Zhao. "Shanghai Labor: Gender, Politics, and Tradition in the Making of the Chinese Working Class, 1911–1949." Ph.D. diss., Queen's University, Kingston, Ontario, 1995.

Meisner, Maurice. "Utopian Socialist Themes in Maoism." In *Marxism, Maoism and Utopianism*, 28–75. Madison: University of Wisconsin Press, 1982.

———. "Marx, Mao, and Deng on the Division of Labor in History." In *Marxism and the Chinese Experience*. Edited by Arif Dirlik and Maurice Meisner, 79–116. Armonk, N.Y.: M. E. Sharpe, 1989.

———. *Mao's China and After: A History of the People's Republic*. 3d ed. New York: Free Press, 1999.

Milward, Alan S. *War, Economy and Society, 1939–1945*. Berkeley: University of California Press, 1977.

Montgomery, David. *The Fall of the House of Labor: The Workplace, the State, and American Labor Activism, 1865–1925*. Cambridge: Cambridge University Press, 1987.

———. *Workers' Control in America: Studies in the History of Work, Technology, and Labor Struggles*. Cambridge: Cambridge University Press, 1979.

Moore, Barrington, Jr. *Injustice: The Social Bases of Obedience and Revolt*. White Plains, N.Y.: M. E. Sharpe, 1978.

Morris-Suzuki, Tessa. *The Technological Transformation of Japan: From the Seventeenth to the Twenty-first Century*. Cambridge: Cambridge University Press, 1994.

Nanfangju dangshi ziliao zhengji xiaozu zuzhi, ed. "Zhonggong Nanfangju zuzhi xitong gaikuang" [The organizational situation of the Southern Bureau]. *Zhonggong dangshi ziliao* 12 (1984): 21.

Nanfangju dangshi ziliao zhengji xiaozu, ed. *Nanfangju dangshi ziliao* [Historical materials of the Southern Bureau]. 6 vols. Chongqing: Chongqing chubanshe, 1990.

Naughton, Barry. "*Danwei*: The Economic Foundations of a Unique Institution." In *Danwei: The Changing Chinese Workplace in Historical and Comparative Perspective*. Edited by Xiaobo Lü and Elizabeth J. Perry, 169–94. Armonk, N.Y.: M. E. Sharpe, 1997.

Nelson, Daniel. *Managers and Workers: Origins of the Twentieth-Century Factory System in the United States, 1880–1920*. 2d ed. Madison: University of Wisconsin Press, 1995.

Nimura Kazuo. *The Ashio Riot of 1907: A Social History of Mining in Japan.* Translated by Terry Boardman and Andrew Gordon. Edited by Andrew Gordon. Durham, N.C.: Duke University Press, 1997.

Oestreicher, Richard J. *Solidarity and Fragmentation: Working People and Class Consciousness in Detroit, 1875–1900.* Urbana: University of Illinois Press, 1986.

Overy, Richard J. *War and Economy in the Third Reich.* New York: Oxford University Press, 1994.

Palmer, Bryan D. *Descent into Discourse: The Reification of Language and the Writing of Social History.* Philadelphia: Temple University Press, 1990.

Parish, William. "The View from the Factory." In *The China Difference,* edited by Ross Terrill, 183–98. New York: Harper & Row, 1979.

Park, Soon-Won. *Colonial Industrialization and Labor in Korea: The Onoda Cement Factory.* Cambridge, Mass.: Harvard University Press, 1999.

Pavone, Claudio. *Una guerra civile: Saggio storico sulla moralità nella Resistenza.* Turin: Bollati Boringhieri, 1991.

Pepper, Suzanne. *Civil War in China: The Political Struggle, 1945–1949.* Berkeley: University of California Press, 1978.

———. *Radicalism and Education Reform in Twentieth-Century China: The Search for an Ideal Development Model.* Cambridge: Cambridge University Press, 1996.

Perry, Elizabeth J. *Shanghai on Strike: The Politics of Chinese Labor.* Stanford: Stanford University Press, 1993.

———. "Labor Divided: Sources of State Formation in Modern China." In *State Power and Social Forces: Domination and Transformation in the Third World,* edited by Joel S. Migdal et al., 143–73. New York: Cambridge University Press, 1994.

———. "Labor's Battle for Political Space: The Role of Worker Associations in Contemporary China." In *Urban Spaces in Contemporary China: The Potential for Autonomy and Community in Post-Mao China,* edited by Deborah S. Davis, Richard Kraus, Barry Naughton, and Elizabeth J. Perry, 302–25. New York: Woodrow Wilson Center Press and Cambridge University Press, 1995.

———, ed. *Putting Class in Its Place: Worker Identities in East Asia.* Berkeley: Institute of East Asian Studies, University of California, 1996.

———. "From Native Place to Workplace: Labor Origins and Outcomes of China's *Danwei* System." In *Danwei: The Changing Chinese Workplace in Historical and Comparative Perspective,* edited by Xiaobo Lü and Elizabeth J. Perry, 42–59. Armonk, N.Y.: M. E. Sharpe, 1997.

Peukert, Detlev J. K. *Inside Nazi Germany: Conformity, Opposition, and Racism in Everyday Life.* Translated by Richard Deveson. New Haven, Conn.: Yale University Press, 1987.

Porter, Robin. *Industrial Reformers in Republican China.* Armonk, N.Y.: M. E. Sharpe, 1994.

Qi Wu. *Kang Ri Zhanzheng shiqi Zhongguo gongren yundong shigao* [A draft history of the Chinese labor movement during the War of Resistance against Japan]. Beijing: Renmin chubanshe, 1986.

Qin Dequan et al., eds. *Erjiuba changzhi* [Annals of Factory No. 298]. Kunming: n.p., 1988.

Rancière, Jacques. "Ronds de fumée (Les Poètes ouvriers dans la France de Louis-Philippe)" [Smoke rings: Worker-poets in France under Louis-Philippe]. *Revue des sciences humaines* 61, no. 190 (Apr.–June 1983): 31–47.

Rawlinson, John L. *China's Struggle for Naval Development, 1839–1895.* Cambridge, Mass.: Harvard University Press, 1967.

Rawski, Evelyn Sakakida. *Agricultural Change and the Peasant Economy of South China.* Cambridge, Mass.: Harvard University Press, 1972.

Rawski, Thomas G. *Economic Growth in Prewar China.* Berkeley: University of California Press, 1989.

Richman, Barry M. *Industrial Society in Communist China.* New York: Random House, 1969.

Riefs, Rolf. "Werner Sombart Under National Socialism." In *Werner Sombart (1863–1941): Social Scientist,* vol. 1: *His Life and Work,* edited by Jürgen G. Backhaus, 193–204. Marburg: Metropolis-Verlag, 1996.

Rimlinger, G. V. "Labour and the State on the Continent, 1800–1939." In *The Cambridge Economic History of Europe,* vol. 8, *The Industrial Economies: The Development of Economic and Social Policies,* edited by Peter Mathias and Sidney Pollard, 549–606. Cambridge: Cambridge University Press, 1989.

Roediger, David R. *The Wages of Whiteness: Race and the Making of the American Working Class.* New York: Verso, 1991.

Rong Gaotang. "Guanyu Nanfangju de zuzhi jigou he Nanfangju zuzhi de qingkuang" [The circumstances regarding the Southern Bureau organization]. *Zhonggong dangshi ziliao* 12 (1984): 61–65.

Roux, Alain. *Le Shanghai ouvrier des années trente: Coolies, gangsters et syndicalistes.* Paris: L'Harmattan, 1993.

Saich, Tony, ed. *The Rise to Power of the Chinese Communist Party.* Armonk, N.Y.: M. E. Sharpe, 1996.

Said, Edward W. *Orientalism.* New York: Vintage Books, 1978.

Schurmann, Franz. *Ideology and Organization in Communist China.* 2d ed., enlarged. Berkeley: University of California Press, 1968.

Scott, James C. *Weapons of the Weak: Everyday Forms of Peasant Resistance.* New Haven, Conn.: Yale University Press, 1985.

Selden, Mark. *The Yenan Way in Revolutionary China.* Cambridge, Mass.: Harvard University Press, 1971.

———. "The Proletariat, Revolutionary Change, and the State in China and Japan, 1850–1950." In *Labor in the World Social Structure,* edited by Immanuel Wallerstein, 58–120. Beverly Hills, Calif.: Sage Publications, 1983.

Sewell, William H., Jr. "Artisans, Factory Workers, and the Formation of the French Working-Class, 1789–1848." In *Working-Class Formation: Nineteenth-Century Patterns in Western Europe and the United States,* edited by Ira Katznelson and Aristide R. Zolberg, 45–70. Princeton, N.J.: Princeton University Press, 1986.

Shaffer, Lynda. *Mao and the Workers: The Hunan Labor Movement, 1920–1923.* Armonk, N.Y:. M. E. Sharpe, 1982.

Shen, Yu. "SACO: An Ambivalent Experience of Sino-American Cooperation During World War II." Ph.D. diss., University of Illinois at Urbana-Champaign, 1995.

Shi Hua. "Xiao Zekuan tongzhi tan Chuandong dixiadang" [Comrade Xiao Zekuan talks about the underground party of eastern Sichuan]. In Chongqingshi zonggonghui gongyunshi ziliao yanjiuzu and Xinan shifan daxue lishixi, comps., *Chongqing gongyunshi yanjiu ziliao huibian*, vol. 2 (Apr. 1982), 20–38.

Shih Kuo-heng. *China Enters the Machine Age: A Study of Labor in Chinese War Industry*. Cambridge, Mass.: Harvard University Press, 1944.

Shum, Kui-Kwong. *The Chinese Communists' Road to Power: The Anti-Japanese National United Front, 1935–1945*. New York: Oxford University Press, 1988.

Sichuan kaojituan baogao [Report of the Sichuan survey team]. Nanjing: Zhongguo gongchengshi xuehui, 1935.

Sichuan shinian wenxue yishu xuanji bianji weiyuanhui, ed. *Sichuan gongchang shi zuopin xuan*. [Selections from the history of Sichuan industries]. Chengdu: Sichuan renmin chubanshe, 1960.

Sichuansheng dang'anguan, ed. *Sichuan gongren yundong shiliao xuanbian* [Selections of historical materials on the Sichuan labor movement]. Chengdu: Sichuan daxue chubanshe, 1988.

Smith, Merritt Roe. *Harpers Ferry Armory and the New Technology: The Challenge of Change*. Ithaca, N.Y.: Cornell University Press, 1977.

Smith, Steve A. "Workers and Supervisors in St Petersburg, 1905–1917, and Shanghai, 1895–1927." *Past and Present* 139 (May 1993): 131–77.

———. "Workers Against Foremen in Late-Imperial Russia." In *Making Workers Soviet: Power, Class, and Identity*, edited by Lewis H. Siegelbaum and Ronald G. Suny, 113–37. Ithaca, N.Y.: Cornell University Press, 1994.

———. "Workers, the Intelligentsia and Marxist Parties: St Petersburg, 1895–1917, and Shanghai, 1921–1927." *International Review of Social History* 41 (1996): 1–56.

———. *Like Cattle and Horses: Nationalism and Labor in Shanghai, 1895–1927*. Durham, N.C.: Duke University Press, 2002.

Somers, Margaret R. "Workers of the World, Compare!" *Contemporary Sociology* 18, no. 3 (May 1989): 325–29.

Speier, Hans. *German White-Collar Workers and the Rise of Hitler*. New Haven, Conn.: Yale University Press, 1986.

Steinberg, Mark D. "Vanguard Workers and the Morality of Class." In *Making Workers Soviet: Power, Class, and Identity*, edited by Lewis H. Siegelbaum and Ronald G. Suny, 66–84. Ithaca, N.Y.: Cornell University Press, 1994.

———. "The Injured and Insurgent Self: The Moral Imagination of Russia's Lower-Class Writers." In *Workers and Intelligentsia in Late Imperial Russia: Realities, Representations, Reflections*, edited by Reginald E. Zelnik, 309–29. Berkeley: International and Area Studies, University of California at Berkeley, 1999.

———. *Voices of Revolution, 1917*. New Haven, Conn.: Yale University Press, 2001.

Strain, Harry A. "More Steel for Free China." *US Steel News* 10, no. 3 (July 1945): 10–12.

Stranahan, Patricia. *Underground: The Shanghai Communist Party and the Politics of Survival, 1927–1937*. Lanham, Md.: Rowman & Littlefield, 1998.

Sun Benwen. *Xiandai Zhongguo shehui wenti* [Social issues of contemporary China], vol. 4, *Laozi wenti* [Issues of labor and capital]. Chongqing, 1943.

Taira, Koji. "Economic Development, Labor Markets, and Industrial Relations in Japan, 1905–1955." In *Cambridge History of Japan*, vol. 6: *The Twentieth Century*, edited by Peter Duus, 606–53. Cambridge: Cambridge University Press, 1988.

Tang Runming. "Shishu Sichuan Kang Ri genjudi de ceding" [Determining when Sichuan became chosen as a base for the War of Resistance against Japan]. In *Zhongguo Chongqing kangzhan peidu shi guoji xueshu yantaohui lunwenji* [Collected papers from the international symposium regarding the history of the Chinese wartime capital, Chongqing], edited by Gu Leguan, 117–29. Beijing: Huawen chubanshe, 1995.

Tang Zhong. "Mou gongchang zhi gongzi zhidu diaocha baogao." *Binggongshu zai Dian gechangchu kuaiji tongxun*, Sept. 1, 1944, 23–24.

Teng Ssu-Yu and John K. Fairbank. *China's Response to the West: A Documentary Survey 1839–1923*. Cambridge, Mass: Harvard University Press, 1954.

Terrill, Ross. *Madame Mao: The White-Boned Demon*. New York: Simon & Schuster, 1992.

Thompson, Edward P. *The Making of the English Working Class*. New York: Vintage Books, 1966.

Tilly, Louise A. *Politics and Class in Milan, 1881–1901*. New York: Oxford University Press, 1992.

Tong Zhicheng. "Mantan fuli" [Speaking of welfare]. *Taosheng tekan* [special issue of the Sound of Great Waves], Jan. 1, 1945, 4.

Tsang Chih. *The Post-War Market of China: A Preliminary Estimate*. New York: Institute of Pacific Relations, 1944.

Van Slyke, Lyman P. *Enemies and Friends: The United Front in Chinese Communist History*. Stanford: Stanford University Press, 1967.

———. "The Chinese Communist Movement During the Sino-Japanese War, 1937–1945." In *The Cambridge History of China*, vol. 13, *Republican China, 1912–1949*, edited by Denis Twitchett and John K. Fairbank, 609–722. New York: Cambridge University Press, 1986.

Wakeman, Frederic, Jr. *Policing Shanghai, 1927–1937*. Berkeley: University of California Press, 1995.

Walder, Andrew G. *Communist Neo-Traditionalism: Work and Authority in Chinese Industry*. Berkeley: University of California Press, 1986.

Waldron, Arthur. *From War to Nationalism: China's Turning Point, 1924–1925*. New York: Cambridge University Press, 1995.

Wales, Nym. *The Chinese Labor Movement*. New York: John Day, 1945.

Wang Dexiu. "Kangzhan shiqi qian Chuan de binggong danwei" [The Relocation to Sichuan of the ordnance work units during the War of Resistance]. In *Kangzhan shiqi neiqian Xinan de gongshang qiye* [The relocation of industries and enterprises to the southwest during the War of Resistance], edited by Guo Songying, 124–33. Kunming: Yunnan renmin chubanshe, 1988.

———. "Houfang binggongchang de huopao zhizao" [Artillery manufacture in the Rear Area arsenals]. In *Kangzhan shiqi xinan de keji* [Technology in south-western China during the War of Resistance], edited by Chen Guozhi, 252–59. Chengdu: Sichuan kexue jishu chubanshe, 1995.

Wang Guoqiang. *Zhongguo binggong zhizaoye fazhan shi* [The historical development of China's armament manufacturing industry]. Taipei: Niming wenhua shiye gongsi, 1987.

Wang Qinghua and Li Hua, eds. *Heilao shibian: Baigongguan, Zhazidong geming lieshi shiwenji* [Selected poems and writings from the dark prison: Poems and letters of Baigongguan and Zhazidong revolutionary martyrs]. Chongqing: Chongqing daxue chubanshe, 1990.

Wang Qitai. "Huchang ying jiefang" [Factory protection responding to liberation]. In *Huiyi Sichuan jiefang (xubian)* [Remembering Sichuan's liberation], edited by Li Hengfu, 283–87. Chengdu: Sichuan jiaoyu chubanshe, 1989.

Wang Zhenghua. *Kangzhan shiqi waiguo dui Hua junshi yuanzhu* [Foreign military aid to China during the War of Resistance]. Taipei: Huanqiu shuju, 1987.

Wei Yingtao. *Jindai Chongqing chengshi shi* [Modern Chongqing's urban history]. Chengdu: Sichuan daxue chubanshe, 1991.

Wei Zhenfu. *Zhongguo junshi shi, juan 1: bingqi* [China's military history, vol. 1: Weaponry]. Beijing: Jiefangjun chubanshe, 1983.

Wen Fuping and Xiao Mingqiang, eds. *Kangzhan shiqi Chongqing de xinwenjie* [The Chongqing press during the War of Resistance]. Chongqing: Chongqing chubanshe, 1995.

Wen Xianmei. "Riji dui Chongqing de 'zhanlue hongzha' he Chongqing de fankong xidongzheng" [Japanese planes' "bombing strategy" of Chongqing and Chongqing's resistance struggles]. In Chongqingshi zonggonghui gongyunshi ziliao yanjiuzu and Xinan shifan daxue lishixi, comps., *Zhongguo Chongqing kangzhan peidushi guoji xueshu yantaohui lunwenji* [Collected papers from the international symposium regarding the history of the Chinese wartime capital, Chongqing], edited by Gu Yueguan, 222–34. Beijing: Huawen chubanshe, 1995.

Weng Zhiyuan, ed. *Tongji daxue shi* [History of Tongji University]. 2 vols. Shanghai: Tongji daxue chubanshe, 1987.

Westad, Odd Arne. *Decisive Encounters: The Chinese Civil War, 1946–1950*. Stanford: Stanford University Press, 2003.

White, Lynn T., III. *Careers in Shanghai: The Social Guidance of Personal Energies in a Developing Chinese City, 1949–1966*. Berkeley: University of California Press, 1978.

———. "Bourgeois Radicalism in the 'New Class' of Shanghai, 1949–1969." In *Class and Social Stratification in Post-Revolution China*, edited by James L. Watson, 142–74. Cambridge: Cambridge University Press, 1984.

White, Theodore H., and Annalee Jacoby. *Thunder Out of China*. New York: William Sloane Associates, 1946.

Whyte, Martin K., and William L. Parish. *Urban Life in Contemporary China*. Chicago: University of Chicago Press, 1984.

Williams, Trevor, ed. *The Twentieth Century, c. 1900 to c. 1950*. Vol. 6, part 1, of *A History of Technology*, ed. Charles Singer et al. Oxford: Oxford University Press, 1982.

Willson, Perry R. *The Clockwork Factory: Women and Work in Fascist Italy*. Oxford: Oxford University Press, 1993.

Wolfe, Joel. *Working Women, Working Men: São Paulo and the Rise of Brazil's Industrial Working Class, 1900–1955*. Durham, N.C.: Duke University Press, 1993.

Woollacott, Angela. *On Her Their Lives Depend: Munitions Workers in the Great War*. Berkeley: University of California Press, 1994.

Wou, Odoric Y. K. *Mobilizing the Masses: Building Revolution in Henan*. Stanford: Stanford University Press, 1994.

Wright, Tim. *Coal Mining in China's Economy and Society, 1895–1937*. Cambridge: Cambridge University Press, 1984.

———. "A Method of Evading Management: Contract Labor in Chinese Coal Mines Before 1937." *Comparative Studies of Society and History* 23, no. 4 (1981): 656–78.

Wu Dange. "Sichuan sheng de difang tanpai" [Local levies in Sichuan province]. *Sichuan jingji jikan* 1, no. 2 (Mar. 15, 1945): 174–98.

Wu Taichang. "Guomindang zhengfu de yihuo changzhai zhengce he Ziyuan weiyuanhui de kuangchan guanzhi" [Nationalist government's barter trade policy and controls over the industries and mines of the National Resources Commission]. *Jindaishi yanjiu*, no. 3 (Beijing: 1983): 83–102.

Wu Yuexing, ed. *Zhongguo Kang Ri Zhanzheng shi dituji* [Historical atlas of China's War of Resistance against Japan]. Beijing: Zhongguo ditu chubanshe, 1995.

Xiao Shaobin et al. "Baizhe bunao, zhandou buzhi: Tan Jianxiao tongzhi zhuanlue" [Biography of Tan Jianxiao, indomitable warrior]. In Chongqingshi zonggonghui gongyunshi ziliao yanjiuzu and Xinan shifan xueyuan lishixi, comps., *Chongqing gongyunshi yanjiu ziliao huibian*, vol. 5 (Oct. 1983), 23–33.

Xiao Yunxi. "Guomindang shiqi Jiangbei xian binyi nuemin jianwen" [Tales of press-ganging during the Nationalist period in Jiangbei County]. In *Jiangbei xian wenshi ziliao* [Jiangbei County historical materials], edited by Zhongguo renmin zhengzhi xieshang huiyi Jiangbei xian weiyuanhui wenshi ziliao yanjiu weiyuanhui, 3: 25–30. Chongqing: Chongqing wenxian chubanshe, 1988.

Xiao Zekuan. "Chuandong ji Chongqing diqu gongren yundong de huiyi" [Recalling the labor movement in Eastern Sichuan and Chongqing]. *Chongqing gongyunshi: Yanjiu ziliao huibian* 10 (Nov. 1983): 1–7.

Xie Fang. "Kangzhan shiqi Sichuan xiaonong jingji yu shehui bianqian" [Small-peasant economy and social change in Sichuan during the War of Resistance]. In *Qingzhu kangzhan shengli wushi zhounian liang an xueshu yantaohui lunwenji* [Collected papers from the cross-straits symposium celebrating the fiftieth anniversary of the War of Resistance victory], 783–808. Taipei: Zhongguo jindai shi xuehui, Lianhebao xi wenhua jijinhui, 1995.

Xinan shifan xueyuan lishixi and Chonggangshi bianxie xiaozu, ed. *Chongqing gangtie gongsi de ershi nian.* Chongqing, 1959.

Xinhua ribao (New China Daily) (Chongqing). 1938–47.

Xinmin bao (New People's Daily) (Chongqing).

Xu Chaojian et al., eds. *Chongqing da hongzha* [The great bombing of Chongqing]. Chongqing: Xinan shifan daxue chubanshe, 2002.

Xu, Xiaoqun. *Chinese Professionals and the Republican State: The Rise of Professional Associations in Shanghai, 1912–1937.* Cambridge: Cambridge University Press, 2001.

Xu Youchun et al., eds. *Minguo renwu da cidian* [Biographical dictionary of Republican China]. Shijiazhuang: Hebei renmin chubanshe, 1991.

Xuexi (Study) (Chongqing). 1945.

Yang Jixuan. "Fuyuan qizhong Chongqing de gongchao" [Labor unrest in Chongqing during demobilization]. *Sichuan jingji huibao,* June 25, 1948, 63–64.

Yeh, Wen-hsin. *The Alienated Academy: Culture and Politics in Republican China, 1919–1937.* Cambridge, Mass.: Council on East Asian Studies, Harvard University Press, 1990.

———. "Corporate Space, Communal Time: Everyday Life in Shanghai's Bank of China," *American Historical Review* 100, no. 1 (Feb. 1995): 97–122.

Yick, Joseph K. S. *Making Urban Revolution in China: The CCP-GMD Struggle for Beiping-Tianjin, 1945–1949.* Armonk, N.Y.: M. E. Sharpe, 1995.

Yu Dawei. Official technical papers of General Yu Dawei, compiled as *Zhanshu yu jishu* [Tactics and technology]. 16 vols. Historical Bureau, Ministry of National Defense, Taipei. File 155.2/8022.3, 1931–39.

Yu Zhuozhi. "Wo zai 21 binggongchang de yixie jingli" [My experiences at Arsenal No. 21]. In Chongqingshi zonggonghui gongyunshi ziliao yanjiuzu and Xinan shifan xueyuan lishixi, comps., *Chongqing gongyunshi yanjiu ziliao huibian,* vol. 4 (May 1983), 28–44.

Zahavi, Gerald. *Workers, Managers, and Welfare Capitalism: The Shoeworkers and Tanners of Endicott Johnson, 1890–1950.* Urbana: University of Illinois Press, 1988.

Zelin, Madeleine. "The Rights of Tenants in Mid-Qing Sichuan: A Study of Land-Related Lawsuits in the Baxian Archives." *Journal of Asian Studies* 45, no. 3: 483–526.

Zelnik, Reginald E. "Before Class: The Fostering of a Worker Revolutionary: The Construction of His Memoir." *Russian History* 20, nos. 1–4 (1993): 61–80.

Zhang Xiaomei. *Sichuan jingji cankao ziliao* [Reference materials on the Sichuan economy]. Shanghai: Zhongguo guomin jingji yanjiusuo, 1939.

Zhang Zhiang. "Kang Ri Zhanzheng shengli qianhou zai Nanfangju lingdao xia de Chongqing gongyun diandi" [The labor movement under the leadership of the Southern Bureau during and after the War of Resistance]. In *Chongqing dangshi yanjiu ziliao,* edited by Zhonggong Chongqing shiwei dangshi ziliao zhengji weiyuanhui, 12: 21–24. N.p., 1982.

Zhang Zhichun. "Jieshao di 21 Chang" [Introducing Arsenal No. 21]. *Binggong yuekan* 1, no. 3 (1941): 68–69.

Zhang Ziqiang. "Hechuan jingji gaikuang" [Survey of Hechuan's economy]. *Sichuan jingji jikan* 1, no. 1 (Dec. 15, 1943): 362–66.

Zhao Zhizhong. "Li Chenggan zhuanlue" [Biography of Li Chenggan]. In *Jiangsu wenshi ziliao* [Historical materials of Jiangsu], vol. 28, *Binggong shilue*, 123–30. Jiangsu: Jiangsusheng zhengxie wenshi ziliao weiyuanhui, 1989.

Zheng Hongquan. "Aiguo binggong zhuanjia Li Chenggan" [The ordnance industrial patriot, Li Chenggan]. In *Chongqing wenshi ziliao* [Historical materials of Chongqing], Xinan shifan daxue chubanshe (Chongqing), no. 35 (1991), 116–36.

———. "Binggong zhuanjia Li Chenggan" [Ordnance expert Li Chenggan]. In *Peidu renwu jishi* [Biographies from the wartime capital], edited by Chongqing kangzhan congshu bianzuan weiyuanhui, 351–62. Chongqing: Chongqing chubanshe, 1995.

———. ed. *Huainian yu zhufu: Jinian Li Chenggan xiansheng tingchen 110 zhounian ji gonghe Yu Zhouzhi xiansheng 90 huating zhuanji* [Remembering and celebrating: Biographies in commemoration of Li Chenggan's 110th birthday anniversary and Yu Zhouzhi's 90th birthday]. Chongqing: Chongqing Chang'an qiche youxian zeren gongsi, 1998.

Zheng Youkui. "Wo guo jinshi nianlai guoji maoyi pingheng zhi yanjiu: 1925–1934" [Research on my country's balance of trade in recent years, 1925–34]. *Shehui kexue zazhi* [Quarterly review of social science] 6, no. 4 (Dec. 1935): 521–71.

Zhonggong Chongqing shiwei dangshi gongzuo weiyuanhui bian, ed. *Zhongguo laodong xiehui zai Chongqing* [The Chinese Association of Labor at Chongqing]. Chongqing, 1984.

Zhonggong Chongqingshi weiyuanhui zhengce yanjiushi, ed. *Jiefang qian Chongqing gaikuang* [Chongqing's situation prior to liberation]. Chongqing, 1950.

Zhonggong Sichuan shengwei dangshi gongzuo weiyuanhui, ed. *Zhonggong Sichuan difang dangshi dashi nianbiao, 1921–1949* [Chronicle history of the Sichuan local Communist Party]. Chengdu: Sichuan renmin chubanshe, 1985.

Zhonggong Sichuan shengwei tongzhanbu, comp. *Sichuan tongyi zhanxian renwu lu* [Records of the Sichuan united front figures]. Chengdu: Sichuan kexue jishu chubanshe, 1993.

Zhongguo di'er lishi dang'anguan. *Zhong-De waijiao midang, 1927–1947* [Sino-German foreign relations: Confidential archives, 1927–47]. Guilin: Guangxi shifan daxue chubanshe, 1994.

Zhongguo gongchengshi xuehui, ed. *Sichuan kaojituan baogao* [Sichuan survey report]. Nanjing: n.p., 1935.

Zhongguo Guomindang zhongyang zhixing weiyuanhui xuanchuanbu. *Kangzhan liunian lai zhi junshi* [Military affairs of the past six years during the War of Resistance]. N.p., 1943.

"Zhongguo jindai bingqi gongye dang'an shiliao" bianweihui, comp. *Zhongguo jindai bingqi gongye dang'an shiliao* [Historical and archival materials re-garding modern China's armaments industry]. 4 vols. Beijing: Bingqi gongye chubanshe, 1993.

Zhongguo Renmin Jiefangjun yanjiushi, ed. *Xinan zhi binggong* [Southwestern China's ordnance]. N.p., 1949.

Zhonghua Minguo zhongyao shiliao chubian—dui Ri kangzhan shiqi xubian [Important historical sources of the Chinese Republic: The War of Resistance against Japan, Introductory edition]. Taipei: Zhongguo Guomindang Zhong-yang weiyuanhui dangshi weiyuanhui, 1981.

Zhongyang ribao (Central Daily) (Chongqing). 1940s.

Zhou Maobo. "Houfang jiqi gongye ji qi tiaozheng wenti" [The problem of the Rear Area machine industry and its reform]. *Xinan shiye tongxun* 6, no. 1 (1942): 9–12.

Zhou Weihan. "Shanxi binggong shiliao" [Historical materials on Shanxi ord-nance]. *Shanxi wenshi ziliao* 9 (1983): 22–35.

Zhou Yong. *Chongqing: Yi ge neilu chengshi de jueqi* [Chongqing: The rise of an inland town]. Chongqing: Chongqing chubanshe, 1989.

Zhu Bangxing et al., eds. *Shanghai chanye yu Shanghai zhigong* [Shanghai in-dustries and Shanghai workers]. 1939. Reprint. Shanghai: Shanghai renmin chubanshe, 1984.

Zhu Jiahua. *Zhongguo gongyun yu gongxun* [China's labor movement and train-ing of labor]. Chongqing: Zhongyang zuzhibu, 1943.

Zhu Senliang. "Zizhong jingji gaikuang" [Survey of Zizhong's economy]. *Sichuan jingji jikan* 2, no. 2 (Apr. 1, 1945): 305–13.

Zhuan Jintao. "Xichong jingji gaikuang" [Survey of Xichong's economy]. *Si-chuan jingji jikan* 2, no. 2 (Apr. 1, 1945): 329–31.

Zuo Mingde. "Pin bo, chuangzao tupo fandongpai de fengsuo: qian tan *Xinhua ribao* de faxing gongzuo" [Risking struggle, creating and breaking the reac-tionaries' blockade: recalling the distribution work of *Xinhua ribao*]. In *Xin Hua zhi guang* [Light of *New China Daily*]. Edited by *Xinhua ribao, Qun-zhong zhoukan* shixue huibian, 379–92. Chongqing: Chongqing chubanshe, 1993.

Zuo Yongzhong and Ye Mao. "33 niandu Sichuan zhi nongye" [Sichuan agricul-ture in 1944]. *Sichuan jingji jikan* 2, no. 2 (Apr. 1, 1945): 44–54.

Interviews

The following people, most of them identified here by pseudonym, were interviewed by the author:

Du Liang. Chemical plant apprentice in Chongqing; activist in the Chinese Association of Labor, 1940s. Chongqing, Dec. 6, 1993, and Feb. 24, 1994.

Feng Junren. Arsenal machinist since the mid 1940s. Chongqing, Sept. 26, 1994.

Gu Weiyun. Arsenal technician, late 1940s. Chongqing, Sept. 20, 1994.

He Qiuping. Apprentice and arsenal lathe turner, 1940s. Chongqing, Nov. 30, 1994.

Li Guosun. Graduate of Tongji University's mechanical engineering department. Arsenal technician from the mid 1940s on. Chongqing, Sept. 26, 1994.

Li Jiesun. Arsenal cartridge worker, late 1940s. Chongqing, Sept. 26, 1994.

Liu Feng. Arsenal apprentice and machinist, 1940s. Kunming, Feb. 10, 1994, and July 27, 1997.

Qian Rui. Graduate of the Ordnance School; arsenal technician, 1940s. Taipei, Aug. 19, 1997.

Sun Zhiguang. Graduate of Tongji University; arsenal technician, 1940s. Kunming, Feb. 6, 1994.

Wang Xianglong. Employed in Chongqing's retail and transport trade; steel plant worker, 1940s. Chongqing, Apr. 4, 1994.

Xie Lin. Apprentice and foundry worker in Chongqing Arsenal, 1940s. Chongqing, Sept. 20, 1994, and Nov. 30, 1994.

Yang Jinhua. Steel mill worker, 1940s. Chongqing, Apr. 24, 1994.

Yang Yiyan. Activist, SACO prisoner, author. Chongqing, July 3, 2002.

Ye Xiuquan. Graduate and instructor of an arsenal skilled workers' training school; mechanical draftsman, 1940s. Chongqing, Apr. 24, 1994.

Zhang Dongqiang. Arsenal engineer, 1940s. Taipei, July 5 and 12, 1997.

Zhang Ping. Arsenal apprentice and lathe turner, 1940s. Chongqing, Nov. 30, 1994.

Zhu Rong. Steel mill machinist, 1940s. Chongqing, Dec. 6, 1993, and Feb. 24, 1994.

Glossary

Binggong Shu 兵工署

Binggong zhuanmen xuexiao 兵工專門學校

Bingyi Shu 兵役署

Chen Cheng 陳誠

Chen Yi 陳儀

Cheng Zijian 程子健

chumen ren 出門人

dachun 大春

Dahoufang 大後方

dahui 搭會

dayaji 打牙祭

Dai Li 戴笠

daiyu 待遇

dangongzi 單工資

danghua 黨化

diangong 點工

dong shuitian 冬水田

Du Yanqing 杜延慶

duiban 對板

duzhe yuandi 讀者園地

fanggong, xiangong, ronggong 防共限共溶共

fulishe 福利社

Gangtiechang qianjian weiyuanhui 鋼鐵廠遷健委員會

gongjiang 工匠

gongwuchu 工務處

He Yingqin 何應欽

Hong Zhong 洪中

jianqiang jianfei budui 堅強劍匪部隊

jixie bing 機械兵

jixie shi 機械士

jiao dixia ren 腳底下人

jintie gongzi 津貼工資

judian 據點

junmi 軍米

Juntongju 軍統局

Junzhengbu 軍政部

junzi budang 君子不黨

kaoji 考績

Laogongke 勞工科

Laozhengke 勞政科

Li Chenggan 李承干

Li Daichen 李待琛

lianjia 廉價

Liao Zhigao 廖志高

Liu Guoding 劉國定

Liu Zonglin 劉宗林

Liu Xiang 劉湘

Lu Zuofu 盧作孚

Luo Shiwen 羅世文

maipao zaodan 買炮造單

mi daijin 米代金

Nanfangju 南方局

Pan Zinian 潘梓年

Paoge 袍哥

pingjia 平價

putong gongren 普通工人

qiantao 潛逃

rangwai bi xian annei 讓外必先安內

sanhua 三化

sanqin 三勤

sanyang 三陽

shangjiang ren 上江人

shiye jiuguo 實業救國

sishu 私塾

Tan Jianxiao 談建嘯

tanpai 攤派

taowang 跳亡

tiaochang 跳廠

Tiechuang shishe 鐵窗詩社

tougong 偷工

Tongji daxue 同濟大學

Wang Ming 王明

weichi fei 維持費

wenguanzhi 文官制

Weng Wenhao 翁文灝

Wu Qinlie 吳欽烈

Wu Yuzhang 吳玉章

xiajiang ren 下江人

xiaochun 小春

xiaogong 小工

Xie Wanquan 謝万全

Yang Jizeng 楊繼曾

yangban 樣板

yanggewu 秧歌舞

yidang 異黨

youli youli youjie 有理有利有節

Yu Dawei 俞大維

Yu Zusheng 餘祖胜

Zhang Qun 張群

Zhang Yintang 張陰堂

Zhazidong 渣滓洞

zhengdui 整對

zhenggong 正工

zhengqu yiren 爭取異人

zhiyuan 職員

zhizao suo 製造所

Zhongguo binggong gonghui xinanqu weiyuanhui 中國兵工工會西南區委員會

Zhongguo jiqi gongren lianyihui 中國機器工人聯誼會

Zhongguo laodong xiehui 中國勞動協會

Zhou Zixin 周自信

Zhu Xuefan 朱學範

Index

In this index an "f" after a number indicates a separate reference on the next page, and an "ff" indicates separate references on the next two pages. A continuous discussion over two or more pages is indicated by a span of page numbers, e.g., "57–59." *Passim* is used for a cluster of references in close but not consecutive sequence.

Absenteeism, 137, 180, 189f
Advisors: German technical and China's industrial development, 8, 11, 29f, 367; German technical and weapon standardization, 33, 47; pullout from China, 44; American in China, 76ff, American impact on arms industry, 77f, 140, 367
Age: of arsenal workers, 177–78
Air raids, 127–29; defense against, 61, 128f; and nationalism, 129f
All-China Federation of Trade Unions, 343
American Federation of Labor, 251
American War Production Mission, 74, 76–79, 142
Anarchism, 316
Anderson, Benedict, 247
Anti-Duhring, The (Friedrich Engels), 244
Applied Chemistry Research Institute, 37
Apprentices, 94f, 110, 225. *See also* Training programs
Armaments: China's imports of, 24, 40–42; domestic production of, 24, 34, 39; standardization of, 25, 32–34; quality of, 25, 379n7; shortages of, 43, 76
Armaments industry: during the Qing dynasty, 20f; state control over, 20–21, 26–27, 53; dependence on foreign technology, 21f; during the 1920s, 22–25; relocation of, 55–59 *passim*; production during anti-Japanese war, 42f, 51, 72–75, 141; size of labor force, 65, 182; monopoly over resources, 65f; and private sector, 78; civilian conversion plans

for, 79–80; production during Chinese civil war, 81, 144; labor costs of, 97, 113, 152; social welfare programs, 148–53, 154f. *See also* Chongqing; Ordnance Department; Strikes; *and individual arsenals by name*
Arms Embargo Agreement (1919–29), 24, 375n17
Arsenal No. 1, 140, 211
Arsenal No. 2, 80
Arsenal No. 10, 116, 140, 143, 157, 162, 241, 244, 290; labor strife at, 117, 164, 180, 275–87; labor turnover at, 174–76. *See also* Factory 152
Arsenal No. 20, 61, 132, 136, 150f, 163, 230, 241; workers' income at, 105, 144, 183f; tenure of employment, 113, 179–80; separations at, 176, 189. *See also* Factory 791
Arsenal No. 21, 61, 77, 113, 129, 177, 306, 331; wages at, 100, 142; labor disputes at, 117, 261f, 293–94, 385n43; worker fatalities at, 130, 132; social welfare at, 150, 153; factory protection movement at, 296–97
Arsenal No. 23, 61, 103; labor organizing at, 120–22; Communist organizing at, 231f
Arsenal No. 24, 59, 67, 93, 140, 154, 178, 240, 296; medical visits at, 131; labor turnover at, 174; gang presence at, 289
Arsenal No. 25, 107f; strike at, 263f
Arsenal No. 26, 80f

67. *See also* Armaments industry; Yu
Dawei
Overtime work, 135, 137

Palmer, Bryan, 5
Pan Zinian, 239
Paobingchu, 178
Paoge, *see* Gelaohui
Partification, *see Danghua*
Peng Ji'an, 275ff
People's Liberation Army, 297; Second
Field Army, 333
Perry, Elizabeth, 4–5, 9, 117, 374n34
Petty capitalists, 185–86
Piecework, 10, 141–42; effect on workers,
143, 146. *See also* Wages
Poaching, 169, 182–84
Political campaigns: of early 1950s, 1, 14,
329–30, 332, 349, 353. *See also* Democ-
racy Reform Investigation Movement;
Five Antis campaign; Three Antis cam-
paign
Political Consultative Conference, 251,
263
Popular fronts, 229, 298
Population: of Chongqing, 87, 89
Productivity, 144
Proletarianization, 10, 358–59
Promotions, 111–15; periodic evaluations
(*kaoji*), 111–13. *See also* Hierarchies;
Social mobility
Punishments, 135–36, 170, 173, 188ff,
206, 285–86

Qi Wu, 3, 137, 358
Qing dynasty, 20–21
Qingnian shenghuo (Young Lives), 244
Qunzhong, 245

Rancière, Jacques, 317
Ran Yizhi, 333
Rao Zuobao, 232
Rawlinson, John, 21
Raw materials: and industrial strategy, 35,
52–53; German imports of, from China,
43–44, 46; Chinese imports of, 74. *See
also* Barter; *and individual metals by
name*
Reading societies, 242–43
Recalling Bitterness Meetings, 207
Recreational activities, 150–51, 199
Recruiting, job, 96, 107, 204
Rectification campaigns, 326
Red Crag (*Hong yan*, by Luo Guangbin
and Yang Yiyan), 157, 303
Regionalism, 85–86, 104, 119; and divi-

sion of labor, 86, 104–8, 116–17, 161;
and class formation, 161, 324, 357. *See
also* Identity; Native place associations;
Native place ties
Resistance, 136, 143–44; mobility as form
of, 170, 180, 191
Resolute Sichuan-Kang Army to Extin-
guish Bandits (*jianqiang jianfei budui*),
295–96
Returned students (from Moscow), 235
Reverse engineering, 19, 33f, 39
Rice riots, 293–95
Rice stipends, 137, 140, 145, 292. *See also*
Wages
Richman, Barry, 332
Riehl, Alois, 29
Roosevelt, Franklin D., 74, 76
Roux, Alain, 177

Saijin Prince (Japanese Chief of Staff), 127
Sanhua (three transformations), 235
Sanpō Federation, 204
Sanqin (three diligences), 235
Sanqingtuan (Guomindang Youth Corps),
211
Saodang bao, 246, 403n60
Schurmann, Franz, 330
Scientific management, 125, 141–42. *See
also* Taylor, Frederick W.
Scott, James C., 144, 170
Secret societies, *see* Gelaohui; Green Gang
Seeckt, Hans von, 29, 33
"Self-Ridicule" (Lu Xun), 309–10
Self-strengthening movement, 20
Separations, 174, 176, 180, 185. *See also*
Layoffs
Severance pay, 80, 190, 251, 259, 279ff,
287
Sexual division of labor, 99–100. *See also*
Women
Shandong, 287–88
Shanghai, 55, 63, 345, 348; and labor
movement, 4–5, 233
Shanghai arsenal, 26f
Shanghai steel plant, 22, 27
Shangjiang ren, *see* Upriver people
Shen Gengzu, 275, 280ff, 287
Shen Qichang, 240, 283, 286
Shen Yongfa, 277, 286
Shenyang arsenal, 19
Shih Kuo-heng, 158, 228
Shunchang Iron Mill, 183–84
Sichuan, as wartime base, 52–53; agrarian
economy of, 89–92, 384n18; feminiza-
tion of rural economy, 101; jobs of
workers from, 101, 108–11, 115–16,